The Scientific Foundation of Neuropsychological Assessment

The Scientific Foundation of Neuropsychological Assessment

With Applications to Forensic Evaluation

Elbert W. Russell
Retired Chief of the Neuropsychological Laboratory
VA Medical Center, Miami, FL, USA

ELSEVIER

AMSTERDAM • BOSTON • HEIDELBERG • LONDON • NEW YORK • OXFORD
PARIS • SAN DIEGO • SAN FRANCISCO • SINGAPORE • SYDNEY • TOKYO

Elsevier
32 Jamestown Road, London NW1 7BY
225 Wyman Street, Waltham, MA 02451, USA

First edition 2012

British Library Cataloguing-in-Publication Data
A catalogue record for this book is available from the British Library

Library of Congress Cataloging-in-Publication Data
A catalog record for this book is available from the Library of Congress

ISBN: 978-0-323-16542-6

This book has been manufactured using Print On Demand technology. Each copy is produced to order and is limited to black ink. The online version of this book will show color figures where appropriate.

Dedicated to Ralph M. Reitan,
the founder of Scientific Neuropsychology

Contents

Preface

Not often, even in the history of science, does a person realize that he or she has made a new important discovery or has begun a new era in a field. This realization, creates a form of elation and vivid remembrance of the event.

Reitan's Grand Experiment

This happened to Ralph Reitan and his compatriots several times over a period of years during the 1950s and 1960s. At one point in an unpublished writing (Reitan, circa 2000), he states, "I still recall the tremendous excitement I experienced when I first realized that verbal intelligence was consistently impaired with left cerebral lesions and performance intelligence was even more consistently impaired with the right lesions" (p. 9).

In this regard, in September 2006, I sent Ralph a critique I had written of the Lezak review of his work that was presented in the fourth edition of her book, which was written with two other neuropsychologists (Lezak, Howieson, & Loring, 2004). I asked Ralph to review my paper for errors that I had made in describing his methodology and the work in this first laboratory. [Lezak et al. (2004) had emphasized this work in their critique.] Ralph returned the manuscript with suggested changes, and he added several pages describing the first years of work in his laboratory. He correctly considered this time to be a "great experiment" in understanding the relationship between brain functioning, pathology, and neuropsychological tests, because this work not only made many discoveries but also transformed the nature of neuropsychological assessment.

The formal presentation of his laboratory work (Reitan, 1966) is provided in the chapter titled "A Research Program on the Psychological Effects of Brain Lesions in Human Beings" that he contributed to Norman R. Ellis (Ed.), *International Review of Research and Mental Retardation* (pp. 156–218). My formal criticism of the Lezak et al. (2004) critique is presented in Chapter 13, "In Defense of the Halstead–Reitan Battery—Revisited."

At this point, I would like to quote in full Ralph's description of those first years in which he and his colleagues developed the Halstead–Reitan Battery (HRB) methodology and made his initial contributions to neuropsychology. This long quote was obtained from a handwritten copy of Reitan's description of his early research. It was apparently dictated to Deborah Wolfson. (The only substantial change I have made was changing the personal pronouns from the academic third person to the first person because this retains the personal quality of this writing.) This description captures the care that was exercised in regard to his methodology, the contributions of supporting surgeons, and the general feeling of discovery that accompanied those years. Reitan wrote:

> *I made a very deliberate attempt to be sure that the results of neuropsychological testing were not influenced by knowledge of the patient's history or neurological diagnosis. One assistant in my laboratory, who did no testing and had no contact with patients, worked with the referring physician (usually a neurologist or neurosurgeon) to complete a full record of the history, neurological findings, and diagnosis (including whether or not the diagnosis was firmly and unequivocally established). The neurological surgeons routinely completed a diagrammatic representation of the lesion they had observed and treated at surgery. I had research funds, which permitted me to hire a fully trained neurological surgeon to complete chart reviews and record a summary of the complete medical record of many of the patients that were tested. Neuropathologists also completed diagrams of brain lesions and a summary of their findings at the autopsy, which were then included in my files for each patient. There probably has been no comparable effort to obtain full neurological information for correlation with neurological test results. In fact, when I moved to the University of Washington, even though a Professor in the Department of Neurological Surgery, I was not able to elicit a comparable degree of effort by physicians and surgeons specifically directed to promote such neurological-neuropsychological correlations.*
>
> *My laboratory was begun even before the term "clinical neuropsychology" was in use. I and the cooperating physicians and surgeons were a closely knit group. I had worked closely with Robert F. Heimburger, M.D., now chief of neuropsychological surgery at the Indiana University Medical Center, while Dr. Heimburger and I had both been working in Halstead's laboratory at the University of Chicago (I was a graduate student and Dr. Heimburger was there because, as he said, he wanted to know more about what brains were really for when he operated on them). Together, we developed a plan for a grand research endeavor that we expected to take years to accomplish.*
>
> *Dr. Heimburger would be responsible for providing the neurological information and I would do the neuropsychological assessments. The validity of the neuropsychological assessments would be evaluated on the basis of their accuracy in predicting the neurological findings. Obviously, this plan required that the two sources of information on each patient be kept entirely separate until I had completed both the testing and a written interpretation of the test results. This written report was entered in each patient's medical chart, but everyone concerned with the patient's care was informed that the Neuropsychological Report was done blindly, without any knowledge of the patient's history, complaints, or any medical or surgical findings and was to be considered and evaluated on this basis. Thus, the Neuropsychological Report was recognized as an assessment of intellectual and cognitive abilities, and that inferences regarding brain disease or damage were experimental in nature.*
>
> *At the beginning, the Neuropsychological Reports included only limited inferences regarding the patient's brain. However, after all information on a patient was complete, the neurological findings and the neuropsychological test results were*

Iowever, the brain's functioning and its pathology are complex, and such brain ditions remain largely unexplored. Ralph states, "Even though I was routinely ly successful in differentiating patients with brain damage and control subjects, ound that I could not go a great deal further in respect to references about brain thology." This was true of almost all psychology at that time.

However, he continued comparing the relationship between test results, which ere obtained in a blind-analysis fashion, and the reports from the neurosurgeons, ith a growing recognition that there was a relationship between test results and different brain conditions. Examination of the test results without neurological knowledge of the patient other than age and sex began to demonstrate patterns of test results. From blind analysis of the data, Reitan found that he could create research hypotheses that could be examined using groups of patients in a research paradigm. It is this excitement, which often approaches euphoria, that often occurs at the point where scientists suddenly realize that they have made a discovery that is new not only for them but also for human science.

The Purposes of This Book

In a general sense, the purpose of this book is to continue the work—both the methodology and the making of discoveries—that were begun by Ralph Reitan. Descriptions of neuropsychological tests and psychometric methods designed for single tests are well represented in neuropsychology textbooks, but the methods for neuropsychological analysis are largely neglected. This is Reitan's legacy. He taught us how to use a battery of tests to obtain an accurate interpretation.

The first specific purpose of this writing is to lay the theoretical foundation for the use of test batteries. Although the entire behavior of humans, both cognitive and affective, is derived from the brain and its organization, for a long period psychology ignored the brain in developing its discipline. The field of neuropsychology, which was traditionally called the "study of brain–behavior relationships," is the bridge between psychological procedures such as tests and the functioning of the brain. This relationship has been inadequately examined from a theoretical point of view. Thus, one purpose of this writing is to extend our understanding of the theoretical relationship between brain functioning and psychological testing procedures.

The second purpose of this book is to examine the scientific foundation of neuropsychological assessment. In part, this emphasis is the result of the neuropsychologist's lack of awareness of the scientific basis for neuropsychological interpretation. Although I am not a statistician, I am among the many neuropsychologists who have acquired some intuitive sense concerning the relationships of tests and batteries to brain functioning. This has been achieved in the context of my unyielding devotion to the scientific method.

Overall, the history of neuropsychology is the history of advancement in scientific instrumentation and methodology. There has been a gradual progress from subjective clinical analysis derived from experienced observation of a patient's behavior to single tests and from there to more formal complex methodologies. Subjective analysis *carefully studied and compared. In some instances, gross mistakes wer as concluding that the testee was a control, who had been sent for te much as Reitan needed controls who had been fully evaluated neurolo found to have no evidence of brain damage or disease) when in fact the p undergone an amputation of a normal right anterior temporal lobe made by the old growth of a meningioma. I have commented that I learned more j mistakes than I did when the neurological findings confirmed my inferences.*

On the basis of knowledge gained on a patient-by-patient basis, tests wer to the battery additionally represented by Halstead's 10 tests. Many of the tes not included in the final battery because they either lacked a satisfactory deg consistent sensitivity to brain damage or they appeared to add little to the infer based on the rest of the tests. (For example, I devised a series of visual tests, g in a totally dark room, involving bisection and trisection of lines at various an and figures of various sizes, but these tests were too often performed poorly by con subjects. Tests of kinesthesia were [proficient] in localization of differences in the t sides of the body, but the size/or standardization of the needed equipment made the impractical.) Other tests, such as those developed by me and Kløve to evaluate sen sory-perceptual abilities, were included. Finally the battery was considered to be com plete when controls were correctly identified in the "blind" reports and brain damage, as well as its various characteristics (diffuse versus focal; left versus right; progressive versus chronic static; and type of lesion) were also usually correctly inferred.

The "grand" experiment was carried out over a course of approximately 17 years, with a focus on correlation of neuropsychological test results with definitive neurological findings and diagnoses. The next phase of the "grand" experiment was to use the results of the test battery to predict, based on the defects shown by the test battery, blindly, the type of [affective] symptomatology that the patient would experience. Considerable progress was made in this phase, but it became apparent that the imprecision in recording or rating the patient's environmental (behavioral) problems, as contrasted with identification and description of brain damage or disease, was an extremely difficult problem and that a plan for formal testing of the accuracy of such prediction could not be developed satisfactorily. This problem stems from the weakness of clinical psychology in developing precise methods of identification, classification, and measurement of the components of emotional disturbances. I and my colleagues had a definite interest in this area and published in the papers, beginning in 1955, using the results of the MMPI to correlate with both neurological diagnosis and neuropsychological test results. Many other studies of this type have been published, which have contributed significantly to knowledge regarding emotional correlates of brain disease and damage, but an MMPI profile can hardly be accepted as a complete description of emotional problems experienced by the individual brain-damaged patient.

Complex Brain-Behavior Assessment

By 1951, when Ralph began his work, the assessment of the existence of brain damage was already a relatively accurate procedure for neuropsychology. The accuracy of single tests to determine the existence of brain damage was approaching the accuracy of current methods almost a half century later (Spreen & Benton, 1965).

of individual observation was replaced by the creation of psychometric tests and from single tests into batteries. Generally, the advance is from more intuitive or clinical judgment approaches to more psychometric formal methods. *Formal methodology* refers to objective and quantitative methods as opposed to clinical judgment or intuition. As assessment methods have become more formalized, they have become more scientific as well as more complex. For instance, recent work has begun the use of automated assessment methodologies.

Unfortunately, as the history of neuropsychology demonstrates, this changing methodology has often resulted in a schism between the more subjective clinical approach and the more formal psychometric approach. Although there is general agreement on many issues in neuropsychology, this division, which was there at the beginning of professional neuropsychology (Goldstein & Scheerer, 1941), continues to the present. When I was a student, the argument was between simply observing a patient's "whole" behavior in performing the tests and using the results of psychometric tests. Eventually, psychometric tests became accepted as the primary basis for neuropsychology because of their validity and accuracy, which could be tested. With the work of Halstead and Reitan, the tests themselves began to be used in a battery as a uniform procedure for interpretation. This writing continues in that direction.

The third purpose of this writing is to provide guidance as to the methods used in assessment. There is little detailed emphasis on how to use tests as a group in order to obtain a full interpretation of brain functioning. The general assumption in traditional neuropsychology is that if neuropsychologists know a lot of tests and some neurology, their clinical judgment is sufficient to enable them to derive understandings of patients' neurological condition. As a result, new neuropsychologists have difficulty in analyzing test results so as to obtain interpretative patterns for medical and forensic purposes. This writing will attempt to provide some guidance on how to organize one's thinking in regard to test battery results so as to obtain an accurate interpretation.

The fourth purpose is to provide neuropsychologists and attorneys with material to use in forensic practice. Much of this information may be obtained from the section on justification.

There will be no attempt in this book to deal with the neurology of the brain. This is accomplished by the neuroscientists and neurologists. Their work at this time is far more advanced than that of neuropsychology. This writing will emphasize assessment. In doing so, it will attempt to establish a bridge between traditional psychological testing and brain functioning. Further work can then be used to expand that bridge in order to provide more scientific and accurate methods of assessment.

Organization of This Book

To handle the various aspects of a scientific approach to neuropsychology, this book is divided into five sections.

In Section I, "Scientific Neurological Basis for Assessment," the nature of science is explored. Because this book is an attempt to apply the scientific method to neuropsychological assessment, a full description of the nature of science is essential, particularly as it is applied to neuropsychology. Thus, Chapter 1 provides an introductory but brief history of the development of scientific assessment batteries in neuropsychology.

Chapter 2 discusses the essence of science. Particular emphasis is placed on instrumentation, because the basis of neuropsychology is its instrumentation. This instrumentation was derived from psychology, although the form of the instrumentation in neuropsychology pertains to testing procedures related to brain functioning. The basis of testing procedures is often neglected in neuropsychology textbooks.

Section II, "The Theoretical Foundation of Neurological Assessment," examines the theoretical basis for the relationship between brain functioning and assessment procedures. This is not directly concerned with the neurological basis of neuropsychology, but it will emphasize the relationship in assessment between neuropsychological testing and brain functioning. In spite of the huge collection of neuropsychology studies that has accumulated over the years, this theoretical basis has seldom been directly examined. The discussion initially involves two aspects of science: discovery and justification (Toulmin, 2006).

Discovery involves that aspect of science in which concepts and theories are created. However, the creative products even in science are not always correct. As such, the theories and methodology must be justified before they can be accepted. Justification is the second but most essential aspect of science. Chapter 3 is concerned with the theoretical relationship between brain functioning and neuropsychological testing. This relationship has recently received a great augmentation by the introduction of scanning techniques in neurology. However, although scanning determines the location of a function, it does not determine the nature of that function. This nature of a function is determined by the form of neuropsychological tests. The test is a task that the brain is required to perform and that demonstrates the function of a particular area of the brain. Thus, the relationship between neuropsychological tests and brain functioning can be determined with greater precision than previously.

Chapter 4 deals with the methods used in neuropsychology to examine brain functioning. The emphasis is on the use of test batteries, because psychometrics has examined individual tests to a far greater extent than this work can deal with. It will examine the way a neuropsychological assessment battery should be constructed in order to model the functioning of the brain. This presents the basic psychometric theory for constructing an assessment battery.

Chapter 5 is devoted to a relatively brief examination of the formal methods used in neuropsychology. These include computerized testing, which appears to be a major aspect of the next phase of neuropsychological assessment.

Chapter 6 is concerned with assessment patterns used for neuropsychological interpretation. There is general agreement that the function of a battery is to enable the investigation of patterns of relationships related to brain functioning. Consequently, this chapter discusses various types of patterns and presents some initial work in this area that may be used for interpretation.

Section III, "Justification of Formal Procedures," is concerned with scientific justification of assessment procedures in order to ensure the reliability of neuropsychological procedures. Justification is the fundamental process used by science to validate its theories, concepts, and methodology. Such validation is the basis for scientific reliability. The justification of assessment procedures, particularly test batteries, will be examined.

Chapter 7 was originally published as a paper in 2005 and contains the essence of justification for a standardized battery. The following chapters present a more detailed elaboration of justification procedures.

Chapter 8 elaborates the nature of justification. It emphasizes the distinction between research in basic theoretical neuropsychology and assessment research. It deals with the concepts used to justify unstandardized batteries, including the difference between medicine and neuropsychology. Finally, it deals with the requirements for a standardized battery, including norming and validation. A battery may be validated by either clinical judgment or psychometric procedures.

Chapter 9 is a crucial discussion of the accuracy of various formal methods that have been used in neuropsychology. It attempts to be as thorough as possible in its selection of procedures to examine. Nevertheless, this examination is restricted to procedures that have developed from the HRB. Accuracy is another way of stating the rate of error for a procedure. The major examined procedures are indexes, decision-tree algorithms, discriminate analysis, and clinical judgment. It also deals with the criticism that neuropsychologists have applied to these formal methods. Finally, it briefly discusses some of the newer methods of creating formal procedures.

These studies indicate that the HRB continues to be as accurate a determination of the existence of brain damage as has been developed. It certainly has more research supporting its validity than any other neuropsychological assessment method.

Section IV, "Application to Forensics," deals with implications of the scientific approach to various issues in neuropsychological assessment to forensics. Chapter 10 is written by attorneys and examines the relationship between neuropsychological testing and the *Daubert* criteria. It finds that formal neuropsychological methodologies are crucial for forensic examinations.

Chapter 11 is written by two neuropsychologists who have utilized the Halstead–Russell Neuropsychological Evaluation System—Revised (HRNES-R) in their forensic practice for many years. Using several case studies, they demonstrate that the use of a standardized battery was critical in the settlement of these cases. This demonstrates the application of standardized batteries to court proceedings.

Section V, "Formal Neuropsychological Methods," examines several critical studies that concern the use of formal psychometric methods, particularly batteries. Chapters 12 and 13 consist of two papers that are critiques of Lezak's criticism of the HRB and the HRNES–R (Lezak, 1995, pp. 709–715). Lezak's method has been considered to be the model for the flexible form of neuropsychological assessment, whereas the HRB was the model for a fixed-battery approach. The HRNES–R consisted of the most advanced standardized and thus co-normed assessment procedure that had been constructed. Chapter 12 is a republication of the first paper defending the HRB against criticism by Lezak. This critique demonstrated that Lezak confused clinical judgment used with a fixed battery, the HRB, with clinical judgment utilized in her method. Chapter 13 is a critique of the newest criticisms of the Reitan method by Lezak and her associates (Lezak et al., 2004, pp. 670–677). In their critique, she and her associates confuse Reitan's scientific method, which is perhaps the most rigorous methodology that has been used in neuropsychology, with his method of assessment. Thus, these papers constitute a dialogue between these two approaches to neuropsychological assessment.

Chapter 14 examines the research on volunteer norms used for studies with the HRB and finds that they are all almost one standard deviation above normal, which means they are inappropriate as control groups for neuropsychology. Chapter 15 presents the six major attempts to norm the HRB and some issues that are involved in norming.

Conclusion

The intention of this book is to cover the basic theory and assessment methods related to the use of neuropsychological batteries, with some discussion of the standing of standardized batteries in forensics. It is the author's belief and hope that the scientific development of neuropsychology assessment will continue to develop in both its accuracy and coverage of human brain functions and that the instrumentation for assessment will continue to improve in both accuracy and efficiency.

Author's Note

In this writing, for the most part, the aspects of psychometrics that are emphasized are those that have concerned my own work. Here I can write with some authority. In other areas, I am only repeating what others have created or discovered. Science is an ongoing process in which various people "standing on the shoulders of giants" make further contributions. These contributions will remain the foundation blocks in the edifice that we are building, particularly in the science of neuropsychological assessment.

Acknowledgments

Because those people who have contributed to the concepts that are expressed in the various papers in this book have influenced me throughout my career, I can best express my appreciation of these contributions in historical order.

Although I was a biology major in college, my first contact with neuropsychology came at the University of Kansas when I had my introductory course in neuropsychology. Initially, it was taught by Dr. Martin Scheerer, the leading exponent of the gestalt approach to neuropsychology. He was a brilliant clinician. Unfortunately, he died during the semester of a heart attack. However, his protégés, some of whom were on the faculty, continued teaching the Scheerer–Goldstein method (Goldstein & Scheerer, 1941).

References

Goldstein, K., & Scheerer, M. (1941). Abstract and concrete behavior: an experimental study with special tests. *Psychological Monographs, 53*(2) Whole No. 239.

Lezak, M. D. (1995). *Neuropsychological assessment* (3rd ed.). New York: Oxford University Press.

Lezak, M. D., Howieson, D. B., & Loring, D. W. (2004). *Neuropsychological assessment* (4th ed.). New York: Oxford University Press.

Reitan, R. M. (1966). A research program on the psychological effects of brain lesions in human beings. In N. R. Ellis (Ed.), *International review of research and mental retardation* (pp. 156–218). New York: Academic Press.

Reitan, R. (circa 2000). The best laid plans—and for guarantees of circumstantial events. Unpublished manuscript.

Russell, E. W., Neuringer, C., & Goldstein, G. (1970). *Assessment of brain damage: A neuropsychological key approach.* New York: Wiley.

Russell, E. W., & Starkey, R. I. (1993). *Halstead–Russell Neuropsychological Evaluation System.* Los Angeles: Western Psychological Services. [Manual and computer program]

Spreen, O., & Benton, A. L. (1965). Comparative studies of some psychological tests for cerebral damage. *Journal of Nervous and Mental Disease, 140*, 323–333.

Toulmin, S.E. (2006). Discovery and rationality. In Philosophy of Science. *Encyclopaedia Britannica.* Retrieved March 3, 2007, from *Encyclopaedia Britannica 2006, Ultimate Reference Suite DVD.*

At this time, I also started my internship at the Veterans Administration hc Topeka, Kansas, where I began working with Gerald Goldstein, who was chie neuropsychology laboratory. He had recently learned a version of the HRB ap that was being used by Phillip M. Rennick. Rennick had apparently worke both Halstead and Reitan. He developed a slightly different version of the HR that employed by Reitan. For my dissertation, based on a taxonomic method learned in an undergraduate biology class, I developed a method to use data this fixed battery to determine the existence of damage and to lateralize it. It called the *neuropsychological key*. Dr. Charles Neuringer was my faculty advisor helped a great deal to develop the ideas that became my dissertation. He was parti larly helpful in his insistence that we use a completely objective method in desig ing the program. In Rennick's method, the aphasia test and the perceptual disorde tests were rated. Under Neuringer's insistence, Gerald Goldstein and I worked o an objective method for scoring these tests. This requirement ensured that the entir algorithm was objective. I have retained the ideal of complete objectivity for neu ropsychological procedures throughout my work.

This key was placed into a computer program by Carolyn Shelly (Later Carolyn Goldstein). The result was that technicians could administer the key and place the results into the program that determined whether the patient had brain damage and whether it was diffuse or lateralized to the right or left hemisphere, without any input from any neuropsychologists. Gerald Goldstein and Charles Neuringer were instrumental in getting our book published (Russell, Neuringer, & Goldstein, 1970). Gerald Goldstein was a major contributor in helping me design and complete the initial neuropsychological key. He and Carolyn Shelley Goldstein, during her life, remained my friends and supporters throughout my career.

After graduation, I became a neuropsychologist at the Cincinnati Veterans Administration hospital. During that time, I visited Reitan's laboratory on many occasions and developed a great admiration for his work. That friendship has remained to this day. Thus, I first want to acknowledge the invaluable contribution of Ralph Reitan in his development of a major aspect of the field of neuropsychology with the help of other neuropsychologists, particularly Deborah Wolfson.

It was evident that the neuropsychological key had several problems that I later attempted to correct. Computer technology developed rapidly during this period so that an automated scoring program could be developed. Using such methods, the HRNES was developed (Russell & Starkey, 1993). Without the help of Regina Starkey, who designed the system's format, and the encouragement of her husband, Tim, I would not have been able to complete this program. In 1993, I was fortunate enough to have it published by Western Psychological Services. This company, particularly the work of Anthony Gerard, provided great help in creating and publishing both the original and the revised version of the HRNES.

In regard to publishing a number of papers, I would like to thank editors of the *Archives of Clinical Neuropsychology*, and especially William Gouvier for both his encouragement and helping me to appreciate writing style.

Finally, in regard to this current book, I would like to thank Elsevier Insights team Lisa Tickner, Erin Hill-Parks, and Tracey Miller.

Foreword

Dr. Elbert W. Russell (Bert) has afforded me the tremendous honor of writing the foreword to his remarkable book. Bert has been widely known in the field for many years but perhaps not always as fully appreciated as his capabilities and accomplishments merit. He has been an unwavering and steadfast champion of science and its extraordinary value in the grounding, extension, and advancement of neuropsychology. His book is the natural culmination of this deep appreciation for science and its unequalled benefits for our field.[1]

There is no question about the intent of this book. Bert sets out to establish the scientific roots of the field, which he then connects theoretically and concretely to neuropsychological practice. He distinguishes between clinical activities that do and do not have adequate scientific grounding, advocates powerfully for the advantages of the former, argues that clinical practice has too often strayed from its needed scientific roots, and calls for greater reliance on and accountability to scientific method and scientific evidence. There is nothing half-hearted about this book and its powerful message, with an unmistakable objective being to provide strong medicine for practices that arguably undervalue or even outright neglect scientific principles and foundations. Bert is one of the few individuals who posses the historical perspective and scholarly breadth to attempt such a wide-ranging treatment of the field, and readers owe themselves the intellectual favor of discovering what he has to convey about these matters.

Some may be taken aback, if not offended, by various strong positions in this book, in particular assertions that in many ways progress in clinical neuropsychology has been stalled, or even reversed, by an all-too-frequent disregard for science. For example, Bert observes that a variety of common assessment methods lack anything approaching sufficient scientific foundations. His criticisms of heavy reliance on subjective (or clinical) judgment, although congruent with a massive body of research on decision making, fly in the face of what is sometimes an almost Jamesian overbelief in its power. At the other end of the spectrum, some will find various descriptions of science too traditionally empiricist. For example, contemporary philosophy of science has all but replaced the search for Truth with a capital T with the search for truth-likeness or verisimilitude. However, I think details of this sort are neither of particular importance or essential to Bert's message, which is to

[1]This foreword is directed solely to Bert's contributions because he has written the great bulk of the material, and this exclusive focus is by no means intended to slight the contributions of the other chapter authors.

use science as fully as possible in our field, not as an "obligation" but because it is the best-known method for advancing knowledge and because the gains that result will benefit our patients and promote human welfare.

If one studies the history of science, one often finds commonalities as fields advance. For example, instrumentation is frequently developed that extends human senses and achieves more accurate measurement. Methodology is applied to the collection and interpretation of data that compensates for the frailties of subjective judgment, attenuates the impact of bias and preconception, and assists in the integration of information. Quantification, formalisms, and theories are often central means to these ends. To provide a familiar example, we can review, say, a body of 150 studies by subjective methods or undertake a meta-analysis. Is there any question that when properly developed and applied, these methodological triumphs over the limits of the unaided human mind can deliver many advantages? This is in no way to detract from human accomplishment. The human mind can still achieve remarkable things that as yet cannot be duplicated otherwise, such as aspects of discovery and theory generation. Furthermore, the development and extension of science is obviously a human accomplishment and at times an act of genius.

Bert Russell has written this book to appeal to our scientific conscience and has done us a great service in doing so. He is an accomplished and compelling voice for this all-important message. He is not an ideologue advocating for one or another particular test or method but a true scientist presenting a position that retains applicability regardless of the specific neuropsychological battery or process one prefers or to which one adheres. Science and true knowledge credentials are of no greater or lesser importance whether one favors more or less structured approaches, for example, or emphasizes tests scores or processes. As Bert reminds us, neuropsychology was founded on science and can benefit greatly from an unwavering commitment or recommitment to the scientific method. Bert has done a magnificent job laying out the argument and rationale, and it behooves us all to lend him an ear.

David Faust
Department of Psychology, University of Rhode Island, Kingston, RI;
and Department of Psychiatry and Human Behavior, Alpert Medical School of
Brown University, Providence, RI
October 6, 2011

Section I

Scientific Neurological Basis for Assessment

1 Introductory Scientific History to Neuropsychological Assessment

However, it appears to the President of this division (Division 40) that we are not actually making as much progress as we are inclined to believe, and that this is true both in absolute terms and in comparison with the progress made in other clinical neurosciences.... Now it is true that the newer tests have the advantage of updated norms, and, in some cases, technical problems have been resolved. However, it is debatable if any of these newer procedures have provided either substantively different approaches or significant neuropsychological advantages over the earlier forms of the same tests. Are we fooling ourselves into believing that we are actually making progress in these areas when we are not?

From presidential address for Division 40 (neuropsychology)
(Dodrill, 1997, pp. 1–2)

Behemoths: Among various Jewish legends, one relates that the righteous will witness a spectacular battle between Behemoth and Leviathan in the messianic era and later feast upon their flesh.

Encyclopaedia Britannica, 2010

We learn from history that we do not learn from history.

Georg Friedrich Wilhelm Hegel

In the last few years, a new neuropsychological assessment method made its appearance. This is the computerized neuropsychological testing program. Several of these programs have been developed and validated. However, the program that appears to be the most challenging to traditional clinical neuropsychology assessment is the MindStreams program (Simon, Doniger, & Amit, 2000). This program is designed for medical practice and requires no neuropsychologist. Technicians with minimal training monitor the patient, who is administered the program by a computer. The results of the program include measures of the amount of impairment for various major cognitive domains. These results are delivered to the physician in a printout "immediately" after the patient is tested. The printout is designed so that a doctor, such as a neurologist, can quickly issue a report on the cognitive status of the individual.

Although MindStreams will be discussed in another chapter, the program appears to meet the general neuropsychological requirements for validation and reliability. As such, it is an acceptable program for medical purposes. It is being rapidly expanded, apparently with the support of strong financing. The procedure seems to

The Scientific Foundation of Neuropsychological Assessment. DOI: 10.1016/B978-0-12-416029-3.00001-4

have obtained diagnostic codes that allow its use to be reimbursed through medical insurance companies. In any case, the cost would be far lower than an equivalent human examination, which would require hours of work by an expensive neuropsychologist. The result is that this program appears to have combined in computerized form of the administration, scoring, and preliminary interpretative report that are sufficient for a doctor's needs. In addition, no expensive neuropsychologist is necessary. Ironically, the field of neuropsychology was quite capable of creating such computerized programs at least two decades ago.

As such, MindStreams is not unique. A number of other validated computerized testing programs are now in use in the military and in many hospitals. Consequently, the field of computerized assessment is developing rapidly and could displace traditional neuropsychological assessment in many situations. It is the most recent development of a long history of refining the methods of neuropsychology. This progress and the obstacles to it are quite apparent in the history of the clinical neuropsychology.

The Contemporary Situation in Neuropsychology Assessment

Historically, computerized testing is the end result of a process that started in the 1940s and 1950s led primarily by Ward C. Halstead (1947) and Ralph Reitan (1955). It represents the progressive development of formalized testing. It now apparently poses a threat to traditional neuropsychological assessment.

About 30 years ago, neuropsychology was on the edge of discovering a new formal assessment methodology. This was a computerized assessment scoring and basic interpretation program (Russell, Neuringer, & Goldstein, 1970). This could have been integrated with computer technology (Kane & Kay, 1992; Russell, 1995). However, this computerized scoring was so severely criticized that, beginning in the 1980s, automated scoring along with standardized ("fixed") assessment of a neuropsychological battery was largely rejected by the field of clinical neuropsychology (Russell, 1995).

Since the 1980s, with the exception of some relatively unrecognized work by a few neuropsychologists, the field has been dominated by the clinical or flexible method that uses flexible batteries and clinical judgment as the basis for assessment. During that time, neuropsychology continued to become a large and well-recognized branch of psychology. This recognition was especially important in forensic neuropsychology. In spite of its growth, the discipline of neuropsychology demonstrated remarkably little progress in the development of scientific assessment methodology. The exception was an increased ability to predict a patient's premorbid ability and in the evaluation of their assessment motivation.

How this situation occurred is a matter of neuropsychology history. This chapter summarizes this history from a scientific perspective. The rest of the book is devoted to the issues, methodology, and problems that are related to restoring the discipline from this stagnation. This new direction is that of formal and automated assessment in both general practice and forensic neuropsychology.

Neurological knowledge and test descriptions are well represented in neuropsychology books, but the methods for neuropsychological analysis are largely neglected. There is little detailed emphasis on how to apply tests to the patient in order to obtain an interpretation. The general assumption in neuropsychology is that clinical judgment is sufficient to enable the neuropsychologist to derive an understanding of a patient's neurological condition from test results and the neuropsychologist's understanding of neurology. As a result, students are generally at a loss about how to analyze test results.

Although there is general agreement on most issues in neuropsychology, the variation in general approaches to assessment has produced a considerable amount of contention. Superficially, these approaches appear to concern whether one should design an assessment battery of tests to answer referrals by means of a flexible battery or to cover the functioning of the entire brain through a standardized battery. However, at a more basic level, these methods reflect a difference in neuropsychological assessment methodology that is quite fundamental. It is the difference between clinical judgment and formal assessment methods. Thus, the primary purpose of this book is to present a theory and methodology for creating and validating assessment methods that model brain functioning. Applications of this theory to medical and forensic conditions are examined in some detail.

Formalization of Neuropsychological History

The history of psychological assessment began with Binet's testing in 1905 (Guilford, 1967, pp. 4–6), more than 100 years ago. During the 20th century, the entire science of psychometrics was developed. In this first century of its existence, psychometrics was primarily concerned with the statistics and methodology related to individual tests.

Such a concentration on individual tests may be somewhat unexpected because even Binet used a group of tests for his analysis. However, the group was combined into a single score that was, in essence, an index. Subsequently, tests have been used in groups to form indexes for intelligence assessment. However, these indexes were treated as individual tests. This is understandable because most tests are indexes of individual items.

The assessment aspect of neuropsychology originated during World War II. The number of veterans with head injuries and brain damage required a form of assessment that could be provided by psychological tests in addition to a neurological examination. Psychological tests almost from their beginning were more accurate in determining the cognitive condition of the individual than a mental status examination. After the war, the Veterans Administration (VA) hired neuropsychologists to help neurology in evaluating patients. Consequently, the VA was the primary catalyst in the development of neuropsychological assessment.

The assessment methods of clinical psychology were not initially derived from neurology but from psychological test methods. Until the 1950s, the proportion of psychologists who were particularly devoted to the study of brain pathology and neurological behavioral functions was quite limited.

Perhaps this concentration of psychology on individual tests is understandable. Historically, neuropsychology has demonstrated a gradual progress from subjective clinical judgment of unintegreated tests toward more formal methodologies (objective and quantitative) and from individual items to combining items in tests. With time, assessment methods became more formalized and thus more scientific.

Nevertheless, throughout its history, this situation has resulted in a schism between the more subjective clinical approach and the more formal psychometric approach. Neuropsychological development has been moving from a subjective examination of a patient's behavior based on the examiner's experience to the recent use of computerized analysis. However, the field is gradually becoming more formalized. The history of neuropsychology demonstrates this movement.

The Holistic Period

In the early part of the 20th century, psychologists such as Kurt Goldstein (1939), Lashley (1929), and Hebb (1949) began to study brain functioning. Many of them adopted a holistic approach. This theory believed that the brain functions as a whole and that different areas did not have special functions.

Thus, more than 60 years ago, two of the primary advocates of neuropsychological assessment were neurologist Kurt Goldstein and psychologist Martin Scheerer (1941). They established the first organized group of tests that were used extensively in neuropsychological assessment. The holistic neuropsychologists believed that there was only one primary effect of brain damage: the damaged patient lost the "abstract attitude" and used a more concrete approach to solving problems (Walsh, 1978).

For instance, one of their tests used discs that had both different colors and different shapes. The test instructions asked the patient to "group the discs" using either a form or a color category. After the patient had grouped them in one way, he or she was asked to group the discs in a different manner. Brain damage was assessed by how the particular patient dealt with the test materials rather than the level of functioning obtained by a test score. Brain damage was indicated if the patient had difficulty in shifting the abstract category used to group the discs. There was no scoring system. The assessment was based instead on the subjective evaluation of the patient's behavior. Thus, the individual test was qualitative and flexible. The test "battery" had several tests that were all administered in the same manner. This clinical judgment approach to an individual test was taught at a majority of universities in the 1950s and 1960s.

In Russia during this time, Luria (1973) took a qualitative but not a holistic approach to neuropsychology. He created his own tests in an extremely informal manner. These he used to explore the brain functioning produced by localized brain damage. His methods were later formalized largely as assessment tests by Anne-Lise Christensen (1984). During this time, it gradually became evident that a properly designed test could measure the same process or function that was examined with the qualitative approach.

Development of Assessment Testing

A more formalized form of neuropsychological assessment originated during World War II. Many veterans with brain damage required a form of assessment that could be provided by psychological tests in addition to a neurological examination. Almost from their beginning, psychological cognitive tests were more accurate in determining the cognitive condition of the individual's brain functioning than a mental status examination.

One-Test Brain-Damage Diagnoses

Initially, psychological assessment methods were more related to behavioral or psychological functioning than to neurology. Until the 1960s, part of every clinical psychological examination was an attempt to separate "organicity" or brain damage from affective disorders. As such, single tests were thought to be sufficient to determine brain damage (Lezak, Howieson, & Loring, 2004, pp. 17–18).

However, during the clinical psychology area of the 1940s and 1950s, the qualitative approach to assessment gave way to the use of individual psychometric tests, many of which could be scored such as the Benton Visual Retention Test (Benton, 1974), the Graham-Kendall Memory for Designs (1960), and the Bender Gestalt (Bender, 1938). These tests accepted the concept of a single entity called *brain damage* (Lezak et al., 2004, pp. 17–18). Even so, they were fairly accurate. In a review of the literature, Spreen and Benton (1965) found that the average prediction of the existence of brain damage made by a single test was 71% correct, whereas a battery of several measures gave an 80% correct prediction. However, a single test provided no knowledge about the nature of the damage.

Although rejecting holism, the qualitative method of the 1950s was conceptually similar to the process approach of Kaplan (1988). In describing her method, she referred to H. Werner (Kaplan, 1988, p. 129), a holistic neuropsychologist, as emphasizing the type of qualitative process approach that she advocated. In this regard, the assessment method had changed little in more than 50 years.

Nevertheless, the tendency toward formalization was evidenced in that Kaplan (1988) and her colleagues have attempted to quantify the processes of the process approach. An elaborate scoring system and a normative database were developed for the California Verbal Learning Test (CVLT; Delis, Kramer, Kaplan, & Ober, 1987) and several other tests. In so doing, the CVLT has become primarily a psychometric test.

The "European" School

Another division in neuropsychology was that between what might be called the "European" school of neuropsychology and the "American" school. Although the European school disparaged the American emphasis on quantitative assessment, which was particularly directed at the Halstead–Reitan approach, the European school was more research oriented than assessment oriented. It was particularly adept at using single tests to examine cognitive functions and it made a great many contributions to neuropsychology.

Luria's Approach

Another approach that has strongly affected American neuropsychological assessment is that of the Russian neuropsychologist Alexander Luria (Luria & Majovski, 1977). Luria (1973) took a qualitative but not a holistic approach to neuropsychology. He created his own tests in an extremely informal manner and used these to explore brain functioning. His methods were later formalized as assessment tests largely by Anne-Lise Christensen (1984). One major flaw in his approach is that he largely ignored the right hemisphere (Luria, 1973).

This effect continues to the present in its effect on Lezak's work. In describing the differences between Russian and American clinical neuropsychological approaches, Luria characterized the American psychometric approach as atheoretical whereas the Russian neuropsychological approach was built on a foundation of neurological theory. Although he specifically mentioned the Halstead–Reitan approach as exemplified in the work of Russell et al. (1970), he included all psychometric approaches by implication. In much of the published material it is true that, with the exception of localization (Reitan, 1964), little in the way of a theoretical foundation for the American psychometric approach has been published. Writings in the psychometric area have been devoted largely to the exploration of the parameters of single psychometric tests related to various types of organicity. However, experienced neuropsychologists who are working in the field are aware of a body of clinical knowledge or lore that is far more extensive than the published research indicates. This knowledge uses several principles of interpretation that appear to be accepted rather widely by clinical neuropsychologists but that have seldom been made explicit.

Development of Psychological Batteries

From the beginning, the measurement of intelligence has used groups of tests. It was thought that intelligence was best measured by a set of tests that sampled various aspects of intelligence, thus an index of results was created. A group of brief tests were first used in the Stanford-Binet (Terman & Merrill, 1973). This use of several tests was designed to provide a more accurate measure of general intellectual ability at each age level. Because different subtests were used for each age, it was difficult to compare a particular cognitive ability across age levels. An intelligence quotient (IQ) was obtained by comparing the test scores as a "mental age" to the child's chronological age.

Wechsler's innovation was to use the same subtests for all age levels and combine the scores to obtain an index: the IQ. The Wechsler subtests were not designed to be compared to each other but to be combined to form an index of intelligence (Wechsler, 1944). It is interesting that more recently Lezak (1988) attempted to turn this conception on its head—that is, she emphasized the comparative relationship between tests and stated that the index was meaningless (Lezak, 1988).

Another indication of the growing formalization of neuropsychology is that, starting in the 1950s, the Wechsler intelligence scales began to be used as part of neuropsychological test batteries, particularly by Reitan (Reitan, 1959). Now the most commonly used batteries of tests in neuropsychology are the Wechsler Adult Intelligence Scales (Butler, Retzlaff, & Vanderploeg, 1991). Currently, the fourth generation of such scales, the WAIS-III (Wechsler, 1997), is being used by a large portion of the neuropsychologist, and the fifth generation, the WAIS-IV (Wechsler, Coalson, & Raiford, 2008), has been published. The general form of the Wechsler test battery remained largely the same from the Wechsler-Bellevue in 1939 until the WAIS-III. The WAIS-IV has been largely transformed (Russell, 2010). Nevertheless, all of the Wechsler subtests have remained co-normed, which permitted the comparison of one subtest with another.

Halstead–Reitan Battery

The formal approach applied to a whole battery was introduced into neuropsychology by Halstead (1947) and Reitan (1955) in the 1950s as the Halstead–Reitan Battery (HRB) (Reitan & Wolfson, 1993). The change in neuropsychological assessment that Reitan (1955) introduced was to begin the application of the psychometric science to an entire battery of neuropsychological tests. Assessment had been developed for individual tests during a period of a century. Reitan realized that patterns derived from a test battery could locate and diagnose brain damage. This use of an entire battery greatly extended the usefulness of a neuropsychological battery. Instead of being relegated to determining the existence of damage, it could now provide evidence of the location of damage, diagnosis, and the extent of damage from the test results alone.

In this writing, the Halstead–Reitan Battery is not specifically defended because currently it is not the only scientifically established neuropsychological test battery and it will not remain the primary standardized battery. Rather, by developing the principles applied to the construction of a standardized battery, Reitan has established many of the basic principles necessary to create a scientifically determined assessment methodology. Although history demonstrates that no particular methodology is unending, the scientific principles used in creating such a methodology endure. Progress in the development of a methodology is inevitable in science. As such, this book is as much dedicated to progress in neuropsychological assessment methodology as to laying a foundation for adequate forensic assessment in neuropsychology.

In this regard, Reitan became aware from his research that one cannot study a relationship between tests unless the battery remains constant during the research. He realized that this was also true of assessment. One cannot adequately develop the understanding necessary to assess brain functioning if the tests are continually being changed.

The test battery must also cover the whole brain. If the whole brain is adequately covered using a fixed battery, then each pathology will produce a different pattern of test results. These patterns can be compared, studied, and learned. If the tests are continually changed, this pattern cannot be observed. Although Reitan did not use scale scores, he standardized his battery by using a consistent—that is, standard—group of tests. As such, the relationship between the tests remained invariant or fixed. To achieve this consistency, Reitan followed Halstead in developing a procedure that could be validly administered by technicians in a uniform manner. The procedure was so standardized that it could be given by any person with a high school or college education who was adequately trained in administration even though he or she had little or no understanding of neurology.

The advantage of this fixed battery was that comparisons between tests could be used to provide information concerning the nature of brain lesions. This is also true of the Wechsler tests (Barron & Russell, 1992). However, comparisons are not possible using individual tests with different normative bases. In addition, it enabled the HRB to build up a body of information and clinical lore that remains unmatched by any other neuropsychological procedure.

When Reitan began his work, neuropsychology had no accurate methods of localizing or diagnosing types of damage. Nevertheless, various neurological procedures could accurately localize pathological conditions. For instance, a certain form of a massed blood vessels seen on an arteriogram could indicate the existence of a tumor. Reitan and his students demonstrated that, with a high degree of validity, the location and major types of diagnoses could be derived from the test results alone (Reitan, 1964). Thus, the ability of HRB to localize damage with a noninvasive procedure was of great help to neurologists and neurosurgeons. With the advent of the scanning techniques for most purposes, this localization ability of the HRB was only rarely needed. Concerning determining the existence of brain damage, the HRB when used by experts has retained a level of accuracy that at best has been only occasionally matched in a some studies.

Neuropsychological Computer Interpretation Programs

The next step in formalization of neuropsychological assessment procedures was to automate the scoring and interpretation. The Reitan methodology was precise enough that it approached automation.

The Neuropsychological Key

In 1968, Russell created an automated procedure for scoring and producing the basic interpretations for determining the existence and lateralization of brain damage. It was called the *neuropsychological key*. It essentially was a decision-tree algorithm based on the biological method for keying species in taxonomy manuals.

This method was published by Russell et al. (1970). A computer program written by Carolyn H. Shelley placed the scoring and the preliminary interpretation of test results into an automated program. This permitted these basic interpretations to be achieved by a person with no formal training in neuropsychology. For instance, the person who entered the original scoring for the neuropsychological key was a patient who had a cerebellar tumor and knew nothing about the Halstead–Reitan Battery (Russell et al., 1970, p. vii).

Rapid Development of Scoring Programs

Soon several other programs (Russell, 1995) were developed. In the 1970s, at least four full programs for assessment of the existence and lateralized brain damage were developed (Adams, 1975; Finkelstein, 1976; Russell et al., 1970; Swiercinsky, 1978).

Thus, the decade was quite productive in creating neuropsychology scoring computer programs, and it appeared that this would be the direction in which neuropsychology would develop. Once the program had been developed in its basic form, it could be expanded to include any pattern that was discovered and validated.

Butcher describes this progress in the introduction to his book *Computerized Psychological Assessment* (1987): "The rate at which computers are being adopted to clinical settings is astounding and stands as one of the most significant developments to appear in clinical practice over the past quarter century" (1987, p. xvii). Along with this general development, neuropsychological assessment had made an early and propitious beginning.

The Regression of Neuropsychology Assessment Methodology

However, in contrast to other areas of psychology (Butcher, 1987), in neuropsychology by the 1990s there had occurred a reversal in this development of assessment methods. Computerized scoring and interpretation had almost ceased to develop. From the 1980s to the present, only two new fully developed scoring programs have been published, one by Reitan (1991) and another by Russell and Starkey (1993, 2001a). The one by Russell and Starkey was a continued to improve the previous neuropsychological key (Russell, 1984). Reitan's the Neuropsychological Deficit Scale (NDS) program contains a procedure to lateralize damage (Reitan, 1991), and Russell (1984) designed the lateralization index that modified the original neuropsychological key. Thus, in 30 years from 1980 to the Meyers battery in 2000 (Volbrecht, Meyers, & Kaster-Bundgaard, 2000), only two published advances in computerized interpretation were created in neuropsychology (Reitan, 1991; Russell & Starkey, 2001b).

Nevertheless, co-norming continued to develop in other areas of neuropsychology, including test administration and scoring of single tests. Unfortunately, this has been a sideline to neuropsychology in general. For most of neuropsychology, the assessment methods have retreated to the type of judgmental intuitive approach used during the 1950s.

This raises the question of why the field of neuropsychology has lagged so far behind in interpretative programs, when it generally has better criteria for deciding the nature and existence of mental conditions than other areas of psychology.

The primary reason for this stalemate appears to be a psychological obstacle that has prevented further development in neuropsychology. The consequence is a general pessimism concerning the field. Even Faust (Faust, Ziskin, & Hiers, 1988), who is a champion of the actuarial approach to psychology, has noted this difficulty in creating a computer program for neuropsychological evaluations. The basis for this pessimism is the prevailing idea in neuropsychology that computer programs are not accurate and cannot be designed to be accurate. By contrast, clinical evaluations were portrayed as being quite accurate.

This doubt concerning the adequacy of computer scoring programs was voiced at least 13 times in the 1980s in major writings (Adams, 1986; Adams & Brown, 1986; Adams & Heaton, 1985, 1987; Adams, Kvale, & Keegan, 1984; Anthony, Heaton,

& Lehman, 1980; Faust, Ziskin, & Hiers, 1988; Golden, 1987; Heaton & Adams, 1987; Heaton, Grant, Anthony, & Lehman, 1981; Honaker & Fowler, 1990; Incagnoli, 1986; Long & Wagner, 1986; Robbins, 1989). Based on the number of times this judgment has been repeated, this skepticism appears to be warranted.

Problems with the Critique

However, if this situation is examined carefully, it is evident that the belief in the "failure" of the computerized method is not justified. Note that the major review articles that disparaged computer usage in neuropsychology were written by only two people, Adams and Heaton. Adams reiterated the critique of computer programs in six articles from 1984 to 1987, and Heaton did so in three papers during the same time period (Adams, 1986; Adams & Brown, 1986; Adams & Heaton, 1985, 1987; Adams et al., 1984; Heaton & Adams, 1987). The other writers simply referred to these authors.

On further examination, it is apparent that the basis for the contention that clinical judgment is superior to computer programs is almost unsupported by any adequate research. There are two reasons for this conclusion. First, the design of the few studies that were used to support this contention were questionable. Second, the authors completely ignored two studies that produced contrary results.

In regard to the adequacy of supporting research, the conclusion that computer scoring programs are not sufficiently accurate for clinical interpretation was based on only two studies, one completed in Heaton's laboratory (Anthony et al., 1980; Heaton et al., 1981) and one performed by Adams (Adams & Brown, 1986; Adams, et al., 1984). (The two Adams references appear to refer to the same study that was published twice.) The other writers have merely cited these studies (Faust et al., 1988; Golden, 1987; Honaker & Fowler, 1990; Incagnoli, 1986; Long & Wagner, 1986; Robbins, 1989).

Studies Opposed to Computer Scoring

Examination of these studies finds that only Heaton et al.'s (1981) study was an adequate study. The adequacy of Adams's study (Adams et al., 1984) is highly questionable. Although it compared three programs, it had no normal control group. It used a limited type of subjects, those with transient ischemic attacks (TIAs) and residual ischemic neurological deficits (RINDs) as subjects; neurology, however, does not classify these events as conditions that produce brain damage. TIAs by definition resolve in 24 hours, and a RIND usually totally resolves within 3 weeks. For both conditions, functional recovery is essentially total (Netter, Jones, & Dingle, 1986, p. 54). Thus, it is not surprising that the programs did not adequately lateralize on any of the programs. Consequently, this study ascertained nothing concerning the accuracy of any of the three computer programs to detect lateralized brain damage. As such, the results of this study were inapplicable to evaluating the accuracy of any computer programs, including the key.

The study by Heaton et al. (1981) was basically acceptable, although it had minor problems and exaggerated results. The study employed only two judges, both of whom were "experts" but unidentified. As such, they could have worked with these cases in Heaton's laboratory. These examiners' clinical judgment of lateralization as presented was more accurate than the neuropsychological key (Heaton et al., 1981). The key designated 57% correctly whereas the judges' average was 69%. (The three groups—right, left, and diffuse—had a 33.3% random chance of being right.)

Consequently, the entire conclusion concerning the accuracy of clinical judgment, which has been accepted for almost three decades, is based on the results derived from two unidentified "expert" judges. There has been no cross validation of this study. In addition, these conclusions run contrary to the experience in every other area of psychology (Faust, 1984, pp. 43–55; Grove & Meehl, 1996; Grove, Zald, Lebow, Snitz, & Nelson, 2000; Kleinmuntz, 1987; Meehl, 1954) in which the actuarial approach has been equal or superior to the clinical judgment.

Unreferenced Contrary Evidence

Even more damaging than the questionable evidence criticizing the accuracy of the key was the fact that none of the reviews of this subject by Adams and Heaton mentioned the studies that strongly questioned their results. Goldstein and Shelly (1982) reanalyzed the Anthony et al. (1980) study and demonstrated that the overall percentage of agreement between the original neuropsychological key study (Russell et al., 1970) and the cross validation was approximately equal when both sensitivity and selectivity are considered. This supported rather than disparaged the validity and utility of a computer program.

In addition, these authors did not mention two studies by Wedding (1983a, 1983b) that demonstrated that the key was almost as accurate as an experienced neuropsychologist 63% to 60% and was more accurate than all but two of 13 neuropsychologists (Garb, 1989; Russell, 1998). These inexperienced neuropsychologists averaged 54%, which was definitely below that of the key at 60%. Note that the expert in this study, at 63% correct, was not as accurate as the experts in the Heaton et al. (1981) study, which averaged 69%, even though the program was always 100% reliable.

These findings contradict the conclusion by Anthony et al. (1980) and echoed by Lezak that the neuropsychological key's accuracy was "unacceptably low for clinical purposes" (Lezak, 1995, p. 710). [Nowhere in her book or the most recent version of that book (Lezak et al., 2004) does Lezak provide any information concerning the accuracy of her method for clinical purposes.]

These analyses by Goldstein and Shelly (1982) and Wedding (1983b) demonstrated that there was almost no difference between clinical judgment and the key even for lateralization. The 1983 study by Wedding indicated that the neuropsychological key was almost as accurate as a very experienced neuropsychologist was and more accurate than less experienced neuropsychologists.

Neither study was mentioned in the subsequent papers by Adams and Heaton (Adams, 1986; Adams & Brown, 1986; Adams & Heaton, 1985, 1987; Adams et al., 1984; Heaton & Adams, 1987). Thus, this review demonstrates that at least one neuropsychology actuarial program, the key, is more accurate than nonexpert clinical judges using only test scores.

Thus, the conclusion concerning the relative accuracy of clinical evaluations and this automated interpretation program was based on only one acceptable study (Heaton et al., 1981) in which there were only two judges, both called "experts" but unidentified. This conclusion also ignored other relevant studies that demonstrated that the accuracy of the computerized program was closely equivalent to that of expert neuropsychologists while being more accurate than most nonexperts. Russell (1984) later demonstrated that improved algorithms could be more accurate than the clinical judgment. However, none of these studies has been cross validated.

Apparently, partly as a result of the Heaton and Adams writings, most clinical neuropsychologists have abandoned any interest in developing formalized or computer methods of neuropsychological assessment. Evidently, neuropsychologists felt that a formal algorithm was a threat to their way of assessment and accepted whatever evidence supported their bias. This bias is still present because only one computerized scoring program (Reitan, 1991) has been published since 1980 and there have been almost no cross-validation studies comparing formal methods such as indexes, much less computer programs.

Neuropsychological Deficit Scale

Reitan (1991; Reitan & Wolfson, 1993) developed his own computerized battery: the Neuropsychological Deficit Scale. The NDS automated the neuropsychology scoring method used with the HRB almost without modification. In this respect, it is a remarkable program. This program was designed to make scoring of the HRB more efficient and accurate and to provide a score for the existence of brain damage and a separate score for each hemisphere that could be combined into a lateralization score (Reitan, 1991). In their 1993 manual *The Halstead–Reitan Neuropsychological Test Battery: Theory and Clinical Interpretation* (2nd ed.), Reitan and Wolfson use the NDS in most of the illustrated studies they present. Subsequent evaluations have indicated that it is as accurate as Halstead's Index and any other program or index that has been compared to it. It may have some problems with older people in that it is not age corrected, but even then the studies that have been done indicate that it is accurate.

Era of the Behemoths

In the future, the current period of neuropsychological development will probably be labeled the "Era of the Behemoths." Instead of creating and testing formal methods in the years after 1985, huge amounts of published research have been collected. They contain mountains of research that has been done in the area of neuropsychological assessment. This type of research has resulted in a series of huge books that catalog studies done for various tests. Various authors appear to have attempted the cataloging of all the neuropsychological research that has been published. For instance, the Lezak, Howieson, and Loring (2004) work (the fourth edition of Lezak's book) is about twice the size of most books in neurology. It contains almost 1,000 pages. Not to be outdone, the third edition of *A Compendium of Neuropsychological Tests* (Strauss, Sherman, & Spreen, 2006) contains 1,216 pages. There is also the *Handbook of Normative Data for Neuropsychological Assessment* by Mitrushina, Boone, and D'Elia (2005), which has 531 pages devoted to 17 tests. A second version of this handbook (Mitrushina, Boone, & D'Elia, 2005) has recently been published with 1,029 pages.

These major "textbooks" in this area devote almost no space to brain function analysis but instead consist of catalogs of test studies. Some catalog tests (Strauss et al., 2006) will occasionally mention neurological conditions to which they are related. Others catalog neurological conditions with the tests that are related to them (Adams, Parsons, Culbertson, & Nixon, 1996).

What do neuropsychologists receive from all of this material other than an expensive and heavy series of books that will need to be thrown away when the next version is published? The problem is that this research is largely unconnected. They may be helpful if one wishes to have all of the studies that have been published on a particular test, but they do not help much in assessing a neuropsychological patient, with the exception of determining whether he or she does or does not have brain damage.

Almost all of this material consists of the one-test, one-condition, one-interpretation type of research. Later in discussing double-disassociation methodology, it will be demonstrated that this type of research is relatively useless to those who would assess brain damage. Because a test has not been formally associated to any other tests, it cannot be compared or even combined with other tests except by using speculative judgment.

Let us look at Lezak's tome to examine how helpful it is for neuropsychological assessment. The first section is a repetition of neurological knowledge from a neurology text presenting a considerable amount of information that is of little use to neuropsychological assessment. Then there is a section on brain analysis in which the practitioner is told to use hypothesis testing without describing what hypothesis testing is or how to do it.

Example: Alzheimer's Disease

To see how the book helps assessment, let's examine the section on Alzheimer's disease (AD) (Lezak et al., 2004). One of the major problems in neuropsychology is to distinguish AD from other dementing processes. Other than head trauma, this is probably the most studied neuropsychological condition.

The discussion of AD assessment in Lezak et al. (2004) uses 13.5 double-column pages (pp. 207–220). Seven pages (pp. 212–218) are devoted to diagnosis and contain 267 references to various studies related to that neurological condition.

The assessment first requires an examination of the entire history of a patient, including the neurological examination and neuroradiographic studies. This provides the neurological basis for the assessment. However, this may not be too helpful because 86% to 100% of the neurological diagnoses are based on biopsies or autopsies. Otherwise, the diagnosis is provisional. Nevertheless, Lezak et al. (2004) state, "Yet much of the diagnosis will ultimately rely on the quantitative pattern and qualitative characteristics of cognitive functioning elicited by neuropsychological assessment" (p. 212). Obviously, the neuropsychological examination must be highly inaccurate in distinguishing this from other dementias.

In this regard, the differentiation of multi-infarct dementia (MID) from AD is the most common differential problem related to AD (Nixon, 1996, p. 66). In Lezak et al.'s (2004) book (pp. 201–202), there is almost no discussion as to how to separate MID from AD other than to state, "In some cases the manifestations of MID are sufficiently like those of Alzheimer's disease that it has been mistaken for it" (p. 202). Thus, the brief neuropsychological test results would not enable a neuropsychologist to separate MID from AD.

The differentiating cognitive characteristics of AD are later described. These include visual dysfunction (p. 213), olfactory impairment, and complex motor task impairment. There is loss of spontaneity. Nearly all aspects of attention and orientation are impaired. Almost all types of memory are impaired (Table 7.5, pp. 215, 216). Verbal functions are impaired, including word generation, confrontation naming (p. 216), speech organization, reading, writing, and arithmetic. Verbal memory deficiencies may show up several years before dementia is obvious (p. 214). Concerning visuospatial functions, complex functions are impaired including constructional abilities (p. 217). There are apraxias. Thinking and reasoning become impaired from the earliest stages of the disease, as do executive functions including self-awareness. Thus, almost every mental function is impaired.

This was similar to the finding by Mathias and Burke (2009) who used meta-analysis to examine 81 studies. They found that only two rather obscure tests differentiated Alzheimer's dementia from vascular dementia. One of these tests (emotional recognition) was given in only two studies. The other (delayed story recall) was more common. The general conclusion was that it was extremely difficult for neuropsychological tests to separate these conditions.

Thus, in spite of all of their discussion, Lezak et al. (2004) apparently provide no information as to how to separate Alzheimer's disease from any other neurological condition other than to examine the neurologist's diagnosis in the hospital record. In other words, the book contains almost no information helpful to a neuropsychologist who is concerned with distinguishing AD from other neurological conditions, especially MID, by means of neuropsychological test results alone.

Patterns for Alzheimer's Disease

However, two patterns of test results distinguish AD from other neurological conditions, neither of which is mentioned in Lezak et al.'s (2004) lengthy discussion that catalogs a huge number of studies devoted to AD. What is even more astounding is that the diagnostic patterns that distinguish these conditions are presented in the studies by Lezak et al. (2004) but are unrecognized.

The first pattern is the relatively well-known fluidity pattern (Barron & Russell, 1992; Russell, 1979, 1980). It is discussed in several other places. Basically, well-learned material, including digit span forward, is retained but functions that require novel cognitive processing such as solving puzzles (e.g., block design) are impaired.

An examination of those functions that Lezak et al. (2004, pp. 212–218) described as being less impaired by AD generally fit this crystallized versus fluid intelligence pattern. Although this pattern applies to many different, diffuse neurological conditions, it is highly characteristic of AD. However, by itself it would not differentiate many conditions such as separating MID from AD.

The second pattern is that pure motor functions and sensory functions that do not contain much cognitive involvement are almost unaffected by AD until late in the development of this disease. The finding that a pattern in which pure motor functioning is almost unimpaired was published by Hom in 1992. Completely independently, this pattern was described by Russell and Polakoff in 1993. (For an unknown reason, the severe alcoholic pattern is almost the same as the AD pattern.) The paper describing this pattern even provided a formula for distinguishing AD from MID. This formula is included in the Halstead–Russell Neuropsychological Evaluation System—Revised (HRNES-R) scoring program (Appendix F, p. 26) (Russell & Starkey, 2001a, Appendix F., p. 26). It is also more thoroughly discussed later in this book. (A typographical error gave the cut point as 14 instead of 1.4.)

Although the retained motor ability was primarily an AD pattern, Lezak et al. (2004) mention that MID often impairs motor functioning, which is part of the pattern that distinguishes AD from MID. What is even more remarkable is that the AD pattern is described in Lezak et al. (2004) in this manner, "Contrasting with the dismal picture of memory and learning … is evidence that learning ability for simple motor and skill tasks is relatively preserved" (p. 216). Thus, the distinguishing feature between AD and MID can be stated in a paragraph but was not in Lezak et al.'s (2004) tome.

Summary

In summary, the discussion concerning AD is characteristic of these giant volumes that catalog neuropsychological testing. They provide little aid to the neuropsychologist who is attempting to use test batteries to assess hospitalized or forensic subjects. In general, they present large numbers of studies and sets of norms related to AD without providing information as to how they are used to distinguish AD from most other types of brain damage in actual assessment.

In all of these behemoths there is currently almost no test patterns or information to guide assessment in neuropsychology other than to separate brain-damaged from normal subjects. Although there is a highly developed theory of neurology, there is almost no neuropsychological theory that connects psychological or neuropsychological tests to neurology that could contribute to neurological diagnosis.

Comparison to Neurology Textbooks

If one compares these tomes to textbooks in neurology, we find that the basic instrumentation used in neurology is discussed in one small section and that the research basis for a neurological examination is not presented. There may be a review of anatomical neurology, but it will be limited. The assumption is that microanatomy is better described in other books. The major portion of the neurology textbook is devoted to the description of pathological conditions in terms of diagnostic patterns. The vast literature concerning medical conditions and the research supporting these conditions is neither presented nor discussed. The conditions are described as *syndromes* in such a way that they can be identified and discriminated from each other. The emphasis is placed on recognizing and diagnosing the conditions.

As an example, a neurology textbook designed for regular medical students and general practitioners is *Modern Practical Neurology* (1977) by Peritz Scheinberg, the previous chairman of the University of Miami Medical School's neurology department. It is only 247 pages long but summarized the entire field of neurology. As an example of a neurology textbook, Chusid's (1985) *Correlative Microanatomy and Functional Neurology* (19th ed.), which covered the field of neurology in some detail, contained 513 pages. It contained almost no references to studies and only described the neurological instrumentation briefly.

By comparison, in neuropsychology textbooks, there are hundreds of tests that are related to various neuropathologies, but the relationships between different tests are seldom discussed in any formal manner. No patterns of relationships between tests are presented. In fact, although vaguely aware that such patterns do exist, neuropsychology has no formal recognition of any patterns. Even in regard to the diagnosis of brain damage, usually one group of tests in a battery will indicate damage and another will not. Not even here does traditional neuropsychology have any reliable method to separate brain-damage from normal subjects. Such separation can only be reliably and validly accomplished by means of indexes, which are lacking in the flexible battery approach.

Contemporary Neuropsychology

Since the 1980s, neuropsychological assessment has entered a static period. Its basic methodology has not improved in the last half century with the exception of two areas. These areas are predicting premorbid ability and determining whether a patient is malingering or at least intentionally underperforming ["poor motivation" or "symptom validity testing" (SVT)]. Although most neuropsychological reports, particularly forensic reports, provide a considerable number of interpretive details concerning a patient's neurological condition in addition to whether he or she is brain damaged, almost none of these "interpretations," even including the diagnosis of brain damage, is based on evidence that is validated. The reliability of this information is based on the "education," "experience," and, in many cases, the certifications the neuropsychologist has received. There is no evidence that any of these three "indications of ability" makes the neuropsychologist's interpretations or forensic opinions any more accurate than that of any other neuropsychologist (Garb, 1998, pp. 166–170). In fact, except for individual tests in the neuropsychologist battery, there is no evidence that the interpretations of the existence of brain damage have any validity. The evidence in a battery is often contradictory because the same battery may have both impaired and unimpaired tests. Almost all tests that are used by neuropsychologist are validated, but there is almost no validation of their accuracy as part of a battery.

Thus, at present, confusion appears to dominate this field. One approach to clarify this situation might be to use the admonition of Reitan (1962) and Matarazzo (1972) that "brain damage" is not a single entity: "Failure by many psychologists and others to understand the vast clinical complexities associated with this seemingly simple diagnosis led to a myriad of confusing research findings in psychological literature during the past several decades" (Matarazzo, 1972, p. 378). This conclusion has not appreciable changed since it was published in 1972. The different types of damage might be expected to produce different patterns of effects, and consequently the selection of proper groups of tests becomes crucial to demonstrate those effects.

In spite of all of the tomes, neuropsychological assessment is still largely an intuitive process in which each neuropsychologist uses his or her own intuition. The assessment ability of neuropsychologists, when tests are flexibly selected, has no demonstrated reliability or validity beyond the fact that individual tests indicate brain damage (Garb, 1998, pp. 157, 168–170), and almost every battery has both normal and impaired tests.

Areas of Progress

The major areas in which there has been progress is in the development of methods to estimate a subject's premorbid ability and methods for determining whether a patient is malingering or at least intentionally underperforming. These, of course, are necessary in order to compare a subject's current functioning to his or her estimated previous level of functioning and to determine whether the subject is putting forth his or her best effort after brain damage may have occurred. Both are necessary in evaluating a patient's current functioning. Although these are crucial in evaluating the validity of test results, they are well covered in other writings and will be mentioned only briefly.

Premorbid Estimates

One major requirement for an integrated neuropsychological battery is that it correct or adjust for basic human characteristics of age, gender, and premorbid ability level. Because brain damage affects cognitive ability levels, the assessment must estimate the patient's premorbid cognitive ability level in some manner. Cognitive ability is usually determined by IQ, so the measures of premorbid ability are essentially measures of premorbid IQ.

In the last few years, a great deal of work has been accomplished on this characteristic. Several formal methods, particularly formulas, have been proposed to estimate premorbid IQ levels (Schinka & Vanderploeg, 2000). This is one area in which formulas are well accepted in neuropsychology. Although educational level is probably the single best estimate of premorbid ability, it is only moderately accurate and other methods have been devised that are somewhat more accurate. These methods are thoroughly discussed, along with advice about how to use them, in Schinka and Vanderploeg's (2000) chapter "Estimating Premorbid Level of Functioning." They discuss various formal methods and formulas as well as present their own.

In this regard, note that because most neuropsychologists use a flexible method of determining what tests to use, in most assessments neuropsychologists are generally unable to consistently estimate premorbid ability levels of the tests in their batteries. Although it is possible to make the proper adjustments to each test in the extensive battery, it would be a very time-consuming task. Only the HRNES-R (Russell & Starkey, 2001b, pp. 39–67) can incorporate the results of a premorbid ability formula directly into the program. The program corrects all scores for the cognitive ability of the individual based on prior testing, educational level, or premorbid estimation formula.

Although the Heaton, Miller, Taylor, and Grant (2004) Revised Comprehensive Norms for an Expanded Halstead–Reitan Battery (RCNEHRB) have corrections for age, the correction for IQ is derived from education level alone so that it is less adequate than when other factors are also included.

Malingering Patterns

An adequate assessment of malingering or at least intentionally underperforming ("poor motivation," "invalid test results," or SVT) requires two parts to the assessment. The first is an impaired score on at least one well-validated SVT; the second is a patient's invalid test pattern.

Concerning the SVT, today a test of motivation is a required test for any assessment, particularly for an assessment to have any forensic credibility. However, a discussion of SVTs will not be attempted in this book because there is an extensive literature (Larrabee, 2005, pp. 92–158), much of which is excellent, and this field is rapidly changing.

Two methods that use test results are effective in determining invalid assessment patterns. One is to examine the pattern of tests in a single administration of a battery. The other is to compare the results of a test and retest for the same person.

When using a single administration, in their well-known study of malingering, Heaton, Smith, Lehman, and Vogt (1978) used a battery consisting of the WAIS, HRB, and the Minnesota Multiphasic Personality Inventory. It was found that, although the level of impairment was equivalent for the brain-damaged and normal subjects who were attempting to malinger, blind evaluations by 10 judges who were trained neuropsychologists were almost unable to separate the groups. Their accuracy varied between zero and 20% correct. By contrast, discriminant function separated 100% of the normal subjects who attempted to malinger from the brain-damaged subjects. This accuracy for clinical judgment is obviously not sufficient for clinical purposes. However, because the overall level of impairment was the same for the two groups, the distinction that the discriminant function found was the result of a different pattern of impairment.

Reitan (Reitan & Wolfson, 1997) observed, "It is difficult to avoid concluding that the accuracy could have been improved if the judges had used an approach that evaluated the interrelationships of test results rather than an approach that reviewed tests essentially as independent measures. One of the major advantages of using a test battery is that it yields scores whose relationships can provide critical interpretive information" (p. 15).

brain-function analysis. In fact, most neuropsychologists would have great difficulty in making an assessment if they had to use blind analysis.

For neuropsychology to make a contribution to medicine or other disciplines related to the mental condition of humans, neuropsychology needs to be able to analyze brain functioning in isolation. It must be able to describe brain functioning in addition to determining whether damage exists and do so entirely from neuropsychological assessment batteries.

Although Reitan and his students were able to diagnose many types of pathologies, their clinical judgment technique was not well described in the literature. It was mostly presented by means of case histories rather than by describing established patterns in a formal manner (Reitan & Wolfson, 1993, pp. 405–823). In addition, it required comparisons that generally used a fixed or standardized battery, and a great deal of experience or training with an expert was necessary to develop the expertise required by the procedure. In this regard, there have been almost no adequate studies of the accuracy of neuropsychological assessment using blind analysis in the last few decades.

Limited Ability of Batteries

The result was that the ability to diagnose conditions and perform differential diagnosis in particular is beyond the capacity of flexible batteries. With the exception of a few people who have had great experience in the area, most neuropsychologists are unable to separate types of pathologies.

In addition, the neuropsychologist may make some estimate as to how well a patient can function and the amount of improvement that may be expected. However, this estimate is still a rather crude clinical judgment. Basically, most neuropsychologists are "flying by the seat of their pants" in using their knowledge of what the tests apparently are measuring.

Consequently, a neuropsychological battery currently has little function other than to determine the existence of brain damage. Because it only requires a few accurate tests (Spreen & Benton, 1965) to determine the existence of brain damage, there is a real question as to why a large battery is needed. In forensics, the primary function is to determine the existence of brain damage. How did the field become so stagnant?

The only area in which the neuropsychologist has a particular expertise is in assessing impairment of cognitive functioning and, to a lesser extent, affective functioning. This is done through using tests. This analysis using tests is what I have delineated as *brain-function analysis*. As a result, it is the area that neuropsychologists should be able handle without recourse to areas that are more properly those of neurology and psychiatry. These other areas consist of the context of an examination.

Dependency on Context

Unfortunately, a majority of neuropsychologists who claim that one is unable to adequately examine brain functioning without knowledge of the neurological and psychiatric examination results. This is the claim that one can obtain no information concerning brain functioning from tests without the context.

In actual malingering or attempted malingering, it is very difficult for a p even a "sophisticated" person (trained by an attorney or a student) to avoid pr ing an "unnatural" pattern or a pattern on a test battery that is inconsistent wit form of brain damage. Thus, the primary cue of "poor motivation" is a pattern "does not make neurological sense." In regard to such patterns, most naive m gerers (including many intelligent professionals) do not know, which patterns any battery of neuropsychological tests are believable and which are not. They not know that some tests in such a battery are "hold" tests that are less affected brain damage and others are "don't hold" tests. It is not uncommon for a subj with questionable motivation to do well on tests sensitive to brain damage while pr viding scores on other tests that would categorize the subject as severely demente Consequently, it is extremely important for the examiner to know various patholog cal patterns in order to distinguish the spurious ones.

The lack of pattern soundness is much more obvious on a standardized battery than on an ad hoc battery. With a standardized battery, experience teaches the neuropsychologist which patterns are and are not expected for various pathologies. Experience is extremely difficult to attain unless the examiner uses a consistent battery for all examinations. Finally, with an integrated battery the invalid patterns can be taught to other neuropsychologists when the various neuropsychologists use the same group of tests.

The second means of using patterns in a neuropsychological examination is to present the same battery of tests to a patient twice at different times. This is the method championed by Reitan and Wolfson (1997). This method uses inconsistent individual comparisons, thus, "using the subject as [his or her] own control" (p. 25). This method is based on the concept that subjects who are not putting forth their best effort respond in a less-consistent manner than subjects who are motivated to do their best, even when they are brain damaged. There is a rather strong pattern consistency for a brain-damaged patient even though the pattern may be very abnormal. This method is well described in Reitan and Wolfson's (1997) book *Detection of Malingering and Invalid Test Scores*. It also includes several tables and validation procedures. Although this method is quite valid, a description of it is beyond the scope of this writing.

In this regard, I tested a patient whose tactile performance test had initially indicated right-hemisphere damage but a year later indicated left-hemisphere damage.

Areas of Stagnation

Probably the major difficulty in neuropsychology today is that neuropsychological assessment appears to have no particular validated function other than diagnosing the existence of brain damage. Beginning with the work of Reitan, the earlier argument between the quantitative and qualitative approaches to neuropsychology became the argument between "fixed" and "flexible" approaches.

When the medical history of a person is read before testing, a neuropsychologist can make rather accurate appraisals of the person. However, most of the information needed for the appraisals comes from the patient's history and not from

Most neuropsychologists with such a background of dependence on the results on neurologists and psychiatrists would be completely helpless if they had to perform a blind analysis on neuropsychological assessment data. The blind analysis, of course, removes the context (except the patient's age, gender, and education) and requires the neuropsychologists to obtain all of his or her information from test results alone. Although the final interpretation requires integration of brain functions with the context, a remarkable amount of information can be derived from test results alone.

Neurological Scanning Techniques

Probably the major new technology in neurology that has most affected neuropsychology is the development of various scanning techniques, particularly the magnetic resonance imaging. For many kinds of neurological pathologies, these techniques are highly accurate in determining the existence of brain damage and its location. These techniques also provide information that aids in diagnosing the type of pathology. Consequently, much of the advantage of neuropsychological techniques was removed.

However, in various areas, particularly head trauma, the scanning techniques are still not highly accurate because of the diffuse nature of the lesion. In addition, scanning techniques cannot accurately determine the amount of impairment and thus, in many cases, the prognosis of the brain condition. It is in these areas where neuropsychological procedures may still make a major contribution. This is particularly true in the forensic area because so many of the litigation cases involve head trauma or diffuse conditions such as anoxia or carbon monoxide brain damage. However, in most cases, the size of the battery that is necessary to determine the existence of damage is far too large. Moreover, in forensic reports many neuropsychologists elaborate on the damage in ways that are reliably impossible.

Revival of Formal Methodology

One historical characteristic of science is that if a procedure or concept that has been validated but is then repudiated or ignored so that it has largely disappeared from scientific intercourse, it will reappear. This is because when a procedure or information is validated, it is grounded on the character of the real world and is therefore "truth." Such reality remains constant, and thus validated methods or information is rediscoverable.

Reintroduction of Co-Normed Batteries

Quite recently, there has been a "return of the repressed." At least five co-normed standardized batteries have been published and validated. The first of these methods was a further development of the neuropsychological key. In 1993, Russell and Starkey published the Halstead–Russell Neuropsychological Evaluation System (HRNES) which has been revised as the HRNES–R (Russell & Starkey, 2001b). It appears to be as accurate and relevant for testing today as it has been for a number years. Although the Heaton et al. (2004) Revised Comprehensive Norms for an Expanded Halstead–Reitan Battery (RCNEHRB) provide a highly extensive set of norms, these are only partially co-normed. The Neuropsychological Deficit Scale (Reitan, 1986) computerizes Reitan's method quite exactly and is as accurate as any other method even today.

Although other computer programs have been developed for scoring co-normed neuropsychological batteries, several co-normed batteries have been produced. These include the Meyers Neuropsychological Battery (MNB) (Meyers & Rohling, 2004; Volbrecht et al., 2000) and the Neuropsychological Assessment Battery (NAB) (Stern & White, 2001). Subsequent work by Russell and Starkey on the HRNES-R (2001c) has created a battery that appears to be as accurate as clinical judgment. It is also far more comprehensive than any other standardized battery that has been developed. However, these new methods have never formally compared the methods to clinical judgment.

Computerized Assessment

Another major development that has not yet been completely coordinated with the rest of neuropsychology is the development of computerized assessment. Beginning in the early 1980s (Kane & Kay, 1992; Reeves, Winter, Bleiberg, & Kane, 2007), several neuropsychologists, particularly those in the military, began to develop batteries of tests that were administered by computers (Kane & Kay, 1992). These computerized assessment batteries have advanced fairly rapidly to the present (Kane, 2007).

Computers have several advantages over individually presented tests. First, they can present an entire process of testing from administration to interpretation (which is currently fairly limited) in one program. The results of the administration can be obtained within a brief time after the patient has completed testing. All of these processes are objective and can be easily repeated. Second, computer administration is highly standardized and therefore less subject to the idiosyncrasies of an administrator. Third, the scoring is 100% reliable because it is repeated by automation. Fourth, except for a moderately trained technician to monitor the test administration, no neuropsychologists is required. As previously mentioned, at least one program—MindStreams (Simon et al., 2000)—produces a printout that provides a medical doctor with the information that he or she needs about the cognitive abilities of the tested individual.

Several other batteries have been developed for specialized purposes, and some of these major batteries have been reviewed recently (Crook, Kay, & Larrabee, 2009). One of these major batteries is the Automated Neuropsychological Assessment Metrics (ANAM) (Reeves et al., 2007), which was originally developed for the Department of Defense 20 years ago. The battery has a number of variations and was developed for many uses. MicroCog is another of these computerized batteries (Powell, Kaplan, Whitla, Weintraub, Catlin, & Funkenstein, 1993). This general neuropsychology instrument was originally designed to identify the cognitive status of physicians and other professionals. Five major domains are assessed, but it cannot score motor ability. Its validity was determined by correlating the tests with known regular known neuropsychological intelligence tests. This validity seems to be reasonable.

CogScreen (Kay, 1995) was developed to detect changes in cognitive function of pilots, and it has been used extensively for the purpose. It measures a fairly wide spectrum of domains. Now it is being used by some hospitals as well as the Federal Aviation Administration.

The Psychologix Battery (Larrabee & Crook, 1991) was designed as a memory battery using everyday stimuli rather than traditional stimuli. Stimuli that are immediately relevant to everyday memory are used to test various types of memory that are usually used by neuropsychologists. Like many memory tests, it is sensitive to age and many conditions that affect memory.

In some ways, considering the vast potential of computerized testing, its development has been rather slow. The reasons are partly a lack of funding and partly that fewer neuropsychologists are involved in developing each particular battery. Also, with the exception of a few batteries such as ANAM, there appears to be little progress in the development of the battery once it has been established. None of the batteries appears to be a thorough measure of the same functions that are found in established traditional batteries. To some extent, this is because it is difficult to translate the standard types of tests into computerized versions.

At this point in neuropsychology, computerized assessment has not become prevalent. Apparently, it is not used in forensic evaluations. In part, this may be because neuropsychologists are reluctant to adopt new procedures for assessment. In addition, there appears to be limited funding for such tests, with the exception of the military and a few limited agencies. Again, an exception is MindStreams, which appears to have a great deal of funding support and is also designing its application to appeal to the medical profession rather than neuropsychologists. However, when the proper methods for transforming standard neuropsychological methods into a computerized form are developed, this method should be found to be as reliable as the standard methods. It is obviously more effective and less expensive than standard methods.

The Future of Neuropsychological Assessment

As mentioned at the beginning of this chapter, in the history of science one principle holds that once a valid scientific discovery or method has been produced, no matter how thoroughly it has been rejected, it will eventually be rediscovered or re-created.

What this means for the history of scientific neuropsychological assessment is that the formal methods that have been developed to this point but which have been largely rejected by the majority of neuropsychologists will inevitably be reintroduced to the field of neuropsychological assessment. They are based on a scientific foundation that does not change. We have already seen instances of this reintroduction. Thus, although largely ignored by present-day neuropsychologists, the work of Reitan and the creation of co-normed, integrated, and comprehensive automated batteries will be perceived by future generations as comprising the true developmental road of scientific neuropsychological assessment.

References

Adams, K. M. (1975). Automated clinical interpretation of the neuropsychological test battery: An ability based approach. *Dissertation Abstracts International, 35*, 6085B. (University Microfilms No. 75-13, 289).

Adams, K. M. (1986). Concepts and methods in the design of automata for the neuropsychological test interpretation. In S. B. Filskov & T. J. Boll (Eds.), *Handbook of clinical neuropsychology* (Vol. 2, pp. 561–575). New York: John Wiley & Sons.

Adams, K. M., & Brown, G. G. (1986). The role of the computer in neuropsychological assessment. In I. Grant & K. M. Adams (Eds.), *Neuropsychological assessment of neuropsychiatric disorders* (pp. 87–99). New York: Oxford University Press.

Adams, K. M., & Heaton, R. K. (1985). Automated interpretation of neuropsychological test data. *Journal of Consulting and Clinical Psychology, 53*, 790–802.

Adams, K. M., & Heaton, R. K. (1987). Computerized neuropsychological assessment: Issues and applications. In J. N. Butcher (Ed.), *Computerized psychological assessment* (pp. 355–365). New York: Basic Books.

Adams, K. M., Kvale, V. I., & Keegan, J. F. (1984). Relative accuracy of three automated systems for neuropsychological interpretation. *Journal of Clinical Neuropsychology, 6*, 413–431.

Adams, L. R., Parsons, O. A., Culbertson, J. L., & Nixon, S. J. (Eds.), (1996). *Neuropsychology for clinical practice: Etiology, assessment, and treatment of common neurological disorders*. Washington, DC: American Psychological Association.

Anthony, W. Z., Heaton, R. K., & Lehman, R. A. W. (1980). An attempt to cross-validate two actuarial systems for neuropsychological test interpretation. *Journal of Consulting and Clinical Psychology, 48*, 317–326.

Barron, J. H., & Russell, E. W. (1992). Fluidity theory and the neuropsychological impairment in alcoholism. *Archives of Clinical Neuropsychology, 7*(2), 175–188.

Behemoths, *Encyclopaedia Britannica. Ultimate Reference Suite*. Chicago: Encyclopaedia Britannica.

Bender, L. (1938). A visual motor Gestalt and its clinical use. American Orthopsychiatry Association, Research Monograph 3.

Benton, A. L. (1974). *Revised Visual Retention Test* (4th Ed). New York: Psychological Corporation.

Butcher, J. N. (Ed.). (1987). *Computerized psychological assessment*. New York: Basic Books.

Butler, M., Retzlaff, P., & Vanderploeg, R. (1991). Neuropsychological test usage. *Professional Psychology: Research and Practice, 22*, 510–512.

Christensen, A. L. (1984). The Luria method of examination of the brain-impaired patient. In P. E. Logue & J. M. Shear (Eds.), *Clinical neuropsychology: A multidisciplinary approach* (pp. 5–2849). Springfield, Ill: Charles C. Thomas.

Crook, T. H., Kay, G. G., & Larrabee, G. J. (2009). Computer-based cognitive testing. In I. Grant & K. M. Adams (Eds.), *Neuropsychological assessment of neuropsychiatric disorders* (3rd ed.). New York: Oxford University Press.

Chusid, J. G. (1985). *Correlative neuroanatomy and functional neurology* (19th ed.). Los Altos, CA: Lang Medical Publications.

Delis, D. C., Kramer, J. H., Kaplan, E., & Ober, B. (1987). *CVLT: California Verbal Learning Test–Research edition*. New York: Psychological Corporation.

Dodrill, C. B. (1997). Myths of neuropsychology. *Clinical Neuropsychologist, 11*, 1–17.

Faust, D. (1984). *The limits of scientific reasoning*. Minneapolis, MN: University of Minnesota Press.

Faust, D., Ziskin, J., & Hiers, J. B. (1988). *Brain damage claims: Coping with neuropsychological evidence*. Los Angeles: Law and Psychology Press.

Finkelstein, J. N. (1976). BRAIN: A computer program for interpretation of the Halstead–Reitan Neuropsychology Test Battery. (Doctoral dissertation, Columbia University.) Dissertations Abstracts International, 37, 5349B. (University Microfilms No. 77-8, 8864).

Garb, H. N. (1989). Clinical judgment, clinical training, and professional experience. *Psychological Bulletin, 105*, 387–396.

Garb, H. N. (1998). *Studying the clinician: Judgment research and psychological assessment*. Washington, DC: American Psychological Association.

Golden, C. J. (1987). Computers in neuropsychology. In J. N. Butcher (Ed.), *Computerized psychological assessment* (pp. 344–354). New York: Basic Books.

Goldstein, K. (1939). *The organism*. New York: American Book Company.

Goldstein, K., & Scheerer, M. (1941). Abstract and concrete behavior: An experimental study with special tests. *Psychological Monographs, 53*(2) Whole No. 239.

Goldstein, G., & Shelly, C. H. (1982). A further attempt to cross-validate the Russell, Neuringer, and Goldstein neuropsychological keys. *Journal of Consulting and Clinical Psychology, 50*, 721–726.

Graham, F. K., & Kendall, B. S. (1960). Memory-for-Designs test: Revised general manual. *Perceptual and motor skills, 11*(Suppl. No. 2–VII), 147–188.

Grove, W. M., & Meehl, P. E. (1996). Comparative efficiency of informal (subjective) impressionistic and formal (mechanical, algorithmic) prediction procedures, The clinical-statistical controversy. *Psychology, Public Policy, and Law*, 2(2), 293–323.

Grove, W. M., Zald, D. H., Lebow, B. S., Snitz, B. E., & Nelson, C. (2000). Clinical versus mechanical prediction, A meta-analysis. *Psychological Assessment, 12*(1), 19–30.

Guilford, J. P. (1967). *The nature of human intelligence*. New York: McGraw-Hill.

Halstead, W. C. (1947). *Brain and intelligence*. Chicago: University of Chicago Press.

Heaton, R. K., & Adams, K. M. (1987). Potential versus current reality of automation in neuropsychology: Reply to Kleinmuntz. *Journal of Consulting and Clinical Psychology, 55*, 268–269.

Heaton, R. K., Grant, I., Anthony, W. Z., & Lehman, R. A. W. (1981). A comparison of clinical and automated interpretation of the Halstead–Reitan Battery. *Journal of Clinical Neuropsychology, 22*, 121–141.

Heaton, R. K., Miller, S. W., Taylor, M. J., & Grant, I. (2004). *Revised comprehensive norms for an expanded Halstead–Reitan Battery*. Odessa, FL: Psychological Assessment Resources. [Manual and Computer program].

Heaton, R. K., Smith, H. H., Lehman, R. A. W., & Vogt, A. T. (1978). Prospects for faking believable deficits on neuropsychological testing. *Journal of Consulting and Clinical Psychology, 46*, 892–900.

Hebb, D. O. (1949). *Organization of behavior: A neuropsychological theory*. New York: John Wiley.

Hom, J. (1992). General and specific cognitive dysfunctions in patients with Alzheimer's Disease. *Archives of Clinical Neuropsychology, 7*, 121–133.

Honaker, L. M. & Fowler, R. D. (1990). Computer-assisted Psychological Assessment. In G. Goldstein & M. Hersen (Eds.), *Handbook of psychological assessment* (pp. 521–546). New York: Pergamon.

Incagnoli, T. (1986). Current directions and future trends in clinical neuropsychology. In T. Incagnoli, G. Goldstein & C. G. Golden (Eds.), *Clinical application of neuropsychological test batteries* (pp. 1–44). New York: Plenum.

Kane, R. L. (2007). Editorial: Introduction to this supplement. *Archives of Clinical Neuropsychology, 22S1*, S3–S5.

Kane, R. L., & Kay, G. G. (1992). Computerized assessment in neuropsychology: A review of tests and test batteries. *Neuropsychology Review, 3*, 1–117.

Kaplan, E. (1988). A process approach to neuropsychological assessment. In T. Boll & B. K. Brynt (Eds.), *Clinical neuropsychology and brain function: Research, measurement, and practice* (pp. 125–168). Washington, DC: American Psychological Association.

Kay, G. G. (1995). *Cog-Screen: Aeromedical edition.* Odessa, FL: Psychological Assessment Resources. [Professional manual].

Kleinmuntz (1987).

Larrabee, G. J. (Ed.). (2005). *Forensic neuropsychology: A scientific approach.* New York: Oxford University Press.

Larrabee, G. J., & Crook, T. H. (1991). Computerized memory tested in clinical trials. In E. Mohr & P. Brouwers (Eds.), *Handbook of clinical trials: The neurobehavioral approach* (pp. 293–306). Amsterdam: Swets & Zeitlinger.

Lashley, K. S. (1929). *Brain mechanisms and intelligence.* Chicago: University of Chicago Press.

Lezak, M. D. (1988). IQ: R.I.P. *Journal of Clinical and Experimental Neuropsychology, 10*, 351–361.

Lezak, M. D. (1995). *Neuropsychological assessment* (3rd ed.). New York: Oxford University Press.

Lezak, M. D., Howieson, D. B., & Loring, D. W. (2004). *Neuropsychological assessment* (4th ed.). New York: Oxford University Press.

Long, C. J., & Wagner, M. (1986). Computer applications in neuropsychology. In D. Wedding, A. M. Horton & J. Webster (Eds.), *The neuropsychology handbook* (pp. 548–569). New York: Springer.

Luria, A. R. (1973). *The working brain.* New York: Basic Books.

Luria, A. R., & Majovski, L. V. (1977). Basic approaches used in American and Soviet clinical neuropsychology. *American Psychologist, 32*, 959–968.

Matarazzo, J. D. (1972). *Measurement and appraisal of adult intelligence* (5th ed.). Baltimore: Williams & Wilkins.

Mathias, J. L., & Burke, J. (2009). Cognitive functioning in Alzheimer's and vascular dementia: A meta-analysis. *Neuropsychology, 23*(4), 411–423.

Meehl, P. E. (1954). *Clinical versus statistical prediction: A theoretical analysis and a review of the evidence.* Minneapolis: University of Minnesota Press.

Meyers, J. E., & Rohling, M. L. (2004). Validation of the Myers short battery on mild TBI patients. *Archives of Clinical Neuropsychology, 19*(5), 637–651.

Mitrushina, M. N., Boone, K. B., & D'Elia, L. F. (2005). *Handbook of normative data for neuropsychological assessment* (2nd ed.). New York: Oxford University Press.

Netter, F. H., Jones, H. R., & Dingle, R. V. (1986). *The Ciba collection of medical illustrations. Vol. 1: Nervous system. Part II Neurologic and neuromuscular disorders.* West Caldwell, NJ: Ciba.

Nixon, S. J. (1996). Alzheimer's disease and vascular dementia. In L. A. Russell, O. A. Parsons, J. L. Culbertson & S. J. Nixon (Eds.), *Neuropsychology for clinical practice: Etiology, assessment, and treatment of common neurological disorders* (pp. 65–105). Washington, DC: American Psychological Association.

Powell, D. H., Kaplan, E. F., Whitla, D., Weintraub, S., Catlin, R., & Funkenstein, H. H. (1993). *MicroCog: Assessment of cognitive functioning*. San Antonio, TX: Psychological Corporation. [Manual and Computer program].

Reeves, D. L., Winter, K. P., Bleiberg, J., & Kane, R. L. (2007). ANAM genogram: Historical perspectives, description, and current endeavors. *Archives of Clinical Neuropsychology, 22S*, S15–S37.

Reitan, R. M. (1955). Investigation of the validity of Halstead's measures of biological intelligence. *Archives of Neurology and Psychiatry, 73*, 28–35.

Reitan, R. M. (1959). The comparative effects of brain damage on the Halstead impairment index and the Wechsler-Bellevue scale. *Journal of Clinical Psychology, 15*, 281–285.

Reitan, R. M. (1962). Psychological deficit. *Annual Review of Psychology, 13*, 415–444.

Reitan, R. M. (1964). Psychological deficits resulting from cerebral lesions in men. In J. M. Warren & K. Akert (Eds.), *The frontal granular cortex and behavior* (pp. 295–312). New York: McGraw-Hill.

Reitan, R. M. (1986). *The Neuropsychological Deficit Scale for adults*. Tucson: Neuropsychology Press. [Computer program].

Reitan, R. M. (1991). *The Neuropsychological Deficit Scale for adults computer program, in the Manual from Traumatic Brain Injury Vol. II: Recovery and Rehabilitation*. Tucson: Neuropsychology Press.

Reitan, R. M., & Wolfson, D. (1993). *The Halstead–Reitan neuropsychological test battery: Theory and clinical interpretation* (2nd ed.). Tucson: Neuropsychology Press.

Reitan, R. M., & Wolfson, D. (1997). *Detection of malingering and invalid test scores*. Tucson: Neuropsychology Press.

Robbins, D. E. (1989). The Halstead-Reitan Neuropsychological Battery. In M. D. Franzen (Ed.), *Reliability and validity in neuropsychological assessment* (pp. 91–107). New York: Plenum.

Russell, E. W. (1968). Neuropsychological keys for assessing the localization and process status of cerebral damage. PhD dissertation University of Kansas. Dissertation Abstracts International, 68, 17,448 (University Microfilms No. 68-17, 448).

Russell, E. W. (1979). Three patterns of brain damage on the WAIS. *Journal of Clinical Psychology, 35*(3), 611–620.

Russell, E. W. (1980). Fluid and crystallized intelligence: Effects of diffuse brain damage on the WAIS. *Perceptual and Motor Skills, 51*, 121–122.

Russell, E. W. (1984). Theory and developments of pattern analysis methods related to the Halstead–Reitan Battery. In P. E. Logue & J. M. Shear (Eds.), *Clinical neuropsychology: A multidisciplinary approach* (pp. 50–98). Springfield, IL: Charles C. Thomas.

Russell, E. W. (1995). The accuracy of automated and clinical detection of brain damage and lateralization in neuropsychology. *Neuropsychology Review, 5*(1), 1–68.

Russell, E. W. (1998). In defense of the Halstead–Reitan Battery: A critique of Lezak's review. *Archives of Clinical Neuropsychology, 13*(1), 365–381.

Russell, E. W. (2010). The "obsolescence" of assessment procedures. *Applied Neuropsychology, 17*(1), 60–67.

Russell, E. W., Neuringer, C., & Goldstein, G. (1970). *Assessment of brain damage: A neuropsychological key approach*. New York: Wiley Company.

Russell, E. W., & Polakoff, D. (1993). Neuropsychological test patterns in men for Alzheimer's and multi-infarct dementia. *Archives of Clinical Neuropsychology, 8*, 327–343.

Russell, E. W., & Starkey, R. I. (1993). *Halstead, Russell neuropsychological evaluation system*. Los Angeles: Western Psychological Services. [Manual and Computer program].

Russell, E. W., & Starkey, R. I. (2001a). *Halstead–Russell neuropsychological evaluation system—revised*. Los Angeles: Western Psychological Services. [Appendix F].

Russell, E. W., & Starkey, R. I. (2001b). *Halstead–Russell neuropsychological evaluation system—revised*. Los Angeles: Western Psychological Services. [Manual and Computer program].

Scheinberg, P. (1977). *Modern practical neurology*. New York: Raven Press.

Simon, E., Doniger, G. M., & Amit, S. (2000). *MindStreams*. Newark, NJ: Neurotrax.

Schinka, J. A., & Vanderploeg, R. D. (2000). Estimating premorbid level of functioning. In R. D. Vanderploeg (Ed.), *Clinician's guide to neuropsychological assessment* (pp. 39–67) (2nd ed.). Mahwah, NJ: Lawrence Erlbaum Associates.

Spreen, O., & Benton, A. L. (1965). Comparative studies of some psychological tests for cerebral damage. *Journal of Nervous and Mental Disease*, *140*, 323–333.

Stern, R. A., & White, T. (2001). *Neuropsychological assessment battery (NAB)*. Lutz, FL: Psychological Assessment Resources.

Strauss, E., Sherman, E. M. S., & Spreen, O. (2006). *A compendium of neuropsychological tests: Administration, norms, and commentary* (3rd ed.). New York: Oxford University Press.

Swiercinsky, D. P. (1978, September). Computerized SAINT: System for analysis and interpretation of neuropsychological tests. Paper presented at meeting of the American Psychological Association, Toronto.

Terman, L. M., & Merrill, M. A. (1973). *Stanford-Binet intelligence*. Boston: Houghton Mifflin. [Manual for third revision, Form L-M]

Volbrecht, M. E., Meyers, J. E., & Kaster-Bundgaard, J. (2000). Neuropsychological outcome of head injury using a short battery. *Archives of Clinical Neuropsychology*, *15*, 251–265.

Walsh, K. W. (1978). *Neuropsychology: A clinical approach*. Hillsdale, NY: Churchill Livingstone.

Wechsler, D. (1944). *The measurement of adult intelligence* (3rd ed.). Baltimore: Williams & Wilkins.

Wechsler, D. (1997). *WAIS-III, WMS-III*. San Antonio, TX: Psychological Corporation. [Technical manual]

Wechsler, D., Coalson, D. L., & Raiford, S. E. (2008). *WAIS-IV technical and interpretive manual*. San Antonio, TX: Pearson.

Wedding, D. (1983). Clinical and statistical prediction. *Clinical Neuropsychology*, *5*, 49–55.

Wedding, D. (1983). Comparison of statistical and actuarial models for predicting lateralization of brain damage. *Clinical Neuropsychology*, *4*, 15–20.

2 The Nature of Science

> *None of the methods for settling doubts we have examined so far is free from human caprice and willfulness. As a consequence, the propositions which are held on the basis of those methods are uncertain in the range of their application and in their accuracy. If we wish clarity and accuracy, order, and consistency, security and cogency, in our actions and intellectual allegiances we shall have to resort to some method of fixing beliefs whose efficacy in resolving problems is independent of our desires and wills. Such a method, which takes advantage of the objective connections in the world around us, should be found reasonable not because of its appeal to the idiosyncrasies of a selected few individuals, but because it can be tested repeatedly and by all men.*
>
> ***Cohen & Nagel, 1962, p. 195***

Because this book is primarily concerned with the scientific foundation of neuropsychological assessment, it is first necessary to understand the essential nature of science. Consequently, it is important first to discuss the fundamentals of science.

The Essence of Science

Although an enormous literature concerning the methodology of science extends back to the ancient Greeks, the essence of that methodology is simple.

"Show Me"

Although simple in essence, in elaboration, science is both complex and dependent on how it is employed. In essence, scientific methodology is as simple as the challenge attributed to the citizens of the state of Missouri in the United States. This challenge to any contention was "Show me" (Westermann & Rafferty, 2010). All of the primary characteristics of science are represented in those two words. In scientific language "show me" means that a proposed procedure or information must be confirmed by scientific methodology in order to be accepted as reliable. Although the core scientific methodology remains consistent, the specific form of the methodology is dependent upon the particular field of study. In this case that field is neuropsychological assessment.

The Scientific Foundation of Neuropsychological Assessment. DOI: 10.1016/B978-0-12-416029-3.00002-6

As the classical textbook on the nature of scientific method by Cohen and Nagel (1962) states:

> *If we look at all the sciences not only as they differ among each other but also as each changes and grows in the course of time, we find that the constant and universal feature of science is its general method, which consists in the persistent search for truth, constantly asking: Is it so?—that is, what general conditions or considerations determine it to be so? … From this point of view scientific method is simply the way in which we test impressions, opinions, or surmises by examining the best available evidence for and against them.* (p. 192)

Science is, thus, an enormous elaboration on the simple statement "Show me."

Testing

"Show me" means that the "truth" of scientific concepts or theory must be demonstrated and that the only reliable method of demonstrating an idea is to test it. Thus, the essence of science is the methodology used to test its theories. Testing involves making a prediction and then demonstrating that the prediction was correct. The methodology of testing either manipulates a phenomenon to demonstrate a predicted result or consistently and repeatedly predicts an objectively observed phenomenon, such as the movement of the planets. It is this testing methodology of information that determines its reliability. It is the methodology of science that ensures the reliability or truth of its information. If the phenomena can be manipulated, then it must be tested as a form of experimentation. The proposed causal relationships between objects are tested by means of experiment or hypothesis testing.

If the phenomenon cannot be directly manipulated, then it is "tested" by predicting a result and repeatedly demonstrating that prediction by means of public observation of the predicted phenomenon. The primary essence of such observations is a prediction that can be observed by any unbiased person with training and appropriate instrumentation.

Practical Foundation

Science is accepted by non-scientists because its results can be trusted. It enables humans to obtain reliable results from their activities. As such engineering as a general occupation is the ultimate triumph and defense of science. When the information is reliable it can be trusted as the method of creating goods and designing activities of life. Such information grows food and enables manufacturing, medicine, transportation and communication. It is crucial for expert witnesses in court. The modern world is built on science because its method creates reliable information. Science is the only means for creating and verifying such information.

Components of Science

From a functional perspective, science has two major components: empirical and conceptual. The empirical component is concerned with *data*—that is, the observations that are made by the neuropsychologist or are derived from tests. The conceptual component consists of concepts—or, in psychology, *constructs*—that constitute neuropsychological theory. Each component will be discussed.

Describing Phenomena

Empirically, there are also two major methods of describing phenomena in science (Nunnally & Bernstein, 1994, pp. 3–5, 27). One consists in the measurement of attributes, as in scaling. This is empirical science. The other consists in defining whether objects belong to the same or different categories, as in classification. In a formal sense, the empirical method involves the quantification of differences, and the second method, classification, involves qualitative differences. *Qualitative* refers to observable distinctions that separate objects and phenomena into categories. These are precisely described in taxonomies. Such taxonomies classify and organize the entities in a field so as to eliminate as much vagueness or overlap of categories as possible.

Quantitative applies to levels or amounts of any particular attribute of a category or entity. Attributes are characteristics of a category or object. The qualitative aspects of observation often comprise taxonomies that order categories. However, in many areas of knowledge, types of entities are quite distinct, relatively infrequent, and obvious enough so that a formal taxonomy is not developed. This is generally true in physics. In contrast, taxonomies constitute an essential aspect of biology that is composed of a multitude of different types of entities (organisms).

In neuropsychology, the various functions in the brain appear to form different qualitative categories (Ardila & Bernal, 2007). However, the various qualitative or categorical distinctions are far from clear. Even such gross concepts as "cognitive," "affective," and "executive" are vague and often confused. Consequently, other than the relationship of some functions to particular areas of the brain, these functions have not been placed into a taxonomic system (Ardila & Bernal, 2007; Russell, 1986, pp. 59–61). The taxonomic problem involving brain functions will be discussed at another point in this writing.

Empirical Methodologies

As described by the philosophers of science (Cohen & Nagel, 1962; Toulmin, 2009) empirical science involves two major forms of methodology: observation and experimentation (Toulmin, 2009, "Empirical data," para. 1). Observation means that the phenomena can be observed and usually measured but are not manipulated. These phenomena include such occurrences as the motion of planets in astronomy, land mass movements in geology, and certain brain pathologies.

In experimentation, the phenomena can be manipulated to produce and verify results. This primarily involves testing hypotheses derived from theories. A particular concept or hypothesis is logically derived from a theory, and an experiment is designed that will demonstrate that the predicted manipulation will produce an effect. A null hypothesis—that the manipulation will produce no effect—is adopted. If the experiment does produce an effect, then the null hypothesis is disproved and the predicted effect is accepted. The effect must be great enough to be significant according to the experimenter's criterion. The experiment almost always uses instrumentation as part of the testing procedure.

Divisions of Science

Science, as a whole, has three major divisions: (1) a body of knowledge, which may be called *theory*; (2) a methodology of inquiry that is designated as *discovery* or *investigation*; and (3) a methodology that is concerned with the "justification" of procedures and theoretical concepts (Cohen & Nagel, 1962, p. 249).

Although the great body of "scientific" knowledge constitutes a part of science, it is a derivative product of the methodology and therefore is not the basis of science. Although a small part of the theory has not been validated, the major proportion of such "theory" consists in information that has been so well validated that it may be considered to be fact or knowledge.

The distinction between discovery and justification is also quite well accepted (Cohen & Nagel, 1962, p. 249; Toulmin, 2009, "Discovery and rationality" paragraph). Both forms of methodology are essential to science in that discovery creates theories, concepts, and procedures, and justification validates these theories, concepts, and procedures.

Theory

The body of knowledge constituting science consists of its theories. Theory is crucial to both observation and testing. In regard to observation, theory is necessary in order to direct observation to a particular phenomenon and to design specific instruments. Most instruments have a narrow range of observation. That range is determined by the theory basic to the purpose of the instruments. For instance, the range of a microscope is limited to very small objects. In regard to theory, even when scientists discover new phenomenon, they realize its importance because they understand the theory related to the phenomenon. That understanding, of course, constitutes his or her theoretical conceptualization of the area of interest (Cohen & Nagel, 1962, pp. 215–219).

Discovery

Discovery in science refers to inquiry that results in the creation of new concepts and theories as well as in originating and developing various scientific procedures. The essence of discovery is creativity, although it must use other aspects of science such as previously validated information, observation, experimentation, and mathematics. As a crucial part of science, discovery creates the theories of science and the methodology to test and apply those theories.

However, although discovery is necessary, it is not sufficient. It does not constitute the necessary essence of science because creative thought is as much a part of many forms of culture as it is of science. In addition, "discovery" may, and often does, produce concepts or methodologies that are inaccurate and even fallacious. Thus, even though discovery and its creativity produce the theories and methods from which scientific knowledge is derived, the generality and unreliability of the initial discovery process means that, although necessary, discovery cannot be the foundation of science.

Historically, the greater proportion of beliefs that were once thought to have been scientific have been disproved or replaced by more valid concepts (Finger, 1994). Undoubtedly, this is still true, and many of the concepts now accepted will prove to be false when scientific justification methods are applied to them. On the other hand, when thoroughly validated and not later disproved or displaced by more effective theories and methods, such concepts and methods become ageless in their acceptance. Almost five centuries after Copernicus's initial proposal, Earth still rotates around the sun.

Justification

As described previously, justification consists in the application of scientific methods to ensure the validity and thus the reliability of the methods and the information that discovery produces. No other area of human endeavor contains such a stringent method of ensuring reliability except for logic and mathematics, and these are part of science. Thus, the justification methodology of science constitutes the unique basis of science. In this regard, scientific justification is the only means that humans have developed that can ensure the reliability of knowledge or theories (Nagel, 1961, pp. 1–14). The essence of science is justification. It is the ultimate response to "Show me."

Consequently, the foundation of science consists in the justification methodology used to ensure the reliability or truth of the information that is being investigated. The purpose of science, which distinguishes it from other disciplines, is to replace fallible subjective human judgment and common-sense ideas (Cohen & Nagel, 1962, pp. 1–14) with a methodology that produces objective reliable knowledge. This methodology is based on a nonhuman process. In other words, the formal process of scientific justification does not obtain credibility from human opinion or judgment at any point in the decision or verification process, although the application of justified knowledge may require judgment. The great advantage of the scientific method is that the method is not influenced by human emotions, biases, or prejudices. As such, neither "authority" nor "general acceptance" constitutes a necessary or sufficient requirement for scientific justification methodology.

Basic Criteria for Scientific Justification

The methods for justification are universally accepted as the criteria for science. However, they are accepted because—and only because—the methods produce reliable information.

Although these methods are often used in discovery, they are essential for justification. Although all three divisions of science use these scientific criteria, such criteria are crucial for justification—that is, discovery must use these criteria for all of the concepts and procedures that it ensures. In addition, the support for the various concepts in the body of scientific knowledge is generally described in terms of these technical criteria.

The criteria that are necessary for both observational and experimental forms of scientific methods are observability, repeatability, testability, and predictability in some combination. In a manner, all of the criteria are involved in predictability. Although observation initially does not require prediction, to justify an observation it must be repeatable as predicted. It is rather obvious that testing requires predictability in that the nature of a hypothesis is a prediction that if a certain procedure is performed (testing) a certain result will be obtained.

Each of these criteria will be examined briefly because they constitute the basis of the rest of science, especially the empirical component of science.

Objective Observability

Observable indicates that information derived from a procedure is objectively observable—that is, "public." This means that the information can be "shown" or demonstrated to any competent observer using the appropriate instruments. *Observable* also means that the procedures and information are recordable, measurable, teachable, and publishable. The means for observation include measurement, formal and statistical, and physical instruments for accurate detailed observation.

Observation may be formalized, which increases its reliability, by means of logic, taxonomy, measurement, and mathematics. Observation is an essential component of the other aspects of science methodology.

Repeatability

Repeatable means that the same observations can be obtained whenever the same conditions and instruments are used—that is, any unbiased trained person can repeat the observations or procedures and obtain essentially the same results. Recording the data obtained from scientific investigations is crucial for ensuring the repeatability of the observation of a phenomenon. The recording and publication should be in a form that allows repeating the research. This repeatability is ensured by instruments that act as recording devices, such as writing, record keeping, and photography, and by an enormous number of other instrumental recording devices. Because recording of observations is central to repeatability in science, it is a requirement even if no instruments other than written descriptions are used.

Testability

When possible, testability is generally considered the preferred basis of science. *Testable* means that, when specified procedures are applied, the results predicted by a particular hypothesis are obtained (observed). Testing is generally accomplished by instruments. In psychology and neuropsychology, the instruments are normally tests or batteries of tests. In general, testing requires measurement, and measurement requires instruments of some form. An instrument is usually a method of transforming an observation into a measurement.

Prediction is the basis of experimentation in that the test determines whether certain predicted results occur. A hypothesis is essentially a prediction—that is, the predicted relationship that is logically derived from a theory. Often the relationship is a causative relationship. In essence, experimental prediction is the hypothesis of what will occur if certain manipulations are employed. Both type I and type II errors are different types of prediction failures. Thus, prediction underlies almost all other criteria.

Using Karl Popper's terminology, in science the prediction of a relationship or entity must be falsifiable (Faigman, Saks, Sanders, & Cheng, 2008), that is, the relationship or entity can be demonstrated to be false. If, because of the nature of a concept, it is not possible to demonstrate that, using scientific criteria, the concept cannot be demonstrated to be false, the concept is not a subject for science. Its existence cannot be proved or disproved by science or, in fact, any other method.

In court, testable means that the evidence will either have been tested scientifically or the veracity of the evidence can be logically inferred from information that has been tested. In regard to phenomena that are only observable, *testable* means that the phenomena are recordable or repeatable and involve outcomes that can be or have been predicted.

Predictability

The final major criterion of science is predictability. Although predictability underlies all of the other criteria, it is often overlooked. For those types of science that deal with nonexperimental phenomena, such as astronomy, predictability is the primary criterion of reliable information. In essence, predictability takes the place of testability when the phenomena are not testable. However, they are predictable, and in astronomy they are highly predictable. This is particularly obvious in the guidance of space probes that use a planet's gravitational field to "sling" a probe on a predetermined course to the next planet or asteroid. All of this is permitted by mathematical prediction.

Prediction is also a major aspect of the other scientific criteria. In observation, one predicts what will be observed. A failure in such observation questions either the information or the instrumental procedure. Obviously, repetition is a matter of repeating the same observations. As described, testability is a matter of verifying a prediction.

In neuropsychology, one of the major types of validation is prediction (Nunnally & Bernstein, 1994, pp. 94–100). It is also a primary component of construct validity. Any time a predicted consequence of a construct is not supported by apparently appropriate statistical analysis, then either the construct must be changed or the methodology must be questioned.

In summary, if the procedure or information derived from the procedure is scientific, the information is objectively observable (or recordable), repeatable, and has been tested or is predictable. The term *scientific* pertains to procedures that meet these criteria and the information derived from such procedures. Such information is acceptable evidence for "evidence-based" practice or for forensic testimony.

The term *scientific* does not pertain to any other known methods or to information derived from other methods. The final criterion for all science is that scientific information is created by scientific methods (Faigman et al., 2008, p. 141).

Measurement

These criteria for science are the basis for formal—that is, quantitative—representation of a theory or procedure. Thus, the basis of scientific formal methods is measurement.

"Measurement is the process of associating numbers with physical quantities and phenomena" (Measurement, 2006, p. 1). It is the mathematical bridge between abstract mathematics and an attribute. As Nunnally and Bernstein (1994) state, "The term 'attribute' in the definition indicates that measurement always concerns some *particular* feature of objects" (p. 4). One measures attributes of physically existing objects. At some point, the attribute must be represented by a physical form or it cannot be measured. In psychometrics, this physical form is usually some type of test.

Quantification permits the application of formal or mathematical analysis to the physical or psychological world. "Measurement always concerns numbers relatable to the physical world, ... as its purpose is to quantify the attributes of real objects" (Nunnally & Bernstein, 1994, p. 8). The attribute must exist as a quality of a real entity or it cannot be measured. In almost all cases, measurement is achieved by means of physical instruments.

"Before the factors determining the psychological characteristics of individuals can be systematically examined, those very characteristics must be described. This is the purpose of psychological measurement. Measurement essentially is concerned with the methods used to provide quantitative descriptions of the extent to which individuals manifest or possess specified characteristics" (Ghiselli, Campbell, & Zedeck, 1981, p. 2). The authors call these descriptions "quantitative descriptions, or scores, given by the various operations of measurement.... " (Ghiselli et al., 1981, p. 2).

In science and psychology, many terms have been used to indicate various objective methodologies in addition to measurement. Meehl (1954) used the term *actuarial* prediction to indicate such objective methodologies. However, this term greatly limits the extent of the types of scientific methodologies that may be included. For instance, it does not include decision-tree algorithms, which can be just as objective as statistical predictions. Consequently, this present writing will use the term *formal* to indicate objective scientific methodologies, such as indexes, formulas, or decision-tree algorithms.

Instrumentation

Although seldom emphasized, measurement requires instrumentation. Objective observation by means of instruments is the method of obtaining precise measurement of a phenomenon. Precise measurement in astronomy long predated the development of telescopes, but it still required instruments such as the astrolabe. The telescopes enabled far more accurate observation than could be accomplished using only the human eye.

Most books on neuropsychological psychometric assessment deal with the properties of scales and statistics, but these writings seldom adequately examine the way in which measurement is related to instruments, which is largely by means of test design. Apparently, it was thought that test design is self-evident if you understand the statistical aspects of psychological instrumentation. For instance, Nunnally and Bernstein

(1994, p. 7) discuss concepts such as "rules" that are necessary to produce measures, but they do not indicate that these rules apply to instruments and constitute test design. A test is an instrument with a design and instructions. These constitute the rules for neuropsychological measurement. Ghiselli et al. (1981, p. 15) mention "operations" needed to create variables, but they also do not specifically deal with these operations in a general manner. Even Anastasi and Urbina (1997) emphasize that "a psychological test is essentially an objective and standardized measure of a sample of behavior. Psychological tests are like tests in any other science insofar as observations are made on a small but carefully chosen *sample* of an individual's behavior" (p. 4). However, their discussion does not explain *how a test changes a behavior into a measure.* Although statistical aspects are examined, these authors do not discuss the procedures that an instrument uses to connect the "observations" of behavior to a measure of brain functioning. Especially for neuropsychology, the instrumental relationship between the brain's functioning and measurement is crucial.

Initially, instrumentation was a method to extend the senses as in the development of microscopes or telescopes. However, instruments such as the telescope permitted one to see objects not visible to the naked eye such as the moons of Jupiter.

Thus, instruments soon were able to observe aspects of nature that are not observable to the human senses, such as electricity and the electromagnetic waves that are not within the human visual range. Instruments often were necessary to enable one to measure objects indirectly. Almost all psychological measurements of mental entities like anxiety or vocabulary are observed objectively and accurately only by instruments, although we may be grossly aware of them subjectively.

In science and neuropsychology, the instrument and its design is absolutely critical. Until there is an accurate validated instrument to demonstrate the existence and amount of a psychological attribute, that attribute cannot be examined by scientific objective methods.

In other words, although we may subjectively experience or believe we observe a particular psychological attribute or phenomena, it is impossible to either perform research or assess that attribute until it has been quantified and transformed into formal information by an instrument (or, in some cases, validated clinical judgment). Thus, for most of psychology, until there is a test for a psychological attribute, that attribute does not objectively exist (Nunnally & Bernstein, 1994, pp. 6–7).

Instrumentation and Language

Although instrumentation is a nonlinguistic aspect of science, it is the aspect that made modern science possible. Since the ancient Greeks, Western society has been dominated by the concept that language is the most superior function that humans possess. As a consequence, the nonlanguage aspects of culture were neglected. Even today, in general, only certain scientists, engineers, and technologists are intrinsically interested in the nonlanguage aspects of the world. The result has been that, in the philosophy of science, the emphasis is on theories and hypotheses deduced from the theories and upon hypothesis testing. In contrast, the physical tools of science, its instruments, have been relatively neglected (see Cohen & Nagel, 1962; Toulmin, 2009), even though, it is these tools that make science and measurement possible.

For all of their verbal brilliance, the ancient Greeks were so contemptuous of "manual" labor and "tools related to such labor"—that is to the nonlinguistic aspects of culture—that they completely failed to create an adequate science. Modern science itself was largely developed by people who were not averse to manipulating the physical world with tools and instruments.

No science or measurement would be possible in any field, including neuropsychology, without objective observations made by means of instruments.

The scientific instruments used in neuropsychology are usually "tests," although they may include entire batteries such as the Wechsler scales. It is these procedures that create information, quantify it, and ensure the reliability of that information. In other words, the instrumentation provides a reliable basis for interpretation. (Currently, the physical instruments of neurology, such as scanning methods, are greatly increasing the interest of neuropsychologists in instrumentation.)

Psychometrics is the field of mathematics that is concerned with the statistical description of instrumental data as variables and with the inferential statistical description of the relationships between variables. Statistics is used to examine how variables produced by instruments are similar, as in correlations, or how they are different, as in analyses of variance (ANOVAs) or *t*-tests. Experimentation primarily involves hypothesized differences between instrumental variables that may be examined statistically. Often the methodology is the quasi-experimental method of comparing two naturally occurring groups, such as "normal" subjects to a group that has sustained head trauma.

For the most part, classical psychometrics will not be discussed in this book because there are many excellent books on noninstrumental psychometrics (Anastasi & Urbina, 1997; Bland, 2000; Ghiselli et al., 1981; Gouvier, 2001; Nunnally & Bernstein, 1994; Retzlaff & Gibertini, 2000). Rather, the issue of instrumentation, which tends to be neglected, will be examined.

Physical Basis of Instrumentation

Initially, it should be recognized that the entire process of measurement is as much physical as linguistic. Even if the content of the test takes the form of language, such as a vocabulary test, it requires a physical instrument, such as a booklet, paper and pencil, or computer screen (Kane, 2007). In a vocabulary test, the measure is the physical number of words correctly identified. No scientific procedure can use measurement until the procedure is operationalized into a physical form required by an instrument. The physical nature of block design or the category test are obvious examples.

Thus, quantification is always achieved by means of a physical instrument that is related to a form of measurement by certain rules (Nunnally & Bernstein, 1994, p. 7). This measurement instrument is the basis of objective science. The instrument bridges the gap between a psychological attribute, its measurement, and interpretation.

Criteria of Science and Instruments

In neuropsychological assessment, the validation of psychometric assessment procedures enables assessment and research to conform to the characteristics of science

(Cohen & Nagel, 1962; Toulmin, 2009). These include objectivity and repeatability, which produces standardization. It also includes experimental testing and thus predictability. Objectivity of observation is provided for science by instrumental measurement. In assessment, the instrumental procedures are objective and published and become available to any qualified neuropsychologist. Their results are repeatable in that they produce essentially the same results for any neuropsychologist who adheres to the instructions (if a subject complies with the instructions to the extent of his or her capability). These two comprise standardization. Finally, any psychometrically acceptable procedure must be predictable and have been experimentally tested in research studies to demonstrate that it measures the abilities that it purports to measure. These operations make the results of the instrument predictable, which is another way of stating that they are reliable.

Thus, the scientific process of validation produces instruments that are reliable for medical or forensic purposes. Their reliability enables them to be the basis of scientific testimony by expert witnesses in court.

Aspects of Instruments

"Measurement essentially is concerned with the methods used to provide quantitative descriptions of the extent to which individuals manifest or possess specified characteristics" (Ghiselli et al., 1981, p. 2). The instruments transform attributes into measurements. Various instruments are designed to produce the desired transformation. Nevertheless, this transformation process involves several procedures.

Measurement is the mathematical bridge between abstract mathematics and an attribute. As Nunnally and Bernstein (1994) state, "Measurement always concerns numbers relatable to the physical world, … In particular, scaling, … always concerns some form of numerical statement of how much of an attribute is present, as its purpose is to quantify the attributes of real objects" (pp. 8–9). At some point, the attribute must be represented by a physical entity or it cannot be measured. In psychometrics, this physical form is usually some type of test. Quantification permits the application of formal or mathematical analysis to the psychological process. The attribute must exist as an attribute of a physical entity or it cannot be measured. As such, the aspects of instruments will now be elaborated.

Sampling the Attribute

The initial process performed by an instrument is to physically sample an attribute of an object. This involves detecting the object and its attribute. In psychology, this object and attribute is a specific type of behavior. The procedure uses a physical apparatus to detect the specific behavior. For instance, a thermometer detects the temperature of an object or a person. The physical design of the instrument determines the way the attribute is detected and measured. A vocabulary test can detect the size of a person's vocabulary by systematically increasing the "difficulty" of the words. The size of the person's vocabulary is determined by the maximum level of difficulty at which a subject can accurately "define" the words.

Specification

A primary operation of an instrument is specification—that is, the instrument isolates the attribute or function from other attributes or functions. As such, it distinguishes the attribute or function from other attributes in the context in which it exists. The thermometer distinguishes the attribute of temperature from other attributes of a person. A test for depression separates this emotion from the panorama of a person's other emotions, such as anxiety, by means of specific questions that concern depression but not anxiety. Thus, the instrument isolates a specific entity from other entities.

Proportional Transformation

For this detection to become a measurement, the instrument must perform a proportional transformation; this is termed *quantification*. The attribute being measured produces a physical effect on the detection instrument, which then transforms the initially detected information into a form, usually physical, that indicates a quantity. The measurement is accomplished by a reference device or gauge. The gauge or quantification instrument is designed so that the effect on the gauge is proportional to the quantity of the attribute. In other words, the gauge transforms an attribute, action, motion, or behavior into a physical indicator that provides a measure of the amount of the attribute. For instance, rising temperature causes the mercury in a thermometer to increase in volume. This increase is proportional to the increase in the thermometer's ambient temperature so that the thermometer's calibration directly indicates an object's temperature. Consequently, the instrument will provide a proportional quantitative representation of the temperature attribute.

An instrument may be very simple—the measurement of steam pressure in a boiler, for example. A small pipe transmits the pressure in the boiler through a vertical tube that pushes up a plunger of a certain weight. The greater the pressure in the boiler, the higher the plunger will be pushed. The measurement is determined by marking a scale on the pipe that indicates the position of the plunger on the scale.

The type of measure itself may be simple, such as indicating whether or not some attribute exists. This is a *nominal* form of measurement, which is the basis of both taxonomy and a form of quantification. (More complex forms of measurement are discussed in various books—see Nunnally & Bernstein, 1994, pp. 11–19.)

In psychology, the instrument, which is usually a test, transforms a psychological attribute, such as the feeling of anxiety, which cannot be observed, into a form, such as the number of items passed or accepted that are recorded. These are counted, or the time to complete a task is recorded. This count is the initial raw measure.

The scores that are directly derived from proportional transformation are raw scores, such as the number of items in a test that are correct. Raw scores can be used for many purposes, in research and assessment. The Halstead–Reitan Battery (HRB) uses raw scores (Reitan, 1966) in the assessment and research studies in which it is used.

Scaling and Norming

Measurement is achieved by using a physical scale that is derived by a proportional transformation. In neuropsychology and psychology, a further process is often used to provide meaning and to transform the test raw scores into a battery of scales that are equivalent. This is norming and scaling, which are parts of the process of standardization. Standardization will be discussed at greater length later in this book.

The transformation of raw scores into some form of scale scores is generally advantageous for two reasons. First, in psychological assessment, a raw score has no meaning in itself (Anastasi & Urbina, 1997, p. 48). Consequently, for most psychology tests, the meaning of a test score is provided through comparing the raw scores to a standard or norm that provides meaning to the scale score. In psychology, this generally may be accomplished by one of two methods. First, raw scores may use a specific score as a criterion reference score or cut point to indicate the existence of an attribute such as depression or brain damage.

Although this provides an indication of the existence of the attribute, it does not provide any graded "measure" of the level or strength of the attribute. In many areas of psychology, such as intelligence, the level is either crucial or it provides the meaning of the attribute score. A scale score is a graduated scale standardized against a criterion, which is usually the distribution of a relevant population, such as the normal population of a country. This comparison provides meaning to the scale score.

Second, scale scores provide equivalent measures for all tests in a battery. Such equivalent scores can be directly compared or combined without requiring mental or formal transformation of raw scores. This permits the application of formal methods such as ratios with minimal difficulty.

In addition, this equivalency enables scale scores to provide certain advantages over raw scores in a battery of tests. First, the interpretation of a battery using either clinical judgment or formal methods is considerably easier and usually more accurate with scale scores than raw scores. Second, the application of a formal method is considerably simpler than when raw scores are used. Finally, equivalent scale scores (based on co-norming) permit groups of tests to be separated from the whole battery without requiring the administration and use of an entire battery. Scale score relationships between all of the battery tests are "fixed" by co-norming and not by repeating the battery as a whole.

Recording

Another important aspect of instruments is their ability to record the results of a procedure. Thus, an instrument contains a system for recording information and measurements. In psychology, the test sheet or computer memory serves as a raw score or scale score data record. There are many possible storage mechanisms. Physical transmission of the recorded data may be another component of the instrument. The instrument stores the information derived from the measurement process and may transmit the information in some form to any place on Earth.

The Value of an Instrument

Finally, note that the particular physical design of a test determines what it measures. The function of psychometrics is to enable both the design (discovery) and validation (justification) of these instruments. Thus, the entire discipline of psychometrics is concerned with physical instruments. When validated, complex instruments, such as batteries, provide reliable information concerning the existence, the level of each psychological function, and the relationships between functions.

The Conceptual Component

In psychology, the conceptual component, as opposed to the instrumental component, is generally emphasized as the basis for interpretation and research. This conceptual component is usually discussed in the form of *constructs* or score patterns. These constitute neuropsychological theory. Historically, the concept of a construct (Cronbach & Meehl, 1955) was applied to the functional relationships between measures of behavior. It was the measurement of these behavioral relationships that was validated (Nunnally & Bernstein, 1994, pp. 84–87).

New neurological methods, especially those related to brain scanning, have added an entire new understanding to the science of neuropsychology. Conceptual components can now be related to brain functioning with an understanding and accuracy that was unimaginable only a few years ago. A considerable proportion of the writing in the following chapters will examine these new neuropsychology conceptual components in the form of brain functioning.

Applied Science

The field of science takes two forms: *pure* and *applied.* In the physical sciences, the pure form is composed of physics, chemistry, and a number of other sciences. *Applied* usually refers to engineering.

The biological and behavioral forms of science also have pure and applied divisions. In the area of biology, medicine is the applied form. In psychology, a major portion of the applied aspect concerns assessment. (Therapy is another form of applied psychology, but it is not within the scope of this writing.)

Of the two major types of science, pure science is concerned with developing an understanding of an area of knowledge—that is, with creating general theories. Applied science is concerned with the application of scientific knowledge to human affairs. Although both pure and applied sciences are forms of science, their methods may differ.

In regard to brain functioning, the pure science, which is generally called *neuroscience*, uses various types of instrumentation rather than psychometrics to develop and understand brain functioning in the form of theory. Clinical neuropsychology is generally an applied science equivalent to engineering in the physical sciences.

Applied neuropsychology generally consists in the use of psychometric methods to examine the brain functioning of humans and to develop procedures for assessment. This may involve "discovering" theory or the assessment of a particular individual in order to explain a subject's brain functioning. The methodology used to assess an individual often differs from psychometric methods used in neuropsychological research designed to understand brain functioning in general. This book is concerned with applied neuropsychology and assessment of normal and pathological brain functioning, especially as related to individual assessment. This scientific nature of this application will be discussed in the following chapters.

Science and Neuropsychological Batteries

The psychometrics related to assessment, research, and its application in assessment is concerned with both discovery (creating) and justifying (validating) accurate assessment procedures [American Educational Research Association (hereafter AERA et al.), American Psychological Association & National Council on Measurement in Education, 1999, pp. 9–24]. The psychometric standards for constructing reliable individual tests have been developed over 100 years and are well established. In general, tests have a known dependability when administered according to standardized instructions. Most neuropsychological writing concerns individual tests and their statistical requirements. These have been well explicated by numerous writers (Anastasi & Urbina, 1997; Ghiselli et al., 1981; Gouvier, 2001; Nunnally & Bernstein, 1994).

In contrast, there has been relatively little work concerning the construction and justification of batteries in the field of neuropsychology. Standards (AERA et al., 1999) have seldom been specifically applied to test batteries as integrated batteries. Instead, batteries such as the Wechsler scales (Anastasi & Urbina, 1997, pp. 214–222; Wechsler, 1997) are treated as if they were single tests (AERA et al., 1999, pp. 49, 123–124) in which the index score represents the entire battery as an individual test.

Because this current writing would add little to the work of these writers on the design of individual tests, it will generally be devoted to the design and justification of the relationship of batteries to brain functioning.

References

American Educational Research Association (AERA), American Psychological Association, & National Council on Measurement in Education. (1999). *Standards for educational and psychological testing*. Washington, DC: American Educational Research Association.

Anastasi, A., & Urbina, S. (1997). *Psychological testing* (7th ed.). Upper Saddle River, NJ: Prentice Hall.

Ardila, A., & Bernal, B. (2007). What can be localized in the brain? Toward a "factor" theory on brain organization of cognition. *International Journal of Neuroscience*, *117*, 935–969.

Bland, M. (2000). *An introduction to medical statistics* (3rd ed.). New York: Oxford University Press.

Cohen, M. R., & Nagel, E. (1962). *An introduction to logic and scientific method*. New York: Harcourt, Brace. (Original work published 1934)

Cronbach, L. J., & Meehl, P. E. (1955). Construct validity in psychological tests. *Psychological Bulletin*, *53*, 281–302.

Faigman, D. L., Saks, M. J., Sanders, J., & Cheng, E. K. (2008). *Modern scientific evidence, standard statistics and research methods (2008 student edition)*. Eagan, MN: Thompson & West.

Finger, S. (1994). *Origins of neuroscience: A history of explorations in brain function*. New York: Oxford University Press.

Ghiselli, E. E., Campbell, J. P., & Zedeck, S. (1981). *Measurement theory for the behavioral sciences*. San Francisco: W. H. Freeman.

Gouvier, W. D. (2001). Are you sure you're telling the truth? *NeuroRehabilitation*, *16*, 215–219.

Kane, R. L. (2007). Editorial: Introduction to this supplement. *Archives of Clinical Neuropsychology*, *22S1*, S3–S5.

Measurement. (2006). *Encyclopaedia Britannica. Ultimate Reference Suite*. Chicago: Encyclopaedia Britannica.

Meehl, P. E. (1954). *Clinical versus statistical prediction: A theoretical analysis and a review of the evidence*. Minneapolis: University of Minnesota Press.

Nagel, E. (1961). *The structure of science: Problems in the logic of scientific explanation*. New York: Harcourt, Brace.

Nunnally, J. C., & Bernstein, I. H. (1994). *Psychometric theory* (3rd ed.). New York: McGraw-Hill.

Reitan, R. M. (1966). A research program on the psychological effects of brain lesions in human beings. In N. R. Ellis (Ed.), *International review of research and mental retardation* (pp. 156–218). New York: Academic Press.

Retzlaff, P. D., & Gibertini, M. (2000). Neuropsychometric issues and problems. In R. D. Vanderploeg (Ed.), *Clinician's guide to neuropsychological assessment*, (2nd ed.). Mahwah, NJ: Lawrence Erlbaum Associates, pp. 277–299.

Russell, E. W. (1986). The psychometric foundation of clinical neuropsychology. In S. B. Filskov & T. J. Boll (Eds.), *Handbook of clinical neuropsychology* (Vol. 2, pp. 45–80). New York: Wiley.

Toulmin, S. E. (2009). Philosophy of science. *Encyclopaedia Britannica. Ultimate Reference Suite*. Chicago: Encyclopaedia Britannica.

Wechsler, D. (1997). *WAIS-III, WMS-III, technical manual*. San Antonio, TX: Psychological Corporation.

Westermann, E. J. & Rafferty, M. D. (2010). Missouri. *Encyclopædia Britannica. Ultimate Reference Suite*. Chicago: Encyclopædia Britannica.

Section II

Theoretical Foundation of Neurological Assessment

3 The Neuropsychological Basis of Assessment

Before the factors determining the psychological characteristics of individuals can be systematically examined, those very characteristics must be described. This is the purpose of psychological measurement. Measurement essentially is concerned with the methods used to provide quantitative descriptions of the extent to which individuals manifest or possess specified characteristics" (Ghiselli, Campbell, & Zedeck, 1981, p. 2). They call these descriptions "quantitative descriptions, or scores, given by the various operations of measurement....

Ghiselli et al. (1981)

Neuropsychology is concerned with providing an understanding of the interrelationships between brain functioning and psychological behavioral attributes. A neuropsychological assessment produces information that is concerned with how the brain of an individual is functioning. Currently, this primarily concerns cognitive and pathological attributes. The only reliable method of obtaining this information is by means of scientific methodology and instrumentation. Neuropsychological tests now constitute the primary psychometric instrumentation for research and assessment.

Although a century has been devoted to the development of psychological and neuropsychological tests, the exact relationship between brain functioning and test design remains largely unexamined. This examination, of course, would require an understanding of how brain functioning is represented by a test score.

When this process is examined, we discover that the complexity of brain functioning, which is much better understood by neurology, requires a form of neuropsychological instrumentation that is not well developed. A single neuropsychological test is far too limited as an adequate representation of the brain's complicated functioning and pathology (Lezak, Howieson, & Loring, 2004, pp. 17–18). Rather, an adequate representation of that functioning requires an integrated group of tests constituting a battery.

The Neurological Basis for Neuropsychological Tests

To understand neuropsychological testing one must examine the relationship between the brain and psychometrics. It is rather strange that even though the testing of brain functions consisting of cognition is almost a century old, the way in which the brain is related to a test is still not well understood. Much of the following material is derived from well-accepted neurology theory but is applied here to neuropsychological assessment theory.

The Scientific Foundation of Neuropsychological Assessment. DOI: 10.1016/B978-0-12-416029-3.00003-8

The Black Box Problem

During the behavioral era, psychologists paid little attention to brain functioning. For the behavioral approach, it was thought that the brain was not needed to understand the psychological behavior of an organism. One well-known psychologist was reported to have said something like "As far as psychology is concerned the skull might as well be filled with corn flakes." As psychology developed and began to emphasize cognitive abilities and genetics, the activities of the central nervous system (CNS) became increasingly relevant. Psychologists began to realize that psychological theory needed to take the brain into consideration.

However, one impediment to relating brain processes to psychological activities was the so-called *black box problem*. In neuropsychology, the age-old problem has been the opinion that brain processes were not observable. Thus, the attempt to study the brain's workings has been compared to trying to understand what is happening inside a black box to which psychologists had no direct access.

Concept of a "Construct"

An established solution to the black box problem has been the concept of a *construct*, which was first proposed in detail by Cronbach and Meehl (1955). It was called a *construct* because a concept was constructed to represent an area of psychological study that cannot be directly observed (Nunnally & Bernstein, 1994, p. 85). Science develops measures of constructs by psychometric means. The construct represents the functional relationships between the construct measures. A construct is theoretically unrelated to the brain.

Nunnally and Bernstein (1994, pp. 104–107) emphasized that the construct was an abstract concept that in itself had no reality (Nunnally & Bernstein, 1994, pp. 104–107.) It was used to explain the correlation of various "observations"—that is, test results. These observations provide measures that were statistical correlated but distinct from other groupings. The correlated groups constituted the phenotype of a construct, whereas the construct itself was an abstract genotype. For Nunnally and Bernstein, a construct was entirely defined by statistical procedures, such as factor analyses that correlate and isolate a group of measures. However, the construct was usually named, such as "anxiety" or "intelligence", and is usually part of neuropsychological theory.

The Nature of a Brain Construct

In assessment, this writing proposes that a construct represents a brain function, at least for cognitive abilities. As such, the assessed constructs provide the foundation for an interpretive statement concerning brain functions. Although not phrased in construct language, an interpretation is a description of the meaning of a construct in terms of the ability levels, such as IQs, or its relationships to other constructs. For instance, a pattern of test results may indicate left-hemisphere brain damage. The interpretive statement that a subject has had left-hemisphere damage is derived from a number of tests in a construct provided by neurological and psychometric theory.

"There is more impairment to verbal than to spatial relations tests" is a description of the test results obtained from the construct related to lateralized damage and strokes.

In assessment and neuropsychological research, constructs are delineated by using psychometric methods. However, in neuropsychology, they can now also be identified by using various functional scanning methods. Thus, in neuropsychology, a construct may be delineated by both psychometric and neurological procedures.

Lack of Unity Within Theories and Constructs

One primary difficulty in neuropsychological and psychological theory and constructs is that no overall theory unifies them. This is true even for cognition. The field of psychology can be divided into cognition, affect, and possibly executive types of functions. Factor analysis and other similar types of statistics have brought some coherence to cognitive functions (Carroll, 1993), but there is less coherence concerning affect and executive functions.

One area that has showed progress in regard to theory is the transformation of Wechsler intelligence scales, adult and child, into a four-factor structure that appears to be fairly substantial (Tulsky, Saklofske, & Zhu, 2003). The WAIS, WAIS-R contained two major factors: verbal and performance. Several tests—Digit Symbol, Digit Span, and Arithmetic—were residuals that were lumped into what was sometimes called the "freedom from distractibility" factor (Tulsky et al., 2003, p. 46). In the WAIS-III, two tests were added that separated these remaining tests into two additional factors. This new construct appears to be fairly substantial. However, considering the number of tests that have been used in neuropsychology to measure different types of functional domains, psychology has a long way to go to integrate all of these tests.

The area of affective psychology, including emotions, motivations and personality, still lacks a major theory, although the five-factor concept of primary personality components (Costa & Widiger, 2002) appears to have begun the process of bringing coherence to personality theory.

The situation with constructs is even more fragmented. Nunnally and Bernstein (1994, pp. 104–106) use the term *construct* for every process in psychology from "intelligence" to "anxiety." Although the statistical methods have been relatively well developed for studying psychology and affective psychology, these have not resulted in a unifying theory for this area of psychology.

Nature of a Brain Function

To eliminate the black box problem, the relationship between tests and brain functioning must be examined. To design a test that assesses a brain function, the general nature of such a function must be known. Every organ of the body has a function—or, occasionally, several functions. The function of an organ is what it does. A function is an activity that an organ performs with a specific purpose that supports the operations of the whole organism. In medicine, a function may be defined as the "special, normal, or proper action of any part or organ" (*Dorland's Illustrated Medical Dictionary*, 1967, p. 589).

A major difference between brain functions and those of other organs is that, except for the brain, the functions of the body's organs are relatively specific.

The Brain's Control Function

A simplistic statement of the brain's functioning is that brain functioning is what the brain does. Although the brain has many specific functions, overall it is usually accepted that its major function is control. It is the control center for an organism. This control encompasses both internal and external control. Internal control primarily regulates the body's vegetative and maintenance processes.

External control consists in the brain's control of the entire organism's behavior. This involves acts of the whole body or person. A brain senses the external world along with the person's body within that world. Based on its motivation and using its perception and cognition, it regulates and integrates the movements of the body to fulfill a multitude of psychological purposes.

A Brain Function as a Construct

As proposed earlier, in general a construct is usually a brain function. As an organ, the brain has many control functions, including such activities as motor speed, cognition, and motivational and emotional processes along with vegetative processes. These are usually called *domains*. When examined from a psychological point of view, the cognitive processes of the brain in particular consist of what psychologists have called *constructs*. The most obvious of these is intelligence. The term *construct* was used in part because, until recently, psychologists had no way of connecting overt behavior to neural structures. This writing reflects the beginning of a new understanding of this relationship between neural structures and mental phenomena.

A construct has at least two aspects related to brain functions. A brain function is both a process and an ability. The process is a particular activity, such as memory for words, and the ability is how well the brain performs that activity, such as how many words a person has learned (the vocabulary).

As such, a construct has two aspects. One is its particular function, and the second is the level or strength of that function, which is called an *ability*. The construct of motor functioning involves not only motor activity but also the speed of that activity. A measure represents the motor construct's ability level. It is the magnitude of a function's ability that is measured by a test, whereas it is the design of the test that determines the particular function that is being measured. When various functions are related to each other, this relationship is described psychometrically by the similarities and differences between ability measures. A person's vocabulary may be greater than block design. If the difference is statistically significant, then the difference may be interpreted as indicating that the person's verbal ability is probably more developed than his or her spatial ability.

The Neuropsychological Method's Bridge

Neuropsychological methods now bridge the gap between physiological brain processes and psychological attributes and processes in terms of the location of functions. These methodologies include many medical techniques such as x-rays, electroencepholograms, angiograms, neurosurgery, and autopsies.

Throughout its history, neurological methods have to some extent bridged the location gap between physiological brain processes and psychological attributes or processes. However, new functional scanning techniques have greatly increased the ability to relate psychological processes to brain structures. They provide another more refined method of studying the relationship of brain functions to psychological processes.

The black box problem is one reason for the enthusiasm of neuropsychologists for functional brain scans and other functional neuroimaging procedures. It was thought that such methods would finally enable psychologists to "see" into the black box. There are now at least several neuroimaging methods that indicate the part of a brain that is active when the brain is performing a certain task. It appeared that finally science had opened the black box. However, an unexpected result of scanning is the demonstration that brain functioning as such is not revealed by functional scanning.

Levels of Brain Functioning

A complete understanding of brain functioning requires an understanding of the neurological and psychological theoretical levels existing in the total psychological analysis of any process or attribute related to brain functioning. Although these levels are well known to psychologists, they provide a heuristic framework for understanding the forms of psychological and physical relationships involved in neuropsychological analysis. Consequently, they need to be briefly discussed.

It should be understood that these "levels" represent only rough descriptions of the various relationships between the psychological and physical constituents of brain functioning. Many neurologists and psychologists would disagree with this organization in that they might believe that certain levels are left out or do not constitute separate levels. In addition, most research and assessment involves two or more of these levels. In summary, these are the levels beginning with the psychological and proceeding toward the more organic levels.

Behavioral Test Level

Initially, there is the behavioral level of test results. This is the phenotype level for constructs in which the subject performs one or more tasks that constitute a test. It is the level of psychometrics and test construction. This level applies measurement to psychological behavior using such techniques as factor analysis and operational characteristics of psychological procedures.

Construct Level

Second, there is the level of theory and constructs. This describes psychological relationships in the form of constructs and theories. They are the psychological genotypes for tests in research and assessment. The primary form of statistical analysis at this level is factor analysis and similar methods to provide a psychological structure.

These are also the basis of psychological and neuropsychological interpretations.

The Transition

Historically, there has been a gap between physiology and psychology as behavior. Initially, psychology as behaviorism had almost no relationship to physiology, although psychological tests were an aid to medicine as well as education. Neuropsychology developed from the interaction of psychology with medicine. In the area of neuropsychology, there are two aspects—research and assessment. Assessment applies the findings of research neuropsychology to individual human assessment.

Brain Structure and Physiological Level

The next level is neurology, the biological and medical study of the brain's physiological functioning. The neurology level is concerned with the physiological aspect of brain functioning, but it only grossly and usually only indirectly evaluates the behavioral aspects of the cognitive and affective functioning of an individual as a whole.

Research at this level involves brain structures and functioning, functional anatomy, magnetic resonance imaging, and so forth. The study of brain pathology occurs at this level. Medicine is applied physiology, just as engineering is applied physics and chemistry. This is the area of neuroscience, which combines neurophysiology and psychology to the study of brain behavior.

Brain Chemistry Level

The next level is chemical that provides an understanding of brain hormones and the mechanisms of impulse movement along a nerve and synaptic transmission. It is directed by genetics.

Genetics Level

The most primary organic level is genetics, which is basic to the organization of the brain and its functioning.

The Interaction of Levels

All of these levels of science contribute to an understanding of the brain's functioning. In addition, there is a great overlap between levels. As such, neurological research must use at least two levels. Most neurological as well as neuropsychological research uses both the psychological level and one or more of the neurological levels.

In this stratigraphic presentation of brain functioning, neuropsychology combines neurology, neuropsychological testing, and psychometrics. Neuropsychology is concerned with providing an understanding of the interrelationships between brain functioning and psychological behavioral attributes.

For neuropsychology, the term *brain function* applies to the nonphysiological aspect of a brain's functioning—that is, it examines how the brain regulates the behavior of the organism.

This previously discussed process, which proceeds from brain physical structure and physiology to psychological processes, is the basis of the brain function theory of psychological processes. The brain function theory unites the physical/physiological structure of the brain to the psychological behavior of an individual. It does this by demonstrating the relationship between the structure of the brain, its function, and the psychological processes or attributes that the function produces.

The Neuropsychological Measurement Procedure

In neuropsychology, the instrument is usually some form of a test given manually or by a computer. The test requires the brain to perform a task. It is the task that connects a particular brain function of an area or areas to a psychological measure. The test is designed as a numerical representation of the ability level of a function. In other words, the concrete task relates brain functioning to an abstract formal numerical description of a particular brain function.

The Task

To determine the function that an active part of the brain is performing, a specific behavior or act must be linked to the active area. In themselves, scans do not reveal what function any area of the brain is performing. It only locates an area of neural activity. Thus, scanning alone is useless in determining the function of a particular part of the brain.

To understand what function is being represented by a particular brain location, the brain's activity needs to be linked to a task that the subject is performing. The scan demonstrates which part of the brain is performing the activity required by the task—that is, the task requirements compel the brain to perform a specific function or functions. These functions use specific areas of the brain.

It is the design of the task, not the scan, that indicates the function that the brain is performing. Thus, the task represents a particular function. A task might be as simple as wiggling a finger on command. However, the subject needs to move the finger and have that movement recorded, at least as an observation to correlate that movement with the area of brain activity found on a scan. This helps determine the function of that area of the brain.

Consequently, specific tasks indicate the functions within the black box. These functions are represented in an overt and objective manner by the task. This representation has been true of psychology throughout its history. Thus, the way we know that a function exists is to have the brain perform a particular task. As such, one can study brain functioning by studying the tasks the brain performs (Nunnally & Bernstein, 1994, pp. 21–24). The black box is opened by means of the design of a task.

Operations of the Task

The design of a particular task requires the subject to use a particular function or set of functions localized in the brain, which the brain uses to accomplish that task. Thus, a task represents a particular brain function or set of functions.

Stimulation and Sampling

The task performs several operations in regard to brain functioning. First, the task stimulates the performance of a particular function, which is part of a system. In this way, it samples the function. The requirements of a task are designed to induce a particular response, such as finger tapping or defining words. Because that response is performed by a particular function, the function is represented or sampled by the task.

Task Limits the Function

Second, the task limits the brain's performance to one function or set of functions. Every function is part of a system in the brain. Speaking a word or sentence that has been read requires the use of vision, the posterior verbal reception area, transference to Broca's area, and then the vocalization motor strip. These are only parts of the system. To perform this act requires the use of many individual functions in the system. However, the task limits the brain's activity to one system and to a function or functions.

The Test: Representation of a Brain Function

The neuropsychological test, at least with a cognitive test, is usually composed of a task or a series of versions of the tasks such that they form a graduated complex task. When correctly designed, this graduated task is a test. The test transforms the subject's performance into a measure of a brain function's ability level. The design of the test, which may take a wide variety of forms, is determined by the function that the test is measuring (Anastasi & Urbina, 1997).

The assumption underlining a test is that a function is activated by a task in a graduated manner by the test. The ability level of brain functions are represented by test scores. By means of testing, brain functions are observed and recorded. With tests, the functioning of the brain becomes manifest and the contents of the black box become observable.

In neuropsychology and cognitive testing generally, the name for the function is often provided by the name of the task—for example, a vocabulary test measures a vocabulary function—or by what activity psychologists think the task is performing, such as spatial relations for block design. In some cases, a domain is named for the general type of tests that constitute the domain such as language tests.

Importance of the Test

The importance of a test is that its information represents a brain function and its level of ability in an accurate, objective, and reliable form. A clinically subjective impression does not provide scientifically reliable information concerning such an activity. In contrast, a test objectively reflects both the process and ability level of a brain function. Consequently, if there is no test for a brain function or condition, then there is no objective evidence that it exists. Thus, there is no assurance that a brain function or condition exists until there is a test for it.

The Type of Test

Unlike most medical laboratory methods, to measure a brain function the subject must actively perform a task. Such an examination is not something that is done to the person; it is something the person does. Performing a task takes time, and performing many tasks requires a considerable amount of time. Thus, an adequate neuropsychological examination demands the administration of many tests, and this requires a considerable amount of time. One problem in designing a test battery is to increase efficiency while retaining accuracy (Russell, 2000, p. 475).

Operations of the Test

A test adds several operations to that of a task. These include isolating the function and quantifying the function.

Isolating the Function

The design of a test must isolate a function for the test to be meaningful. Although the task stimulates a function, the function is part of a system. The performance of the person is not limited to one function until it is performed by a test. The test isolates a function in two ways. First, a system uses only a particular set of functions in the brain. Because the test is measuring a function or functions in that system, the system separates those functions from other areas of the brain.

Second, the test isolates a function from other components of the system by means of its design. This design emphasizes or stresses only one component of the system. The other components are sufficiently general and elementary, so they are not isolated.

For instance, the visual acuity examination uses a system that requires many activities such as listening and understanding particular instructions, holding one's head in a particular position, fixing the eyes on a particular screen. However, only the function related to visual acuity is stressed by the process of serially identifying smaller and smaller objects or letters. The rest of the functions in the system, such as hearing instructions and looking at a particular object, are not stressed, so they are not tested.

Quantifying the Function

The second operation of a test is quantifying a function's ability. This procedure also requires stressing the function. Although a task stimulates a function, a test is designed to stimulate the function progressively up to the maximum that a particular person can perform the function. A test places increasing stress on a particular brain function. This determines the ability level of the function because the test uses psychometrics to quantify each ability level. The raw score is the maximum ability level of a function that an individual can obtain. (Of course, this assumes that the subject is expending his or her maximum effort.) As such, a test represents how well the brain can perform a certain function.

A simple example of this operation is again the visual acuity test used by opticians. In this test, the individual is required to identify smaller and smaller pictured objects at a set distance. The objects are quantified by a designed gradient of decreasing size. The score is the smallest object that the person can correctly identify. This procedure provides a quantitative measure of the individual's visual acuity function.

The various procedures in which a test performance is changed into a measurement are described for individual tests in textbooks and manuals (Anastasi & Urbina, 1997). This part of testing is generally well known and well described in psychometrics. Test measures are usually either *speed* or *power* tests. Speed tests measure the time required to complete test of a specific length or how many items are completed in a designated time. Power tests consist of a series of similar subtasks or items that increase in difficulty. Measurement is obtained by a metric that quantifies the increasing difficulty of these items.

Thus, the design of the test places a stress on a particular function of the brain. This transforms the brain function's ability into a quantified physical entity: the test or computer score. As such, the score represents a brain function's ability.

Components of a Test

A test is designed to fulfill several components that constitute the requirements of the instrument. In an assessment situation, these include instructions as to how to perform the test, commands to initiate and end the test, and a recording device.

Instructions

The instructions are crucial because they are aspects of the test that determine which particular functions are tested. These instructions place constraints and requirements on the subject's behavior such that an instrument is used correctly. The instructions closely control the patient's behavior on a test and thus help determine how the brain is functioning.

Recording Device

The performance of the individual is recorded in some manner—by marking test materials, by an examiner's timer, or by a computer. This transforms the behavior into an objective record that may be observed, reproduced, or repeated. There are various forms of scores that involve either speed or performance.

Standardization

A final aspect of a test is standardization. The term *standardization* has several meanings that must be distinguished. One major meaning is that all conditions accept the condition required by testing are held constant. This means that administration procedures are constant whenever the test is administered.

Second, standardization means that the scores are compared to criteria that provide meaningful norms (Nunnally & Bernstein, 1994, p. 6). The *norms* may be as simple as a raw score cut point between normality and pathology or as elaborate as a full battery with co-normed scaling with adjustments for demographic characteristics.

For research purposes, the test may not need standardization other than those necessary to obtain raw scores. For many purposes, especially research, raw scores may be used for statistical analysis. However, even such raw scores are standardized in that they remain constant from one testing to another. They are, in fact, absolute scores, as long as the test itself is not changed. Each method has an advantage for research and assessment.

For assessment in which the scores of individuals are used, norms act as a *control group* for the test. They provide a standard for comparison. The comparison also provides a meaning for the scores, such as this person's score is average, below average, and so on. Thus, "Measures based upon well-developed rules, usually include some form of norms that describe the scores obtained in populations of interest, are called 'standardized'" (Nunnally & Bernstein, 1994, p. 6). In other words, to transform a subject's brain functioning into a meaningful measurement, the record of the subject's performance is compared to a standard. The requirements for standardization will be discussed presently.

The Psychometric Nature of a Test

For most psychologists, the nature of a test appears to be self-evident, but for many statisticians this is not the case. In fact, some statisticians use the word *measure* rather than *test* because of certain ambiguities in the term *test* (Ghiselli et al. 1981, p. 2; Nunnally & Bernstein, 1994, p. 3). This difficulty may be seen in the definition proposed by Adkins and Fiske (2009). "The word 'test' refers to any means (often formally contrived) used to elicit responses to which human behavior in other contexts can be related" (p. 1). A more complex definition by Nunnally and Bernstein (1994) is almost as inclusive: "Although tomes have been written on the nature of measurement, in the end it boils down to two fairly simple concepts: 'measurement' consists of rules for assigning symbols to objects so as to (1) represent quantities of attributes numerically (scaling) or (2) define whether the objects fall in the same or different categories with respect to a given attribute (classification)" (p. 3). Apparently, by "rules" Nunnally and Bernstein mean the design of a test or other measurement procedures.

Ghiselli et al. (1981) were more explicit in including combinations of tests as measures. For instance:

> *Many of the tests and other operations we use in measuring individuals are complex, being composed of a series of items, subtests, or other kinds of parts or components that are added together. Consequently we must examine the implications of combining diverse components into composites.* (p. 3)

Thus, on examination, none of the definitions, including that by Anastasi and Urbina (1997, p. 4), would exclude groups of tests, which are often called *subtests*, from being a *test*. Therefore, they do not exclude an entire battery, as long as the battery is used to obtain a single measure or is interpreted by means of clinical judgment.

Because of this ambiguity in the definition of a test or measure, this writing will attempt to distinguish two types of measurement operations. The traditional test is an operation that is derived from a combination of correlated items or from a timed task. Alternatively, the assessment method may be derived by combining or comparing tests in a battery. In this case, it will be called a *procedure*. In either case, the test or procedure produces scores or measure that may be used in an interpretation.

The Nature of Brain Functioning

Both the form of scientific methodology and the nature of the phenomenon to be assessed, determine the design of assessment procedures. As such, it is essential to examine the way the brain operates in order to design assessment procedures. This subsequent explanation of brain functioning is a cursory summary of those aspects of brain functioning, particularly cognitive functioning, that are now generally accepted. In addition, this discussion will be limited to those aspects of brain functioning which have a bearing on the development of neuropsychological assessment methodology.

Usual Body Organ Functioning

There are crucial differences between the way the brain and most other organs in the body function. Most other organs have a restricted physiological function that is relatively independent of other functions, even though they all contribute to the health and existence of the whole body. Some organs may have more than one function, but often such organs are separated into parts, each of which is related to a distinct function. An abnormality has a particular significance that is only concerned with a particular aspect of a subject's physiological functioning.

Second, because of homeostasis, the normal hormonal and chemical levels in the human body are generally restricted to a relatively narrow range. Consequently, only a narrow range of scores is required, and only the normality or abnormality of the function needs to be considered in a syndrome.

Brain Functioning

In contrast, brain functioning has certain characteristics that are distinct from the functioning of other body organs. The primary function of the brain and the CNS is control. No other organ functions as a control mechanism except in a limited manner. This control represents a different kind of functioning than that of other organs. Control by the brain is an extremely complex procedure that involves a large number of components.

All parts of the brain contribute to this control system. Using a computer analogy, the brain acts as a controller program that regulates the rest of the body. Each area of the brain has a different function that contributes to its overall control function. (Of course, there may be redundancies, although there is no known major area without a function.) This is one basic assumption of neuropsychology. This assumption is that each area of the brain has some mental function—cognitive, affective, or vegetative.

Functional Variations

Normal brain function includes both a general ability related to the whole brain and specific abilities related to certain areas. Probably the most inclusive description of normal brain functioning is that by Carroll (1993), who discusses the argument between advocates of a general IQ factor and advocates of several intelligences. This argument appears to be resolved, at least on a practical level. Both a general and specific intelligences exist. The concept of a general intelligence factor (g factor) is well known and generally accepted. People's overall intelligence varies from person to person so that some people have a higher general level of ability than others (Carroll, 1993). However, each area of the brain has its own functioning ability that may vary independently from other areas in its degree of ability. As such, the characteristics that have been identified as composing brain functioning are the g factor and many elementary functions that are related to different areas of the brain. These normal cognitive characteristics provide a baseline for neuropsychological assessment.

Specific Functions

In addition to this general ability, the brain has many specific abilities. These are related to various areas of the brain. These abilities vary in amount from person to person and within an individual. For instance, certain types of learning disabilities are evidently produced by inherited, relatively poor verbal functions in the left parietal area (for most right-handed people). This apparently results from an isolated underdevelopment of that area of the brain. It is probable that every area of the brain varies in its development to some extent, and that is likely also with the general level of development of the whole brain. This means that different cognitive functions will vary naturally for each person.

Obviously, this premorbid situation becomes important in neuropsychological interpretations. Because brain functions are related to areas of the brain, consideration must be given to both types of function and the location of functions. A brain-function model locates functions in various areas of the brain as shown in neurological diagrams.

Normal Distribution

One major difference between cognitive functions and other body organ functioning is that cognitive functions are not regulated by homeostasis. This is reflected in the difference between laboratory panel testing and neuropsychological testing.

Because homeostasis restricts normal function to a narrow range, an abnormality appears in a panel when a function is operating at a level that is either too high or too low; both are identified by cut points.

Brain functioning ability does not have narrow limits. A normal adult's brain functioning ability varies according to the normal distribution—that is, from an ability level well below average to one well above average. All levels are normal. Although a low ability is usually less desirable socially, it cannot be called "abnormal," because it falls within the normal distribution. An above-average ability level would not be called abnormal because it is usually considered to be desirable.

In addition, cognitive ability varies with age. According to some informal studies, the IQ of a 5-year-old is probably about 10 standard deviations (SDs) below the normal adult average. This may depend on the function and how it is measured. An average ability level of a 5-year-old is not considered abnormal even though it is far below that of the average adult. Thus, if all ages are taken into consideration, human intelligence evidently varies as much as 14 SDs without being abnormal. Within any given age, the distributions follow the normal curve in which about 2/3 of the subjects fall within 1 SD of the mean.

Premorbid Ability

In assessing brain damage, the interpretation must consider that the subject's overall ability level is affected by brain damage. Thus, the premorbid ability of the person must be estimated using one of several means. Several formulas are designed to provide this estimate (Schinka & Vanderploeg, 2000). Of the components in these formulas, education level is usually the most accurate predictor. If no formula is available, then under usual conditions education is the best estimate of intellectual ability. However, under certain circumstances, such as prematurely leaving school, education level becomes a poor indicator of intelligence; other means such as occupation level must be used.

An actual measurement of premorbid ability may often be obtained or estimated from school records and previously administered intelligence tests. Finally, when education does not provide a valid measure of a person's ability, the actual measured IQ of the subject, who is being examined for possible brain damage, may be used as a base-level estimate. This provides a minimal estimate of the subject's premorbid ability. A reasonable rule is that a person's ability is at least as good as its measurement, unless there is a practice effect. Note that the *Halstead–Russell Neuropsychological Evaluation System—Revised* is the only battery that provides the possibility of using any means other than educational level to predict premorbid intellectual level (Russell & Starkey, 2001, p. 24).

General Classification of Functions

In distinguishing brain functions, the various cognitive operations of the brain may be separated into structural and process aspects. The process aspect consists of systems. The structural aspect represents the various parts of the brain related to different functions. In spite of a considerable amount of plasticity, functions in a normal person appear to be related to relatively specific brain structures. Neurological scanning methods are now beginning to demonstrate how these structures are related to each other.

Structural Functions

The classification of functions (taxonomy) is now only preliminary. However, an overall general set of categories may be identified. These compose the structural taxonomy of the brain's functioning.

Elementary Functions

Most brain theories, such as the modularity theory (Gazzaniga, Ivry, & Mangun, 2002), assume that various functions are related in some manner to relatively specific brain areas. Following Luria's (1973) conception of a neural system in the brain, the functions in the brain can be roughly conceptualized into various units that are related to various areas and domains. In cognitive psychology, the term *ability* is often used instead of *function*. However, a function has an ability level.

The most basic aspect of Luria's concept of brain functioning was that of basic components (Luria, 1973). These basic components of cognitive functions may be called *elementary functions*. From a neurological and psychometric point of view, such elementary functions may be defined in two ways. First, they could be psychometrically distinguished from other functions (abilities) using psychometric means such as factor analysis. An elementary function would be a factor composed of tests that are intercorrelated and cannot be further subdivided into other factors. In the past, there has been a considerable amount of study in this area (Carroll, 1993).

Second, an elementary function would be related to a relatively specific area of the brain. This can be identified using various neurological methods such as the f-MIR or focal brain damage. This area would be relatively constant across the human species, although plasticity may permit a change in location under certain unusual circumstances.

Consequently, when these two methods agree and tests of the function cannot be further divided, then the evidence would indicate that an elementary function has been determined.

Compound Functions

Most tests that are now used in neuropsychology are not tests of pure elementary functions. Rather, the tests are influenced by several of these elementary functions. Because methods of isolation have not been thoroughly used to "purify" tests, the existing tests are largely multidimensional. As such, the usual tests are measures of a *compound function*. Note that the compound function measured by a test might even involve distant areas of the brain. Nevertheless, a good test will contain one or only a few dominant elementary functions.

One major endeavor of neuropsychological and cognitive research should be to conduct studies designed to separate compound functions into their elementary components. This can be done by several methods such as component analysis.

Domains

The next larger taxonomic classification is that of a *domain*. A domain may also be called a *capacity* or an *area function*. It consists of several functions—ideally, elementary functions—that are functionally related. They compose a general form of cognitive functioning that may be separated from other domains. Language, of course, is the most thoroughly delineated. The language domain appears to be more completely understood, primarily because of the analysis of aphasia over about one and a half centuries. The results of research on aphasia indicate that the language domain may be separated into receptive, expressive, and several other subdomains.

A domain should be distinguished from a compound function. The tests in a domain are functionally related in some manner, but they are tests of separate constructs. By contrast, compound functions may simply be two parts of a system that has not yet been separated into its elementary functions.

A domain is primarily defined by factor analysis and similar statistical methods. When groups of elementary functions are intercorrelated but not to other factors, they form a general domain. Another attribute of a domain is that it is generally related to a particular and rather large area of the brain that is separated from areas having other functions. Language is usually "located" in parts of the anterior and posterior sections of the left hemisphere.

Currently, it is a rather arbitrary decision as to what constitutes a domain. Probably the best initial division of domains is the four-factor model that forms the basis of the Wechsler intelligence tests. The first major division of domains is derived from lateralized abilities, in that a domain primarily exists in one or the other hemispheres.

Probably the most complete survey of factor analytic studies to date is that done by Carroll in his book *Human Cognitive Abilities* (1993). He identifies nine major clear-cut domains and a 10th domain that is composed of miscellaneous abilities. These domains are presented as chapters in his book. His general theory of intelligence is composed of domains that have a hierarchical arrangement. This theory generally conforms to Cattell's divisions of intelligence. This arrangement includes Spearman's g or general intelligence, fluid intelligence, crystallized intelligence, visualization, auditory or language intelligence, perceptual speed, fluency and memory (Carroll, 1993, pp. 585–584). Nevertheless, currently the concept of a domain is so vague and extensive that it would be difficult to select tests representing each domain. Other cognitive psychologists would divide domains somewhat differently (Gardner, 1983; Guilford, 1967).

Whole Brain Functioning

The most general level of structural organization is the whole brain. The normal whole brain acts through systems that involve areas of the whole brain when a number of functions are used to perform an act. That is, brains operate through systems of functions. Within systems, various functions vary in ability. The neuropsychological examination of a normal person will find both a general level of ability and variation in individual functions. Even for normal people, an area may be underdeveloped while the rest of the brain functions normally or even at an above-normal level.

Systems

The brain operates as a complex unit in which various functions are organized into systems. These systems are brought into play when certain types of activities are performed. To complete an act, the brain assembles many various parts into a system that performs the act. These areas are composed of elementary functions that may belong to several domains. The system does not use the entire brain but only those parts that are necessary to perform the act.

The Language System

The language system is the best-known brain system because of several centuries of studying aphasia. As an example of this system, consider the act of speaking a written word. The system begins with visualization of the reading matter. This information is transferred to the receptive language (Wernicke's area) in the left temporal parietal area (which translates visual symbols into meaningful words). These are transferred to the left frontal area (Broca's area) that places the visual symbols into grammatically meaningful statements. These are transferred to the motor area of the cortex, which "speaks" the words using the vocalization area of the motor system. This is a brief schematized illustration of the system. The assumption is that in a system each area's function contributes to the system. Although many areas of the brain are used by a system, there are areas that are not involved. For instance, the right hemisphere may not be involved in the speaking process. Second, a system varies with each act. For instance, if the act was to speak a heard sentence, the system would begin with the auditory area of the brain and not the visual area. The language components of the system belong to the language domain, which will be discussed. Other parts of the brain tend to form systems that are interrelated. Only a few systems are known to any great extent. Two that have been identified will be discussed.

Lateralized Functional Systems

In humans, the major division in types of cognitive functions is related to lateralization. In general, language functions are lateralized to the left hemisphere whereas spatial relations functions are lateralized to the right hemisphere in right-handed individuals.

Through extensive research, Mishkin, Ungerleider, and Macko (1983) have localized the visual processing of information in monkeys into two routes or systems that extend from the occipital lobes through the parietal lobes. The evidence indicated that the superior route processes information that was related to the location of objects in the individual's space. Mishkin et al. (1983) labeled this is the *where* system. The inferior route processed information that identified the nature of an object. In other words, it tended to categorize objects according to various forms of meaning such as use or relation to a particular set of objects. He labeled this the *what* system.

Although Mishkin et al.'s (1983) work indicated that these two routes occurred in both hemispheres of monkeys, the description of the functions in the two routes corresponds rather closely to the different types of functions that are lateralized in humans. The spatial relations or the where system in humans is largely localized in the right hemisphere, whereas the what system corresponds to conceptual formation and the functions that language performs. Language provides names for various categories of objects related to the function and description of objects. The primary localization of spatial relations in the right hemisphere and the localization of conceptual understanding in the left hemisphere is exactly what was found in a recent PET-scan study (Ventre-Dominey et al., 2005).

One might speculate that during the evolution of humans, to obtain more intellectual capacity for a brain with limited size, these two laterally redundant systems could have evolved into lateralized functional systems. Such lateralization would provide more space in each hemisphere for the particular system that was localized to that hemisphere.

The Nature of Intelligence

Probably more has been written in the attempt to define intelligence than any other subject in psychology. Intelligence exists somewhere between total brain functioning and a domain, because several processes such as motor and sensory processes are only weakly correlated with IQ measures (Carroll, 1993, p. 596; Guilford, 1967, pp. 6–7). However, neuropsychology along with factor analysis provides a definition that is relatively straightforward.

Factor analysis provides a solution to the definition of intelligence by demonstrating the existence of a g factor along with many subfactors (Carroll, 1993, pp. 577–628). Apparently, genetics is involved in forming different areas of the brain such that, even though brain functioning as a whole varies in ability, every brain also has some functions that are more developed than others. For instance, savants and many geniuses are evidently produced by a genetic factor that is related to an area of the brain. Neuropsychologists have often found that there are general tests that are impaired when there is damage almost anywhere in the brain (Reitan & Wolfson, 1993, pp. 9–19, 27). These are often tests of high-level functions that appear to be related to the g factor. However, certain types of activities, such as acrobatics and sports, are related to factors that are not highly correlated with the g factor (Carroll, 1993, pp. 577–628). Thus, intelligence is the ability level of the general brain functions that are primarily measured by the g factor.

A neuropsychological examination, in fact, appears to be an expanded examination of intelligence (Ardila, 1999). Certainly, most intelligence tests are incomplete. The primary intelligence tests do not cover many areas covered by a neuropsychological examination. Future work using test development and brain-scan techniques will undoubtedly expand our understanding of what the g factor covers. As such, intelligence will be defined as how well the g factor abilities of the brain are functioning.

This would solve most of the arguments concerning the nature of intelligence because various functions or abilities would be related to different functions as well as the general functioning of the brain. For instance, most verbal aspects of intelligence tests appear to be academic ability tests and may have less relevance to other kinds of activities. Consequently, other activities would involve different functions and require different tests, even though there is a general factor.

References

Adkins, D. C., & Fiske, D. W. (2009). Psychological testing. *Encyclopaedia Britannica. Ultimate Reference Suite*. Chicago: Encyclopaedia Britannica.

Anastasi, A., & Urbina, S. (1997). *Psychological testing* (pp. 45–51) (7th ed.). Upper Saddle River, NJ: Prentice Hall.

Ardila, A. (1999). A neuropsychological approach to intelligence. *Neuropsychological Review*, *9*(3), 117–136.

Carroll, J. B. (1993). *Human cognitive abilities: A survey of factor-analytic studies*. New York: Cambridge University Press.

Costa, P. T., & Widiger, T. A. (Eds.). (2002). *Personality disorders and the five-factor model of personality* (2nd ed.). Washington, DC: American Psychological Association.

Cronbach, L. J., & Meehl, P. E. (1955). Construct validity in psychological tests. *Psychological Bulletin*, *53*, 281–302.

Dorland's illustrated medical dictionary. (1967). (24th ed.). Philadelphia: W. B. Saunders.

Gardner, H. (1983). *Frames of mind: The theory of multiple intelligences*. New York: Basic Books.

Gazzaniga, M. S., Ivry, R. B., & Mangun, G. R. (2002). *Cognitive neuroscience: The biology of the mind* (2nd ed.). New York: Norton.

Ghiselli, E. E., Campbell, J. P., & Zedeck, S. (1981). *Measurement theory for the behavioral sciences*. San Francisco: W. H. Freeman.

Guilford, J. P. (1967). *The nature of human intelligence*. New York: McGraw-Hill.

Lezak, M. D., Howieson, D. B., & Loring, D. W. (2004). *Neuropsychological assessment* (4th ed.). New York: Oxford University Press.

Luria, A. R. (1973). *The working brain*. New York: Basic Books.

Mishkin, M., Ungerleider, L., & Macko, K. (1983, October). Object vision and spatial vision: Two cortical pathways. *Trends in Neuroscience*, *6(2)*, 414–417.

Nunnally, J. C., & Bernstein, I. H. (1994). *Psychometric theory* (3rd ed.). New York: McGraw-Hill.

Reitan, R. M., & Wolfson, D. (1993). *The Halstead–Reitan neuropsychological test battery: Theory and clinical interpretation* (2nd ed.). Tucson: Neuropsychology Press.

Russell, E. W. (2000). The cognitive-metric, fixed battery approach to neuropsychological assessment. In R. D. Vanderploeg (Ed.), *Clinician's guide to neuropsychological assessment* (pp. 449–481) (2nd ed.). Hillsdale, NJ: Lawrence Erlbaum Associates.

Russell, E. W., & Starkey, R. I. (2001). *Halstead–Russell Neuropsychological Evaluation System—Revised (Manual and computer program)*. Los Angeles: Western Psychological Services.

Schinka, J. A., & Vanderploeg, R. D. (2000). Estimating premorbid level of functioning. In R. D. Vanderploeg (Ed.), *Clinician's guide to neuropsychological assessment* (pp. 39–67) (2nd ed.). Mahwah, NJ: Lawrence Erlbaum Associates.

Tulsky, D. S., Saklofske, D. H., & Zhu, J. (2003). Revising a Standard: An evaluation of the origin and development of the WAIS-III. In D. S. Tulsky, D. H. Saklofske, R. K. Heaton, R. Bornstein & M. F. Ledbetter (Eds.), *Clinical interpretation of the WAIS-III and WMS-III* (pp. 7–41). New York: Academic Press.

Ventre-Dominey, J., Bailly, A., Lavenne, F., Lebars, D., Mollion, H., & Dominey, P. F (2005). Doubled disassociation in neural correlates of visual working memory: A PET study. *Cognitive Brain Research*, *25*(3), 747–759.

4 Brain-Function Analysis

There is no certainty in science
Where one of the mathematical sciences
cannot be applied,
or which are not in relation
with these mathematics.

(Leonardo da Vinci) *Notebooks, sections on philosophical maxims*
(Klein, 1988, p. 190)

In the United States, though we are reputed to be the most scientifically and technically advanced among nations, ancient and illogical units are retained in every day use … all derived from ancient British units.

(Klein, 1988, pp. 26–27)

Chapter 2 examined the relationship of brain functioning to testing, emphasizing the relationship between a brain function and a single test. However, a single test is related to only a limited portion of brain functioning. A neuropsychological interpretation usually involves the entire brain unless a specific area such as aphasia is being investigated. Consequently, the investigation of an entire brain requires the use of many tests.

This chapter examines the relationship between brain functioning as a whole and the psychometric aspects of assessment. These measurements, which constitute an examination of the entire brain, comprise a neuropsychological battery. Almost all neuropsychological interpretations use entire batteries. This chapter is devoted to an examination of the psychometric principles and relationships that are used in the construction of a battery.

The emphasis will be on the discovery process in the design of a battery. The justification process will be examined in a later chapter. When the discovery aspect of science is applied to assessment procedures, it includes the construction of assessment methods as well as research methods. Research methods have been extensively discussed in textbooks, but assessment procedures, especially when applied to test batteries, have rarefy been examined in depth. This and the next chapters will be devoted to a discussion of such construction methodology.

The Scientific Foundation of Neuropsychological Assessment. DOI: 10.1016/B978-0-12-416029-3.00004-X

The Purpose of Neuropsychological Assessment Procedures

From the preceding theoretical discussion, it is evident that the purpose of neuropsychological assessment is to describe the psychological functioning of the brain and its pathology as accurately and reliably as possible.

A neuropsychological evaluation yields information describing the functioning of an individual's brain as manifested in the person's behavior. For neuropsychology, the term *brain functioning* applies to the nonphysiological aspect of a brain's activity—that is, the behavior of the organism. Neurology is concerned with the physiological aspect of brain functioning, but it only grossly and indirectly evaluates the brain's behavioral functioning.

The methods of neuropsychology assessment are specifically designed to examine and describe the behavioral results of an individual's brain functioning. The purpose of both research and assessment is to produce reliable knowledge about brain functioning.

The methods of assessment are based on scientific principles and the science of neurology and psychology. The relationships of these scientific methods are somewhat complex, so they will be examined first.

The Scientific Study of Brain Functioning

Although the basis of science remains constant, the particular methodology of constructing procedures, especially for brain-function analysis, varies even within the study of brain functioning. From the perspective of neurological science, brain-function analysis has three primary levels.

The first level is pure neurological research or neuroscience, which may include some research in neuropsychology. The second level constitutes applied neuropsychology. This aspect may be termed *brain-function analysis*. This deals with creating, validating, and using methods for the behavioral assessment of human brain functioning. Applied neuropsychology is to neuroscience what engineering is to physics. Engineering science creates the methods that practicing engineers use to build physical structures. Engineering also has its own research methods devoted to the application of the physics theory to practical problems. The third level is assessment, which applies the findings of applied neuropsychological research to the examination of an individual.

"Pure" Research Methodology

Neuropsychological research methodology may be either a pure form of neuroscience or an applied methodology. As a form of neuroscience, it is designed to investigate how the brain functions and to demonstrate the existence of theoretical neurological functions or relationships. For the most part, such pure neuropsychological research methods are not within the scope of this book.

Applied Neuropsychology Methodology

The second and third levels of methodology constitute applied neuropsychology and are designed for the evaluation of an individual human subject's brain functioning. This applies to both as research and as individual assessment. In these levels, both discovery and justification procedures are employed.

Neuropsychology Research and Assessment

Although applied neuropsychology is designed to study brain functioning from a behavioral or psychometric standpoint, its two levels are (1) research on assessment procedures and (2) assessment of individuals. The research level is devoted to relating brain functioning to psychometric assessment procedures. This form of psychometrics is well known to neuropsychologists because it is the type of neuropsychology methodology that is usually taught in graduate schools. The statistical methods such as *t*-tests, analyses of variance (ANOVAS), and correlations are research methods designed to compare groups of individuals with different conditions to examine the effect of the conditions on behavior or tests.

Assessment Procedures

Finally, there is the third level, which is the practitioner level; it involves the assessment of an individual. This applies psychometric procedures in the assessment of a subject to determine the brain condition of an individual. Often such assessment is used to answer a referral, which may ask whether a person has a particular condition.

The primary difference between general applied neuropsychological research and assessment is whether a test measures a particular condition or indicates a particular condition affecting an individual. The traditional assumption in clinical neuropsychology was that when the relationship of a specific test to a condition was established by research, then that test could be used to determine whether an individual has that condition.

However, as will be discussed later, in most cases an evaluation requires more than a single test to determine the existence of a condition because there are many alternative reasons for impairment to any single test. A single test cannot distinguish these reasons. Thus, as a minimum, the examiner must use additional tests to rule out alternatives. In an assessment, tests are used in a unit, such as a battery, to determine the condition of an individual person. Thus, assessment usually involves an analysis of an individual's total brain functioning.

Brain-Function Analysis and Context

In addition to the battery of tests, a complete neuropsychological assessment has two parts: the *brain-function analysis* and its *context*. The brain-function analysis is that part of an assessment evaluation that is derived from psychometric procedures alone.

It is the information that would be obtained from a blind analysis of the battery results.

The *context* includes all of the information used in a complete interpretation that is not derived from the brain-function analysis. This context of an evaluation elaborates the meaning of the information obtain from analyzing the functioning of the brain in terms of the patient's situation. The context includes the patient's medical history, diagnosis, affective condition, academic history, relevant social history, and any other material that might be relevant to an assessment. Such material is necessary to integrate the psychometric results into a dependable and complete interpretation of an individual's neurological condition. The component that is derived from test results provides an assessment of the patient's brain functioning at a particular time, whereas the context specifies the meaning of this brain functioning in terms of the patient's situation.

The brain-function analysis part of the evaluation may be completely scientific because it is based on validated information. However, in a specific assessment case, particularly in forensic cases, the information that can be derived from brain-function analysis is only part of the information used to derive the full interpretation. In the practice of most neuropsychologists, the context may be almost as important as the analysis.

Although information derived from brain-function analysis is distinct from that derived from the context, many neuropsychologists confuse these two processes, so it is difficult to know whether their conclusions were obtained from brain-function analysis or the context. If the context is obtained first, then it may easily bias the analysis. For the most part, the concern of this chapter will be restricted to psychometric processes used in brain-function analysis. The non-neuropsychological training of a clinical neuropsychologist is important in understanding the context of the examination.

Neuropsychological Examination Results

The practice of neuropsychological assessment is dependent on the accuracy of the assessment psychometrics that is used along with a thorough understanding of the context of the assessment. The particular form of the assessment depends on the purpose of the assessment or the referral question. In a few cases, the referral question will be quite specific, in which case the neuropsychologists applies the requisite tests and submits the report.

However, often the neuropsychologists may be able to expand the request through providing a more thorough testing of the patient's brain functioning. Lezak, Howieson, and Loring (2004) indicate that making such suggestions is one of the functions of the neuropsychologist (p. 11). This, of course, would require a test battery that includes the entire brain.

Forensic neuropsychology is fairly limited in the type of "referral" questions that are appropriate. Although this will be discussed later, the questions are largely concerned with (1) whether there is brain damage, (2) whether there is an affective component in the situation, (3) the amount of impairment, (4) the prognosis (including possibly a lifetime prognosis), and in many cases (5) an opinion as to the cause of the impairment.

Theoretical Basis of Brain-Function Analysis

The rationale for the construction of individual tests is well known, but the rationale for the design and construction of batteries is not well understood. The scientific approach to psychometric methodology involved in an assessment, which uses a battery, began with the work of Teuber (1955) and Reitan (1955). In the 1950s, both Reitan (1955) and Teuber (1955) developed methods to localize lesions with neuropsychological tests.

Teuber's Double Disassociation

Teuber (1955, 1975) described and designated this procedure as the method of *double dissociation*. The method of double disassociation needs to be presented in some detail, because it has become a major method for neuropsychological research (Dunn & Kirsner, 2003). More relevant, for assessment it is the basis for the battery method that is used by neuropsychological assessment. Although it is rarely mentioned in writings on neuropsychological assessment, most formal neuropsychological assessment methods are constructed on the fundamental procedure.

The Method

The method of double dissociation was first used to determine the lateralization of a lesion by neuropsychological tests. This procedure involves a comparison of the results of at least two tests for lateralizing damage applied to each of the two hemispheres. Historically, other arrangements had been used to associate a test to an area of the brain. The four major types of arrangements used to lateralize damage are presented in Table 4.1.

Table 4.1 Double Dissociation Applied to a Right-Hemisphere Lesion

Methods	Brain-Damage Type		
	Right Hemisphere	**Left Hemisphere**	**Control**
1. Test A	Impaired	—	Not impaired
2. Test A	More impaired	Less impaired	Not impaired
3. Test A	More impaired	—	Not impaired
Test B	Less impaired	—	Not impaired
4. Test A	More impaired	Less impaired	Not impaired
Test B	Less impaired	More impaired	Not impaired

In this table, this method is illustrated by studies that are used to locate right-hemisphere damage. The initial method of determining localization of a lesion is to use only one test. It is presented in Table 4.1 as method 1. In this method, the impairment of test A was thought to indicate impairment of the right cerebral hemisphere because patients with right-hemisphere damage performed more poorly on the test than normal subjects. Obviously, the difficulty here is that almost any kind of brain damage, not just right-hemisphere damage, may produce impairment on test A. This type of procedure may be called the *one-test, one-condition* type of study.

As an illustration, research may demonstrate that the category test is impaired by Alzheimer's disease. This method would imply that an impaired category test indicates Alzheimer's disease. Although the faulty logic is obvious, it is amazing that a large proportion of the research being published today concerning diagnoses still uses this form of procedure.

In method 2, patients with right- and left-hemisphere damage are compared using a single test. This research study found that test A is more impaired with right-hemisphere damage than with left-hemisphere damage. The study concluded that test A is primarily a right-hemisphere test. Again, if this test is impaired in assessment, then it is concluded that the patient has a right-hemisphere lesion. Although this method is a somewhat more accurate procedure, it still contains two problems. First, test A may be more impaired by subjects with right-hemisphere damage because the damage is greater for the subjects with right-hemisphere damage than left-hemisphere damage. Second, it may be impaired by diffuse damage.

In method 3, the previous problem may be overcome by utilizing two tests: A and B. When test A is more impaired for right-hemisphere damage than B, the researcher concludes that A is more sensitive to right-hemisphere lesions, and so impairment of Test A in assessment indicates a lesion in the right hemisphere. However, the error here is that A may simply be more sensitive to brain damage in general than B.

In the history of neuropsychology, this type of error was evidently the basis of the concept that alcoholism produced more right-hemisphere damage than left (Parsons & Farr, 1981). Previously, several studies had found that Wechsler Performance subtests were more impaired by right-hemisphere damage and verbal tests were more impaired by left-hemisphere damage. However, using a complex method of double disassociation, Barron and Russell (1992) demonstrated that the Wechsler Performance tests were more impaired by alcoholism because the performance tests tended to be fluid intelligence tests that are more sensitive to damage in general than verbal tests. In contrast, the verbal tests measured crystallized ability that is less impaired by diffuse or generalized damage. Thus, the greater impairment of performance tests in alcoholism resulted from fluidity and not lateralization (Barron & Russell, 1992; Russell, 1979, 1980a).

Method 4 illustrates double disassociation. Double dissociation is the procedure that most unequivocally demonstrates lateralization (Teuber, 1955, 1975). Double dissociation is effective because different tests have known differing sensitivities to different locations or brain conditions (Reitan & Wolfson, 1993, pp. 23–54). It is the ratio between test scores that is crucial for localization of lesions or diagnosis of a brain condition and not the absolute score.

The difference between the two tests is indicated when research demonstrated that test A is more impaired for right-hemisphere damage than test B, whereas test B is more impaired for left-hemisphere damage than test A. There is a disassociation of test scores in addition to a disassociation in the known lateralization of the damage. Consequently, in assessment when these tests are compared, one can be confident that when test A is significantly more impaired then the person has right-hemisphere impairment; and when test B is significantly more impaired, the major damage is in the left hemisphere. It is only this comparison methodology that reliably indicates lateralization or localization of damage.

Finally, the double-disassociation procedure may be applied to the discrimination of many conditions other than the location of damage, such as pathologies (Dunn & Kirsner, 2003). When verbal fluency tests are more impaired, left frontal damage is indicated but only when primary verbal tests such as vocabulary and similarities are relatively intact. Thus, this method of double disassociation uses both research and assessment methods. Research establishes the relationships, whereas assessment uses the known relationships to determine the location of damage or diagnosis of damage in an individual.

Importance of Double Dissociation

The concept of double dissociation is crucial for neuropsychological assessment, because it is the basis for the methods that produce reliably batteries. Single tests are only capable of examining single dissociations (methods 1, 2, and 3 in Table 4.1). Individual tests are usually one-dimensional in that they provide a single score that has a single interpretation, which in neuropsychology is restricted to the conclusion that this person does or does not have brain damage somewhere.

In addition, double dissociation demonstrates that unimpaired tests are as important in brain-function pattern analysis as are deficits. A poor score on one test that is sensitive to an entity (location, function, or pathology) only demonstrates the abnormal functioning of that entity, which may be a result of a number of causes, including general brain damage. Thus, two or more tests are needed to distinguish types of pathologies or locations.

Psychometric Requirements for Double Disassociation

To be reliable, double disassociation has certain psychometric requirements that are seldom discussed because they are usually taken for granted. However, when applied to whole batteries, these requirements become important.

Procedural Uniformity

First, double disassociation requires procedural uniformity—that is, the tests and administration procedures must be uniform across testings. The criterion for consistency is specified in the test instructions. This requirement applies to both assessment procedures and research.

Invariance of Tests

Next, in double dissociation, for the results to be reliable, the same tests must be used for each assessment. This means that the tests in double dissociation must be invariant from one administration to another. Although this is obvious on this elementary level, the implications for more complex assessments are often overlooked.

This invariance requirement means that the test scores must be standardized so that the differences between scores will remain invariant. This provides the same fixed difference or ratio between tests each time the tests are administered. Equating may be accomplished in one of two ways. Either the raw scores are fixed or equivalent scale scores are created.

There is a naive belief that if tests are derived from the same domain, then they are measuring the same function and thus are interchangeable. Because of the variability of tests within a domain, such double dissociation can only be obtained through statistical methods that equalize individual pairs of specific tests.

Research to Validate the Comparison

Obviously, the major requirement for using double disassociation in assessment is that research must have previously demonstrated that one test is more sensitive to the condition under consideration—localization, pathology, or function—whereas other tests in a battery are less sensitive. Such a study establishes the initial validity of the relationship between the tests but not the validity of individual tests used alone.

Criterion for Comparison

Finally, a fixed cut point or ratio between the tests must be obtained. This cut point will indicate a significant difference between test results. The cut point must be determined by research studies, which are usually the same studies that validate the comparison. Thus, a standard criterion is established to determine at what point the difference between the tests is sufficient to indicate a significantly greater probability of impairment of one test. This significance indicates the existence of a particular condition.

Reitan's Battery

At the same time that Teuber proposed the concept of double disassociation, Reitan independently found that he could localize brain lesions by the comparison of tests using a complex form of double disassociation (Reitan, 1964). He found that a minimum of two tests, which have an invariant relationship to each other and differing sensitivities to an area of damage and opposed sensitivities to other areas, were required to accurately localize lesions. The invariant relationship was needed to provide a fixed ratio between the scores. This was also true of other brain conditions.

Multiple Dissociation

Although Reitan specified four methods in his assessment methodology (Reitan & Wolfson, 1993, pp. 28–29), two methods—the level of performance and pathognomonic

Table 4.2 Multiple Dissociation

Tests	R Frontal	R Parietal	L Frontal	L Parietal
Test A	XXX			
Test B		XXX		
Test C			XXX	
Test D				XXX

Note. Tests are related to the area of the brain marked with "XXX." For multiple dissociations, possible combinations indicating locations of brain damage.

1. Tests A, B, C, D not impaired = No Damage.
2. Tests A, B, C, D impaired = Diffuse.
3. Tests A and B more impaired, tests C, D less impaired = R hemisphere.
4. Tests C and D more impaired, tests A, B less impaired = L hemisphere.
5. Tests A and C more impaired, tests B, D less impaired = bifrontal damage.
6. Tests B and D more impaired; tests A, C less impaired = biparietal damage.
7. Test A more impaired, tests B, C, D less impaired = R frontal.
8. Test B more impaired, tests A, C, D less impaired = R parietal.
9. Test C more impaired, tests A, B, D less impaired = L frontal.
10. Test D more impaired, tests A, B, C less impaired = L parietal.

signs—may use individual tests. However, the other two methods—intra-individual comparisons and comparisons of functions on two sides of the body—require comparisons that are essentially forms of double dissociation. Reitan's battery was a relatively large number of double dissociations, which are generally used in many comparisons. Often several tests would be used redundantly to indicate the area or type of lesion.

Expanded to cover a whole battery, the double-dissociation method is essentially a multiple dissociation of tests (Russell, 2000, pp. 469–465). The more tests that are known to be sensitive to a location and are used in conjunction with tests that are not sensitive to the same location or condition, the more accurate is the assessment of the lesion's location or condition. Consequently, multiple dissociation is an extension of the double-dissociation method and has all of the requirements that apply to double dissociation. This method may be explained using Table 4.2.

In this illustration, the method will be simplified so that the explanation using Table 4.2 will be restricted to demonstrate the method of determining the location of brain damage that can be obtained from the interaction of four tests in relationship to four areas of the brain. These are the right and left, frontal, and parietal areas.

It is assumed that previous research has particularly related these tests to these four areas of the brain. In this table, the known location of a test is indicated by the XXX's in the table. The notes for the table indicate the various patterns that may be obtained from these tests.

Requirements for Multiple Dissociation

Because multiple disassociation is a complex form of double disassociation, the basic requirements for double disassociation also apply to multiple disassociation. However, the application of these requirements is more complex. As with double dissociation, multiple disassociation can be used only with a group of tests in which the interrelationships between all of the tests have been psychometrically equated by standardization. In addition, the particular tests, the content of a battery, must remain invariant, at least during standardization.

Because Table 4.2 illustrates only a few relationships, in practice the more tests there are in a battery, the more possible combinations exist. These combinations provide the basis for pattern analysis. Pattern analysis is thus composed of various combinations of test results made possible by a multiple application of the double-dissociation method.

In addition, redundancy is increased when there is more than one test for an area. The more tests that are known to be sensitive to a location or condition used in conjunction with tests that are not sensitive to the same location or condition, the more reliable is the assessment.

Although the method of multiple dissociation was initially established for locating a lesion, the method may be used for many kinds of interpretations. For instance, Russell and Polakoff (1993) and Russell and Starkey (2001b, p. 36) employed a disassociation method for distinguishing Alzheimer's dementia from cerebral vascular dementia with an accuracy rate of 95% on cross-validation. The same method may be used to separate Alzheimer's disease from most other forms of brain damage, with the exception of alcoholism. Nevertheless, independent cross-validation is needed.

The amount of research in neuropsychology that is based on multiple dissociation is scanty. Neuropsychological studies in assessment have seldom dealt with the interaction of tests. The majority of research has examined the relationship of one test to one condition. There is more research on indexes, but it is still minimal. The research on differences between tests related to various neurological conditions is almost nonexistent.

The Brain-Function Model

From a neuropsychological perspective, a test battery uses multiple dissociation to create a brain-function model. A model is an abstract representational form in which each component has a specified relationship to the entity being modeled. It is standard practice for engineers and scientists to employ physical and mathematical models to represent complex structures and processes. In psychology, mental models have been used to represent aspects of cognition (Pellegrino, 1988; Reitan & Wolfson, 1986, pp. 63–71).

Just as a single test represents a specific brain function, so an integrated battery is a brain-function model that represents the functioning of the entire brain. (A specific integrated battery, such as an aphasia battery, may be designed for a specialized area such as language.) This model provides patterns of impaired functions that may represent various brain locations and conditions.

Test: Representing a Single Brain Function

In almost all textbooks on neuropsychology, a test represents a single construct (Nunnally & Bernstein, 1994, pp. 104–105). In neuropsychology, the construct is usually a cognitive ability or attribute. In this theoretical presentation, the construct of a single test represents a single brain function. The function may be compound, but it is measured by a single test. The ideal test, of course, measures an elementary function.

An index such as an IQ is not a single test but a measure derived from a combination of tests that represents a process like intelligence. The distinction is important when interpreting test results.

The Distinctions Between a Test and an Integrated Battery

The distinction between a single test used in a group and a battery of tests is crucial for neuropsychological assessment. As used in this writing, a battery is any group of tests used in an interpretation. This includes flexible as well as standardized batteries.

A group of tests in which each test is used to obtain an independent interpretative conclusion is not an integrated battery. If a person is administered a reading, a spelling, and an arithmetic test and the conclusions are that he or she is poor in reading, spelling, and arithmetic, then this is an unintegrated group of test results. However, if the conclusion is that the person is a poor student, all three tests were used to form the single interpretation. Consequently, this group of tests constitutes an integrated battery.

Although both an item test and a battery of tests with an index score such as an IQ may be included under the same term such as *test* or *procedure*, there are psychometric differences between them. Essentially, an item test is measuring one attribute or brain function, whereas a battery is measuring a number of attributes simultaneously. Psychometrically, a test is an index consisting of a unit of items, all measuring the same entity. The internal consistency (internal reliability) for a test should be high because the items are intended to measure a single neuropsychological attribute.

In contrast, a battery is composed of a number of tests that are measuring different neuropsychological attributes. Consequently, the correlations between tests in a battery should be relatively low. Obviously, internal consistency measures do not apply to a battery. Test–retest reliabilities can be obtained for a battery as for the individual tests in a battery.

In an ideal battery, each test or designated group of tests would be related to a separate domain. The primary criteria for a psychometric domain is a stable factor derived from factor-analysis studies or equivalent methods of separating the tests into groups, each of which is measuring a different entity.

Currently, the various domains of cognitive functions have not been adequately distinguished. Consequently, accurate psychometric interpretative results need to be provided by individual tests rather than a domain presumably represented by a test. Tests usually represent a function that can be named.

From a neurological perspective, a test is ideally a measure of an elementary function. However, because there appear to be almost no pure measures of elementary functions, in practice a single test usually represents a compound function. At best, a test is a measure that is limited to a small number of elementary functions or a group that is related to a dominant elementary function. The number of elementary functions in a compound function should be as limited as possible.

A single test provides an interpretation that is limited to a single limited conclusion. In neuropsychology, this conclusion is often limited to whether a person does or does not have brain damage. In addition, a single test cannot account for the many alternate effects that may influence a test score. In research, most of these effects are considered random error, which is nullified in part by a control group. However, in assessment, these alternative effects are only slightly reduced by standardization. Generally, they must be ruled out by reference to other tests or even by the non-neuropsychological context.

Norms Represent Human Brain Functioning

As described earlier, the basic neuropsychological assessment question is how well the brain functions in a particular individual are performing—that is, what is the ability level of a particular brain function, or a group of brain functions, which may include the entire brain? Thus, the most fundamental "population" of neuropsychological assessment is the functioning of the human brain. In other words, the ultimate direct concern of neuropsychological assessment is not the behavior of an individual but the functioning of that individual's brain. In a forensic case, the court is not directly concerned with the behavior of an individual, as it would be in a robbery case, but in the functioning of the brain. "Is this person's brain damaged"? "How severe is the impairment?" "Which functions are impaired?" And so forth.

Of course, the test is measuring behavior. However, the behavior is of a particular kind that is measured by the ability to perform a specific task (the test). The task represents brain functioning. Thus, the basis of neuropsychological theory is that all humans have the same basic genetics that create their brains' functioning, which is normally distributed.

Although the genetic basis, or as Halstead would call it the *biological intelligence* of humans, is the ideal basis for a neuropsychological assessment, in reality learning has such a powerful effect on all forms of cognitive functioning that separating biological from learned brain functioning is extremely difficult. Consequently, neuropsychology now must assess the brain functioning that is composed of both genetic and learned functions. When learning is included, the population to be sampled is restricted to a particular culture. Consequently, the norms represent the human brain functioning of individuals within a particular culture.

An Adequate Integrated Brain-Function Model

As mentioned previously, a battery models brain functions in two ways: (1) psychometric characteristics and (2) content characteristics. About psychometric characteristics, the model assumes that the brain is relatively invariant in certain psychometric or formal respects. This involves standardization. About content, the model assumes that the locations of various abilities, particularly elementary functions, are relatively invariant.

The design of a battery may model brain functioning adequately or poorly. A major characteristic of an adequate integrated brain-function model is a well-designed battery. A battery is adequately integrated when all of the tests are co-normed—that is, it has been standardized (Nunnally & Bernstein, 1994, p. 4) so that the relationships between tests are either invariant or equivalent. In such a battery, the tests can psychometrically be reliably combined and compared (Anastasi & Urbina, 1997, p. 49; Lezak et al., 2004, pp. 153–155; Reitan & Wolfson, 1993; Russell, 1998, 2000; Russell, Russell, & Hill, 2005).

The same score will mean the same amount of impairment or level of functioning for all tests that constitute the battery or set of tests. Thus, such an integrated battery requires standardization. A central concept related to a standardized brain-function model is that of a *constant background* (Russell, 2000, pp. 456–458). In a constant background produced by standardization, the tests remain equivalent within a battery and are invariant from one subject to another. With a constant background, the differences in scales reflect differences in the subjects and not differences in the way the tests were normed.

An analogy may be made with a mirror. In a sense, a set of tests is a mirror of a person's functioning. If the mirror is constant or even in that the glass does not vary from one point to another and the complete mirror is used each time, the reflected image is true and can be trusted. However, if different parts of the glass vary in angle, as with different norms, so that the surface is uneven, then one does not know whether the shape of the perceived image results from variations in the object or variations in the medium—that is, the mirror.

Thus, the psychometric relationships between tests are standardized by means of co-normed scale scores. As such, these relationships are invariant across time and administrations.

Content of the Battery

The second major component of an integrated battery is that the tests used in an interpretation remain the same from one administration to another. Integration includes both the content of the tests as well as standardization of the battery. The test content should systematically represent the entire brain. This model will demonstrate how well the different parts of a brain are functioning. The content of the battery remains constant from one testing to another. Thus, a standardized battery forms a constant background against which a person's particular strengths and weaknesses become evident (Russell, 2000, pp. 456–458). The battery itself is a fixed standard, a model, against which the variation in the individual patient's examination results are apparent as patterns.

Test Relationships

Because a standardized battery is an integrated group of tests, it primarily concerns the relationships between tests. Usually, the relationships between tests enable the examiner to reach an accurate interpretative conclusion. The standardization of relationships enables a battery to accurately combine and compare tests. The relationships form the patterns that provide an interpretation.

Basis of Pattern Analysis

In an assessment, the relationships between tests in an integrated battery form a pattern that is distinctive for each subject. This is the basis for an interpretation derived from the examination. As a brain model, this pattern represents the pattern of brain functioning. The pattern models the functional condition of the brain.

It is the understanding of these patterns that enables the neuropsychologist to not only determine the existence of brain damage but also establish its type, location, and prognosis. About the importance of patterns, Lezak et al. (2004, pp. 153–154) were correct. Currently, this understanding of patterns is in an embryonic stage. Formal research on patterns is almost nonexistent.

A pattern of test results is produced by the multiple dissociations between tests in a battery. When observed as a unit, these test dissociations represent the relationship between tests in the form of a pattern. A double disassociation is a primary, simple pattern that enables the examiner to determine the laterality of damage or the existence of a number of other conditions. Multiple disassociations represent a complex form of double disassociation. When taken as a unit, multiple disassociation represents the way that the entire brain is functioning. This pattern of relationships between test scores may be analyzed in different ways to determine various conditions of the brain. Patterns will be discussed more fully in a later chapter 6. However, the multiple dissociation patterns are produced by the combinations and comparisons of tests. These are derived from neuropsychological measurement.

Standardization of Batteries

Although standardization of a battery is a major concern of this chapter, much of the discussion applies to individual tests as well as whole batteries. For this reason, the standardization of individual tests as a separate entity will not be discussed.

Measurement in Science

Measurement in science involves two different components. These are the components that relate a measure to the attribute being measured and the method designed to make those measures reliable. In regard to the component that relates the measure to the attribute, Nunnally and Bernstein (1994) designate the relational aspect of measurement procedures as *rules*: "'measurement' consists of rules for assigning symbols to objects so as to … represent quantities of attributes numerically (scaling) …" (p. 3). The rules refer to the design of tests and procedures. They determine what attributes are being measured and how they are measured. In neuropsychology, the attribute being measured is generally a brain function or brain-function pathology. This consists of the contents of a test or battery, which will be discussed later.

The second component of measurement consists of the characteristics of the measurement that make a measure accurate, reliable, and valid. In most cases, this consists of the standardization process.

Standardization of Scales

For the most part, the requirements to ensure reliability are aspects of standardization and validity. The methods for standardization and validation are different and will be discussed separately. Although the specific term *standardization* is not regularly used in neuropsychology books, it includes such central procedures as norming and scale design.

A Basis for Scale Measurement

The purpose of standardization is to ensure objectivity and repeatability—that is, consistency—across measurements. An entity must be objective to be repeatable. "The basic point about standardization is the users of a given instrument should obtained similar results" (Nunnally & Bernstein, 1994, p. 4). A standard is a criterion for ensuring the reliability of repeated measurement. As such, the method must be fixed so that a test gives the same results every time it is repeated.

Basis for Meaning

A standard is a means to provide a measure that has a specific meaning. The measure is derived from a consistent external entity: the standard. Without a comparison with a meaningful standard, the results of a measurement are simply meaningless numbers. For instance, the standard for a thermometer is the freezing and boiling points of water (at sea level). A standard generally is based on a stable quantifiable aspect of the universe to which scoring can be referred to gain consistency, meaning, and utility.

With a scale, adequate standardization has three parts. The standard is anchored at a minimum of two points, which are fixed by external criteria and are known to be constant. The third part is a scale with intervals that are arbitrary as long as they are constant. However, they are more meaningful if an established number is used to determine the intervals between the anchors. In the metric system, the number is 10 or 100. Thus, these points may be the basis for a system of degrees or scale points established by the anchors to form the scale. The scale scores generally continue beyond both anchors. (A ratio scale has zero as the anchor point.)

Currently, in psychological psychometrics a standard score interval scale is anchored by a population mean and by the population's *standard deviation* (SD). The SD is also the basis for the scale intervals. The distance between the mean and the SD provides the basis for most psychological scales. The scale intervals between the mean and the SD have varied. They have included at least 15, 10, and 3 intervals. The actual mean and SD of the population are determined by a sample. Thus, the adequacy of a scale is dependent on the adequacy of the sample. (Percentile scores use another method that will not be discussed at this point.)

Advantages of Standardizing Batteries

Many of the advantages of standardization that apply to individual tests also apply to the standardization of a battery. These include objectivity (Nunnally & Bernstein, 1994, pp. 6–8).

This eliminates, as much as possible, the subjectivity that occurs in a brain-function analysis with an unstandardized battery. Any procedure and resulting patterns that were obtained are repeatable. However, the difference between standardization of a single test and a battery is derived from the concept of multiple disassociation, which is the basis for neuropsychological batteries. The requirements for a standardized battery are directly derived from the requirements for double disassociation and multiple disassociation. In other words, disassociation requires that (1) the same tests must be used for each assessment and (2) the test scoring must be fixed or equated so that the differences between scores will remain invariant. This procedural standardization applies to both assessment and research.

This is related to another major advantage, which is objectivity. Standardization creates an objective group of relationships that permits the creation of multiple objective relationships consisting of combinations and comparisons among the battery tests. These consistent measures permit the use of mathematical or formal methods of analyses that are essential for the creation of formal assessment patterns and their validation.

In addition, standardization is the basis of scientific generalizations. Consequently, relationships in a battery must be invariant for the results to be generalized from research to an assessment procedures. Unless the results of research studies on batteries can be generalized to a single patient's test results, those results cannot be reliably interpreted (Nunnally & Bernstein, 1994, pp. 6–8).

Finally, validation of any testing procedure requires standardization. The statistical methods used in validation depend on consistent measures. Batteries or formal sets of relationships within batteries used for interpretations can be validated only when there is consistency or equivalency between the measures in a battery that has been standardized.

Unique Information

In addition, the use of standardized batteries provides information that cannot be obtained from individual tests used singly or from unstandardized batteries, which are collections of unintegrated groups of tests. The reliable information from an integrated battery is derived using consistent formal relationships between tests. When the tests and their relationships are changed with each administration or from one administrator to another, clinical lore and research knowledge cannot be accumulated. As such, there is no possibility of creating the large body of reliable information on brain functioning for any variable battery.

The aspect that most differentiates the Halstead–Reitan Battery (HRB), the Halstead–Russell Neuropsychological Evaluation System—Revised (HRNES-R), and other standardized batteries from unstandardized batteries is not their increased accuracy of diagnosing brain damage. In fact, their accuracy is only slightly greater than what can be obtained from almost any highly sensitive individual neuropsychological test. This is evident on examination of the differential ability of the HRNES-R indexes when compared to the most sensitive individual tests in the battery (Russell, 2004).

The Table 3 in this study by Russell (2004) demonstrates that the predictive power of the average impairment score (AIS) was 85% correct and the percent impaired index (PPI) was 83%. By contrast, the percentage correct for the tactile performance test (TPT) total time was 82; Trails B was 78; and the Digit Symbol was 78. Thus, even though the indexes were slightly more accurate, the difference was small. Studies with other populations could easily obtain higher accuracy than the HRNES-R.

Instead of increased accuracy, the HRB, the HRNES-R, and other standardized batteries provide reliable detailed knowledge of the patient's neurological condition. This can be observed in the case studies presented in the handbook by Reitan and Wolfson (1993, pp. 417–823). The standardized battery permits patterns of brain functioning and pathology to be revealed and validated.

Standardization Procedures

Although Anastasi (1988) uses the terms *standardization sample* (p. 72) and *standardization* (p. 25), they only mean "uniformity of procedure" (p. 25). The term *standardization* as used in traditional science includes the entire process of forming measures. Scaling and norming constitute major aspects of standardization.

Although he term *standardization* is used in several ways in neuropsychology, the common aspect of standardization is consistency (Nunnally & Bernstein, 1994, pp. 3–4). The consistency of an assessment procedure from one administration to another is ensured by standardization.

A *standard* is any specified rule or set of rules and methods that apply to the norming procedure. It is designed to ensure consistency of the entire procedural performance. The different aspects or types of standardization are discussed by many authors (Anastasi & Urbina, 1997, pp. 6–7; Ghiselli, Campbell, & Zedeck, 1981, pp. 63–74; Nunnally & Bernstein, 1994, pp. 3–8).

The components of standardization are well established in neuropsychology and psychology in general. The emphasis in this presentation is that standardization applies to the entire measurement procedure in neuropsychology. The components of such procedures include administrative procedures, norming procedures, and content consistency.

Administrative Procedures

First, there is procedural uniformity. According to Anastasi and Urbina (1997), "Standardization implies uniformity of procedure in administering and scoring the tests" (p. 6). In other words, the tests and administration procedures are uniform or consistent across testings. The criteria or standards for consistency are the test instructions and a consistent environment.

Norming Procedures

A measurement procedure, either a test or a battery, has two general aspects other than administration instructions: (1) the content or attributes of a brain function that is being measured and (2) the set of procedures used to create an accurate reliable measure.

The norms provide two major advantages in psychology (Anastasi & Urbina, 1997, p. 6). First, norms provide a way to understand the meaning of a test score. The primary methods for providing this meaning are either cut points that separate groups or the comparison of a score to a population in terms of a population mean, standard deviation (z-score equivalents), or percentiles.

Second, norms provide a method of comparing and combining a subject's scores on different tests. This enables the creation of score indexes and patterns. However, unless a battery is standardized the relationships between tests cannot be adequately determined. Standardization of a battery may be obtained either by having an invariant (fixed) battery or by means of scale scores.

Invariant Raw-Score Batteries

The "fixed" raw-score battery is standardized because all of the scores in the battery are invariant from one administration to another. The battery itself is the standard. When the tests remain invariant, the relationships between tests are invariant. The prime example of this type of battery is the HRB (Reitan & Wolfson, 1993). In this raw-score battery, the tests and their relationships remain consistent so that the interpretations that are based on the tests and relationships are consistent. The interpretations are derived from criteria such as cut points or ratios that are established by research and experience. Clinical judgment patterns, which are derived from the experiences of the many users of a battery, comprise the lore of such a battery. Research and validation studies obviously must have content constancy.

The advantage of such a battery is that the tests and scores remain constant and absolute. They are absolute because they do not change over time. Unless it can be demonstrated by means of published studies that conditions have changed, then research that was performed years ago is still valid. In addition, the use of this battery by many people over time creates a lore and expertise that enables the clinical judgment of those with experience using the battery to be highly reliable. This reliability can be and has been validated on numerous occasions (Chapter 9). As such, no other battery is demonstrably as well validated and as reliable as the HRB.

Disadvantage of a Fixed Battery

Although a fixed battery has the advantages of consistency, it also has certain problems. Raw scores provide no measure of the relative difficulty of test scores (Anastasi & Urbina, 1997, p. 49). To interpret a raw-score battery clinical judgment based on extensive training, experience and research are required to set informal cut points. This experience provides knowledge of the relative difficulty of scores on different tests and the informal cutting points for an abnormal performance. Such training requires an extensive period of apprenticeship with an expert in the system.

Another problem is that because raw scores do not have equivalent scales, the expected ratios and differences between the raw-score scales created by different brain conditions vary from one pair of scales to another. As such, each of the informal numeric relationships used in a battery must be learned. This requires lengthy experience or considerable training with a neuropsychologist who is experienced in using this technique.

The consequence of this need for extensive experience is that many neuropsychologists without this training are not able to obtain the same results as the experts. Consequently, they tend to abandon the battery and reject the concept of a fixed battery.

Scale Score Standardization

The second method to standardize a battery is to equate scores with a standard or norm to produce scale scores. This type of battery is usually called a *standardized battery*. In this method, raw scores are transformed into equivalent scale scores. As such, the scale relationships between scores remain equivalent for all scores. This permits direct depiction of test patterns without mentally transforming each raw score into its scale score equivalent. Intelligence tests such as various Wechsler tests have used scale score standardization for many years.

Requirements for Scale

There are several requirements for constructing a scale score battery: a common metric (type of scale), a normative method, and the test content. The scaling and norming compose the psychometric aspect of the standardization, and the content consists of the tests that measure brain functions. The requirement for a battery to have a common metric is universally accepted (Lezak et al., 2004).

Common Metric

Initially, the most obvious requirement for standardization and one that is recognized by almost all neuropsychologists is that a battery of uniform scale scores requires a common metric (Lezak et al., 2004, pp. 28–146; Mitrushina, Boone, & D'Elia, 2005; Strauss, Sherman, & Spreen, 2006). Such scale scores may take one of a number of forms.

Scaling Problems

Batteries using scale scores obviously require a consistent type of scale or some common metric. However, as compared to the physical sciences, the scaling methods in psychology are in a disordered state.

Attainment and Error Scores

Initially, particularly when raw scores or flexible batteries are used, a major problem has been mixing attainment scores with error or impairment scores. This is not a great problem when the method of analysis is clinical judgment because the difference in score directions can be readily taken into consideration.

Only when we begin to formalize a battery of tests does the direction of the scales become a problem. For instance, the factor analysis of a raw-score battery requires that about half of the negative signs (for impairment scores) in the matrix be reversed, even for clinical interpretive purposes. Obviously, when scores are combined or graphed, the direction of the test scores must be taken into consideration.

The tradition in the physical sciences for tables and graphs is that the values in vertical scores increase in an upward direction and the horizontal scores increase to the right. Transforming all scores into scale scores using the traditional directions of attainment scores solves this problem.

Types of Scales

The situation with matrixes in psychology, including neuropsychology, from its origin has been confused both as to interpretation and statistically. Many metrics are used in neuropsychology, including percentiles, IQ scores, *T*-scores, and *C*-scores (Russell & Starkey, 2001a, pp. 32–34) which is a source of confusion. The comparison tables in several textbooks concerned with neuropsychological assessment, such as Figure 6-3 (p. 142) in Lezak et al. (2004), demonstrate that the scaling systems in neuropsychology are confusing. Nine different scales are listed in the HRNES-R (Russell & Starkey, 2001a).

Although one can obtain a rough judgment as to the difference between scales using such comparison tables, it is often quite difficult to compare an exact number from one type of measurement with another. Exact numbers are normally required for formal analysis. For instance, since their initiation, the Wechsler scales have used two different kinds of scales: one for IQs and another for subtests (Wechsler, 1939). Since the WAIS, the IQs have a mean of 100 and an SD of 15, whereas the subtest scores have a mean of 10 and an SD of 3. It is rather difficult to numerically transform one of these scales into the other for comparison purposes. The recent version of these scales, the Wechsler VI (Wechsler, Coalson, & Raiford, 2008), advises the examiner that the comparison between the subtest scores and composite scores should not be made because they have different SD (p. 45). They do not explain how subtest scores can be mathematically compared to the full-scale intelligence quotient (FSIQ) or composite scores if this is needed.

This has been the situation with all previous versions of the Wechsler (1944) scales. The mean for the Wechsler scales was initially set at 100, as was customary practice. The score interval was set at 1 probable error (PE) with 10 points between 1 PE and 100 (Wechsler, 1939, pp. 34–36). Using this scale, the SD was 14.69. Later the scale was based on a mean of 100 and an SD of 15 (Wechsler, 1981, p. 9). Thus, Wechsler began by using a metric scale and then switching to a SD scale with 15 points.

The subtest scores used Hull's method of a 20-point scale with 10 as the mean and 3 as the SD (Wechsler, 1944, p. 117). Apparently, this scale best fit the data. A number of the original tests had a limited raw-score range. However, the two systems were not readily convertible.

Another type of scale is the percentile scale. From the point of view of a battery in which scales are combined or compared, percentile scaling is useless. This type of scale may be helpful to psychologists who wish to know how a score is related to the work of other people. However, the intervals vary in size so that they are difficult to compare to other scores even using clinical judgment, and it would be almost impossible to use them numerically in a battery.

The different metrics have different characteristics. However, they can often be transformed into the other metrics because most metrics are based on *z*-scores. Percentiles and standard scores are the two major types of scales that are somewhat difficult to transform into each other (Anastasi & Urbina, 1997, pp. 48–76; Russell, 2000; Russell & Starkey, 2001a, pp. 32–35).

Metric Scales

Standard score scales are derived from *z*-scores in which the mean is 0 and the standard deviation is 1. These are inconvenient for scoring because the numbers below the mean are negative. Consequently, there is general agreement that *z*-scores themselves are not used as the scale in tests. Over the years, there have been a number of methods of transforming *z*-scores into different types of standard scores (Lezak et al., 2004, p. 142).

An alternative method is to use decimal scales. This type of scale has been used in almost all areas of science except the human sciences. Exact combinations require minimal mathematical manipulation. Second, the scale can be subdivided into an infinite number of subdivisions. For instance, with measures of length, a meter can be divided into centimeters and then into millimeters or expanded into kilometers. There is nothing equivalent to this in psychology.

Decimal scales in which the mean is 100 and the standard deviation is 10 could be applied to psychological measurement. This scale would be called a *D-scores scale* for decimal scales. If one needs to increase the finesse of the scale, then decimal points can be used. The scale becomes quite flexible without requiring complex calculations or conversions.

This is similar to *T*-scores that use the number 50 for the mean and 10 for a standard deviation. The *D*-scores scale uses scores in which the mean is 100 and the standard deviation is 10 points. The advantage of changing the mean from 50 to 100 is that it allows sufficient "basal" for tests that have brain damage and for scales that include children's scores (Russell & Starkey, 1993, 2001a, p. 34). This is equivalent to a metric system and can be applied to both the total scores and the subscores of a battery (Russell & Starkey, 2001a, pp. 32–34).

Other neuropsychological measurement procedures. There are many as yet largely unrecognized differences between normal and neuropsychological (largely pathological) formal procedures. These differences were not noticed when clinical judgment is used with neuropsychological tests that were developed from patients who had abnormal brain conditions. Neuropsychologists simply ignored the differences. For instance, many tests for brain damage use impairment scales whereas normal psychology universally uses achievement scales. (The WAIS-III and WAIS-IV are recent exceptions.)

These "brain-damage tests" work adequately with patients who had lost cognitive ability when clinical judgment was used and the only judgment was whether the person had brain damage. However, impairment tests are difficult to integrate with standard normal achievement scales when formal statistical procedures are applied to whole batteries and more nuanced interpretations using patterns are attempted. For instance, Wechsler adult scales did not and do not have a sufficiently low base for many brain-damage patterns (Wechsler, 1981; Wechsler et al., 2008).

In addition, almost all statistical methods and conclusions that are used in neuropsychology are derived from the study of normal populations, which were then applied to brain-damaged populations. Often 1 SD is used as an indication of impairment produced by brain damage. This is an invalid indicator of brain damage. In valid brain-damage studies, the definition of impairment is determined by a separation point between a normal group and a brain-damaged group. Thus, in neuropsychological studies, "impairment" caused by brain damage is being measured as not impairment as indicated by 1 SD in a normal group.

Another problem with using 1 SD from a so-called normal group as an indication of impairment is that in almost all cases the control group is composed of volunteers, not patients suspected of having brain damage that were found to be normal by neurologists. Consequently, there was no validated cut point between brain-damaged and normal patients. In one review study (Russell, 2005), almost all "normal" volunteer subjects were found to have a mean FSIQ that was essentially 1 SD above the average for the United States. This would imply that half of all normal people are impaired.

Perhaps the most obvious example that is seldom discussed in neuropsychological literature is that brain-damaged populations are usually skewed and in some cases extremely skewed (Dodrill, 1987; Russell, 1986, p. 53; Russell, 1991, p. 404). This is because of both the way the tests are constructed and the nature of the population. [In unpublished work, the distributions of almost every neuropsychology test in the HRB and HRNES-R (Russell & Starkey, 2001a) were skewed.]

Co-normed Scale Scores

The standardization of scale scores in a battery ensures that the scales are psychometrically equivalent. Neuropsychologists thoroughly understand the norming of individual tests, so only the aspects of norming that are relevant to batteries will be discussed.

The primary difference between individual tests and a scale-score integrated battery are the requirements for scale scores. These scores are primarily equated by using co-norming, which may be called *coordinated norming*. Because the co-norming method applies the same sample of subjects to all tests in the battery, their scale scores have the same means and standardization. This equates both the tests and the relationships between tests (Ghiselli et al., 1981, pp. 37–40).

In a co-normed battery, any single test or group of tests can be compared to any other test or group. Thus, a powerful analytic system has been created in which various patterns between the various tests are produced. Many of these patterns are meaningful and can be discovered and analyzed.

Although almost all intelligence test batteries are co-normed, only a few neuropsychological batteries use co-norms, although the number is growing. Some of the co-normed batteries include the Meyers Neuropsychological Battery (MNB); the Neuropsychological Assessment Battery (NAB) (Stern & White, 2001); Volbrecht, Meyers, and Kaster-Bundgaard (2000); the Reynolds Intellectual Assessment Scales (RIAS) (Reynolds & Kamphaus, 2003), and the *Halstead–Russell Neuropsychological Evaluation System—Revised* (Russell & Starkey, 2001a). [Heaton, Miller, Walden, Michael, and Grant's (2004) *Revised Comprehensive Norms for an Expanded Halstead–Reitan Battery* is not fully co-normed.]

Calibration

There is the difficulty of adding tests to a co-normed battery and retaining the equivalency. Lezak et al. (2004, p. 677) questioned the complete co-norming of the HRNES-R battery (Russell & Starkey, 2001a) because the more recently added tests had different *N*'s from the original group. Apparently, none of the authors read the manual because it explains how new tests can be added or batteries can be joined while retaining their equivalency. There are several methods to unite other groups of tests with the co-normed battery without losing the equivalency between all of the tests. These processes may be called *calibration*.

Direct Calibration

The simplest method of joining tests in a battery so they retain their co-normed equality can be used when the SDs of the tests to be joined are essentially the same. Then only the test means for one of the groups needs to be adjusted. This is accomplished by adding or subtracting the mean of the new group to make it equal that of the original group. Russell (1992) used this method to convert the WAIS to the WAIS-R so the groups could be combined. Apparently, Dodrill (1987) used the same method to combine his Wechsler scores.

Bridging Statistics

An alternative to complete co-norming that is statistically acceptable is what may be called *bridging statistics*. Generally, this is a form of linear regression or linear transformation. In either case, a small sample of subjects (preferably at least 100) is required to make a dependable bridge. If a co-normed battery has an index with scale scores derived from the battery, then a new test scale scores may be added using linear transformation. If an earlier version of a test such as the WAIS is to be incorporated with a later version, then linear transformation based on the FSIQ difference between the two versions may be used (Russell, 1992). In this way, new tests may be made compatible with a set of existing co-norms, thus creating a larger overall set of co-norms. There are, of course, a number of issues to be discussed concerning bridging statistics, but this is beyond the scope of this chapter.

Reference Scale Norming

There is, however, another method of producing relatively coordinated norms. This method may be designated as *reference scale norming* or *index norming*. In addition, it helps solve the problem of different distributions of the various brain-damaged scales in a battery because of widely varying skews in test construction (Dodrill, 1987; Russell, 1987). When the distributions of the scales are skewed, it is difficult to create scale intervals that are equivalent from one scale to another. There are now no commonly used types of scales that provide both equal scale intervals and measurements of equal amounts of ability at all parts of a skewed scale. This is because two problems prevent equivalency of scales when *z*-scores are used. These are variability in fluidity and variability in test construction, which may create a varying *z*-score range (Russell, 1987). *Fluidity* means that some tests are more affected by brain damage than other tests, and *z*-scores may vary from test to test, depending on the characteristics of the tests (Russell, 1987). Normalized *t*-scores (Anastasi & Urbina, 1997, pp. 62–63) alleviate the problem of equivalency concerning skewness, but it does not produce coordinated norming.

Essentially, the creation of equivalency is accomplished by constructing an index of representative measures based on *z*-scores. They are derived from a normal population sample. The index is a mean composed of about 10 of the most sensitive scores in the battery. The brain-damaged raw scores are then transformed into the index *z*-score equivalents by linear transformation or linear regression. Thus, the entire brain damaged set of scores are transformed into the equivalent of normal *z*-scores. The effect of skewness as well as variations among raw scores are eliminated. The use of these reference scale scores means that the same scale score indicates the same amount of ability or impairment for each test at each level of ability without normalization. The scale scores retain the skewed scores produced by brain damage. In contrast, normalization eliminates the variation between tests that is required for an adequate pattern analysis. Assessment statistics, such as operating characteristics, can be applied to the brain-damaged scores without being distorted by their abnormal distribution.

This same method can be used to calibrate any new scores so they are equivalent to the original co-normed battery index. The new score or scores should have an *N* of at least 100 (20 is sufficient to provide an estimate) to reduce the standard error to a usable level. However, the enlarged battery will have usably equivalent scale scores. This method was used to equate the WAIS, the WAIS-R, and WAIS-III (Russell & Starkey, 2001b, pp. 1, 11).

This problem was used to solve the nominative problem of the skewed brain-damaged tests for the HRNES-R (Russell & Starkey, 2001a). All of its scores are equated by use of reference scale norming (Russell, 1987).

Linear Transformation to an Index

A third and relatively simple to use method is linear transformation to an index. This method was used to add tests to the HRNES-R battery (Russell & Starkey, 2001b, pp. 1, 11) and to create the new HRNES-R scales.

Demographic Corrections

Next to scale scores, the most important aspect of a complete neuropsychological battery of tests is some method of correcting for demographic differences in a population. Although such corrections are used for individual tests, they are required for batteries because various tests are affected differently by such differences. Such methods should use linear regression to predict the appropriate scale for a particular age and ability level. The various attempts to provide age and IQ adjustments will be examined in a later chapter 15.

Universal Norms

Three characteristics of test battery norms are important when batteries are examined: universal norms, absolute norms, and premorbid ability. They have important implications for neuropsychology tests and batteries. The subject of malingering or inadequate motivation has been thoroughly examined in recent literature and will not be discussed to any extent in this book.

Range

One major difference between neuropsychological analytic and normal population studies concerns the extended range of scores for neuropsychological patients. Almost always a group of patients with neuropathology has a skewed range in which the bottom of the range extends to or beyond the normal adult standard distributions. This was the primary reason why neuropsychological impairment tests such as the Boston Naming Test (Goodglass & Kaplan, 1983) often had a low ceiling and an extended basal. This was one of the main problems when using the Wechsler batteries with neuropathology patient's particularly older ones. The impairment of patients' scores would often reach beyond the limits of scale ranges, so that scores could not be accurately compared with the scores of other brain functions.

The characteristics of *t*-scores illustrate some of the problems related to range. Again, this is an instant in which the basis for a statistical procedure was based on normal subjects but was not appropriate for brain-damaged subjects. The *t*-scale was given a mean of 50 for a normal distribution. This mean of 50 allows for 5 SDs on either side of the mean between the numbers of 0 and 100 (Guilford, 1965, pp. 518–524). Patients with relatively severe neuropathological conditions often reach the bottom of the scale and are not accurately measurable. This, of course, would be particularly true of older patients. An adult cognitive test using *t*-scores also cannot apply to children.

In this regard, the concept a universal scale will be discussed. A universal scale is one that covers the entire range of brain functions from zero (theoretically) to the full adult range. Such tests have an extended range from childhood to superior adult or from an IQ equivalent of 0 to 160 (or the ceiling of the scale). Zero is usually unattainable in psychological scoring, so the bottom or basal of a scale is the lowest score in which a reliable score can be obtained. In some areas, such as memory, a zero is obtainable. Using the SD with adults, the Wechsler (1997) adult scales have a practical range of 6 SDs, which is from a FSIQ of approximately 55 (percentile 0.1) to 145 (percentile 99.9). Obviously, a few subjects score above 145. The WAIS-III (Wechsler, 1997) extends the scale to 160 and the basal to 45 to accommodate the older age group. To do so, it turned the scale upside down. This was probably the most irrational thing that has been perpetuated on the Wechsler scales. They could have retained 100 as the normal population mean and changed the SD to 10 as in the *t*-scales. Then the range would be changed to 13 or 14 SDs.

Advantage of Universal Scales

Universal scales have many advantages. People with significant brain damage or dementia often will score below the basal of the scales on many tests used to assess brain damage. In the area of neuropsychology, there is an awkward position between a Wechsler Adult Scale used with brain-damaged patients and the dementia batteries. Because the level of functioning varies greatly around the juncture between moderate brain damage and dementia, it would be of great help to extend the standard test range into the dementia range by producing universal scales. In fact, because brain impairment often reduces the performance of adults to a point well below the average adult range, all neuropsychology tests should be a full range of universal scales. On the other hand, intelligent people who have brain damage may have an ability range that is higher than that of most brain-damage tests.

Age

Another major advantage of universal scales is that they cover the entire range from early childhood to old age. This enables one to measure on a single scale the ability level of the individual at any age with any impairment because of a neurological condition.

Although Wechsler (1944) initially was concerned with children, the method of testing children appeared to be distinct from that of adults, and subsequently he separated the adult Wechsler test (1981) into a children's test and an adult's test. The original Stanford–Binet intelligence test (Terman & Merrill, 1973), although a children's test, extended into the adult range. Currently, many if not most of the newly developed tests for intelligence, other than the Wechsler scales, cover the entire range from at least 5 years to 80 or 90 years of age. Often, children's abilities below the age of 5 are thought to be too variable to be included in a universal age examination.

Brain Damage

Many neuropsychology adult tests that are customarily used for neuropsychological assessment do not have a sufficient ceiling. For instance, using the Boston Naming Test (Goodglass & Kaplan, 1983), a person with a normal intelligence can usually reach the ceiling or be very near it so that the measurements are distorted. This means that people with unusually high intelligence (probably above 110) cannot be adequately evaluated in terms of their impairment compared to their premorbid ability. To counter this result, the HRNES-R has incorporated the Expressive Vocabulary Test (Williams, 1997) for people whose premorbid ability was above average. The design of this test is equivalent to that of the Boston Naming Test, but the distribution of scores covers the normal range.

Universal Scoring Methods

The major disadvantage of universal scales is that the scoring could require more time for administration than the currently existing scales. However, statistical means have been developed to reduce the time needed to administer the universal scores. For many years, the basal-ceiling method of scoring has been used, so it is quite well developed (see manuals for *Peabody, Picture Vocabulary Test—Third Edition* (Dunn & Dunn, 1997) and the *Wide Range Achievement Test, Manual* (Jastak, Jastak & Wilkinson, 1984).

However, there are computer methods beyond the basal and ceiling scoring. [See manuals for PPVT (Dunn & Dunn, 1981) and WRAT (Jastak, Jastak, & Wilkinson, 1984).] Choca, Laatsch, Garside, and Arnemann (1994) introduce another method for shortening a long test, the Adaptive Category Test (ACAT). It is an interactive program that contains a set of rules that determine when sufficient information has been gathered by subtest items to predict an accurate score. The score sheet gives the predicted score for each of the original tests or subtests in a battery. From a methodological point of view, this general method could be used with universal scales for almost any test and for batteries.

Premorbid Ability

The premorbid ability of the patient is another factor in addition to demographic corrections that must be accounted for by some form of correction or adjustment. Almost all brain-damage evaluations and forensic evaluations in particular compare the current ability of the patient to some estimate of their premorbid ability. The amount of damage is equivalent to the impairment provided by these two measures of ability.

In practice, the major premorbid ability of the person is formally determined by the basic demographic characteristics of age, gender, and ability level (as measured by education or other means). These are generally estimated using one or more of various formal procedures such as education level or by a more complex formula (Schinka & Vanderploeg, 2000). If the person's background is sufficiently different from that of most patients or clients, this must be taken into consideration but primarily by clinical judgment because the specifics of norms do not exist. Notice that this is one area of neuropsychology that uses formulas or other formal procedures extensively.

The development of methods for estimating premorbid ability has been one of the major areas of progress in neuropsychology over the last two decades. So much has been published on this subject that this book will not attempt to examine this area. Instead, such writings as *Estimating Premorbid Level of Functioning* by Schinka and Vanderploeg (2000) and *Assessment of Malingering* by Larrabee (2005) should be read.

Absolute Scales

Perhaps the major problem in standardizing any test or battery among the human sciences is to produce an absolute standard. An absolute scale is one that does not change over time or with any other condition. Within the Wechsler (1981) tests, the reference scale operated as an absolute scale. However, the entire scale was changed with every new version that was published. Almost any norming aspect of psychology or other human sciences is variable over time. It now appears from the apparent plateau of the Flynn effect (Flynn, 1999) that even the major standard for psychology, which is the normal distribution, is not consistent over time. The population appears to be changing [although there is rather strong evidence (Russell, 2010) that the change in overall intelligence has plateaued, even in the United States].

A Sample Is Never Exact

The problem is that a sample is only a sample and the entire population can never be sampled. Consequently, the sample will vary in an unknown manner from the actual population. This variation becomes apparent when test norms are compared. A sample is never exact, and samples may vary widely because of many factors.

This is especially true if any screening to eliminate possible brain-damage subjects is performed to "make the sample more normal." This distortion of normality has been found to be true for volunteer subjects used in the neuropsychological samples. In all samples using volunteers for a neuropsychological normal group who have been screened for possible brain damage, the Wechsler intelligence scale of the sample indicates that the sample has an intelligence that is approximately 1 SD above the average IQ (Russell, 2007, 2010). Apparently, the process of screening eliminates subjects with any form of brain-function impairment that reduces intelligence. Because such individuals are an integral part of the US population, the sample is a supernormal and not average sample.

Note that the last two Wechsler tests, the WAIS-III (Wechsler, 1997) and WAIS-IV (Wechsler et al., 2008), were carefully screened to remove patients with any indication of neuropathology. Consequently, it is highly probable that the mean for those two scales is well above the average IQ for the US population (Russell, 2007, 2010). These are only two indications that a sample may not represent the average population. Because there are many other problems incurred in obtaining adequate samples of a population, creating an absolute standard is a major problem among the human sciences. The lack of an absolute standard calls into question the reliability of almost every study of cognitive abilities performed in neuropsychology as well as the entire field of psychology. Almost any aspect of psychology or other human sciences is variable over time.

Measurement Issues in Science

Because several issues involved in the standardization of scientific measurements were encountered almost two centuries ago, a brief discussion of the development of an absolute measurement system in the physical sciences will better enable one to understand a number of the psychometric problems involved in measurement.

The Metric System

The metric system was adopted in 1791 during the French Revolution. Before the revolution, the measurement systems in France and the rest of Europe were so inconsistent and irregular that it became obvious to scientists that a new system was needed. The system thus created became the metric system that the entire world uses today except for the United States. The only type of metric system that is used in the United States for domestic purposes is money, which uses the decimal system.

The basis of the metric system is the meter (Klein, 1988, pp. 122–123). It was initially defined as 1/10 millionth part of the meridian from the north pole to the equator. It was believed that Earth's dimensions would provide a standard for measurement. This measurement was incorporated into a bar of platinum of exactly that length; the bar is still held in Paris. The two points of the standard are the ends of the meter, and the scale consists in decimal multiples or parts of the meter. All other measures of length were derived from the meter. For instance, a kilometer is 1,000 m.

Later it was discovered that the length of the meter was slightly larger than the original measurement. However, attendees to an international convention concerned with measurement decided that the measurement of a meter would be based on the physical object, the bar, and not on the original measurement definition that led to the establishment of the meter. Once the standard had been set as a physical bar of a certain length, it was irrational to insist that the length of the bar be changed to fit the definition. This would have required an incredible amount of adjustment throughout science and the world. The important point to notice is that the standard was essentially arbitrary. Any other consistent dimension of the universe could have been chosen as the initial standard. As such, it was only rational that the measurement instrument remain absolute rather than changing it whenever the original criterion concept was found to be slightly inaccurate. This conclusion should be applied to the creation of cognitive tests, particularly new versions of intelligence tests.

The metric system has several advantages. A completely standardized system is based on a single standard or norm, the meter. The decimal system allows us to deal with different length measures by simply changing the decimal point. Although it began as a standard of length, the decimal system has since been extended to cover area, volume, weight, and money (Klein, 1988, pp. 97–115). The advantage of the metric system is that all measures of a certain type such as length are incorporated into a single scale as multiples of the standard. This permits measurement and mathematics to be much simpler and more accurate.

Scientific Absolute Scales

The history of the meter emphasizes two characteristics of a standard. First, a standard is essentially arbitrary. It may be based on a physical attribute of the universe, primarily to give it meaning. Second, however, the important aspect of a standard is that it remains absolute, once it has been established. In this regard, the history of the development of temperature measurement is also informative.

This development demonstrates that, to a certain extent, the initial reference object on which the measurement is based and other natural parameters are arbitrary as long as they represent the attribute. Ultimately, the parameters are chosen for mathematical convenience not in any apparently external stable relationship.

In regard to temperature, a number of preliminary studies completed before the 1700s had suggested various constant temperature points related to water. Following Roemer, Daniel Fahrenheit about 1694 accepted what he thought was the coldest possible point in nature, the freezing point of salt and water. Other constant points were the freezing point of pure water, the human body temperature, and the boiling point of water. For his scale degrees, Fahrenheit adopted Roemer's scale of 60 points between the lowest cold point and the human body temperature. Later studies demonstrated that the scale was wrong on all points (Klein, 1988, pp. 296–305). However, Fahrenheit also invented the closed tube thermometer using mercury as the temperature indicator. This created an instrument that was accurate in terms of degrees and convenient to use. As such, it is still used in United States, although the scale was illogical and erroneous (Klein, 1988, pp. 298–304).

In Europe the accepted scale was developed by Celsius in 1741. The scale corresponded to the metric system. The Celsius scale (°C) had 100 degrees between the freezing and boiling points of pure water at sea level.

The ultimate scientific temperature scale was the Kelvin scale. At the end of the 1800s, Lord Kelvin proposed a temperature unit that began at absolute zero, which is –273.16 (°C). Nevertheless, he retained the Celsius scale units. More recently, the Kelvin scale (K) has been accepted as the primary scientific method of measurement (Klein, 1988, pp. 324–336). The commercial and practical temperature scale is the Celsius scale for all nations in the world except for the United States.

The examination of these scales used in the physical sciences indicates some characteristics of an absolute scale. For instance, the boiling point temperature of water decreases as the height above sea level increases because of decreased air pressure. However, science does not change the measurement form of the thermometer every thousand feet but simply makes corrections for the height above sea level or air pressure as needed.

In part the acceptance of absolute measures in the physical sciences is because of the relative lack of variability of physical phenomena. The economic, sociological, and psychological sciences have much greater variability. This means that the social sciences may need to use somewhat different methods for creating scales. However, an absolute scale should remain the ideal because a variable scale requires a change in methods and the reworking of previous data for many purposes every few years (Russell, 2010). At times, it requires a change in social concepts based on those data. A variable scale that changes at certain intervals greatly increases the difficulty in comparing previous research findings with the newer research.

Absolute Scales in Neuropsychology

The creation of an absolute scale in neuropsychology and psychology as a whole is quite possible. The basis for an absolute scale is the concept that human brain functioning does not change genetically from one generation to another, so it is constant across all genetic groups. However, this genetic basis may be changed by exogenous factors such as learning and nutrition. These factors may change the distribution of brain functioning for different populations. There is a need for a universal absolute (culture-free) measure of human ability. However, because of these exogenous factors, such a genetic absolute measure cannot currently be constructed. However, what can be developed is an absolute standard based on one population as an absolute standard.

With this requirement for absolute consistency as a major characteristic, it would be appropriate for neuropsychology to accept the norming schemes of intelligence tests to be used as the absolute basis for all other cognitive scales. Earlier in this discussion it was demonstrated that almost any scale could be equated to an absolute scale using one or another method of calibration. Consequently, it would be relatively easy to create an absolute scale of intellectual ability. Other brain functions could be calibrated to be equivalent to that scale once it has been accepted.

If neuropsychology and even psychology as a whole, developed and employed a set of absolute scales, changes such as the Flynn effect could simply be added to the scales as corrections. Both absolute and corrected scales could be presented in the norm tables, such that the psychologist could use either scale. Apparently, this was in fact the concept that Wechsler (1944) originally proposed. Subsequently, the reference scale, which was the scale for ages 28–34, was presented as an absolute measure of intelligence, whereas the other age-group scales were age-corrected scales. These two scales were in the manual up through the WAIS-R.

Advantages of Absolute Psychological Scales

Absolute scores have the advantage of being unaffected by changes in time or population because the norms do not change. Consequently, the scores always indicate the same amount of ability. As such, the absolute scales could be used to compare groups and populations across time. The tests may be designed so that the time and population may affect cutting points, but this would not affect the scales themselves.

Absolute scales have many other advantages. In many situations, neuropsychologists may want to know how well a person can perform a function regardless of his or her age. For instance, few people would want to determine the competency of commercial airline pilots using age-comparison norms. We want to know how well the pilot can fly the airplane, not how well in comparison to people 70 years of age. Psychological testing may soon be used to determine retirement rather than age, in which case absolute norms will be necessary.

Types of Absolute Psychological Scales

Currently, there are at least two types of absolute neuropsychological or cognitive scales. First, it should be noted that raw scores are absolute scores. In other words, tests or batteries using raw scores are fixed such that the tests and their relationships are determined by the construction of the battery without reference to norms. Consequently, the test and battery scores are unaffected by time or any particular population.

Probably the best example of a well-validated single test employing absolute scores is the Progressive Matrices (Raven, 1982). There is no overall set of norms for this test. Rather, a person's score is compared against norms that are considered to represent the population typical of that person for a particular purpose. It was largely the characteristic that enabled the discovery of the Flynn effect (Flynn, 1999) because that test was used throughout Europe. The change in the mean scores of the test over time indicated a change in the population, not the test. It was also this absolute characteristic that indicates that the Flynn effect may have plateaued, at least in parts of Europe and possibly in the United States (Russell, 2007). Whatever caused the increase in intellectual ability has reached its apex in nations that protect the physical welfare of its entire population.

This is also why research on the HRB remains relevant over time, whereas a vast amount of research on the Wechsler tests must be discarded every time the battery is renormed. Over time, this renorming has rendered about 10,000 studies useless because they are considered obsolete by changes in the Wechsler scales (Russell, 2010). On the other hand, the HRB studies done in 1955 (Reitan, 1955) remain relevant.

Absolute-Scale Score Norms

Although raw scores are absolute scales, as has been discussed, there are many advantages to using an absolute-scale score battery. Scale scores require norms. As such, the norms must be absolute to serve as a basis for a scale-score battery. As has been discussed, the effects of extraneous factors on brain functioning are so strong that there appears to be no way, at least currently, to derive norms that are representative of cerebral genetic factors that are not influenced by extraneous factors.

As was amply demonstrated when discussing the scientific standardization of physical scales, the standard itself is arbitrary, although the characteristics of usefulness and simplicity and initial meaningfulness are also important. However, the primary characteristic of any standard is consistency over time and space.

An absolute scale would provide unity to neuropsychology and even psychology as a whole. All other intellectual and even various neuropsychological tests would be calibrated against such an absolute measure so that their scale scores would be equivalent throughout the entire field of psychology. It would permit comparisons with almost any brain-function test (at least neuropsychological tests) to this absolute measure. Several batteries are now using co-norming. so almost any test could be compared with any other neuropsychological test with the proper bridging techniques. This would permit the development of reliable brain-damage patterns not only within co-normed batteries but also across batteries

Another proposal for an absolute measure would be for a major organization such as the American Psychological Association to take on the development of absolute norming criteria as a major project. It would require the formation of a committee and a considerable amount of money along with possibly the cooperation of a number of companies. However, such a project is highly improbable, so the advice that is the most practical is simply to use one of the existing intelligence batteries that combines the adult and children's scales. As such, the test battery would be both an absolute and a universal scale. This would be the first absolute and universal scale developed by the human sciences.

If the APA and the company owning such a scale do not want to take on this project, then several other excellent intelligence scales are quite capable of being the basis for such a project. In fact, their cooperation in developing such a scale (and sharing the profits) would be extremely beneficial to the entire field of psychology.

Content Characteristics

An integrated battery includes test content, which consists of the particular set of tests that compose a battery. An integrated battery is standardized in regard to its content as well as its statistical method. The content is, of course, a crucial element in a battery. The interpretation of the functioning and condition of the brain depends on the tests and the relationship between tests that a battery contains.

Content Domains

Concerning content, although most of the neuropsychological reports are currently written in terms of domains, the concept of a domain is at best a hazardous concept for assessment. There are several reasons for this. With the exception of language, the domains in neuropsychology are vague. They are primarily demarcated by factor analysis, which is still quite inexact, in delineating groups of tests as factors. In addition, almost every test used in neuropsychology is a compound test with aspects of several domains. At this point, neuroscience has not separated the various domains, nor does it know how they interact. Finally, because domains are very vague, they cannot be used in the actual assessment process, that is composed of tests and not domains.

A number of years ago in his presidential address to the neuropsychology division, division 40 of the APA, Carl Dodrill (1997) discussed the "Myths of Neuropsychology." One of the myths was "we know what our tests measure" (p. 1). He correlated the various tests in his neuropsychological battery, which was an extended HRB, with tests that represent the general grouping of tests in what would be called a *domain*. Then he correlated them across groups. He used both normal groups and brain-damaged groups. The correlations were slightly higher for the brain-damaged groups than the normal groups. However, the correlations within groups were slightly higher than those of the cross groups, which was not significant. The correlations within groups should have been higher than across groups.

Dodrill summarized his findings by stating, "The above information clearly shows that we need to face up to the fact that our fundamental tools of trade are not behaving in ways that we conceptualize them." If we are mistaken on such a fundamental point, then how can we hope to progress scientifically? Also clinically, how can we progress if the vast majority of us divide the results section of our reports according to headings such as "memory," "perceptual," "problem-solving," "attention," and so forth? "There is little scientific basis for such divisions, and they create a false impression both about our knowledge and about what our tests are actually measuring. Far better is an integrated report in which we combined the results of brain sensitive measures into coherent and concise series of conclusions" (p. 5). It does not appear that our science, particularly with an emphasis on domains, has progressed to any great extent since 1997.

Current Localization

A second issue related to content is the status of the concept of localization. Recently, many major neuropsychologists have denigrated the concept of localization on the basis that brain scans are much more accurate. This is only partly true. Scans are more accurate with focal lesions but still cannot distinguish many of the more diffuse diagnostic entities such as head injury damage. However, there is one great advantage of knowing localization. The work with functional scans is demonstrating that brain functions are usually related to location in the brain. This relationship is complex and only beginning to be understood but still indicates that the location of damage is important. Textbooks on functional neuroanatomy and neuropsychology (Kolb & Whishaw, 2009) appear to be very much concerned with the location of various functions.

In addition, some of the neuropsychologists who disparage localization are emphasizing the frontal localization of executive functions. The test Delis–Kaplan Executive Functions System (D-KEFS) (Delis, Kaplan, & Kramer, 2001) emphasizes that these tests, which are supposed to be a measure of executive function, or frontal tests. There is very little substantial research to support these tests, which presumably measure executive functions. Certainly, the tests selected have very little support for their unique relationship to the frontal lobes. Our own experiences have only found fluency tests to be fairly adequate indicators or frontal damage and only then when the posterior components of the compound tests, such as word ability, are demonstrated to be intact. (The research supporting the current issue is too voluminous to be referenced in this book.)

Content Consistency

Several requirements for content must be considered when constructing or evaluating a battery (Russell, 2000). The major requirements are consistency or invariance and comprehensiveness of coverage. Standardization requires that the content of the procedure remain the same. Just as the items in a test must remain constant, the tests in a battery should be consistent from one administration to another (Russell, 2000, p. 457). Consistency applies to either an invariant raw-score battery or equivalent scale scores. This ensures that the battery will provide the same pattern of scores each time it is given. This requirement is based on the concept of multiple disassociation.

Content Comprehensiveness

The content must be comprehensive for the specific needs of the battery. For most batteries that represent the entire brain, the content must adequately represent the brain's overall functioning (Reitan, 1991, pp. 98, 100). Coverage follows the principle that one cannot determine whether a function is impaired unless that function is tested.

For particular requirements, the particular content of a battery will depend on the purposes for which the battery is used. In a hospital with specific requirements, batteries may be designed for that function. Batteries have been designed for aphasia or epilepsy. In these cases, the content of the battery needs to be comprehensive only for that requirement. When only the existence or nonexistence of brain damage is required, then a relatively short battery may be used, because fewer than 10 tests can usually make that distinctions as reliably as a larger battery. However, in most situations and especially in forensic situations both the utmost reliability and dependability is required as well as complete coverage of brain functioning. This enables the battery to provide not only maximum reliability as to the existence of brain damage but also information as to the extent and type of impairment. This is determined by the pattern of test results, which requires a larger battery.

Coverage

To obtain comprehensive coverage in a battery, several principles must be used (Russell, 2000, pp. 465–471). Coverage is determined by the principle that one cannot know whether a function is impaired unless that function is tested. As a brain model, a set of tests should be designed to cover all areas of the brain and all cognitive functions in as much depth as efficiency allows.

Most assessment batteries are used to delineate the existence and type of pathology of brain functioning. For such situations, a comprehensive examination of the entire brain's functioning is necessary. To be comprehensive, a battery requires full coverage of the brain's major functional domains (Russell, 2000, pp. 465–469).

There are an almost infinite number of ways in which the tests in a battery can be combined and compared. The investigation of such relationships requires a selection of tests based on research. The particular selection of tests constitutes the major component of an integrated battery.

Types of Coverage

Two types of coverage are important in neuropsychological assessment: (1) coverage by areas of the brain and (2) coverage by types or domains of cognitive functioning.

Anatomic Area

Neuropsychological test batteries have traditionally attempted to fashion complete coverage by selecting tests that cover all of the various anatomical areas of the brain. This approach has been used from the time that it was realized that different areas of the brain have different functions. A proper selection of tests helps determine the localization of the damage (Reitan, 1964). In addition, the diagnosis of a pathology is dependent on the areas that are impaired.

The most thoroughly recognized division of functions related to area is that of lateralization (Matarazzo, 1972; Russell, 1972, 1974, 1979). Any well-organized test battery today will have tests that are related to both hemispheres of the brain, ideally in a balanced or equal proportion (Russell, 1980b). Coverage by area is well known in that large sections of textbooks have been devoted to it (Kolb & Whishaw, 1985).

Cognitive Functions

In recent years, there has been a tendency for neuropsychologists to downplay coverage by area and emphasize coverage by function or domain. This change in emphasis has occurred since the mid-1970 s when the CAT scan began to localize focal lesions more exactly than was possible using neuropsychological tests.

Because of this situation, some neuropsychologists have argued that the detection of brain damage is passé (Mapou, 1988) and that neuropsychologists should concentrate on assessing cognitive functions (Lezak et al., 2004, pp. 5–11). Ironically, since Mapou's 1988 paper, two events have nullified his contention. First, neuropsychology has become a major means of determining the existence of brain damage, primarily because it is able to demonstrate relatively mild impairment. This is particularly true in forensics because none of the scanning procedures can adequately specify the existence or amount of cognitive impairment because of a pathological brain condition. Currently, this is still especially true of brain trauma. This often escapes detection by any scanning methodology unless there is hemorrhage (Bigler, 1991).

Second, in most cases, the relationship between brain-function locations and cognitive functions has been entirely reversed. This is particularly obvious in research, but it also applies to assessment. As discussed in Chapter 1, although the brain-scanning technologies have been able to locate the area of focal damage or of a function much more exactly than previously neurological methodologies, they cannot determine the particular function of a brain location. It is neuropsychology that examines and determines the various mental functions of the brain. Currently, whereas neurological techniques determine a location, neuropsychology determines its function. As such, if anything, neuropsychological methods are more important now than when Mapou (1988) published his paper.

Thus, there is a unique contribution that neuropsychology can make in both the research and applied fields. In research, neuropsychology is able to study the differential effects that brain damage produces. In fact, one major concern should be to determine what the human cognitive functions are and then categorize them (Rourke, 1991) so they can be localized. In the clinical setting, neuropsychologists understand the effects of specific lesions and brain conditions on human abilities. This is important for medical, legal, and psychological activities.

Principles of Coverage

Several principles are important when designing the coverage of a battery, including completeness, balance, redundancy, and efficiency.

Completeness

As much as possible, a battery of tests (except for a specialized battery) should contain tests related to all areas of the brain and all known functional domains in order to be complete or thorough. An integrated battery is designed to have as adequate coverage as possible for both area and function. Currently, this subdivision of the brain by area may generally be refined to lobes and in some cases to parts of a lobe.

This is required because, in spite of scanning methodologies, major types of functions such as memory, verbal abilities, and spatial relations are related to particular areas of the brain. Consequently, complete coverage of the brain's areas is also complete coverage of the brain's functions. This is especially important if a purpose of the battery is to estimate the amount of impairment produced by brain damage to a person's individual functions as well as his or her total functioning.

A huge battery probably would be required to cover both areas and cognitive functions of the brain. However, because generally different areas are related to specific functions, the same tests simultaneously cover both aspects. As such, an integrated battery should be designed over a period to contain thorough coverage of both areas and functions. A flexible battery, one that is put together for each new patient, may very well have critical lacunae in various areas of coverage. Thus, problems may be missed that a well-designed integrated battery would reveal (Rourke & Brown, 1986).

Balance

Balance simply means that an equal number of tests are devoted to each major area of the brain and to each major type of function. Balance related to area is best understood in terms of hemispheric lateralized functions. One criticism of the Luria–Nebraska Neuropsychological Battery is that it lacks balance (Russell, 1980b).

As with all of Luria's work (1973), the emphasis was primarily on left-hemisphere verbal functions. Consequently, the Luria–Nebraska is very heavily weighted in the verbal area. Alternately, the HRB (Reitan & Wolfson, 1993) and HRNES-R (Russell, 1980b) are quite well balanced concerning lateralization.

In as much as possible, balance also should apply to the difference between anterior and posterior parts of the brain, as well as to localized areas. The principle is that every area should be represented by tests but not overrepresented. In constructing a battery, it is preferable to add a test related to an uncovered area rather than duplicate tests within areas even when the added test is well known.

Balance also concerns different types of functions such as *crystallized* versus *fluid* abilities (Barron & Russell, 1992; Horn, 1976; Kaufman & Kaufman, 2004; Russell, 1979, 1980a). For instance, one should not overload a battery with verbal as opposed to spatial relations tests (Russell, 1980b).

Our lack of understanding of the function of areas and the difficulty in finding tests related to various areas often has meant not only that balance is lacking but also that we may not even know it is lacking. For instance, most neuropsychological batteries lack tests of social intelligence or what Guilford (1967) called *behavioral abilities*. Such social intelligence tests may be critical in understanding certain types of functioning such as that required by businesspeople.

Redundancy

Redundancy has been less emphasized than completeness and balance (Russell, 2000, p. 468). One characteristic of any cognitive test is normal variability. This variability can lead to false identification of the existence of brain damage or descriptions of impaired functions simply because some extraneous occurrence interfered with a patient's functioning on a particular test. The seasoned neuropsychologist does not trust a single incidence of a particular phenomenon. When several tests that are all impaired are related to the same area or function, then one has more confidence that there is indeed an impairment in that area.

Efficiency

In some ways, efficiency is the opposite of coverage and redundancy. It is obvious that a test battery cannot be of infinite length. Currently, so many tests are available that one could presumably test a person for 100 hours without running out of tests. Consequently, the number of tests must be limited at some point. To some extent, efficiency may be retained even though there is redundancy. This is accomplished by using overlapping tests. Efficiency means that within the limits imposed by both thoroughness of coverage and redundancy, the length of a battery should be as short as possible.

Known Tests

The final principle in determining the creation of a battery is that known tests are preferable to unknown tests. Known tests have known reliability, validity, and information concerning their actions. One's understanding of the effects of damage on known tests is greater than for unknown tests. A new test should be added to an otherwise well-designed battery only when there is an obvious lack in a particular area of coverage and no known tests are adequate. This is the rationale for adding mostly familiar tests to extend the HRNES-R.

Another reason for using known tests is that information can be more readily transmitted to other clinicians. When one reads a report based on a set of unknown tests, the clinician will not be able to determine how well the testing has been done or how well it has been interpreted.

Validation and Discovery

Although validation is the essential aspect of justification (Nunnally & Bernstein, 1994, p. 83), it also has a place in discovery because it determines the degree to which the assessment procedure measures what the procedure purports to measure (Anastasi & Urbina, 1997, p. 8; AERA, 1999, p. 9). As such, it is the final stage in the discovery process. In essence, validation is a testing process. It consists in the psychometric testing of a research or assessment procedure. Thus, validation ensures that these assessment procedures produce reliable information. In general, the validation methods in discovery are the same as in justification, consequently their examination will be reserved for the chapters on justification.

References

AERA (American Educational Research Association), American Psychological Association & the National Council on Measurement in Education, *Standards for educational and psychological testing*. Washington, DC: American Educational Research Association.

Anastasi, A. (1988). *Psychological testing* (6th ed.). New York: Macmillan.

Anastasi, A., & Urbina, S. (1997). *Psychological testing* (7th ed.). Upper Saddle River, NJ: Prentice Hall.

Barron, J. H., & Russell, E. W. (1992). Fluidity theory and the neuropsychological impairment in alcoholism. *Archives of Clinical Neuropsychology*, *7*(2), 175–188.

Bigler, E. D. (1991). Neuropsychological assessment, neuroimaging, and clinical neuropsychology: A synthesis. *Archives of Clinical Neuropsychology*, *6*(3), 113–132.

Choca, J., Laatsch, L., Garside, D., & Arnemann, C. (1994). *CAT: The computer category test.* Toronto: Multi-Health Systems. (Manual and program).

Delis, D. C., Kaplan, E., & Kramer, J. H. (2001). *D-KEFS: Delis-Kaplan executive functions system (Examiner's manual).* San Antonio, TX: Psychological Corporation.

Dodrill, C. B. (1987). *What constitutes normal performance in clinical neuropsychology?* Paper presented at the 97th Annual Convention of the American Psychological Association, Atlanta, Georgia.

Dodrill, C. B. (1997). Myths of neuropsychology. *The Clinical Neuropsychologist*, *11*, 1–17.

Dunn, J. C., & Kirsner, K. (2003). What can we infer from double disassociations? *Cortex, 39*(1), 1–7.

Dunn, L. M., & Dunn, L. M. (1981). *Peabody, picture vocabulary test—revised.* Circle Pines, MI: American Guidance Service. (PPVT-R) (Manual).

Dunn, L. M., & Dunn, L. M. (1997). *Peabody, picture vocabulary test—third edition.* Circle Pines, MI: American Guidance Service. (PPVT-III) (Manual).

Flynn, J. R. (1999). Searching for justice: The discovery of IQ gains over time. *American Psychologist, 54*(1), 5–20.

Ghiselli, E. E., Campbell, J. P., & Zedeck, S. (1981). *Measurement theory for the behavioral sciences.* San Francisco: W. H. Freeman.

Goodglass, H., & Kaplan, E. (1983). *Boston naming test—booklet.* Philadelphia: Lea & Febiger.

Guilford, J. P. (1965). *Fundamental statistics in psychology and education* (4th ed.). New York: McGraw-Hill.

Guilford, J. P. (1967). *The nature of human intelligence.* New York: McGraw-Hill.

Heaton, R. K., Miller, S. W., Taylor, M. J., & Grant, I. (2004). *Revised comprehensive norms for an expanded Halstead–Reitan Battery: Demographically adjusted neuropsychological norms for African American and Caucasian adults.* Odessa, FL: Psychological Assessment Resources. (Professional manual and computer program).

Horn, J. L. (1976). Human abilities: A review of research and theory in the early 1970s. *Annual Review of Psychology, 31*, 437–485.

Jastak, J. F., Jastak, S. R., & Wilkinson, G. S. (1984). *Wide range achievement test—revised (WRAT-R).* Wilmington, DE: Jastak Associates. (Manual).

Kaufman, A., & Kaufman, N. (2004). *Kaufman brief intelligence test* (2nd ed. (KBIT-2)). Los Angeles: Western Psychological Services.

Klein, H. A. (1988). *The science of measurement: A historical survey.* New York: Dover Chicago Press.

Kolb, B, & Whishaw, I. Q. (1990). *Fundamentals of Human Neuropsychology* (3rd ed.). New York: W. H. Freeman.

Kolb, B, & Whishaw, I. Q. (2009). *Fundamentals of Human Neuropsychology* (6th ed.). New York: W. H. Freeman.

Larrabee, G. J. (2005). A Scientific approach to Forensic Neuropsychology. In G. J. Larrabee (Ed.), *Forensic Neuropsychology: A Scientific Approach* (pp. 3–28). New York: Oxford University Press.

Lezak, M. D., Howieson, D. B., & Loring, D. W. (2004). *Neuropsychological assessment* (4th ed.). New York: Oxford.

Luria, A. R. (1973). *The working brain.* New York: Basic Books.

Mapou, R. L. (1988). Testing to detect brain damage: An alternative to what may on longer be useful. *Journal of Clinical and Experimental Neurology, 10*, 271–278.

Matarazzo, J. D. (1972). *Measurement and appraisal of adult intelligence* (5th ed.). Baltimore: Williams & Wilkins.

Mitrushina, M. N., Boone, K. B., Razani, J., & D'Elia, L. F. (2005). *Handbook of Normative Data for Neuropsychological Assessment* (2nd ed). New York: Oxford University Press.

Nunnally, J. C., & Bernstein, I. H. (1994). *Psychometric theory* (3rd ed.). New York: McGraw-Hill.

Parsons, O. A., & Farr, S. R (1981). The neuropsychology of alcohol and drug use. In S. B. Filskov & T. J. Boll (Eds.), *Handbook of clinical neuropsychology* (pp. 320–365). New York: John Wiley & Sons.

Pellegrino, J. W. (1988). Mental models and mental tests. In H. Wainer & H. I. Braun (Eds.), *Test validity* (pp. 49–59). Hillsdale, NJ: Erlbaum.

Raven, J. C., (1982). Revised manual for Raven's Progressive Matrices and Vocabulary Scale. Windsor, UK: NFER Nelsson.

Reitan, R. M. (1955). Investigation of the validity of Halstead's measures of biological intelligence. *Archives of Neurology and Psychiatry, 73*, 28–35.

Reitan, R. M. (1964). Psychological deficits resulting from cerebral lesions in men. In J. M. Warren & K. Akert (Eds.), *The frontal granular cortex and behavior* (pp. 295–312). New York: McGraw-Hill.

Reitan, R. M. (1991). *The neuropsychological deficit scale for adults computer program.* Tucson: Neuropsychology Press. (User's manual).

Reitan, R. M., & Wolfson, D. (1986). *Traumatic brain injury: Vol.1. Pathophysiology and neuropsychological evaluation.* Tucson: Neuropsychology Press.

Reitan, R. M., & Wolfson, D. (1993). *The Halstead–Reitan neuropsychological test battery; Theory and clinical interpretation* (2nd ed.). Tucson: Neuropsychology Press.

Reynolds, C. R., & Kamphaus, R. W. (2003). *Reynolds intellectual assessment scales.* Los Angeles: Western Psychological Services. (RIAS).

Rourke, B. P. (1991). Human neuropsychology in the 1990s. *Archives of Clinical Neuropsychology, 6*, 1–14.

Rourke, B. P., & Brown, G. G. (1986). Clinical neuropsychology and behavioral neurology: Similarities and differences. In S. B. Filskov & T. J. Boll (Eds.), *Handbook of clinical neuropsychology* (Vol. 2, pp. 3–18). New York: Wiley.

Russell, E. W. (1972). A WAIS factor analysis with brain damaged subjects using a criterion measure. *Journal of Consulting and Clinical Psychology, 39*, 133–139.

Russell, E. W. (1979). Three patterns of brain damage on the WAIS. *Journal of Clinical Psychology, 35*(3), 611–620.

Russell, E. W. (1980). Fluid and crystallized intelligence: Effects of diffuse brain damage on the WAIS. *Perceptual and Motor Skills, 51*, 121–122.

Russell, E. W. (1980b). *Theoretical bases of the Luria-Nebraska and the Halstead-Reitan Battery.* Paper presented at the 88th Annual Convention of the American Psychological Association, Montreal.

Russell, E. W. (1986). The psychometric foundation of clinical neuropsychology. In S. B. Filskov & T. J. Boll (Eds.), *Handbook of clinical neuropsychology* (Vol. 2, pp. 45–80). New York: Wiley.

Russell, E. W. (1987). A reference scale method for constructing neuropsychological test batteries. *Journal of Clinical and Experimental Neuropsychology, 9*, 376–392.

Russell, E. W. (1991). A reference scale method for constructing neuropsychological test batteries. In B. P. Rourke, L. Costa, D. V. Cicchetti, K. M. Adams & K. J. Plasterk (Eds.), *Methodological and biostatistical foundations of clinical neuropsychology* (pp. 399–415). Berwyn, PA: Swets & Zeitlinger.

Russell, E. W. (1992). Comparison of two methods for converting the WAIS to the WAIS-R. *Journal of Clinical Psychology, 48*, 355–359.

Russell, E. W. (1995). The accuracy of automated and clinical detection of brain damage and lateralization in neuropsychology. *Neuropsychology Review, 5*(1), 1–68.

Russell, E. W. (1998). In defense of the Halstead–Reitan Battery: A critique of Lezak's review. *Archives of Clinical Neuropsychology, 13*(1), 365–381.

Russell, E. W. (2000). The cognitive-metric, fixed battery approach to neuropsychological assessment. In R. D. Vanderploeg (Ed.), *Clinician's guide to neuropsychological assessment* (pp. 449–481) (2nd ed.). Hillsdale, NJ: Lawrence Erlbaum Associates.

Russell, E. W. (2004). The operating characteristics of the major HRNES-R measures. *Archives of Clinical Neuropsychology*, *19*(8), 1043–1061.

Russell, E. W. (2005). Norming subjects for the Halstead–Reitan Battery. *Archives of Clinical Neuropsychology*, *20*(4), 479–484.

Russell, E. W. (2007). The Flynn effect revisited. *Applied Neuropsychology*, *14*(4), 262–266.

Russell, E. W. (2010). The "obsolescence" of assessment procedures. *Applied Neuropsychology*, *17*(1), 60–67.

Russell, E. W., & Polakoff, D. (1993). Neuropsychological test patterns in men for Alzheimer's and multi-infarct dementia. *Archives of Clinical Neuropsychology*, *8*, 327–343.

Russell, E. W., Russell, S. L. K., & Hill, B. (2005). The fundamental psychometric status of neuropsychological batteries. *Archives of Clinical Neuropsychology*, *20*(6), 785–794.

Russell, E. W., & Starkey, R. I. (1993). *Halstead, Russell neuropsychological evaluation system*. Los Angeles: Western Psychological Services. (Manual and computer program)

Russell, E. W., & Starkey, R. I. (2001a). *Halstead, Russell neuropsychological evaluation system—revised*. Los Angeles: Western Psychological Services. (Manual and computer program).

Russell, E. W., & Starkey, R. I. (2001b). *Halstead, Russell neuropsychological evaluation system—revised*. Los Angeles: Western Psychological Services. (Appendix F).

Schinka, J. A., & Vanderploeg, R. D. (2000). Estimating premorbid level of functioning. In R. D. Vanderploeg (Ed.), *Clinician's guide to neuropsychological assessment* (pp. 39–67) (2nd ed.). Mahwah, NJ: Lawrence Erlbaum Associates.

Strauss, E., Sherman, E. M. S., & Spreen, O. (2006). *A compendium of neuropsychological tests: Administration, norms, and commentary* (3rd ed.). New York: Oxford University Press.

Stern, R. A., & White, T. (2001). *Neuropsychological assessment battery*. Lutz, FL: Psychological Assessment Resources. (NAB)

Terman, L. M., & Merrill, M. A. (1973). *Stanford-Binet Intelligence: Manual for the third revision, Form L-M*. Boston: Houghton Mifflin.

Teuber, H. L. (1955). Physiological psychology. *Annual Review of Psychology*, *6*, 267–296.

Teuber, H. L. (1975). Recovery of function after brain injury. In Ciba Foundation Symposium 34, *Outcome of severe damage to the central nervous system* (pp. 159–190). Amsterdam: Elsevier.

Volbrecht, M. E., Meyers, J. E., & Kaster-Bundgaard, J. (2000). Neuropsychological outcome of head injury using a short battery. *Archives of Clinical Neuropsychology*, *15*, 251–265.

Wechsler, D. (1939). *The measurement of adult intelligence*. Baltimore: Williams & Wilkins. [Manual for the Wechsler-Bellevue Intelligence Scale].

Wechsler, D. (1944). *The measurement of adult intelligence* (3rd ed.). Baltimore: Williams & Wilkins.

Wechsler, D. (1981). *WAIS-R, Wechsler adult intelligence scale—revised, manual*. San Antonio, TX: Psychological Corporation.

Wechsler, D. (1997). *WAIS-III, WMS-III, technical manual*. San Antonio, TX: Psychological Corporation.

Wechsler, D., Coalson, D. L., & Raiford, S. E. (2008). *WAIS-IV technical and interpretive manual*. San Antonio, TX: Pearson.

Williams, A. D. (1997). Fixed versus flexible batteries. In R. J. McCaffrey, A. D. Williams, J. M. Fisher & L. C. Laing (Eds.), *The practice of forensic neuropsychology: Meeting challenges in the courtroom* (pp. 57–70). New York: Plenum.

5 Formal Analytic Methodology

> *"Measurement always concerns numbers relatable to the physical world, and the legitimacy of any measurement is determined by data (facts about the physical world). In particular, scaling, but not classification, always concerns some form of numerical statement of how much of an attribute is present, as its purpose is to quantify the attributes of real objects. The measure may be intended to fit a set of measurement axioms (a model), but it's fit to the model can be determined only by seeing how well the data fit the model's predictions". "... the various types of validity for psychological measures all require data rather than purely mathematical deductions."*
>
> **Nunnally & Bernstein (1994, pp. 8–9).**

An area of neuropsychology that has been neglected is the construction of formal assessment methods. The term *formal* applies to any completely objective method for making psychometric or logical interpretive decisions. These methods have the scientific characteristics of objectivity, repeatability, validity, and predictability. Formal methods provide information that is quantitative or logical. In neuropsychology, they provide an objective, quantitatively accurate description of a relationship between aspects of brain functioning.

Formal battery methods are more complex than formal individual test methods. This section will discuss some of the methodology that is used to construct formal battery methods. Like neuropsychological testing, batteries must be standardized and validated. Ultimately, such validation of formal procedures provides greater reliability than can be obtained from clinical judgment.

Ideally, science would require a completely formalized neuropsychological battery for assessment. In such a battery, all three major aspects of assessment would be formalized and automated: administration, scoring, and interpretation. At this point, each of these three has been computerized to a certain extent, but these methods are largely unintegrated. The work in the area of computerized neuropsychology has combined these three aspects, although incompletely thus far. Most of the work in the field of computerized neuropsychological assessment has emphasized the development of administration methodology. Computerized testing also scores and interprets the data, but the interpretive aspect has general been designed for specific purposes. Consequently, the construction of a general computerized battery is underdeveloped. Concerning scoring, a number of programs score batteries and the

The Scientific Foundation of Neuropsychological Assessment. DOI: 10.1016/B978-0-12-416029-3.00005-1

number finally seems to be increasing. Almost all major intelligence tests now have computerized scoring. In addition, many individual neuropsychological as well as some affective tests are computerized.

In neuropsychology, the area that has not been formally developed is that of battery interpretation. Nevertheless, almost all scoring systems, such as Reitan's Neuropsychological Deficit Scale (NDS) (Reitan & Wolfson, 1993, pp. 347–397), the Halstead–Russell Neuropsychological Evaluation System—Revised (HRNES-R) (Russell & Starkey, 2001a), or the Revised Comprehensive Norms for an Expanded Halstead–Reitan Battery (RCNEHRB) (Heaton, Miller, Taylor, & Grant, 2004), provide basic interpretive functions. These include an index for the existence of brain damage and a method to lateralize the damage. A few extend beyond basic indexes to provide a score for other functions such as lateralization or even for a diagnosis such as Alzheimer's disease (AD) (Russell & Starkey, 2001b, Appendix F, p. 27). Otherwise, more complex interpretive patterns have not been attempted.

In a neuropsychological examination, the various scores may be entered into a scoring program that provides a gross interpretation of the existence of brain damage. This is helpful to neuropsychologists who can use the score to help in medical or forensic settings.

However, such scoring systems require a formalized type of neuropsychological analysis in which tests belong to a standardized battery and are compared using formal procedures. The type of written report that is provided by the Minnesota Multiphasic Personality Inventory (MMPI-2) (Butcher et al., 1989) or the Millon Clinical Multiaxial Inventory-III (MCMI-III) (Millon, 1997) inventories is completely lacking in neuropsychology. (For the most part, these MMPI-2 and MCMI-III interpretive reports have not been validated because they remain secrets of the companies.) In light of this situation, this chapter will be devoted to examining the possibilities that exist for formalized neuropsychological analysis and how these can be applied to computerized analysis.

Characteristics of Formal Methods

Most of the psychometric procedures involving formal methods are generally variations of the methods commonly used with single tests. Concerning batteries, however, formal procedures apply to the relationships between tests as well as to individual tests. Formal methods enable one to make decisions and to supply information used in interpretations without the use of subjective judgments. This is essentially the same process as that provided by a test score. Neither requires clinical judgment. The term *formal* includes procedures such as tests, indexes, ratios, formulas, algorithms, and taxonomies.

In Meehl's (1954) well-known studies, he demonstrated the generally equal or greater accuracy of actuarial—that is, formal—methods compared to clinical judgment. The examination of this difference was brought up to date in several papers (Dawes, Faust, & Meehl, 1989; Grove & Meehl, 1996; Grove, Zald, Lebow, Snitz, & Nelson, 2000). The results were the same as Meehl (1954) had initially discovered.

In regard to neuropsychological batteries, formal procedures require a fixed or standardized battery. This standardizes or fixes the relationships between tests. As such, reliable information may be derived from validated tests or validated relationships between the tests.

Formalized Procedures in Neuropsychology

Although formalized procedures, other than tests such as indexes, had been used elsewhere in psychology, the earliest use of such mathematical procedures in neuropsychology appears to have been Halstead's Index (HI). Originally, the HI consisted of 10 scores (Reitan, 1955). Research and experience found that just 7 of the 10 tests provided accurate indications of brain damage. As such, the seven-test form of the HI became the only form that has been used. Loring and Larrabee (2006) apparently did not realize this in their criticism of the Halstead–Reitan Battery (HRB) (Russell, 2008). With the reduction of the HI to seven tests, this index indicated the existence of brain damage quite accurately. It has remained at least equal to any other measure of the existence of brain damage (Russell, 1995) for almost 70 years. The cutting point for each score in the HI had been determined in Halstead's original study (1947). Surprisingly, the overall cutting point has remained remarkably accurate over time in validating studies (see Chapter 9).

Pattern Analysis

Pattern analysis is the method of examining the pattern of relationships between tests of a battery. The method draws interpretative conclusions from various types of patterns indicated by relationships between the tests rather than from individual test results. Pattern analysis combines or compares test results. As a result, normal test performances are as important as deficit performances.

This pattern-analysis methodology, although not in its formal mode, is almost universally accepted (Lezak, Howieson, & Loring, 2004, pp. 17–18). Pattern analysis may be used by either clinical judgment or formal methodology. Using clinical judgment, an experienced neuropsychologist examining an integrated battery, such as the Wechsler Adult Intelligence Scale—Revised (WAIS-R) or the HRB (Reitan & Wolfson, 1993), will recognize and interpret certain patterns of test results in the test matrix (Reitan & Wolfson, 1993, pp. 405–823).

When used by clinical judgment, pattern analysis is a subjective process that is often difficult to teach or learn by experience. It is possible for pattern analysis to be used with a flexible battery. Nevertheless, this presents severe difficulties for the reliability of the interpretation, because the batteries are continually changed and the norms are variable or often undisclosed in forensic situations. Because the discussion of different patterns and types of patterns is discussed in other chapters, its details will not be further examined here.

However, it should be emphasized that patterns involve the whole brain. As such, pathology patterns may involve many functional systems. A lesion in the occipital cortex may destroy a person's ability to read because the person cannot see.

Nevertheless, his or her language system may remain intact. One area of research that is most needed for assessment is that which delineates the various patterns and types of patterns that may occur in various brain-function pathologies.

Pattern Analysis with Formal Methods

Patterns that may be recognized subjectively in clinical analysis can be converted into a formal procedure such as an index or a formula. These are objective and can be validated. In addition, a pattern may be portrayed by any number of graphic methods. The pattern is often portrayed as a profile of test scores in which the comparative heights of the scales indicate how well the subject performed on each test. If the tests use equivalent scale scores such as co-normed *z*-score equivalents, then the pattern is a direct representation of the relationships between the tests' ability levels. This method was used to examine the Alzheimer's disease pattern on HRNES-R (Russell & Polakoff, 1993).

Pattern analysis is the essence of formal analysis using a battery. It is concerned with the overall variations in brain functioning. As Reitan realized, the primary function of a battery of tests is to reveal the characteristics of brain functioning and pathology (Reitan & Wolfson, 1993, pp. 23–32). Thus, a formal pattern is any set of relationships in a battery that represents a brain-functioning process, normal or pathological, in a *psychometric manner*—that is, the test relationships are equated, numerical, and invariant.

Multiple disassociation is the basis of pattern analysis. Because the brain is an integrated unit that functions as a system with subsystems, it is possible for multiple disassociation patterns between tests to model brain functioning. When accurate, a pattern represents the functioning and pathologies of the brain. The relationship between those functions may indicate a neurological condition or the location of a pathology. For instance, the pattern in which vocabulary and information is more impaired than similarities and digit span often indicates left temporal damage (Russell & Russell, 1993).

Formal Assessment Procedures

Many formal procedures may be used in pattern analysis. A number of these methods will be considered.

Taxonomic Methods

There are two general types of formal methods: taxonomic and mathematical (Nunnally & Bernstein, 1994, pp. 3–4, 27). Taxonomy includes classification of entities that describe and distinguish different categories. A taxonomy orders classes in some manner, usually in a hierarchical form. Formal taxonomic classification systems require an exact objective description of an entity so that the class identifications are observable and repeatable. There are few taxonomic systems in neuropsychology although a number of such systems exist in cognitive psychology such as Guilford's structure of the intellect model (Guilford, 1967). The most comprehensive review of this field was Carroll's (1993) book *Human Cognitive Abilities*. A rather gross system of brain functions that includes elementary functions, domains, and systems is described in Chapter 3.

The taxonomic methodology is intimately involved with the mathematical methodology in that a taxonomy identifies and organizes the various kinds of functions in brain processing. These functions are represented by abilities in psychometrics that can be quantified.

In neuropsychology, a category is a function. Each taxonomic category is mathematically represented by a nominal scale, although categories also can be represented by more complex scales (Nunnally & Bernstein, 1994, p. 27). Mathematical analysis, such as factor analysis, is used to examine the relationships between these processes or functions. For instance, brain functions are largely lateralized—that is, they are separated into right- and left-hemisphere functions or verbal and spatial functions. Once research has determined the distinction or lateralization of functions, assessment procedures using pattern analysis can lateralize that function to a particular hemisphere or place it into a particular domain.

Mathematical Methods

Quantitative or mathematical formal methods apply mathematical processes to the attributes of processes (functions) represented by tests and to the relationships between the functions (Ghiselli, Campbell, & Zedeck, 1981; Nunnally & Bernstein, 1994). As discussed initially, abstract mathematical constructs used in science are applied to entities (such as brain functions) by means of measurement instrumentation. Thus, in science formal methods may apply mathematics to neuropsychological data.

Validity and Reliability

A major characteristic of formal psychometric methods is that their validation usually provides a measure of accuracy, which is a rate of error. Although most statistical methods apply to formal methods, operating characteristics are currently the most used measure of the rate of error applied to neuropsychological assessment methods (Retzlaff & Gibertini, 2000; Russell, 2004; Slick, 2006).

Formalized methods are simply more accurate methods of placing a subject into a category such as brain damage than clinical judgment. Judgment has relatively unknown reliability, but the reliability of formal methods is represented by their rate of error. When Heaton, Grant, Anthony, and Lehman (1981) examined the accuracy of the formal neuropsychological key (Russell, Neuringer, & Goldstein, 1970), they measured the correspondence between the examiners as an indication of reliability. However, they did not measure the psychometric reliability of the key because the formal key would provide the same results each time the same scores were entered into it. In other words, its reliability was 100%, so that test–retest measures are superfluous.

Advantages of Formal Methods

There are advantages to formal methods other than accuracy and reliability. First, formal methods can be changed to improve their accuracy. Contrary to what most clinicians appear to believe, a formal method is not set in concrete but may easily be changed both in form and in its score cutting point. By contrast, clinical judgment cannot be changed. Judgment may be improved with experience, but the improved experience can seldom be verbalized. As such, it is difficult to teach judgment without direct experience with a mentor. In contrast, a formalized method does not require teaching or experience. One simply applies the method.

Secondly, an unexpected advantage of formalized methods is that they enable the generation of interpretations that are not possible with clinical judgment because of the complexity of the procedure to be judged. Thus, advanced formal methods such as decision trees would enable the field of neuropsychology to develop scientifically far beyond what would be possible if it remains dependent on clinical judgment. Currently, the field of clinical neuropsychological assessment, which is dependent on clinical judgment, is largely stagnant.

Types of Formal Methods

The most basic form of a formal method is the ubiquitous item test. It is so well accepted that most psychologists do not realize that it is a formal method. There are many other types of formal procedures, generally using tests, that have been developed in neuropsychology. Except for the index, most of these methods are seldom employed. Each procedure involves the combination or comparison of a number of test scores in order to come to a conclusion expressed in a single score. (At least in the current developmental stage of psychology, only one score per procedure can be validated.)

The Test

The test is a formalized method of making a judgment. Instead of judging that a person is intelligent, the intelligence test may give the subject a full-scale intelligence quotient of 130. The psychometric methods that have been thoroughly developed are presented in many textbooks (Anastasi & Urbina, 1997) and have been codified in the Standards (AERA et al., 1999). They are well known to neuropsychologists. Consequently, an examination of the characteristics of a test is beyond the scope of this writing.

Indexes

Other than tests, the most used formal procedure derived from standardized batteries is the index, in particular the impairment or brain-damage index. Several of these indexes have been constructed, and they provide a major indication of the validity of a battery. Currently, the indexes employing the HRB and its derivative batteries have accumulated a substantial documentation of their validity (Franzen, 2000, pp. 116–132; Reitan & Wolfson, 1993; Russell, 1995, 1998). These indexes include the HI (Reitan & Wolfson, 1993, p. 92), the NDS (Reitan, 1986; Reitan & Wolfson, 1993, pp. 93, 347–397), the Average Impairment Rating (Russell et al., 1970), the Average Impairment Score (AIS), and the Percent Impaired Index (PII) (Russell & Starkey, 2001a, pp. 19, 38). The Global Deficit Score (Heaton et al., 2004, pp. 14–15) has been partially validated.

The Total NAB Index Score is another validated index score based on a co-normed battery, the Neuropsychological Assessment Battery (NAB) (Stern & White, 2001). In addition, the discriminant function in the Meyers Neuropsychological Battery (MNB) (Meyers & Rohling, 2004; Volbrecht, Meyers, & Kaster-Bundgaard, 2000) is also a validating index. Further methods of analysis in this battery discriminate degrees of severity of the pathology (Rohling, Meyers & Millis, 2003).

Several indexes that indicate whether brain damage is lateralized to one or the other hemispheres of the brain have also been developed for the NDS and HRNES-R (Russell, 1995; Russell & Starkey, 2001a).

Ratios

Ratios are probably used in clinical judgment more than any other method, although they are seldom formalized. If the tapping speed of the left hand is half as fast as the right hand (corrected for the normal difference), then a neuropsychologist would normally entertain the existence of a right-hemisphere brain lesion. Of course, in clinical judgment there is no specific cutting point.

An example of a formal ratio was derived from a study designed to separate AD from cerebral vascular dementia (CVD) (Russell & Polakoff, 1993, Russell & Starkey, 2001b, p. 27). The possibility of AD rather than CVD (Russell & Starkey, 2001b, p. 27) is indicated if the scale-score average tapping speed is 1.2 greater than an average derived from the Wechsler (1974) verbal and figural memory scores. (A typographical error in the original paper gave the ratio as 14, instead of 1.4.)

Triangulation

Another formal method may be called *triangulation*. It is the formalization of a psychological assessment method for making certain diagnostic decisions that commonly use clinical judgment (Russell & Russell, 2008, p. 156). In contrast to clinical judgment, this formal procedure provides an exact measure of the accuracy of the decision. Using two tests, the MMPI and a brain-damaged test, this procedure was initially delineated by Watson (1977) to make a differential diagnosis between brain damage and schizophrenia. Nevertheless, the same method applies to making many types of differential neuropsychological assessments.

The concept of *triangulation* is analogous to the concept of triangulation employed in surveying. Using trigonometric data concerning spatial relationship, lines drawn between two points enable a person to locate the position of a third point. This third point could not be located by lines drawn from either of the first two points alone. For instance, in the forestry service, fire towers determine the location of a fire through triangulation. This requires the cooperation of two towers. The direction and distance between the two towers are known. If a line is drawn on a map to the smoke from a fire from each of the two towers, then the angle of intersection precisely locates the fire.

The triangulation method used in formal assessment enables us to obtain information from two tests that is not obtainable from either test alone. Concerning the differentiation of schizophrenia and brain damage, the difficulty is that both schizophrenia and brain damage impair neuropsychological tests (Goldstein, 1986; Watson, Thomas, Anderson, & Felling, 1968). In addition, the MMPI-2 is not sensitive to brain damage (Gass, 2006; Russell & Russell, 2008). To overcome this dilemma, the method is to administer both a neuropsychological battery and an objective test of schizophrenia such as the MMPI-2.

Comparison of scores from these will produce a differentiation between normal, schizophrenic, and brain-damaged subjects:

1. If the neuropsychology battery indicates impairment and the psychopathology tests are relatively benign, then the patient probably has an organic condition.
2. If the neuropsychological battery is impaired and the psychopathology tests indicate schizophrenia, then the diagnosis is probably schizophrenia.
3. If neither is impaired, then the patient is probably normal.

This description was formalized in a preliminary study by Brown (1987), who compared a neuropsychological battery and the MMPI. The algorithm's overall separation of normal, organic, and psychiatric (largely schizophrenic) cases was 73%. The chance probability for making a separation between three categories is only 33.3%.

Formulas

Advanced forms of statistical mathematics are used in neuropsychology research, but neuropsychological assessment, as currently conducted, is almost completely unmathematical—that is, almost no mathematical procedures have been developed to represent a relationship between neuropsychological test scores. Instead, formulas are often viewed with contempt by many neuropsychologists. Although formulas have been developed and accepted, particularly for estimating premorbid intelligence (Schinka & Vanderploeg, 2000, pp. 39–110). They have also been developed to predict Alzheimer's disease (Fuld, 1984; Russell & Polakoff, 1993).

Formulas and Science

By contrast, the hard sciences generally use mathematical formulas to represent the relationships between variables because a formula permits the application of mathematics to complex relationships.

In neuropsychology using a standardized battery, especially with scale scores, such relationships can be represented by formulas (Russell & Polakoff, 1993; Russell & Russell, 1993). This can be done for the simple reason that the equated scores have invariant numerical values, which can be represented by mathematical formulas. Such a formula produces a score that enables this quantitative relationship to be predicted and tested.

Formulas and Neuropsychology

In neuropsychology, a formula is a formalized way of quantifying a particular pattern, primarily by using algebraic notations. Neuropsychology is too undeveloped at this point to use more than simple algebraic formulas. However, as such, pattern analysis could often be expressed in formulas.

If correctly constructed, the formula would select out of all of the confusion of test scores those results that are particularly relevant for a certain diagnosis or assessment condition. It would also assign a specific numerical relationship between test scores in a formalized pattern. This suggests the strength of the relationship in terms of the probability that the condition exists. A cut-point value for the particular condition or relationship between brain functions could be obtained. All of these aspects are illustrated in at least three studies (Russell & Polakoff, 1993; Russell & Russell, 1993; Russell & Starkey, 2001b, p. 26). These values represent the probability that certain types of brain damage exist, as well as lesion locations. Such formulas could be computerized so that a formula would determine whether the battery results contain a particular pattern. A few such formulas have been incorporated into the HRNES-R (Russell & Starkey, 2001b). The formulas can be validated, which, of course, provides the probability that the designated relationship exists.

Nature of Formulas

A formula is only a formalized description of how the interrelationships between test results may be used for diagnosis or assessment. It formalizes the same reasoning that is used in an accurate clinical judgment. The results section of most neuropsychology research papers only provide a verbal description link to the relationship between a test and a condition. It is often difficult to transform such a description into a clinical judgment, much less a quantitative form. Formulas are simply more exact than the informal verbal descriptions that are found in the literature. The formula states the quantitative relationship between test results in a form that can be validated and with its accuracy determined. As such, it can be used dependably in an assessment. Note that there is nothing sacred about a particular cut point derived from one experiment. The position of most cut points may be improved by further research.

There is the suspicion that the true reason neuropsychologists dislike formulas is that they are afraid a formula would not support their clinical judgments.

Advantage of a Formula

The advantage of a formula is exactly the same as the advantage of using a test rather than judgments derived from observations of a patient's informal behavior. The difference is that formulas apply to complex brain relationships indicated by the tests in a battery, whereas a test usually applies to only one function. Most of the same validation methods that apply to a test also apply to a formula's cut point. The operational characteristics of a cut point can be determined for a formula with the same exactness as for a test score. Thus, the various patterns derived from a battery can be validated and their numerical accuracy can be established. In this regard, formulas greatly increase the accuracy of confirming the existence of a condition or the location of damage.

Instead of recognizing this value, neuropsychologists have customarily ridiculed formulas. For instance, the accuracy of Fuld's (1984) formula for determining the existence of Alzheimer's disease has been calculated in several studies (Russell & Polakoff, 1993). Based on the results, it has been criticized as not being accurate enough for assessment purposes. However, those who have criticized it have proffered *no* evidence that their clinical judgment was even as accurate as Fuld's (1984) formula. No study has compared the formula against blind clinical judgment.

The advantage of a formula is that its accuracy can be determined; in the case of Fuld's (1984) formula, it was about as accurate as another formula using the WAIS but not nearly as accurate as a formula derived from the HRNES-R (Russell & Polakoff, 1993; Russell & Starkey, 2001b, p. 26). To the present, apparently, the accuracy of clinical judgment in assessing the existence of AD is untested and unknown. Note that a study by Hom (1992) found the same relationship between motor tests and other neuropsychological tests as was demonstrated in Russell and Polakoff's 1993 study, but Hom did not express it in a formula.

Existing Validated Formulas

A complex index formula for determining the lateralization of brain damage is provided in the HRNES-R, Appendix F (Russell & Starkey, 2001b, p. 26). An earlier version that bridged the gap between the Russell et al. (1970) key approach and the 2001 formula was published by Russell in 1984. The 1984 study provided the most accurate separation between right, left, and diffuse brain damage that has so far been published.

In regard to formulas, in addition to Fuld's (1984) formula, an example of a formula for Alzheimer's disease (AD) was derived from a research study by Russell and Polakoff (1993). It is the following, using the scale scores from the HRNES-R:

$$\frac{\left[(\text{TapR}+\text{TapL})/2\right]}{\left[(\text{MemV2}+\text{MemF2})/2\right]} > 1.2 = \text{AD}$$

where

TapR = tapping test, right hand
TapL = tapping test, left hand
MemV2 = Wechsler verbal memory scale, ½ h (logical memory)
MemF2 = Wechsler figural memory scale, ½ h (visual reproduction)

(A typographical error in the original study indicated a cut point of 14 when it should have been 1.4. A more recent unpublished study found the most accurate cutting point was >1.2 (Russell & Starkey, 2001b, p. 26).

This formula was 97% accurate in separating cerebral vascular disease patients who had not had a stroke or major transient ischemic attack from those with AD. The formula considers the concept that motor functions in AD are not greatly impaired until late in the disease and compares that with motor functions that are impaired early in cerebral vascular disease. Both diseases impair memory, although almost all cognitive functions are relatively more impaired in AD.

Although this formula separates these two conditions, it is primarily relevant to AD because the CVD subjects were less impaired. Consequently, it was placed in the HRNES-R as an indication of AD in general (Russell & Starkey, 2001b, p. 26).

Further unpublished studies also found that alcoholic brain damage demonstrates almost exactly the same pattern, as does AD. Consequently, the patient's history must be used to separate these conditions.

Finally, as another example, a formula was developed on the basis of several cases of focal damage that indicated the existence of left temporal lobe damage (Dobbins & Russell, 1990; Russell & Russell, 1993). This formula essentially compares the WAIS-R Information and vocabulary to digit span and similarities subtests. Several cases had strongly indicated that information and vocabulary are more related to the left temporal lobe whereas digit span and similarities are related to the left parietal lobe. Although this formula works primarily with those having left-hemisphere damage, the Russell and Russell (1993) study found that this pattern did not occur for damage in any of the other major lobes of the brain.

Algorithm Decision Trees

The method of triangulation is a simple form of a decision-tree algorithm. Such algorithms often formalize the way that neuropsychologists analyze a protocol using clinical judgment. A decision-tree algorithm consists in a hierarchy of decision points that progressively differentiate the specific component or components of a generalized system (Kleinmuntz, 1968)—that is, a series of questions determine decision points. Answering each question leads to another that further reduces the possibilities in an assessment.

However, at times a decision point may lead to an increase in possibilities. For instance, an alternative that implies that the impairment is the result of an affective disorder opens the algorithm to all of the possible affective disorders that produce mental impairment.

The first published form of such an algorithm in neuropsychology was the neuropsychological key (Russell et al., 1970). Historically, such decision-tree algorithms have been used in biological taxonomy almost from its beginning. They were called *taxonomic keys* (Russell et al., 1970). They were used to determine the species that a biologists was examining.

Using a standardized battery and the algorithm, the key, could determine whether a person had brain damage, whether the damage was lateralized, and, if so, to which hemisphere. There was no input from clinical judgment at any point in the process from input of test scores to interpretive results. (The administration of the tests could be performed by technicians.) The most recent and complete examination of the various studies comparing the key to clinical judgment (Goldstein & Shelly, 1982; Russell, 1995, 1998) found that the key was almost as accurate as the three expert neuropsychologists in these studies and was more accurate than nonexperts (Chapter 9).

Several years after the initial development of the neuropsychological key was published, a more complete or extensive form of the key algorithm program was designed (Russell, 1992). This new method included a number of steps. These included administering a brief screening test and eliminating affective disorders using the MMPI before determining the existence of brain damage.

In this system, using cutting points derived from research, a patient's neuropsychological functioning was first separated into normal subjects and those with impairment. From the impaired patients, the schizophrenic patients were then distinguished from patients with brain damage. Finally, those with brain damage were separated into patients with right hemisphere, left hemisphere and diffuse damage.

The algorithm was partially validated by Brown (1987) but never published. This preliminary study used a neuropsychological battery and the MMPI. (The MMPI-2 would require changing the cut points.) When the most accurate cutting points were employed, the algorithm's overall separation of normal, organic, and psychiatric (largely schizophrenic) cases was 73%. This was quite adequate because the probability of making a separation between three categories is only 33.3%. In terms of the separate categories, 69% of the organics, 94% of the schizophrenic subjects, and 89% of the normal subjects were correctly identified. The lateralization part of the decision tree was not tested.

Computerized Assessment

Over the last 30 years, the military has been developing computerized testing of neuropsychological conditions (Reeves, Winter, Bleiberg, & Kane, 2007) and has made considerable progress in developing such programs. At this point, various computerized programs are a legitimate form of neuropsychological assessment.

Fundamentally, formal procedures are ideal methods for computerized assessment. Each of the three major aspects of assessment—administration of the examination procedure, scoring, and interpretation—can be computerized and united into a single procedure. The computer program administers tests to which it can apply formal scoring and interpretation. The programs simply require the construction of neuropsychological assessment programs that are applicable to computer processing. Again, with a computerized program the test–retest reliability is 100%. These computerized formal programs must be validated by research in the same way as any neuropsychological procedure.

Formalization enables the entire neuropsychological assessment procedure to be combined into a single unified system that is completely operated by a computer process (Russell et al., 1970). Clinical judgment is not required at any point. However, the use of automated assessment for the entire assessment procedure necessitates the complete use of formal neuropsychological psychometric methods. Currently, each of the three major aspects of assessment—administration, scoring, and interpretation—have been computerized to some extent, but this progress is erratic and without any attempt at designing a unified procedure. Apparently, the neuropsychologists who are applying computer methodology to the administration of neuropsychological procedures have proceeded the furthest in creating a unified formal system.

History of Computerization in Neuropsychology

The first attempt at automating neuropsychological testing was apparently made by Halstead (1947) in the late 1950s or early 1960s. There appear to be no published references to this attempt. However, several neuropsychologists who used the HRB in the late 1950s remember this device. According to descriptions by his contemporaries, Halstead designed a single console that would contain all of the major tests in the HI and record the results. Apparently, it never worked very well and most of the machines were returned. Nevertheless, Halstead recognized the possibility and value of completely automating neuropsychological tests. The students of Halstead, especially Reitan, developed the clinical administration of the test battery, but there seem to have been no further attempts to automate the administration procedure.

Subsequently, Reitan demonstrated that the procedure could be validly administered by technicians in a manner so uniform that it approached automation. The procedure was so standardized that it could be given by any person with a high school or college education. They needed little or no understanding of neurology but were adequately trained to administer the procedure.

Computerization of Scoring and Interpretation

The next step in reducing the variability inherent in clinical judgment would be to create a computer program that would provide basic aids for interpretations. Initially, these might determine the existence of brain damage and its lateralization. As the science progressed, these interpretation aids could become more detailed. The neuropsychological key by Russell et al. (1970) placed the scoring and preliminary interpretation of test results (existence of brain damage and lateralization) in a form that could be accomplished by a person with no formal training in neuropsychology. The person who "ran" the original scoring for the neuropsychological key was a patient, James K. Majors, who had a cerebellar tumor and knew nothing concerning the HRB or neurology (Russell et al., 1970, p. vii). The neuropsychological key program was transformed into the Fortran computer language by Carolyn H. Shelly. The value of a computer in scoring a protocol was immediate evident, and many users continued to score them by computer.

The accuracy of this method was challenged in a study by Heaton et al. (1981) and by a relatively invalid study by Adams, Kvale, and Keegan (1984; see also Russell, 1995). These seem to indicate that clinical judgment was more accurate than the neuropsychological key. However, a study by Goldstein and Shelly (1982) that reanalyzed the Heaton et al. (1981) data using both sensitivity and selectivity found that the "overall percentage of agreement between localization key predictions and neurological criteria achieved approximately equal accuracy levels in both the original study and the cross validation" (Goldstein & Shelly, 1982, p. 721). The evaluation of Heaton and Adams's work is further examined in Chapter 9.

Contemporary Situation

In the last few years, considerable progress is being made in the area of formalizing assessment. Three major areas of formal assessment that are being developed are co-norming, automated administration, and automated interpretation. There has been some work in all three areas.

Computerized Scoring

Computerized scoring has now been developed by several authors (Reitan & Wolfson, 1993; Russell, 2000a, 2000b). In fact, most major tests, including batteries with multiple subtests, now have scoring programs. As such, no psychologist is necessary to score the tests. This increases efficiency while reducing errors to those made during the test administration and in data entry.

The primary advantage of computerized scoring is that the scoring is completely objective. As such, the psychometric aspects of the test scoring must be objective. In those few cases where a qualitative methods are used, the results are usually transformed into objective scores. Because most tests in neuropsychology already use objective scoring, there is generally no difficulty in transforming the objective scoring method for a battery into a computerized system (Russell, 1995). Obviously, the same psychometric requirements for the development of test scores apply to tests that are computerized.

Co-Normed Batteries

Quite recently, there has been a "return of the repressed." At least five co-normed standardized batteries have been published and validated. The first of these methods was a further development of the neuropsychological key. In 1993, Russell and Starkey published the Halstead–Russell Neuropsychological Evaluation System (HRNES), which has been revised as the HRNES-R (Russell & Starkey, 2001a). It appears to be as accurate and relevant for testing today, as it has been for many years. Although the Heaton et al. (2004) Revised Comprehensive Norms for an Expanded Halstead–Reitan Battery (RCNEHRB) provides a quite extensive set of norms, these are only partially co-normed. The NDS (Reitan, 1986) computerized Reitan's method quite exactly and is possibly more accurate as any other method even today (Chapter 9).

After the HRNES study in 1993 (revised in 2002 as the HRNES-R) and the Comprehensive Norms for an Expanded Halstead–Reitan Battery (CNEHRB) study in 1991 (revised in 2004 as the RCNEHRB), no other major co-normed computer programs were developed until 2000 when the MNB (Meyers & Rohling, 2004; Volbrecht et al., 2000) was first published. This is known as a *semiflexible battery*. The primary battery was completely co-normed and fixed, so a test could not be removed without destroying the validity that had been established, although apparently the authors believed that tests could be added to the battery, which made it semiflexible. The authors validated the core of tests without taking into consideration any additional tests so that the core was a fixed battery. Of medium length, it took approximately 3 h and used different tests from the HRB with the exception of the trail-making test and tapping. This battery was able to separate traumatic head injury patients from normal controls using discriminant analysis with 90% sensitivity and 98.9% selectivity. Considering that this battery was considerably higher than most studies, it needs to be cross validated and compared to other batteries.

A second co-normed battery, the Neuropsychological Assessment Battery (NAB) (Stern & White, 2004), has been recently created. It is composed of several batteries or units that compose a total battery. One is a general screening battery that requires the presence or absence of possible abnormal or impaired performance. It contains modules that are designed to cover seven major functional domains such as language and memory and sensory functions. Each dimension is covered with a screening test of less than 45 min. It covers a high range of ability from well above average by adding items to a normal range of functioning. It also includes the Reynolds Intellectual Screening Test (RIST) (Reynolds & Kamphaus, 2003). It is entirely co-normed. The norms are demographically corrected for age, education, and sex. It appears to be well validated compared to a normative sample of 1,400. These appear to be the primary neuropsychological examinations using co-norms that have appeared in recent years.

Computer Administration

Another aspect of computerized assessment is that of automated test administration and scoring. This adds another link to the computerization of the total assessment procedure. A number of individual tests are already administered by a computer. However, only a small group of neuropsychologists has devoted their energies to the development of computer battery administration. The review by Crook, Kay & Larrabee (2009) discusses the major completed computerized batteries in more detail than we are able to do in this discussion.

The first of these tests was the MicroCog (Powell et al., 1993). This is a general neuropsychology instrument. It was originally designed to identify the cognitive status of physicians and other professionals. Five domains are assessed: attention, memory, reasoning, spatial relations, and reaction time. The attention includes span tests forward and backward and a continuous performance task. Memory is assessed for immediate and delayed recall of two stories. It cannot score motor ability. It could be administered in a long form that takes an hour or a short form that takes 30 min. There is one alternate form. The reliability of this test appeared to be typical, which had reliabilities that ranged from 0.52 to 83 at the end of 3 months. Validity was determined by correlating the tests with known regular neuropsychological in intelligence tests. This validity seems to be reasonable. Data are provided as a percentage of correct classification for several different clinical groups, including dementia, depression, and schizophrenia.

Another test that is in fairly wide use is MindStreams (Simon et al., 2006), which is sold by NuroTrax. It consists of fairly traditional neuropsychological tests administered and scored by computer. It has a brief interpretive section. A moderately trained technician oversees the computer administration. Otherwise, no neuropsychologist is involved. The data are presented directly to the referring physician, usually within a very short time after the patient has finished testing. The test consists of a battery of mostly traditional neuropsychological tests. These are downloaded over the Internet and scored by the company. A global assessment battery includes information, memory problem solving, a Stroop type test, finger tapping, and processing speed. The cognitive scores can be applied to different types of brain conditions, depending on the referral from a doctor. These include Alzheimer's disease, multiple sclerosis, Parkinson's disease, and attention deficit hyperactivity disorder. The reliability and validation appear to be equivalent to those of other neuropsychological batteries. Most of the validation work has been published in foreign journals. However, the test presents a method of providing physicians with neuropsychological test results rapidly and without the expense of retaining a neuropsychologist.

CogScreen (Kay, 1995) was developed to attempt to examine changes in cognitive functions among pilots, including slow reaction time and critical flight situations. It measures perceptual, cognitive, and information-processing abilities. It focuses on attention concentration and information along with immediate memory and working memory. The entire battery requires about 45 min for administration. It now has versions for recent versions of Windows. Its validity is obtained by its correlation to special neuropsychological tests such as the Wisconsin Card Test and the trail-making test. This battery has proven to be a good predictor for pilot success with strengths in the area of attention and information-processing speed. It is now been expanded for use with nonpilot patients. However, its memory measurements are rather limited, so it may be administered along with a memory battery.

A battery that has been designed primarily for military evaluations is the Automated Neuropsychological Assessment Matrix (ANAM) (Reeves et al., 2007), which is now commercially available. It is quite flexible in the use of various tests. However, the tests have been co-normed and form scale scores. The battery covers most of the major neuropsychological domains, including motor speed (tapping test), logical reasoning, cognition, and memory. The battery has been validated on a number of conditions, including hypothermia, Alzheimer's disease, multiple sclerosis, and traumatic brain injury. It appears to be an excellent test and could be used for psychological examinations by the general public.

Psychologx (Crook, Kay & Larrabee, 2009, pp. 94–96) is a computer-stimulated battery designed to measure various forms of memory. A unique characteristic is that the tests are designed to resemble those found in everyday life. It has undergone extensive standardization and psychometric analysis. It has been validated by comparing it to various psychological tests such as the Wechsler Memory Scale (Wechsler, 1974). It has been thoroughly factor analyzed. The normative data extend from ages 18 to 90.

Characteristics of Computerized Assessment

Although many of the problems related to computerized administration have been solved, a number of problems remain. Many of these solutions and problems are well reviewed in a special issue of *The Archives of Clinical Neuropsychology* (Kane, 2007). These problems were particularly well described by Reeves et al. (2007).

Computerized administration of neuropsychological test batteries is both similar and different from manual administration. It is similar in that it generally uses the same basic test methodology as other formal methods. It is different in that it pushes formalized methods to their limits. Some of the particular characteristics of computerized administration will be described.

Consistency

Consistency is obtained by administering the tests in precisely the same way each time. With traditional manual testing, the examiner's administration may unintentionally vary from one subject or testing to another. This is an important advantage of computerized testing because it ensures the consistency of administration. However, this does not mean that automated testing is not adjustable. In certain situations, the test program may allow or require certain changes to fit or correct particular examination conditions. For instance, on the block design test the computer program may allow unlimited time for the task. Time and accuracy could then be distinguished. An older person may be slow but still able to construct the design correctly.

Obviously, formalized testing must be used. All of the previous requirements for standardization would apply to computerized test administration.

Efficiency

The efficiency of computerized administration is obvious. A single technician or guide may give the same battery of tests to several or many people using a group of computers simultaneously rather than individually.

Manual Equivalency

Almost any test that can be given manually can be given by computer. This is obvious for verbal tests, but it may require a some transformation of methodology for nonverbal tests. However, nonverbal tests have been given in groups since World War I, so it is quite possible to automate them. Incidentally, gaming methodology may provide methods for handling spatial relations problems.

Measurement of Speed

One great advantage of computerized testing is the ability to measure the speed of mental operations. The ANAM test provides 10 types of responses (Reeves et al., 2007). Of these, eight are various forms of speed measures. This enables computerized testing to examine the relationship between speed and the ability to perform various brain functions.

However, one of the first major discoveries in the history of cognitive psychology was that correlations were extremely low between various kinds of cognitive abilities and sensory and motor speed. The tests in James M. Cattell's battery that were designed to measure intelligence were primarily composed of sensory and motor speed functions. These did not correlate to any great extent with the grades of college students (Guilford, 1967, p. 6). Thus, there appeared to be little relationship between physical speed and intelligence. Nevertheless, tests such as the digit symbol are highly related to brain damage (Russell & Starkey, 2001a, p. 38). Consequently, the relation of speed to different types of brain-functioning abilities should be explored using computerized testing.

Interpretation

Computerized testing also opens the possibility of great developments in the third area of neuropsychological assessment: interpretation. This is particularly true for formalized procedures. The primary reason that almost no progress has been made in the area of interpretation, with the exception of determining premorbid ability and the motivation of patients, is that almost no research is being published that examines formal neuropsychological and patterns that are related to interpretations.

The first interpretative formal methodology to have been placed into a computer program was the neuropsychological key (Russell et al., 1970). This included a lateralization scale as well as an index for determining the existence of brain damage that used a different method than the HI (p. 14). Since then, several basic interpretation programs have been created. Reitan's NDS identifies the existence of brain damage and determines whether it is lateralized (Reitan, 1986).

In contrast, the HRNES-R contains two indexes of the existence of brain damage and one related to the probability of damage. It also has a lateralization index and formulas for identifying both Alzheimer's disease and left temporal lobe damage (Russell & Starkey, 2001b).

The HRNES-R procedure incorporates these indexes and formulas into its program. As such, it demonstrates that computerized assessment that includes interpretation is possible for almost any interpretation that can be reliably made by clinical judgment. A subject may answer questions, manipulate forms, and solve mechanical puzzles presented by a computer, and interpretations can be printed out.

However, even more important, such interpretations can be created that have a reliability and validity that are impossible to obtain by means of clinical judgment or even manual formal testing. Although many neuropsychologists have been attacking the conception of formalized processing, especially the use of formulas, for 20 years (Russell, 1995), the form and accuracy of a computer program can nevertheless be continually refined, which is difficult for human judgment because such judgment depends on rather unreliable memory (Reeves et al., 2007).

Although there is relatively little neuropsychological research in this area now, a new group of neuropsychologists (Crook et al., 2009; Kane, 2007; Kane & Kay, 1992; Reeves et al., 2007) is already devoting its energies to developing such methods. This would eventually demonstrate that the finding of Meehl (1954) and his associates (Dawes et al., 1989; Grove & Meehl 1996; Grove et al., 2000)—that formal methods are as accurate or more accurate than clinical judgment—also applies to neuropsychology.

Algorithms

Decision-tree algorithms are another major method for employing neuropsychological scores to obtain an interpretation. The computer is an ideal instrument for using this formal method. Algorithms may be developed in many forms, all of which could be incorporated into computer programs. Such algorithms would employ the input scores and, by using various indexes and formulas, would provide a computerized description of the patient's brain functioning, including affective pathologies. Such programs already exist in regard to the MMPI-2 and the MCMI-III. Unfortunately, the algorithm programs in both of these programs have not been published or validated.

A computerized program for neuropsychology could also be constructed. Already, the operational characteristics of the major HRNES-R tests have been published (Russell, 2004). The computerized programs could be updated as new research is obtained. A program could be designed for assessment that would provide different interpretive results. The neuropsychological key was validated and determined to be accurate (Russell et al., 1970; Chapter 9). A more extensive form of such an algorithm program was designed (Russell, 1992) and partially validated by Brown (1987), but it was never published.

Integrating a Computerized Battery

Thus, a completely developed computerized assessment procedure that fully integrates all aspects of neuropsychological assessment into a formal methodology can now be developed. It could be expanded, and its accuracy could be improved almost indefinitely without losing its formal quality (Kane, 2007; Kane & Kay, 1992). Clinical judgment has human limitations that limit its extent and accuracy (Faust, Grimm, Ahern & Sokolik, 2010; Franzen, 2000; Garb, 1998), but computerized and automated methods do not.

Full Development of Computerized Methodology

Rather than being a rigid and unchanging method, computerization is actually a never-ending process that nevertheless retains its formal qualities (Reeves et al., 2007). There is no need to retain a fixed battery indefinitely. The standardization process allows a battery to be modified and new tests or procedures to be added. Bridging statistical methods (as previously described) can be used to extend norming to new tests and procedures.

As has been noted, although automated testing has been extremely helpful in certain limited areas such as human engineering and evaluating people for particular jobs and assessing particular pathologies (Kane, Roebuck-Spencer, Short, Kabat, & Wilken, 2007), no one has yet developed a type of wide-ranging battery that would be used for the generalized type of assessment needed in forensic cases.

Thus, considering the vast potential for computerized testing, its development has been rather slow, partly because of a lack of funding and partly because few neuropsychologists are involved in developing these batteries. Also, with the exception of a few batteries such as the ANAM, there appears to be little progress in the development of a battery once it has been established. None of the batteries appear to be thorough measures of the same functions that are found in established traditional batteries. To some extent, this is because of the difficulty of translating the standard types of tests into computerized versions.

An exception is that of MindStreams, which appears to have a great deal of funding support. It is also designed to appeal to the medical profession rather than neuropsychologists. When the proper methods for transforming standard neuropsychological methods into computerized forms and those methods are found to be as reliable as the neuropsychological methods, it is a psychometrically acceptable procedure. In addition, it is obviously more efficient and less expensive for the medical profession than neuropsychological methods.

Conclusion

In conclusion, computerized assessment is able to put all three stages of the assessment process into one procedure. A computer can administer tests, score them, and generate at least preliminary interpretations. In addition, computerization has many advantages. It is extremely good at performing certain kinds of tests, particularly those that require accurate timing such as reaction time tests. Its efficiency is obvious: one psychologist or even a technician can oversee the testing of a half-dozen subjects simultaneously. Another advantage is in the computation of scores. A program can do this more accurately and deal with complex types of scores more efficiently than can humans. There is almost no limit to the complexity of scoring that could be programmed into this format. Consequently, computerized testing has many advantages over manual testing and opens an entire new area for neuropsychological test battery development.

Surprising as it may sound to some neuropsychologists, most of the future development in neuropsychology will probably involve formal computerized procedures that apply to the whole process of brain-function analysis. Such development will require assessing the interrelations of tests. This will require complex formal methods which permit the development of accurate procedures. Such procedures are difficult for clinical judgment. Thus, the greatest importance of the formal methods for neuropsychology is that it promotes a great advance of neuropsychological assessment methodology. This is the possibility of applying mathematical procedures, such as formulas and decision-tree algorithms, to neuropsychological functioning. Such formal quantitative methodology has previously been limited to the hard sciences. Currently, neuropsychological clinical judgments are subjective and undeveloped. However, if widely accepted, the use of formal methods, especially when automated, would raise neuropsychological analysis to a whole new level of scientific sophistication and accuracy.

References

Adams, K. M., Kvale, V. I., & Keegan, J. F. (1984). Relative accuracy of three automated systems for neuropsychological interpretation. *Journal of Clinical Neuropsychological, 6*, 413–431.

AERA, et al. (1999) *Standards for educational and psychological testing*. Washington, DC: American Educational Research Association. (American Educational Research Association, American Psychological Association & the National Council on Measurement in Education).

Anastasi, A., & Urbina, S. (1997). *Psychological testing* (7th ed.). Upper Saddle River, NJ: Prentice Hall.

Brown, J. (1987). *A screening key to differentiate normals from organics and patients with functional disorders*. Unpublished doctoral dissertation, Nova University, Fort Lauderdale, FL. (Advisor E. W. Russell).

Butcher, J. M., et al. (1989). *Minnesota Multiphasic, Personality Inventory: MMPI-2*. Minneapolis: Minnesota Press.

Carroll, J. B. (1993). *Human cognitive abilities: A survey of factor-analytic studies*. New York: Cambridge University Press.

Crook, T. H., Kay, G. G., & Larrabee, G. J. (2009). Computer-based cognitive testing. In I. Grant & K. M. Adams (Eds.), *Neuropsychological assessment of neuropsychiatric disorders* (pp. 94–96) (3rd ed.). New York: Oxford University Press.

Dawes, R. M., Faust, D., & Meehl, P. E. (1989). Clinical versus actuarial judgment. *Science, 243*, 1668–1674.

Dobbins, C. T., & Russell, E. W. (1990). Left temporal lobe brain damage pattern on the Wechsler Adult Intelligence Scale. *Journal of Clinical Psychology, 46*, 863–868.

Faust, D., Grimm, P. W., Ahern, D. C., & Sokolik, M. (2010). The admissibility of behavioral science evidence in the court room: the translation of legal to scientific concepts and back. *Annual Review of Clinical Psychology, 6*, 49–77.

Franzen, M. D. (2000). *Reliability and validity in neuropsychological assessment* (2nd ed.). New York: Kluwer Academic/Plenum.

Fuld, P. A. (1984). Test profile of cholinergic dysfunction and of Alzheimer's-type dementia. *Journal of Clinical Neuropsychology, 6*, 380–392.

Garb, H. N. (1998). *Studying the Clinician: Judgement research and psychological assessment*. Washington, DC: American Psychological Association.

Gass, C. S. (2006). Use of the MMPI-2 in neuropsychological evaluations. In J. N. Butcher (Ed.), *Computerized psychological assessment: A practical guide* (pp. 301–326). Washington, DC: American Psychological Association.

Ghiselli, E. E., Campbell, J. P., & Zedeck, S. (1981). *Measurement theory for the behavioral sciences*. San Francisco: W. H. Freeman.

Goldstein, G. (1986). The neuropsychology of schizophrenia. In I. Grant & K. M. Adams (Eds.), *Neuropsychological assessment of neuropsychiatric disorders* (pp. 147–171). New York: Oxford University Press.

Goldstein, G., & Shelly, C. H. (1982). A further attempt to cross-validate the Russell, Neuringer, and Goldstein neuropsychological keys. *Journal of Consulting and Clinical Psychology, 50*, 721–726.

Grove, W. M., & Meehl, P. E. (1996). Comparative efficiency of informal (subjective) impressionistic and formal (mechanical, algorithmic) prediction procedures, The clinical-statistical controversy. *Psychology, Public Policy, and Law, 2*(2), 293–323.

Grove, W. M., Zald, D. H., Lebow, B. S., Snitz, B. E., & Nelson, C. (2000). Clinical versus mechanical prediction, A meta-analysis. *Psychological Assessment, 12*(1), 19–30.

Guilford, J. P. (1967). *The nature of human intelligence*. New York: McGraw-Hill.

Halstead, W. C. (1947). *Brain and intelligence*. Chicago: University of Chicago Press.

Heaton, R. K., Grant, I., Anthony, W. Z., & Lehman, R. A. W. (1981). A comparison of clinical and automated interpretation of the Halstead–Reitan Battery. *Journal of Clinical Neuropsychology*, *22*, 121–141.

Heaton, R. K., Miller, S. W., Taylor, M. J., & Grant, I. (2004). *Revised comprehensive norms for an expanded Halstead–Reitan Battery: Demographically adjusted neuropsychological norms for African American and Caucasian adults*. Odessa, FL: Psychological Assessment Resources. [Professional manual and computer program].

Hom, J. (1992). General and specific cognitive dysfunctions in patients with Alzheimer's Disease. *Archives of Clinical Neuropsychology*, *7*, 121–133.

Kane, R. L. (Ed.), (2007). *Archives of Clinical Neuropsychology* (22S, pp. S1–S144)

Kane, R. L., & Kay, G. G. (1992). Computerized assessment in neuropsychology: A review of tests and test batteries. *Neuropsychology Review*, *3*, 1–117.

Kane, R. L., Roebuck-Spencer, T., Short, P., Kabat, M., & Wilken, J. (2007). Identifying and monitoring cognitive deficits in clinical populations using automated Neuropsychological Assessment Metrics (ANAM) tests. In R. L. Kane (Ed.) (2007), Supplement: DoD contributions to computerized neurocognitive assessment: The ANAM Test System. *Archives of Clinical Neuropsychology*, S2S1, S115–S126.

Kay, G. G. (1995). Cog-Screen-Aeromedical Edition. *Professional Manual*. Odessa, FL: Psychological Assessment Resources.

Kleinmuntz, B. (1968). The processing of clinical information by man and machine. In B. Kleinmuntz (Ed.), *Formal representation of human judgment* (pp. 149–186). New York: Wiley.

Lezak, M. D., Howieson, D. B., & Loring, D. W. (2004). *Neuropsychological assessment* (4th ed.). New York: Oxford University Press.

Loring, D. W., & Larrabee, G. J. (2006). Sensitivity of the Halstead and Wechsler test batteries to brain damage: Evidence from Reitan's original validation sample. *Clinical Neuropsychologist*, *20*(2), 221–229.

Meehl, P. E. (1954). *Clinical versus statistical prediction: A theoretical analysis and a review of the evidence*. Minneapolis: University of Minnesota Press.

Meyers, J. E., & Rohling, M. L. (2004). Validation of the Myers short battery on mild TBI patients. *Archives of Clinical Neuropsychology*, *19*(5), 637–651.

Millon, T. (Ed.). (1997). *The Millon inventories: Modern clinical and personality assessment* (2nd ed.). New York: Guilford.

Nunnally, J. C., & Bernstein, I. H. (1994). *Psychometric theory* (3rd ed.). New York: McGraw-Hill.

Powell, D. H., Kaplan, E. F., Whitla, D., Weintraub, S., Catlin, R., & Funkenstein, H. H. (1993). *MicroCog: Assessment of cognitive functioning. [Manual and computer program]*. San Antonio: Psychological Corporation.

Reeves, D. L. , Winter, K. P., Bleiberg, J., & Kane, R. L. (2007). In R. L. Kane (Ed.). (2007). Supplement: DoD contributions to computerized neurocognitive assessment: the ANAM Test System. *Archives of Clinical Neuropsychology*, *22S*, S15–S35.

Reitan, R. M. (1955). An investigation of the validity of Halstead's measures of biological intelligence. *Archives of Neurology and Psychiatry*, *73*, 28–35.

Reitan, R. M. (1986). *The Neuropsychological Deficit Scale for Adults: Computer program*. Tucson: Neuropsychology Press.

Reitan, R. M., & Wolfson, D. (1993). *The Halstead–Reitan Neuropsychological Test Battery; Theory and clinical interpretation* (2nd ed.). Tucson: Neuropsychology Press.

Retzlaff, P. D., & Gibertini, M. (2000). Neuropsychometric issues and problems. In R. D. Vanderploeg (Ed.), *Clinician's guide to neuropsychological assessment* (pp. 277–299) (2nd ed.). Mahwah, NJ: Lawrence Erlbaum Associates.

Reynolds, C. R., & Kamphaus, R. W. (2003). *Reynolds Intellectual Assessment Scales (RIAS)*. Los Angeles: Western Psychological Services.

Rohling, M. L., Meyers, J. E., & Millis, S. R. (2003). Neuropsychological impairment following traumatic brain injury: A dose-response analysis. *Clinical Neuropsychologist*, *17*, 289–302.

Russell, E. W. (1984). Theory and developments of pattern analysis methods related to the Halstead–Reitan battery. In P. E. Logue & J. M. Shear (Eds.), *Clinical neuropsychology: A multidisciplinary approach* (pp. 50–98). Springfield, IL: Charles C. Thomas.

Russell, E. W. (1992). *Development of a neuropsychology step key*. Miami, FL: VA Medical Center. Unpublished manuscript.

Russell, E. W. (1995). The accuracy of automated and clinical detection of brain damage and lateralization in neuropsychology. *Neuropsychology Review*, *5*(1), 1–68.

Russell, E. W. (1998). In defense of the Halstead–Reitan Battery: A critique of Lezak's review. *Archives of Clinical Neuropsychology*, *13*, 365–381.

Russell, E. W. (2000). The application of computerized scoring programs to neuropsychological assessment. In R. D. Vanderploeg (Ed.), *Clinician's guide to neuropsychological assessment* (pp. 483–515) (2nd ed.). Hillsdale, NJ: Lawrence Erlbaum Associates.

Russell, E. W. (2000). The cognitive-metric, fixed battery approach to neuropsychological assessment. In R. D. Vanderploeg (Ed.), *Clinician's guide to neuropsychological assessment* (pp. 449–481) (2nd ed.). Hillsdale, NJ: Lawrence Erlbaum Associates.

Russell, E. W. (2004). The operating characteristics of the major HRNES-R measures. *Archives of Clinical Neuropsychology*, *19*(8), 1043–1061.

Russell, E. W. (2008). Commentary on Loring and Larrabee's reanalysis of Reitan's original studies. *Clinical Neuropsychologist*, *22*(3), 519–523.

Russell, E. W., Neuringer, C., & Goldstein, G. (1970). *Assessment of brain damage: A neuropsychological key approach*. New York: Wiley Company.

Russell, E. W., & Polakoff, D. (1993). Neuropsychological test patterns in men for Alzheimer's and multi-infarct dementia. *Archives of Clinical Neuropsychology*, *8*, 327–343.

Russell, E. W., & Russell, S. L. K. (1993). Left temporal lobe brain damage pattern on the WAIS, Addendum. *Journal of Clinical Psychology*, *49*, 241–244.

Russell, E. W., & Starkey, R. I. (2001). *Halstead–Russell Neuropsychological Evaluation System—Revised*. Los Angeles: Western Psychological Services. [Manual and computer program].

Russell, E. W., & Starkey, R. I. (2001). *Halstead–Russell Neuropsychological Evaluation System—Revised*. Los Angeles: Western Psychological Services. (Appendix F)

Russell, S. L. K., & Russell, E. W. (2008). Using the MCMI-III in neuropsychological evaluations. In T. Millon (Ed.), *The Millon inventories: Modern clinical and personality assessment* (2nd ed.). New York: Guilford.

Schinka, J. A., & Vanderploeg, R. D. (2000). Estimating premorbid level of functioning. In R. D. Vanderploeg (Ed.), *Clinician's guide to neuropsychological assessment* (pp. 39–67) (2nd ed.). Hillsdale, NJ: Lawrence Erlbaum.

Simon, E. S., Harel, Y., Appleboim, N., Doniger, G. M., Lavie, M., & Achiron, A. (2006). Validation of Mainstream Computerized Cognative Battery in multiple sclerois. *Neurology*, *66*, A239.

Slick, D. J. (2006). Psychometrics in neuropsychological assessment. In E. Strauss, E. M. S. Sherman & O. Spreen (Eds.), *A compendium of neuropsychological tests:*

Administration, norms, and commentary (pp. 3–43) (3rd ed.). New York: Oxford University Press.

Stern, R. A., & White, T. (2001). *Neuropsychological assessment battery (NAB)*. Lutz, FL: Psychological Assessment Resources.

Volbrecht, M. E., Meyers, J. E., & Kaster-Bundgaard, J. (2000). Neuropsychological outcome of head injury using a short battery. *Archives of Clinical Neuropsychology*, *15*, 251–265.

Watson, C. G. (1977). Brain damage tests in psychiatric settings. *INS Bulletin*, March, 10–12.

Watson, C. G., Thomas, R. W., Anderson, D., & Felling, J. (1968). Differentiation of schizophrenics from organics at two chronicity levels by use of Reitan–Halstead organic test battery. *Journal of Consulting and Clinical Psychology*, *32*, 679–684.

Wechsler, D. (1974). *Wechsler Memory Scale*. San Antonio, TX: Psychological Corporation.

6 Neuropsychological Battery Patterns

The medical need for CER (comparative effectiveness research) arises from a fact that few patients realize and fewer doctors acknowledge: the scientific basis for many medical treatments is often flimsy or even nonexistent. More than half the guidelines issued by the Infectious Disease Society of America, for instance, are based on "expert opinion" alone and not an actual comparative data, let alone a clinical trial.

Begley (2011, p. 52)

Modern data graphics can do much more than simply substitute for small statistical tables. At their best, graphics are instruments for reasoning about quantitative information. Often the most effective way to describe, explore, and summarize a set of numbers—even a very large set—is to look at pictures of those numbers. Furthermore, of all methods of analyzing and communicating statistical information, well-designed graphics are usually the simplest and at the same time the most powerful.

Tufte (1983, p. 8)

Although the primary use of neuropsychological batteries currently is to determine the existence of brain damage, this is not the only important function of a battery. The second major use of neuropsychological batteries is to determine patterns that indicate neurological conditions through diagnosis, location, and prognosis.

Pattern Analysis

Pattern analysis provides an examination of how the brain is functioning. In addition to a general effect, various forms of pathology may have different effects on the brain so that they form patterns of impairment. Different patterns will be produced by the type of damage and the process of the lesion. In addition, a battery may help in determining the prognosis, treatment, and postaccident life skills of a patient. Consequently, a large battery is often required to characterize adequately the nature of a brain lesion as well as its existence.

Because there are many conditions that may affect a test of brain functioning, the impairment of an individual test is not diagnostic. At some point, any test will

The Scientific Foundation of Neuropsychological Assessment. DOI: 10.1016/B978-0-12-416029-3.00006-3

be impaired by brain damage such that an individual test will seldom indicate much about aspects of the brain's condition. The only value of an individual test is to help estimate whether a particular brain function is impaired. A single test provides almost no information concerning the type of pathology or its location (Russell, 1976).

Only the use of a neuropsychological test battery can provide information about the brain-damage patterns that are related to various neurological conditions (Lezak, Howieson, & Loring, 2004, pp. 153–155). Thus, the question is not whether a battery of tests is necessary for neuropsychological assessment but rather how it should be constructed to provide the most accurate information about the various types of brain functioning and pathology.

As described previously in this book, in the early 1950s, Reitan, working with Kløve at the University of Indiana's medical school (Reitan, 1966, pp. 156–218), used a battery of tests based on Halstead's (1947) original work. With this battery, he discovered that the localization and often the diagnosis of various kinds of neurological disorders could be determined by neuropsychological tests alone. His method used clinical judgment applied to a group of tests that were constant across administrations. These assessments of a brain's condition were obtained by examining the consistent relationships between various tests in the battery. These relationships may form a pattern that indicates the condition of the brain's functioning.

The pattern of results was crucial to determining the characteristics of brain damage. These characteristics could often be derived from neuropsychological testing without reference to information obtained from external sources. Lezak et al. (2004, pp. 17–18) agreed with the need for a battery of tests, because only a battery permits the observation of patterns of tests that are able to elucidate various types of lesion characteristics.

Although Lezak et al. (2004, pp. 4–11, 153–144) often mention the need for batteries to observe patterns, such patterns are almost never discussed in their book. Nor are patterns examined to any extent in any other neuropsychology books, except those by Reitan. Thus, there is general agreement that the function of a battery is to provide patterns of test results that enable the examiner to determine characteristics of brain functioning. Some of the various brain-damage effects are well known to experts in neuropsychology, but they are seldom studied as distinctive patterns in graduate-school assessment programs.

Almost no neuropsychological reports describe validated patterns of test results that support an interpretation. Thus, there is little or no scientific information or even clinical lore supporting many of the interpretative conclusions that are derived from neuropsychological examination results. Rather, commonly neuropsychological interpretations depend more on the context of the assessment than on the examination results. Only the work derived from Reitan's battery is concerned with pattern analysis, and it is difficult to learn without direct experience of his methodology provided by practitioners trained by Reitan.

Consequently, this chapter is designed to provide an elementary and preliminary introduction to various kinds of pattern analyses. It describes both how to obtain and use some patterns for research and assessment purposes.

Reitan's Four Methods of Analysis

The classical methods of brain-function analysis are best described by Reitan and Wolfson (Reitan, 1964; Reitan & Wolfson, 1986, 1993). Reitan uses every neuropsychology method, even though he employed a fixed battery. Reitan was one of the first neuropsychologists to propose a theory as a basis for methods that went beyond interpreting a single test score. He delineated four methods of interpretive inference (Reitan & Wolfson, 1986, pp. 28–29): (1) level of performance for individual tests, (2) differential patterns of ability, (3) comparisons between the two sides of the body, and (4) pathognomonic signs. It is clear that the first is the conventional method of examining individual tests. The next two interpretive methods are forms of pattern analysis, and the fourth is the qualitative approach.

Level of performance is the beginning of pattern analysis. Using an index of individual tests such as the Halstead Index (HI) provides an average level of performance that itself is a type of pattern created by combining tests. The second method is the pattern of performance. Patterns are simply combinations of levels of performance for several tests. In Reitan's actual practice, the patterns appear to be largely confined to the Wechsler Adult Intelligence Scale (WAIS), at least on the variables presented in the General Neuropsychological Deficit Scale (GNDS; Reitan, 1991). On examination, the third method, comparison of right and left sides of the body, is also a type of pattern analysis. This is the pattern of test results that occurs when the tests that are related to each side of the body are compared, a form of double dissociation that is routine in neurology. Finally, this leaves pathognomonic signs as the only method that does not involve a form of pattern analysis. The signs themselves are actually qualitative signs that indicate types of brain-damage conditions. In practice, as demonstrated by the GNDS, Reitan uses signs only in regard to the Aphasia Screening Test (Reitan, 1991). Many of the answers on the aphasia examination are written or drawn. Consequently, they can be observed qualitatively without examining the patient directly. Reitan was able to derive a large amount of information from a small number of items on this test using this sign approach (Reitan, 1984).

In the Russell version of the Halstead tests, the Halstead–Russell Neuropsychological Evaluation System—Revised (HRNES–R; Russell & Starkey, 1993, 2001), the number of items that are failed are counted and therefore quantified instead of examining signs as related to particular pathologies. Hence, this sign approach itself has been quantified, and the score for the Aphasia Screening Examination becomes part of the patterns used in the total test battery. Of course, one can still use the Aphasia Screening Test qualitatively when it is helpful.

Nature of a Pattern

In neuropsychology, there are only two ways to obtain interpretive information directly from test results without using contextual material such as a patient's medical history: (1) from the results of a test and (2) from the relationships between tests.

Although both methods provide information, the information provided by a single test in a blind analysis is quite limited. In contrast, the information provided by relationships between tests is abundant, and it increases as more tests are added to a battery. Every pair of tests in a battery has a relationship, and three tests provide four relationships. The number of relationships increases geometrically with the number of tests in the battery. Consequently, the number of relationships in even a moderately sized battery is extremely large. Each relationship and each group of relationships constitute a pattern or part of a pattern. Consequently, a battery has as many patterns as there are relationships between tests within the battery. However, in practice, only certain relationships can provide meaningful interpretations. These meaningful relationships must be discovered and validated. Currently, very few of them have been identified formally, although many are part of the Halstead–Reitan Battery (HRB) lore, and most neuropsychologists who have not been trained in the Halstead–Reitan tradition have no ability to recognize them.

Definition of a Pattern

In this book, a meaningful *pattern* is defined broadly as "a specific fixed set of relationships between two or more scores in a battery or procedure (tests, indexes, etc.) that indicate a specific interpretation." Such interpretations are not obtainable from a single test or even a group of tests that does not have a fixed set of relationships as in an index. This is similar to a definition of a *pattern* in Merriam-Webster (2002): "a discernible coherent system based on the intended interrelationship of component parts." It is the consistency of the test relationships that enables a meaningful pattern to exist and become known. If relationships within a battery change from one administration of a battery to another, only chaos exists in the relationships between tests.

Basis of Patterns

A consistent pattern derived from a battery of tests is a formal procedure that is created by combining or comparing tests or procedure scores. A procedure is any method of obtaining a score such as a test, an index, a ratio, or a formula. These patterns may be recognized referentially by those experienced with a consistent or fixed battery, but they only constitute lore and not objective patterns that may be published and taught. Some of the patterns may be formalized in various ways that will be described later in this chapter. As a formal procedure, each of these process patterns must be validated in the same manner as an individual test.

Patterns and Domains

In assessment, patterns are formed between tests and not between domains. (When a domain is formalized as an index, such as in an IQ or HI, the index score is treated as a test score.) Almost all research and assessment use tests and not domains. Domains may be helpful in describing test results, but they are relatively useless in research and pattern analysis. The reason for this is that a domain is a very inexact concept.

The particular tests that constitute a domain are generally only vaguely known because the differences between domains have seldom been delineated by research except through factor analysis. In contrast, a test or procedure is exact—to the extent that measurement may be applied to it.

Some years ago, in a presidential address, Dodrill challenged the concept that neuropsychologists "have good knowledge of the constructs that our tests measure" (Dodrill, 1997, pp. 3–5). First, he separated the tests in the HRB into eight traditional conceptual groupings that composed what would now be called world *domains*. These groups were generally accepted as indicating distinct types of cognitive abilities. He examined the correlations between commonly accepted groupings of tests and compared them to the correlations within the groups. For the control group of 120 subjects, the mean correlation within groups was 0.42, whereas the between-group mean correlation was 0.34. The 120 neurological subjects had a slightly higher mean within-group correlation of 0.52, but the mean across correlations increased to 0.44. The difference between the controls and brain-damaged groups was not significant for either controls or neurological patients. Consequently, Dodrill was unable to demonstrate the existence of individualized domains for the various tests in this battery. Apparently, this study has not been repeated.

Another problem with the concept of a domain is that, as has been recognized by many neuropsychologists, most tests are compound tests that are composed of many different brain-function domains. Pure elementary tests are rare; even when they exist, they have seldom been demonstrated to be elementary.

Finally, from the point of view of patterns, domains cannot be quantified. Because mathematics and statistics cannot be applied to them, they cannot be handled in a scientific manner. Consequently, the relationships between domain entities cannot be specified with any precision.

In a pattern analysis, this difficulty with the vagueness of the domains related to individual tests is multiplied by the use of many relationships between tests. If it is not known which domains are being compared or even combined in an index, then an understanding of the domains that are being measured is almost impossible. When their components have no precision, domains will remain vague phantoms, loosely connected by intuition and fad to an inexact and varying group of tests that are used in overgeneralized interpretations.

Factor analysis can define domains as factors, as was accomplished by Cattell (1971), Guilford (1967), and others (Carroll, 1993, pp. 30–72). However, factor analysis is now often more confusing than helpful in determining the constituents of domains. The analysis of factors in terms of brain functioning has only just begun. [Some excellent definitive work has been accomplished for the Wechsler battery, especially WAIS–III and WAIS–IV (Wechsler, 1997; Wechsler, Coalson, & Raiford, 2008).] Other than this, the use of domains in neuropsychology lacks any specificity in relationship to brain functioning.

As a result, at least at this stage of neuropsychology development, research and assessment must be largely confined to patterns found between specific individual tests and not domains. When neuropsychologists interpret their findings or publish study abstracts, they may indulge themselves in describing the results in terms of domains, but this is largely to exhibit the impression that they know more about brain functioning than is known about the field.

The Psychometric Requirements for Patterns

The psychometric requirements for a battery of tests were previously discussed at some length. These requirements are the same as those needed to create and understand patterns, because patterns are derived from a battery of tests. Consequently, these requirements will only be discussed briefly and with specific reference to patterns.

The first requirement for any pattern is that the relationships between tests, which compose the pattern, must remain consistent from one administration to another. They must be standardized so that they retain the same metric, the same norms, the same construction of scale scores (co-norming), and the same correction for demographic characteristics of the population. In other words, the methodology, which validates certain relationships in research, must apply to those relationships in the assessment of an individual.

Coverage

Finally, it should be rather obvious that the content of the test battery or validated pattern of tests must remain the same because a pattern involves a consistent relationship between specific tests that have a particular content.

An integrated battery is designed to assess the functioning of the entire brain in order to assess conditions operating within the whole brain. Patterns usually involve the whole brain or at least a part that is related to the rest of the brain. Thus, the psychometric patterns in which both impairments and assets are related to each other represent the way in which an individual brain is functioning. As such, a well-designed battery of tests that covers the entire brain presents an observable model of how a particular brain is functioning. Using sets of tests, the functioning of the brain becomes manifest so that the functions in the black box become observable.

In this regard, the requirement for a fully integrated battery is that the major functions of the brain must be covered. It is perhaps here that the concept of domains may be relevant, because the tests that are selected for the battery should represent all known domains.

As discussed elsewhere, coverage is of two major types: (1) that of content or domains and (2) that of location. The advantage of using locations, even in this world of magnetic resonance images (MRIs), is that the concept of locations has been more fully developed than the concept of domains. Because domains of brain functioning are related to specific areas of the brain, when the various areas of the brain are covered then it is highly probable that most of the domains are also covered.

The reason for this full coverage is that if an area or domain is not included in the battery then it cannot be part of any pattern, and as such it cannot be assessed. Consequently, to obtain as full coverage of patterns as possible, the greatest coverage of the brain functions and locations is required.

Table 6.1 WAIS Subtests Using Age-Corrected Scores for Two Forms of Neurological Pathology

Tests	***Cases***	
WAIS Subtests (Age-Corrected)	**E0362**	**E0363**
Information	9	9
Comprehension	10	8
Arithmetic	4	8
Similarities	11	9
Digit span	7	6
Vocabulary	11	8
Digit symbol	0	0
Picture completion	4	8
Block design	0	0
Picture arrangement	0	2
Object assembly	0	1
Tapping test (raw scores) (taps/10 s)		
Tapping, right	40	21
Tapping, left	33	0

Illustrations of Pattern Coverage

An adequate assessment of the diagnosis of a neurological condition generally requires a specific set of tests—that is, a battery. Without certain tests, patterns such as those derived from Wechsler scales often cannot be established. The following case study illustrates this lack of diagnostic differentiation because of a lack of particular tests. The two cases in this illustration were tested in our laboratory.

One patient had a stroke or a cerebrovascular accident (CVA), and the other had Alzheimer's disease (AD). These two cases are presented in Table 6.1.

Without the use of tests other than the WAIS subtests to complete the pattern, the two cases could not have been separated in a blind analysis. However, by including the tapping test (raw scores) in the pattern, the diagnoses can be distinguished.

The first case (E 0362), which actually has a stronger verbal versus performance difference, was the Alzheimer's case. This AD patient had no significant motor problems, so his tapping speed with both hands was almost normal. In contrast, the second case (E 0363) has a tapping rate of zero for the left hand, which indicates a paralysis. Consequently, this patient had the CVA. Thus, the tapping score enabled the examiner to distinguish the diagnosis of the two cases, whereas the Wechsler scale patterns alone would not allow this separation. In addition, patterns are useful in the prognosis and treatment of patients. This use of neuropsychological assessment almost always requires the use of a number of tests for accurate interpretations. As an example, a young man tested in our laboratory (Russell, 1981) had developed cerebral encephalitis from herpes simplex, which was concentrated in the left temporal lobe, according to a neurological radioisotope brain scan. A neuropsychological examination indicated left-temporal-lobe damage, producing a severe chronic reading disability with other milder verbal problems. This reading disability persisted as an area of chronic focal damage. After rehabilitation, he was able to function as an automobile mechanic but was unable to perform work that involved reading. Thus, the pattern found on the neuropsychological examination was able to help determine this patient's rehabilitation. In this case, although neurology determined that the patient had a severe, localized encephalitis that caused left-temporal brain damage, it was the neuropsychological examination that determined the type of impairment and its implications for the patient's rehabilitation.

As a final note, recognize that neuropsychology probably does not use tests that cover certain important functions or areas of the brain. A function that should be covered but for which there is no common test is that of social intelligence as defined by Guilford (1967). He called this ability *behavioral intelligence*. Although there is considerable academic research work in the area of brain functioning, no adequate tests have been developed for neuropsychology or are in common usage. (It is quite possible that the reason neuropsychology or cognitive psychology in general has failed to discover the crucial elements necessary for assessing a successful businessperson is that such success requires a high level of social intelligence. Cognitive psychology and neuropsychology do not now have social intelligence measures.)

Descriptive Patterns

Having discussed the various requirements for creating or recognizing patterns, two of the most generally accepted patterns will be described. Although these are evident in many forms of neuropsychology batteries, they were primarily recognized on the Wechsler scales. As such, they will be described on the basis of research performed on those scales. There will be emphasis on the interaction and recognition of these patterns.

Fluidity Pattern: Generalized Intelligence Fluid and Crystallized

The first neuropsychological pattern to be definitely defined is the concept of fluidity. This has been a major pattern in neuropsychology that was conceptualized in different ways by several people during the 1940s. At that time, Hebb (1941), Cattell (1943), and Halstead (1947) all postulated the existence of two general forms of intellectual abilities. One form was strongly affected by brain pathology, and the other was less affected. The roots of this theory can be found as early as 1930 when Babcock demonstrated that some tests, such as vocabulary, were less impaired by brain damage than tests that require a more actively deductive thought process. The Shipley Institute for Living Scale (Shipley, 1940) and the Hunt–Minnesota Test for Organic Brain Damage (Hunt, 1943) for brain damage were based on this concept. More recently, Kaufman and Kaufman (2004) have developed an intelligence test based on this distinction.

Apparently, Hebb (1941) was the first neuropsychologist to clearly identify these two forms of intellectual abilities, but it was Cattell (1943, 1963) and later Horn

(1966, 1968) who developed the concept and demonstrated its importance. Hebb (1949) called these abilities *Intelligence A* and *Intelligence B*. Halstead (1947) proposed a similar theory that contrasted *psychometric* to *biological intelligence* (Barron & Russell, 1992). Biological intelligence, which was inherent in the organism, was different from learned psychometric or IQ intelligence. Because biological intelligence was directly related to neural tissue, Halstead thought that it should be more affected by brain damage than psychometric intelligence. Consequently, the tests that are particularly sensitive to brain damage should be the most direct measures of biological intelligence.

This concept appears in factor analysis as two factors that have been repeatedly obtained. Cattell (1943) described this theory in terms of *fluid* and *crystallized* intelligences. The terms *fluid intelligence* and *crystallized intelligence* are descriptive terms derived from a chemistry analogy that involves the crystallizing process of a material. He called the two types of intelligence *Gc* and *Gf* for "generalized intelligence crystallized" and "generalized intelligence fluid." The basic concept is often called *fluidity*.

Cattell (1943) proposed that they reflected different phases of the learning process. Fluid intelligence involves the active mental processing of new material such as problem solving, which uses minimal amounts of prior learning. When the process is composed of well-learned or overlearned abilities, it is called *crystallized*. In regard to brain functioning, fluid abilities are those that require active brain processing of novel material, whereas crystallized intelligence only requires the brain to retrieve well-remembered material.

Thus, included in this theory of fluidity was the postulation that brain damage would impair fluid abilities more than crystallized abilities. Cattell (1943) suggested the relationship of his theory to the effects of brain damage. Horn (1976) was instrumental, along with Hebb (1949), in emphasizing the neurological underpinnings of fluid abilities. However, unlike Halstead's theory, the fluidity hypothesis was not tested by Hebb, Cattell, or Horn using brain-damaged subjects.

In addition to these three psychologists, Wechsler (1955) proposed the concept that aging produced a differential effect or pattern on the various subtests of the Wechsler batteries such that some test scores deteriorate more rapidly than others. The subtests that do not deteriorate so rapidly with aging (vocabulary, information, object assembly, and picture completion) were called *hold* tests. Those that appear to deteriorate more rapidly (digit span, similarities, digit symbol, and block design) were called *don't hold* tests (Matarazzo, 1972; McFie, 1960). This same concept was applied to the assessment of brain damage. Later studies (Barron & Russell, 1992; Russell, 1979, 1980) demonstrated that Wechsler was incorrect in the tests that deteriorate. All of the verbal tests were hold tests, and only picture completion was not a fully don't hold test among the performance tests. Apparently, Wechsler wanted an equal number of hold and don't hold tests among the verbal and performance tests.

Thus, this concept of two types of intelligence related to the effect of aging and brain damage was proposed by four of the most respected neuropsychologists and was accepted widely into the 1950s. A large discrepancy of 15 or more points between verbal and performance IQ (PIQ) traditionally has been used to indicate brain damage

(Matarazzo, 1972). This discrepancy often was thought to be especially indicative of an organic condition if the performance IQ was below the verbal IQ (VIQ).

However, this concept of fluidity was largely abandoned by neuropsychology in the 1960s. Because lateralization findings had become so well supported in the literature, Matarazzo (1972) concluded that lateralization was the major effect of brain damage on the Wechsler scales. Consequently, it is understandable that a difference between VIQ and PIQ would be attributed to lateralized hemispheric damage, even though the existence of fluidity was repeatedly demonstrated under different names (Cullum, Steinman, & Bigler, 1983; Finlayson, 1977; Fitzhugh, Fitzhugh, & Reitan, 1964; Horn, 1968, 1976; Horn & Cattell, 1966, 1968; Kaufman, 1979; Reed & Reitan, 1963; Russell, 1974, 1979, 1980). In contrast, apparently, there has never been a study that has challenged the existence of a fluidity effect (a thorough library and computer search did not locate any such study).

Although the fluidity effect was abandoned by neuropsychology in the 1950s and 1960s, by the 1970s it had become one of the major organizing principles in gerontology (Botwinick, 1977) to explain the effects of aging. Subsequently, Horn (1976) and Kaufman (1979) directly related the concept of fluid and crystallized intelligence to the Wechsler intelligence tests. Today, fluidity is again a major principle in neuropsychology that should be taken into consideration in most neuropsychological research and in all clinical interpretations (Russell, 1986).

Lateralization

Beginning in the 1950s, but based on concepts that were much older (Matarazzo, 1972), other research had found that a major effect of various forms of brain damage on the Wechsler tests was a lateralization effect in which verbal abilities were more impaired by left-hemisphere damage and nonverbal or performance abilities were more impaired by right-hemisphere damage. The Wechsler tests reflected this difference. Research repeatedly demonstrated that lateralized damage would produce a differential pattern of Wechsler test scores.

Reitan (1966, pp. 177–185) was among the first neuropsychologists who realized that the right and left hemispheres served different types of functions. In general, the left hemisphere contained verbal functions whereas the right hemisphere contained nonverbal or performance functions. Beginning as early as 1955, Reitan (1955a), his colleagues, and then others provided the research that demonstrated this effect (Kløve, 1974; Matarazzo, 1972; Reitan, 1962).

It rapidly became accepted that, in right-dominant people, the verbal IQ and verbal subtests were more affected by left-hemisphere damage, whereas right-hemisphere damage affects the performance subtests to a greater extent. This differential was particularly evident in acute damage and does not hold as well in chronic damage (Fitzhugh, Fitzhugh, & Reitan, 1962; Kløve, 1974; Matarazzo, 1972; Russell, 1972a, 1972b). Reviews and acceptance of this effect can be located in classic texts such as Lezak (1983) and Matarazzo (1972).

Other studies had indicated that verbal tests were more left-hemispheric measures whereas performance tests, except digit symbol and picture completion, measured right-hemispheric abilities (Russell, 1972a).

Combined Effect of Patterns

From the literature so far reviewed, there appears to be at least two major patterns of brain damage that affect the Wechsler scales and possibly all cognitive abilities. These are the effect of fluidity and of lateralization. One would expect that these two effects would be recognizable in Wechsler batteries of tests. As has been demonstrated, both effects have been found to be related to the Wechsler tests in research. Consequently, their effects should interact in a Wechsler battery. This interaction effect was demonstrated in two different studies by Russell (1979, 1980; Barron & Russell, 1992). The results are more evident in the second study.

Research could demonstrate these effects through the careful selection of subjects. The subjects who should best support the fluidity principle would be those who have organic conditions that are not lateralized and are slowly progressive, primarily dementias. In the first study (1979), the dementias consisted of a number of different forms of degenerative disease but primarily Alzheimer's disease. In the second study (Barron & Russell, 1992), the dementia cases were those produced by chronic alcoholic encephalopathy. (The study was also designed to test the effects of alcoholism on cognitive abilities.)

In regard to the lateralization principle, acute patients need to be selected (Fitzhugh et al., 1962). Intrinsic tumors and CVAs appear to be more lateralized or even localized in their effect than most other conditions. Thus, they would be expected to produce the most definite lateralizing effect. The Russell (1979) and Barron and Russell (1992) studies were designed to investigate the effects that these types of organic conditions produce on the WAIS and Wechsler Adult Intelligence Scale–Revised (WAIS–R).

The effect of these conditions on adult Wechsler tests is most clearly illustrated by the Barron and Russell (1992) study, as demonstrated in Figure 6.1. This study used four groups of 40 subjects who were matched for age and education. The groups

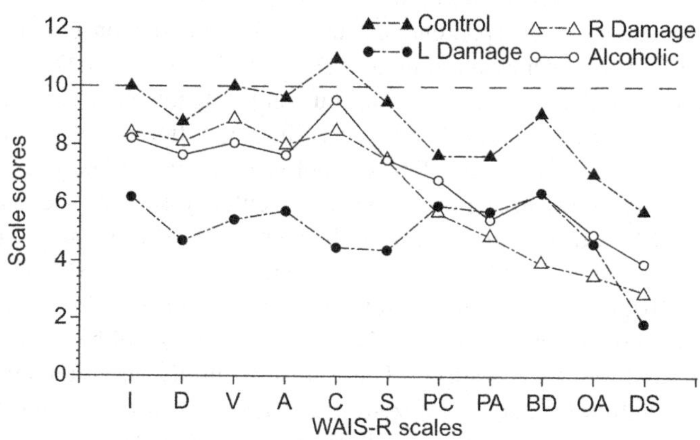

Figure 6.1 WAIS–R mean subtest profiles for alcoholic, control, and left- and right-hemisphere brain-damaged groups of subjects. The dashed line in the middle of the diagram at scale-score 10 is the reference group score for all scales.

were composed of subjects with (1) diagnosed alcoholism, (2) right-hemisphere damage, and (3) left-hemisphere damage, along with (4) a normal control group.

In regard to patterns of test results, this study essentially found five WAIS subtest patterns. The first is not immediately apparent because it consists in the mean of the reference group for the WAIS–R, which were scale scores for the 20–34 age group. It produces a straight mean line across all of the tests, against which the other scales were compared. In this diagram, it is seen as the dotted line across the mean.

The second pattern was an aging pattern produced by the older control subjects. They had a mean age of 51.75. The figure profile demonstrates a pattern in which the verbal tests are almost equivalent to the reference tests, but there is a moderate reduction of ability for the performance tests with the exception of block design. These are generally fluid tests. Digit symbol, a speed test, was also moderately impaired. This pattern is a modified form of the fluidity pattern and is evidently because of the age difference between the mean age of this group, which was almost 53, and the age of the reference group, which was composed of subjects ages 20 to 34.

The third and fourth patterns are almost identical and are found in two groups: the degenerative brain-damaged group and the right-hemisphere-damage group. This profile pattern was that of relatively high verbal subtest scores and relatively low performance scores. Only block design demonstrates a major difference between right-hemisphere damage and alcoholic encephalopathy. However, it appears to be abnormally high in all groups and may be an artifact. In any case, these two patterns on the Wechsler scale could not be distinguished in a blind analysis.

The fifth pattern was that of the left-hemisphere patients. The performance subtests, except for digit symbol, were somewhat higher than the verbal subtests, but the difference was not great enough to produce a significant difference between the verbal and performance tests. In Russell's 1979 study, the *F*-test differences between the left-hemisphere cases and the other two brain-damaged groups were large and highly significant for verbal subtests, but only two of the 10 performance subtest comparisons between left-hemisphere damaged subjects and either right-hemisphere or degenerative cases reached significance.

From these studies, it is apparent that there is an interaction effect between the fluidity effect and the lateralization effect. The verbal tests are both left-hemisphere tests as well as crystallized function tests. Thus, in left-hemisphere damage, these two effects tend to cancel each other. The result is that the difference between verbal and performance tests is not great. The digit symbol is an exception because it is impaired by any damage that slows down brain functioning, either left or right hemisphere.

Conversely, block design, object assembly, and, to a lesser extent, picture arrangement are not only don't hold tests but also right-hemisphere tests. Thus, in right-hemisphere damage these two effects reinforce each other, which produces a strong difference between the verbal tests and the performance tests of block design, picture arrangement, and object assembly. These results imply an interaction between the principles of fluidity and lateralization that accounts for different patterns that have been found in the WAIS, the WAIS–R, and probably the more recent versions of the Wechsler scales.

There are several practical implications of these results. First, and most obviously, this study reaffirms the concept that there is no single pattern for all types of brain damage on the Wechsler scales. The most common pattern is the fluidity or deterioration pattern. This pattern appears in most generalized brain damage, but it is most clearly observed in the degenerative conditions.

Right-hemisphere damage apparently has almost the same pattern as this diffuse degenerative damage pattern, although it may be more exaggerated. Left-hemisphere damage (and some other forms of brain damage that were not investigated in this study such as head trauma) apparently does not have a differential pattern. Rather, such damage may have a pattern in which there is little or no difference between verbal and performance tests, and all tests are relatively depressed. As such, this WAIS pattern cannot be differentiated from the usual form of mental retardation on Wechsler tests.

Consequently, these results are important for clinical practice. In determining the lateralization of damage, one should take the effect of fluidity into account before the focality of damage can be designated. As demonstrated previously, the Wechsler tests (probably all of them) by themselves cannot adequately assess either the existence or lateralization of brain damage. Assessment must be supported by other tests that are designed specifically to determine the existence and location of damage. This was apparent in the first study, as indicated by the difference between a degenerative disease and a right CVA. However, this does not mean that the WAIS is of no importance in the assessment of brain damage. On the contrary, when used along with other tests of brain damage, it often makes a necessary contribution. Thus, its widespread use in brain-damage assessment is quite justified.

The Structure of the Classic Adult Wechsler Scales

Finally, this study demonstrates some aspects of the structure of the Wechsler adult scales at least up to the WAIS–III. When the Wechsler tests were first constructed, there was little in the way of psychological theory to guide the construction of the tests (Benson, Hulac, & Kranzler, 2010). In view of this, it was remarkably well designed. Although research has supported the separation of verbal and performance test factors, in the light of fluidity findings it now appears that the Wechsler scales, at least up through the WAIS–III, had some major defects from the point of view of neuropsychological assessment. All of the verbal tests were to some extent crystallized ability tests. Thus, these Wechsler scales did not contain any verbal tests that were fluid, and so they were highly sensitive to the generalized dementia form of brain damage. Arithmetic is only slightly more sensitive to damage than the other verbal tests. On the other hand, only picture completion is somewhat of a nonverbal crystallized test, and it is not a strong crystallized test. Thus, the left-hemisphere verbal tests are almost all crystallized tests, and right-hemisphere tests are largely fluid ability tests. As has been demonstrated, this lack of symmetry evidently has produced some of the confusion related to the effects of brain damage on these Wechsler scales.

Recent Wechsler Scales

Apparently, some of the more recent intelligence tests have taken these conditions into consideration such as Kaufman intelligence tests (Kaufman & Kaufman, 2004). The WAIS–IV made some attempts in that direction (Benson et al., 2010), but the matrix reasoning test apparently does not lateralize. Although the Wechsler test may be developing to correspond to factor analytic studies, especially Cattell's system (1971), it has yet to demonstrate any better correspondence to neuropsychological theory than previous versions.

In regard to patterns, an examination of the WAIS–III and Wechsler Memory Scales–III (WMS–III) (Wechsler, 1997) and WAIS–IV (Wechsler et al., 2008) manuals does not add much to the findings that have already been discussed. In these manuals, there was a considerable description of some neurological syndromes and a description of impaired test findings. However, there was very little description or comparison of patterns between the scales or with tests not in the Wechsler battery. Thus, differential diagnosis would be difficult if not possible using these Wechsler scales. This was partly because almost all studies compared the test results of a particular pathology to a normal control group and not to groups having different disorders.

There was almost no discussion of lateralization in either manual, although the effect of lateralization on Wechsler scales has been dramatic and long-standing. This may have resulted from studies of localization now being out of fashion (Russell, 2010). Because it is accepted that all brain functions are related to localization, even if the test results are generalized, and that localization contributes to patterns of diagnosis (for instance, diagnosing a CVA), this lack is quite detrimental to any attempt at pattern analysis with recent Wechsler scales.

In regard to the patterns described in the WAIS–III–WMS–III (Wechsler, 1997) manual, these were primarily concerned with degenerative diseases. The referenced research studies were primarily of studies done with the previous versions of the adult Wechsler scales and therefore would be considered to be outdated by the American Psychological Association (Russell, 2010). As such, they do not apply to the WAIS–IV. The research studies that were described used *N*'s that were so small that the results are hardly generalizable. A close examination of the results finds that—in spite of distinguishing conditions such as Alzheimer's disease and Huntington's disease—the general pattern described for all degenerative conditions was that of fluid versus crystallized intelligence accompanied by memory loss.

The manual for the WAIS–IV (Wechsler et al., 2008) was even less informative than the WAIS–III–WMS–III (Wechsler, 1997) manual. The findings were similar to those found in previous research by other authors on previous forms of the Wechsler tests. In conclusion, the recent Wechsler scales, although improving their factor structure, have not contributed much additional information to our understanding of neuropsychological patterns and so provide little additional aid in assessment beyond the previous versions of the Wechsler scales.

Alcoholism

To demonstrate how these patterns may help solve a neuropsychological problem, alcoholism will be discussed. The pathology of severe alcoholism is intimately involved with both the concept of lateralization and fluidity. It was known that chronic alcoholism, particularly when it was severe enough to approach creating a Wernicke's syndrome, had a particular effect on the Wechsler adult scales. This effect of alcoholism is described in more detail elsewhere (Barron & Russell, 1992; Ellis & Oscar-Berman, 1989; Parsons & Farr, 1981), but briefly it is as follows. In chronic alcoholism, the verbal scaled scores were relatively normal, but the performance scaled scores were impaired (Fitzhugh, Fitzhugh, & Reitan, 1965). This finding was so common that it was considered to be a "classic" pattern (Matarazzo, 1972). Parsons and Farr (1981) cite 15 alcoholism studies that compared the WAIS verbal and performance IQ scores (VIQ and PIQ), as well as a few tests from the Halstead–Reitan Battery. With the exception of one study, all of the studies indicated lower PIQ than VIQ scores.

There were four major theories concerning the causation of this pattern: the frontal-lobe damage theory, the premature-aging theory, the right-hemisphere theory, and the fluidity effect theory. The frontal-lobe hypothesis assumes that Wechsler performance tests were more frontal than the verbal tests. The premature-aging theory relies on the knowledge that performance tests in aging deteriorate faster than verbal tests. In gerontology, the premature-aging theory has now been incorporated into the fluidity theory (Botwinick, 1977). The frontal-lobe theory and the premature-aging theory quickly lost credibility because of contradictory neuropathological research data (Goldstein, 1987).

The right-hemisphere-damage theory contended that alcoholism results in significantly greater biological damage to the right hemisphere than to the left hemisphere. This theory has received considerable attention (Ellis & Oscar-Berman, 1989; Parsons & Farr, 1981).

Previous research had found that the major effect of various forms of brain damage on the WAIS was the lateralization effect, in which verbal abilities were more impaired by left-hemisphere damage and performance abilities were more impaired by right-hemisphere damage. Reviews and acceptance of this effect can be located in classic texts such as Lezak (1983) and Matarazzo (1972). Consequently, when alcoholics demonstrated a similar pattern on the WAIS, it was logical to generalize from the established clinical interpretation.

However, in the early 1980s, this hypothesis began to be seriously criticized by Goldstein (1987; Goldstein & Shelly, 1982). Ellis and Oscar-Berman (1989) thoroughly reviewed this entire controversy concerning the possible greater affect of alcoholic damage on the right hemisphere. Although they did not find support for a right-hemisphere effect, they did not offer an alternative explanation for the source of the so-called classic alcoholic pattern.

However, as described, the fluid and crystallized intelligence or fluidity effect proposed by Cattell (1943) and demonstrated by Russell (1979, 1980) would explain this chronic alcoholism pattern as resulting from the fluidity effect. To test this hypothesis, Barron and Russell (1992) constructed a study using double dissociation. Right-hemisphere-damaged, left-hemisphere-damaged, chronic alcoholism, and control groups composed of 40 subjects each. They were matched on the variables of age and education. The subjects were administered the WAIS–R, along with four sensory and motor measures that measured right and left impairment: the tapping test (TAP), the finger agnosia test (FAT), the fingertip writing test (FTW), and the tactile performance test (TPT). These tests were sensitive to lateralized damage but not to fluidity.

In this comparison, the alcoholic group demonstrated the classic Wechsler pattern of a lower performance than verbal scores, as can be observed in Figure 6.1. Although for the right-hemisphere-damaged group, the left-hand scores on the sensory and motor tests were significantly more impaired than the right-hand scores, they were not for the alcoholic group. Thus, these results did not support the right-hemisphere theory. Rather, as hypothesized, the pattern was essentially the same as Russell's 1979 and 1980 studies in which both fluidity and lateralization were demonstrated to affect the adult Wechsler test. Thus, the alcoholic pattern was most adequately explained by the fluidity theory. Thus, chronic alcoholism damages the brain in the same manner as a degenerative disease.

To test whether this pattern of mean scores was significant, a chi-square statistic was applied the mean score pattern as seen in Figure 6.1. The WAIS–R subtest mean scores were divided at the median (7.53) for all scales. It was predicted that those above the median would be crystallized and those below the median would be fluid. Fisher's exact test was used, which was significant at a probability level of 0.002.

The above finding supported the contention that the classic alcoholic pattern on the WAIS or WAIS–R is produced by the fluidity effect and not right-hemisphere damage. It also lends credence to the Russell (1979, 1980, 1986) contention that the existing WAIS and WAIS–R format of verbal and performance tasks confounds actual hemispheric damage with the loss of fluid and crystallized ability.

In the manuals describing the Wechsler patterns for alcoholic disorders (in WAIS–III and WMS–III; Wechsler, 1997, pp. 161–164), it was found that if patients with Korsakoff's syndrome are retested, particularly after a period of abstinence, the results are relatively normal. In this case, the researchers removed patients with severe chronic damage, so naturally the subjects demonstrated little evidence of severe chronic brain damage. The Korsakoff results (pp. 164–165) were those found by Barron and Russell (1992), with the exception that memory (which had not been measured) was impaired. The WAIS–IV manual does not discuss chronic alcoholism.

This impaired memory in dementia was demonstrated in the Russell and Polakoff (1993) study. The primary effect found for tests that were not Wechsler subtests was the retention of motor abilities. Thus, chronic alcoholism apparently acts like Alzheimer's disease and some other degenerative pathologies, at least as long as the person continues to drink. Because crystallized functions and motor abilities appear to be better sustained over time, an individual may seem to be competent when he or she actually is cognitively slipping quite severely. Thus, in the early stages there may be the illusion of competency as long as the alcoholic, or individual with a degenerative disease, remains within the parameters of his or her area of expertise. At this stage, the major difficulties appear in their inability to handle new problems and cognitive changes.

Informal Analytic Types of Pattern Analysis

Patterns may be presented in many ways. These range from a verbal descriptions derived from clinical judgments to algebraic formulas. They vary from very "intuitive" to highly formal methods. The major forms of these methods will now be discussed.

Clinical Judgment

Narrative descriptions of patterns based on clinical judgment may be very sophisticated or quite ingenious. The level of sophistication tends to be related to the reliability of a clinical judgment. Although this will be discussed elsewhere in this book, the level of accuracy in clinical judgment depends in part on the type of methodology that forms the basis for the clinical judgment. Judgments based on a variable set of tests are quite different in their accuracy from those derived from a well-constructed consistent set of tests. If the scores are simply scribbled onto a sheet of paper and are not even collected into a table, then they do not present an adequate basis for clinical judgment. On the other hand, the type of table derived from a well-constructed and well-validated battery provides an adequate basis for clinical judgments. The following example may illustrate an adequate basis for clinical judgment.

Almost all discussions of neuropsychological assessment, whether using clinical judgment or a more formal methodology, advise the examiner to construct a table of scores for each subject (Reitan & Wolfson, 1993, p. 418; Strauss, Sherman, & Spreen, 2006, pp. 32–43). As an example of tables, the HRNES–R table (Figure 6.2) used for an interesting client (GR03) in a forensic case, will be examined.

Subject GR03 was a 41-year-old right-handed woman with 16 years of education who was tested with the HRNES–R. She had had a "mild" head trauma from a motor vehicle accident in which she hit the right side of her head against the car frame. There was only a brief loss of consciousness and some relatively minor physical injuries. The current testing occurred 4 years after the accident so that her brain condition had become chronic.

Before the accident, she had been a librarian. She had no difficulty graduating from a reputable college, as an A and B student with a GPA of 3.5. She had been given a WAIS–R in high school that demonstrated an IQ in the high average range, with no indication of verbal problems. After the accident, she found it extremely difficult to perform her job as a librarian and was having great trouble completing a master's degree.

The table in Figure 6.2 provides the scores obtain from the HRNES-R. The tests used in the table are completely described in the HRNES–R manual (Russell & Starkey, 2001) and in Russell (2004). In addition, a graphic portrayal is presented later in this chapter, where many items that are not familiar will be explained. Note that the scale scores, called *C*-scores, are equivalent to *t*-scores, but with a mean set at 100 instead of 50. Consequently, to obtain a *C*-score equivalent to a *t*-score,

Halstead Russell Neuropsychological Evaluation System-R (HRNES-R)

Name__GR________________ ID Code RG03______ **Summary form**

Age_41_ Education__16_ Gender__M__ Dominance: HAND: R

INDEXES

Average Index Score (AIS)	98
Percent Impaired Index (PII)	40%
Probability of Brain Damage	18%
Lateralization Index: 337	Left, Weak

INDEX TESTS	Raw	C-Score
Category	33	105
Trails B	78	100
Tapping Av.	41	102
Digit Symbol	11	100
TPT - Total (min)	23.2	95
TPT - Memory	7	95
Speech Perception	16	87
Block Design	9	95
Aphasia Screening	4	97
Perceptual Disorders	4	102

Verbal Ability		
PPVT - R, [III]	CND	55
Expressive Verbal Test	___	___
Analogies	___	___
WRAT- R, 3		
Reading	517	82
Spelling	516	82
Arithmetic	520	87
Boston Naming Test,		
Named	___	___
Known Ratio	___	___
Memory		
Digits Forward	9	82
Digits Backward	5	65
Corsi Board	12	112
MSLT - Immediate	5	85
MSLT - Long Term	8	97
MSLT - ½ Hour	7	92
MSLT - Recognition	11	102
Wechsler Memory Test	Orig.	R, [III]
Verbal Immediate	7	85
Verbal ½ Hour	10	95
Verbal % Retained	100	112
Figural Immediate	10	95
Figural ½ Hour	10	97
Figural % Retained	68	112
TPT		
Dominant Hand (Min)	9.8	92
Nondominant Hand	8.1	97
Both	5.3	97
Memory	7	95
Location	6	105
Spatial Ability		
Trails A	20	105
Cross Drawing	3	97

[Centile Score: M = 100, SD = 10]

WAIS- R, [III]	Raw	Age	C-Score
VIQ	47	87	82
PIQ	50	99	92
FSIQ	96	91	85
Information	42	9	90
Digit Span	9	5	77
Vocabulary	42	9	90
Arithmetic	12	9	90
Comprehension	NG		
Similarities	16	7	85
Picture Comp.	16	7	87
Picture Arrang.	17	13	107
Block Design	32	9	95
Object Assem.	NG		
Digit Symbol	75	11	100
L-N Sequenc.	___	___	___
Matrix Reason.	___	___	___
Symbol Search	19	6	85

Rhythm (err)	7	85
Fluency		
H-Words	14	85
FAS Total	___	___
FAS - F	___	___
FAS - A	___	___
FAS - S	___	___
Design Fluency	___	___
Motor Ability		
Grip Strength - Dom (Kg)	45	100
Grip Strength - Non	40	100
Tapping - Dom/10sec	43	100
Tapping - Non	39	100
Pegboard - Dom	64	102
Pegboard - Non	82	95
Write Name - Dom	NG	
Write Name - Non	NG	
Psychomotor Speed		
Trials Speed (sec)	9	105
Digit Symbol	11	100
Perceptual Disorders		
Total Disorder Score	4	102
Suppression R	2	
Suppression L	0	
Finger Agnosia R	0	100
Finger Agnosia L	0	100
Finger Tip Writing R	2	100
Finger Tip Writing L	0	107
Field Cuts R_NG L___		
Visual Gestalt		
Gestalt - Objects	___	___
Gestalt - Words	___	___

Figure 6.2 Copy of the score sheet for GR03. It is in the format for scores that used in the HRNES–R. The scale scores are *C*-scored in which the mean is set at 100 and the standard deviation at 10. These data are also presented in Figures 6.3 and 6.4.

subtract 50 from the score. The four index scores used in the HRNES–R are provided in the upper left-hand side. Both raw scores and scale scores are provided.

On examination, it is evident that it would be difficult to understand the pattern that the scores present if only the raw scores were used. In the right upper-left side are the WAIS–III scores. (These scores—labeled VIQ, PIQ, and FSIQ—are provided under the column called *raw scores*, which may be confusing.) Notice that not all of the tests in the HRNES–R were administered. This is quite acceptable when using scale scores because these scores were co-normed. Such scale scores are derived by the same method as those used in most intelligence tests, including the Wechsler tests.

Graphic Methods of Presenting Patterns

Many graphic methods present either individual cases or groups of cases used for research and assessment of neurological conditions. These methods generally illustrate patterns in a more vivid manner than do numbers on a table. Although the pattern may be extricated from the table, the particular pattern demonstrated is often more easily observed when graphically presented.

Localization Diagrams (Neural Maps)

One form of pattern presentation that is found in almost all neurology textbooks is a diagram of the brain in which various functions are localized to areas of the brain. These functions form patterns in the brain that may be presented in localization diagrams. Damasio (2003) describes these as *neural maps* (pp. 7, 351). In the HRNES–R manual (Russell & Starkey, 2001, p. 22), various tests are placed at various locations in the brain. The locations are stated to be approximate and are based on both research and clinical lore, which is too extensive to describe here.

To illustrate the utility of localization diagrams, the diagrams in Figures 6.3 and 6.4, which were used in a forensic case, are presented. These were derived from the table in figure 6.2. The diagrams are of patient GR03's right and left hemispheres. Most of the tests that were administered to her are presented in the boxes, with lines indicating the area of the brain to which the test is related (Figures 6.3 and 6.4). The colors of the boxes and their text indicate the level of the scale scores. (These scale scores are HRNES–R *C*-scores, in which a standard deviation is 10 points 100 is equivalent to the mean of people with similar age, gender, and intellectual ability, generally as indicated by educational level.) Blue indicates a score in the normal range, which is above a scaled score of 95. Orange scores indicate mild impairment, with scale scores from 95 through 90. Red scores indicate moderate to severe impairment, with scores below 90.

As is evident from this diagram and the preceding table, these scores indicate a pattern of left parietal severe impairment, whereas other parts of the brain vary from mild impairment to normality. This is the classic pattern for a contra-coup lesion from a right-sided blow to the head. There appears to be some additional mild impairment in the right hemisphere. These results clearly explain this patient's difficulty in dealing with verbal material after the accident. The area of maximum impairment is

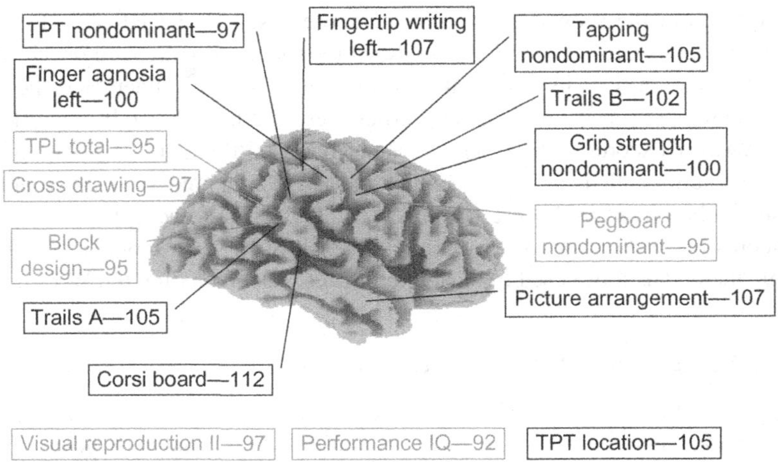

Figure 6.3 The right hemisphere of GE03. The HRNES–R scale scores of tests are placed in the boxes with lines leading to the area of the brain where the tests are estimated to be located. Blue is normal (scores >95), orange is mild impairment (scores 90–95), and red is severe impairment (scores <90). (For interpretation of the references to color in this figure legend, the reader is referred to the web version of this book.)

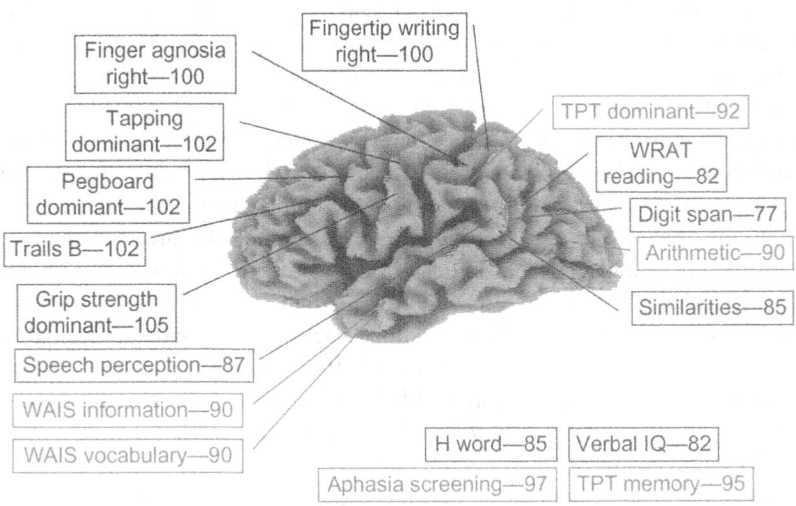

Figure 6.4 The left hemisphere of GE03. The HRNES–R scale scores of tests are placed in the boxes with lines leading to the area of the brain where the tests are estimated to be located. Blue is normal (>95), orange is mild impairment (scores 90–95), and red is severe impairment (scores <90). (For interpretation of the references to color in this figure legend, the reader is referred to the web version of this book.)

exactly that area, which is related to verbal ability. Incidentally, her symptom validity tests (SVTs) indicated that she was applying full effort to her assessment.

Note: Although uncommon, there are cases when head trauma results in a focal area of damage without great loss of consciousness. It is presumed that if the reticular activating system in the brain stem is not impacted by the trauma, then damage may occur with minimal loss of consciousness. It has been reported that as many as 20% of soldiers in battle, who sustained penetrating wounds to the brain, did not lose consciousness.

Although in head trauma the pattern of test results is seldom crucial to the case because patterns are highly variable, in this case the forensic conclusion is that this patient had a specific area of brain damage, this interpretation, which was compatible with her reported postaccident problems, would probably have not been possible except for the neuropsychological pattern. This pattern indicated a definite focal area of damage that was consistent with her history of verbal deficit.

This case indicates that use of patterns in neuropsychological assessment may be critical, even in those cases where the primary conclusion is the existence of brain damage. In this case, the pattern indicated both the existence of damage and its location, which explained the patient's symptomatology.

Criticism of Location Diagrams

In spite of its obvious usefulness in assessment and the fact that the general locations of many tests are known through both research and clinical lore, there are critics of such location diagrams. For instance, Lezak (1995, p. 714; Lezak et al., 2004, p. 677) attacks similar diagrams in the HRNES–R manual, which indicate the approximate location for the various tests in the battery (Russell & Starkey, 1993, 2001, p. 22), as being "phrenology." Because her critique is well answered in Russell's papers reviewing Lezak in Chapters 12 and 13 of this book, a further defense of this method need not be repeated.

However, in this regard, the HRNES–R manual is careful to state that these locations indicate approximate areas of the brain even though a test name, by necessity, must be placed in a specific area. Obviously, as research, especially using the *f*-MRI and other localizing tools, provides exact locations for various tests, the vagueness of their location will decrease. Also note that many of the tests used in neuropsychology now are compound tests or even tests of generalized brain functioning. As such, they may be related to several locations or hemispheres, or even to the entire brain.

Scattergrams

Scattergrams are regularly used in neuropsychological research to indicate relationships between tests and their various characteristics. Linear regression or even curvilinear regression may be illustrated with this graphical method. These scattergrams provide information about the relationships between test scores and various influences such as age, education, and gender. Tests can also be compared to each other, such as comparing a test to the index for brain damage.

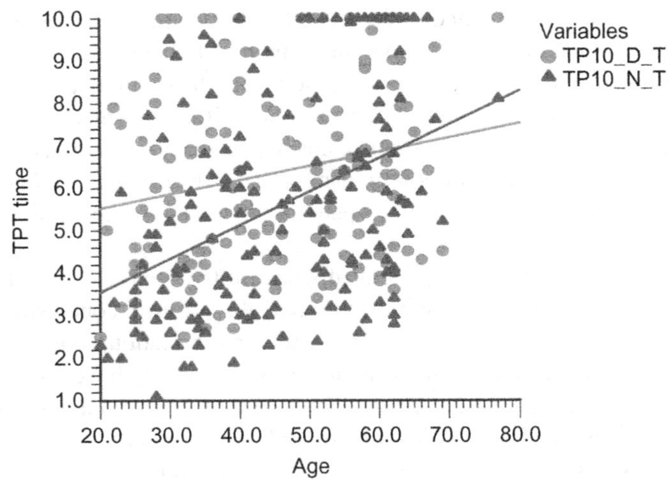

Figure 6.5 Effect of age on the dominant and nondominant tactual performance test control group's raw time scores.

Unpublished scattergrams were used to understand many of the interrelationships for tests in the HRNES–R. Some of these studies found relationships of special interest. As an example, see the scattergram in Figure 6.5. This study compares the raw time scores of the HRNES–R (Russell & Starkey, 2001) control group scores for the TPT dominant and nondominant hands against age. The score is the time in minutes required to place all of the blocks.

This comparison demonstrated an unexpected relationship between the times for the TPT dominant and nondominant hands. This relationship was also published in a paper by Thompson and Heaton (1991). As a person ages, the difference in time between TPT hands is reduced until, at about age 60, the dominant hand becomes faster than the nondominant hand. Apparently, the nondominant hand, which is always given second, is faster at younger ages because the subject remembers the position of the blocks. Then the person can insert them more rapidly the second time that he or she does the test. As the person ages, memory becomes less acute and consequently it is less of an aid to the procedure. However, the scaling process for the HRNES–R, which corrects for age, eliminates this effect so that the difference between scores remains constant for all ages.

Test Score Profiles

Another method of analyzing patterns is profile analysis. The graphic profile provides a visual means for examining patterns that may be extremely important in understanding the relationship between tests. The interpretation of a profile is referential or intuitive even though the profile is derived from quantitative data. However, a profile may be the basis for creating a more formal method of stating a relationship. Figures 6.6 through 6.8 illustrate profiles that contain far more information than can be provided in the text.

A method of profile pattern analysis, which will be presented later, is derived from a previous study (Russell & Polakoff, 1993) that compared AD with multi-infarct dementia (MID). [A more detailed discussion of this study may be found later in this chapter and in the original study by Russell and Polakoff (1993).] This profile is provided in Figures 6.7 and 6.8. Because this study was published before the methodology used in the HRNES–R was completed, the profile used *z*-scores. Impairment is indicated by high scores.

The first of these profiles was composed of the index tests in the HRNES (with the exception of block design). It included the average of the dominant and nondominant tapping test scores, as well as the average of the perceptual scores (see Russell & Starkey, 2001). The second profile presents the individual tapping, grip strength, and perceptual disorders tests and the Wechsler memory scores.

From these profiles, it was evident that only simple motor tests such as tapping and grip strength exhibited a significant difference between the two subject groups. The motor tests were significantly less impaired for the AD subjects (Russell & Polakoff, 1993). Because memory deficits have been identified as a major symptom of AD, the memory tests were included in this profile. However, they were not more impaired than other cognitive tests. The trail-making tests A and B also demonstrated a large difference, but unfortunately this difference was overlooked in this study.

Formal Analytic Types of Pattern Analysis

Pattern methods that are completely formal are those that place the relationships between tests into a mathematical, algebraic, or logical form. Theoretically, almost any mathematical or classification methodology that is used in science could be applied to psychology or neuropsychology. However, because the human science fields are relatively undeveloped as sciences, only basic arithmetic and algebraic methods can be adequately applied to the data in a formal manner for assessment.

Concerning this, there are two basic procedures for creating formal methods in neuropsychology: (1) combining scores and (2) comparing scores. Combining scores usually involves either the addition or multiplication of specified test scores. Comparisons ordinarily apply subtraction or division. Division often takes the form of ratios. Finally, combinations and comparisons may be united to create a formula.

For most purposes, a formal procedure will produce a single final score, just as a simple test does. A formal method, even if it involves a mixture of combinations and comparisons, is still a single procedure that eventuates in a single score for interpretation. The final score is generally expressed through either a cut point or a graduated scale. As with single tests, a battery pattern must demonstrate the interpretive validity of its score through a research study.

Combining Scores

In neuropsychology, the methods for combining scores are usually termed *indexes*. There are many forms of indexes from the simple (e.g., summing scores) to the complex (e.g., creating a weighted score index).

Indexes

Currently, determining the existence of brain damage is the most important function of a neuropsychological battery. Consequently, more indexes have been developed for this purpose than for any other aspect of neuropsychological assessment. All of these brain-damage indexes and their validity are examined in some detail in Chapter 9, so they will not be discussed much here.

The Halstead Index (Halstead, 1947) was the first index to be developed. Initially, it was composed of 10 tests. The existence of brain damage was indicated when more than half of the component tests were in the brain-damage range. However, further research found that three of these tests were not very sensitive to brain damage (Reitan, 1955b), so only seven of the original tests are now used in the HI. These seven have consistently remained among the most accurate indicators of brain damage (Chapter 9). Although other indexes may be slightly more accurate in some studies, the HI is still the gold standard for neuropsychological indexes.

The average impairment rating (AIR), which was originally developed by P. M. Rennick, was modified by Russell and Goldstein (Russell, Neuringer, & Goldstein, 1970, pp. 13–14). It used a different method than the HI to create an index. It averaged the scores of 12 tests selected from the HRB and WAIS tests. Nevertheless, its accuracy and validity has remained equivalent to the HI (Chapter 9).

The average index score (AIS) was the primary index for the HRNES and later the HRNES—Revised (HRNES–R) (Russell & Starkey, 1993, 2001). It revised the AIR to include only the eight tests from the HRB and two from the adult Wechsler tests. Studies have found that it is equivalent to the original AIR in accuracy even though it uses fewer tests. The operational characteristics of this index, along with the percent impaired index and the other tests in the Halstead Index have been determined. Operational characteristics include measured of validity. (Russell, 2004).

Reitan also developed a Neuropsychological Deficit Scale that formalizes his four methods of analysis. It appears to be somewhat more accurate than the HI. Several more indexes are discussed in some detail in Chapter 9.

Lateralization Indexes

Another area of neuropsychological assessment in which several indexes have been developed is that of lateralized brain damage. These include the *lateralization key*, which was part of the neuropsychological key (Russell et al., 1970). This was greatly improved and formalized as a separate scale that was part of the HRNES–R, the *HRNES–R lateralization index* (Russell, 1984; Russell & Starkey, 1993, 2001). Although the key was originally a decision-tree algorithm, it was transformed into an index.

Part of Reitan's Neuropsychological Deficit Scale consisted of separate scales for each hemisphere that formed a lateralization index when combined (Reitan & Wolfson, 1993, pp. 315–346). Several other scales are also discussed in Chapter 9.

Test Comparisons

In general, the comparison of scores is used for differential diagnoses. Consequently, they are the basis for most complex formal pattern analyses. Research, especially in recent years, has compared many tests, but few of these studies have proceeded further than describing the differences. They have not attempted to place them into a more formal method such as ratios. Ratios are critical in pattern analysis because they constitute the basis for most comparisons. Mathematical manipulation of the comparisons requires the use of formal methods.

Double Disassociation

As the basis for neuropsychological assessment, double disassociation was discussed in Chapter 4. Double disassociation is the difference between two tests (first disassociation) that have been demonstrated to be related to different brain areas or diagnoses (second disassociation). If this difference meets certain criteria, then it indicates there is greater impairment to one of the two areas. This difference provides a diagnoses or assessment interpretation such as right-hemisphere damage.

Essentially, double disassociation is the basic form for pattern analysis. Combining these forms multiple dissociations, which are the primary basis for brain-functions patterns. The pattern of double dissociation primarily consists in the amount of difference between the different tests, which is a ratio. As such, it requires a fixed relationship between the tests that is determined by research and is described in Chapter 4. The fixed relationship is essential for the tests to represent an interpretable pattern. The assessment may be made either by clinical judgment of the difference between the two tests or by a formal method in which a cutting point or a graduated scale for the ratio between the tests has been determined by research.

Triangulation

Triangulation is a form of pattern analysis. It is a formalization of the psychological assessment method for making certain diagnostic differentiations commonly used in clinical judgment. In contrast to clinical judgment, this formal procedure, when quantified, provides an exact measure of the accuracy of the differentiation.

In the 1970s, research demonstrated that schizophrenia, with the possible exception of paranoid varieties, could not be separated from brain damage using neuropsychological tests (Goldstein, 1986). (One "solution" was that schizophrenia was a form of brain damage. Nevertheless, it needed to be treated as a different form of damage.) Thus, a method for separating brain damage from schizophrenia was required and was sought. Although several methods were suggested, the most accurate procedure for this differential diagnosis was delineated by Watson (1977). He found that schizophrenia could be separated from brain damage by comparing two tests. Although this method was designed to distinguish schizophrenia and brain damage, the same method could be applied to differentiating various disorders.

The method used by Watson (1977) may be called *triangulation*. The concept is analogous to the term employed in surveying. Using trigonometry, lines drawn between two points enable one to locate a third point if the distance between the two points is known. This third point could not be located by lines from either of the first two points alone. For instance, in forestry services, fire towers determine the location of a fire by means of triangulation. If the direction and distance between two towers is known, then the angles of intersection drawn on a map to the fire or smoke from each of the two towers precisely locates the fire.

By analogy, the triangulation method used in psychological measurement enables one to obtain information from two tests that is not obtainable from either test alone. As used in regard to the assessment of schizophrenia, the method is to administer both a neuropsychological battery and an objective test of psychopathology. Comparison of the results from these two tests will differentiate normals, schizophrenics, and organic subjects. This method is presented in Table 6.2.

The steps in deriving this interpretation are the following:

1. Using research-determined cut points, if the neuropsychology battery indicates impairment and the schizophrenia test is negative, then the patient has an organic condition.
2. If the neuropsychological battery is impaired and the psychopathology test indicates schizophrenia, then the diagnosis is schizophrenia.
3. If both the neuropsychological battery and the psychopathology test are within the normal range, then the patient is normal.

In support of this concept, a preliminary study by Brown (1987) was designed to use an algorithm based on the preceding method. This method used a neuropsychological battery and the Minnesota Multiphasic Personality Inventory (MMPI). When the most accurate cutting points were used, the algorithm's overall separation of normal, organic, and psychiatric (largely schizophrenic) cases was 73%. (The probability of making this separation between three categories is only 33.3%.) In terms of the three separate categories, 69% of the organics, 94% of the schizophrenic subjects, and 89% of the normal subjects were correctly identified.

Triangulation is a form of double disassociation applied to the differential diagnosis of an affective disorder from brain damage. It could be used to provide a more valid and accurate basis for many forms of differential diagnosis. However, almost

Table 6.2 Triangulation Method for Differential Diagnosis of Normal, Brain-Damaged, and Schizophrenic Subjects[a,b]

AIS		MMPI-2, SC[c]		Diagnosis
>95	Unimpaired	<75	Normal	Normal
<95	Impaired	<75	Normal	Brain-damaged
>95	Unimpaired	>76	Abnormal	Schizophrenia
<95	Impaired	>76	Abnormal	Schizophrenia

[a]Schizophrenia may or may not impair the AIS.
[b]Cut points are included.
[c]SC indicates the schizophrenia scale.

no further work has been published concerning the differentiation of schizophrenia brain damage since the 1970s.

Multiple Disassociation

The nature of multiple disassociation, including its characteristics, was also discussed previously. This is essentially double disassociation between many different tests that have been related to brain functioning by research. The advantage of multiple disassociation is that this permits the observation of many different patterns related to both localization and diagnosis. Each relationship must be validated. Again, this disassociation requires a set of fixed or standardized relationships between all of the tests involved. As described previously, this standardization may be produced either by a battery of raw scores that is completely fixed or consistent from one administration to another or by scale scores that have been standardized by a co-norming procedure.

Formulas

As has been discussed, neuropsychological assessment is commonly based on examining patterns between tests. However, descriptions of patterns are generally vague and, consequently, difficult to apply using judgment. One method to describe a pattern that is more exact is to create a formula. A formula specifies exact quantitative and mathematical relationships between test scores. This permits the pattern to be precisely transmitted to other clinicians. Formulas can be tested for their accuracy, and they can be modified by subsequent research to assess the condition more exactly.

Although uncommon in neuropsychology, over time several formulas have been designed to provide a formal determination of the existence of a neuropsychological condition. Although most of the formulas have been created to determine the premorbid intelligence or for SVT measures, a few have been created to determine the location or diagnosis of a neurological condition. Almost none appear to have been published for these purposes in the last decade. Several formulas for diagnosis will be presented.

Localization Formulas

As discussed elsewhere, localization procedures are out of fashion currently, but they still present a precise methodology that could be well used in neuropsychology assessment. A major problem is the rapid revision of major tests so that enormous amounts of research have been lost (Russell, 2010). Nevertheless, previous tests often can be transformed to use the formal methods developed for previous versions of tests and batteries.

Wechsler IQ Lateralization Formula

Although there had been a few attempts at designing formulas for neuropsychological tests such as Hewson's ratios (Hewson, 1949), these were apparently not based on adequate research and consequently were not accurate (Wheeler & Wilkins, 1951). Because of their lack of accuracy, many neuropsychologists have contemptuously rejected all formulas. This is related to a general rejection of any formalized methods other than tests.

However, formulas were again introduced into neuropsychology as part of the neuropsychological key (Russell et al., 1970, pp. 39–40). A WAIS lateralization formula was described in Russell et al. (1970, pp. 39–40). It was designed to provide a more accurate indication of lateralization than the WAIS IQ scores alone. This index was designed using the concept that selecting the most highly lateralized tests from the WAIS would provide a more accurate measure of lateralization than using all of the subtests. Consequently, three verbal subtests—vocabulary, similarity, and digit span—were selected for the verbal measure, and two performance subtests—block design and object assembly—were selected for the performance measure. A cutting point divided the Wechsler tests into symmetrical divisions.

The first formula to be presented in this section was derived from the WAIS VIQ and PIQ. In this study, Russell (1984, pp. 80–81) compared the subtest formula against simple verbal versus performance IQ scores and found that the IQ scores were somewhat more accurate. Therefore, the subtest formula was discarded for an IQ formula. The IQ formula was simply subtracting PIQ from VIQ, so the scores were equivalent to IQ points.

The accuracy of the separation of these groups using these WAIS IQ points was demonstrated using *t*-test studies, which compared right, left, and diffuse groups. The numbers of lateralized cases were relatively small, but the total numbers of brain-damaged cases were 191. The number of subjects used in this study was 37 right, 32 left, and 88 diffuse damage groups.

The separations between groups using IQ scores were all significant beyond the 0.0001 level. The comparison of right versus left had a *t*-score of 7.40, which was beyond the 0.0001 level. The right-versus-diffuse comparison did not give as high a *t*-score. The WAIS IQ *t*-score was 3.96, with a probability level of 0.0001. In regard to the difference between left versus diffuse, the IQ gives a *t*-score of 6.48, which was significant beyond the 0.0001 level. Thus, the IQ and the Index scores were also essentially the same.

Further research found that in addition to establishing cutting points that separated the three subject groups, left, diffuse and right damage, asymmetrical cutting points would be required. A symmetrical criterion, with the mid point for the cutting points separating Verbal and Performance IQ scores at the IQ score equivalent to 100, was incorrect because the effect of fluidity meant that too many diffuse cases would be classified as right-hemisphere-damaged cases (Barron & Russell 1992; Russell, 1979).

The percentage distributions for these three groups were compared to each other using the WAIS Verbal and Performance IQ scale points. Because the *N* varied so greatly between groups the distributions are composed of scores that were derived from the proportion (percents) of the subjects in the group. This equalizes the *N* for each group. This division is demonstrated in the profile presented in Figure 6.6.

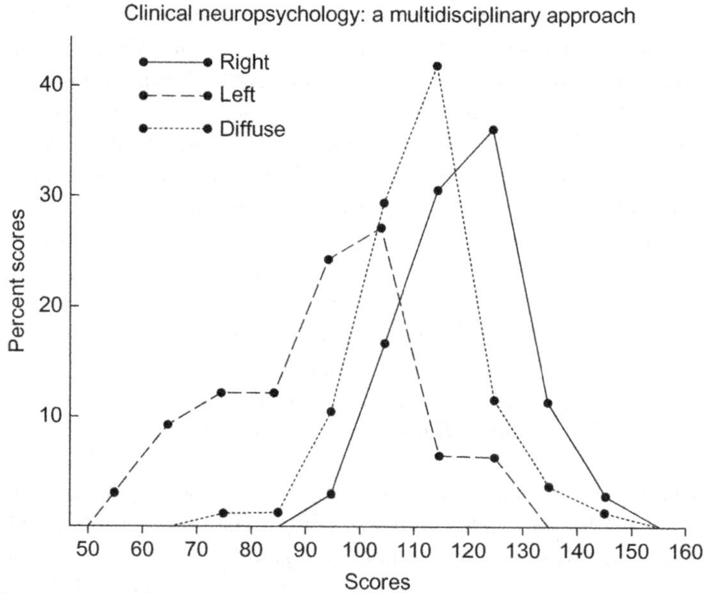

Figure 6.6 VIQ–PIQ lateralization index composed of VIQ minus PIQ scores. The index uses equivalent frequency distributions (percentage of group) for right- and left-hemisphere and diffuse brain-damaged subjects.

This figure demonstrates that the IQs of right- and left-brain-damaged subjects are separated into the accepted verbal and performance groups. However, it also demonstrates a shift of the subjects' IQs toward the PIQ tests. These performance tests are, of course, more fluid and so were more impaired than verbal tests.

A formula was derived to compare the VIQ with the PIQ scores. In this formula, the PIQ was subtracted from the VIQ scores. One hundred was added to this to provide positive base scores. This is the formula:

$$(\text{VIQ} - \text{PIQ}) + 100 = \text{IQ lateralization index score}$$

Using this formula, subjects with impaired performance scores had a higher scores than did subjects with impaired verbal scores. The greater the difference, the higher the score.

Cutting Points

To determine the correct and incorrect portion of classifications using this index scale, cutting points were established by means of the distribution profile in Figure 6.6. The cutting points were the two points where the group distributions intersected. Because of the asymmetrical affect of brain damage on the WAIS, the cutting point that separates left from the diffuse was set at 100, and the cutting point that separates right hemisphere from diffuse was set at 120. Finally, the point that separated the right from left impairment was set at 110. These cutting points produced the greatest number of correct classifications for all three groups of subjects. In addition, two other cutting points were added to indicate strength of lateralization. A cutting point was placed at 90, indicating damage strongly lateralized to the left; a cutting point was placed at 130 indicating strong lateralization to the right.

Summary of Cutting Points

$$
\begin{aligned}
<90 &= \text{Strongly lateralized to the left} \\
<100 &= \text{Lateralized to the left} \\
9-119 &= \text{Diffuse damage} \\
>120 &= \text{Lateralized to the right} \\
>130 &= \text{Strongly lateralized to the right}
\end{aligned}
$$

In determining its accuracy, the IQ lateralization index with the cutting points designed to account for the fluidity shift was fairly accurate in separating right, left, and diffuse types of brain damage in the sample. In regard to right-hemisphere cases, the IQ lateralization index score with the revised cutting points of 100 and 120 correctly classified 20 of the 37 right-hemisphere-damaged cases, falsely classified as left hemisphere one of these cases, and falsely classified as diffuse 16 of these cases. In regard to the 32 left-hemisphere subjects, this IQ index correctly classified 20 as left-hemisphere cases. It falsely classified only one as a right-hemisphere case, and it falsely classified as diffuse nine of the cases. Finally, in regard to diffuse damage, the index cut points correctly classified 63 of the 88 cases. It incorrectly classified 11 cases as left hemisphere and 14 cases as right hemisphere. Note that even though the IQ index can separate the groups fairly well, it is probably not sufficiently accurate to be used for clinical judgment alone.

The newest version of the Wechsler adult intelligence scale does not include a VIQ or a PIQ, so this formula would not be appropriate (Loring & Bauer, 2010). However, a similar formula could probably be derived from the WAIS–VI verbal comprehension and the perceptual reasoning factors. However, it is unlikely that such research will be attempted any time soon with the current antiformalization attitude in neuropsychological assessment.

Area Localization Formulas

Expert neuropsychologists, particularly those who use a standardized or fixed battery, are aware of localization patterns that are more restricted than lateralization. These apply to areas the size of lobes or at least quadrants of the brain. Decades ago and using clinical judgment, Reitan demonstrated that he could localize damage to the quadrants of the brain at a significant level (Reitan, 1964). No one has attempted to cross validate this study, although such accuracy has been demonstrated unofficially many times.

Although many informal patterns have been proposed for the localization of types of damage that involve smaller areas than lateralization cases, only one has been placed into a formula. This is the following left-temporal-lobe formula.

Left-Temporal-Lobe Focal Impairment

In an initial study (Dobbins & Russell, 1990), a unique pattern of WAIS subtests was shown to be related to damage in the left temporal lobe. In this pattern, the WAIS information and vocabulary subtests were considerably more impaired than the similarities subtest when there was left-temporal-focal damage. Because the usual pattern is for the vocabulary and information to be less impaired than similarities, it was only suspected when assessing a man who had a motorcycle accident that crushed the left side of his skull and brain. In debriding the lesion, the surgeon removed a section of the left temporal lobe. Soon after this the same pattern appeared in a woman who had had a tumor removed from her left temporal lobe. This pattern would not have been suspected except that the same battery of tests was given repeatedly so that this unusual pattern was readily recognizable.

An examination of the literature found that this pattern had been previous suggested by several neuropsychologists (Coughlan & Warrington, 1978; McFie, 1975; Russell, 1987). Subsequently, the pattern was placed into a formula that compared the WAIS vocabulary and information to similarities. Left-temporal-lobe damage was indicated when the average of vocabulary and information was more impaired than similarities. A chi-square analysis, $\chi^2(2, N = 36) = 6.24$, was significant at $p < .05$.

Later, the second author realized that digit span had been found by Warrington, Logue, and Pratt (1971) to be related to the left parietal lobe. If this association were correct, then the addition of digit span to the formula would improve its predictive power. Consequently, a second study was undertaken (Russell & Russell, 1993) in which the digit span was added to the formula. The new formula compared the average of vocabulary and information to the average of digit span and similarities using WAIS scale scores. The formula was as follows:

$$\frac{(V + I)}{2} \quad \frac{(D + S)}{2} < 0.0 = \text{LTD}$$

where V = vocabulary, I = information, D = digit span, S = similarities, and LTD = left-temporal-lobe damage

This meant that if the average of vocabulary and information scale scores is more impaired than the average of digit span and similarities, then left-temporal-lobe focal damage is indicated. The previous study assumed that the formula would be valid only if left-hemisphere damage had already established. Experience using this formula with clinical cases indicated that it would assess left-temporal-lobe damage even when left-hemisphere damage had not been thoroughly established before applying the formula. For this reason, it was decided to examine this formula with subjects who had focal right-frontal, right-temporal, and right-parietal or occipital damage, as well as the left-hemisphere-damage groups.

The subjects were patients with focal damage in one area. The three left-hemisphere groups included 12 left-frontal, 12 left-temporal, and 12 subjects in a group that contained both left-parietal and occipital subjects. (Because there were only two occipital subjects, they were combined with 10 parietal lobe subjects.) The three right-hemisphere groups of subjects included 10 frontal, 10 temporal, and 10 subjects with parietal and occipital focal damage. Again, there were only two subjects with lesions limited to the occipital lobe.

These subjects were selected carefully to possess damage limited to a specific lobe. The selection was based on computed tomography (CT) scan, surgery, and autopsy reports. The diagnostic reports were written by doctors of the University of Miami Medical School. Duncan's Multiple Range Test indicated small but significant differences in mean age between the temporal groups and the parietal occipital groups. There were no significant educational differences among the groups. All of the subjects were right-handed. The patients were predominately white males.

A mean of the scores for each group was obtained by applying the previously given formula to the WAIS data from each subject. The mean group scores and standard deviations for the six groups are given in the paper. The table also included a matrix of the significant differences derived from Duncan's Multiple Range Test. Among the formula index scores of all of the groups, only the index score for the left temporal lobe was negative. Thus, in all other lobes the vocabulary and information tests were less impaired than in the left-temporal-lobe group. The analysis of variance (ANOVA) across all of these groups was significant, $F(5,60) = 3.55, p < .007$. Duncan's Multiple Range Test indicated that the significant differences were between the left-temporal group and every other group including the right-temporal group. There were no significant differences among any of the other groups.

The results of this study support the validity of a score for left-temporal-lobe damage derived from a formula. Evidently, the addition of digit span increased the accuracy of the formula to some extent because the *F*'s across all of the group were somewhat more significant than the results of the previous study (Dobbins & Russell, 1990), even though the three right-hemisphere groups had been added.

The main finding of this study was that left-temporal lesions are associated with a WAIS subtest pattern of a more impaired information and vocabulary score than similarities and digit span scores. Consequently, these findings supported the validity of this formula.

This pattern of lower information and vocabulary scores than similarities and digit span scores is rather unusual (Russell, 1979). Information and vocabulary evidently involve more crystallized intelligence than does similarities. Nevertheless, Milberg, Greiffenstein, Lewis, and Rourke (1980) reported that temporal-lobe epileptics showed greater impairment on WAIS information and vocabulary than on similarities. Their formula, consisting of

$$\frac{\text{Vocabulary} + \text{Information}}{2} - \text{Similarities}$$

was nearly 80% successful in discriminating between generalized and temporal-lobe seizure patients. The temporal-lobe epileptics had a negative index score. In a replication of Milberg et al.'s (1980) study, Bolter, Venerlasen, and Long (1981) also found a tendency of temporal-lobe epileptics to score more negatively on the formula, although not to a statistically significant degree.

The current study used essentially the same formula that was used by Milberg et al. (1980), with the addition of digit span. Also, because the purpose of this study was to investigate focal lesions, the subject population was not composed of seizure patients, but patients with focal damage.

The addition of digit span to the formula also supported Warrington's contention that the primary area of the brain related to the digit span is the left parietal lobe (Warrington et al., 1971; Warrington & Weiskrantz, 1973).

This research also supports the concept that the left temporal lobe is particularly involved with the verbal semantic memory processes—that is, the storage and retrieval of well-learned verbal information. These appear to be largely assessed by information and vocabulary. For example, word comprehension and word retrieval (naming) tasks, which are involved in the storage and retrieval of semantic memory, may be particularly associated with dominant temporal-lobe lesions (Coughlan & Warrington, 1978; Goodglass, 1980). Thus, the left temporal lobe may be a location for verbal semantic memory store, such that damage to this area may impair these memory traces. Specifically, the temporal part of Wernicke's area seems to play an important role in word storage. Damage to temporal portions of Wernicke's area is associated with persistent word comprehension and naming deficits (Goodglass, 1980; Knopman, Seines, Niccum, & Rubens, 1984).

Note that this pattern, in which the vocabulary and information subtests are lower than similarities and digit span, can occur in conditions other than left-temporal focal damage. Clinical experience indicates that both children and adults with a history of learning disabilities may display this pattern. Possibly such a learning disability is produced by a congenital underdevelopment of the left temporal lobe. In addition, both children and adults with certain types of personality problems may show this pattern when there is no evidence of brain damage. Presumably, this is the result of poor motivation for academic work.

Finally, this is an example of the value of a formula. There do not appear to be any other studies using formulas. Nevertheless, further studies could help us understand the functioning of the brain. Location is important because location is related to function.

Diagnostic Formulas

Diagnostic formulas are even less common than localization formulas. However, as we will demonstrate, formulas can be applied to diagnosis and may be more useful than localization formulas.

This research presents a group of interrelated studies concerned with the development and validation of two types of formulas designed to separate AD from cerebrovascular or MID conditions. Each type of formula concerns a major set of tests that are used in neuropsychology: the WAIS–R and the HRB. In addition, a well-known formula for assessing AD, the Fuld formula, was compared to the WAIS–R formula.

Distinguishing Alzheimer's Disease from Multi-infarct Dementia

Almost every neuropsychologist who has studied dementia states that the primary distinction between types of dementia is between AD and MID (Nixon, 1996). Nevertheless, currently there are evidently almost no neuropsychological methods that have adequately separated AD from cerebrovascular conditions such as MID in spite of the extensive discussion of these conditions in the literature.

There have been several reviews of the literature (Mathias & Burke, 2009; Nixon, 1996; Russell & Polakoff, 1993). All of them found that, despite considerable success in separating AD and MID from normal subjects, studies have not been very successful in isolating neuropsychology test patterns that differentiate AD from MID. For instance, Loring, Meador, Mahurin, and Largen (1986) found that even though both conditions produced the familiar verbal versus performance difference on the WAIS, no significant differences between AD and fairly severely impaired MID subjects were found on tests of memory, visual-spatial perception, and measures of sustained concentration. The familiar WAIS pattern was apparently the fluidity pattern described elsewhere in this chapter.

In their section on vascular dementia, Lezak et al. (2004, p. 202) attempted to differentiate between MID and AD primarily on the basis of memory. However, a person with severe MID would have more impaired memory than a person with mild AD. There is no discussion of a differentiation of the test patterns of MID and AD that would not result from a difference in severity of the conditions. In the section on AD in Lezak et al. (2004, pp. 207–220), there is a long discussion of the testing that has been done with AD patients. However, reading this section gives the impression that all mental functions are impaired.

The most thorough description of the distinction between AD and MID is that by Nixon (1996, pp. 65–105). She states, "studies have suggested that, despite differences in etiology, there are considerable similarities in the two disease states" (p. 66). She then says that she will describe the distinctions between the various dementias as they were discussing the characteristics of the diseases. Her conclusion was that the primary scale for assessing MID was Hachinski's Ischemic Scale (p. 79). Many studies have used that scale (Nixon, 1996, p. 79), to differentiate the groups. However, the most powerful discriminator on the scale is a history of a stroke (Nixon, 1996, p. 80). This method is of little help in distinguishing patients who have not yet had a stroke. Obviously, patients who had had both AD and MID cannot be separated (Nixon, 1996, p. 80). This indicates that Hachinski's Ischemic Scale is insufficiently sensitive to warrant its use in differential diagnosis (Nixon, 1996, pp. 79–80). Consequently, if a patient has not had either a stroke or a transient ischemic attack (TIA), the instrument is fairly useless.

Recently, a study using a meta-analysis of previous studies (Mathias & Burke, 2009) failed to find any major distinguishing differences between the AD and MID groups using any neuropsychological test. Although the authors claimed to have included all studies of neuropsychological tests comparing the AD to MID subjects, they failed to include the Russell and Polakoff (1993) study. Their study found that "motor" tests did not distinguish these groups. However, the only motor tests examined were reaction time and ideomotor apraxia tests—that is, they did not include tests of simple motor functions such as tapping and grip strength, which do demonstrate a difference. In addition, they did not consider the overall great difference in impairment of AD and MID patients who have not had a stroke. Of course, if a subject has had a TIA or stroke, there is no problem in distinguishing the conditions, except for the few patients who have both pathologies. If the right tests are not included, no distinguishing pattern can be found.

Formulas Separating AD and MID

In spite of these discouraging studies concerned with distinguishing AD and MID, several formulas appear to have some validity. Three patterns of test performance on the Halstead–Reitan Battery and the Wechsler Adult Intelligence Scale–Revised, including Fuld's formula, differentiated Alzheimer's disease from cerebrovascular disease, especially multi-infarct dementia. The three methods were the Fuld formula, a WAIS–R formula created in this study, and a formula derived from the HRNES–R. This research, which consisted of three studies, was abbreviated from a study by Russell and Polakoff (1993).

Fuld's formula was one of the few attempts to find a pattern of results that characterizes AD that would distinguish it from MID (Fuld, 1984, 1986) [the formula is also provided in Nixon (1996, p. 70)]. It was moderately successful. Initial results indicated that it correctly classified slightly more than half of the AD subjects and almost all of the non-AD subjects. Several reviews of the studies examining its accuracy with various groups were completed (Nixon, 1996, pp. 70–72; Russell & Polakoff, 1993). Although the author suggested that the formula was designed to detect scopolamine-induced patterns, it was actually a formula to detect AD. Some studies found that about 40% of the patients classified as AD were false-positives. Several other studies indicated that even though it is not highly accurate, the formula might have utility in identifying AD cases. There was a general conclusion that the Fuld formula was not accurate enough for clinical purposes (Massman & Bigler, 1993; Nixon, 1996, p. 71), even though no study compared the formula against clinical judgment. It is quite probable that clinical judgment is no more accurate than this formula. A major value of a formula is that its accuracy can be determined.

A WAIS–R deterioration profile pattern was created for this study to compare AD subjects with TIA subjects. As mentioned previously, the difficulty has been to differentiate AD patients from vascular disease patients who have not had a major CVA. A solution to this difficulty is selecting patients with TIAs because TIAs are indicative of a definite vascular condition before a subject has had a frank stroke. However, TIA subjects had considerably less impairment than AD subjects. The severity of the impairment between groups was equated by subtracting the mean difference between the two groups from the TIA subjects so that patterns unaffected by severity could be compared.

The AD subjects had a distinctive pattern that appeared to be different from that of the TIA subjects. The vocabulary and information subtests showed the greatest separation from the picture arrangement and block design. The difference between these tests was examined by averaging vocabulary and information as well as picture arrangement

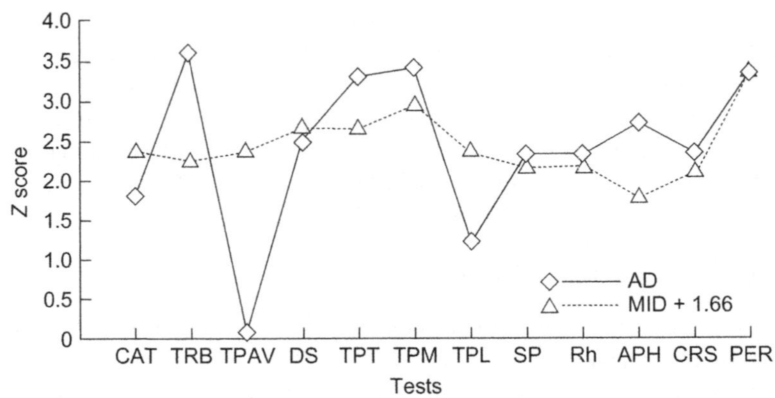

Figure 6.7 Profile consisting of the HRNES–R index test scores (plus TPT location and the cross drawing) in the form of *z*-scores. High scores indicate impairment, and low scores indicate less impairment. CAT = category test, TRB = Trails B, TPAV = tapping mean of the two hands, DS = digit symbol, TPT = tactile performance test, TPM = TPT memory, TPL = TPT location, SP = speech perception, Rh = rhythm test, APH = aphasia test, CRS = cross drawing, PER = perceptual disorders.

and block design. These two averages were found to be significantly different: $F(1, 23) = 12.24$, $p < .001$. This difference for the AD patients—but not for the TIA patients—indicated a different pattern of test results for these two types of dementia.

The following WAIS–R formula was created from the WAIS–R profile:

$$\left[\frac{(V + I)}{2}\right] - \left[\frac{(BD + PA)}{2}\right] > 1.5 = \text{AD and not CVD}$$

The best cutting point between scores of these two groups was found to be >1.5. Thus, if the mean of vocabulary and information is greater than the mean of block design and picture arrangement by more than 1.5, then the subject was predicted to be a AD subject; if not, then the diagnosis was CVD. The WAIS formula was moderately accurate. This is basically a form of the fluidity pattern. [A number of the "scales" listed in Nixon, (1996, pp. 81–82) are versions of this fluidity pattern.]

However, as discussed previously, this pattern in itself would not separate dementia from right-hemisphere lateralized brain damage (Barron & Russell, 1992; Russell, 1979, 1980, 1984).

The Alzheimer's Z-Score Formula

To create a formula that would separate AD and MID patients, two profiles were created that compared scores for these two groups. These profiles are presented in Figures 6.7 and 6.8. In Figure 6.7, the HRNES–R index tests are presented using *z*-scores.

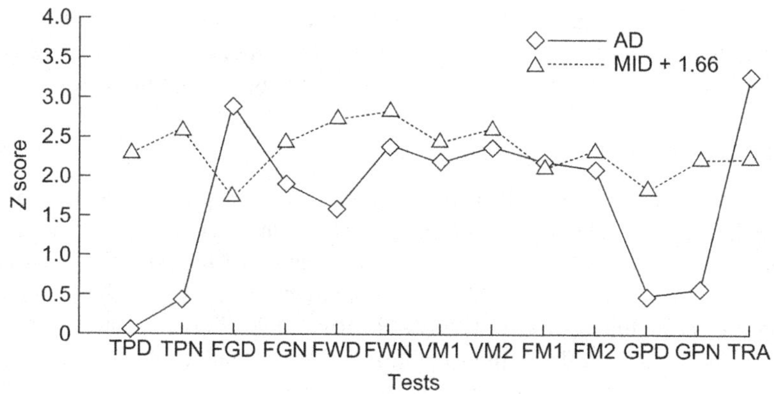

Figure 6.8 Profile consisting of the HRNES–R sensory, motor, and Wechsler memory tests in the form of *z*-scores. High scores indicate impairment, and low scores indicate less impairment. TPD = tapping dominant, TPN = tapping nondominant, FGD = finger agnosia dominant, FGN = finger agnosia nondominant, FWD = fingertip number writing dominant, FWN = fingertip number writing nondominant, VM1 = verbal memory first, VM2 = verbal memory one-half hour, FM1 = figural memory first, FM2 = figural memory one-half hour, GPD = grip strength dominant, GPN = grip strength nondominant, TRA = Trails A.

Next, to equate the scale scores for the AD and MID groups, the mean *z*-score for each group was obtained. The difference in the score means (1.66) between the two groups was added to each of the MIA subtest scores. All statistical calculations were performed on the equated groups.

When these profiles for Figures 6.7 and 6.8 were examined, the major finding concerning the differences between the AD and MID patterns was that pure motor performances were significantly less impaired in the AD group. In the MID group, motor performance is equally as impaired as were cognition and memory. A study by Storrie and Doerr (1981) using finger tapping as one of the discriminatory measures found similar results. Lezak et al. (2004, p. 214) noted some motor preservation but did not indicate that these had any diagnostic value. Nixon (1996) emphasized that at least two studies had noted the lack of impairment on pure motor tests (pp. 81–82) but then did not use pure motor ability as a means for distinguishing AD and MID. None of these studies attempted to use pure motor ability in differentiation patterns.

It was Hom (1992) who identified this pattern of relatively little impairment of pure motor tests even when memory was severely impaired as the distinguishing feature of Alzheimer's dementia. In contrast, MID had an equal or greater impairing effect on motor tests.

Thus, with the exception of the motor tests, none of the cognitive tests demonstrated a significant difference between the AD and TIA groups when the groups are equivalent for overall amounts of impairment. Although finger tip writing and finger agnosia tests were less impaired in the AD patients, with equalized scores, the degree of impairment did not reach statistical significance. The relationship between the two groups for the WMS–R tests were also examined. Memory deficits, as in all studies, were identified as a major symptom of AD and as being impaired in MID.

Formula Construction

These major differences found in the profiles were then placed into the form of a formula. In the original study, two formulas were constructed. One was a raw-score formula, and the other used *z*-scores. With the creation of the HRNES–R (Russell & Starkey, 2001), *C*-scale scores replaced *z*-scores without changing the formula. This AD formula is included in the HRNES–R (Russell & Starkey, 2001, Appendix F, p. 26) as one of the "Aids to Interpretation." Consequently, the raw-score formula appeared to be redundant, so it is not repeated in the HRNES-R Appendix F.

On the basis of these profiles, it was postulated that only the motor tests—tapping and grip strength—would show a significant difference between the two subject groups, with the motor tests being less impaired for the AD subjects (Russell & Polakoff, 1993). ANOVAs demonstrated a significant difference between groups in regard to tapping for both the dominant hand [$F(1, 23) = 32.38$, $p = <.001$] and the nondominant hand [$F(1, 23) = 42.30$, $p = <.001$]. Grip strength also showed significance differences between groups for both hands.

The relationship between the two groups for the memory tests were also examined, because memory deficits have been identified as a major symptom of AD. The memory tests used were the WMS–R verbal one-half hour memory (logical memory) and figural one-half hour memory (figural reproduction). However, when the groups were equated, neither the ANOVA for verbal memory nor the ANOVA for figural memory was significant.

The formula that was derived compared the tapping and memory tests. Because the results with tapping and grip strength in this study were quite similar (except that the tapping tests were somewhat less affected by AD), only tapping was used in the formula.

The *z*-score formula compared the average tapping speed scale score for the two hands with the average memory scale score for verbal and figural memory. Provided a ratio of TapAv/MemAv, the TapAv was the average tapping scale score for the dominant and nondominant hands. The MemAv was the average WMS–R, HRNES–R scale scores for the verbal and figural one-half hour memory test. The full formula is:

$$\left[\frac{(\mathrm{TapD} + \mathrm{TapN})/2}{(\mathrm{MemV2} + \mathrm{MemF2})/2}\right] > 1.2 = \mathrm{AD}$$

where

TapD = tapping dominant hand, TapN = tapping nondominant hand, MemV2 = memory verbal (Logical Memory) one-half hour, MemF2 = memory figural (Figural Reproduction) one-half hour

This HRNES–R AD formula is included in the HRNES–R program so that the computer computes the score and determines whether AD is indicated. This program is also considered to be a program for assessing severe alcoholism, such as in Wernicke's syndrome. The formula in the HRNES–R (Russell & Starkey, 2001, Appendix F, p. 26) has a slightly different form:

$$\frac{\text{AD}}{\text{AL}} = \frac{(\text{TapD} + \text{TapND}) \times 0.5}{(\text{MemV2} + \text{MemF2}) \times 0.5}$$

Either formula will work, although the one provided previously is easier to understand. The cut point is the same: >1.2.

A cutting point was determined by comparing the scores of the two groups and locating the score that most accurately separated the two groups. A cutting point of >1.2 = AD appeared to be stable and provide the best separation. It is quite probable that somewhat different cutting points would work better with other subjects' samples, but the general formula is ostensibly adequate. [In the original study (Russell & Polakoff, 1993), a typographical error gave the cutting point as 14 rather than 1.4.]

Results of the AD Formulas

To test this formula, the predicted classification of AD and MID subjects was compared to the diagnosed AD and TIA subjects in a 2 × 2 matrix for each formula and cutting point. This matrix was then subjected to a chi-square analysis, and the percentage of correctly predicted cases for AD, MID, and total groups was obtained. Because the *N* was less than 40, the significance level was found by using Fisher's exact test. The scale-score formula, using cutting points of >1.2 and >1.5, separated the AD subjects from cerebrovascular subjects at a high level of significance ($p < 0.0001$). The formulas correctly predicted 92% of the total number of subjects in both cases. These results are given in Table 6.3 as the HRNES–R study.

To determine whether the formulas that had been developed on TIA vascular subjects would apply to patients with MID, a third study (the cross-validation study) was undertaken. In this study, the formulas were applied to an entirely new group of 28 subjects, all of whom had MID as indicated by a diagnosis of cerebral vascular disease. Thus, this study also represents a partial cross-validation study.

By definition, the TIA subjects have no permanent gross neurological deficit, although they apparently often have mild deficits on neuropsychological examinations (Delaney et al., 1980). To test this formula on an MID population, a sample of MID subjects was selected. To reduce the amount of obvious focal pathology, subjects without severe lateralizing deficits were selected. Twenty-eight MID subjects met this criterion. These represent the type of CVD subjects who are difficult to differentiate from AD subjects because they do not have an obvious focal vascular impairment. After screening for confounding conditions, there were 11 AD subjects.

The mean age and education level of the AD subjects were not significantly different from the MID subjects. Because the subjects were drawn from population of Veterans Administration (VA) patients, who are mostly men, the three women in the original pool were removed. Although there were no African Americans in the AD group, there were four African Americans in the MID group.

The cross-validation assessment of the subjects followed the same procedures and formulas as was used in the original sample (Russell & Polakoff, 1993). All subjects were diagnosed by members of the University of Miami Medical School's neurology department who also worked at a VA medical center. The AD subjects had a diagnosis that was considered to be as definitive as possible by neurological methods without a brain biopsy or autopsy. The diagnoses of MID was based on neurological examinations and either CT scans or arteriograms. To reduce the amount of obvious focal pathology, subjects without severe lateralizing deficits were selected. Because the MID subjects had impairment that was equivalent to the AD patients, no equating of the groups was attempted. The WAIS–R, the Fuld formula, and HRNES–R scale score were all examined with this sample. The number of subjects was great enough to obtain a chi-square coefficient.

The results of this study are given in Table 6.3 under the column heading "Cross Validation." Although the HRNES–R scale-score formula held up quite well, the WAIS–R formula did not. The WAIS–R formula with the cutting point of >1.5 could not significantly separate the two groups. However, if the cutting point was shifted to >1.7, the chi-square, using Fisher's exact test, did reach significance, $\chi^2(1, n = 39)$, $p < 0.03$, with 72% of the total sample being correctly identified.

The Fuld formula was somewhat more accurate for this MID sample than the WAIS–R formula with the original cutting point. It correctly identified 71% of the

Table 6.3 Comparison of the Fuld, WAIS–R, and Z-Score Formulas for Alzheimer's Disease and Cerebrovascular Conditions Using Number, Percent Correct, and Chi-Square Significance

	Studies					
	1 WAIS–R and Fuld		2 HRB	3 Cross Validation		
	WAIS–R	Fuld	Z-Scores	WAIS–R	Fuld	Z-Scores
AD Group	$N = 12$		$N = 12$	$N = 11$		
Number Correct	11	8	11	7	7	11
Percent Correct	92	66	92	64	64	100
TIA or CVD Group	$N = 13$		$N = 13$	$N = 28$		
Number Correct	10	11	12	17	20	27
Percent Correct	77	85	92	61	71	96
Total	$N = 25$		$N = 25$	$N = 39$		
Number Correct	21	19	23	24	27	38
Percent Correct	84	76	92	61	69	97
χ^2 $P<$	0.001	0.015	0.000	0.284	0.068	0.000

Note: All studies used Fisher's exact test.

28 MID subjects. However, this did not quite reach a 0.05 level of significance. Thus, it performed somewhat better with this sample than the WAIS–R formula using a 1.5 cutting point but not as well as this formula using the best cutting point of 1.7.

By contrast, the HRNES–R scale-score formula was highly accurate—as accurate in this MID study as in the original study. The *z*-score cut point was 1.5. The HRNES–R scale-score formula correctly identified all of the 11 AD subjects and 27 of the 28 (96%) MID subjects with a total of 97% correct identifications.

The two formulas developed by this research—the WAIS–R formula and the *z*-score formula—varied in their accuracy in separating AD and CVD subjects. (In this study, a *z*-score of 1.5 is equal to an average impairment score of 95.) The *z*-score formula and cutting points were highly accurate in both the TIA and MID cross-validation studies. Although the WAIS–R formula was acceptable in the first study, its results did not reach significance in the MID study until the cutting point was changed. Although the results of the Fuld formula reached significance in the TIA study, they were not quite significant in the MID study. In separating AD and MID patients, the accuracy of the WAIS–R formula and the Fuld formula were barely significant, whereas the HRNES–R scale-score formula was highly accurate in separating 97% of the AD and MID subjects. Thus, when the correct combination of tests is used, a pattern separating AD and MID patients can be highly accurate. This AD-versus-MID formula is undoubtedly more accurate than clinical judgment.

Experience with this *z*-score formula (now the HRNES–R formula) indicated that it was primarily an AD formula that separated AD from most other neurological conditions. The exception was chronic severe alcoholism. To make this separation, the patient's history must be examined to rule out severe alcoholism.

Nonbrain Damage Formulas

The neuropsychological areas of predicting premorbid ability and determining whether a patient is malingering or at least intentionally underperforming have been two areas in which "formulas" and patterns are accepted. However, even though they are crucial in evaluating the validity of test results, they do not directly concern patterns of brain functioning. Consequently, they will only be briefly mentioned.

Premorbid Ability Estimation

One major requirement for an integrated neuropsychological battery is correction or adjustment for the basic human characteristics of age, gender, and premorbid ability level. Because brain damage affects one's cognitive ability levels, the assessment must somehow estimate the patient's premorbid cognitive ability level. Cognitive ability is usually determined by IQ; as such, the measures of premorbid ability are essentially measures of premorbid IQ.

In the last few years, a great deal of work has been accomplished on this characteristic. Several formal methods, particularly formulas, have been proposed to estimate premorbid IQ levels. Although educational level is probably the best single estimate of premorbid ability (Schinka & Vanderploeg, 2000), it is only moderately accurate, and several other methods have been devised that are somewhat more accurate. These methods are probably most thoroughly discussed, with advice concerning how to use them in Schinka and Vanderploeg's (2000) chapter on "Estimating Premorbid Level of Functioning." They discuss various formal methods and formulas as well as present their own.

In this regard, note that most assessments by neuropsychologists are generally unable to consistently estimate premorbid ability levels of the tests in their batteries because they use a flexible method of determining which tests to use. Although it is possible to make the proper adjustments to each test in an extensive battery, it would be a very time-consuming task. Only the HRNES–R (Russell & Starkey, 2001, pp. 39–67) can incorporate the results of a formula directly into the program. The program corrects all scores for the cognitive ability of the individual based on prior testing, educational level, or a premorbid estimation formula. While the Heaton, Miller, Taylor, & Grant (2004) *Revised Comprehensive Norms for an Expanded Halstead–Reitan Battery* only corrects for educational level.

Malingering or Symptom Validity Testing Patterns

To assess malingering—or, at least, intentionally underperforming, "poor motivation," or "invalid test results"—symptom validity testing (SVT) is used. It requires two parts. First is an impaired score on an SVT test; second is a patient's invalid test pattern.

In regard to the SVT, today a test of motivation is a required test for any assessment, particularly for an assessment that is to have any forensic credibility. However, a discussion of SVT tests will not be attempted in this book because there is an extensive literature (Larrabee, 2005, pp. 92–158), much of which is excellent, and the field is rapidly changing.

Two methods of determining invalid assessment battery patterns have been developed. One is to examine the pattern of tests in a single administration of a battery. The other is to compare the results of a test and retest for the same person.

In their well-known study of malingering, Heaton, Smith, Lehman, and Vogt (1978) used a single test battery of the WAIS, HRB, and the MMPI. They found that, although the level of impairment was equivalent for the brain-damaged and normal subjects who were attempting to malinger, blind evaluations by 10 judges, all trained neuropsychologists, were almost unable to separate the groups. Their accuracy varied between zero and 20% correct. By contrast, discriminant function separated 100% of the normal subjects who attempted to malinger from the brain-damaged subjects. This clinical judgment accuracy is obviously not sufficient for clinical purposes. Because the overall level of impairment was the same for the two groups, the distinction that the discriminant function found was because of a different pattern of impairment.

As Reitan (Reitan & Wolfson, 1997, p. 15) observed,

> *It is difficult to avoid concluding that the accuracy could have been improved if the judges had used an approach that evaluated the interrelationships of test results rather than an approach that reviewed tests essentially as independent measures. One of the major advantage is of using a test battery is that it yields scores whose relationships can provide critical interpretive information.*

In actual malingering or attempted malingering, it is very difficult for a person, even a "sophisticated" person (trained by an attorney or a student) to avoid producing an "unnatural" or invalid pattern on a test battery. Thus, the primary cue of "poor motivation" is a pattern that "does not make neurological sense." In regard to such patterns, most naive malingers (including many intelligent professionals) do not know which patterns on any battery of neuropsychological tests are and are not believable. They do not know that some tests in such a battery are hold tests that are less affected by brain damage and that other tests are don't hold tests. It is not uncommon for a subject with questionable motivation to do well on tests sensitive to brain damage while providing scores on other tests that would categorize the subject as severely demented. Consequently, it is extremely important for the examiner to know various pathological patterns in order to distinguish the spurious ones.

The lack of pattern soundness is much more obvious on a standardized battery than on an ad hoc battery. With a standardized battery, experience teaches the neuropsychologists which patterns are and are not expected for various pathologies. Experience is extremely difficult to attain unless the examiner uses a consistent battery for all examinations. Finally, the invalid patterns can be taught to other neuropsychologists when the various neuropsychologists use the same group of tests.

The second means of using patterns in a neuropsychological examination is to present the same battery of tests to a patient twice at different times. This is the method championed by Reitan and Wolfson (1997). This method uses inconsistent individual comparisons, thus, "using the subject as [his or her] own control" (p. 25). This method is based on the concept that subjects who are not putting forth their best effort respond in a less-consistent manner than subjects who are motivated to do their best, even when they are brain-damaged. There is a rather great pattern consistency for a brain-damaged patient even though the pattern may be very abnormal. This method is well described in their book *Detection of Malingering and Invalid Test Scores* (Reitan & Wolfson, 1997), including the a number of tables and validation procedures. Although this method is quite valid a description, it is beyond the scope of this writing.

Unformalized Patterns

Many effects of various types of brain pathology are known but have not been formalized. Many of these patterns concerning the HRB may be seen in the case studies presented in Reitan and Wolfson's (1993) manual and in Bradford's (1992) interpretive manual. When other tests are included to make a more extensive coverage of the brain, such as in the HRNES–R, far more patterns are observable.

The various patterns produced by various types of pathologies have not been investigated to any great extent. Obviously, at this point neurology and neuropsychology are just beginning to understand how various pathologies produce patterns of brain functioning. Such patterns are only readily observable and amenable to research when standardized fixed batteries are used. Most of these patterns are found in the neuropsychological lore of practitioners who use a standardized battery.

Although these patterns have not been validated or published, a few of them will be presented in the following pages. Note that these have not been cross validated even though many of them are based on research findings. When the supporting research exists, it will be presented. Many of the pattern characteristics of neuropsychological assessment, however, may be inferred from a knowledge of neurology. For instance, it is obvious that a stroke will have a focal affect that is related to the part of the vascular system that is compromised. If one knows the approximate area that a test represents, then the area of focal damage can be located. Thus, neurological knowledge is essential.

Test and Battery Characteristics

The other aspect of neuropsychology—the tests and test patterns—is also of critical importance. Obviously, this is what distinguishes neuropsychologists from neurologists. Consequently, neuropsychologists should be aware of the characteristics of tests in regard to patterns. In other words, neuropsychologists must not only recognize the characteristics of the test and relationship to the brain but also the test's relationships to other tests.

An example involves the use of finger tapping (Lezak et al., 2004, p. 643). These authors do not indicate that even though the finger tapping test is not a highly accurate indication of brain damage, it is the most accurate test of lateralization when the damage is in the midportion of the brain. Consequently, as with any test, it should not be used in isolation to determine any interpretation. As another example, a normal tapping rate with a very poor memory and cognitive testing is a pattern that is normal for alcoholics as well as AD patients (Russell & Polakoff, 1993).

Another example is the TPT. This test is probably the most underrated test in neuropsychology, except for examiners who use the HRB. Of course, it is boring to administer, but it is probably the most useful test in neuropsychology. Lezak et al. (2004, pp. 470–471) criticize the test for "the enormous discomfort experienced by many patients when blindfold" (p. 471). Her reference to Russell's 1985 study completely misrepresents the conclusions of that study. The study was designed to permit adults to use the 6-hole form board with patients who were too impaired to use the normal 10-hole board. Only a fraction of our patients have actually needed to use the 6-hole board. However, that board enabled us to obtain accurate TPT scores when the patients' impairment was too severe to handle the usual adult board. Our experience over 40 years and thousands of administrations is that most patients have no particular discomfort with the test in either form. Rather than the patient's feeling of discomfort, it is often an uncomfortable or boring test for an examiner to administer. However, a trained technician can give it quite accurately.

In evaluating the TPT's worth in the neuropsychological battery, first it is probably the most sensitive test for brain damage in existence (Russell & Starkey, 2001, pp. 37, 38; Russell, 2004). In various studies, it is usually a little better than the category test, but not always. Both the memory and location tests are also highly diagnostic (Russell & Starkey, 2001, pp. 37, 38; Russell, 2004). However, the TPT has many other attributes. The total test time is sensitive to lateralized right-hemisphere damage (Russell, 1972a), while each hand is sensitive to contralateral damage. All of these are among the most accurate of neuropsychological tests (Russell & Starkey, 2001, pp. 37–40).

The TPT is also very informative when it comes to the patient's motivation. My admiration for the test began early in my career when I tested a high-school teacher with a possible left-hemisphere stroke. The patient had previously been given all of the HRB, except for the TPT. The results, particularly a very slow tapping for the left hand, indicated to the previous examiner that the patient had had a mild left-hemisphere stroke. (The patient was also stuttering to some extent.) I repeated the entire Halstead–Reitan Battery, including the TPT. When blindfolded, the patient's right hand worked completely normally. My diagnosis was *hysteria*. Under hypnosis, the patient could use his right hand perfectly normally, and 6 months of intensive therapy essentially cured the condition. Since then, I and my colleagues have had hundreds of such cases where the TPT was either supportive or crucial to an interpretation.

There is not enough time to discuss the various attributes of each of the approximately 60 tests in the HRNES–R battery, including subtests. However, the conclusion of these examples is that one needs to know the characteristics of the individual tests because they are related to the other tests in the battery for an accurate interpretation.

General Effects of Brain Damage

Any brain damage can and usually does produce a general impairment effect (Reitan & Wolfson, 1993, pp. 27, 52), such that almost all functions are impaired, although some tests are more sensitive to general damage than others. The general effects of brain damage can be manifested in several ways. First, there is the effect produced by damage to the part of the neural system that controls consciousness, alertness, and psychomotor speed. This may include shock or damage to the reticular activating system or to other systems that are related to the general activity level of the brain as a whole. A shock to these systems that control the brain's general activity level may be severe enough to produce unconsciousness. The effect may last for any length of time—from a few seconds to a continuous coma. Acute moderate damage may produce unconsciousness or amnesia of limited duration, whereas chronic damage may reduce general psychomotor speed for a lifetime. Both the length of amnesia and the length of unconsciousness are related to the severity of impairment. The general effects, particularly in acute or progressive damage, include reduced alertness and reduced psychomotor speed.

The brain is supplied and supported by many physiological components such as the vascular system. Its disruption may produce either focal effects or generalized effects. Certain vascular conditions produce a generalized dementia. Disruption or blockage of the primary arteries that supply the brain may produce strokes that involve large areas.

Because brain damage usually affects a person's intellectual ability, the effect of brain damage is to change the range of a person's ability. For brain-damaged people as a group, the range of intelligence scores is greatly increased, both immediately and chronically. This range of brain-damage scores extends from the above-average range or about 140 when there is almost no impairment to complete impairment as in loss of consciousness or death. In practice, this range for brain-damaged adults may extend more than five standard deviations below the normal mean. This applies to the entire brain functioning, all areas of the brain, and all measures of brain functioning.

Fluid and Crystallized Effect

Another generalized effect of brain damage is that produced by fluidity or the difference between fluid and crystallized intelligence (Cattell, 1963; Russell 1986, pp. 63–64).This was thoroughly discussed previously and need not be discussed here. However, note that there has been a general and long-accepted concept that brain damage produces a tendency for the individual to shift from abstract to concrete thinking (Goldstein & Scheerer, 1941; Walsh, 1978). This effect may, in fact, represent a tendency for brain-damaged individuals to change from a more fluid form of thinking to a more crystallized form (Russell, 1986, p. 60). Because crystallized intelligence remains more intact, it is a more reliable means of dealing with problems when the brain's functioning is impaired.

Distant Effects (Diaschisis)

Another type of brain effect that is fairly well known is the distant effect of focal brain damage. A lesion in one area will suppress the functioning of the brain at some distance from the lesion. This has been called *diaschisis* (Luria, 1973, p. 104; Russell, 1981, 1986, p. 65). It may be related to spreading depression. This effect is strongest in the acute stage of a lesion and may disappear in the chronic phase (Russell, 1981).

Thus. the effects of a lesion in the cortex often extend beyond the boundaries of the lesion itself. This distant effect (Riese, 1959) of a lesion first was described in detail by von Monakow (1911, 1969), who first called this effect *diaschisis*. Smith has discussed this phenomena in considerable detail (1975, pp. 70–73) and presented many studies and research that support this phenomena. Apparently, this effect is distinct from the generalized effects produced by such conditions as increased intercranial pressure, edema, or compression (Smith, 1975, p. 70). This effect not only spreads through gray matter but also may travel along neural tracks to the opposite hemisphere from the original lesion (Smith, 1975, pp. 71–73).

In most cases, diaschisis tends to resolve as the lesion becomes static (Smith, 1975, p. 71; von Monakow, 1969). This effect is supported further by the finding that at times the removal of a diseased hemisphere has eliminated a chronic disfunctioning of the opposite hemisphere. Thus, the individual, after the removal of a hemisphere, functions better than with the diseased hemisphere (Smith, 1972). Finally, another excellent example of this distant effect is presented by Luria (1973, p. 136). His study demonstrated that phonemic hearing is impaired primarily by lesions in the left temporal lobe. However, damage that is distant from this area also produces impairment that decreases as the distance from the temporal lobe increases.

The distant effect (diaschisis) principle states that a lesion may affect functions in a distant undamaged area of the cortex. The pattern of spread is not known, but it appears to decrease in strength with distance (Luria, 1973, p. 136). The effect evidently spreads most easily through the gray matter within a hemisphere, but it may cross the corpus callosum into the opposite hemisphere (Smith, 1975, pp. 70–71). This principle may explain why some lateralized lesions affect functions in the opposite hemisphere (Smith, 1975, pp. 70–71).

In general, fluid tests are more easily affected by damage at a distance, whereas crystallized functions that are more focal are less affected by damage at a distance.

Process Effects

Brain damage may be either progressive or resolving. Each condition has a different effect on patterns. Progressive lesions such as those produced by dementia or tumors have a number of effects on brain functioning. Each may have a particular pattern of damage. However, the impairment gradually increases.

In resolving lesions, such as those caused by head trauma or a stroke, the effect is worse immediately after the accident and gradually lessens (Goldstein, Shemansky, Beers, George & Roberts, 1996). The acute stage is variable but seldom lasts more than 3 months and demonstrates rapid recovery of functions. The static stage is generally thought to last from the end of the acute stage to about 2 years. During this stage, there is still improvement in functioning but at a gradually decreasing rate. In the chronic stage, for the most part the maximum improvement in functioning has been reached and little improvement is expected. However, both improvement and a mild decrease in functioning have been reported.

The Chronicity Effect

Another effect generally occurs during the acute and static stages, what may be called the *chronicity effect* (Russell, 1981). Distant effects interact with other characteristics of lesions to produce various patterns of test results. One of the major sets of patterns is that related to a resolving lesion. Clinical experience and some studies (Russell, 1981) indicate that as diaschisis resolves, the distant effects gradually are reduced so that there is a return of functions in areas that are not related to the damaged areas. Accordingly, as the lesion resolves, there is a changing pattern of test results.

In a localized resolving lesion, over a period of time those tests that are not related directly to the area of damage gradually will return to normal, whereas functions directly related to the area of the cortex that was destroyed will remain permanently impaired. There may be some initial improvement of functions related to the damaged area, but this improvement will plateau within the impaired range. Thus, with a resolving, relatively limited focal lesion, one would expect that initially many functions would be impaired, whereas after a period of time only those functions related to the area of tissue destruction would be impaired.

There is a decelerating return of functions such that impaired functions improve rapidly initially and then more slowly with time. Most of the return of functions will have occurred within the first year, according to our clinical experience and the study by Russell (1981), although in some cases the return of some functioning may continue for some years.

Finally, in the static phase, only the focal effects of damage remain, with elementary functions primarily impaired—that is, the diffuse or remote effects drop out as the lesion becomes static. This introduces what may be, called a *punched-card effect* because the measured functions of an individual with static damage tend to look like a computer punch card in which most of the brain functions are normal, whereas the few functions that are related directly to the area of damage are "punched out" or impaired. Note that this focal effect of static damage applies only to functions largely existing in the damaged area. Functions that are complex and consequently cover many areas of the brain obviously will be less affected. Thus, some complex functions will remain mildly impaired.

Implications of Resolving Lesions

The most important implication for assessment of resolving and especially chronic lesions is that a patient's overall functioning may be essentially normal, especially for someone with higher initial levels of ability, whereas debilitating damage remains for a particular type of function or functions. This creates a particular difficulty in assessing patients with chronic damage. Because chronic damage only impairs functions related to a few specific areas, several tests directly related to the particular area must be impaired in order to demonstrate this focal static damage. If the group of tests that are administered does not cover the particular elementary functions that are impaired, then the lesion will be missed.

In a flexible battery, the damage may be missed or considered to be the consequence of the expected rate of error because of normal probability. In a standardized battery, a general index of brain damage may be within the normal range. A definite pattern of impairment derived from a comprehensive battery must demonstrate the area in which all related functions are impaired. This type of chronic lesion was previously illustrated in the section titled "Localization Diagrams (Neural Maps)."

The way to overcome this problem is to use tests for complex functions and a battery with complete coverage and sufficient redundancy. Standardized batteries with scale scores that are designed to cover the whole brain and provide finer discriminations are more accurate in defining such lesions.

Another implication of chronicity is an explanation of the long-standing finding that the Wechsler intelligence tests are often lateralized with acute lesions, but not for chronic lesions (Fitzhugh et al., 1962; Russell, 1971, 1972a). If we assume that the lateralized impairment of the Wechsler adult scales includes distant effects as well as the direct effect of a lesion, then the test scores not directly impaired by the damage should return to normal functioning as the lesion ages and the diaschisis gradually resolves.

Finally, in regard to research, it should be obvious that static focal lesions are the most appropriate type to use in studying the localization of a function. If static lesions are used, then we do not have to account for remote effects.

On the other hand, if we wish to study the effects of lateralization, then acute forms of damage are more relevant. In investigating lateralization effects, such as in most of the Wechsler lateralization studies, the influence of remote effects is desirable because distant effects affect lateralized tests within one hemisphere and are not as strong in the opposite hemisphere. Thus, the principle of chronicity provides us a basis for determining which forms of damage are the most appropriate for different types of research studies.

Specific Neurological Conditions

To emphasize the patterns involved with neurological conditions, some of the more usual diagnostic categories will be examined. These are only a few examples of patterns related to neurological conditions. They are derived from clinical studies, so their reliability is not as great as validated formal results. Conditions that have already been explored will not be discussed.

Brain-damage patterns can be separated into four types: diffuse, focal, scattered, and peripheral.

Diffuse Lesions

Diffuse damage involves brain functions covering much of the brain in a relatively uniform manner. They are usually produced by a degenerative condition. The fluidity effect is expected. Occasionally, a specific form of diffuse pattern may be found. Although generally Alzheimer's disease is a diffuse condition, lateralized cases occasionally occur (Martin et al., 1986). If the AD is lateralized, the neuropsychological assessment examination requires a more careful analysis to rule out other conditions than if the condition is bilateral. In regard to other degenerative patterns, although several of these have been studied in the literature, almost no specific patterns have been cross validated.

Focal Lesions

Focal lesions are those that involve functions related to a specific area of the brain. The two major types of focal lesions are strokes and tumors. However, other focal lesions may occur such as gunshot wounds. In general, crystallized functions provide more accurate localization for focal lesions than fluid functions because generally crystallized functions produce fewer distant effects.

Strokes may be hemorrhagic or thrombotic (Goldstein et al., 1996). Either can produce extensive impairment. Thrombotic strokes involve the areas of the brain that are "upstream" to a clogged artery. They usually form focal impairment. Hemorrhagic strokes are more diffuse and may not produce a focal lesion. In the acute stage of either type of stroke, the impairment is widespread, whereas the impairment may involve only a limited area in the chronic stage.

Certain types of strokes produce fairly consistent patterns. For instance, internal capsule strokes produce dense motor paralysis but less impairment to cognitive functions even on the equilateral side.

Tumors

Although there are a number of types of tumors with different effects, tumors usually produce more exact focal effects than many other neurological conditions. They can produce pressure effects or can extend beyond one hemisphere. If there are two metastatic tumors of different sizes, then the neuropsychological examination could indicate either lateralized effects related to the larger tumor or bilateral effects. Tumors tend to produce milder and less lateralized motor impairment than strokes.

Scattered Lesions

A third general form of lesion may be called *scattered lesions*. These consist of unevenly distributed focal lesions, often small, that form no consistent pattern in the brain. With diffuse lesions, the impairment is relatively evenly distributed and affects test results with a particular diffuse pattern, which is usually the fluidity pattern. Scattered lesions occur when the agent that produces the lesions itself lacks focus and damages the brain, often in a random manner. As a result, no specific patterns are related to scattered lesions, although certain pattern characteristics may be related to particular forms of pathology. In almost all cases, there will be a general background of brain impairment that particularly affects psychomotor speed. Two forms of scattered lesions will be presented.

Closed Head Injury

Perhaps the most common form of brain damage that neuropsychologists now encounter, especially those in forensics, is closed head injury (CHI) (Reitan & Wolfson, 1986, 1988; Williamson, Scott, & Adams, 1996, pp. 9–64). It is also the most treacherous type of brain damage to use as a neuropsychological criterion in assessment or research. No matter what the neurological evidence is for a particular focal effect, the effect on cognitive tests will generally vary from the expected location. As such, normally its location cannot be predicted. The CT or MRI scan may show a hematoma in the right hemisphere, and the neuropsychological examination finds bilateral damage. Because of some sobering experiences, my rule of thumb is to never use CHI cases in a lateralization or localization study and discount the results of any research study on localization that used very many CHI cases. Usually, the cross-validation studies with a large proportion of CHI subjects do not find the localization effects that other studies have found.

Even in assessing the existence of brain damage, the mere history of a head injury is insufficient. Head injuries could be relatively slight—for example, a person having been slightly dazed for a few seconds with minimal tissue damage to death. Consequently, the severity of neurological injury must be ascertained. The history must be supported by other evidence of brain injury, such as the length of unconsciousness, amnesia, or the score on the Glasgow Coma Scale.

After malingering or poor motivation has been ruled out, almost any pattern of impairment may be found. At times, focal impairments may occur as in a contrecoup lesion. Even the length of time that a person is unconscious is not an invariable indication of the severity of damage. My assumption is that unless the brainstem has been shocked in the trauma, which it usually is, the severity of damage is not related to the length of unconsciousness. Bullets may produce wounds that pass through the brain without a loss of consciousness (Williamson et al., 1996, p. 12). (In my files, I had half a dozen attempts at suicide that destroyed part of the brain but did not kill the person.) Particularly if there is a CHI, the Glasgow Coma Scale is probably the best indication of the amount of brain damage. Almost always, measures of psychomotor speed such as the digit symbol will be impaired in the acute stage and often into the static stage.

In spite of their excellent chapter on head trauma, Williamson et al. (1996, pp. 18–42) do not present any diagnostic patterns or the lack of patterns related to head trauma, other than a slowing of digit symbol. They indicate that the most common form of head trauma occurs in the inferior frontal lobes and anterior temporal, yet they provide no discussion of impairment to frontal tests. Of the major tests they suggest that are related to this area, the category test was largely ruled out in a study by Reitan and Wolfson (1995). Using a huge database, they found no difference between the effects of frontal and nonfrontal damage on either the category test or Trails B. Our own experience has been that the fluency tests appear to be the only consistently frontal tests. The fluency tests are accurate only after the component of the tests related to the posterior part of the brain, such as the left-hemisphere verbal area, has been found to be unimpaired.

The result of this heterogeneous nature of traumatic damage is that neuropsychological testing is often more useful in describing the cognitive assets and deficits resulting from head trauma than in assessing its existence. Of course, noncognitive tests are necessary to determine the validity of the testing and occasionally the affective results of the trauma.

Cerebrovascular Disease

Cerebrovascular disease is another common scattered form of damage. Thus, arteriosclerosis can produce lateralized impairment without a stroke or even physical evidence from the CT or MRI. Thus, it is quite possible to show lateralized effects on neuropsychological testing when the neurological diagnosis is that of a diffuse condition such as vascular dementia.

By the nature of the diagnosis, neither subjects with a transient ischemic attack nor an episode of reversible ischemic neurological deficit should be used as the criterion in accuracy studies. By definition, these are patients who neurologically recover from their episodes (Netter, Jones, and Dingle 1985). Although neuropsychological studies have found that some of these patients have mild residuals (Lezak, 1983, p. 178), the neurological criterion diagnosis is that of complete recovery.

Peripheral Damage

Another way in which a program or clinical judgment can make mistakes concerning impairment is derived from peripheral damage. There may occasionally be impairment that is wrongly attributed to the cortex but actually results from peripheral damage. Peripheral damage may be suspected when there is motor or sensory impairment but little evidence of cortical impairment in neuropsychological assessment. Currently, it is difficult to distinguish central impairment from peripheral damage. Only a few clinicians can do this with even modest reliability without seeing the patient's neurological record

Conclusion

Unfortunately, as far as I am aware, the formal assessment patterns presented in this chapter constitute almost all of the published patterns that neuropsychology has produced. There are probably some that are not widely known and have been missed. There are also many patterns that are part of the assessment that were not presented because of lack of space and validation (Bradford, 1992). In addition, the literature offers a great many studies that have the potential for creating formal patterns that could be cross validated but have not yet been examined by neuropsychologists.

Rather, the major textbooks in neuropsychology, such as those by Adams, Parsons, Culbertson, and Nixon (1996), Lezak et al. (2004), and Strauss et al. (2006), while cataloging mountains of studies, mostly of the one-test, one-condition type, describe almost no differential patterns, much less validate them. As such, these huge textbooks are of almost no practical assistance to the student or neuropsychologist in forming a differential diagnosis. Their utility is largely limited to determining the existence of brain damage. As mentioned previously, this can be reliably accomplished with indexes employing between 5 and 10 carefully selected tests.

References

Adams, L. R., Parsons, O., Culbertson, J. L., & Nixon, S. J. (Eds.), (1996). *Neuropsychology for clinical practice: Etiology, assessment, and treatment of common neurological disorders*. Washington, DC: American Psychological Association.

Babcock, H. (1930). An experiment in the measurement of mental deterioration. *Archives of Psychology*, *18*(117), 1–68.

Barron, J. H., & Russell, E. W. (1992). Fluidity theory and the neuropsychological impairment in alcoholism. *Archives of Clinical Neuropsychology*, *7*, 175–188.

Begley, S. (2011, July). The best medicine. *Scientific American*, *305*, 50–55.

Benson, N., Hulac, D. M., & Kranzler, J. H. (2010). Independent examination of Wechsler Adult Intelligence Scale—Fourth Edition (WAIS–IV): What does the WAIS–IV measure? *Psychological Assessment*, *22*(1), 121–130.

Bolter, J., Venerlasen, J., & Long, C. J. (1981). Investigation of WAIS effectiveness in discriminating between temporal and generalized seizure patients. *Journal of Consulting and Clinical Psychology*, *49*, 549–553.

Botwinick, J. (1977). Intellectual abilities. In J. E. Birren & J. W. Schaie (Eds.), *Handbook of the psychology of aging* (pp. 58–565). New York: Van Nostrand Reinhold.

Bradford, D. T. (1992). *Interpretive reasoning and the Halstead–Reitan Tests*. Brandon, VT: Clinical Psychology Publishing.

Brown, J. (1987). *A screening key to differentiate normals from organics and patients with functional disorders.* Unpublished doctoral dissertation, Nova University, Fort Lauderdale, FL. (Advisor E. W. Russell)

Carroll, J. B. (1993). *Human cognitive abilities: A survey of factor-analytic studies.* New York: Cambridge University Press.

Cattell, R. B. (1943). The measurement of adult intelligence. *Psychological Bulletin, 40,* 153–193.

Cattell, R. B. (1963). Theory of fluid and crystallized intelligence. *Journal of Educational Psychology, 54,* 1–22.

Cattell, R. B. (1971). *Abilities: Their structure, growth, and action.* New York: Houghton-Mifflin.

Coughlan, A. K., & Warrington, E. K. (1978). Word-comprehension and word-retrieval in patients with localized cerebral lesions. *Brain, 101,* 163–185.

Cullum, C. M., Steinman, D. R., & Bigler, E. D. (1983). Relationship between fluid and crystallized cognitive functions using the Category Test and WAIS scores. *The International Journal of Clinical Neuropsychology, VI*(3), 172–174.

Damasio, A. R. (2003). *Looking for Spinoza: Joy, sorrow, and the feeling brain.* New York: Harcourt.

Delaney, R. C., Wallace, J. D., & Egelko, S. (1980). Transient cerebral ischemic attacks and neuropsychological deficit. *Journal of Clinical Neuropsychology,* 2, 107–114.

Dobbins, C., & Russell, E. W. (1990). Left temporal brain damage pattern on the Wechsler Intelligence Scale. *Journal of Clinical Psychology, 46,* 863–868.

Dodrill, C. B. (1997). Myths of neuropsychology. *Clinical Neuropsychologist, 11,* 1–17.

Ellis, R. J., & Oscar-Berman, M. (1989). Alcoholism, aging and functional cerebral asymmetries. *Psychological Bulletin, 106,* 128–147.

Finlayson, M. A. J. (1977). Test complexity and brain damage at different educational levels. *Journal of Clinical Psychology, 33,* 221–223.

Fitzhugh, K. B., Fitzhugh, L., & Reitan, R. (1962). Influence of age upon measures of problem solving and experimental background in subjects with long-standing cerebral dysfunction. *Journal of Gerontology, 19,* 306–310.

Fitzhugh, K. B., Fitzhugh, L., & Reitan, R. (1964). Influence of age upon measures of problem solving and experimental background in subjects with long-standing cerebral dysfunction. *Journal of Gerontology, 19,* 132–134.

Fitzhugh, L., Fitzhugh, K. B., & Reitan, R. (1965). Adaptive abilities and intellectual functioning of hospitalized alcoholics: Further considerations. *Quarterly Journal of Studies on Alcoholism, 26* 411–412

Fuld, P. A. (1984). Test profile of cholinergic dysfunction and of Alzheimer's-type dementia. *Journal of Clinical Neuropsychology, 6,* 380–392.

Fuld, P. A. (1986). Pathological and chemical validation of behavioral features of Alzheimer's disease. In L. W. Poon (Ed.), *Handbook for clinical memory assessment of older adults* (pp. 302–306). Washington, DC: American Psychological Association.

Goldstein, G. (1986). The neuropsychology of schizophrenia. In I. Grant & K. M. Adams (Eds.), *Neuropsychological assessment of neuropsychiatric disorders* (pp. 147–171). New York: Oxford.

Goldstein, G. (1987). Etiological considerations regarding the neuropsychological consequences of alcoholism. In O. A. Parsons, N. Butters & R. E. Nathan (Eds.), *Neuropsychology of alcoholism.* New York: The Guilford Press.

Goldstein, K., & Scheerer, M. (1941). Abstract and concrete behavior: An experimental study with special tests. *Psychological Monographs, 53*(2) Whole No. 239.

Goldstein, G., & Shelly, C. (1982). A multivariate neuropsychological approach to brain lesion localization in alcoholism. *Addictive Behaviors*, *7*, 165–175.

Goldstein, G., Shemansky, W. J., Beers, S. R., George, T., & Roberts, K. (1996). A clarification of the Russell, Neuringer, and Goldstein process key: Implications for outcome. *Archives of Clinical Neuropsychology*, *11*(7), 581–587.

Goodglass, H. (1980). Disorders of naming following brain injury. *American Scientist*, *68*, 647–655.

Guilford, J. P. (1967). *The nature of human intelligence*. New York: McGraw-Hill.

Halstead, W. C. (1947). *Brain and intelligence*. Chicago: University of Chicago Press.

Heaton, R. K., Miller, S. W., Taylor, M. J., & Grant, I. (2004). *Revised comprehensive norms for an expanded Halstead–Reitan Battery: Demographically adjusted neuropsychological norms for African American and Caucasian adults*. Odessa, FL: Psychological Assessment Resources. [Professional manual and computer program].

Heaton, R. K., Smith, H. H., Lehman, R. A. W., & Vogt, A. T. (1978). Prospects for faking believable deficits on neuropsychological testing. *Journal of Consulting and Clinical Psychology*, *46*, 892–900.

Hebb, D. O. (1941). Clinical evidence concerning the nature of normal adult intelligence. *Psychological Bulletin*, *38*, 593.

Hebb, D. O. (1949). *Organization of behavior, a neuropsychological theory*. New York: Wiley.

Hewson, L. R. (1949). The Wechsler-Bellevue scale and the substitution test as aids in neuropsychiatric diagnosis. Part 2. *Journal of Nervous and Mental Disease*, *109*, 246–265.

Hom, J. (1992). General and specific cognitive dysfunctions in patients with Alzheimer's disease. *Archives of Clinical Neuropsychology*, *7*, 121–133.

Horn, J. L. (1966). Intelligence—Why it grows, why it declines. *Transaction*, *4*, 23–31.

Horn, J. L. (1968). Organization of abilities and the development of intelligence. *Psychological Review*, *75*, 242–259.

Horn, J. L., & Cattell, R. B. (1968). Refinement and test of the theory of fluid and crystallized general intelligences. *Journal of Educational Psychology*, *5*, 253–270.

Horn, J. L. (1976). Human abilities: A review of research and theory in the early 1970s. *Annual Review of Psychology*, *31*, 437–485.

Horn, J. L., & Cattell., R. B. (1966). Age differences in primary mental ability factors. *Journal of Gerontology*, *21*, 210–220.

Hunt, H. F. (1943). A practical clinical test for organic brain damage. *Journal of Applied Psychology*, *27*, 375–386.

Kaufman, A. S. (1979). *Intelligent testing with the WISC-R*. New York: Wiley.

Kaufman, A. S., & Kaufman, N. (2004). *Kaufman Brief Intelligence Test* (2nd ed.). Los Angeles: Western Psychological Services. (KBIT-2)

Kløve, H. (1974). Validation studies in adult clinical neuropsychology. In R. M. Reitan & L. A. Davison (Eds.), *Clinical neuropsychology: Current status and applications*. New York: Wiley.

Knopman, D. S., Seines, O. A., Niccum, N., & Rubens, A. B. (1984). Recovery of naming in aphasia: Relationship to fluency, comprehension, and CT findings. *Neurology*, *34*, 1461–1470.

Larrabee, G. J. (2005). Assessment of malingering. In G. J. Larrabee (Ed.), *Forensic neuropsychology: A scientific approach* (pp. 92–158). New York: Oxford University Press.

Lezak, M. D. (1983). *Neuropsychological assessment* (2nd ed.). New York: Oxford University Press.

Lezak, M. D. (1995). *Neuropsychological assessment* (3rd ed.). New York: Oxford University Press.

Lezak, M. D., Howieson, D. B., & Loring, D. W. (2004). *Neuropsychological assessment* (4th ed.). New York: Oxford University Press.

Loring, D. W., & Bauer, R. M. (2010). Testing the limits: Cautions and concerns regarding the new Wechsler IQ and memory scales. *Neurology, 74*(8), 685–690.

Loring, D., Meador, K., Mahurin, R., & Largen, J. (1986). *Neuropsychological performance in dementia of the Alzheimer type and multi-infarct dementia.* Paper presented at the 14th Annual Meeting of the International Neuropsychological Society, Denver, CO, pp. 1–20.

Luria, A. R. (1973). *The working brain.* New York: Basic Books.

Martin, A. et al. (1986). Towards a behavioral typology of Alzheimer's patients. *Journal of Consulting and Experimental Neuropsychology, 8*, 594–610.

Massman, P. J., & Bigler, E. D. (1993). A quantitative review of the diagnostic utility of the WAIS–R Fuld profile. *Archives of Clinical Neuropsychology, 8*, 417–428.

Matarazzo, J. D. (1972). *Measurement and appraisal of adult intelligence* (5th ed.). Baltimore: Williams & Wilkins.

Mathias, J. L., & Burke, J. (2009). Cognitive functioning in Alzheimer's and vascular dementia: A meta-analysis. *Neuropsychology, 23*(4), 411–423.

McFie, J. (1960). Psychological testing in clinical neurology. *Journal of Nervous and Mental Disease, 131*, 383–393.

McFie, J. (1975). *Assessment of organic intellectual impairment.* New York: Academic Press.

Merriam-Webster, *Collegiate dictionary.* Springfield, MA: Merriam-Webster. Computer version 2.5.

Milberg, W., Greiffenstein, M., Lewis, R., & Rourke, D. (1980). Differentiation of temporal lobe and generalized seizure patients with the WAIS. *Journal of Consulting and Clinical Psychology, 48*, 39–42.

Netter, F. H., Jones, H. R., & Dingle, R. V. (1985). *The Ciba collection of medical illustrations.* West Caldwell, NJ: Ciba.

Nixon, S. J. (1996). Alzheimer's disease and vascular dementia. In L. A. Russell, O. A. Parsons, J. L. Culbertson. & S. J. Nixon (Eds.), *Neuropsychology for clinical practice: Etiology, assessment, and treatment of common neurological disorders* (pp. 65–105). Washington, DC: American Psychological Association.

Parsons, O. A., & Farr, S. R (1981). The neuropsychology of alcohol and drug use. In S. B. Filskov & T. J. Boll (Eds.), *Handbook of clinical neuropsychology* (pp. 320–365). New York: Wiley.

Reed, H. B. C., & Reitan, R. M. (1963). Changes in psychological test performance associated with the normal aging process. *Journal of Gerontology, 18*, 271–274.

Reitan, R. M. (1955). Certain differential effects of left an right cerebral lesions in human adults. *Journal of Comparative and Physiological Psychology, 48*(6), 474–477.

Reitan, R. M. (1955). Investigation of the validity of Halstead's measures of biological intelligence. *Archives of Neurology and Psychiatry, 73*, 28–35.

Reitan, R. M. (1962). Psychological deficit. *Annual Review of Psychology, 13*, 415–444.

Reitan, R. M. (1964). Psychological deficits resulting from cerebral lesions in men. In J. M. Warren & K. Akert (Eds.), *The frontal granular cortex and behavior* (pp. 295–312). New York: McGraw-Hill.

Reitan, R. M. (1966). A research program on the psychological effects of brain lesions in human beings. In N. R. Ellis (Ed.), *International review of research and mental retardation* (pp. 156–218). New York: Academic Press.

Reitan, R. M. (1984). *Aphasia and sensory-perceptual deficits in adults*. Tucson: Neuropsychology Press.

Reitan, R. M. (1991). *The Neuropsychological Deficit Scale for adults computer program: Users Manual*. Tucson: Neuropsychology Press.

Reitan, R. M., & Wolfson, D. (1986). *Traumatic brain injury: Vol. 1 . Pathophysiology and Neuropsychological evaluation*. Tucson: Neuropsychology Press.

Reitan, R. M., & Wolfson, D. (1988). *Traumatic brain injury: Vol. 2. Recovery and rehabilitation*. Tucson: Neuropsychology Press.

Reitan, R. M., & Wolfson, D. (1993). *The Halstead–Reitan Neuropsychological Test Battery: Theory and clinical interpretation* (2nd ed.). Tucson: Neuropsychology Press.

Reitan, R. M., & Wolfson, D. (1995, February). Category test and trail making test as measures of frontal lobe functions. *Clinical Neuropsychologist*, *9*(1), 50–56.

Reitan, R. M., & Wolfson, D. (1997). *Detection of malingering and invalid test scores*. Tucson: Neuropsychology Press.

Riese, W. (1959). *A history of neurology*. New York: M. D. Publications.

Russell, E. W. (1971). A reexamination of Halstead's Biological Intelligence Factors. *Proceedings, 79th Annual Convention of the American Psychological Association*, *6*, 461–462.

Russell, E. W. (1972). The effect of acute lateralized brain damage on a factor analysis of the Wechsler-Bellevue Intelligence Test. *Proceedings, 80th Annual Convention of the American Psychological Association*, *7*, 421–422. Honolulu

Russell, E. W. (1972). A WAIS factor analysis with brain damaged subjects using a criterion measure. *Journal of Consulting and Clinical Psychology*, *39*, 133–139.

Russell, E. W. (1974). The effect of acute lateralized brain damage on Halstead's Biological Intelligence Factors. *Journal of General Psychology*, *90*, 101–107.

Russell, E. W. (1976). The Bender-Gestalt and the Halstead-Reitan Battery: A case study. *Journal of Clinical Psychology*, *32*, 355–361.

Russell, E. W. (1979). Three patterns of brain damage on the WAIS. *Journal of Clinical Psychology*, *35*(3), 611–620.

Russell, E. W. (1980). Fluid and crystallized intelligence: Effects of diffuse brain damage on the WAIS. *Perceptual and Motor Skills*, *51*, 121–122.

Russell, E. W. (1981). The chronicity effect. *Journal of Clinical Psychology*, *37*, 246–253.

Russell, E. W. (1984). Theory and developments of pattern analysis methods related to the Halstead–Reitan Battery. In P. E. Logue & J. M. Shear (Eds.), *Clinical neuropsychology: A multidisciplinary approach* (pp. 50–98). Springfield, IL: Charles C. Thomas.

Russell, E. W. (1985). Comparison of the TPT 10 and the TPT 6 hole form board. *Journal of Clinical Psychology*, *41*, 68–81.

Russell, E. W. (1986). The psychometric foundation of clinical neuropsychology. In S. B. Filskov & T. J. Boll (Eds.), *Handbook of clinical neuropsychology* (Vol. 2, pp. 45–80). New York: Wiley.

Russell, E. W. (1987). A reference scale method for constructing neuropsychological test batteries. *Journal of Clinical and Experimental Neuropsychology*, *9*, 376–392.

Russell, E. W. (2004). The operating characteristics of the major HRNES–R measures. *Archives of Clinical Neuropsychology*, *19*(8), 1043–1061.

Russell, E. W. (2010). The "obsolescence" of assessment procedures. *Applied Neuropsychology*, *17*(1), 60–67.

Russell, E. W., Neuringer, C., & Goldstein, G. (1970). *Assessment of brain damage: A neuropsychological key approach*. New York: Wiley.

Russell, E. W., & Russell, S. L. K. (1993). Left temporal lobe brain damage pattern on the WAIS, Addendum. *Journal of Clinical Psychology*, *49*, 241–244.

Russell, E. W., & Polakoff, D. (1993). Neuropsychological test patterns in men for Alzheimer's and multi-infarct dementia. *Archives of Clinical Neuropsychology, 8*, 327–343.

Russell, E. W., & Starkey, R. I. (1993). *Halstead–Russell Neuropsychological Evaluation System.* Los Angeles: Western Psychological Services. [Manual and computer program]

Russell, E. W., & Starkey, R. I. (2001). *Halstead–Russell Neuropsychological Evaluation System—Revised.* Los Angeles: Western Psychological Services. [Manual and computer program].

Schinka, J. A., & Vanderploeg, R. D. (2000). Estimating premorbid level of functioning. In R. D. Vanderploeg (Ed.), *Clinician's guide to neuropsychological assessment* (pp. 39–67) (2nd ed.). Hillsdale, NJ: Lawrence Erlbaum.

Shipley, W. C. (1940). A self-administering scale for measuring intellectual impairment and deterioration. *Journal of Psychology, 9*, 371–377.

Smith, A. (1972). Dominant and nondominant hemispherectomy. In W. L. Smith (Ed.), *Drugs, development and cerebral function*. Springfield, Ill: Charles C Thomas.

Smith, A. (1975). Neuropsychological testing in neurological disorders. In W. J. Friedlander (Ed.), *Advances in neurology* (pp. 49–110). New York: Raven.

Storrie, M. C., & Doerr, H. O. (1980). Characterization of Alzheimer Type Dementia utilizing an abbreviated Halstead-Reitan battery. *Clinical Neuropsychology, 2*, 78–82.

Strauss, E., Sherman, E. M. S., & Spreen, O. (2006). *A compendium of neuropsychological tests: Administration, norms, and commentary* (3rd ed.). New York: Oxford University Press.

Thompson, L. L., & Heaton, R. K. (1991). Pattern of performance on the tactual performance test. *Clinical Neuropsychologist, 5*(4), 322–328.

Tufte, E. R. (1983). *The visual display of quantitative information.* Cheshire, CN: Graphics Press.

von Monakow, C. (1911). Localization of brain functions. *Journal of Psychology and Neurology, 17*, 185–191.

von Monakow, C. (1969). Diaschisis. In K. H. (1969). Pribram (Ed.), *Brain and behavior* (Vol. 1). London: Penguin. (Original work published 1914)

Walsh, K. W. (1978). *Neuropsychology, A clinical approach.* Hillsdale, New York: Churchill Livingstone.

Warrington, E. K., Logue, V., & Pratt, R. T. C. (1971). The anatomical localization of selective impairment of auditory verbal short-term memory. *Neuropsychologia, 9*, 377–387.

Warrington, E., & Weiskrantz, L. (1973). An analysis of short-term and long-term memory defects in man. In J. A. Deutsch (Ed.), *The physiological basis of memory* (pp. 365–395). New York: Academic Press.

Watson, C. G. (1977). Brain damage tests in psychiatric settings. *The INS Bulletin*, March 10–12.

Wechsler, D. (1955). *Wechsler adult intelligence scale. Manual.* New York: Psychological Corporation.

Wechsler, D. (1997). *WAIS–III, WMS–III: Technical manual.* San Antonio, TX: Psychological Corporation.

Wechsler, D., Coalson, D. L., & Raiford, S. E. (2008). *WAIS–IV technical and interpretive manual.* San Antonio, TX: Pearson.

Wheeler, J. I., & Wilkins, W. L. (1951). The validity of the Hewson ratios. *Journal of Consulting Psychology, 15*(2), 163–166.

Williamson, D. J. G., Scott, J. G., & Adams, R. L. (1996). In L. A. Russell, O. A. Parsons, J. L. Culbertson & S. J. Nixon (Eds.), *Neuropsychology for clinical practice: Etiology, assessment, and treatment of common neurological disorders* (pp. 9–64). Washington, DC: American Psychological Association.

Section III

Justification of Formal Procedures

7 The Fundamental Psychometric Status of Neuropsychological Batteries

Elbert W. Russell, Sally L.K. Russell and B. Hill

The controversy between different approaches to the construction and use of assessment batteries is a major area of contention in clinical neuropsychology today. This debate often centers on a comparison between fixed or standardized batteries and flexible or heterogeneous approaches. Many researchers have contended that both methods are acceptable and equally adequate for assessment (Bauer, 2000; Franzen, 2000, pp. 2–4; Goldstein, 1997; Incagnoli, 1986; Kane, 1991; Lezak, Howieson, & Loring, 2004; Mitrushina, Boone, & D'Elia, 1999, pp. 23–24). The main contention of these neuropsychologists is that one or the other method may have slight advantages under certain circumstances, but it is generally agreed that the acceptance of the standardized or flexible method is primarily a matter of personal preference.

However, to adequately address this controversy requires an understanding of the most fundamental basis of assessment. The discussions previously mentioned have seldom dealt with two fundamental concepts related to neuropsychological assessment, although they are often implied. The first of these is the concept of dependability. The second concerns the application of psychometric methods to interpretations derived from batteries of tests [American Educational Research Association, American Psychological Association, & National Council on Measurement in Education, 1999 (hereafter AERA, 1999); Anastasi & Urbina, 1997]. These two concepts will be the focus of this chapter.

Dependability

The most fundamental concept related to the application of scientific methodology can be designated as *dependability*. Dependability means that information will be invariant from one situation to another. The justification for all standardized scientific procedures is the assurance of dependability. The basic purpose of the neuropsychological assessment is to provide dependable information concerning the functioning of the human brain for both forensic and medical purposes. It is generally accepted that validated psychometric procedures ensure that the information derived from neuropsychological assessment can be dependably generalized to the person tested as a basis for interpretation. The concept of dependability is especially

The Scientific Foundation of Neuropsychological Assessment. DOI: 10.1016/B978-0-12-416029-3.00007-5

important in forensic situations. As neuropsychologists have become increasingly involved in forensic cases, the dependability of their information has been increasingly challenged.

The preeminent standard by which dependability is now assessed in forensic situations is *Daubert v. Merrell* (1993). This standard specifies that dependability, which is termed *reliability* by the court, is derived through the use of the scientific method. The *Daubert* standard states that information presented in legal settings must have been tested and validated. This eliminates information that fails to meet these criteria even if it is apparently correct. In *Chapple v. Ganger* (1994), the *Daubert* standard was applied to neuropsychological assessment. The judge's ruling was that the results of a fixed battery as a whole could be accepted as evidence but that the results of only some tests were acceptable from a flexible battery (Reed, 1996). This is because the flexible battery has not been tested and validated as a whole. The *Chapple* application, as this ruling has since been called, does not specifically eliminate the use of flexible batteries. Instead, the emphasis is on the dependability, or reliability, of the expert's testimony.

The question that has been forced on us is, how do we ensure the dependability of neuropsychological interpretations? In neuropsychological assessment, scientific methodology is, for all practical purposes, psychometric methodology (AERA, 1999; Anastasi & Urbina, 1997). In other words, psychometrics, with all its limitations, is the only assessment procedure that currently can produce dependable information for interpretation. Qualitative and inferential interpretation may, however, begin where psychometric analysis leaves off. The purpose of psychometric validation is to confirm that a procedure actually provides dependable knowledge as opposed to assuming it is accurate without evidence. A concept may be correct, but if it has never been proven to be correct using psychometric validation methods, then it cannot be considered to be dependable. Therefore, neuropsychological knowledge is dependable if, and only if, it has been validated using psychometric methods. However, although the application of dependability has been well established for individual tests, it has not been applied to test batteries to any great extent.

Test Batteries

From a psychometric point of view, there is a difference between a group of tests and a battery. A *battery* is defined as two or more tests that are related by an assessment method, such as by combination or comparison, that is used for a neuropsychological interpretation. In other words, if one uses the relationship between two or more tests to reach an interpretative conclusion, then one is employing a battery. The advantages of using a testing battery for neuropsychological assessment are well known (Lezak et al., 2004; Mihushina et al., 1999). A battery provides information about a person that cannot be obtained from individual tests used alone. This information comes from combinations and patterns that are derived from the relationships between the tests.

Many neuropsychologists contend that the validation of batteries is unnecessary because the individual tests used have already been validated. This contention is correct when tests are only used individually without relating them to each other. This is done when a hypothesis-testing format is employed and a single test is used to answer the hypothesis. However, heterogeneous or flexible-battery users, as observed in forensic cases, almost never consistently use a hypothesis-testing format. They often gain much of their information from the entire battery in a manner that could not be derived from the individual tests. When used in this way, statistical constraints apply to the interpretation of the battery results.

Standardization of a battery generally applies the procedures that are used for standardizing individual tests to the whole battery (Anastasi & Urbina, 1997, pp. 6–7). Batteries should be validated as thoroughly as individual tests for three reasons. First, interpretations derived from tests are validated, not the tests themselves (AERA, 1999, p. 9). When interpretations are derived from batteries, the whole battery must be validated. Second, batteries produce information that is uniquely different and impossible to obtain from individual tests. The results of the battery are not simply the sum of the individual tests. Third, the use of test batteries creates certain psychometric difficulties that reduce the effectiveness and accuracy of the individual tests that comprise the battery (Rosenfeld, Sands, & van Gorp, 2000; Russell & Russell, 2003). In other words, using individual tests in a battery places constraints on the validity of the results from the individual tests. This last caveat is particularly important and will be discussed in greater detail.

Capitalizing on Chance

The major problem with using interpretations derived from a single test in a battery is that tests do not statistically operate the same in a battery as they do individually. When used alone, a test has a certain probability that it is correct. For instance, if 1 standard deviation (SD) is used as a cutting point for impairment, then an individual test with a normal distribution will be impaired about 1/6 of the time. Consequently, it is relatively safe to state that impairment on the test indicates brain damage. The clinician will be correct about 5/6 of the time.

However, when a test is used in a battery, the probability of correctly identifying impairment is transformed into a percentage of the total number of tests that are generally impaired (Ingraham & Aiken, 1996). If all of the tests in the battery have a normal distribution, then using 1 SD as the indication of impairment will mean that about 1/6 of the tests in the battery will probably fall into the impaired range. A random error of 1/6 of the tests means that in a battery of 12 test scores, 2 scores can be expected to fall in the impaired range simply by chance. In a battery of 24 test scores, 4 scores should be expected to fall within the impaired range when no impairment is actually present. In forensic practice, it is common for neuropsychologists to employ batteries containing many more than 24 test scores. This phenomenon is similar to what occurs in research when one examines conclusions from many different tests. There is a certain probability that a test result will be significant because of random variation. Researchers are taught to avoid capitalizing on chance by instituting statistical controls in their analyses, such as the Bonferroni correction method or the Scheffé test (Gravetter & Wallnau, 2000). Unfortunately, many clinical neuropsychologists fail to extend this same logic to their assessment procedures.

Battery Interpretation

The implication of this psychometric battery characteristic is that the clinician cannot interpret the impairment of any single test score in a battery as an indication of brain damage. The flexible battery provides no psychometric justification for selecting any particular test results in the impaired range to support the hypothesis that a person has brain damage. Consequently, using a flexible battery provides dependable knowledge concerning whether a particular impaired test score indicates brain damage.

Another implication is that the proportion of impaired test scores that are required to indicate the existence of brain damage varies among batteries, depending on the tests selected for the battery. There is no way of knowing how many impaired test scores in any battery are required to indicate the existence of brain damage unless there is a validated index. Consequently, the user of a flexible battery has no way of knowing how many impaired results are necessary to reliably constitute a finding of brain damage because no indexes have been created. In addition, these indexes probably cannot be obtained for the flexible battery because its construction varies among clinicians. Dependability is sacrificed.

Conversely, a standardized battery has validation studies and indexes to dependably determine the number of impaired test results that are necessary to indicate brain dysfunction. The psychometric reliability of indexes in standardized batteries appears to be sound (Franzen, 2000, pp. 121–123, 140–141; Goldstein & Watson, 1998; Russell, 1992). An index also has a significant advantage over individual tests because, when properly constructed, the index is generally more accurate than any single test in a battery (Russell, 1995). In conclusion, a validated index from a standardized battery is more accurate and dependable in assessing the existence of brain dysfunction than any other psychometric method.

Using a flexible battery that has not been validated also presents other problems. Perhaps the most significant one is that the validity of the battery as a whole is no better than the single most valid test in the battery. Flexible batteries that have not been subjected to validation have no method for combining test scores other than clinical judgment. From a psychometric point of view, the examiner may as well only administer the single most valid test because he or she has no data to show that the additional tests increase the validity of the flexible battery.

Another concern is that the user of the flexible battery has no demonstrated dependable means of determining which tests correctly assess brain damage when the test results contradict each other. The clinician who interprets the impaired results while ignoring results in the normal range is capitalizing on chance and engaging in bad science. The only way to avoid this is to know both the relative accuracy of the various tests in the battery and the relative accuracy of any group of tests in the battery. The most accurate test or, usually, group of tests will provide the most accurate assessment. This information has been derived for the Halstead–Reitan Battery (HRB) and Halstead Russell Neuropsychological Evaluation System—Revised (HRNES–R; Russell & Starkey, 1993) but not for most other neuropsychological tests.

The Logic of Test Batteries

Shortly after 1950, both Reitan and Teuber developed methods to localize lesions with neuropsychological tests. Essentially, they both applied a similar method, which was to compare functions by means of two or more tests. Previously, assessment had depended on the score from single tests. Teuber (1955, 1975) developed the method of double dissociation, which involves a comparison of the effects of at least two tests as applied to the two hemispheres of the brain to determine the relationship between tests and the hemispheres. This method can be expanded into multiple dis-associations for global brain assessment (Russell, 1999, pp. 461–464).

At about the same time, Reitan independently began using comparisons of tests to localize brain lesions. He found that a minimum of two tests, which have an invariant relationship with each other and differing sensitivities to the area damaged, were required to localize lesions accurately. The invariant relationship was needed in order to provide a fixed ratio of their scores. This method works because different tests have differing sensitivities to different locations and brain conditions. Although focal brain damage may affect both tests to some degree, it will affect the test most sensitive to the damaged area more than tests that are less sensitive to the affected area. Thus, it is the ratio between test scores that is crucial for localization of injury, not the absolute score. This assessment relationship may be referred to as *Reitan's rule*. This method is essentially the multiple dissociation of tests. The more tests that are known to be sensitive to a location that are used in conjunction with tests that are not sensitive to the same location, the more accurate the assessment of localization. In this method of comparison, tests that are less sensitive to lesions in a specific area are just as important as tests that are more sensitive to damage in the same area. This same technique also can be applied to differential diagnosis (Russell & Polakoff, 1993).

The Problem of Stability

To compare scores from tests, the test scores must either be invariant or equivalent (Anastasi & Urbina, 1997; Ghiselli, Campbell, & Zedeck, 1981). Invariance creates stability or consistency across time. The relationship (ratio) between tests remains stable with a fixed battery of raw scores. Comparisons using raw scores can therefore occur in fixed batteries because the test scales are invariant and so retain the same relationship from testing to testing. In fact, much of the multivariate research in psychology has used raw scores that remain fixed during the research (Nunnally, 1978). This invariance in fixed batteries has the same stabilizing effect as equating the tests. The same cannot be said of flexible batteries.

The Problem of Equivalence

Even with fixed batteries, however, equivalent scores are desirable. Fixed raw scores do not have equivalent scales, so the expected ratios between the raw-score scales vary from one relationship to another. Because of the differences in scale units, the relationship between tests varies from pair to pair. For instance, a ratio of 0.5 may indicate that one pair of tests is impaired but another pair of tests may be normal. As such, each ratio used in a battery must be learned, which may require years of experience.

Equivalency ensures that the relationships between all test scales in the battery are the same. The same score indicates an equivalent amount of ability for all tests. A score such as 100, which indicates an average ability, will be the same for every test. Equivalency is obtained by means of standardized scale scores. The following are necessary for standardization: (1) the relationship between test scores must be invariant; (2) the norms must be derived from the same normative sample (co-norming) or equated by some method; and (3) there must be common metric units.

Unlike flexible batteries, tests in standardized batteries are co-normed. This procedure norms all of the tests in a battery simultaneously by employing the same sample and the same norming procedure. The "fixed" status of the battery is established by the norming process. Once the tests have been co-normed, they may be used individually or in groups without losing their fixed status because the norming process establishes the consistency of the relationships.

Because norms are so critical to a battery, the concept of standardization deserves more detailed examination. Different types of norms have been created for various fixed batteries. When choosing a set of norms to use, care should be taken to ensure that the norms are truly representative (Russell, 1997, pp. 15–65). Three methods are used to create norms for a standardized battery. The first method is to use stratified scores in which a proportion of the total sample was represented in each of the various demographic variables included in the battery. The second method is to use linear regression to predict the mean scores for the demographic variables of each subgroup or cell. The third method, which was used by Reitan to set norms for the Neuropsychological Deficit Scale (NDS; Reitan, 1986), is to derive scale norms from experience rather than from statistical data. The NDS has since been thoroughly validated (Russell, 1995). The primary problem that neuropsychologists have when using the various sets of norms occurs when the norms are not stratified or adjusted for age and education.

In flexible batteries, when different norms for each test are used, the assumption is that the norms for the different tests are equivalent regardless of their norming sample. Most methods of placing tests in flexible batteries assume that the various test norm samples all represent the entire United States. However, no neuropsychological sets of norms have come close to representing the whole average population of the United States, with the exception of the Wechsler tests (Russell, 1997). This assumption of normative equivalence is contrary to all of the rules of standardization in the literature (AERA, 1999, pp. 49–60; Anastasi & Urbina, 1997, pp. 66–70; Ghiselli et al., 1981, pp. 37–55). The assumption of normality is especially questionable for "voluntary" norms (Russell, 2005). So far, two of the criteria necessary for equivalency have been satisfied by fixed batteries but not flexible batteries. We will now look at the final criteria, the common metric.

Initially, standardization requires a common metric such as z-scores or t-scores. Standardized batteries contain a common metric for the scale scores. To overcome this limitation in a flexible battery, Lezak et al. (2004) and Mitrushina et al. (1999) have advocated transforming scores to standard scores. This would provide the common metric or scale scores for the tests. One such method of using *z*-scores to combine test results is the Rohling Interpretative Method (RIM; Miller & Rohling, 2001). It is a definite advancement in establishing an equivalency between tests in neuropsychology that could be used in a flexible manner. However, at this point, the primary problem with RIM is that the scores from various tests do not have equivalent nouns (Ghiselli et al., 1981, pp. 37–55). In fact, for equating tests, adequate common norms are more important than equivalency of metric units (Anastasi & Urbina, 1997, pp. 66–70). Dependable knowledge can only be produced by batteries if they are either fixed or standardized, which currently means that they are co-normed. Co-norming on its own overcomes most of the problems of equating tests. It would be difficult to find a flexible battery that is composed entirely of co-normed tests. By comparison, fixed batteries such as the Luria–Nebraska Neuropsychological Battery (Golden, Purisch, & Hammeke, 1991) and the group of standardized versions of the HRB all use either simultaneous norming or co-norms. Having failed all three criteria for equivalence, the information derived from the flexible battery cannot be considered dependable.

Clinical Judgment

An alternative validation method to formal psychometric analysis is clinical judgment. Many neuropsychologists who use flexible batteries claim that they are not concerned about the formal psychometric requirements for combining and comparing tests in a battery because clinical judgment is the basis for any forthcoming interpretations. Although it is not a formal psychometric method, clinical judgment can be subject to validation in the sense that the accuracy of such judgments may be validated using accepted psychometric methods. Consequently, a complete examination of the psychometric status of neuropsychological batteries requires a discussion of clinical judgments. The most complete examination of clinical judgments has been published in book form by Garb (1998), who also published an article looking specifically at clinical judgments in neuropsychology (Garb & Schramke, 1996). Garb found good interrater reliability between clinical judgments when fixed batteries were used. However, he found no evidence that clinical judgments using flexible neuropsychological batteries were reliable. He was also able to locate interrater reliability data for flexible batteries related to regular psychological tests. The results of these studies found very poor reliability between test raters (Garb, 1998, p. 13).

Many studies have examined the validity of clinical judgments in neuropsychology. A meta-analysis by Garb and Schramke (1996) found an overall hit rate of 84% for standardized batteries assessing the existence of brain damage and a hit rate of 89% for studies comparing right- versus left-hemisphere damage. Conversely, no validation studies of clinical judgment using a flexible battery have been published (Garb, 1998, pp. 157–162). The information derived from flexible batteries using clinical judgment must consequently be considered undependable.

Many neuropsychologists claim that it is their experience that allows them to interpret the results from flexible batteries. In regard to experience, the few studies in the area that have been published indicate that, beyond the graduate-school level, there is almost no relationship between the amount of experience of the clinician and the accuracy of his or her assessment (Garb, 1998, pp. 167–169; Garb & Schramke, 1996). This is true of all psychologists. In addition, as far as expertise is concerned, neuropsychologists certified by the American Board of Professional Psychology have not been found to be more accurate than neuropsychologists without this accreditation (Garb, 1998, pp. 169–244).

Conclusion

Testing batteries must be examined and found valid in order to produce dependable information. For psychometric validation, published studies have demonstrated that all major fixed and standardized batteries are valid, but there are no studies in the literature that support the validity of flexible batteries. Flexible batteries often rely on the interpretation of individual tests, but some test results in a battery will fall in the impaired range simply because of random variation rather than being a reflection of brain dysfunction. Because there is no known method that can determine which specific tests in the flexible battery are truly indicative of brain damage, the clinician who interprets these results is capitalizing on chance and cannot dependably diagnose brain injury.

Further, localization and diagnostic assessments use test comparisons. Dependable comparisons of tests requires a standardized battery in which tests are invariant, have equivalent norms, and share a common metric. Studies have validated the ability to accurately compare tests in a standardized battery but not in flexible batteries. In addition, only standardized batteries have been demonstrated to foster reliable and valid clinical judgments.

In summary, in forensic situations, the expert witness who uses a standardized battery is the only psychologist who can provide dependable testimony interpreting psychometric test data as a whole to the court. The expert witness who uses a flexible battery cannot provide dependable evidence derived from the battery as a whole, although he or she may present the results of individual tests. Overall, this review supports the continued development of standardized batteries and challenges those who use flexible batteries to validate their work with empirical methods.

Summary

Dependability is a fundamental requirement for neuropsychological assessment. Neuropsychological knowledge is dependable only if it has been validated using psychometric methods. Because batteries are used for interpretations, the psychometric validation methods that are acceptable for individual tests must be applied to batteries to produce dependable information. Although the standardized battery has been validated, the flexible battery has not. Because of the probability that some tests will be impaired by chance, a flexible battery cannot produce dependable interpretations by selecting or combining test results. Localization and diagnostic assessments are obtained by comparisons. Comparisons require that the tests in a battery are invariant or have equivalent norms along with a common metric. Standardized batteries meet these criteria, but flexible batteries do not. Consequently, clinical judgment applied to a flexible battery cannot provide dependable knowledge beyond that which could be provided by a single validated individual test.

References

American Educational Research Association, American Psychological Association, & National Council on Measurement in Education (AERA). (1999). *Standards for educational and psychological testing*. Washington, DC: Author.

Anastasi, A., & Urbina, S. (1997). *Psychological testing* (7th ed.). Upper Saddle River, NJ: Prenctice Hall.

Bauer, R. M. (2000). The flexible battery approach to neuropsychological assessment. In R. D. Vanderploeg (Ed.), *Clinicians guide to neuropsychological assessment* (pp. 419–448) (2nd ed.). Hillsdale, NJ: Lawrence Erlbaum Associates.

Chapple v. Ganger, 851F. Supp. 1481 (E.D. Wash., 1994).

Daubert v. Merrell, Dow Pharmaceuticals, Inc. 113S. CT. 2786 (1993).

Franzen, M. D. (2000). *Reliability and validity in neuropsychological assessment* (2nd ed.). New York: Kluwer Academic/Plenum.

Garb, H. N. (1998). *Studying the clinician: Judgment research and psychological assessment.* Washington, DC: American Psychological Association.

Garb, H. N., & Schramke, C. J. (1996). Judgment research and neuropsychological assessment: A narrative review and meta-analysis. *Psychological Bulletin,*, *120*, 140–153.

Ghiselli, E. E., Campbell, J. P., & Zedeck, S. (1981). *Measurement theory for the behavioral sciences.* San Francisco: W.H. Freeman.

Golden, C. J. ., Purisch, A. D., & Hammeke., T. A. (1991). *Luria–Nebraska neuropsychological battery: Forms I and 11. [Manual].* Los Angeles: Western Psychological Services.

Goldstein, G. (1997). The clinical utility of standardized or flexible battery approaches to neuropsychological assessment. In G. Goldstein & T. M. Incagnoli (Eds.), *Contemporary approaches to neuropsychological assessment* (pp. 67–91). New York: Plenum.

Goldstein, G., & Watson, J. R. (1998). Test–retest reliability of the Halstead–Reitan Battery and the WAIS in a neuropsychiatric population. *Clinical Psychologist*, *3*(3), 265–273.

Gravetter, F. J., & Wallnau, L. B. (2000). Statistics for the behavioral sciences (5th ed.). Belmont, CA: Wadsworth/Thompson Learning.

Incagnoli, T. (1986). Current directions and future trends in clinical neuropsychology. In T. Incagnoli, G. Godstein, & C. G. Golden (Eds.), *Clinical application of neuropsychological test batteries* (pp. 1–44). New York: Plenum.

Ingraham, L. J., & Aiken, C. B. (1996). An empirical approach to determining criteria for abnormality in test batteries with multiple measures. *Neuropsychology*, *10*, 120–124.

Kane, R. L. (1991). Standardized and flexible batteries in neuropsychology: An assessment update. *Neuropsychology Review*, *2*, 281–339.

Lezak, M. D., Howieson, D. B., & Loring, D. W. (2004). *Neuropsychological assessment* (4th ed.). Oxford, NY: Oxford University Press.

Miller, L. S., & Rohling, M. L. (2001). A statistical interpretive method for neuropsychological test data. *Neuropsychology Review*, *11*(3), 143–169.

Mitrushina, M. N., Boone, K., & D'Elia, L. F. (1999). *Handbook of normative data for neuropsychological assessment*. New York: Oxford University Press.

Nunnally, J. C. (1978). *Psychometric theory* (2nd ed.). New York: McGraw-Hill.

Reed, J. E. (1996). Fixed vs. flexible neuropsychological test batteries under the Daubert standard for admissibility of scientific evidence. *Behavioral Science and Law*, *14*, 315–322.

Reitan, R. M. (1986). *The Neuropsychological Deficit Scale for adults: Computer program*. Tucson: Neuropsychology Press.

Rosenfeld, B., Sands, S. A., & van Gorp, W. G. (2000). Have we forgotten the base rate problem? Methodological issues in the detection of distortion. *Archives of Clinical Neuropsychology*, *15*(4), 349–359.

Russell, E. W. (1992). Reliability of the Halstead Impairment Index: A simulation and reanalysis of Matarazzo et al. (1974). *Neuropsychology*, *6*, 251–259.

Russell, E. W. (1995). The accuracy of automated and clinical detection of brain damage and lateralization in neuropsychology. *Neuropsychology Review*, *5*(1), 1–68.

Russell, E. W. (1997). Developments in the psychometric foundations of neuropsychological assessment. In G. Goldstein & T. Incagnoli (Eds.), *Contemporary approaches to neuropsychological assessment* (pp. 15–65). New York: Plenum.

Russell, E. W. (1999). The cognitive-metric, fixed battery approach to neuropsychological assessment. In R. Vanderploeg (Ed.), *Clinician's guide to neuropsychological assessment* (2nd ed.). Hillsdale, NJ: Lawrence Erlbaum Associates.

Russell, E. W. (2005). Norming subjects for the Halstead–Reitan. Battery. *Archives of Clinical Neuropsychology*, *20*(4), 479–484.

Russell, E. W., & Polakoff, D. (1993). Neuropsychological test patterns in men for Alzheimer's and multi-infarct dementia. *Archives of Clinical Neuropsychology*, *8*, 327—43.

Russell, E. W., & Russell, S. L. K. (2003). Twenty ways and more of diagnosing brain damage when there is none. *Journal of Controversial Medical Claims*, *10*(1), 1–14.

Russell, E. W., & Starkey, R. 1. (1993). *Halstead–Russell Neuropsychological Evaluation System [Manual and computer program]*. Los Angeles: Western Psychological Services.

Teuber, H. L. (1955). Physiological psychology. *Annual Review of Psychology*, *6*, 267–296.

Teuber H. L. (1975). Recovery of function after brain injury. In *Ciba Foundation Symposium 34, Outcome of Severe Damage to the Central Nervous System* (pp. 159–190). Amsterdam: Elsevier.

8 Justification of Neuropsychological Batteries

If we look at all sciences . . . , we find that the constant and universal feature of science is its general method, which consists in the persistent search for truth, constantly asking: is it so? To what extent is it so? Why is it so?—that is, What general conditions or considerations determine it to be so?

(Cohen and Nagel, 1962, p. 192)

[In regard to the diagnosis of the minimal conscious state and vegetative state:]

The other new tool was the JFK Coma Recovery Scale. This consists of more than 20 clinical tests and is reckoned not only to enable doctors to distinguish patients in a vegetative state from those with minimal consciousness, but also to identify those who were previously in a minimally conscious state but have emerged from it. It is widely accepted as giving an accurate diagnosis of these conditions. But is it being adhered to?

The work by the Liege team suggests not. They compared the diagnoses of 103 patients according to the consensus opinion of the medical staff looking after them with that determined by the coma recovery scale. Of the patients they looked at, 44 had been diagnosed by a staff as vegetative. The coma scale, however, disagreed. It suggested 18 of those 44 were in a minimally conscious state . . . error rate around 40%. . . . It also suggested that four of the 40 patients whose consensus diagnosis was "minimally conscious state" had actually emerged from that state.

Dr. Laureys's measured conclusion is that neurologists do not like their skills to be replaced or upstaged by a scale.

(The Economist, Diagnosing comas, 2009)

This chapter is concerned with the justification of neuropsychological methodology. Neuropsychological assessment is an applied form of science that uses psychometric methods to create reliable information concerning a subject. In essence, to be reliable and thus acceptable, particularly in forensic cases, any statement concerning the science of neuropsychology must be derived and supported by a validated methodology. As discussed previously, only justification by scientific procedures produces reliable methods and information. In neuropsychology, scientific methods are primarily psychometric methods.

However, there is a division of opinion as to whether scientific (psychometric) principles in assessment should apply to the entire assessment battery or only

The Scientific Foundation of Neuropsychological Assessment. DOI: 10.1016/B978-0-12-416029-3.00008-7

to individual tests within a battery. Currently, the majority of neuropsychologists believe they are using scientific methodology when they use psychometrically valid individual tests (American Academy of Neurology, 2007). As such, the major controversy in neuropsychology now concerns the application of psychometric principles to batteries of tests (Bauer, 2000).

The contention of this book is that scientific (psychometric) principles apply to the entire brain-function analysis in assessment—that is, the *testing* process. (This does not include the context of testing, which is the nonpsychometric information that a neuropsychologist may use to support his or her opinions.) As such, the brain-function analysis process includes all interpretative results derived from neuropsychological psychometric procedures in the assessment of an individual, not simply individual test results. The purpose of this chapter is to support this contention.

There is no major argument in neuropsychology concerning the application of psychometrics to individual tests. The AERA et al. standards (American Educational Research Association, American Psychological Association, & National Council on Measurement in Education, 1999) for creating, validating, and determining their accuracy have been developed over the last century (Anastasi & Urbina, 1997; Ghiselli, Campbell, & Zedeck, 1981; Lezak, Howieson, & Loring, 2004; Nunnally & Bernstein, 1994).

However, these standards have seldom been specifically applied to test batteries as integrated batteries in which the relationships between tests are used. Rather batteries such as the Wechsler scales (Anastasi & Urbina, 1997, p. 214–222; Wechsler, 1997) are treated as if they were single tests (AERA et al., 1999, pp. 49, 123–124) in which the index score represents the entire battery. As such, they are single procedures. Otherwise, the relationships of tests to each other in a battery have not been examined. This is rather surprising because major writings in neuropsychology advocate the use of batteries as a procedure rather than individual tests (Lezak et al., 2004, pp. 17–18). In neuropsychology, a battery is used as a single procedure.

In this regard, factor analysis has been used to divide the tests in a battery into factors, which are essentially domains. This provides more clarity concerning the brain functions that are being measured. Nevertheless, the relationships between factors, as represented by tests, have hardly been examined in neuropsychological studies. Patterns of relationships are still largely unknown outside of the Halstead–Reitan Battery (HRB) lore and practitioners of that approach. The relationship of batteries to justification has not been studied to any great extent.

Even in this regard, there is general agreement that an adequate evaluation of brain functioning requires a battery of tests (Lezak et al., 2004, pp. 17–18). The problem involves the way in which psychometrics is applied to the justification and interpretation of a battery. Consequently, the emphasis in this chapter will be primarily on test batteries.

Discovery and Justification

As discussed in previous chapters, the methodology of science distinguishes two major aspects of science: *discovery* and *justification* (Toulmin, 2006, p. 34). Discovery is the creative process that innovates new concepts, theories, and procedures.

This chapter will deal with the justification of neuropsychological assessment methods. In doing so, it is an expansion of Chapter 7, "The Fundamental Psychometric Status of Neuropsychological Batteries." This chapter will be concerned with a detailed examination of the methodological issues involved in neuropsychological justification related to neuropsychological assessment.

Nature of Justification

Justification is the process of ensuring the reliability of a method or procedure such that the information derived from that procedure is also reliable. A product of discovery may be innovative and brilliant, but until it has been justified or validated it can neither be accepted as part of the body of scientific knowledge and methods for further scientific development nor for practical use such as forensics.

Although the concept of *justification* is central to philosophy, it is seldom used in neuropsychology, except as presupposed by terms such as *validation* and *standardization*. Much of the basis for this discussion has been examined as components of science. Here the scientific basis of neuropsychology will be briefly examined again, with an emphasis on neuropsychological assessment.

Assessment, Discovery, and Justification

This distinction between discovery (investigation) and justification is crucial in obtaining an understanding of the assessment procedures, particularly as applied to forensic neuropsychology. Many of the assessment procedures may be quite applicable as discovery procedures, but if they have not been justified, they have no scientific reliability.

Concerning the various levels of neuropsychological science, the relationship between discovery and justification is somewhat different for each level. For neuroscience, discovery produces theory and new methodologies that are often different from psychometrics. However, for the theory to be accepted, the scientific theory must be justified. For the most part, applied neuropsychology depends on justified theory and methodology derived from neuroscience, but it has its area of specialization, which is derived from psychometrics.

At the level of applied neuropsychology, both research and individual assessment use discovery and justification, whereas research methods involve discovery in the development of procedures and creating information and theory. For assessment procedures to be scientifically acceptable, however, they must be justified. A great deal of the work in neuropsychological research consists in this justification process. This process consists in the examination, standardization, and validation of those procedures.

As such, the interrelationship between the two forms of applied neuropsychology, research and assessment practice, is quite close. The practitioner uses the procedures created and justified by the researches. In fact, often in neuropsychology the researchers who discover new procedures are also practitioners. This provides an experience and knowledge basis for the development of procedures.

As applied to assessment practice, discovery may uncover the apparent condition of a patient. Discovery in itself may be sufficient in a hospital setting, where the object is to discover a neurological condition or support a presumed condition as in "rule out" some pathology. However, discovery or investigation does not ensure the reliability of an apparent condition, a methodology, or a concept. Consequently, justification is necessary when it is important that the information concerning a condition be reliable or dependable. In forensics, justification is crucial for determining the reliability or dependability of information used in court proceedings. Justification in forensics is equivalent to what medicine is now advocating as evidence-based treatment (Bland, 2000, p. 1). Forensics, however, has always been evidence based.

Reliability

In science, it is the justification of procedures that creates reliable knowledge. The justification methodology of science is used to ensure that the information derived from a methodology is reliable (*Daubert v. Merrell*, 1993; Nagel, 1961; Russell, Russell, & Hill, 2005). As previously demonstrated, the essence of science is its methodology to justify the reliability of information. Thus, justification is the use of scientific methodology to ensure the reliability of information or methodologies in research and assessment.

Reliability[1] means that information will be invariant from one equivalent situation to another. Consequently, validated information or theories can be used in assessment with confidence in the reliability of that information or theories. The justification by means of psychometrics for all standardized scientific procedures is the assurance of invariance in test and battery construction. The basic purpose of the neuropsychological assessment is to provide reliable information concerning the functioning of the human brain for both forensic and medical purposes. Consequently, validated psychometric procedures ensure that the information derived from neuropsychological assessment can be reliability generalized to the person tested as a basis for interpretation.

In neuropsychology, psychometrics is the only assessment procedure that can currently produce reliable information for interpretation (AERA et al., 1999; Anastasi & Urbina, 1997). Qualitative and inferential interpretation may be the means of discovery, but the purpose of psychometric justification is to confirm that a procedure actually provides reliable knowledge. A concept may be correct, but if it has never been demonstrated to be correct using psychometric justification, then it cannot be considered reliable. Therefore, neuropsychological knowledge is reliable if, and only if, it has been justified using psychometric methods.

The concept of reliability is especially important in forensic situations. In forensics, reliability is the assurance that the information presented by an expert witness

[1] In psychology, the term *reliable* as used in its general sense is easily confused with a commonly used specific meaning of that term. In psychometrics, reliable is used to indicate that a test is consistent internally or consistent from one administration to another. Consequently, to prevent confusion, this chapter will attempt to specify when *reliable* is used in its psychometric sense.

is true—that is, it correctly represents the situation it is supposed to represent. In addition, validated research usually provides a measure of the accuracy of the information derived from the procedure.

The standard by which reliability is now assessed in forensic situations is *Daubert v. Merrell* (1993). This standard specifies that scientific reliability be derived by the scientific method. The *Daubert* standard states that scientific information presented in legal settings must have been tested and validated. In this regard, *Daubert v. Merrell* (1993) stipulates that the purpose of science is to replace general acceptance with the *testing* process that is more reliable. Methods that are generally accepted within a field of science are only acceptable when they were justified by established scientific procedures. This is the reason the *Daubert* statement gives for using the scientific method in court ["Requirement under Federal Rule of Evidence that expert's testimony pertain to 'scientific knowledge' establishes standard of evidentiary reliability." Fed. Rules Evid., Rule 702, 28 U.S.C.A. (*Daubert v. Merrell* (1993)]. To be admissible in court, scientific knowledge must be derived from a scientific method that is both reliable and relevant.

Requirements for Justification

To demonstrate scientifically the reliability of a procedure or a theory, several scientific requirements are universally accepted. As discussed in Chapter 1, these are objectivity, repeatability, and testability. When applied to neuropsychology assessment research, these scientific requirements become procedure development, standardization, and validation.

Objectivity

As previously discussed, a primary requirement for scientific observation is methodological objectivity. The methodology and the results must be public—that is, they can be observed by any qualified person using the appropriate instruments. Because they are objective, they are teachable and publishable. One problem with clinical judgment is that it is seldom objective and consequently is often difficult to teach and its results seldom publishable. In forensics, because clinical judgment is not objective, its reliability is dependent on the "expertise" of the expert witness.

Objectivity is primarily related to the creation of neuropsychological instruments, tests, and batteries. One major requirement for objectivity is that the observations can be quantified. In science generally, and especially in neuropsychology, the requirement for objectivity implies the existence of instrumentation or procedures. In neuropsychology, instrumentation largely consists of tests and test batteries. These instrumental procedures are necessary to transform clinical observations into quantitative measures. Quantification concerns how much of an attribute is present in a phenomenon (Nunnally & Bernstein, 1994, p. 5). Instruments create a proportional transformation of the amount of some ability into a form of measurement. This may be transforming a person's spatial relations ability into a form of measurement such as the block design score. In psychology, the instrument transforms a subjective attribute or phenomena into an objective measurable entity.

Testability

Another major aspect of science is testability. As an applied science, neuropsychology assessment uses testability in the justification of procedures as well as a means to support a theory. Basically, testing consists of demonstrating that a predicted concept or methodology is correct. (A correct methodology is one that performs or measures what it is purported or designed to do.)

The process of demonstrating—that is, testing—the correctness of a concept or procedure becomes complex, however, when one examines what *demonstration* means. A *test* or *testing procedure* has several parts.

1. The first is the question. For instance, does a test indicate the existence of brain damage because of head trauma?
2. The procedure or test to be examined, such as a proposed test for brain damage, is selected or created.
3. The question is framed as a hypothesis that predicts that this procedure is sensitive to brain damage because of head trauma.
4. The hypothesis requires a criterion that is predicted. In this example, the criterion is the known existence of brain damage because of head trauma.
5. The correctness of the criterion is ensured by a history of head trauma along with various other validated medical tests such as the Glasgow Coma Scale, electroencephalograms, and brain scans.
6. The testing process is then applied. It consists in selection of two groups of subjects—one with brain damage and one without. (Ideally, all of the subjects would be randomly assigned to the two groups and the experimental process would be applied to one group. However, in the case of brain damage, random assignment obviously is not possible. Consequently, the two groups must be equated in some manner to demonstrate their similarity.)
7. Finally, a statistical method is used to determining whether the test procedure can separate a group of brain-damaged subjects from an equivalent group of normal subjects to a significant degree. This method establishes a null or possibly false hypothesis that the procedure cannot separate the two groups and the statistical method demonstrates that the null hypothesis is false.

Thus, when examined closely, the simple concept of a test becomes complex if it is a reliable method.

In regard to psychometric justification, testability of an assessment procedure involves test and battery creation as well as standardization. Testing, whether in general practice or in forensics, only applies to a single score from a validated test or other validated procedure.

In psychometric science, however, testability is validation. In other words, validation is testing a procedure or a concept to determine whether it is reliable. The accuracy of the score from the procedure is validated. When validation is regarded as hypothesis testing, the hypothesis is that an instrument's score measures what it purports to measure or provides accurate score information concerning a predicted attribute or phenomenon. Validation ensures that the information derived from the procedure's score is reliable because it has been tested and found to be reliable.

The types of validation procedures will be discussed later, but in one way or another they all involve *predictability*. Predictability is one of the accepted methods of validation. Construct formation is a method of creating concepts that, like theories, may be tested as hypotheses and whose results are predicted by hypotheses.

Repeatability

Another requirement of scientific observation is *repeatability*—that is, the phenomenon and methodology can be repeated by anyone who is qualified and has the instruments to make the observations. *Repeatable* applies to testability in that to be scientifically acceptable, a procedure must be consistent to be repeatable. Thus, in neuropsychology, repeatability is made possible by the requirement for consistency (Russell, 2000b, pp. 456–458).

The primary method of ensuring consistency of neuropsychological procedures is *standardization*. The purpose of standardization is to ensure that if the test or procedure is repeated and the subject's brain function is the same, then the procedure will produce the same result.

Cross Validation

In this regard, a primary requirement of testing or validation is *cross validation*. If a concept has not been cross validated or the test that supports the concept has not been repeated, then the concept is as much discovery as justification. In mathematics or science, there is a saying that is roughly, "Say it three times and it is true." In other words, if a procedure is checked and the result is different from the first time the procedure was performed, then one does not know whether the initial trial or the checked result is correct. The method of determining the correctness is to check the procedure the third time. If it agrees with one of the trials, then that trial is correct. This implies, of course, that when there is disagreement between test results, the only solution is to compare the two tests using the same group of brain-damaged and normal subjects. The only large study of this kind that has been reported is in the manual for the Halstead–Russell Neuropsychological Evaluation System—Revised (HRNES-R) (Russell & Starkey, 2001a, pp. 38–41). More studies of this type would solve many disputes in neuropsychology.

Justification in Applied Research and Assessment

In applied scientific neuropsychology, the difference between research and assessment is quite simple. In research, two groups—an experimental group and a control group—are statistically compared to examine a hypothesis represented by the experimental group. The null hypothesis is that there is no difference between the two groups. Statistics are used, such as *t*-tests, analyses of variance (ANOVAs), and effect-size measurements that compare groups. If there is a significant difference between the experimental and control group, this rejects the null hypothesis and thus supports the experimental hypothesis.

By contrast, in assessment an individual is examined, possibly using assessment hypothesis testing or pattern analysis, in order to explain the individual's condition by a theory or concept. The procedures may indicate the probability of the existence of the condition. Although related, applied research and assessment often require different methods.

This also applies to the difference between discovery and justification. Research and assessment may use either discovery or justification. In research discovery, a neuropsychologist's experience with any test or group of tests may reveal new information or the possibility of a new procedure. Further work may eventuate in the construction of a new test procedure. In contrast, justification applies to the validation of that procedure.

In assessment, discovery applies to the initial conjecture or hypothesis as to the condition of a subject, whereas justification requires using validated procedures to reliably determine the existence of the condition. Obviously, discovery and justification overlap, and complete justification is seldom if ever possible. On the other hand, discovery procedures are not applicable beyond the initial supposition phase and must be justified to be accepted as reliable.

The Assessment Problem

Almost all assessment involves an N of 1 or the examination of a single individual, whereas research is based on at least a moderately large sample because a large number of subjects reduces random fluctuations. The assessment problem is how to examine an individual reliably when there is only $N = 1$. The solution has been developed over the history of psychometrics. It involves norms and a proportional transformation.

In assessment, the equivalent of a control group consists of norms. These provide the "random" sample of a population that the single subject represents. It also provides a measure—random error—of the expected accuracy of the test. In part, this solves the problem of single-subject assessment using a single test.

Data Transformations of Statistical Status

Because of the psychometric methods that constitute the basis for assessment procedures, a subtle transformation occurs in the nature of the data or information as one proceeds from research to assessment with individual tests and finally to assessment using test batteries. These changes will have different effects on the statistical justification methods used for each type of process. These changes will be briefly described so that they may be recognized in each of the following different psychometric conditions.

The transformation is from the proportion of subjects in research versus normal groups to the assessment probability that a subject belongs to a particular diagnostic group using a single test. Finally, in a group of tests, the probability changes into the number of tests in a battery that may be impaired by chance.

Research Studies

In research studies that compare two groups, the nature of the data that are used is the proportion of subjects in each group. For instance, in comparing brain-damaged to normal subjects, the concern is with the number or proportion of subjects in each of the overlapping distributions. Standard statistics, such as ANOVAs or correlations, are employed to determine whether the two distributions are significantly different or significantly similar in correlations. Various statistics may be applied to determine such differences or similarities.

Assessment Methodology

In assessment with a single test used for a single individual, the proportion of subjects in each group becomes a matter of an individual probability. In other words, when the research findings are applied to the assessment of individual patients, the proportional status is changed into a probability. For instance, the 80% portion of brain-damaged subjects in the research brain-damaged group is transformed into an 80% chance that the subject falls into the brain-damaged range. As such, there is also an 80% chance that the individual will be diagnosed correctly.

The primary method for determining these probabilities is through the operating characteristics (Retzlaff & Gibertini, 2000) for an individual (Bayesian statistics). This includes measures such as sensitivity, selectivity, and predictive power. Another way to state this is through the proportion of false and true negatives and positives (Slick, 2006, pp. 20–24).

Operating characteristics more accurately evaluate an individual condition occurring in assessment than more traditional research statistics such as *t*-tests or ANOVAs. These traditional methods are not specifically designed to help the clinician's situation in which the *N* is 1 (Retzlaff & Gibertini, 2000, pp. 277–299). Because traditional research statistics compare an entire group with another group to determine the existence of a significant difference, the patients at the extremes of the groups as well as those that are close to the cut point exert an effect on the statistic. In fact, generally the effect exerted by a score increases the further from the cut point the score lies. This becomes especially problematic in a skewed distribution, which characterizes almost all brain-damage distributions (Dodrill, 1987; Russell, 1987). Thus, the conventional statistics may give the impression that the scale is more accurate in assessing an individual than it is.

When a neuropsychologist is dealing with a specific individual, the examiner wants to know whether that patient falls within one group or another, such as within a brain-damaged or a control group. The cut point is crucial. When using operating characteristics the severity of impairment has no effect on the statistic other than determining which side of a cut point the subject falls. All members of a group on each side of the cut point are statistically treated equally no matter how extreme is their impairment. Consequently, for clinical purposes, in which the question is determining the existence of a condition, statistics based on the operating characteristics of a cut point are more accurate (Retzlaff & Gibertini, 2000).

These cut points only specify which group, such as brain-damaged or no brain-damaged, an individual belongs. However, although it has almost never been done, the probability for having brain damage may be set up as a range of scores, using intervals on a scale as cut points. Then a particular score would indicate the probability that the person has that particular attribute (Russell & Starkey, 2001b, Appendix F, p. 26). This, of course, would increase the reliability of a diagnosis, such as brain damage. A higher score would indicate a higher probability of damage.

Use of Batteries

From a psychometric point of view, there is a difference between using a single test and using a single test in a group of tests. In hypothesis testing, when more than one test is used, the tests become a battery of tests and new constraints apply. As the number of tests in a battery increases, the probability that a test is impaired by chance increases. This introduces several problems, one being that there is no statistical method of determining whether a single test is impaired by chance or by a neurological condition.

Forensic Application

In forensic cases, these probability characteristics are particularly important. One major criterion of the *Daubert* standard for determining whether an expert's testimony was based on scientifically reliable studies was whether a technique considered "known or potential rate of error, and existence and maintenance of standards controlling the technique's operation" (*Daubert v. Merrell*, 1993, vol. 28, 2789). In a neuropsychological or medical setting, the primary method for demonstrating potential rate of error is by means of operating characteristics.

Psychometric Method Versus Application

Concerning the neuropsychological development of assessment psychometrics, the complexity of statistical analytic methods has far outstripped the development of the clinical methods for creating and employing tests in neuropsychology, as well as in other parts of psychology. It is of little use to have complex statistics when the normally used test procedures remain in a primitive state. Regardless of the sophistication of the statistics, the old saying that was applied to computers is equally applicable to neuropsychological analysis: "GIGO," or "garbage in, garbage out."

Base-Rate Problem

Base rates (classification statistics) are examples of a situation in which statistics has developed beyond practice. Theoretically, the advocates of base rates are correct in that the base rate should be taken into consideration in achieving the most accurate operational characteristics (Larrabee, 2005, pp. 13–16). However, for practical reasons this is seldom possible in research, much less in assessment (Russell, 2004).

The first and primary reason for this difficulty is that base rates are highly variable. For instance, the base rate of head trauma in the general population is so low that the examiner should always choose the normal group to classify a person. In contrast, the base rate in a hospital trauma unit would require one to always choose the pathology. Second, the base rate for small populations such as in hospitals changes almost daily, and the cut points would need to be changed daily. Finally, if each test has its own base rate, then the tests cannot be compared. Because of these problems, the best solution is to use a base rate of 0.5, which is the same for both experimental and normal groups (Russell, 2004).

Interpretation and Context

Before dealing with the justification of batteries, an aspect of a neuropsychological examination especially relevant to a forensic report needs to be addressed. A complete neuropsychological assessment has two parts that are often not distinguished during the assessment process. The first part describes the functioning of the brain at the time of the assessment by means of a brain-function analysis. Brain-function analysis is that part of assessment that is derived from psychometric procedures and psychometrics alone.

The second part specifies the meaning of this brain functioning in terms of the patient's context. Although contextual information derived from a referral, medical situation, and history is not derived from testing, such information is necessary to integrate the psychometric results into an accurate, complete interpretation of an individual's condition.

Contextual factual material and neuropsychological analysis results are logically integrated to form a complete interpretative opinion. At times, the context may require modification or qualification of the psychometric analysis because of the particular circumstances of the individual and the incident.

This distinction is necessary to clarify many of the issues related to neuropsychological assessment. Brain-function analysis includes research for developing and validating psychometric assessment instruments as well as the application of those instruments in the assessment of an individual subject. Thus, brain-function analysis indicates that the information was obtained exclusively from neuropsychological testing.

The term *context* includes all information used in a complete interpretation that is not derived from the brain-function analysis. This includes the patient's medical history, diagnosis, affective condition, academic history, relevant social history, and any other material that might be relevant to an assessment of the individual patient.

This distinction is crucial because most of the psychometric research on assessment procedures applies specifically to brain-function analysis with no direct reference to the context. In a specific assessment case, the information that can be derived from brain-function analysis is distinct from that derived from the context. Many neuropsychologists confuse these two processes, so it is difficult to know whether their conclusions were derived from brain-function analysis or the context.

The Limits of Science

In any assessment, the methodology only extends to a certain point in determining the probability of an attribute. In clinical assessment, including forensic cases, the answers to questions related to the context of an event may not be obtainable through psychometric, that is, scientific methods. Either the procedures to obtain such answers have not been developed or aspects of the particular situation are idiosyncratic so that no formalized procedures are applicable. In such situations, one must depend on methods that are not strictly scientific, such as unvalidated clinical judgment, logic, common sense, individual observation, and rational inferences.

Context and Clinical Judgment

At the limits of science, clinical judgment becomes crucial in determining an assessment. For instance, a patient who does very poorly on neuropsychological tests may be genetically mentally retarded rather than brain damaged. In this case, the history of the patient becomes crucial in the clinical judgment that the patient, who received low scores on tests, was mentally retarded. In addition, a patient may have a limited but important impairment because of brain damage, particularly with a chronic focal condition, such that his overall brain-damage index score may be within the normal range. Nevertheless, for a particular type of occupation the person has been impaired by a focal brain injury. This type of focal injury can occur without evidence of the lesion on any neurological scanning technique. At times, such a focal injury can be determined using clinical judgment by examining the pattern of damage on a neuropsychological battery.

Consequently, the examiner must keep in mind the limits of the procedures that he or she is using and place those results within the context, neurologically and historically, of the individual being examined. The more that neuropsychology is developed, the more reliance the individual neuropsychologist can place on the test results and the less he or she will need to use context. One danger, however, is that a neuropsychologist will use contextual information rather than test results even when the test results are more accurate. In general, within their scope, test results are more accurate than judgment, but that scope must be known through training and experience.

The general rule that is applicable to this situation is that available scientific evidence normally takes precedence over other kinds of information. A complete interpretation, of course, integrates the results of brain-function analysis with information gathered from contextual sources. Scientific reliability is largely limited to the results derived from psychometric procedures. As the science of neuropsychological assessment progresses in the future, the more extensive will be the information that can be derived directly from the analysis.

Justification and Flexible Batteries

In neuropsychological assessment, there is general agreement that a battery of tests is necessary to evaluate adequately a neurological condition (Lezak et al., 2004, pp. 111–113). However, the methodological approach used for the evaluation is in dispute. As such, the scientific justification of variable batteries should be examined.

Definition of a Battery

A neuropsychology battery is any group of tests that a neuropsychologist uses in an assessment. As used in this writing, there are two general types of batteries: integrated and unintegrated. The term *integrated* is approximately the same as the term *standardized. Standardization*, however, applies specifically to the psychometric characteristics of a battery, whereas *integration* includes the battery's content or type of tests. (At times, the term *battery* may be used in a way that means integrated battery.)

An unintegrated battery is approximately the same as the procedure that neuropsychologists have designated as a *flexible battery*. This is a battery of tests that were selected without any statistical reference to the other tests. The tests in the battery have no formal—that is, psychometric—relationship to each other, although they may all be selected to examine a particular question or referral. The characteristics of an unintegrated or flexible battery will be examined first.

Approaches to Battery Assessment

There are two major approaches to designing a battery. The battery may be designed (1) to investigate a specific condition, usually posed by a referral, or (2) to determine the condition of the brain as a whole.

Referral Basis for a Battery

The basis of the argument for a flexible battery is that a battery should be designed to fulfill a particular purpose (usually determined by the referral or the plaintiffs' complaint). The typical flexible approach, which is "modeled" on the medical examination, contends that, because the purpose of each neuropsychological assessment referral varies, the battery should be designed to fulfill that purpose.

Such a battery is almost inevitably a flexible battery in which the examiner selects tests that he or she believes to be related to the referral. The interpretative results are almost entirely based on the clinician's judgment derived from the test results. This method is acceptable and may be accurate on a clinical level, particularly in a medical situation, where the medical staff knows and trusts the neuropsychologist's judgment.

In terms of reliability, however, the problem is that the neuropsychologist designing the battery already knows the diagnosis and may (unconsciously) select tests to support that diagnosis. This is one reason why a flexible battery may have questionable validity in forensic cases.

Whole Brain-Functioning Assessment

By contrast, the standardized comprehensive battery approach is based on the contention that, because brain functioning does not very in its essentials (even pathology affects the brain in specific ways), the method for assessing brain functioning should remain invariant and comprehensive. The variability in brain functioning derived from a standardized battery results from differences in subjects and types of pathology that were not in the tests and norms that were used. Thus, reliable information concerning the varying functioning of the brain from one subject to another can only be obtained from a consistent standardized battery (Russell, 2000b, pp. 456–458). The standardized integrated battery is designed to represent the functioning of the brain as a whole. Because it covers the functioning of the entire brain, it can answer most referral questions.

Flexible-Battery Methodology

The flexible-battery approach contends that, beyond an application of necessary individual tests, no psychometric procedures are necessary for interpretation of a battery. In flexible-battery theory, different tests are applied to different subjects either to answer a specific question, such as a referral question or to adapt testing requirements to an individual situation (Lezak et al., 2004, pp. 100–102).

Forms of Flexible Batteries

There are now several forms of flexible-battery procedures (Bauer, 2000). They involve both quantitative and qualitative approaches. In the pure form, each test in a battery is selected for each particular assessment. As such, the composition of the battery is different for each subject and assessment.

Probably the purest form of flexible neuropsychological assessment is that of Luria (Bauer, 2000, pp. 432–434; Luria, 1973). In this method, using his many years of experience, Luria examined each patient and often created his own tests for a particular condition. This was an excellent research method, but it had several difficulties concerning assessment. From reading Luria's accounts, this method was primarily used for focal lesions. These were the types of lesions that scanning techniques are better able to detect than neuropsychological methods. Second, Luria almost completely neglected the right hemisphere (Luria, 1973, pp. 160–168).

A second form of relatively pure neuropsychological investigation is that which has been practiced by the European school or, more exactly, the cognitive neuropsychology school (Bauer, 2000, pp. 434–435). This also is strongly research oriented and has made great contributions to neuropsychological knowledge (Ellis & Young, 1988). However, for assessment, it has the same problems that other flexible batteries demonstrate.

Another major school is that of the so-called Boston process approach (Bauer, 2000, pp. 435–436; Kaplan, 1988). Here the emphasis is on qualitative as well as quantitative methods. These qualitative methods are derived from early holistic neuropsychologists such as Goldstein and Scheerer (1941) and Werner (Kaplan, 1988, p. 129). Although qualitative analysis may add a great deal of richness to an assessment, there is very little evidence in the literature that it increases accuracy or reliability of a neuropsychological assessment.

The more general "flexible" procedure is the *core-battery method* (Bauer, 2000, pp. 421–443). In this method, each neuropsychologist uses a consistent core group of tests with each patient and adds tests as needed that appear to contribute to the assessment. Lezak's battery uses the core-battery approach (Lezak et al., 2004, pp. 3–38, 86–156). Nevertheless, the psychometrics—that is, scientific procedures—are restricted to individual tests, which are interpreted by an inferential examination of test relationships and qualitative aspects of assessment. This means, of course, that in Lezak's method most of the tests are not selected to assess a particular problem or referral question but to test the brain in general. Only a few tests are added to the battery for any particular purpose. As such, this method is the same as that employed by the standardized integrated battery, which is designed to cover the whole brain although tests may be added to deal with special problems.

The final approach is to design a specific specialized *fixed* battery for each particular pathology that is being investigated. Each neuropsychologist would design his or her own battery for a particular condition, such as the study of epilepsy or lead poisoning. As far as I am aware, none of these specialized batteries has been validated for the purpose for which it was designed. Consequently, their validity and even their reliability are unknown.

None of these approaches is consistent from examiner to examiner but remain individualized. The interpretations obtained from the tests in the battery cannot be derived from either the experience of other neuropsychologists or from research that validated the interpretations of the battery. Only in a gross intuitive manner are they related to the relationships between tests in the battery.

Neuropsychologists, using a nonstandardized approach, will insist that the individual tests they use must be standardized and validated, otherwise interpretations are not reliable. However, they change their reasoning when interpreting their battery of tests and insist that such psychometric methods are not necessary for a whole battery because they intuitively know when they are right.

One Test, One Condition

In pure flexible-battery theory, the various test results are only compared to external norms to determine whether a test score is in the normal or impaired range for a particular condition. As such, because a single test is related to only one condition, this is a *one-test, one-condition method.* The term *one-test, one-condition* indicates that a single test is only related to a single condition by validation. In fact, this relationship between tests and conditions can be extended to a *one-test, one-condition, one-interpretation* paradigm. In other words, a test for Alzheimer's disease is only validated for Alzheimer's disease (AD). If a test for brain damage is impaired, then its results are only valid for the diagnosis of brain damage.

Criticism of the one-test, one-condition approach comes directly from the work of Teuber (1955, 1959) and Reitan (1955, 1962) a half century ago. They emphasized the use of double dissociation to counter the problems with using a single test to identify a functional brain condition (see Chapter 4).

The criticism by Teuber and Reitan is primarily that the one-test, one-condition method does not remove the possibility that other conditions can also impair the test. For instance, a single test validated for traumatic head injury may also be impaired by AD or any number of other conditions. In an overall assessment, this means that each test in a flexible battery remains a one-dimensional test. Consequently, the entire group of tests measures various unrelated conditions, each of which may be affected by alternate tests, norms, and conditions. It is only through standardization of a battery that the relationships between tests are established and are uniform. In a flexible battery, the major attempt to deal with this situation is by means of hypothesis testing.

Hypothesis Testing

This hypothesis-testing method of deriving an interpretation from individual tests using a flexible battery is the primary method used with flexible batteries (Larrabee, 2005, p. 4–13; Lezak et al., 2004, pp. 112–113). Neuropsychologists who use the flexible-battery method base their contention that a flexible battery is a form of the classic hypothetico-deductive scientific method by implying that hypothesis testing is a scientific method (Bauer, 2000, pp. 422–424). Depending on the referral question or previous test results, the neuropsychologist, using a flexible method, develops a hypothesis concerning the condition of the patient. Then he or she selects a test designed to support or reject that hypothesis.

Serial Hypothesis Testing

Obviously, the one selected test cannot determine the existence of a type of brain damage such as Alzheimer's disease, because, as indicated above, many other conditions may impair the test. Consequently, a method of assessment that has been called *serial hypothesis testing* was designed to remedy this problem (Bauer, 2000, pp. 422–424; Larrabee, 2005, p. 5; Lezak et al., 2004, pp. 112–114). As these authors indicate, a second hypothesis is accepted that may rule in or out another possible condition. However, this does not answer all of the relevant questions, so another hypothesis is adopted. This process is continued until the examiner is satisfied that the correct condition has been isolated. In an example, Larrabee (2005, p. 5) states five conditions that need to be distinguished. If this is true, then a battery need only be five tests long.

Although hypothesis testing may seem to resolve the difficulty with a one-test, one-condition situation, there are a number of problems with such hypothesis testing. First, the number of other tests that may need to be administered is unknown and may be extremely long. For instance, a subject is thought to have a vascular dementia that is not Alzheimer's disease (Nixon, 1996, pp. 78–95). Both conditions cause dementia. However, AD must be eliminated, so one must select tests that are sensitive to Alzheimer's disease. If these were not impaired, it would indicate that the condition is not AD. But the review by Lezak et al. (2004, pp. 212–218) and the study by Mathias and Burke (2009) indicate that almost all neuropsychology tests are impaired by AD. To complicate the distinction, most tests that are sensitive to Alzheimer's disease are also sensitive to vascular dementia. Thus, using hypothesis testing, it is almost impossible to know that the patient does not have AD and does have vascular dementia.

Scientific Hypothesis Testing

The concept of hypothesis testing has other problems. In particular, there is the question as to whether it is an authentic scientific method of using hypotheses in testing. To examine this question, the form of research hypothesis testing will be examined. Many neuropsychologists who use a flexible method refer to the work of Popper (Bauer, 2000, pp. 422–423; Larrabee, 2005, pp. 4–5). Rather than becoming involved in the philosophical difference between Popper's approach and the standard scientific statistical methods (Cohen & Nagel, 1962), we will simply use the standard methods that are taught psychologists in all graduate schools and therefore serve as a model for science (Anastasi & Urbina, 1997). In addition, there is a real question as to whether Popper's method is essentially any different from the rejection of a null hypothesis that is the standard procedure.

The basic form of scientific neuropsychological research experiment tests a hypothesis that is postulated to reflect a particular neurological condition. A statistical test is administered to a group of subjects who have that condition and a normal group of subjects who do not have the condition. The hypothesis is confirmed when the null hypothesis—that there is no difference between the groups—is statistically rejected at a significant level.

First, note that two groups are compared. In these research studies, a proportional difference validates a theory or test. Second, relatively large groups of subjects are used to reduce the random variance, which can be caused by any number of factors.

Assessment Hypothesis Testing

In assessment, as previously discussed, there is the probability transformation, which was discussed above. In assessment, there is an *N* of 1. This requires a probability transformation from research proportional status to probability status—that is, the research portion of patients in the brain-damaged and control groups become the probability that a particular patient is brain damaged or is not brain damaged.

When we use a single individual in assessment, the question becomes "What is the probability that the individual has a condition?" It does not become "What is the proportion of people who have the condition?" This requires an entirely different form of statistics, which is not the scientific experimental hypothesis-testing method but rather determines the operational characteristics of the condition (Retzlaff & Gibertini, 2000, pp. 277–299; Slick, 2006, pp. 20–24). In operational characteristics, the procedure is to determine the probability that the person is within a group that has a particular condition. This is not hypothesis testing in the scientific sense, although it provides a reliable means of determining the probability that a single individual has a particular condition. Thus, assessment is not hypothesis testing. At best, this may be analogous to hypothesis testing as an analogy with the scientific methodology. However, analogy is not science.

The problem—that impairment in the one-test, one-condition situation could result from a number of extraneous situations—is not resolved. As an *N* of 1, there is no nullification of any extraneous variables by means of randomization. Users of a hypothesis-testing assessment begin to add other tests to eliminate some of the extraneous variables. The norms against which the individual is compared are somewhat equivalent to a control group in research. The norms eliminate some extraneous variables. However, to take advantage of this elimination, the subject should be tested under approximately the same conditions under which the norms were obtained (AERA et al., 1999, Standard 5.4, p. 63). In most neuropsychological testing, this does not occur.

There are also other relevant problems. First, in hypothesis testing, using a new test with a different population in each sequential testing means that the norms vary from testing to testing. This introduces the question as to whether the different tests are measuring the same condition, at least in the same amount.

In addition, this procedure becomes a decision-tree format in which each decision leads to another decision. Any of the serial hypotheses may fail because the norm sample was derived from a population that was different from the sample used in the previous hypothesis or because of an irrelevant condition, such as normal probability would cause a hypothesis to fail. Consequently, if a single test fails to support the hypothesis, then the entire series will fail to support the original hypotheses. To complicate matters, as the series becomes extended, the chance of a wrong hypothesis testing increases (Rourke & Brown, 1986, pp. 6–9).

Another problem with serial hypothesis testing is the amount of time required to do adequate testing. For each hypothesis, a patient must be given a test with results that are analyzed. The results require that a new test be selected and then administered. To adequately test all reasonable alternatives would take an enormous amount of time, most of which is not devoted to actual testing. Evidently, not a single textbook suggests that tests be singularly administered so that the results can be examined before a new hypothesis is constructed and the next test is administered. The major text books on testing, even those emphasizing this method (Lezak et al., 2004, pp. 111–113), suggest that initially at least a moderately sized battery should be administered at one time. This is the core-battery approach (Bauer, 2000, p. 442), which is not too different from a standardized battery to which an individual may add tests if needed. The great exception is that the core battery is unique to an individual examiner and therefore has not developed any lore or research to support it.

In regard to the time necessary for serial hypothesis testing, a neuropsychologist might state that only a certain number of reasonable alternatives need to be tested. However, this adds considerable uncertainty to the procedure because, as is apparent in almost all court cases, another neuropsychologist may not agree with the alternatives. For all these reasons, in a forensic situation there is no way that a neuropsychologist can ensure the reliability of his or her interpretive conclusion using the serial hypothesis-testing method.

Problems Using an Entire Flexible Battery

The method of avoiding this difficulty is thus to administer an entire battery without selecting tests by means of hypothesis testing. The neuropsychologist can then select from the battery those tests that fit his or her hypotheses. Using an entire battery of tests simultaneously from which interpretations are drawn has its own problems, however.

When the individual person is tested by a battery, the probability that the test is correct changes, depending on the number of tests in the battery. The more tests there are in the battery, the less accurate an individual test becomes simply because of chance. In other words, single tests do not operate statistically the same in a battery as they do individually. When not used in a battery, a test has a certain probability that it is correct. If 1 SD is used as a cut point for impairment, an individual test with a normal distribution will be impaired about 1/6 of the time. Consequently, it is relatively safe to state that impairment of the test indicates brain damage. The clinician will be correct about 5/6 of the time. But when a test is used in a battery in accordance with the transformation of proportion of impaired tests into probability, the probability of correctly identifying impairment is transformed into a percentage of the tests in the whole group that are generally impaired (Ingraham & Aiken, 1996).

If all of the tests in the battery have a normal distribution, which they never do (Dodrill, 1987; Russell, 1987), using 1 SD as the indication of impairment will mean that about 1/6 of the tests in the battery will probably fall into the impaired range even if they are "normal." A random error of 1/6 of the tests means that in a battery of 12 test scores, two can be expected to be impaired simply by chance.

The actual rate of impairment in an existing battery has been calculated (Heaton, Grant, & Matthews, 1991, pp. 36–38; Russell & Russell, 2003, p. 4). These statistics demonstrated that, in this battery of 40 tests, more than half the subjects had four tests impaired and almost 20% of the subjects had at least 10 impaired tests. In forensic practice, it is common for neuropsychologists to employ batteries containing many more than 24 test scores.

A related problem that has recently become apparent (Russell, 2005; and Chapter 15 in this writing) is that most volunteer norms and most norms are composed of volunteers have a mean that is about 1 SD above the average population. Because the cutting point that is often set for neuropsychological norms is about 1 SD above the general population mean, the average for the general population is at this cutting point. Consequently, using these norms, one-half of the normal population would be considered impaired.

This phenomenon of an increased probability of occurrence is similar to what occurs in research when one examines conclusions from many different tests. There is a certain probability that a test result will be significant because of random variation. Researchers are taught to avoid capitalizing on chance by instituting statistical controls in their analyses such as using the Bonferroni correction method or the Scheffé test (Gravetter & Wallnau, 2000). Unfortunately, many clinical neuropsychologists fail to extend this same logic to their assessment procedures. Thus, this becomes a basic problem for flexible-battery interpretation.

Flexible-Battery Interpretation

This psychometric battery characteristic of probability means that the clinician cannot interpret the impairment of any single test score in a battery as an indication of brain damage. Consequently, with a flexible battery, there is no way to provide reliable knowledge concerning whether a particular impaired test score indicates brain damage.

Another implication is that the proportion of impaired test scores that are required to indicate the existence of brain damage varies among batteries, depending on the tests and the norms selected for the various tests. In any battery, there is no practical way of reliably knowing how many impaired test scores are required to indicate the existence of brain damage unless there is a validated index. Moreover, a validated index requires a fixed battery. Consequently, the user of a flexible battery has no psychometrically reliable way of knowing how many impaired results are necessary to indicate a finding of brain damage.

There are additional problems with using a flexible battery that has not been validated. Perhaps the most significant of these is that the validity of the battery as a whole is no better than the single most valid test in the battery. Flexible batteries have no method for validly combining test scores other than clinical judgment, which has its own problems as will be discussed. From a psychometric point of view, the examiner may as well only administer the single most valid test because the examiner has no psychometric method to demonstrate that the additional tests increase the validity of the flexible battery.

Another concern is that the user of the flexible battery has no demonstrably reliable means of determining which tests correctly assess brain damage when the test results contradict each other. Almost any battery will have some tests that are within the normal range and others that are impaired. The clinician who interprets the impaired results while ignoring those results that are normal is exploiting chance. The only way to avoid this is to know both the relative accuracy of the various tests in the battery. The most accurate test or group of tests will provide the most accurate assessment. This information has been derived for the Halstead–Reitan Battery and Halstead–Russell Neuropsychological Evaluation System—Revised (Russell & Starkey, 1993a; Russell, 2004) but not for any other group of neuropsychological tests.

Combining and Comparing Tests in a Flexible Battery

The result of these interpretation problems is that often flexible-battery proponents begin to abandon the test-by-test method of assessment and instead combine and compare tests (Lezak et al., 2004, pp. 153–155). They combine tests to gain redundancy and compare tests in order to observe relationships.

The primary problem with attempting to combine or compare scores in a flexible battery is that the various tests are normed on different population samples. An assumption employed by flexible-battery users is that all of the test norms that use a "normal" sample are equivalent (Lezak, 2004, pp. 142–145) in that they accurately represent the entire population of the United States. Lezak (2004) writes, "Although this situation results in less than perfect comparability between the different tests . . . these 'mixed bag' norms generally serve their purpose" (p. 147). As usual, Lezak cites no research to support her claim.

When actual evidence is examined, it is obvious that norms are not equivalent and so cannot be dependably compared or combined. The norms derived from the book by Mitrushina, Boone, and D'Elia (1999) demonstrate the variability of norms. In an example derived from this work (Mitrushina et al., 1999, pp. 6–7) concerning a memory test, the mean raw scores varied from 5.9 to 12.6.

Again, examination of the norms for the Category Test age groups from 19 to 34 showed that the mean varied from 23 to 47 for the United States (Mitrushina et al., 1999, pp. 457–474). Thus, the maximal mean score was more than twice as high as the minimal mean score. For the Grooved Pegboard, the differences between hand speeds for the two genders varied from more than 20 seconds for Bornstein (1986) (Mitrushina et al., 1999, p. 435) to essentially no difference for Heaton et al. (1991) (Mitrushina et al., 1999, p. 437). These conflicting examples could be duplicated for almost every test in the book.

Supporting these examples of variation, a thorough study by Kalechstein, van Gorp, and Rapport (1998) examined the equivalency of sets of norms. In conclusion, they state, "Our findings indicate that interpretation of performance on neuropsychological tests is frequently and dramatically affected by sampling differences across normative data sets." They found that the differences for four of the five tests in their battery would have affected clinical interpretations. Most flexible batteries use at least 20 tests.

In this regard, the examination of all batteries that use the HRB and also provide the average full-scale intelligence quotient (FSIQ) found that all batteries using volunteer norms had a sample FSIQ that was almost 1 SD above normal (See Chapter 14 in this text). These findings explain why the assumption of normative equivalence for flexible norms is contrary to all of the rules of standardization in the literature (AERA et al., 1999, pp. 49–60; Anastasi & Urbina, 1997, pp. 66–70; Axelrod & Goldman, 1996; Ghiselli et al., 1981, pp. 37–55).

The equivalence of norms cannot be known without directly comparing them by using the same sample of real subjects or some other equating method. Consequently, it is clear that with flexibly derived norms the examiner can place little reliance on comparisons between tests made within a battery even when the sample scores use the same metric and supposedly represent the same population (Strauss, Sherman, & Spreen, 2006, p. 76).

Validation of a Flexible-Battery Interpretation

Concerning individual tests, only a specific *fixed* or standardized test can be validated. (An unstandardized test is one in which the selection of items is variable.) The reason that only a fixed or standardized test can be validated is that a test that is changed in any significant aspect is no longer the test that was validated. Psychometric methods do not apply to any variable test because these are not standardized or objective (Anastasi & Urbina, 1997, p. 4). As such, a type of test, approach, or domain cannot be validated because the specific tests within the domain vary. Qualitative data cannot be validated because they are not objective or standardized.

This is also true of batteries. At this point, no flexible battery has been validated because the test must be standardized to be validated.

Problem of Test Selection

Because any single neuropsychological test is only one among hundreds of others, any one of which could be administered in its place, an individual test is, in fact, one of the group of existing neuropsychological tests, even when given singly. Norms vary for each test, consequently the differential accuracy of any two or more tests is unknown until they have been administered to the same group of subjects.

Clinical Judgment

The only method of validation for a nonstandardized battery is clinical judgment. As discussed later, validation of clinical judgment can be used to validate a fixed or standardized battery. In regard to such batteries, evidently clinical judgment now is approximately as accurate as formalized programs, most of which have been computer programs (Russell, 1995; Chapter 9 in this text).

Reports Derived from Flexible Batteries

The result of this dilemma is that, even though hypothesis testing is invariably advocated as the basis of flexible-battery interpretations, it is invariably absent in reports. In practice, hypothesis testing is much too involved to be used in test administration or reviewed in the report. Rather, a prearranged battery of tests is usually presented to the subject as a whole (Bauer, 2000, pp. 427–441; Lezak et al., 2004, p. 111; Strauss et al., 2006, pp. 75–76). This may be followed by a limited number of follow-up tests to examine a few alternatives. The initial battery is often a customized and relatively fixed battery or one of a set of fixed batteries used by an examiner. Such predesigned batteries are incompatible with extensive hypothesis testing because the tests were not individually selected to test a particular hypothesis. However, more critically, neither the tests nor any relationships derived from them have been validated.

A consequence is that flexibly derived neuropsychological reports seldom adequately provide supportable connections between test results and conclusions. One requirement derived from the *Daubert* standard (*Daubert v. Merrell*, 1993) is that there must be a clear connection between the scientific data and expert witnesses' conclusions.

In a deposition or trial, under questioning, adequate reasoning supporting the conclusions often cannot be provided. When the reasoning is elaborated, it is based on clinical judgment, and consequently the neuropsychologist may make psychometrically wrong, unsupported, or unsupportable connections. In particular, an adequate justification for the selection of tests and the selection of the norms can seldom be provided. In a standardized or fixed battery, most of the connections between tests are predetermined. There is only one set of norms. These are validated in the construction of the battery. Consequently, they can be readily and dependably provided.

The Testability of Flexible Batteries

The "key" criterion of a science in scientific theory and in the *Daubert* standards is "whether theory or technique can be, and has been, tested" (*Daubert v. Merrell*, 1993, vol. 24, p. 2787). This need for testing is stated repeatedly in *Daubert*. Certain pseudoscientific theories such as astrology, some personality theories, and Freudian psychosexual stages are not stated in such a manner that they can be readily tested. As such, information based on these theories is not admissible.

There is a question as to whether interpretations derived from any flexible battery are testable. Because batteries are variable and written after the patient's medical history is known, no scientific method can be applied to the interpretation. Using some form of blind analysis, the ability of some neuropsychologists to generate interpretations that correspond to a neurological diagnosis or location of a lesion could be determined. However, this has never been attempted.

Summary of Attempts at Justification

The problem raised by attempts to justify flexible batteries is that reliable interpretations cannot be derived from an unintegrated set of tests when there is no method to determine which test or group of tests is correct. As will be discussed later, even clinical judgments cannot be validated in a variable battery. Clinical judgment has never been validated for a flexible battery. As indicated in forensic situations, the "clinical judgments" of opposing neuropsychologists almost always disagree.

In any battery, some tests are impaired and others are not. Any specific test or group could be impaired by chance. For any variable battery, there is no way to know how many impaired tests are required to indicate brain damage. Because tests and norms in a flexible battery vary without any psychometric relationship to each other, any impairment or pattern of impairments may be the result of random variation. How does the flexible-battery neuropsychologist know and demonstrate that any particular impairment of the tests in a flexible battery has any significance?

Medical Versus Neuropsychological Assessment

A medical physiological examination, which consists in a panel of tests, examines the physiological products of various organs of the body to determine whether they are normal. In this regard, the medical laboratory panel has been cited by the American Academy of Clinical Neuropsychology (2007) as a model for the way in which a neuropsychological test battery should be flexibly designed. The academy contends that if the individual tests are validated, then the battery interpretation is reliable.

Medical Laboratory Methods

Medical laboratory test results such as those for blood work are organized in a list, generally with the test mean and cut points indicating the maximum and minimum limits of a test's normal range. Although there is usually a core group of tests that are usually included, many are chosen according to the patient's problem or to answer specific referral questions. As a result, many of the tests in a panel will vary.

The Medical Analogy

Based on the medical laboratory examination as a model, another "argument" used by the advocates of the unstandardized or flexible-battery use is that their method is the same as that used in the medical profession.

This argument has been partly discussed in Chapter 4, "Brain Function Analysis," but some implications apply to justification. The first and foremost problem with the analogy is that it is not a psychometric method. It merely states a similarity in order to use the reputation that doctors have with the public. An analogy, without supporting psychometric evidence, is not a scientific, psychometric method that could validate the use of any procedure.

Second, in terms of *Kumho Tire v. Carmichael* (1999), medical practice (Faigman, Saks, Sanders, & Cheng, 2008, pp. 48–52) is a type of expertise and not a science. When medical expertise refers directly to validated scientific experimentation, then it is scientific expertise (Faigman et al., 2008, pp. 51–52). However, much of what the medical profession does is a matter of using information derived from studies that used scientific methodology. The test relationships in the panel are generally not directly related, so they are not validated and therefore are not scientific. In other words, medical practice is generally not a science but a technology based on a science. As such, the analogy is wrong if neuropsychologists claim their method is scientific and not that of an expert using a technology.

Crucial Differences

In addition, there are a number of crucial differences between medical laboratory examinations and neuropsychological procedures. These are derived from the differences between the functioning of the brain and other body organs. Because of these differences, which are presented next, the analogy breaks down.

Brain as a Single Organ

First, physiologically the brain is a single organ, whereas a panel of tests covers the many organs in the body. The various tests represent the various different organs. Although they operate together in the whole body, they can often become damaged individually without affecting other organs. In contrast, the brain is a single organ that is closely interactive. Almost any damage will affect the functioning of many parts of the brain, if not its entirety. To determine diagnosis, location of damage, prognosis, and other effects on behavior, the various brain functions must be compared. Comparison requires a well-researched, co-normed, and integrated battery.

Homeostasis

Second, because of homeostasis, the hormonal and chemical levels in the human body and its organs are generally restricted to a limited "normal" range. This may vary slightly, depending on various factors such as the individual's age and sex. Usually, only a score outside of the normal range is considered in a medical examination.

In contrast, the brain's mental or behavioral functions do not operate according to homeostasis. (Of course, most of the brain's physiological processes are controlled by homeostasis.) Consequently, a person's ability anywhere in the entire distribution of behavioral brain functions, which vary from a very low ability level to the genius level, must be considered normal. The exception is impairment because of a pathological condition.

Range of Impairment

Third, this great range of normal functioning becomes greater when the entire life-span range of a human is included. For a normal adult population, the distribution includes more than 6 SDs. When the entire life span of a person is included for cognitive and neuropsychological tests, the range extends from the level of approximately a 5-year-old to an adult IQ of more than 145. Thus, unpublished investigations indicate that the full cognitive range of norms may include at least 13 SDs. These include 10 SDs below an adult IQ of 100 and 3 SDs above 100. (This range needs to be established through good psychometric studies.)

This means that a low score in itself does not indicate impairment of a person's abilities. No score in the entire range of human abilities can be considered impaired unless it has been produced by a pathological condition or event. If the event is not the result of a congenital condition, then impairment represents a reduction of the person's premorbid ability.

Pathology may reduce any brain-function score in the entire range by any amount. Thus, the range of impaired functioning extends from an ability level considerably above average to unconsciousness or death. The impairment resulting from brain damage of a person with superior ability may not reduce the person's ability to the below-average range, but it may mean that a physician, for example, may no longer be able to perform his or her occupation. Unlike assessing most physiological functions, a cognitive brain-function assessment cannot assume that a particular score is "abnormal" without considering the person's premorbid ability. Tests and batteries should be designed to register this variation in ability (Dodrill, 1997).

Interrelationship of Functions

Fourth, both the physiological and behavioral functions of the brain are inherently interrelated because of a number of brain-functioning characteristics. These include physiological characteristics such as a generalized vascular system for the whole brain, the interrelationship of neuron tracks, the tendency for damage in one area to affect the entire brain as in a reduction in consciousness, mental fatigue, and the effects of chemicals that can reduce the total level of ability. In addition, diaschisis may affect parts of the brain that are distant from a focal lesion (Russell, 1981). To disentangle these relationships, a simple group of impaired tests is not adequate. As was described, this may require a set of specific double-dissociation comparisons and combinations of tests. These may form patterns that are related to various brain conditions.

Generalized and Localized Tests

Fifth, in addition, some tests appear to be generalized in that they are impaired by lesions in any area, whereas others are more sensitive to lesions in a specific area. As such, tests that are particularly sensitive to focal areas are not adequate measures of brain functioning as a whole. A complete examination should include tests that reflect both focal and generalized impairment (Reitan & Wolfson, 1993, pp. 27–28).

Panel Tests Unrelated Processes

Sixth, in contrast to a battery, panel test scores generally describe physiological processes that are relatively unrelated to each other physically and statistically. In a panel, scores are not mathematically combined or compared in order to provide significant information. This is not necessary because each abnormal test has a particular significance concerned with a different aspect of the organism's physiological functioning. The standardization of scores would seldom increase their usefulness.

The aspect of a panel that is the most comparable to a neuropsychological battery occurs when a particular group of tests is abnormal. This group may indicate a syndrome consistent with a particular pathology. However, the scores within a syndrome are not sufficiently related to form more than a gross pattern. In medical methodology, the test scales are often raw scores in which only abnormal scores are significant.

Brain Scanning

Finally, the various brain-scanning techniques, such as magnetic resonance imaging (MRI) and computed tomography (CT) scans, have had a dramatic effect on neuropsychology. These methods almost always scan the entire brain, regardless of the referral. This is different from their use for the rest on the body, in that there they are often used to examine parts of the body or specific organs. In contrast, the entire brain is scanned because a diagnosis generally requires the comparison of normal versus abnormal areas of the brain.

In addition, scanning the entire brain may demonstrate pathologies that were not evident on a gross physical medical examination. Such a total examination is not possible unless the entire brain is examined using a method that is consistent from one examination to another. Thus, the various forms of brain scans generally employ a fixed procedure covering the entire brain. This is similar to the use of a fixed or standardized battery.

In all, these are some of the reasons that a neuropsychological examination needs to cover the entire brain, whereas a panel need not cover all of the physiological functions in the body.

Justification of an Integrated Test Battery

When using more than one test, the primary justification problem for any neuropsychological assessment is how to justify the interpretative conclusion drawn from the group of tests. The single test score is validated for only a particular interpretation (AERA et al., 1999, pp. 9–24). However, this is a severely limited interpretation that may be wrong because of the lack of any reliable method for eliminating alternative interpretations. The method for providing a broad range of reliable interpretations related to the assessment of brain functioning and pathology is the integrated neuropsychological battery.

Definition of an Integrated Battery

Integrated batteries are groups of tests that are psychometrically interrelated in such a manner that the tests can be combined or compared (Anastasi & Urbina, 1997, p. 49; Lezak, 1988, pp. 153–155; Reitan & Wolfson, 1993; Russell, 1998, 2000b; Russell et al., 2005). Thus, in this chapter an integrated battery is defined as two or more tests that constitute a single psychometric and content assessment process that is designed to produce reliable interpretations. A group of tests in which each test is used to obtain an independent interpretative conclusion is not an integrated battery. If a person is administered a reading, spelling, and arithmetic test and the conclusions are that he or she is poor in reading, spelling, and arithmetic, then this is an unintegrated group of test results. However, if the conclusion is that the person is a poor student, then all three tests were used to form a single interpretation. Consequently, the group of tests constitutes an integrated battery.

This approach conceives of the brain as a unified or integrated whole; as such, assessment requires an integrated battery that psychometrically models the functioning of the brain. Reliability, in the general sense, requires standardization, comprehensive content, and validation.

An integrated set of tests is standardized by either fixed or equivalent scales. Concerning the formal structure of an integrated battery, the most important requirement of a set of tests is that the scores of all the tests are either fixed or equivalent. To make multiple comparisons, all of the scales should be invariable or equivalent. The term *integrated* implies, among other things, that the system uses the same basic measurement procedure for all tests. The same score must mean the same amount of impairment or level of functioning for every test that constitutes the battery or set of tests. Such equivalency requires that all of the scales be either normed on the same sample or that the samples are equated by some statistical method. Thus, an integrated battery is standardized and validated. The requirements for standardization and validation will be thoroughly discussed later.

An integrated battery involves more than standardization and validation, however. Integration includes test content. The content of the tests constituting the battery is comprehensive in that it covers the entire brain, unless the battery is a specialized battery such as an aphasia battery.

Comprehensive Coverage

In any integrated battery, the selection of tests is an essential aspect of assessment (Russell, 2000b). To some extent, most batteries attempt to cover the entire brain, although there are specialized batteries with specialized coverage such as aphasia batteries. Fixed and standardized batteries are designed to ensure such coverage. Forms of coverage include areas of the brain, types of brain functions, forms of functioning such as fluency, and redundancy (Russell, 2000b, pp. 465–469).

Coverage permits the establishment of localizing relationships between parts of the brain using a single battery. This same technique can also be applied for differential diagnosis of such conditions as Alzheimer's disease (Russell & Polakoff, 1993). Such a battery is designed to permit an interpretation of the functioning and pathology of the whole brain (Reitan & Wolfson, 1993, pp. 23–29; Russell, 2000a, 2000b).

The integrated battery assumes that most referral questions will involve the functioning of the whole brain. For instance, a referral question might be "Does this patient have a lesion in the left hemisphere?" In this case, the flexible examiner might select only tests related to the left hemisphere and thus commit one of the fallacious double-dissociation errors. The integrated battery will provide tests for both hemispheres, thus using double disassociation to answer the referral question. (If a special need occurs, then another test may be added to measure the special need.)

In addition, the test results and thus the interpretation of an integrated battery will be the same even though the examiner knows that diagnosis before testing. The advantage of blind assessment is that it produces an independent conclusion that is not influenced by any context. Nevertheless, the tests composing an integrated standardized battery remain the same whether the examiner knows the diagnosis and context or not.

Psychometrics of an Integrated Battery

Although the same basic psychometric scientific principles that were developed for individual tests must be applied to a battery of tests, in many ways batteries operates differently than do individual tests. Consequently, the correct application of psychometric principles may be different from those that apply to an individual test. Additional methods may apply to the operation of a battery because a battery consists of the relationships between tests that enable the tests to be combined or compared in addition to individual tests.

Forensics and an Integrated Battery

Although the reliability of an integrated battery is desirable in most areas of neuropsychological practice, it is critical in forensic activities. The *Daubert* standard (*Daubert v. Merrell*, 1993) specifies that the criterion for judging the "reliability" of expert testimony is the use of scientific methodology (*Daubert v. Merrell*, 1993; Reed, 1996; Russell et al., 2005). Thus, this standard acknowledges and employs the universally held concept that scientific methodology is the primary means to produce reliable information. The integrated battery is a battery that is constructed to apply scientific methodology to assessment; consequently, validated results derived from it are reliable.

Integrated Battery Methodology

The combination of scores in a battery, which is necessary for a reliable interpretation, may be accomplished by clinical judgment using an integrated battery. Nevertheless, the interpretation is still a subjective opinion. To create a more scientific formal method of interpretation, psychometric combinations of tests are required. The best known of these is the index, which combines a number of scores into a scale that may be validated. The chapter on formal analytic methods (Chapter 5) discusses various other formal methods but does not emphasize their justification.

Indexes

The index is an example of how a formal method may permit a reliable combination of scores that avoids the problems of combining scores in a variable battery. As mentioned previously in this chapter and in Chapter 7, the only way to avoid the problems in dealing with individual tests in a battery is by using a formal method of combining and comparing scores such as in an index. This combines individual tests in a method that produces a single score that may be validated.

The advantage of an index is immediately evident in that its score is statistically treated and validated in the same manner as a single test score. As a rule, this overcomes the problems with using unstandardized, flexible scores in a test battery.

In spite of its obvious advantage, little work has been done using formal methods in neuropsychology, much less psychology as a whole. There is almost no realization that this is the method that can bypass or overcome many of the problems related to batteries. It is only when those problems are recognized as being real that there will be an interest in devising more statistically valid formalized methods.

Standardization of Batteries

Justification of assessment procedures requires the standardization of batteries as well as of individual tests. Because the standardization of individual tests is well described in statistics textbooks, this text will only be concerned with battery standardization.

In batteries, consistency between tests is produced by standardization. This ensures intertest reliability and allows the validation of battery patterns. Standardization is also necessary for the generalization of validated information, especially to an individual being assessed. Without standardization, which creates a consistent battery, validation is not possible, and information derived from an unvalidated procedure is not reliable.

Psychometric Standards Apply to Batteries

In neuropsychological assessment, the use of test batteries is now universally accepted. The advantages of using a battery for neuropsychological assessment has been well expressed (Lezak et al., 2004; Mitrushina et al., 1999; Spreen & Strauss,

1998). To obtain dependable information from these batteries, however, the interpretive problem is to ensure the same psychometric validity when using a battery as has been established for individual tests.

Many neuropsychologists contend that the validation of batteries is unnecessary because the individual tests within the battery have been validated. This contention is correct when the tests are used for individual interpretations without relating them to other tests in a group, but there are at least three reasons why batteries and procedures requiring batteries should be validated as thoroughly as individual tests.

First, interpretations derived from tests are validated, not the tests themselves (AERA et al., 1999, p. 9). Similarly, when interpretations are derived from a whole battery, the battery must be validated.

Second, batteries produce unique information by combining and comparing tests, information that cannot be obtained from individual tests. The results of a battery are not only that which may be derived from individual tests but also information that is derived from the relationships between tests. The accuracy of battery information depends on validating the battery and the relationships between tests within it.

Finally, individual tests in a battery do not operate statistically in the same manner as they do when used individually. The use of test batteries creates certain psychometric difficulties that place constraints on the validity, effectiveness, and accuracy of the individual tests when incorporated in a battery (Kalechstein et al., 1998; Rosenfeld, Sands, & van Gorp, 2000; Russell & Russell, 2003; Chapter 7 in this book).

Advantages of Standardization

The advantages of standardizing a battery are generally the same but more extensive as standardizing individual tests. Standardized measures are necessary for the reliable scientific assessment with a test or battery. Individual tests and batteries use standardization so that the results are objective, consistent, and reliable.

Standardization establishes consistent, uniform relationships between the tests in the battery. The relationships between the tests are objective and repeatable every time the standardized battery is used. Consequently, the results can be replicated and are therefore reliable. Thus, interpretations derived from the relationships between tests in a standardized battery are reliable.

Because standardization establishes consistency for a battery by means of norms and equivalent scores, the battery is repeatable. Consistency provides invariant scores. Consequently, the results can be tested—that is, validated. Thus, standardization, along with validation, fulfills all of the criteria for science in the form of psychometrics. Consequently, standardized measures are necessary for reliable scientific assessment

Pattern Interpretations

The major advantage of an integrated battery is that it is not limited to a one-test, one-condition format because it uses multiple dissociation of tests and the relationships between tests. Consequently, it can distinguish one condition from another.

In the one-test, one-condition paradigm, there is no method of isolating the intended condition from many other conditions that may impair a test.

In contrast, the integrated battery permits the creation of patterns that are specific to various conditions. For instance, Alzheimer's disease impairs almost all cognitive functions except simple motor and sensory tasks (Hom, 1992; Russell & Polakoff, 1993; Russell & Starkey, 2001b, p. 26). With a relatively large battery, almost all of the published known patterns can be obtained and distinguished from conditions that produce other patterns.

Single Tests in an Integrated Battery

The use of a standardized integrated battery does not preclude the use of individual tests to augment battery findings. The requirements for standardization and especially co-norming, as in double and multiple disassociation, apply when information for an interpretation requires the use of combining or comparing tests. When information is derived from a single test that does not require combining or comparing tests within the battery, then a test may be used that is not psychometrically integrated with the battery.

It is acceptable to use tests that are not in the integrated battery to obtain a specific type of information that is not obtainable from the battery. An example is using the Minnesota Multiphasic Personality Inventory 2 (MMPI-2) to evaluate the affective status of a patient.

Norms

In the neuropsychological assessment, norms that are designed to provide a consistency for a test also provide consistency for a battery. This consistency is obtained by basing the standardization on a particular group of people called a *population*. The population is the standard. However, the test norms are derived from a sample that is representative of the population, so it is important to be clear as to the type of population that the test represents. This is particularly true in forensic cases (Anastasi & Urbina, 1997, pp. 48–49; Bush, Connell, & Denney, 2009, pp. 66–67). In neuropsychology, although the whole population is the standard, it is impossible to test an entire population. Consequently, in practice, norms consist of a *sample* from the population that represents the population (Anastasia & Urbina, 1997, pp. 68–70).

Thus, the norms represent the test behavior of a group of people as a distribution of test scores. In neuropsychological assessment, however, the test scores represent brain functioning as is reflected in people's behavior.

Using psychometric methods, the norm distribution provides a range of scores that represent the behavioral characteristics of a particular population (Anastasia & Urbina, 1997, pp. 68–70). As such, norms provide a measure that indicates an individual's relative standing in the normative sample. This permits an evaluation of the subject's performance in reference to others in a group or population. This procedure has been well developed and explained for individual tests (AERA et al., 1999; Anastasi & Urbina, 1997, pp. 48–83).

There are two primary functions performed by standardization. First, it relates scales to a meaningful standard or criterion such as the average of the general population. This provides a meaning for the score.

Second, standardization of a battery permits the direct comparison of the individual's performance on different tests when they are administered to the same person (Anastasia & Urbina, 1997, p. 49). This creates an equivalency between scales so intraindividual test results can be dependably combined and compared.

The Valuation of a Set of Norms

A set of norms is evaluated by examining how accurately it represents the population that it is intended to represent. The procedures for norming are designed to ensure that the sample is an accurate representation of a population. These procedures are described in the AERA et al. standards (1999, pp. 7–60) and in textbooks on test construction (Anastasi & Urbina, 1997). The same conditions apply to the norming of a whole battery.

In evaluating a set of norms, it is important to be aware of information that is normally expected to be presented in the test manual but that is not mentioned. Inadequacies in norming may be obscured by simply not mentioning them. Thus, unmentioned information often indicates an attempt by the test author to conceal weaknesses in the test-norming procedure.

For neuropsychological norms, several major characteristics of a sample determine the quality of its population representation (Anastasi & Urbina, 1997, pp. 68–69). These include size of the sample, the representativeness of the location from which the sample subjects were gathered, the type of subjects (volunteers or neurologically normal subjects), and demographic characteristics such as age, sex, ethnicity, ability level, and gender.

The Size of a Normative Sample

The size of a sample is a major concern for norming and is often emphasized in descriptions of the sample. If other parameters are adequate, then the greater the size, the more accurate the norms. There are no absolute criteria, however, for determining the minimal size for a test or co-normed battery (Anastasi & Urbina, 1997, pp. 68–69). The desirable size depends on the standard error of the sample (Guilford, 1965, pp. 144–146). When the size of the norming sample reaches a fairly large number—for instance, 200 (Strauss et al., 2006, pp. 44–45)—the standard error will not be significantly reduced by further increasing the number of subjects even if the increase is great. For instance, if we are using a standard deviation of 10 as in *t*-scores or digital scores, when the sample *N* is 200 the standard error is 0.71 or slightly less than three-quarters of a score. If the *N* is increased by 300 to 500, the standard error is only reduced to 0.45 or approximately one-half a score. Because the SD scores are 1, one-quarter of a score point would almost never be significant. This is particularly true in comparison to the effect of changing a sample of population.

Consequently, the absolute size above about 200 is not nearly as important as the selection procedure used to obtain the sample. Obviously, a group of 2000 college graduates is not representative of the general population, even if it is a large sample. Thus, the emphasis placed on obtaining a huge normative sample is largely misplaced. The representation of the sample is more important for *N* more than 200.

The Representative Location

The representative location of subjects is crucial to the soundness of a sample. The location from which the subjects are drawn is a major indicator of the population that the sample represents (Anastasi & Urbina, 1997, pp. 68–69; Strauss et al., 2006, pp. 44–45). If a sample is drawn from several locations, then the representation is dependent on the proportion of subjects derived from each location. Consequently, the AERA et al. standards (1999, p. 55) state that the *N* for each location should be provided.

In this regard, the manuals for the Comprehensive Norms for an Expanded Halstead–Reitan Battery (CNEHRB) (Heaton et al., 1991) and the Revised Comprehensive Norms for an Expanded Halstead–Reitan Battery (RCNEHRB) (Heaton, Miller, Taylor, & Grant, 2004) state that these subjects were drawn from 11 locations, including parts of Canada. However, neither manual provides the *N* for the locations. Consequently, the proportion of the subjects derived from each area is either not known or may be too few to be representative of the area.

However, an accurate estimation of the *N* for various locations in the CNEHRB (Heaton et al., 1991) sample is possible (Russell, 1997, pp. 38–40). The evidence is strong that the vast majority of the norming group was derived from only three locations: the University of Colorado, the University of California at San Diego, and the University of Wisconsin. Because no *N* is provided, it is quite conceivable that only one subject was contributed to the total pool from some of the locations and the total from eight locations was probably much too small to be representative of any of those locations.

In the revised version of the CNEHRB, the RCNEHRB (Heaton et al., 2005, pp. 8–9), 148 Caucasians were added to the 486 subjects in the CNEHRB for a total of 634 participatants. The location of their origin was not provided, but it is reasonable to assume that they came from the San Diego area, which is where the author's laboratory was located and where the African American subjects in the same study resided (Heaton et al., 2004, p. 7). Because apparently 181 of the original CNEHRB subjects also came from San Diego as described in the 1986 study (Heaton et al., 1986), more than 300 of the 634 Caucasian RCNEHRB (Heaton et al., 2005) subjects came from this city. Consequently, half of the RCNEHRB subjects came from the San Diego area. Thus, it is reasonable to conclude that the RCNEHRB sample is essentially representative of only the Western United States, especially San Diego, and not the 11 areas spread over the United States and the Canadian province of Manitoba stated in the manual. Southern states are not represented at all.

The Use of Volunteer Subjects

Neuropsychological normal test subjects for norms typically come from one of two sources. They are either volunteer participants or clinical patients who were found to be neurologically normal (Russell, 2005). Many neuropsychologists criticize the use of negative neurological subjects who are not volunteers. In some parts of their book, Mitrushina et al. (1999) selectively eliminated the norms collected by Russell (2003) in part for this reason.

By contrast, Reitan and Wolfson (1993, pp. 33–35) contend that neurologically normal subjects represent the ideal group for neuropsychological assessment controls. These were exactly the subjects from which the neurological patients were distinguished, and consequently they were primarily the group from which they would need to be distinguished in assessment (AERA et al., 1999, Standard 5.4, p. 63).

Neither of the test manuals for the CNEHRB (Heaton et al., 1991) or the RCNEHRB (Heaton et al., 2004) provided any actual information as to the proportion of subjects who were volunteers and not neurologically normal patients. The subjects were called *participants*, not *volunteers*. The subjects were stated to have been screened by a "structured interview" method. This structured interview was probably similar to the interview containing standard questions that Reitan and others use for all of their patients. The "normal" patients used for the norms in the HRNES-R were all neurologically normal patients who were found to lack any neurological disease and not volunteers. They were also given a structured interview. Consequently, the proportion of volunteers in the CNEHRB and RCNEHRB is unknown.

Evidently, the subjects supplied for the CNEHRB (Heaton et al., 1991) by Matthews (1987) were negative neurological patients. Because volunteers are usually paid, and the RCNEHRB (Heaton et al., 2004) stated "most individuals were paid for their participation" (p. 7), as many as 49% of the participants could have been negative neurological patients.

Some neuropsychologists argue that neurologically normal participants may be abnormal because of some undiagnosed pathology or because they were referred to a physician for some reason. This issue was addressed by Russell (1990, 2009) in a study done at the University of Miami Medical School. It described a series of 200 patients who were suspected to have a neurological condition but were found to be normal subjects. They were used to norm the HRNES-R. These subjects were followed for more than a year after their initial presentation and evaluation. More than half were eventually diagnosed with minor psychological or nonneurological physical ailments (Russell, 2009). None in this group showed evidence of neurological problems at any point during the following year. These data suggest that concerns about undiagnosed organic pathology among neurologically normal subjects is largely a red herring that draws attention away from the relevance and importance of using such a group of patients for comparison purposes.

The main argument in favor of using volunteer subjects is their screened and confirmed "normalcy" (Russell, 2005). Unfortunately, this screening also ensures that the selection of volunteer subjects is never truly random. Random selection is a major method to ensure proper statistical representation. Rather, volunteer normative participants select themselves for studies and are customarily encouraged to do so with compensation for participation. Volunteer bias is a well-known phenomenon in medical research (Bland, 2000, pp. 13–14).

One method of determining the normalcy of a sample is to use a well-established neutral method for judging the general ability level of the normative sample, a procedure outlined by Anastasi and Urbina (1997) under the rubric "national anchor norms" (p. 70). Of all the tests in our armamentarium, none is a better candidate for being a universal standard than the Wechsler tests.

In the meta-analysis reported by Stanczak, Stanczak, and Temper (2000), the mean WAIS-R FSIQ score for the volunteer group was almost 112 (111.6) (Stanczak, 2003). Not surprisingly, the volunteer participants averaged nearly 3 years more education than did the referral participants (Russell, 2005). This higher-than-average FSIQ for volunteers was also supported by a reexamination of a review of smaller studies (Steinmeyer, 1986). For the norms in which the IQ scores were reported, all nine volunteer groups had a FSIQ almost 1 SD above normal, with a mean FSIQ of 116.9, whereas the five neurologically normal groups had a FSIQ of 103.6.

The same above-average intelligence level was found in a further study by Russell (See Chapter 14 in this book) of the large-scale normative studies of the HRB, which had Wechsler IQ measures (Wechsler, 1955, 1981). These studies had *N*'s of almost or greater than 200. There were five such studies, including the Heaton et al. (1991) and HRNES-R (Russell & Starkey, 2001a) studies. Of these, only the norms of Russell and Starkey (2001a) were composed of neurologically normal subjects; the remaining four studies presumably used volunteers in their norming. The norms for the CNEHRB (Heaton et al., 1991) were used in this examination because the RCNEHRB manual (Heaton et al., 2004) failed to provide the mean IQs of its Caucasian subjects.

This study (Russell, 2005) found that all of the mean FSIQs of the volunteer subjects in these large samples were approximately one full SD above average, with a total mean of 115. Clearly, then, "normal" volunteer participants were not normal but represented the upper one-sixth of the population in intellectual ability. Only the HRNES-R norms (Russell & Starkey, 2001a), using referred but neurologically normal patients, showed an average IQ of 102.1 (p. 39). A brief review of several of the individual tests reported in Mitrushina et al. (1999) found the same tendency for volunteers to be above average in IQ tests as was found in the studies of the HRB full-battery norms.

As these studies indicate, volunteer subjects are not representative of the "normal" person who undergoes a clinical evaluation. Norms based on volunteer subjects run the risk of an increased false diagnosis of pathology by raising the criteria for what is normal. Reliance on volunteer norms increases the chances that a neurologically normal person of average intelligence will be misdiagnosed as brain damaged. This concern is especially important in forensic settings, because any norms using volunteers for the "normal" controls are suspect.

The possibility of misdiagnosis is one reason that neurologically normal subjects represent the most appropriate norms for most neuropsychological examinations. In this regard, as one of the criteria for norms, the AERA et al. standards (1999) stipulate that norms "should refer to clearly described populations. These populations should include individuals or groups to whom test users will ordinarily wish to compare their own examinees" (AERA et al., 1999, Standard 4.5, p. 55). For almost all neuropsychology assessments, the usual reason for referral is that the subject has symptoms that indicate a possible neurological condition.

In those situations in which a neuropsychologist may need to examine a subject who neither was referred for nor has any suspicion of a pathological brain condition, it is appropriate for the examiner to use norms derived from "normal" volunteers. However, most forensic and hospitalized patients are referred to neuropsychologists exactly because they were suspected of having a neurological condition.

In addition, the AERA et al. standards (1999) stipulate the following: "In general, the testing conditions should be equivalent to those that prevailed when norms and other interpretive data were obtained" (p. 63). Thus, norms should be collected under the same conditions as they will be used. It is important to note that volunteers were not tested to assess their medical condition and they were usually paid, where neurologically normal subjects were tested under exactly the conditions in which the test norms would be used.

The Flynn Effect

Another condition that may affect test norms and should be taken into consideration in assessment is the ability level of the individual. However, in the last decade or so, another effect has dominated assessment to such a degree that it influences the level ability in almost all intelligence testing. This is the Flynn effect.

The Flynn effect (Flynn, 1999) postulates that the average measured intelligence is increasing over time for most Western countries, including the United States. This concept was supported by a remarkable set of studies by James R. Flynn (1999). The rate of increase appeared to be about 0.3 FSIQ points a year for the United States (Flynn, 1999, p. 6). As a result, IQs from the same intelligence test would be expected to increase with each new generation.

Because intelligence testing has now become a major force in our society, any change in measured intelligence will have wide-ranging consequences (Russell, 2007). Concerning test construction, the American Psychological Association has recommended that intelligence tests be renormed at regular intervals in the *Standards for Educational and Psychological Testing* (AERA et al., 1999, p. 59, 4.18) and the *Ethical Principles of Psychologists and Code of Conduct* of the American Psychological Association (APA, 2002, p. 1072).

For instance, because a new version of the Wechsler adult intelligence scale has appeared every 17.2 years, the ability level has been reduced to accommodate this effect for the last two versions.

The authors of the WAIS-III have stated (Wechsler, 1997, pp. 9–10) that measured IQ is increasing at a 0.3 points each year, as it had between 1955 (Wechsler, 1955) and 1981 (Wechsler, 1981, p. 47). This makes "periodic updating of the norms essential" (Wechsler, 1997, p. 9). In accordance, most companies that produce intelligence tests are beginning to do periodic renorming.

However, for biological organisms, as an environment becomes optimal, a plateau in the organisms' maximal growth occurs such that growth is largely determined by genetics and not environmental conditions. Subsequently, organisms reach an asymptote in their growth (Russell, 2007). There is evidence that such a plateau is occurring for intelligence in countries with optimal social environments. Several studies have indicated that there appears to be a plateau effect in several Scandinavian countries that have well-established welfare systems in which the basic physiological needs of all citizens are met (Russell, 2007). Since Russell's study in 2007, at least three new studies have found evidence of this plateauing effect in Europe (Russell, 2010).

In the United States, examination of adult Wechsler test scores between normings indicates that there is a reduction of the FSIQ increase such that the average FSIQ would plateau in approximately 2024 (Russell, 2007). However, the WAIS-III norming process eliminates many types of subjects with possible brain impairment. This probably raises the average FSIQ level. With an increase of only 1 FSIQ point in 16 years, a plateau in the Flynn effect would have been reached in 2004.

Nevertheless, in contrast, the current WAIS-IV manual (Wechsler, Coalson, & Raiford, 2008) presented a comparison of the WAIS-IV and WAIS-III in which the reduction in the IQ levels because of an increase in intelligence was 2.9 for 11 years (or 0.26% per year) (Wechsler et al., 2008, pp. 75–77). This appears to be relatively consistent with the initial prediction of the Flynn effect in the 1980s, which was a 0.3% increase a year.

As indicated in Russell's study (2007), however, the rate of FSIQ increase for the adult Wechsler tests had dropped to 0.18% per year in the 16 years between the WAIS-R (Wechsler, 1981) and the WAIS-III (Russell, 2007; Wechsler, 1997). Consequently, it is somewhat odd that after falling for 16 years the rate of improvement would suddenly increase to 0.26% per year between the WAIS-III (Wechsler, 1997) and WAIS-IV (Wechsler et al., 2008). The authors of the WAIS-IV do not discuss or try to explain this phenomenon. However, they present an extensive list of criteria that were used to eliminate their volunteer subjects (Wechsler et al., 2008, p. 75). Consequently, a considerable number of subjects were eliminated who normally constitute part of the adult population but who had conditions that would have lowered their IQ (Loring & Bauer, 2010, p. 687). Thus, this elimination of subjects probably produced an artificially high average intelligence that could easily have raised the overall FSIQ on the WAIS-IV by 0.26%.

Obsolesce

Perhaps an even greater problem for norming is what might be called the *obsolescence effect* on assessment. The Flynn effect brings this issue into prominence. The concept that obsolescence or being out-of-date makes a test or procedure invalid ("inaccurate," "inappropriate," "not useful," "creating wrong interpretations," etc.) has been widely accepted in psychology and neuropsychology (Russell, 2010). Such obsolescence, which is produced by merely publishing a new version of a test, has been accepted by the American Psychological Association as indicated by statements in the *Standards for Educational and Psychological Testing* (AERA et al., 1999, p. 59, 4.18) and the *Ethical Principles of Psychologists and Code of Conduct* of the American Psychological Association (APA, 2002, p. 1072).

This change resulting from the concept of obsolescence has produced a great amount of damage in the field of psychology. For instance, it has produced an extensive nullification of research effort. Each new test means that the research done on the previous versions is no longer applicable to the newer versions. Examination of the literature (Russell, 2010) indicates that, up to the present, the number of psychological research studies that have been obliterated are probably about 10,000.

The arguments attempting to justify this concept of obsolescence, generally referring to the Flynn effect, mean that the creation of a new version of a test or simply time makes tests obsolete. However, the Flynn effect appears to have plateaued. In psychometric theory, validated tests do not lose their validity because of the creation of newer versions. In addition, time does not invalidate tests because of the improvement of neurological methodology such as the MRI. This assumption is unscientific, unproven, and, if true, would discredit all older neuropsychological and neurological knowledge, including the work by Broca, Wernicke, William James, Luria, Head, Hebb, and Teuber. In science, no method, theory, or information, once validated, loses that validation merely because of time or the creation of another test or procedure. Once validated, a procedure is only disproved or replaced by means of new research that demonstrates the procedure's lack of validity.

The Requirements for Standardization of a Battery

To provide a standard to measure brain functions, a battery must meet the following requirements: it must be composed of a fixed group of tests, have a common metric, have equivalent scales, and should adjust the scores for the major demographic characteristics of the subjects. Although an integrated neuropsychological battery requires comprehensive coverage of the functions and areas of the brain, this is not an aspect of standardization.

The Fixed Battery

Two forms of standardized batteries are recognized: the fixed battery such as the HRB and the scale-score standardized battery. A fixed battery of tests is one in which the relationships between tests are invariant across all tests for all administrations. In the HRB, psychometric scientific methods are applied to the entire battery and not simply to individual tests in the battery. The relationship between tests must meet psychometric requirements just as much as individual tests.

A fixed battery has several crucial advantages. Most important, the patterns derived from a subject become evident against the fixed background of the battery. In a fixed battery, the relationships (ratios) between tests remain constant so that the various patterns of test scores are produced by the individual's responses and not the particular tests or norms that were selected (Russell, 2000b, pp. 456–458). Dependable comparisons using raw scores can be made with fixed batteries. In fact, much of the multivariate research in psychometric psychology has used raw scores that obviously remain fixed during the research (Nunnally & Bernstein, 1994).

Finally, a fixed battery, which is used by many neuropsychologists across time, enables the development of a body of knowledge, both lore and validated information, concerning how the tests interact with each other. This wealth of information is not possible for flexible batteries.

There is, however, a major difficulty in using a fixed raw-score battery. Because raw scores do not have equivalent scales, the expected ratios or differences between the raw-score scales vary from one pair of scales to another. As such, each numeric relationship used in a battery must be learned. This requires years of experience.

The Scale-Score Standardized Battery

This scale-score standardized battery, which is often referred to simply as a *standardized battery*, consists of a battery of tests that have been equated in some manner, usually by co-norming. The entire battery is normed in the same manner that an individual test is normed.

Standardized batteries have several advantages. First, because the tests are equated, the scores for all the tests are equivalent; the same score for each test indicates the same amount of impairment or lack of impairment. Almost all intelligence tests have this format, which is certainly recognized by neuropsychologists as characteristic of the Wechsler scales. This equality permits the direct observation of test patterns that may reflect various brain functions and pathologies. Such test patterns are relatively easy to recognize and remember, whereas it requires years of experience for one to recognize crucial differences between tests in a fixed battery. A second advantage of the standardized battery is that once the scales have been equated through the norming process, they may be used separately or in groups without losing their relationships between the tests. The requirements for a standardized battery are relatively straightforward. This permits the ready use of formal methods from indexes to formulas. Formal methods cannot be developed for a flexible battery because it cannot be standardized.

A Common Metric

To create a consistent battery, all tests must use the same form of scales, which is a common metric. For standardized scoring, the common metric sets the mean and standard deviations of all tests to the same scale numbers. This includes such metrics as *t*-scores, decimal scores, and percentiles (Anastasi & Urbina, 1997, pp. 48–76; Russell, 2000b; Russell & Starkey, 2001a, pp. 32–35).

Note that providing a common metric for the various tests does not make the scores equivalent, because the raw-score means and standard deviations would vary with the test norming sample. In addition, because norm samples are derived from different populations (even if they are all called "normal"), the scales are not equivalent. For instance, a mean set at 10 for a group of high school graduates from Alabama is not the same as for high school graduates from Massachusetts. Thus, a primary problem with scales is the lack of a common metric.

Equivalent Scores

Equivalency for a battery is established when a scale number represents the same amount of ability across all the tests. When equivalent, a number that is set to represent the average subset score, such as the WAIS-R number 10, will indicate an average ability for every scale in the battery. In comparing scores when a person receives a 10 on test A and an 8 on test B, we know that the person's brain is performing at a higher level on test A. Thus, equivalent scores are desirable for ease of interpretation.

The importance of such an analytic method introduces the problem of how to ensure dependable equivalence of scores in a battery. Lezak (1995, pp. 154–157) and several other authors (Mitrushina et al., 1999, pp. 11–17; Strauss et al., 2006) advocate a procedure for dealing with different scores in which a common metric is used but the various tests are not statistically equated because they are derived from different norming groups. Strauss et al. (2006, pp. 28–29, 32–43) offer a profile method of presenting scores flexibly from variously normed tests so that they can be compared. These authors assume that all tests normed on any sample are equivalent.

This is a form of pseudoequivalency because, as has been discussed, the variability between the norms for different tests is so great that accurate comparisons were questionable (Kalechstein et al., 1998) and certainly not dependable. This practice goes against accepted wisdom in psychometrics. "The norms are thus empirically established by determining what persons in a *representative* group actually do on the test" (italics added) (Anastasia & Urbina, 1997, p. 48). Thus, an examiner or expert witness can place little reliance on comparisons between flexibly derived tests even when using the same metric.

Co-Norming

Scale equivalence is obtained by *coordinated norming* or *co-norming*. This is the only statistical procedure that has been demonstrated to produce dependable equivalent scales (Russell, 2000b, pp. 457, 472–475; Russell et al., 2005). Co-norming is an accepted statistical equating procedure that is used by the WAIS-III, the Wechsler Memory Scale–III (Wechsler, 1997), and many other intelligence test batteries (Williams, 1997) including the Stern Neuropsychological Assessment Battery (NAB) (Stern & White, 2001).

This procedure norms all of the tests in a battery simultaneously by employing the same sample and the same norming procedure or bridging statistics. In this way, co-norming statistically transforms all scales so that they are equivalent to a single standard, the norm (Anastasia & Urbina, 1997, pp. 55–73). Scale scores are assigned so that one number—for example, 10—represents the average and other numbers represent degrees of ability. In Wechsler tests, three digits are assigned to each subtest SD so that the number 7 represents 1 SD below the mean. This ensures that the same score indicates an equivalent amount of ability for all test performances.

Co-norming permits direct real comparisons between test results in a battery. This allows the creation of a pattern of relationships within a whole battery of standardized tests. The pattern is produced by the individual's brain functioning and is affected by pathological conditions. Examination of these patterns is *pattern analysis*. Such a pattern analysis depicts the brain's functioning. As such, pattern analysis is a form of brain-function analysis (Chapter 4).

Although co-norming creates "fixed" scales, these fixed scales may be used individually or in groups without losing the fixed relationships between tests. The norming process establishes the consistency of the relationships between tests. In contrast, adding tests to a fixed battery without co-norming changes the battery into a flexible battery in regard to the added tests. Exactly the same problems that bedevil the flexible battery are incorporated into a mixed flexible–fixed battery concerning the new unstandardized tests.

However, it is acceptable to use tests that are not in the integrated battery to obtain a specific type of information that is not obtainable from the battery—for example, using the MMPI-2 to evaluate the affective status of a patient.

Co-Norming for Pathology Assessment

For reliable comparisons of normal subjects and brain-damaged subjects, the co-norms should include both normal and brain-damaged subjects derived from the same source. This ensures that the norms will include equivalent groups that can be compared. This is like randomly assigning subjects from one source to two groups in an experiment and applying a condition to the experimental group but none to the control group. Otherwise, the difference between normal and brain-damaged subjects may be the result of extraneous variables. For instance, if the brain-damaged group was recruited from an institution for mentally retarded individuals, they could not psychometrically be legitimately compared to normal subjects from a high school to distinguish brain-damaged from normal subjects.

This requirement goes beyond creating normal norms and comparing them to a pathology group derived from some other source. Currently, only a few batteries fully meet these consistency standards. These batteries are Reitan's HRB and NDS (Reitan & Wolfson, 1993), the HRNES-R (Russell & Starkey, 2001a), the Meyers Assessment Battery (MAB) (Meyers & Rohling, 2004), and the NAB (Stern & White, 2001).

Representation of Demographic Characteristics

Normative accuracy requires as close a fit as possible between a subject's scores and the norms related to the subject's relevant characteristics (AERA et al., 1999, pp. 54–56; Anastasia & Urbina, 1997, pp. 68–70). Consequently, the subject should be compared to norms with major demographic characteristics that are similar to those of the subject. The more similar an individual is to such a representative subgroup of a population, the more accurate will be the distinction between a normal and an impaired performance. These characteristics include age, intellectual ability (IQ or education), gender, and possibly ethnicity. The AERA et al. standards (1999, pp. 54–56) emphasized the importance of such comparisons (Anastasia & Urbina, 1997, pp. 68–70; Wechsler, 1997, pp. 19–35).

In norming whole batteries, neuropsychologists have used two methods to represent major demographic characteristics: stratification and linear regression. However, because of problems with stratification, the linear regression has major advantages (Russell et al., 2005). The regression method may be used to calculate scale scores for each of the demographic characteristics of age, IQ or education, and gender levels when the number of subjects in some cells is insufficient for accuracy (Russell, 1997). Currently, only two neuropsychological batteries based on the HRB use regression norming: the RCNEHRB (Heaton et al., 2004) and the HRNES-R (Russell & Starkey, 2001a). The use of linear regression for norming has generally been supported in neuropsychology (Crawford & Howell, 1998; Moses, Prichard, & Adams, 1999; Vanderploeg, Axelrod, Sherer, Scott, & Adams, 1997).

Finally, it is true that the effect of severe brain damage impairs test performance to such a great extent that the effects of age and education are largely overwhelmed or confounded, especially in the middle age range (Reitan & Wolfson, 1995). However, accuracy is reduced, especially in the extreme scores of age and ability level, when demographic adjustments are not used. Such adjustments may be needed to separate normal subjects from brain-damaged subjects when the damage is rather mild and when patients are older. Adjustments are particularly important when the subject has higher-than-average intelligence (Dodrill, 1997; Russell, 2001). In these cases, the effect of age and education on test scores may be significant (Heaton, Matthews, Grant, & Avitable, 1996; Russell, 2001). This correction for extreme age and intellectual ability is important, particularly in forensic cases.

Validation

Scientific methodology replaces unreliable sources of justification with methods that validate the procedures for producing information. Thus, validation is the indispensable basis for reliability in that, as stated before, "neuropsychological knowledge is reliable if, and only if, it has been validated using methods generally acceptable in science and psychometrics." These generally accepted methods are the psychometric methods used in all sciences (Anastasi & Urbina, 1997; Bland, 2000; Ghiselli et al., 1981; Nunnally & Bernstein, 1994).

Two Psychometric Methods for Validation

Two general methods can justify a procedure and so provide reliable information: validated clinical judgment and formal psychometric methods.

Clinical judgment bases an opinion on an inferential understanding of a situation or test results. Such judgment may be applied directly to a situation, the results of individual tests, or the results of test batteries. Clinical judgment is reliable when it has been validated using appropriate psychometric procedures.

The alternate way of obtaining reliable information is to use a formal psychometric methodology. Formal psychometric methods are objective methods that provide test result information that is quantitative and logical. These methods do not involve a psychologist's subjective clinical judgment. Tests, indexes, formulas, and algorithms are types of formal procedures. Except for individual tests, these methods usually require a standardized battery.

In trial testimony, reliable opinions of expert witness are based on these two validating procedures. A whole battery and any relationships within it are validated through clinical judgment. In formal methods, each battery must be standardized to form a basis for various formal procedures such as indexes. Although many formal procedures such as indexes of brain-damage existence or lateralization may be obtained from the same standardized battery, each procedure is validated separately.

Validation by Clinical Judgment

Many neuropsychologists who use flexible batteries claim that they are not concerned about the psychometric requirements of a battery, other than the accuracy of the individual tests, because clinical judgment is the basis for their interpretations.

Clinical judgment derives an opinion from an inferential, subjective, understanding of a situation, test or battery results. Although the inferential judgment process is not objective, the results of that process are objective. As such, the results of clinical judgment can be validated in the sense that the accuracy of such judgments may be determined using accepted psychometric procedures.

The most complete examination of the accuracy of clinical judgments in psychology has been published by Garb (1998), who also published an article specifically examining clinical judgment in neuropsychology (Garb & Schramke, 1996).

There are three questions to be examined and validated in the application of clinical judgment to a battery. The first question is, has a particular procedure or battery been validated by clinical judgment? The second is, is the battery or procedure the same as that which was validated? The final question, is a particular neuropsychologist capable of making such a valid clinical judgment using a validated battery?

The Clinical Validity of Batteries

Validating a battery (or even a single test) requires that various clinical judges can obtain the same results. This is measured by any of several means for determining interrater reliability that may be found in statistics textbooks.

Concerning batteries, Garb (1998) found good interrater reliability between clinical judgments when fixed batteries were used. There have been many studies concerning the validity of clinical neuropsychology judgments when fixed batteries were studied (Franzen, 2000, pp. 116–120; Garb, 1998; Russell, 1995). A meta-analysis by Garb and Schramke (1996) found an overall hit rate of 84% for standardized batteries assessing the existence of brain damage and a hit rate of 89% for studies comparing right- versus left-hemisphere damage. By contrast, no validation studies of clinical judgment using flexible batteries have been published (Garb, 1998, pp. 157–162).

Garb (1998) was able to locate interrater reliability data for flexible batteries derived from nonneurological clinical psychological assessment. The results of these studies found very poor reliability between test raters (Garb, 1998, p. 13). Consequently, there is no reason to suppose that the reliability of judgments from flexible neuropsychological batteries would be any better.

Thus, there is no evidence that clinical judgment employing any flexible neuropsychological battery is reliable. The reliability of two neuropsychologists using flexible batteries is unknown. More than a decade later, the situation remains the same. In conclusion, no information derived from neuropsychological flexible batteries using clinical judgment is validated, so this method cannot be considered to be reliable for forensic purposes.

Clinical Judgments in an Altered Battery

The second problem concerning clinical judgment relates to the fixity of the validated fixed battery. Judgment studies are applied to a whole battery because the clinician uses the whole battery to make judgmental interpretations. If the battery has been changed to any substantial extent, then it is not the same battery that was validated. Removal or changing tests in a validated battery creates a different and unvalidated battery. The addition of tests to a validated battery is less of a threat than removal of tests from the fixed battery, because the addition of tests leaves the original battery intact. However, conclusions derived from the relationship of the added tests to the original battery are unvalidated.

A Neuropsychologist's Clinical Judgments

Finally, there remains the question as to whether a particular neuropsychologist is capable of accurate judgments. It is thought that the accuracy of such judgment depends on the examiner's expertise and training. Neuropsychologists who employ batteries claim that their experience allows them to interpret the results of these batteries. However, the few published studies concerning such experience indicate that, beyond the graduate-school level, there is almost no relationship between the amount of experience of the clinician and the accuracy of his or her assessment (Garb, 1998, pp. 166–169; Grab & Schramke, 1996, p. 153). In addition, it should be noted that all of these studies of experience used fixed batteries.

The effect of experience employing flexible batteries is completely unexamined, but obviously it would be no better than using fixed batteries. When a flexible battery is continually changed, experience with a particular set of tests is lacking. Thus, the claim that experience validates a neuropsychologist's opinions derived from a flexible battery is completely unsupported by the literature. Such opinions must be deemed unreliable.

In addition, as far as expertise is concerned, neuropsychologists certified by the American Board of Professional Psychology (ABPP) have not been found to be more accurate than neuropsychologists without this accreditation (Garb, 1998, pp. 167, 244). At this time diplomas were not completely awarded on the basis of an objective examination, as such, its results were no more reliable than any other unvalidated subjective clinical judgment. As Garb states in his book, "The research findings reviewed in this book put severe limitations on what forensic clinicians can ethically state to a court. First, and foremost, expert witnesses should not defend their testimony by saying that their statements are based on clinical experience" (Garb, 1998, p. 246).

In contrast to experience, training on fixed batteries did make a difference in the accuracy of clinical judgment in the few studies that have been examined (Garb, 1998, p. 167). In support of the positive effect of training, all of the studies that have demonstrated valid clinical judgments derived from neuropsychological batteries have employed neuropsychologists trained on fixed batteries (Garb, 1998; Russell, 1995). There have been no studies of the effect of training using flexible batteries.

In conclusion, the studies validating clinical judgment demonstrate that accurate interpretive judgments have only been demonstrated when the judgments are made by persons trained in the use of a fixed battery. No studies have demonstrated that neuropsychologists employing any flexible method can make accurate judgments regardless of experience, certification or training.

Validation of Flexible Batteries

Because of the pressure from neuropsychologists who advocate the validation of batteries, attempts are being made to validate flexible batteries. In this regard, it is important to make a distinction between a flexible battery and a fixed battery that is not the HRB. One attempt to create a battery claimed to represent a partially flexible battery (Volbrecht, Meyers, & Kaster-Bundgaard, 2000) simply validated a fixed battery that was not the HRB. If the same battery of tests is used throughout the validating process, then it is a fixed battery. In addition, if a user of the battery wishes to obtain the same validated results derived from this battery, the psychologist must use the battery that was validated without changing it.

Miller and Rohling (2001) have proposed the most sophisticated method to date for possibly creating a validated flexible battery, the Rohling interpretative method (RIM). The essence of this procedure places into practice the method proposed by both Lezak and Mitrushina et al. (1999), which was to transform scores into standard scores with a common metric and then depend on the assumption that any norms that are derived from a presumably normal population are equivalent. As with all batteries, the validation studies of the RIM (Rohling, Miller, & Langhinrichsen-Rohling, 2004) only apply to that battery and not to flexible-battery assessment in general.

The RIM method has been rather strongly criticized (Palmer, Applebaum, & Heaton, 2004; Russell et al., 2005; Willson & Reynolds, 2004). The primary problem with the RIM is that it violates a primary requirement of norming—that is, "norms are thus empirically established by determining what persons in a representative group actually do on the test" (Anastasi & Urbina, 1997, p. 48). Norms are derived from a single specific sample of subjects. No amount of statistical manipulation can overcome this requirement. These flexible batteries, which combine norms from different samples, cannot be considered reliable (Ghiselli et al., 1981, pp. 38–40). There is no method that can determine the relationships between tests without using a single group of people for norming.

The Validation of Formal Methods

It is because of the problems with subjective procedures, even validated clinical judgment, that formal procedures are used in science (Cohen & Nagel, 1962, p. 195). As described earlier, formal psychometric methods, when validated, provide objective valid score information that does not involve a psychologist's subjective clinical judgment. *Formal* applies to any completely objective method for making decisions or measuring psychological tasks. As such, formal methods include all psychometric methods except clinical judgment. They are objective and repeatable psychometric methods that provide measurement information that is quantitative or logical.

These methods obviously include not only tests but also cut points, indexes, ratios, formulas, taxonomies, and algorithms. In batteries, these procedures apply to the relationships between tests as well as to individual tests. In fixed and standardized batteries, the results of these methods are as objective as the results of tests. As such, when validated these methods are completely scientific and so provide reliable information. They use quantitative measurement such as operating characteristics, standards, rates of error, and significance levels.

The term *formal* applied to psychometric methods is a more inclusive term than *actuarial* or *quantitative* methods, which were used previously. Using the term *actuarial* in his well-known studies, Meehl (1954) demonstrated the generally greater accuracy of actuarial methods compared to clinical judgment in psychology. The examination of this difference was brought up to date in two papers by Grove and Meehl (1996) and Grove, Zald, Lebow, Snitz, and Nelson (2000). The results were the same as Meehl (1954) had initially discovered.

Formal Types: Quantitative and Classification

There are two general types of formal methods—qualitative and quantitative. The primary scientific qualitative method is classification, which forms a taxonomic system. This is the scientific "logical" method of dealing with distinct concepts or entities. Classification requires an exact objective description of an entity so that the identification is observable and repeatable. Where possible, the description distinguishes a class from similar classes of entities. Taxonomy orders classes in some manner, usually a hierarchical form. Classification provides the different entities or components of any area of science such that the different components of the science can be distinguished and manipulated.

Quantitative formal methods include forms of mathematics. Abstract mathematics is related to real entities by means of measurement (Nunnally & Bernstein, 1994, pp. 3–9). As such, formal assessment methods are generally based on measurement. Quantification has several advantages: numbers are objective, and they provide finer detailed descriptions than personal judgments. This enables one to generalize research results to a wide range of situations. In general, the control group parameters of the research or norms in assessment determine the population to which the results can be generalized.

Direct Application to Data

In contrast to clinical judgment, formal measures of validity are applied directly to psychometric data (See Chapters 5 and 8 in this text). Formal methods make decisions used in interpretations without the use of clinical judgment just as a test provides a score without requiring judgment. This is the case even for complex judgments. The neuropsychological key (Russell, Neuringer, & Goldstein, 1970), using a standardized battery and an algorithm, could determine whether a person had brain damage and whether the damage was lateralized, and if so to which hemisphere without input of clinical judgment at any point in the process. The key was almost as accurate as expert neuropsychologists were and more accurate than nonexperts (Russell, 1995, 1998). Further development of such methods would certainly create methods as accurate as expert neuropsychologist's judgments.

Indexes

Other than tests, the major formal procedure derived from standardized batteries is the index and particularly an impairment or brain-damage index. These provide the major objective indication of the validity of a battery.

The use of an index is actually quite old in neuropsychology because it was first created as the Halstead Index (HI) (Halstead, 1947). (Several indexes will be discussed in Chapter 9.) The HI demonstrates one of the many methods for designing an index. It was simply the proportion of the original 10 index test scores that were in the brain-damaged range as determined by cutting points. The cutting point for the HI was set at about 50%, or 5 out of the 10 original scores. When three of the original scores were rejected as being relatively insensitive to brain damage, the cutting point was changed to 3.5 or 4. A score of 4 and above indicated that the patient's score was in the impaired range (Jarvis & Barth, 1984, pp. 22–23). This cutting point has remained stable through all of the studies that have been done on the index since 1955.

The psychometrics for validating an index score are generally the same as those used to validate a single test. One simply compares the number of brain-damaged subjects to the control (non–brain-damaged subjects) and applies the operational characteristics type of statistics or possibly another form of statistics.

However, several indexes employ the HRB and its derivative batteries, including the HI (Reitan & Wolfson, 1993, p. 92), the Neuropsychological Deficit Scale (Reitan & Wolfson, 1993, pp. 93, 347–397), the Average Impairment Rating (Russell et al., 1970), The Average Impairment Score (AIS) (Russell & Starkey, 2001a, pp. 19, 38), and the Percent Impaired Index (Russell & Starkey, 2001a, pp. 19, 38). The Global Deficit Score (Heaton et al., 2004, pp. 14–15) has been partially validated. All of these have accumulated a substantial documentation of their validity (Franzen, 2000, pp. 116–132; Reitan & Wolfson, 1993; Russell, 1995, 1998). In addition to determining the existence of brain damage, these psychometric methods usually provide a measure of accuracy, which is a rate of error (Russell, 2004). A number of indexes indicating whether brain damage is lateralized to one or the other hemisphere of the brain have also been developed (Russell, 1995; Russell et al., 1970).

Other types of formal methods also have been developed, as discussed in Chapter 5.

Types of Validity

For validation, formal psychometric procedures can be applied to fixed and standardized batteries. The validation methods are generally the same as have been developed for single tests. These include construct validity, predictive validity, and content validity (Nunnally & Bernstein, 1994, pp. 83–112). Content validity seldom is used in neuropsychology and will not be discussed.

Construct validity is the accumulation of studies concerning the nature of an underlying entity. It concerns how measures that apply to a construct correlate and do not correlate to those measures pertaining to other constructs (Nunnally & Bernstein, 1994, pp. 83–94). The construct validity of a test is the extent to which the test appears to measure a theoretical entity, trait, or ability (Anastasi & Urbina, 1997, pp. 126–135).

For a neuropsychological battery, construct validity is the accumulation of studies that indicate the extent to which the battery measures the theoretical construct of brain functioning (see Chapter 3). Although this validation process is too complex to be fully examined in detail (Anastasi & Urbina, 1997, pp. 126–135), in the forensic context it is much like the concept of weight of evidence. Construct validity studies are designed to measure how the various brain functions are related to each other and related to the activities that the individual performs. A standardized battery models the construct of brain functioning. The accumulation of the studies supporting a battery provides the construct validity for a battery. Thus, the total supporting research and its psychometric adequacy support its general validity.

Formal predictive validity indicates the effectiveness of a test or battery in predicting a particular criterion (Anastasi & Urbina, 1997, pp. 108–126). A fixed battery using clinical judgment can be validated as a whole by predictive validity. The accuracy of clinical judgment in predicting various brain conditions from the whole battery can be determined. However, using clinical judgment, the prediction of each condition must be individually and specifically validated.

In contrast, a standardized battery cannot be validated as a whole. Rather, standardized scale scores enable various different psychometric formal procedures to be performed using the same battery. Each procedure produces certain specific information, which is validated when the procedure is validated. Each of these procedures can be validated using predictive validity.

For instance, a general impairment index using major tests in the battery may be validated. Many indexes including the HI and AIS have been validated (Russell, 2004; Russell & Starkey, 2001a, pp. 35–41). However, validating an impairment index does not validate a lateralization index, although they both use the same battery. Thus, an advantage of a standardized scale-score battery is that it permits large numbers of formal procedures to be done with the same battery, even though each procedure must be separately validated.

Types of Validating Procedures

There are two general types of statistical procedures that have been used to obtain validated information: distribution statistics and accuracy. Distribution statistics are the traditional research statistical methods that compare the distributions, averages, and SDs of two or more groups of subjects. These methods are thoroughly taught in graduate school and addressed in psychometric literature, so they need not be discussed here.

Classification statistics (Bayesian statistics) is the ability of a procedure to separate subjects into two assessment categories (Slick, 2006, pp. 20–24). Accuracy is obtained through determining the "operating characteristics" of the differentiation procedure (Bland, 2000, pp. 275–279; Gouvier, 1999, 2001; Retzlaff & Gibertini, 2000; Russell, 2004). The method measures the proportion of subjects in groups separated by cutting points. It determines how well a group of subjects can be separated into two categories such as a normal group and a pathology group.

Because operating characteristics require a demonstration that a certain score or cut point on a particular test or index reliably separates two groups, the only completely valid way of setting cut points is to derive them from a comparison of two groups of patients with different conditions (Russell, 2004). Ideally, this means that all of the criterion subjects were derived from one population, such as patients from a single hospital, in which a thorough neurological examination found one group to be normal and the other group to have a neurological condition.

The practice of using 1 SD below the mean to set the cutting point for impairment using norms composed of normal subjects indicates a misunderstanding of psychometrics (Bland, 2000, p. 279). There is no statistical justification for expecting 1 SD in a completely normal sample to be the most accurate cut point, because in this sample all of the subjects below as well as above that point are normal.

In determining the validity and accuracy of a cut point, operating characteristics are more accurate than traditional statistical methods (Bland, 2000, pp. 275–279; Gouvier, 1999, 2001; Retzlaff & Gibertini, 2000, pp. 277–299; Russell, 2004). Traditional statistics compare an entire group with another group such as brain-damaged and normal control subjects, usually employing means and standard deviations, so that the severity of impairment for the various subjects affects the statistic, especially if there is a skewed distribution. The severity of individual test impairment has no effect on operating characteristics other than determining on which side of a cut point the subject falls.

Distribution statistics assume a normal distribution for both groups while operating characteristics do not. The distributions using brain-damage tests are almost never normal (Dodrill, 1987; Russell, 1987). Consequently, for clinical purposes in which the question is determining the existence or nonexistence of a condition, operating characteristics are more accurate (Gouvier, 1999; Retzlaff & Gibertini, 2000, pp. 277–299; Russell, 2004).

Operating characteristics, however, have certain requirements. They may not be reliable when different samples are used to obtain sensitivity from that used to determine specificity. When various operating characteristics are derived from different samples, the subject's characteristics may vary for many reasons other than the effect of the condition being tested. An example of operating characteristics not obtained from the same sample is the operating characteristics provided in the RCNEHRB (Heaton et al., 2004, pp. 9, 23–33). There is no description of the source of the brain-damaged subjects, nor their connection with the normal "participants."

Finally, many neuropsychologists emphasize domains rather than tests. However, as has been discussed previously, the selection of tests for coverage cannot be accurately based on domains, although this is a common practice in flexible-battery neuropsychology. The reason is that there is no consensus in neurology or neuropsychology as to the number of domains or the tests included in each domain. Almost all neuropsychological tests are compound tests that include components from a number of domains, and none clearly identifies a domain (Dodrill, 1997).

Interpretation of Formal Psychometric Results

Along with the advantages of formal psychometric methods is a limitation. In any specific situation, psychometric method results are inflexible and do not in themselves provide for exceptions. Psychometric statistical methods need to be thoroughly understood for accurate interpretation. These methods are statistically derived so that a cut point states the most statistically accurate separation, not an absolute separation between conditions. The cut point generally occurs where two distributions overlap, such as normal and brain-damaged subject distributions (Slick, 2006, p. 20). As such, there will be normal subjects in the brain-damaged range and brain-damaged subjects in the normal range.

As an example, when there are equal numbers of brain-damaged and normal subjects in a HRNES-R battery, an AIS cutting score of 95 is 77% correct in predicting that a person has brain damage and 94% correct in predicting normal (no brain-damaged) subjects (Russell, 2004). Thus, a person who scores above 95 still has a 23% chance of having some sort of brain damage. The clinician must look at additional test indications in the battery as well as history to determine whether a particular person might have a focal area of brain damage even if the general AIS score was above 95. In addition, if the AIS index is below 95, the context is important. For instance, it is now almost obligatory in neuropsychology assessment to use well-validated tests of effort in reaching a conclusion.

To increase accuracy, a scale was developed for the HRNES-R that provides percentage of brain-damage cases for various AIS scores in the total normative sample (Russell & Starkey, 2001b, Appendix F, p. 26). This provides a measure of the probability that a subject has brain damage. For instance, although the cut point for brain damage is 94 or below, there is some probability that a person with a score somewhat above 95 may have brain damage. However, if the subject has a score of 102 or above he or she has almost no probability of having brain damage. Not one subject in the normative sample of 776 subjects with a score that high had brain damage. In contrast, if the AIS is 90 or below, the chance of having brain damage is 92.3%.

Validation and Forensics

In regard to forensics, the conclusion of this review is that, in neuropsychological assessment, the norming and validating procedures used to obtain information must be examined and found to be psychometrically sound in order to produce forensically reliable expert witness information. Such reliability is desirable in most areas of neuropsychological practice, but it is critical in forensic activities.

The defining characteristic of clinical neuropsychology is the analysis of an individual's brain function using psychometric tests. This use of neuropsychological tests distinguishes it from neurology, psychiatry, neuroscience, and other forms of clinical psychology.

The exception to the use of tests occurs when that methodology is inapplicable to parts of the case. In such a situation, logic, common sense, and reliable observation must be used. However, neuropsychologists who base an assessment almost entirely on a mental status examination or history of the patient are not practicing neuropsychology. A full interpretation requires a logical application of reliable psychometric information to the subject's situational context.

Concerning psychometric validation, published studies have demonstrated that all major neuropsychological fixed and standardized batteries have been validated. In contrast, there are no studies in the literature that support the validity of flexible batteries.

Flexible batteries rely on the interpretation of individual tests to indicate a neurological condition. However, a certain number of test results in a battery will fall in the impaired range simply because of random variation rather than being a reflection of brain dysfunction, whereas other tests are unimpaired. Because there is no known method that can determine which specific tests in the flexible battery are truly indicative of brain damage, the clinician who interprets these results is capitalizing on chance and cannot reliably diagnose brain injury.

Further, in a battery, reliable determination of the existence of brain damage as well as localization and diagnostic assessments must use test combinations and comparisons. Reliable combinations and comparisons of tests require a fixed or standardized battery in which tests are invariant and have a common metric, equivalent norms derived from co-norming, and relevant demographic characteristics. Studies have validated the ability of standardized batteries to indicate brain damage accurately but flexible batteries have not been validated. In addition, only standardized batteries have been demonstrated to foster reliable and valid clinical judgments. The advantage of formal psychometric methods in forensic situations is their great reliability. Both the validity and rate of error can be determined.

There are many reasons that the *Daubert* standard provides a means to justify the dependence of testimony on scientific methodology in court ["Requirement under Federal Rule of Evidence that expert's testimony pertain to 'scientific knowledge' establishes standard of evidentiary reliability." Fed. Rules, Evid. Rule 702, 28 U.S.C.A. (*Daubert v. Merrell*, 1993)]. In forensic cases, formal methods provide both an objective method to determine the existence of brain damage but also the potential rate of error. In this regard, the operating characteristics are particularly important (Reed, 1996). One of the major criteria of the *Daubert* standard for determining whether an expert's testimony was based on scientifically reliability studies was whether a technique considered "known or potential rate of error" (*Daubert v. Merrell*, 1993, vol. 28, 2789). In a neuropsychological or a medical setting, the primary method for demonstrating rate of error is obtained by means of operating characteristics.

In summary, the expert witness using a fixed or standardized battery in forensic situations is the only neuropsychologist who can provide reliable testimony interpreting psychometric test data based on a battery of tests. The expert witness who uses a flexible battery can only reliably use evidence derived from one individual test. Such individual tests cannot be reliably combined, compared, or used in a group with other neuropsychological tests. Finally, clinical judgment has never been validated when used to interpret flexible test batteries.

Such validating studies would be a welcome and essential contribution to the field for research on the dependability of flexible batteries to be pursued in earnest and published in neuropsychological peer-reviewed journals.

Summary

The basis of all neuropsychological assessment procedures, including forensics, is *justification*. Justification is derived from general reliability. Neuropsychological assessment knowledge is reliable if, and only if, it is derived from methods that have been validated using psychometric procedures that are generally acceptable in science. Because whole batteries are used for interpretations and provide information different from that derived from individual tests, psychometric procedures must be applied to batteries. Individual tests in a battery are usually not reliable indicators of brain damage because they may be impaired by chance. A flexible battery provides no method for determining which contradictory test is correct. Standardized battery norms represent a sample of the general population. Adequate representation depends on the size of the sample, the location of subjects, and whether they are neurologically normal. Co-norming is necessary to dependably combine or compare scales. Although clinical judgment has been validated for fixed and standardized batteries, it has never been validated for flexible batteries. Thus, formal psychometric procedures that provide dependable objective information cannot be applied to flexible batteries. For this reason, flexible batteries cannot provide dependable knowledge beyond that which could be obtained from a single individual test.

References

American Academy of Neurology Brief. (2007). *Baxter v. Temple brief* 949 A. 2d 167 (NH 2008).

American Educational Research Association (AERA), American Psychological Association, & the National Council on Measurement in Education. (1999). *Standards for educational and psychological testing*, Washington, DC: Author.

American Psychological Association (APA). (2002). Ethical principles of psychologists and code of conduct (5th ed.), *American Psychologist*, 47, 1060–1073.

Anastasi, A., & Urbina, S. (1997). *Psychological testing* (7th ed.). Upper Saddle River, NJ: Prentice Hall.

Axelrod, B. N., & Goldman, R. S. (1996). Use of demographic corrections in neuropsychological interpretation: How standard are standard scores?. *Clinical Neuropsychologist, 10*, 159–162.

Bauer, R. M. (2000). The flexible battery approach to neuropsychological assessment. In R. D. Vanderploeg (Ed.), *Clinician's guide to neuropsychological practice* (pp. 419–448) (2nd ed.). Hillsdale, NJ: Erlbaum.

Bland, M. (2000). *An introduction to medical statistics* (3rd ed.). New York: Oxford University Press.

Bornstein, R. A. (1986). Normative data on selected neuropsychological measures from a non-clinical sample. *Journal of Clinical Psychology, 41*, 651–659.

Bush, S. S., Connell, M. A., & Denney, R. L. (2009). *Ethical practice in forensic psychology: A systematic model for decision-making*. Washington, DC: American Psychological Association.

Cohen, M. R., & Nagel, E. (1962). *An introduction to logic and scientific method*. New York: Harcourt, Brace. (Original work published in 1939).

Crawford, J. R., & Howell, D. C. (1998). Regression equations in clinical neuropsychology: An evaluation of statistical methods for comparing predicted and obtained scores. *Journal of Clinical and Experimental Neurology, 20*, 755–762.

Daubert v. Merrell Dow Pharmaceuticals (1993). 113 Supreme Court Reporter (S.Ct.) 2786.

Diagnosing comas. (2009, July 25). *The Economist, 92*(8641), 76.

Dodrill, C. B. (1987). *What constitutes normal performance in clinical neuropsychology?* Paper presented at the 97th Annual Convention of the American Psychological Association, Atlanta, GA.

Dodrill, C. B. (1997). Myths of neuropsychology. *Clinical Neuropsychologist, 11*, 1–17.

Ellis, A. W., & Young, A. W. (1988). *Human cognitive neuropsychology*. London: Lawrence Erlbaum.

Faigman, D. L., Saks, M. J., Sanders, J., & Cheng, E. K. (2008). *Modern scientific evidence, standard statistics, and research methods (student ed.)*. Eagan, MN: Thompson & West.

Flynn, J. R. (1999). Searching for justice: The discovery of IQ gains over time. *American Psychologist, 54*(1), 5–20.

Franzen, M. D. (2000). *Reliability and validity in neuropsychological assessment* (2nd ed.). New York: Kluwer Academic/Plenum.

Garb, H. N. (1998). *Studying the clinician: Judgment research and psychological assessment*. Washington, DC: American Psychological Association.

Garb, H. N., & Schramke, C. J. (1996). Judgment research and neuropsychological assessment: A narrative review and meta-analysis. *Psychological Bulletin, 120*, 140–153.

Ghiselli, E. E., Campbell, J. P., & Zedeck, S. (1981). *Measurement theory for the behavioral sciences*. San Francisco: W. H. Freeman.

Goldstein, K., & Scheerer, M. (1941). Abstract and concrete behavior: An experimental study with special tests. *Psychological Monographs, 53*, 2. Whole No. 239.

Gouvier, W. D. (1999). Base rates and clinical decision-making in neuropsychology. In J. Sweet (Ed.), *Forensic psychology: Fundamentals and practice*. Lisse, the Netherlands: Swets and Zeitlinger.

Gouvier, W. D. (2001). Are you sure you're telling the truth? *NeuroRehabilitation, 16*, 215–219.

Gravetter, F. J., & Wallnau, L. B. (2000). *Statistics for the behavioral sciences* (5th ed.). Belmont, CA: Wadsworth/Thompson learning.

Grove, W. M., & Meehl, P. E. (1996). Comparative efficiency of informal (subjective) impressionistic and formal (mechanical, algorithmic) prediction procedures: The clinical-statistical controversy. *Psychology, Public Policy, and Law*, *2*(2), 293–323.

Grove, W. M., Zald, D. H., Lebow, B. S., Snitz, B. E., & Nelson, C. (2000). Clinical versus mechanical prediction: A meta-analysis. *Psychological Assessment*, *12*(1), 19–30.

Guilford, J. P. (1965). *Fundamental statistics in psychology and education* (4th ed.). New York: McGraw-Hill.

Halstead, W. C. (1947). *Brain and intelligence*. Chicago, IL: University of Chicago Press.

Heaton, R. K., Grant, I., & Matthews, C. G. (1986). Differences in neuropsychological test performance associated with age, education and sex. In I. Grant & K. M. Adams (Eds.), *Neuropsychological assessment of neuropsychiatric disorders* (pp. 100–120). New York: Oxford.

Heaton, R. K., Grant, I., & Matthews, C. G. (1991). *Comprehensive norms for an expanded Halstead–Reitan Battery [Norms manual and computer program]*. Odessa, FL: Psychological Assessment Resources.

Heaton, R. K., Matthews, C. G., Grant, I., & Avitable, N. (1996). Demographic corrections with comprehensive norms: An overzealous attempt or a good start. *Journal of Clinical and Experimental Neuropsychology*, *18*, 121–141.

Heaton, R. K., Miller, S. W., Taylor, M. J., & Grant, I. (2004). *Revised comprehensive norms for an expanded Halstead–Reitan Battery: Demographically adjusted neuropsychological norms for African American and Caucasian adults [Professional manual and computer program]*. Odessa, FL: Psychological Assessment Resources.

Hom, J. (1992). General and specific cognitive dysfunctions in patients with Alzheimer's disease. *Archives of Clinical Neuropsychology*, *7*, 121–133.

Jarvis, P. E., & Barth, J. T. (1984). *Halstead–Reitan Test Battery; An interpretive guide*. Odessa, FL: Psychological Assessment Resources.

Ingraham, L. J., & Aiken, C. B. (1996). An empirical approach to determining criteria for abnormality in test batteries with multiple measures. *Neuropsychology*, *10*, 120–124.

Kalechstein, A. D., van Gorp, W. G., & Rapport, L. J. (1998). Variability in clinical classification of raw test scores across normative data sets. *Clinical Neuropsychologist*, *12*(3), 339–347.

Kaplan, E. (1988). A process approach to neuropsychological assessment. In T. Boll & B. K. Brynt (Eds.), *Clinical neuropsychology and brain function: Research, measurement, and practice* (pp. 125–168). Washington, DC: American Psychological Association.

Kumho Tire v. Carmichael (1999). 526 U.S. 137.

Larrabee, G. J. (2005). A scientific approach to forensic neuropsychology. In G. J. Larrabee (Ed.), *Forensic neuropsychology: A scientific approach* (pp. 3–28). New York: Oxford University Press.

Lezak, M. D. (1988). IQ: R.I.P. *Journal of Clinical and Experimental Neuropsychology*, *10*, 351–361.

Lezak, M. D. (1995). *Neuropsychological assessment* (3rd ed.). New York: Oxford University Press.

Lezak, M. D., Howieson, D. B., & Loring, D. W. (2004). *Neuropsychological assessment* (4th ed.). New York: Oxford University Press.

Loring, D. W., & Bauer, R. M. (2010). Testing the limits: Cautions and concerns regarding the new Wechsler IQ and Memory scales. *Neurology*, *74*(8), 685–690.

Luria, A. R. (1973). *The working brain*. New York: Basic Books.

Matthews, C. G. (1987). Personal communication.

Mathias, J. L., & Burke, J. (2009). Cognitive functioning in Alzheimer's and vascular dementia: A meta-analysis. *Neuropsychology*, *23*(4), 411–423.

Meehl, P. E. (1954). *Clinical versus statistical prediction: A theoretical analysis and a review of the evidence*. Minneapolis, MN: University of Minnesota Press.

Meyers, J. E., & Rohling, M. L. (2004). Validation of the Myers short battery on mild TBI patients. *Archives of Clinical Neuropsychology, 19*(5), 637–651.

Miller, L. S., & Rohling, M. L. (2001). A statistical interpretive method for neuropsychological test data. *Neuropsychology Review, 11*(3), 143–169.

Mitrushina, M. N., Boone, K. B., & D'Elia, L. F. (1999). *Handbook of normative data for neuropsychological assessment*. New York: Oxford University Press.

Moses, J. A., Prichard, D. A., & Adams, R. L. (1999). Normative corrections for the Halstead Reitan Neuropsychological Battery. *Archives of Clinical Neuropsychology, 14*, 445–454.

Nagel, E. (1961). *The structure of science: Problems in the logic of scientific explanation*. New York: Harcourt, Brace.

Nixon, S. J. (1996). Alzheimer's disease and vascular dementia. In L. A. Russell, O. A. Parsons, J. L. Culbertson, & S. J. Nixon (Eds.), *Neuropsychology for clinical practice: Etiology, assessment, and treatment of common neurological disorders* (pp. 65–105). Washington, DC: American Psychological Association.

Nunnally, J. C., & Bernstein, I. H. (1994). *Psychometric theory* (3rd ed.). New York: McGraw-Hill.

Palmer, B. W., Applebaum, M. I., & Heaton, R. K. (2004). Rohling's interpretative and inherent limitations on the flexibility of "flexible batteries". *Neuropsychology Review, 14*(3), 171–176.

Reed, J. E. (1996). Fixed vs. flexible neuropsychological test batteries under the Daubert standard for admissibility of scientific evidence. *Behavioral Science and the Law, 14*, 315–322.

Reitan, R. M. (1955). Investigation of the validity of Halstead's measures of biological intelligence. *Archives of Neurology and Psychiatry, 73*, 28–35.

Reitan, R. M. (1962). Psychological deficit. *Annual Review of Psychology, 13*, 415–444.

Reitan, R. M., & Wolfson, D. (1993). *The Halstead–Reitan Neuropsychological Test Battery: Theory and clinical interpretation* (2nd ed.). Tucson, AZ: Neuropsychology Press.

Reitan, R. M., & Wolfson, D. (1995). Cross-validation of the General Neuropsychological Deficit Scale (GNDS). *Archives of Clinical Neuropsychology, 10*(2), 125–131.

Retzlaff, P. D., & Gibertini, M. (2000). Neuropsychometric issues and problems. In R. D. Vanderploeg (Ed.), *Clinician's guide to neuropsychological assessment* (pp. 277–299) (2nd ed.). Mahwah, NJ: Lawrence Erlbaum Associates.

Rohling, M. L., Miller, L. S., & Langhinrichsen-Rohling, J. (2004). Rohling's interpretive method for neuropsychological data analysis: a response to critics. *Neuropsychological Review, 14*(3), 155–169.

Rourke, B. P., & Brown, G. G. (1986). Clinical neuropsychology and behavioral neurology: Similarities and differences. In S. B. Filskov & T. J. Boll (Eds.), *Handbook of clinical neuropsychology* (Vol. 2, pp. 3–18). New York: Wiley.

Rosenfeld, B., Sands, S. A., & van Gorp, W. G. (2000). Have we forgotten the base rate problem? Methodological issues in the detection of distortion. *Archives of Clinical Neuropsychology, 15*(4), 349–359.

Russell, E. W. (1981). The chronicity effect. *Journal of Clinical Psychology, 37*, 246–253.

Russell, E. W. (1987). A reference scale method for constructing neuropsychological test batteries. *Journal of Clinical and Experimental Neuropsychology, 9*, 376–392.

Russell, E. W. (1990). *Three validity studies for negative neurological criterion norming*. (Unpublished Paper presented at the 98th annual convention of the American Psychological Association, Boston).

Russell, E. W. (1995). The accuracy of automated and clinical detection of brain damage and lateralization in neuropsychology. *Neuropsychology Review*, *5*(1), 1–68.

Russell, E. W. (1997). Developments in the psychometric foundations of neuropsychological assessment. In G. Goldstein & T. Incagnoli (Eds.), *Contemporary approaches to neuropsychological assessment* (pp. 15–65). New York: Plenum.

Russell, E. W. (1998). In defense of the Halstead–Reitan Battery: A critique of Lezak's review. *Archives of Clinical Neuropsychology*, *13*, 365–381.

Russell, E. W. (2000a). The application of computerized scoring programs to neuropsychological assessment. In R. D. Vanderploeg (Ed.), *Clinician's guide to neuropsychological assessment* (pp. 483–515) (2nd ed.). Hillsdale, NJ: Lawrence Erlbaum Associates.

Russell, E. W. (2000b). The cognitive-metric, fixed battery approach to neuropsychological assessment. In R. D. Vanderploeg (Ed.), *Clinician's guide to neuropsychological assessment* (pp. 449–481) (2nd ed.). Hillsdale, NJ: Lawrence Erlbaum Associates.

Russell, E. W. (2001). Toward an explanation of Dodrill's observation: High neuropsychological test performance does not accompany high IQs. *Clinical Neuropsychologist*, *15*, 423–428.

Russell, E. W. (2003). The critique of the HRNES in the "Handbook of Normative Data for Neuropsychological Assessment." *Archives of Clinical Neuropsychology*, *18*(2), 165–180.

Russell, E. W. (2004). The operating characteristics of the major HRNES-R measures. *Archives of Clinical Neuropsychology*, *19*(8), 1043–1061.

Russell, E. W. (2005). Norming subjects for the Halstead–Reitan Battery. *Archives of Clinical Neuropsychology*, *20*(4), 479–484.

Russell, E. W. (2007). The Flynn effect revisited. *Applied Neuropsychology*, *14*(4), 262–266.

Russell, E. W. (2009). Commentary on Larrabee, Mills, and Meyer's paper "Sensitivity to brain dysfunction of the Halstead–Reitan vs an ability-focused neuropsychology battery." *Clinical Neuropsychologist*, *23*, 831–840.

Russell, E. W. (2010). The "obsolescence" of assessment procedures. *Applied Neuropsychology*, *17*(1), 60–67.

Russell, E. W., Neuringer, C., & Goldstein, G. (1970). *Assessment of brain damage: A neuropsychological key approach*. New York: Wiley Company.

Russell, E. W., & Polakoff, D. (1993). Neuropsychological test patterns in men for Alzheimer's and multi-infarct dementia. *Archives of Clinical Neuropsychology*, *8*, 327–343.

Russell, E. W., & Russell, S. L. K. (2003). Twenty ways and more of diagnosing brain damage when there is none. *Journal of Controversial Medical Claims*, *10*(1), 1–14.

Russell, E. W., Russell, S. L. K., & Hill, B. (2005). The fundamental psychometric status of neuropsychological batteries. *Archives of Clinical Neuropsychology*, *20*(6), 785–794.

Russell, E. W., & Starkey, R. I. (1993). *Halstead–Russell Neuropsychological Evaluation System [Manual and computer program]*. Los Angeles: Western Psychological Services.

Russell, E. W., & Starkey, R. I. (2001). *Halstead–Russell Neuropsychological Evaluation System—Revised [Manual and computer program]*. Los Angeles: Western Psychological Services.

Russell, E. W., & Starkey, R. I. (2001). *Halstead–Russell Neuropsychological Evaluation System—Revised [Appendix F]*. Los Angeles: Western Psychological Services.

Slick, D. J. (2006). Psychometrics in neuropsychological assessment. In E. Strauss, E. M. S. Sherman, & O. Spreen: *A compendium of neuropsychological tests: Administration, norms, and commentary* (pp. 3–43) (3rd ed.). New York: Oxford University Press.

Spreen, O., & Strauss, E. (1998). *A compendium of neuropsychological tests* (2nd ed.). New York: Oxford University Press.

Stanczak, D. E. (2003, March 27). Personal communication.

Stanczak, E. M., Stanczak, D. E., & Templer, D. I. (2000). Subject-selection procedures in neuropsychological research: A meta-analysis and prospective study. *Archives of Clinical Neuropsychology*, *15*(7), 587–601.

Steinmeyer, C. H. (1986). A meta-analysis of Halstead–Reitan test performances on non-brain damaged subjects. *Archives of Clinical Neuropsychology*, *1*, 301–307.

Stern, R. A., & White, T. (2001). *Neuropsychological assessment battery (NAB)*. Lutz, FL: Psychological Assessment Resources.

Strauss, E., Sherman, E. M. S., & Spreen, O. (2006). *A compendium of neuropsychological tests: Administration, norms, and commentary* (3rd ed.). New York: Oxford University Press.

Teuber, H. L. (1955). Physiological psychology. *Annual Review of Psychology*, *6*, 267–296.

Teuber, H. L. (1959). Some alterations in behavior after cerebral lesions in man. In: A. B. Bass (Ed.), *Evolution of nervous control from primitive organisms to man* (pp. 157–190). Amsterdam: Elsevier.

Toulmin, S. E. (2006). Philosophy of science. *Encyclopaedia Britannica*. Retrieved March 3, 2007, from *Encyclopaedia Britannica 2006, Ultimate Reference Suite DVD*.

Vanderploeg, R. D., Axelrod, B. N., Sherer, M., Scott, J., & Adams, R. L. (1997). The importance of demographic adjustments on neuropsychological test performance: A response to Reitan and Wolfson (1995). *Clinical Neuropsychologist*, *11*(2), 210–217.

Volbrecht, M. E., Meyers, J. E., & Kaster-Bundgaard, J. (2000). Neuropsychological outcome of head injury using a short battery. *Archives of Clinical Neuropsychology*, *15*, 251–265.

Wechsler, D. (1955). *Wechsler Adult Intelligence Scale [Manual]*. New York: Psychological Corporation.

Wechsler, D. (1981). *WAIS-R Wechsler Adult Intelligence Scale—Revised [Manual]*. San Antonio, TX: Psychological Corporation.

Wechsler, D. (1997). *WAIS-III, WMS-III [Technical manual]*. San Antonio, TX: Psychological Corporation.

Wechsler, D., Coalson, D. L., & Raiford, S. E. (2008). *WAIS-IV technical and interpretive manual*. San Antonio, TX: Pearson.

Willson, V. L., & Reynolds, C. R. (2004). A critique of Miller and Rohling's statistical interpretative method for neuropsychological test data. *Neuropsychology Review*, *14*(3), 177–181.

Williams, A. D. (1997). Fixed versus flexible batteries. In R. J. McCaffrey, A. D. Williams, J. M. Fisher & L. C. Laing (Eds.), *The practice of forensic neuropsychology: Meeting challenges in the courtroom* (pp. 57–70). New York: Plenum.

9 The Accuracy of Formal Neuropsychological Methods

> *Ordinarily, [the] key question to be answered in determining whether theory or technique is scientific knowledge that will assist trier of fact, and, thus, whether expert testimony is admissible, will be whether theory or technique can be, and has been tested.*
>
> **Federal Rules of Evidence, Rules 104 (a), 702, 28, U.S.C.A.**

> *[A] method's accuracy often should be the most important factor when considering courtroom application or admissibility.... If a method either cannot be tested or has not been tested, there will be no direct scientific information on the method's accuracy.*
>
> **Faust, Grimm, Ahern, and Sokolik (2010, p. 49)**

Having discussed the justification of neuropsychological batteries, which primarily concerns the standardization and validation of neuropsychological procedures, the question then becomes, how accurate are the various neuropsychological batteries? Justification is the method for demonstrating the reliability of a procedure. In neuropsychology, this is accomplished by the accuracy of the procedure in the validation process. Validation always concerns accuracy—that is, the strength of a procedure's validation is the accuracy of the procedure.

Requirements for Battery Accuracy

The Standards for Educational and Psychological Testing [American Educational Research Association, American Psychological Association, and National Council on Measurement in Education (hereafter, AERA et al.), 1999] are quite clear: "Validity refers to the degree to which evidence and theories support the interpretations of test scores entailed by proposed uses of tests" (p. 9).

Consequently, if the tests are used as a whole in a battery to produce an interpretation, then the battery as a whole must be validated. The individual validation of a myriad of unrelated individual tests does not validate this collection of items as a basis for a unified interpretation. Although innumerable studies have testified to the validity of individual tests, the studies validating and determining the accuracy of standardized batteries are limited.

The Scientific Foundation of Neuropsychological Assessment. DOI: 10.1016/B978-0-12-416029-3.00009-9

Many neuropsychologists do not appear to be concerned with the accuracy of whole-battery interpretations, although they insist that whole batteries are necessary for interpretations (Lezak, Howieson, & Loring, 2004, pp. 17–18; Mitrushina, Boone, Razani, & D'Elia, 2005, p. 5).

For instance, in spite of a thorough discussion of factors that affect the assessment of brain damage and an extensive discussion of the accuracy of individual tests, Lezak et al. (2004) do not discuss the overall accuracy of neuropsychological batteries or clinical judgment anywhere in their 1,016-page book, nor do Mitrushina et al. (2005) in their *Handbook of Normative Data for Neuropsychological Assessment* (2nd ed.) or Strauss, Sherman, and Spreen (2006) in their *A Compendium of Neuropsychological Tests: Administration, Norms, and Commentary* (3rd ed.). Neuropsychology appears to be unaware that there are standardized batteries that have been validated and are therefore reliable for forensic and any other purpose. The Halstead–Reitan Battery (HRB) and the Neuropsychological Deficit Scale (NDS) (Reitan & Wolfson, 1993b, pp. 347–397), the Luria–Nebraska Neuropsychological Battery (LNNB) (Golden, Hammeke, & Purisch, 1980), the *Halstead–Russell Neurological Evaluation System—Revised* (HRNES–R) (Russell & Starkey, 2001a), the Meyers Neuropsychological Battery (MNB) (Meyers & Rohling, 2004), the Neuropsychological Assessment Battery (NAB) (Stern & White, 2001), and a number of computerized batteries.

The Importance of Accuracy Studies

The importance of accuracy studies for both clinical judgment and computer programs cannot be overemphasized (Faust, Grimm, Ahern, & Sokolik, 2010). Such research is probably the most important yet one of the least exercised activities in neuropsychology. Without such studies, it is not possible to know whether a test battery interpretation is reliable because its accuracy would have never been tested. Neuropsychologists using a nonstandardized battery may presume that their work is accurate but they have no sound evidence to support this presumption.

There is also no evidence concerning which method or approach is more accurate. For instance, there are no studies comparing the accuracy of more recent batteries, much less the accuracy of any flexible battery. In fact, the only extensive studies related to batteries that have been subjected to validity studies have concerned the HRB, the LNNB, and the HRNES–R. This means that the accuracy of the flexible battery and the Process Approach methods are unknown. Neuropsychologists should take this situation into consideration when performing legal work (Faust et al., 2010; Garb, 1998, pp. 246–247).

Accuracy provides several important characteristics of formal neuropsychological procedures. First, it indicates that a measure is valid because the rate of error is a measure of the validity of a procedure. Second, as such, it is an indication of the amount of reliability that one may place in the procedure. Third, it enables a neuropsychologist to compare the reliability of various procedures. This is useful in most areas of neuropsychology, but it is particularly important in forensics because it provides a means to determine which procedures are the most trustworthy. Finally, rate of error is a major component in most interpretations. In examining interpretations, the results from a highly accurate procedure takes precedent over a less accurate one.

Accuracy in Forensic Assessment

Although accurate procedures are necessary for most uses of neuropsychological examinations, they are especially important in court. In forensics, neuropsychological assessment is now involved in multimillion-dollar litigation and rehabilitation activities. Today, the management of hundreds of millions of dollars is decided by methods of neuropsychological assessment whose validity is generally completely unknown; at best, there is limited information about their accuracy.

Areas of Interest

Two types of accuracy will be examined in this chapter, primarily because they are the only two types that have been investigated to any extent: (1) the accuracy in determining the existence of brain damage and (2) the accuracy concerning the lateralization of the damage. This review will also examine the accuracy or validity of both formal and clinical judgment methods related to the various neuropsychological batteries. Although there have been many studies related to more detailed aspects of brain functioning, most of them have not been cross validated. Some of these studies are discussed in Chapter 6 on neuropsychological battery patterns. However, before neuropsychological studies can be examined, the problems connected with the criteria for neuropsychological conditions need to be examined.

The Criterion Problem

Many studies have examined the accuracy of individual tests related to a particular neurological condition. However, as Reitan indicated almost a half century ago in an interpretation, the alterative possibilities must be excluded (1962, pp. 422–426). Much of his writing in his 1964 paper is concerned with how his laboratory dealt with the criterion problem. To a great extent, the criterion problem is discussed by reference to individual conditions that the neuropsychologist knows through experience. However, this is of little help to the student who is dealing with a new case. Considering the importance of the criterion for validation, it is surprising that it is so seldom discussed, although there have been references to it for a half century.

It is the criterion that generally sets the limits on the accuracy of a procedure. If the neurologist's diagnosis is the criterion and its accuracy is only 80%, then the neuropsychological procedure cannot be greater than 80%. If it is higher, then the neuropsychologist's report is making the same errors as the neurologists. For instance, if a neuropsychology examination was 100% accurate and the criterion was only 80% accurate, then the neuropsychology examination would differ from the criterion on 20% of the cases so that the study would give the procedure only an 80% accuracy.

The importance of the neuropsychologist's reliance on the accuracy of the neurologist's report as a criterion is indicated in a study by Boyar and Tsushima (1975). In this study, there were two groups of brain-damaged patients. One group, designated as *neurological* patients, had a neurological examination that included only x-rays and electroencephalograms (EEGs). The other group, designated as the *neurosurgical* group, consisted of patients undergoing a neurosurgical evaluation. They had findings reported from surgery, brain scans, angiograms, and autopsies. The control group of 40 negative neurological patients was compared to one of the brain-damaged groups, and apparently the same neuropsychologists made both examinations. The findings for the neurological group was an 83% agreement with the neuropsychological evaluation, whereas the neurosurgical group had 100% agreement. In the case of the neurosurgical patients, evidently the diagnosis was quite definite, whereas the diagnoses of the neurological group were primarily based on the neurological physical examination. The importance of this study is that it demonstrates the difference in neuropsychological examination agreement with different criteria. This finding would also explain the 100% agreement between the HRB and neurosurgical findings in the study by Filskov and Goldstein (1974). The authors state that only clear-cut neurosurgical cases were selected.

The Basis for Criteria

In the great majority of the neuropsychological studies, the criterion is the neurological diagnosis using either all relevant methods, such as the final diagnosis of neurologists, or a specific technique such as an imaging method. Anyone who has worked extensively in a medical setting knows that the accuracy of the neurological diagnosis, even when all procedures are used, is far from perfect. It is influenced by the relative proportion of patients who have obvious diagnoses compared to those whose diagnoses are ambiguous. Thus, there is a variation in the general accuracy of the criterion diagnosis. This variation in accuracy is very evident in the cases presented in the tables for this chapter.

The reliance on the neurologists' findings means that the criterion in neuropsychology is usually secondary. The neurologists' findings are primary, because there must be criteria for the neuropsychologists' conclusions. Even when magnetic resonance imaging (MRI) is used as the criterion, it must be interpreted by a neuroradiologist. In this case, the neuropsychological criterion is the neuroradiologist's report.

In this regard, two types of criterion have been used by neuropsychology. The first criterion is the diagnosis by a neurologist or neurosurgeon who has used all of the relevant neurological procedures such as the MRI, computed tomography (CT), and EEGs. The second criterion is for the neuropsychologist to use a particular neurological procedure directly such as the MRI. The problem with using any neurological procedure directly is that none is completely accurate. The MRI, which is highly accurate for focal tissue damage, is unreliable when it is applied to many diffuse conditions such as head trauma or Alzheimer's dementia (AD) (Barth, Gideon, Sciara, Hulsey, & Anchor, 1986; Bigler, 1991, Chapter 7). In almost all cases, a neurologist or neurosurgeon who has been trained in these methods and uses all of the relevant methods to come to a diagnostic decision is more accurate than the selection of a procedure via neuropsychologist. An excellent discussion of this procedure was published by Filskov and Goldstein (1974).

Time and Accuracy

Time is one major criterion that is used as a basis of diagnosis. Almost all lesions have a temporal aspect, and progressive lesions eventually manifest themselves with or without the use of scanning techniques. Once manifest, they can ultimately be accurately diagnosed, even if it is from an autopsy.

This progressiveness provides one method in which neuropsychological testing may be more accurate than neurological procedures. If neuropsychologists can identify a test pattern that relatively accurately predicts a neurological condition before it becomes manifest to neurological procedures, then the neuropsychological procedures may be more accurate than neurological criteria. There have already been attempts to identify AD prior to the appearance of obvious memory problems.

Another relationship of time to accuracy is that almost all brain damage changes over time. Even nonprogressive lesions such as strokes have a time aspect such that they are identified as being acute, static, or chronic (Goldstein, Shemansky, Beers, George, & Roberts, 1996; Russell, 1981). A lesion improves rapidly in the acute stage, which may last 2 to 3 months. The improvement continues at a slower pace to about 2 years when it becomes chronic. Although there may be some further improvement, particularly with learning, the improvement is generally limited. This progression is particularly important in forensic cases, which usually come to court years after an initial incident.

Criterion Accuracy

During the 1970s, there was interest in the relative accuracy of neuropsychological tests, particularly in reference to the CT scan. Examination of references in PsycINFO indicates a current lack of interest by neuropsychologists in the criterion problem. However, several studies during the 1970s (Filskov & Goldstein, 1974; Snow, 1981; Swiercinsky & Leigh, 1979; Tsushima & Wedding 1979) examined the relative accuracy of various psychological and neuropsychological procedures.

The apparent lack of interest in the accuracy of neuropsychological methodology after the early 1980s is not coincidental, because it occurred after a severe critique of formal methods in neuropsychology, including standardized batteries. This leaves neuropsychological assessment with almost no studies since about 1985 that demonstrate the accuracy or validity of neuropsychological batteries or interpretations based on batteries. Many neuropsychologists will say that with the development of the MRI and CT scans, studies concerning the accuracy of neuropsychological methodology are irrelevant (Mapou, 1988). This may be true for many areas of neuropsychology, but it is not true for forensics.

Accuracy of Neurological Procedures

Examining these five studies (Filskov & Goldstein, 1974; Sherer, Scott, Parsons, & Adams, 1994; Snow, 1981; Swiercinsky & Leigh, 1979; Tsushima & Wedding, 1979) provides some idea of the accuracy of various neurological procedures in comparison to certain neuropsychological procedures, primarily the HRB and the HI. The neuropsychological procedures were found to be generally as accurate or more accurate than individual neurological methods. It is obvious that none of these methods is completely accurate compared with a full neurological examination in which all procedures are used by knowledgeable neurologists. The CT scan, which appears in most of the studies after 1974, was evidently the most sensitive neurological instrument. However, it was only 35% accurate in the Tsushima and Wedding study (1979). This study had a high percentage of head traumas, seizures, and degenerative diseases, which are not obvious on CT scans (Bigler, 1991). The MRI is not much better at identifying these conditions than the neurological examination. In this study, the EEG was more sensitive than the CT scan at 53% correct identification, probably because of a high percentage of head trauma and seizure cases.

The study by Swiercinsky and Leigh (1979) had a low hit rate for almost all procedures compared to the CT scan. There was a high number of diffuse and equivocal patients in the data.

More recently, Sherer et al. (1994) attempted to demonstrate that the Wechsler Adult Intelligence Scale—Revised (WAIS–R) was as sensitive to the effects of brain damage as the HRB; they did so by examining the related neurodiagnostic findings of various neurological methodologies. These included the CT scan as well as seven other generally used neurological procedures. The presentation of these procedures was such that it is not possible to determine their sensitivity or specificity to the 65 brain-damaged and 45 non–brain-damaged subjects. However, it was evident that although the most accurate procedure was the CT scan, it apparently missed many of subjects.

Although studies are lacking, my estimate is that the neurological criterion diagnosis is generally between 80% and 90% accurate. The study that provides indirect evidence of this criterion accuracy is Boyar and Tsushima (1975), which was done before the introduction of imaging techniques. In this study, the agreement between the neuropsychological assessment for lateralization was 58% correct for neurological subjects, whereas it was 87% correct for neurosurgical subjects. In the various studies that had CT scans, their accuracy was only about 80%. In the Sherer et al. (1994) study, it was only about 60% correct.

Another way to demonstrate the effect of criterion group variability would be to hold the testing procedure consistent while varying the types of subjects in the criterion. The HI and the neuropsychological key were both formal procedures that were administered without change from one study to another. Table 9.1 shows 13 studies of the HI, with overall predictive powers ranging from 60% to 90%, with an average of 77.2%. In Table 9.2, seven different studies contained the key index for the existence of brain damage. The sensitivity of the key varied from 42.5% to 91.5%, whereas the specificity varied from 61.2% to 100%. The overall predictive power varied from 55.3% to 88.0%. This is a huge variation produced by different criterion groups.

Table 9.1 Halstead Index Studies: Operating Characteristics for Assessing the Existence of Brain Damage[a]

Study	Brain Damage (*N*)	Control (*N*)	Sensitivity (%)	Specificity (%)	Predictive Power (%)		
					Positive	Negative	Overall
Halstead, 1947	171	30	61.4	100.0	100.0	30.1	66.7
Wheeler, Burk, & Reitan, 1963	79	61	89.9	90.2	92.2	87.3	90.0
Wheeler & Reitan, 1963	140	79	85.7	79.9	93.8	78.0	87.2
Vega & Parsons, 1967, p. 622[b]	50	50	76.0	78.0	77.5	76.5	77.0
Goldstein et al., 1973	10	10	80.0	70.0	72.7	77.8	75.0
Kiernan & Matthews, 1976	81	87	59.2	83.9	77.4	68.9	72.0
Tsushima & Wedding, 1979	34	11	61.8	54.5	80.8	54.5	60.0
Anthony et al. 1980	150	100	78.7	85.0	88.7	72.6	81.2
Snow, 1981[c]	64	25	92.2	40.0	79.7	66.7	77.5
Russell, 1984	157	34	87.3	79.4	95.1	57.4	85.9
Fields 1987	53	22	90.6	77.3	90.6	77.3	86.7
Sherer & Adams 1993	61	53	77.0	50.9	64.4	65.8	64.9
Rojas & Bennett, 1995	25	25	60.0	100.0	100.0	71.4	80.0
Average	82.7	45.1	76.9	76.1	85.6	68.0	77.2

[a]These studies used 0.5 as the cutting point to separate brain-damaged from control subjects.
[b]Cut point was reset at 0.7 for this older group of subjects.
[c]Equivocal group not used.

Table 9.2 AIR, AIS, Brain 1, and NDS Operating Characteristics for Assessing the Existence of Brain Damage

Study	Brain Damage (*N*)	Control (*N*)	Sensitivity (%)	Specificity (%)	Predictive Power (%)		
					Positive	Negative	Overall
AIR							
Russell et al., 1970	80	24	91.5	73.5	92.6	69.6	87.5
Swiercinsky & Warnock, 1977	198	62	79.8	61.2	86.8	48.7	75.4
Tsushima & Wedding, 1979	34	11	52.9	90.9	94.7	34.5	62.2
Anthony et al., 1980	150	100	74.6	89	91.0	70.1	80.4
Wedding, 1983a	20	5	85	100	100	62.5	88.0
Russell, 1984	157	34	73.5	91.2	97.5	42.5	76.4.0
Sherer & Adams, 1993	73	41	42.5	78.0	77.5	43.2	55.3
Sum	714	275	499.8	583.8	640.1	371.1	525.2
Average	102	39.3	71.4	83.4	91.4	53.0	75.0
Brain 1							
Anthony et al., 1980	150	100	84.0	71.0	81.3	74.7	78.8

Average Impairment Scale (AIS)[a]							
Russell & Starkey, 2004[a]	100	100	77	94	93	80	85
Percent Impaired Index (PII)[a]							
Russell & Starkey 2004[a]	100	100	81	85	84	82	83
Neuropsychological Deficit Scale							
Reitan & Wolfson, 1993b	79	41	92.4	90.2	94.8	86.0	91.7
Sherer & Adams, 1993	73	41	84.9	46.3	73.8	63.3	71.0
Sherer & Adams, 1993[a]	73	41	84.9	68.3	82.7	71.8	78.9
Wolfson & Reitan, 1995	50	50	96.0	80.0	82.8	95.2	88.0
Rojas & Bennett, 1995	25	25	84.0	100.0	100	86.2	92.0
Average NDS	60	39.6	88.44	76.96	86.82	80.5	84.32

[a]Base-rate prevalence adjusted to 50%.

Summary of Neurological Criteria

These studies demonstrate the great variable of results among test batteries using either an index or clinical judgment. Consequently, no one index or clinical judgment using a battery can be selected as having the strongest indication of accuracy. Comparisons are only adequate when they use the same group of subjects. For instance, Loring and Larrabee (2006) have used a study in which the results of the verbal selective reminding test were equal to the HI to demonstrate that the HI was no better than other indicators of brain damage. However, when a different group of patients were used in the HRNES–R norming sample (pp. 38–39), the average impairment score (AIS) (Russell & Starkey, 2001a, pp. 19–20) was an F of 375.4. In other studies (Tables 9.1 and 9.2), AIS was equivalent to the HI. In this battery, the Miami Selective Learning Test (MSLT), a selective reminding test, had a long-term memory score in which the F was only 20.2. Another study group that compared the selective reminding test to the HI or the AIS with the same group of subjects might have found the verbal selective reminding test to be equal to or superior to the HI, but this appears unlikely.

What is clear from these studies is that the accuracy rate of a neuropsychological procedure is increased by selecting patients for the criterion group who have a definite clear-cut diagnosis. In composing my own research group (Russell, 1984), about a third of the cases were eliminated on the basis of an indefinite or mixed diagnosis. This partly explains the high accuracy of this lateralization study. Thus, part of the variability in the validation studies was because of this difference in selecting patients. Although this variability is well known to neuropsychologists, its consequence for validity studies is often overlooked.

Base Rates

Before examining other aspects of the criterion, the concept of the base rate must be mentioned although it is too complex for a detailed discussion. The base rate of a neurological condition is crucially important in understanding the ability to predict the accuracy of a procedure. This has been well discussed by Faust and Ahern (In press) and by Russell (2004). The base rate determines the possibility of making an accurate prediction. However, the base rate may apply differently to various situations. For instance, if a person comes into a doctor's office and is found to have a fever of 103 °F, there are two ways of looking at base rates. The base rate of a person having a temperature of 103°F and being sick at any one time is probably more than 1,000 to 1, so from a classical point of view one would predict that the person is not sick. However, the base rate of a person who has a temperature of 103 °F is probably the inverse of the population base rate—that is, the probability that he or she is ill with a temperature that high is probably well over 99%. Thus, the base rate that is important is the probability that in a particular situation a particular procedure with a particular score will indicate a particular condition.

The concept of accuracy as related to base rate has been discussed in many articles, but if we want to determine the accuracy of an instrument in general when the particular situation is unknown, the base rate needs to be set at some neutral level; generally, this would be a 50% chance as to whether one does or does not have a condition (Russell, 2004).

"Normal" Control Subjects as a Criterion

Although it is obvious to experienced neuropsychologists that the measured accuracy of a particular procedure varies from one brain-damaged group to another, it is not obvious that the same may be true for samples of the so-called normal population. The accuracy of normal subjects is examined in several places in this book, such as Chapter 14. These studies found that, although the variation is not as great as with brain-damaged samples, there is a considerable amount of variation. In regard to individual tests, neuropsychology now has fairly comprehensive data on a number of the major tests presented in the book by Mitrushina et al. (2005), which used meta-analysis to create more accurate collective norms for 21 tests. Although this is certainly more accurate than trying to depend on any one set of norms, if there are systematic biases across all groups then those norms may be distorted.

The adequacy of neuropsychological norms depends on the characteristics of the subjects in the sample. For the most part, the normal subjects who are used in norming neuropsychological tests belong to one of two groups: volunteers or neurologically negative subjects.

Volunteer Subjects

Volunteer subjects and neurologically normal subjects are both used in many neuropsychological studies. They demonstrate markedly different test performances. In the study comprising Chapter 15 (Russell, 2005), when all of the HRB norming studies with an *N* of approximately 200 or more were examined, the Wechsler full-scale intelligence quotient (FSIQ) scores were about 1 standard deviation (SD) above the national average.

This finding was also true of the volunteers who were collected from norms with smaller numbers of subjects. In the Steinmeyer (1986) study, for the norms with IQ scores, the nine volunteer groups had a mean FSIQ of 116.9, whereas the five neurologically normal groups had a mean FSIQ of 103.6.

The norms from the HRNES–R, which used neurologically normal patients, were essentially average, with an FSIQ of 102 (Russell & Starkey, 2001a, p. 39). Evidently, the exclusion of neurologically suspect subjects from volunteer normative studies led to a bias that was reflected in higher-than-normal levels of performance. This sets inappropriately high assessment cutoffs for impaired performance.

The *Handbook of Normative Data for Neuropsychological Assessment* (2nd ed.) by Mitrushina et al. (2005) generally had the same level of high FSIQs. For example, examination of the category test norms, excluding the negative neurological subjects, found that almost all of the FSIQs were close to 1 SD above average, and none were below 106. The Boston Naming Test was unusual in that almost no IQs were reported out of 28 studies. Those that were reported tend to be considerably above average or considerably below average. This is regrettable for tests that are highly influenced by intellectual ability. When examined, supernormal IQs were characteristic of almost all of the other tests.

These findings almost require the conclusion that volunteer norms are, in fact, not normal but are instead supernormal norms. This means that if one sets the cutting point for brain damage at 1 SD below the sample mean (*t*-score of 40) and the mean of the volunteer norms is a standard deviation above the normal population average, then one-half of normal subjects would fall into the impaired range and thus be designated as brain damaged. This calls into question the results from many studies and assessments using volunteer norms.

Neurologically Normal Subjects

Many studies use negative neurological subjects. Such subjects have been highly criticized by many neuropsychologists because they say that they would not receive a neurological examination unless they had some kind of problem. Consequently, they were not normal. Although this is true, their lack of normality may be the result of such conditions as being worried about their memory, neurosis, or many other factors that might indicate the possibility of brain damage. When thoroughly examined, these subjects have no evidence of brain damage.

There are several reasons for using neurologically normal patients. First, they are not self-selected and not screened, so their intelligence tends to be average rather than above average. Second, as Reitan (Reitan & Wolfson, 1993a, pp. 33–35) has expressed, they are exactly the kind of patients who need to be separated from those who have brain damage. In this regard, the *Standards for Educational and Psychological Testing* (AERA, 1999) advise that norms should refer to populations that "include individuals or groups to whom test users will ordinarily wish to compare their own examinees" (p. 55). Finally, the psychometric requirements for operating characteristics assume that the subjects in the comparison group are derived from the same population as the brain-damaged subjects. This population consists of people who are suspected of having a neurological condition. These subjects with suspected brain damage are separated into normal and neurologically impaired groups by the standard neurological procedures.

Veterans Administration Subjects

Many norming and validity studies have used Veterans Administration (VA) medical center patients as subjects (Russell, 2003). Recently, a number of neuropsychologists have criticized the use of VA patients on the supposed grounds that they are highly likely to malinger. There is no evidence for this. The only study that made this claim (Larrabee, Millis, & Meyers, 2008) used an unvalidated procedure to indicate possible malingering (Russell, 2009). The only set of norms that have been open to public inspection and use are derived from VA patients (Russell & Starkey, 2001a). Recent work by a friend who works at the Miami VA medical center and who is generally using symptom validity tests (SVTs) has found that VA patients demonstrate poor motivation at about the same level as other people (Gass, 2011). About 40% of those who might gain compensation from poor test results fail SVT tests. Those who have nothing to gain do not malinger or show any greater lack of motivation than any other group of people.

Forensic Application

These are some of the reasons why the validity and accuracy of neuropsychological testing is so important in forensic cases, particularly in head trauma cases. Unless there is a hemorrhage, various scanning techniques may not be able to determine the existence of diffusely damaged tissue that may produce dramatic effects in neuropsychological testing. This is particularly true after the acute stage of head trauma when forensic cases usually come to court.

Aspects of Battery Accuracy

There are two general types of measurement in neuropsychology: (1) the amount or strength of a particular brain-function attribute and (2) the rate of error in validating a formal procedure. In most cases, procedures measure the quantitative aspect—that is, the patient does not just have brain damage but has a certain amount of brain damage or more exactly an amount of impairment because of damage. Measurement as to how much ability exists is obviously used in traditional research psychometrics.

However, assessment is generally concerned with classification of a characteristic of brain functioning or a brain condition. If an assessment procedure is a classification method, then the measurement is primarily the rate of error. Accuracy, of course, is the inverse of rate of error and is an essential component of validation because validation does not just refer to the existence of something but how thoroughly that existence can be specified.

The accuracy of a battery or a test is not simply its ability to produce a high level of true positives. In almost any validity study of brain damage or other neurological conditions, there will be a comparison between the neurological condition and a non–brain-damaged group or between two conditions. In such a situation, accuracy is determined not just by the level of true positives but also by the level of true positives, false positives, true negatives (control subjects), and false negatives.

These various forms of accuracy constitute classification statistics or statistical operating characteristics of statistics. Although such terms as *true positives, false positives,* and *sensitivity* have been used for many years in medicine and psychology, it is only recently that the sophisticated and widespread use of this method of accuracy has occurred (Gouvier, 1999, 2001; Retzlaff & Gibertini, 1994; Russell, 2004; Slick, 2006).

An understanding of operating characteristics is necessary for one to be able to adequately evaluate the accuracy and so validity of a study. Although standard statistics are well known, these statistics are generally more applicable to research on theoretical matters than to assessment methods and procedures. Thus, in neuropsychological assessment, accuracy is primarily measured by classification statistics. These are often called *operating characteristics* (Retzlaff & Gibertini, 1994) or *Bayesian statistics* (Slick, 2006, pp. 20–24). Bayesian statistics can become more complicated than is presented here, but the more complex forms are almost never used in neuropsychology.

Operating Characteristics

Although many writings provide a more thorough discussion of operational characteristics, several aspects of operational characteristics need to be emphasized. For the most part, operational characteristics are designed to classify a condition into two groups, usually an abnormal and a normal group. Most often, operational characteristics are used to separate brain-damaged from non–brain-damaged subjects. The primary components of operational characteristics are sensitivity, specificity, and predictive power—positive, negative, and overall. These components are part of a 2×2 classification. In general, one condition of the 2×2 classification is considered to be the criterion. This is most often the diagnosis of brain damage. (This generally refers to the vertical dimension of the 2×2 classification.) The other dimension concerns the procedure or neuropsychological test. (This generally refers to the horizontal dimension.) There are several other aspects of classification statistics. *Sensitivity* refers to how well a test can identify the neurological condition such as brain damage. Obviously, there are two parts to sensitivity the true positives, that proportion (often designated as a percentage) of the brain-damaged subjects who are correctly identified as having brain damage. Just as important as sensitivity is *specificity*, which is the portion of normal subjects who are correctly identified. This second measure, specificity, is also a measure of the accuracy of the test to identify the control group. Obviously, in a forensic situation, it is as important to know how accurately the test can identify those who are normal as those who are brain damaged.

The other aspect of operating characteristics are predictive power statistics. These are measures of how accurate a particular procedure distinguishes two conditions such as brain damage and normality. Positive predictive power is the proportion of subjects in the primary condition, such as brain damage, whom the procedure can identify. Negative predictive power is the proportion of primary condition that the procedure misses. Alternatively, it is a measure of how accurately the procedure measures the second group, usually the non–brain-damaged group. The *overall predictive power* is how well the procedure can distinguish these two groups.

Predictive power is strongly influenced by base rate. However, the problems with base rate are discussed elsewhere in this writing and will not be examined at this point.

In regard to error rate, each aspect has a false positive rate that is equivalent to error rate—that is, if the sensitivity of a procedure is 80%, then its error rate is 20%. Thus, accuracy always includes both positive identification and the error rate. In forensics, it is often as important to know the proportion of subjects or cases that a procedure fails to identify, which is the error rate, as it is to know the proportion that it can identify. Also, keep in mind that sensitivity, sometimes called *hit rate*, is not directly related to specificity, which is the hit rate for non–brain-damaged subjects. Accuracy includes all of these operating characteristics, particularly because sensitivity and specificity are not directly related. A test may have a high hit rate for brain damage but may be quite inaccurate in that it identifies a very high proportion of normals as having brain damage.

Cut Points

A cut point is, of course, the number in a range of numbers that separates one group from another. Cut points are crucial in determining accuracy. A method of determining the optimum cutoff score or *receiver operating characteristics* may be rather complicated, and as such a complicated method is seldom used. The simplest way to set a cut point is to use the score where the two distributions intersect. This is more usable if the proportions of the two distributions are equivalent (Russell, 2004).

Although all neuropsychologists should have some understanding of cut points and operating characteristics, they are often not aware of the sample requirements for these statistics. In neuropsychology, the cut point has been assigned to separate brain-damaged from non–brain-damaged subjects in one of two general ways: (1) using 1 SD of a normal distribution or (2) comparing normal and brain-damaged groups by classification statistics.

In the first method, the norms are entirely derived from a normal population in which all the subjects with histories that suggest the possibility of brain damage are excluded. The use of 1 SD is based on a statistical myth that subjects below 1 SD are abnormal and thus are impaired. (It is a myth because all of the subjects were selected to be normal.) In a normal distribution, about one-sixth of normal subjects fall below 1 SD. In this method, these normal subjects are designated as impaired—that is, brain damaged. The problem with this method is that this does not provide a reliable method to determine whether a person being assessed has brain damage. Because all of the subjects in this distribution are normal, this method provides no valid psychometric method to separate brain-damaged from non–brain-damaged subjects. As such, the method is not reliable.

The other method is to determine the most accurate cut point that separates the brain-damaged and normal distributions, which overlap (Slick, 2006, pp. 20–24). For this method to be valid, the normal or non–brain-damaged and brain-damaged subjects should be derived from the same sample. Such a sample may be composed of subjects who were admitted to a neurology clinic and had undergone a neurological examination. Those who are found to have brain damage are placed into one group, and those without neurological evidence of damage are placed into the negative neurological group. This method is particularly applicable to forensic cases because the plaintiff *always* claims that he or she has brain damage.

This method applies to the determination of operating characteristics because the method assumes that the subjects are derived from the same sample and the procedure to be validated separates the subjects into the brain-damaged and negative neurological groups. If the groups are derived from separate samples, then the method cannot psychometrically distinguish brain-damaged subjects from the alternate group's unrelated norms.

This is the problem with Heaton, Miller, Taylor, and Grant's (2004) use of operational characteristics to "validate" the brain-damage cut point in their *Revised Comprehensive Norms for an Expanded Halstead–Reitan Battery* (RCNEHRB). The location from which the brain-damage subjects came is not provided (p. 9), but it was apparently not derived from the same sample, or even the same location, as the normal subjects. Consequently, the norms for the two samples are different.

In the RCNEHRB, a general index of brain damage, the global deficit scale (GDS) (Heaton et al., 2004, pp. 14–15, 31–33) was introduced. It was basically derived from 21 scores using a scale derived from *t*-scores. The accuracy of the operating characteristics for this index cannot be determined from the manual. Only the "sensitivity" of the GDS scales is provided (p. 33). Although the authors emphasize that the GDS was more sensitive than the AIR, the specificity and predictive power of the GDS and AIR are not provided. Consequently, the GDS overall may not be any more accurate than the AIR that was published 34 years previously (Russell, Neuringer, & Goldstein, 1970). (Only two graphs of the AIR, without numbers, were provided to indicate its operating characteristics—Figures 1 and 2 on pp. 30 and 31.)

Brain-Damage Indexes

The index is most common form of formal neuropsychological methodology. It essentially combines a number of test scores into a single score. Although most indexes have been applied to the existence of brain damage, they have been used for other aspects of neuropsychological evaluations such as lateralization.

There are two reasons to use an index in a neuropsychological battery. First, but not of primary importance, is that indexes are usually more accurate than any single test (Rojas & Bennett, 1995; Russell & Starkey, 1993, pp. 38–39; Spreen & Benton, 1965) . However, the primary reason is that indexes avoid the problems related to the validity of a group of tests in a battery (Chapter 7; Russell, Russell, & Hill, 2005).

Increased Accuracy of Batteries

In regard to the diagnosis of brain damage, batteries are generally only slightly more accurate than the most accurate individual tests. In a study of the operating characteristics of the AIS, which is the primary measure of brain-damage impairment used in the HRNES–R, the AIS had a sensitivity of 77% and a specificity of 94% for an overall predictive power of 85%. However, one test in the battery, the tactual performance total time (TPTT) test, approached that accuracy, with a sensitivity of 80%, a specificity of 85%, and an overall 82% correct prediction. In a study by Rojas and Bennett, the TPTT also performed better than any other single test and at the same level as the HI. Both had an overall accuracy of 80%.

The AIS contained only 10 tests. Consequently, only a relatively small number of tests, 5 to 10, are necessary to provide an accurate indication of brain damage

(Russell, 2004). The discriminant analysis statistical method can examine the increasing accuracy of tests as the proportion of tests (variables) are added to the group formula. In separating brain-damaged from control subjects, the first discriminant analysis of the Halstead battery (Wheeler, Burke, & Reitan, 1963), which included the Wechsler–Bellevue and the trail-making test, found that the Halstead Index, in which only seven tests made substantial contributions, was almost as accurate as using the entire battery of tests. The entire battery was 90.7% correct, whereas the HI was 90% correct. [A later study (Wheeler & Reitan, 1963) found the HI was slightly more accurate, though not significantly, than discriminant analysis.] Approximately the same results have been found from other studies such as Mutchnick, Ross, and Long (1991), who found that 7 tests in a discriminant analysis study were as accurate as 18 tests. Swiercinsky and Warnock (1977) found that 9 variables were as accurate as the maximum number of variables, which was 25. Thus, after the few most accurate tests have been determined, adding additional tests does not increase accuracy but may decrease it.

Also, apparently the accuracy of tests to assess the existence of brain damage has not changed to a great extent since 1965. That year, Spreen and Benton reviewed the studies that had been completed to that time to determine the accuracy of neuropsychological tests and batteries of tests. Their conclusion was that "the average prediction rate for single measures is 71 percent: this figure drops to 62 percent if the test authors' cutting scores are used" (p. 325)—that is, in cross validation. Test batteries are more accurate: "the percentage of correct predictions with a battery of tests can be raised to 80 percent" and "the correct predictions on cross-validation averaged 82 percent" (p. 325).

Avoidance of Group Psychometric Problems

The primary reason for employing an index is to avoid several conditions that render the results from an unrelated group of tests unreliable. Unless these problems are overcome psychometrically, the advantage of using a battery of tests is nullified. At best, clinical judgment must be used in the assessment, and then the problems related to clinical judgment must be overcome.

As discussed in Chapters 7 and 8, a group of individual tests in a battery encounters a number of problems that makes their use unreliable. These problems include random error (which produces impaired tests), deciding which tests with opposing results are correct, and determining the proportion of impaired test scores that are required to indicate the existence of brain damage. Together, these problems produce an unstandardized battery from which it is almost impossible to create a reliable interpretation (Russell et al., 2005). The solution to these problems is an index that can be validated and its accuracy determined. Validation generally includes an accuracy indicator.

Forensic Importance

In forensic cases, indexes are particularly important because they provide validated and thus scientifically reliable information as to the existence of the condition in question. The accuracy of an index can be determined psychometrically. As such, this information indicates the reliability of the procedure. Lacking such validating accuracy, a procedure has no scientific evidence of any reliability. Consequently, the court will not find such information highly credible. To put the case more succinctly, with the psychometric determination of accuracy, we know the extent of a procedure's accuracy; without measures of accuracy, we do not know if the procedure has any accuracy.

In practice, almost all accuracy is derived from the operating characteristics of a procedure. The studies of operating characteristics of various measures are presented in the accompanying tables.

The various indexes that have been created in neuropsychology will be examined. The list is as complete as was possible, although some indexes may have been missed.

Halstead Index

The earliest of the indexes was the Halstead Index (Halstead, 1947). Originally, it was the proportion of Halstead's 10 index tests that were in the brain-damaged range. By research and general agreement in the field, three subtests that were found to be much less accurate (Reitan, 1955) were eliminated (Reitan & Wolfson, 1985). Subsequently, at least seven other formal indexes were devised to assess the existence of brain damage. These will be examined individually and compared.

Halstead's Original Index Study

Halstead's original index research study has been repeatedly criticized, particularly by Lezak (Lezak, 1995, pp. 711–713; Lezak et al., 2004, pp. 670–671). Lezak et al. treated this study as if it was the only norming study for the HI. As is quite clear on reading Halstead's book (1947, pp. 132–136), he had no intention or illusion that this was a norming study. Rather, it was an attempt to demonstrate the feasibility of such an index. This he succeeded in doing. The brain-damaged subjects were composed of those patients whom he had been studying: 147 patients with closed head injuries, 24 patients with lobectomies, and a reference group of 30 control subjects (p. 133). These control patients had an average age of 28.3.

Closed head injury subjects are extremely difficult to categorize either as to the severity of impairment or the location of the lesion. As might be expected, only 55% of the closed head injury patients met the criteria for brain-damage impairment. By contrast, the graph indicates that almost 100% of the lobectomy patients were designated as brain damaged.

Under these conditions, it is rather amazing, as is apparent in Table 9.1, that the cutting point score of 0.5 or more indicates an impaired test; this has remained stable through many validation studies. This is especially true when 3 of the original 10 tests were found to be unreliable and were removed (Reitan, 1955). (With only seven tests, four or more is equivalent to 0.5.)

Validation of the Halstead Index

To examine the validation of the HI, 13 studies were located that examined the accuracy of the HI and presented the data in such a manner that operating characteristics could be determined. (Mutchnick et al., 1991, did not use the usual HI tests). These studies are presented in Table 9.1. This table includes the measures of sensitivity, specificity (Goldstein & Shelly, 1982), and predictive power. In essence, the measures of sensitivity and positive predictive power are concerned with the accuracy of the procedure to measure a brain condition, such as the existence of brain damage. The measures of specificity and negative predictive power concern the accuracy of the non–brain-damaged control group. In an interpretation, one is as important as the other.

In many of these studies, the data used to obtain these measures had to be constructed from the data presented in the study. In Table 9.1, the results of these studies are averaged across the studies for each characteristic and presented at the bottom of the table. Averaging does not take into consideration that some studies are better designed than others, and the *N* differs for each study.

Table 9.1 indicates that there has been considerable variability concerning the HI. In Halstead's original study, the HI was correctly sensitive for 61.4% of the brain-damaged subjects and 100% for the normal subjects. The results of the Wheeler and Reitan studies (Wheeler et al., 1963; Wheeler & Reitan, 1963) provided more balanced results, as did most of the other studies. (So many analyses were presented in the Wheeler et al. studies that the most representative studies had to be selected.)

Vega and Parsons (1967) found that they had to reset the index to 0.7 to obtain a sensitivity rate of 76% correct. However, it is a tribute to Halstead's conception that the index has fared better in other peoples' studies than in his original study.

The results related to the total percent correct are moderately variable and, as such, indicate that the accuracy of this index depends strongly on the criteria sample. The average sensitivity was 76.9% correct, with a range of variability from 59.2% to 92.2%. The average specificity was 76.1, with a range from 40.0 to 100.0. The mean overall predictive power was 77.2, with a range from 60.0 to 90.0.

Because the index remains constant (with the exception of the Vega & Parsons, 1967, study), the variations between samples are the result of differences in the samples. In summary, the HI accuracy for identifying the existence of brain damage is close to 80% correct, especially for the more adequate studies. The specificity tends to be little less than sensitivity, and the overall predictive power is also about 80%.

Alternative Indexes of Brain Damage

Although the HI is the most commonly used index in neuropsychology, several other indexes have been developed. These were often part of a computer scoring program, but they are evaluated here as individual indexes. They are presented in Table 9.2, and some are discussed individually. Although more indexes were created than are shown, Table 9.2 presents the results of all the published studies that could be located, including seven AIR studies, one Brain 1 study, one AIS study, one percent impaired index (PII) study (Russell & Starkey, 1993, pp. 19–20), and five NDS studies.

Table 9.2 summarizes the operating characteristics for the alternative indexes. Three of them—the AIR, the AIS, and the PII—were created by Russell. The NDS was created by Reitan. Brain 1, part of Finkelstein's (1977) computer program, was not published. The cross-validation studies for the AIR and NDS were averaged. The other procedures did not have enough studies for averaging.

Average Impairment Rating

The second index to be introduced into neuropsychology was the average impairment rating. The AIR was part of the neuropsychological key computer scoring program (Russell et al., 1970). The index, which was originally created by Philip Rennick, was adopted and improved by Russell et al. (1970). Philip Rennick used ratings for some of the index tests. Although Russell et al. (1970) transformed all of the tests into scored scales, they retained the term *rating* in the name of the index. The scale was originally accepted from Rennick without knowledge of its psychometric properties. The different levels of impairment in the index, however, ranged from 100% to 61.2%. The average overall predictive power of the AIR was 75.0%. The highest accuracy rate of overall predictive power, which was 88.0, came from Wedding's (1983a, 1983b) study when the data were reanalyzed. The overall predictive power for the Russell et al. (1970) study was 87.5%.

These operating characteristics are approximately the same as the reported accuracy of the HI with an average overall predictive power of 77.2%, whereas the AIR was 75.0%. The AIR index is strongly related to the HI (Russell, 1984), although the HI tended to be somewhat more accurate in this study. When both indexes were used in a studies (Anthony, Heaton, & Lehman, 1980; Russell, 1984; Sherer & Adams, 1993; Tsushima & Wedding, 1979) their accuracy was almost the same. For instance, Tsushima and Wedding (1979) found the HI overall predictive power of their sample to be 60% accurate, whereas the AIR was 62.2%.

In Russell's 1984 study (Table 9.2), which introduced a revised version of the AIR, the brain-damage index. The HI sensitivity was 87.3% (Table 9.1). The specificity was 79.4%, with an overall predictive power of 85.9%. The sensitivity of the new index (Table 9.2) was 73.5%, and the specificity was 91.2%, with an overall predictive power of 76.4%. The HI was still more accurate.

The Neuropsychological Deficit Scale

The NDS was developed by Reitan (1991) as a form of decision-tree algorithm. It is a computerized neuropsychology scoring procedure that uses the HRB methodology without modification. This program was designed to make scoring of the HRB more efficient and accurate. It consists of three subindexes. The name for the base program is the General Neuropsychological Deficit Scale (GNDS) (Reitan & Wolfson, 1993b, pp. 93, 347–397). This scoring program includes more of the HRB tests than did the HI, and as such it may replace the HI. The computer program also includes a Left Neuropsychological Deficit Scale (LNDS) and a Right Neuropsychological Deficit Scale (RNDS) to assess the laterality of damage. The GNDS was created to improve the accuracy of assessing the existence of brain damage. Because it combines the

GNDS, LNDS, and RNDS, this combination appears to increase the accuracy of the NDS.

The four studies that have been performed on the NDS (brain-damage index) are provided in Table 9.2. The original study by Reitan and Wolfson (1993b) found the NDS to be highly accurate at 91.7% correct overall predictive power prediction. In the second study by Sherer and Adams (1993), with an overall predictive power of 71.0%, the GNDS was not found to be as accurate. This reduced accuracy was to be expected with cross validation. In addition, the subjects used by Sherer and Adams apparently were not as clearly diagnosed as in Reitan's studies. Almost all of the scores derived from it are low. This lack of clarity is displayed by the scores on the HI, which was included in the study. Its score was lower than was usually found (Table 9.1).

Sherer and Adams (1993) also used a variation on the usual research method. To counter a base-rate problem—that there was a greater number of brain-damaged subjects than normals—they used percent scores rather than raw scores (Guilford, 1965; Russell, 2004). This adjusted the base rate to 0.50. This method balanced the lower prevalence of the normal subjects to be equivalent to the brain-damaged subjects. It increased the overall rate somewhat as indicated by the average NDS. The averages in Table 9.2 included both methods of scoring the Sherer and Adams (1993) results. The study also compared the NDS with the HI and the AIR. They were found to be approximately equivalent, although the NDS was a little more accurate than the HI and the AIR.

Recently, Wolfson and Reitan (1995) published a cross validation of the NDS. They examined the accuracy of the NDS in assessing the diagnosis of 50 control and 50 brain-damaged subjects. At 96.0% sensitivity, 80.0% specificity, and an overall predictive power of 88.0, this accuracy rate fell in between the other two studies.

The NDS is apparently somewhat more accurate than the HI. In the accuracy studies, it has usually been the most accurate index. This evaluation is given support in a study by Rojas and Bennett (1995), who compared the accuracy of the HI, NDS, and several major HRB tests against the Stroop test. The HI had an overall predictive power of .80%, whereas the NDS was 92%. In contrast, the Stroop at 62% sensitivity was less accurate than either index or most of the HRB tests. The Stroop was hardly better than chance.

Brain 1

Brain 1 (Finkelstein, 1977) was a rather complex program that used Reitan's four methods of analysis (Reitan & Wolfson, 1985) to determine the existence of a lesion, its diagnostic group, its recency, and the lateralization of brain damage. In regard to determining the existence of brain damage in the unpublished version, it initially appeared to be quite accurate by classifying 96% of brain-damaged and normal cases accurately. This accuracy was reduced in the study by Anthony et al. (1980) (Table 9.2) to a sensitively of 84.0%, a specificity of 71.0%, and an overall predictive power of 78.8, which was less than the HI or the AIR in their study. No other study of its accuracy in separating normal subjects from brain-damaged subjects has been published. The NDS (Reitan, 1991), which was constructed by Reitan, is now a better representative of Reitan's method.

The Average Impairment Scale

The average impairment scale was designed to be used with the HRNES (Russell & Starkey, 1993). It was derived from the AIR and first published as part of the Halstead–Rennick–Russell Battery (HRRB) (Russell, Starkey, Fernandez, & Starkey, 1988). Regina Starkey designed the program.

Because unpublished studies indicated that some of the tests in the AIR could be removed without impairing its accuracy, the index was reduced to 10 tests. The construction of the AIS is described in detail in the manual for the HRNES computer scoring program (Russell & Starkey, 1993). Table 9.2 indicates that the accuracy of the AIS is somewhat better than the AIR as indicated by the validation studies performed for the HRNES and also in a study that examined the operating characteristics of the major test in the HRNES–R (Russell, 2004). In this study, it had a sensitivity of 77.0%, but its specificity was of 94.0% and the overall predictive power was 85.0%. The AIR had a sensitivity of 71.4%, a specificity 83.4%, and an overall predictive power of 75.0%.

The Percent Impairment Index

The percent impairment index (Russell & Starkey, 2001a, p. 20; Russell, 2004) is a second index used by the HRNES–R to indicate the existence of brain damage. It is composed in the same manner that the HI was constructed—that is, it consists in the percentage of the 10 impairment tests that are in the brain-damaged range.

As indicated in Table 9.2, which uses the same method of determining operating characteristics as the AIS, the PII is more sensitive to the existence of brain damage, with an 81% correct prediction, than the AIS. However, the PII specificity at 85% is less than that of the AIS. Consequently, if one were seeking to determine the existence of brain damage, the PII would probably be more relevant. Its overall predictive power at 83.0% is less than that of the AIS at 85.0%.

Discussion

From these studies, it is evident that the HI, GNDS, AIR, and AIS have similar accuracies of about 80%. This accuracy is sufficient for clinical purposes and should be taken into consideration even by expert neuropsychologists.

Although indexes are more accurate than single tests, it should be noted that some single tests are also quite accurate (Goldstein & Shelly, 1972; Russell & Starkey, 1993). In the Russell and Starkey (1993) study (Table 6, p. 37), although the AIS was 86% correct, the TPT total time was 83% correct, and both digit symbol and Trails B were 78% correct.

An examination of Table 9.1 demonstrates that the accuracy rate of the HI and other indexes have not increased much over the years. Because the HI has not been changed, there is no reason for it to have improved since it was first published in

1947 (Halstead, 1947) in spite of the development of scanning techniques. Although the NDS (Reitan, 1991; Reitan & Wolfson, 1993b, pp. 347–397) is more accurate, the surprising aspect of this situation is that, after 45 years, only recently have newer and somewhat more accurate formal methods been developed.

Decision-Tree Algorithms

Since 1970 (Russell et al., 1970), indexes have been combined into algorithms that determined whether brain damage existed and if so whether it was lateralized. An algorithm is a formalized step-by-step process for solving a problem. It is well adapted for computer programs, a decision-tree algorithm accomplished through a series of decision rules that separate a problem into two parts at each decision.

For instance, a group of tests are administered to determine whether a subject is impaired. If the tests are passed at a high level and determined by a cut point (developed by research), the person is categorized as normal and the testing is complete. If the person's score falls below the cut point, he or she is considered to be possibly impaired and further tests are administered. The next procedure, such as a Minnesota Multiphasic Personality Inventory 2, might be used to rule out an emotional disorder. If the scores are in the normal range for emotions, then the impairment is classified as possibly resulting from brain damage. Next, new tests or indexes would be given to determine whether the condition is lateralized. If lateralized, then the person is stated to have brain damage. Many variations of this decision-tree procedure could be developed, although each step or decision must be validated. The initial procedure of this sort was the neuropsychological key (Russell et al., 1970). Through the use of a brain-damage index, it initially determines whether a subject has brain damage. If so, then a more complex series of decisions determines whether it is a right-hemisphere lesion or a left-hemisphere lesion. If neither, then the brain damage is considered to be diffuse brain damage. The accuracy of this decision trees, called *keys*, is examined in two places in this chapter. The brain-damage index was previously examined, and the lateralization key will be examined next.

Advantages of Decision-Tree Algorithms

There are several reasons for discussing decision-tree algorithms. They are more than indexes in that they may combine indexes, single tests, or other psychometric procedures into a unified process. Obviously, there are many methods of combining tests into a single processes, but the key has been tried and found to be workable, even if it evidently needed improvement.

First, such a procedure can replace clinical judgment with a method that is entirely formal and objective. As such, the method is completely reliable in that the same scores will always provide the same results. The work of the clinician is to coordinate the battery results with the situational context. This will require a person trained as a clinical neuropsychologist.

Second, such a procedure can be changed and improved. There is nothing permanently fixed about the method. However, it cannot be changed at the whim of the individual neuropsychologist. Rather it must be changed through the psychometric procedures of comparative testing and validation, much as intelligence tests are improved today.

Third, they constitute a major aspect of computerized assessment. The computer can use such algorithms to reach more complex conclusions than simply scoring individual computer-administered tests.

Finally, as such, decision-tree algorithms represent the future of neuropsychology. They will increase reliability and with development will continue to improve. New and revised methods can simply be installed into the program. Nevertheless, such methods must be validated with the same rigor that is now required of individual tests.

The Adequacy of Decision-Tree Algorithms

Although various parts of the neuropsychological key have been examined as indexes of brain damage, the total results will now be discussed. First, the key demonstrated that such an algorithm could be scored by a computer program. The only question was whether it was as accurate as clinical judgment.

The Development of Decision-Tree Algorithms

Decision-tree algorithms began with the book *Assessment of Brain Damage: A Neuropsychological Key Approach.* by Russell et al. (1970). It spawned several computerized programs along with considerable interest in this type of procedure. Then in the 1980s, this type of procedure almost vanished and neuropsychology returned to its previous clinical approach.

Neuropsychological Deficit Scale

The NDS, which was created by Reitan (1991), was the first computerized neuropsychology scoring procedure to include a method to lateralize brain damage. It is also a decision-tree algorithm. The program used the HRB without modification. In addition to the GNDS, it provides the LNDS and RNDS to assesses the laterality of damage.

These three programs are combined to form the NDS score. To examine the accuracy of this program for lateralization, two studies have been performed. These are summarized in Table 9.3. In Reitan's (1991) original study, the accuracy across the three lateralization categories was 62.1%, whereas it was 98.8% accurate for the right and left subjects. The only cross-validation study yet completed was done by Sherer and Adams (1993). It found the accuracy of the LNDS and RNDS to be somewhat less than in the original study. It was 54.8% correct for the three categories and 88.9% correct for the right and left categories alone. This accuracy is comparable to that found for the key.

Conclusion

Although the overall results for the key were mixed, there was enough consistency to obtain a fairly reliable appraisal of its accuracy. The accuracy rate of the overall predictive power in Table 9.3 for the key varied from 46.2% to 64.3%. Although Anthony et al. (1980) severely criticized the lateralization key as being less accurate in their cross-validation study than in the original study, the current study found that the overall predictive power across the three categories was slightly better than when the key was used in Anthony et al.'s cross-validation study.

Lateralization Indexes and Algorithms

The ability to accurately assess the lateralization of brain damage is still an important issue in neuropsychology, because lateralization is a major indication of brain damage. In addition, it helps one to know what cognitive functions of a patient are intact. The indexes to determine the existence of brain damage do not require a full program. Generally, a single index will suffice. Lateralization assessment is a more complicated process and initially required a more extended use of algorithms. Lateralization thus represents the beginning of formalized in-depth analysis and even computerized assessment, because this is the first attribute of brain activity other than the existence of brain damage to be decided.

Contrary to the few studies generally cited in the literature, eight studies using a lateralization key or index are presented. Four concern the neuropsychological key or were derived from it. One was a revision by Russell (1984) of the lateralization method in the key, and two concern the NDS right and left indexes. These are presented in Table 9.3.

Both measures of sensitivity and specificity for right, diffuse, and left locations are presented. The table also presents the overall or total predictive power of the lateralization index, which is the same for all locations. (The table contains enough data to reconstruct the positive and negative predictive powers. Providing them in the table would make it unnecessarily large.)

The sensitivity and specificity operating characteristics were computed for each of the three localization positions—left, diffuse, and right. Specificity was calculated by combining the correct scores of the two positions that were not calculated for sensitivity and dividing that sum by the sum of the *N*'s for those positions. In other words, if left sensitivity had been calculated, then the diffuse and right correct scores were combined and divided by their *N*'s for specificity. This was repeated for each lateralization category. Thus, three sets of operating characteristics, one for each position, were calculated for every study. In evaluating the accuracy of these measures, the probability score for each characteristic was 33.3%, not 50%.

Finally, the table includes a measure of the ability of the scale to indicate right or left damage when the diffuse condition is omitted. This right-versus-left distinction appears to be a more representative indication of the accuracy of a program than

Table 9.3 The Neuropsychological Operating Characteristics of Key, Neuropsychological Deficit Scale, and Lateralization Indexes

Sensitivity (%)			Specificity (%)			Power (%)	Right Versus Left (%)		Total Power
Right	**Diffuse**	**Left**	**Right**	**Diffuse**	**Left**	**Total**	**Right**	**Left**	
Neuropsychological Key (Russell et al., 1970) (Validations and Cross Validations)									
Original Key, Russell et al., 1970, p. 75; N: R = 16, D = 43, L = 21, Total = 80									
46.1	48.4	31.6	46.2	14.0	48.2	46.2	75.0	46.1	57.0
Swiercinsky & Wernock, 1977; N: R = 13, D = 126, L = 19, Total = 158									
46.1	48.4	31.6	46.2	14.0	48.2	46.2	75.0	46.1	57.0
Anthony et al., 1980 (Table 4, p. 322); N: R = 47, D = 29, L = 37, Total = 113									
72.3	34.5	54.0	45.4	65.8	57.9	56.6	91.9	76.9	85.7
Goldstein & Shelly, 1982; N: R = 49, D = 300, L = 41, Total = 390									
67.3	44.7	51.2	45.4	22.7	47.8	48.2	76.7	72.4	75.0
Wedding, 1983b (Table 6); N: R = 3, D = 4, L = 7, Total judges = 14									
66.7	75.0	57.1	63.6	75.0	71.4	64.3	100.0	80.0	85.7

NDS (Reitan & Wolfson, 1991, pp. 347–397)									
NDS: Reitan & Wolfson, 1993, p. 396; Reitan, 1985; N: R = 61, D = 53, L = 55, Total = 170									
63.9	47.2	74.5	61.1	73.4	56.1	62.1	97.5	100	98.8
NDS (RNDS & LNDS): Sherer & Adams, 1993, p. 433; N: R = 26, D = 29, L = 18, Total = 73									
19.2	82.8	61.1	74.5	69.6	52.7	54.8	71.4	100	88.9
Neuropsychological Indexes (Russell)									
New Index (Not Key Index): Russell, 1984, p. 88; N: R = 37, D = 88, L = 32, Total = 157									
79.4	78.8	75.0	77.8	73.9	79.0	78.1	100.0	100.0	100.0
HRNES–R Lateralization Index: Russell & Starkey, 2001; N: R = 142, D = 428, L = 145, Total = 715									
69.7	64.9	63.4	64.6	54.7	66.1	65.6	96.1	97.4	96.9

when the diffuse category is included. Note that the calculation method for the right-versus-left operational characteristics is the same as the sensitivity-versus-specificity calculations. Thus, if the right score is equivalent to sensitivity, the left scores are the same as specificity. For a number of studies, these scores were derived by reworking the original data. Some categories in the original study were excluded, such as the normal category.

In 1984, Russell introduced a new form of the key, the lateralization index, which is included in the table. It demonstrated that the lateralization ability of the key index could be improved. The overall predictive power improved from 54.7% to 78.1%, and the right-versus-left overall power improved from 88.0% to 100%. This improvement is probably partly because of better criteria but nevertheless partly an improvement in the index.

In several studies, the data were not presented in a complete enough form to provide information for all of the categories in Table 9.3. This applied to some studies of the key, the Adams revised program (ARP), and Brain 1 (Adams, Kvale, & Keegan, 1984; Anthony et al., 1980; Ross, Thrasher, & Long, 1990; Wedding, 1983b). These incomplete studies were not included.

Discussion

Table 9.3 contains the validation and cross validation of several lateralization procedures. These are the neuropsychological key (Russell et al., 1970) and the NDS (RNDS and LNDS) (Reitan & Wolfson, 1993b, pp. 347–397), Russell's 1984 lateralization index, and the HRNES–R lateralization index. These studies demonstrate a great deal of variation between studies. However, again remember that the programs or indexes for the scales are constant so that the variation is entirely because of the data sample and not the index.

The diffuse category almost always reduces the accuracy of a lateralization index. Consequently, studies in which there is a large diffuse group, such as the Swiercinsky and Warnock (1977) study, tend to have lower accuracy than those with fewer diffuse subjects. For this reason, the right-versus-left operational characteristics is probably more indicative of the accuracy of an index than the right, diffuse, and left format. The right-versus-left calculations are again variable, but they often exceed 80%, whereas the three category studies never do.

In regard to right-versus-left lateralization, the NDS appears to be the most accurate. In this regard, although its overall predictive power varies, its general accuracy level in two studies was 98.8 and 88.9 (Table 9.3). In contrast, the neuropsychological key's accuracy was 88.0%. The HRNES–R (Russell, 2004) had a right-versus-left total predictive power of 96.9%, which is equivalent to the NDS lateralization procedure.

The accuracy of these indexes is sufficient for clinical purposes. Remember that the accuracy of the neurological criteria was probably in the upper 80s during the time these indexes were developed. Newer indexes such as that included in the NDS and the HRNES–R (Russell & Starkey, 2001b) are undoubtedly somewhat more accurate than the key. The major area in which the CT scans and MRI augmented neuropsychology was in increasing neuropsychological localization accuracy.

Process Key

The neuropsychological key contained a *process key* (Russell et al., 1970) as well as the *lateralization key*. The process key was designed to predict whether the lesion was acute, chronic, or congenital (Russell, 1981). This has been evaluated in three studies. In the initial study, the average classification across these three categories was 86%. However, using only the acute and chronic categories, Anthony et al. (1980) obtained a 69.4% correct prediction. The prediction of the acute category was only 35% correct, whereas the chronic category was 76% correct. Goldstein and Shelly (1982) also examined the process key and obtained results that were substantially the same as those of Anthony et al. (1980). Their overall correct rate was 88%, but this high rate was partly an artifact of the base rate of 334 chronic to 51 acute cases. The correct prediction for the acute cases was only 22%.

In the key, cases were considered to be acute if they were less than 3 months old. Apparently, the acute phase is not that long for many conditions, and the accuracy for assessing acute brain damage is increased when the definition of acute damage includes a shorter period of time (Goldstein, 1993).

Although these results are not spectacular, they did not warrant the castigation that was given by Anthony et al. (1980). In fact, in their study, the process key was more accurate than clinical judgment (Heaton, Grant, Anthony, & Lehman, 1981). It is possible that changes in the process key could improve the accuracy of the acute classification. On reexamining the situation, Goldstein et al. (1996) found that the type of lesion in the acute stage was particularly important. The key tends to correctly classify patients with a recent stroke that is either thrombotic or hemorrhagic. It is less accurate in assessing strokes derived from aneurysms and arteriovenous malformations. Their paper presents an excellent discussion of the progression and impairment expected from various kinds of strokes.

Discriminant Analysis

Another formal method that has been applied to creating accurate test scores is the actuarial method of *discriminant analysis*. In this statistical technique, a weighted combination of indicators is chosen to give an optimal prediction of a criterion. A fairly complex statistical formula (Nunnally & Bernstein, 1994, pp. 610–620) is used to produce a weighted linear combination of indicators. Each test is assigned a weight that is equivalent to the variance that the test contributed to the difference between the two groups. The tests with the greatest prediction of the difference between the groups are selected. The number of tests in the predicting group may vary with each study. In the Wheeler, Burke, and Reitan analysis (1963), only the five most highly predictive tests were needed for optimum prediction (p. 428).

For 30 years, neuropsychologists have been using the discriminant analysis statistic as a formal method of assessing the existence and lateralization of brain damage. However, only six such studies were located. Of these, five were used to predict the existence of brain damage. Four of those plus another study were used to determine the lateralization of damage. The results of these studies are provided in Table 9.4.

Beginning with the often-referenced studies by Wheeler and Reitan (Wheeler et al., 1963; Wheeler & Reitan, 1963), five discriminant analysis studies were found that were concerned with determining the existence of brain damage. The mean overall predictive power was 82.8%, with a sensitivity of 79.6% and a specificity of 87.2%. The mean for the HI studies (Table 9.1) had an overall predictive power of 77.2%, with a mean sensitivity of 76.9% and a mean specificity of 86.1%. For the AIR (Table 9.2), the overall predictive power was 75.0% with a sensitivity of 71.4% and a specificity of 83.4%.

Thus, the discriminant analysis on its first presentation was more accurate than the key or NDS. However, in the studies in which discriminant analysis was directly compared with the HI or AIR the discriminant analyses had about the same accuracy. In Swiercinsky and Warnock (1977), the discriminant analysis's overall predictive power was 57.1%, and the AIR was 75.4%. In Wedding (1983a), discriminant analysis was 95.8% correct, and the AIR was 87.5% correct. Thus, in studies that directly compared the methods, the simple cutting points in the AIR or HI were almost as accurate as the discriminant analysis.

This accuracy of discriminant analysis was essentially the same as the overall predictive power of clinical judgment (Table 9.5), which was 84.4% (Table 9.4). Several discriminant analysis studies had an overall predictive power rate as great as or almost as great as those of the two judges in the Heaton et al. (1981) study, which were 91.2% and 87.6%. These were Wheeler et al. (1963), 90.0%; Wheeler and Reitan (1963), 87.2%; and Rojas and Bennett (1995), 80.0%. The AIR in Russell et al. (1970) was 87.5%, and Wedding (1983a) was 88.0%. Thus, from these studies it appears that discriminant analysis is essentially as accurate as clinical judgment in separating brain-damaged from normal subjects.

Discriminant Analysis of Lateralization

Regarding classifying brain damage into lateralized groups, four studies were located. Of these, one (Ross et al., 1990) compared only right and left lateralized patients. The results of these studies are provided in Table 9.4.

The accuracy of discriminant analysis was somewhat better than the key in lateralizing damage. The predictive power for discriminant analysis was 73.5% correct for the three categories and 85.7% correct for the right and left categories, whereas in the key (Table 9.3) the predictive power was 54.0% correct for the three categories and 78.3% correct for the right and left categories. However, in the two studies that compared the key with discriminant analysis, they were similar. In the Swiercinsky and Warnock (1977) study, they were the same at 46.2%. In the Wedding (1983b) study, the predictive power of the key was 64.3%, and for the discriminant analysis it was 61.1%. The studies that did not directly compare these two methods tended to produce higher scores for discriminant analysis than those that did compare them.

In regard to clinical judgment, there have been almost no studies with a direct comparison to discriminant analysis for either existence of brain damage or

Table 9.4 Discriminant Analysis: Operating Characteristics for Assessing the Existence of Brain Damage

Study	Brain Damage (*N*)	Control (*N*)	Sensitivity (%)	Specificity (%)	Predictive Power (%)		
					Positive	**Negative**	**Overall**
Halstead–Reitan Battery							
Wheeler et al. 1963	79	61	94.9	95.1	96.1	93.5	95.0
Wheeler & Reitan, 1963	79	61	86.1	95.1	95.8	84.1	90.0
Swiercinsky & Warnock, 1977	198	62	46.1	76.0	75.0	46.1	57.1
Wedding, 1983a	18	6	100	83.3	94.7	100	95.8
Mutchnick et al. 1991	93	44	71.0	86.4	91.7	58.5	75.9
Mean	93.4	46.8	79.6	87.2	90.7	76.4	82.8
Meyers Neuropsychological Battery							
Meyers & Rohling, 2004	55	103	96.3	90.3	84.1	97.9	92.4

(Continued)

Table 9.4 (Continued)

Discriminant Analysis Lateralization

Sensitivity %			Specificity %			Power %	Right Versus Left %		Power Tot.
Right	**Diffuse**	**Left**	**Right**	**Diffuse**	**Left**	**Total**	**R (Sensi)**	**Left (spec)**	
(HRB) Wheeler et al., 1963; *N*: *R* = 92, *D* = 84, *L* = 86, Total = 262									
95.7	100.0	91.8	95.9	97.4	91.8	95.6	98.3	100	99.2
(HRB) Wheeler & Reitan, 1963; *N*: *R* = 84, *D* = 96, *L* = 92, Total = 272									
87.1	95.6	92.0	93.8	94.3	90.7	91.1	87.1	93.7	91.1
(Key) Swiercinsky & Warnock, 1977; *N*: *R* = 13, *D* = 126, *L* = 19, Total = 158									
12.5	84.7	15.8	60.9	37.5	55.8	46.2	46.1	76.0	57.1
(Key) Wedding, 1983b (Table 6, p. 19); *N*: *R* = 3, *D* = 4, *L* = 7, Total = 14 judges									
66.7	33.3	83.3	58.3	69.2	50.0	61.1	100.0	100.0	100.0
Ross et al., 1990; *N*: *R* = 38, *L* = 73 (diffuse group not included), Total = 111									
—	—	—	—	—	—	—	84.2	79.4	81.1
The % means for the columns									
65.5	78.4	70.7	77.2	74.6	72.1	73.5	83.1	89.8	85.7

Table 9.5 Clinical Judgment Operating Characteristics for Assessing the Existence of Brain Damage

Study	Brain Damage (*N*)	Control (*N*)	Sensitivity (%)	Specificity (%)	Predictive Power		
					Positive	Negative	Overall
Russell et al. 1970	80	24	70.8	93.7	77.3	91.5	88.5
Goldstein et al., 1973	10	10	100.0	90.0	90.9	100.0	95.0
Boyar & Tsushima, 1975 (neurology)	40		40	82.5	62.5	68.8	78.1
Boyar & Tsushima, 1975 (neurosurgery)	40	40	100	62.5	72.7	100	81.3
Tsushima & Wedding, 1979	34	11	76.5	81.8	92.9	52.9	77.6
Heaton et al. 1981 (Clinician 1)	150	100	90.7	92.0	94.4	86.8	91.2
Heaton et al., 1981 (Clinician 2)	150	100	86.7	89.0	92.2	81.6	87.6
Kane et al., 1981a	23[a]	22	87.0	68.2	74.1	83.3	77.8
Wedding, 1983a (judgments)	204[b]	84	95.3	70.2	89.1	85.5	88.2
Faust et al. 1988 (judgments)	120	35	85.8	60.0	88.0	55.3	80.0
Average (sum/10)	85.1	46.6	87.5	77.0	84.0	81.5	84.0

[a]Calculated from text data.
[b]Minus judgments called schizophrenia.

Clinical Judgment Lateralization

Sensitivity %			Specificity %			Power %	Right Versus Left %		Power Tot.
Right	Diffuse	Left	Right	Diffuse	Left	Total	R (Sensi)	Left (spec)	
Reitan, 1964; *N*: $R = 32$, $D = 48$, $L = 32$, Total = 112									
81.2	95.8	84.4	91.3	89.8	90.0	88.4	92.9	93.1	93.0
Russell et al., 1970; *N*: $R = 16$, $D = 43$ $L = 21$, Total = 80									
68.8	65.0	78.9	69.5	63.4	66.1	69.3	91.7	100	96.3
Wedding, 1983a, 1 Expert; *N*: $R = 4$, $D = 6$, $L = 5$, Total judgments = 15									
67.7	43.7		84.6	67.3	75.6	57.5	67.4	100.0	91.7

lateralization. The only exception is Wedding's 1983 study (Wedding, 1983a, 1983b). For the existence of brain damage, the Wedding (1983a) publication had an overall predictive power for clinical judgment of 88.2%; for discriminant analysis, it was 95.8%. However, the two analyses are quite different in that the discriminant analysis was simply applied to 24 studies using judges, whereas the clinical judgment analysis was applied to the judgments that were made by each judge, who each made 12 judgments. The judgments concerning schizophrenia were removed. Consequently, the results of this study are very tenuous. If only the averages of the various studies are compared, the accuracy of discriminant analysis was almost the same as clinical judgment, with an average overall predictive power of 84.4% for clinical judgment and 82.8% for discriminant analysis.

In regard to lateralization, too few clinical judgment studies had complete data for averages to be obtained. In the only direct comparison, which was Wedding's (1983a) study, the discriminant analysis had a predictive power of 61.1% for three groups of right, diffuse, and left damage. The expert received a predictive power of 80.0%, whereas the nonexperts' predictive power was only 68.8. For right and left groups alone, the discriminant analysis was 100% correct, as was the clinical judgment of the expert. The nonexperts predictive power was 96%.

Thus, the overall predictive power of clinical judgment and discriminant analysis was essentially the same. In regard to sensitivity and specificity, there were not enough data to for the clinical judges, so their relative accuracy could not be determined. Thus, overall it is not possible to reliably compare either discriminant analysis or the neuropsychological key to clinical judgment for lateralization.

Clinical Use of Discriminant Analysis

These results appear encouraging for the use of discriminant analysis in clinical practice in that discriminant analysis was as good or better than clinical judgment and the neuropsychological key when it was first presented. Thus, it is rather curious that, with the exception of Wheeler and Reitan's original studies, none of these programs has been cross validated in new studies, and none has been reported to have been used in clinical practice. Each study developed its own original program. In each case, after the authors describe the accuracy of their program, the program was not mentioned in the literature again.

There is very little discussion in the literature that could explain this phenomenon. The only clinical study that addressed this issue at all was the Ross et al. (1990) study. According to the researchers, "Unfortunately the discriminant analyses reported by these studies could not be readily applied to different sample populations or individual cases" (p. 274). There was no elaboration on this statement.

There are several problems with discriminant analysis. First, its accuracy is generally overestimated in the initial study. In the first study that used discriminant analysis, Wheeler et al. (1963) indicated that discriminant analysis was highly accurate. However, in a cross validation, Wheeler and Reitan (1963) found that it was not much more accurate than the Halstead Index and was certainly much more difficult to administer. In cross validation, there is usually a drop in accuracy because the method takes advantage of the numerical differences that are specific to a particular sample or that result from chance or both. The method may be called *fragile* as opposed to *robust*. When a particular discriminant analysis program is applied to a new sample or an individual in a new sample, it loses some of its accuracy. In addition, these programs contain no redundancy to give the method stability.

Another practical problem with discriminant analysis programs is that it requires some statistical sophistication to transform the printed weights into a usable program. Thus, few clinicians have either the ability or the patience to make this transformation.

Nevertheless, even though discriminant analysis has major weaknesses, when used as a research program for assessing neuropsychological conditions, it may be of great help in designing programs by helping to determine the weights of various tests. By running the program on different samples and making appropriate modifications, discriminant programs could become more robust.

Recent Progress Toward Integrated Batteries

Recent years have seen a revival of interest in co-normed batteries as expressed by Meyers and Rohling (2004) in the introduction to the general discussion of a validation study for a new battery: "Not only do individual tests making up a battery need to be valid and reliable, but the 'whole' of a battery needs to be established, as a test is not interpreted alone but always in context with other tests used in the battery" (p. 646). The new battery, the Meyers Neuropsychological Battery, demonstrates a change in attitude toward recognition of the need for statistically united batteries. Consequently, it is very promising for the future of neuropsychology.

Meyers Neuropsychological Battery

The MNB battery has had several names, including the *semiflexible battery* (Volbrecht, Meyers, & Kaster-Bundgaard, 2000) and *Meyers Short Battery* (Meyers & Rohling, 2004). It is not a "semiflexible battery" because the core tests are always administered in the same order (Meyers & Rohling, 2004, p. 638). In addition, it is not a short battery. Apparently it takes from 2 to 4 h to administer, with an average of about 3 h. The HRB only takes 5 h, which is about the same length of time that the HRNES–R requires. Consequently, this battery will simply be called the *Meyers Neuropsychological Battery*.

The MNB is a reliable battery that is primarily validated on its ability (1) to determine the amount of impairment related to head trauma and (2) to separate head trauma from some other general psychological conditions (it includes the use of control groups). It is primarily composed of tests that are not in the HRB. The exceptions are the trail-making test, tapping, and an abbreviated form of the WAIS–III. The other tests are also relatively well-known tests (Volbrecht et al., 2000).

This battery has been validated, and its reliability has been determined. The Meyers and Rohling (2004) validation was accomplished by using discriminant analysis to separate several types of non–brain-damaged patients from those with brain damage. However it appears to have been primarily used and validated with head trauma patients. Derived from Meyers and Rohling (2004), its operating characteristics were established by discriminant analysis and are presented in Table 9.4. In that study, its sensitivity was 96.3% and its specificity was 90.3%, with an overall predictive power of 92.4%.

These are excellent characteristics, but the accuracy of discriminant analysis tends to be reduced on cross validation, which also happens when the other brain-damaged samples are used. A fairly direct comparison, with the HRB was administered by Dikmen, Machamer, Winn, and Temkin (1995), which used similar patients. In a "Dose-response analysis," Dikmen et al. found that it recorded a similar amount of head injury severity as did the HRB. Undoubtedly, the MNB will remain an excellent usable standardized battery.

Neuropsychological Assessment Battery

Another relatively new co-normed battery is the Neuropsychological Assessment Battery (Stern & White, 2001). It is based on the concept of domains and uses a "normal" sample to form test and index scores. The domains are generally composed of fairly well-known tests. These domains have been created by means of extensive factor-analytic studies. This is an excellent beginning for neuropsychological test construction, but only a beginning.

In neuropsychology, domains have not been well established even though they have been created by factor analysis. Factor analyses may vary, depending on the tests they contain or the samples they use. Tests in a battery are validated, not the domains. Finally, there do not appear to have been any studies that have related domains to particular areas of the brain, although many tests have been related to particular areas. In essence, this was part of the message in Dodrill's presidential address in 1999, and the situation has not improved much in more than a decade. The exception may be the frontal lobe, which is supposed to be the area related to executive functions. However, there is little precise evidence as to what executive functions are and what tests measure them. Neuropsychological testing, including the NAB, uses tests rather than domains.

Unfortunately, particularly for forensics, the NAB indexes which are supposed to represent domains have not been validated using predictive validation methods. Apparently, operational characteristics of NAB indexes such as sensitivity and specificity have not been determined using psychometric methods. As such, their validity for such things as head trauma is unknown. For this reason, the operational characteristics of the NAB could not be included in Table 9.2, which provides the operational characteristics of various indexes of brain damage. Of course, this may change.

Mitrushina et al. 2005

Many neuropsychologists have been using various means to avoid the problems inherent in flexible batteries. One of these is a recent work by Mitrushina et al. (2005).

A huge volume (1,029 pages) presents the collected norms for about 24 tests. Of these, 6 are HRB tests (Reitan & Wolfson, 1993a) and 11 are found in the HRNES–R (Russell & Starkey, 2001a). Much of this information is also in Mitrushina et al.'s first edition. However, new tests were added, and a few of the less well-known HRB tests were removed. The description of various norms is relatively complete for such an extensive review.

As in the previous edition, Mitrushina et al. state that the norms for the HRNES are not included "because the 'normal' group consisted of Veterans Administration patients who presented with symptoms requiring neuropsychological evaluation." This is the exact quote from the previous edition. In a rebuttal article, Russell (2003) indicated, first, that there were 30 other papers using Veterans Administration subjects cited in the book and none of them had been rejected for that reason. Second, 47 other studies were neurologically negative studies "who presented with symptoms requiring neuropsychological evaluations." These were not rejected.

In addition, several of Russell's studies are presented in the book although the same patients were used. Russell's (1987) paper is used to obtain norms. This is a huge mistake in that these norms were being gathered for the HRNES–R in the 1987 study. Its norms are not the same as those presented in this book and are much better developed. Finally, the HRNES–R norms met and continue to meet all of the requirements that the authors stated as conditions for inclusion.

However, overlooking this flaw, the general approach of Mitrushina et al. (2005) was to attempt to overcome one problem with the flexible battery: that it is very difficult to know which set of norms to select when accepting a particular test for a battery. The Mitrushina et al. (2005) solution was to use meta-analysis to form their own norms derived from a number of studies.

This was a painstaking process, but it is better than attempting to select a set of norms from a large unrelated collection. However, it still has several problems. First, if there is a systematic error, the set of norms may be wrong. For instance, it was found that volunteer norms for all previous batteries of HRB tests, as indicated in Chapter 15 of this book, are almost 1 SD above the national population average. A relatively brief examination of this book finds the same is true for most volunteer norms, unless they were obtained for a special purpose such as norming an older population. Second, in some places, such as with the category test, the norms provided in Mitrushina et al. (2005) have age adjustments but no adjustment for intellectual ability. The category test is relatively highly correlated with FSIQ. This is evident in the norms provided by Appendix F for the HRNES–R (Russell & Starkey, 2001b). Finally, and perhaps most important from a psychometric point of view, these metanorms are uncorrelated between tests, so there is no psychometric relationship between the various norms presented in this book. As such, interpretations based on a battery derived from these norms is unreliable. As of this time, the only set of norms using the HRB and many of the other tests in this book that are equivalent to the national population average is found in the HRNES–R (Russell & Starkey, 2001a).

The Accuracy of Clinical Judgment

Much of the initial assessment work on the HRB used clinical judgment. Reitan used clinical judgment along with the HI. After developing the NDS, he made regular use of it along with clinical judgment to create his reports. This may be seen in the examples in Reitan and Wolfson's (1993a) manual (pp. 405–823). Reitan apparently found that the combination of formal decision-theory programs along with clinical judgment was a most appropriate method for neuropsychological assessment. The formal programs are limited in their extent and certainly do not cover the context of the assessment. However, they provide a framework for the assessment.

Much has been said about clinical judgment (Faust, Ziskin, & Hiers, 1988; Faust et al., 1988; Matarazzo, 1990; Meehl, 1954; Wedding & Faust, 1989). Currently, however, there are two major works concerning clinical judgment. The first was written by Garb (1998), *Studying the Clinician: Judgment Research and Psychological Assessment.* The other is *Clinical Judgment and Prediction* by Faust and Ahern (In press). Both cover clinical judgment for the entire field of psychology. Faust and Ahern discuss the various aspects of clinical judgment particularly thoroughly. This current writing is primarily concerned with the accuracy of clinical judgment as portrayed in various studies.

Judging the Existence of Brain Damage

Considering the importance of clinical judgment, only a moderate number of studies have been devoted to the accuracy of clinical judgment, even of the HRB, and almost none since 1990. An examination of the entire literature found only eight studies concerned with the accuracy of clinical judgment used to assess the existence of brain lesions. In regard to lateralization, only three studies had complete enough data to construct the operating characteristics of the procedure.

Table 9.5 presents all of the studies of clinical judgment that could be located in which enough data were available to calculate the sensitivity, specificity, and predictive power for the assessment of the existence of brain damage. Some studies did not present sufficient data to be included. One was a well-known study by Filskov and Goldstein (1974) that claimed a 100% accuracy rate. This rate was opposed to the then existing neuropsychological procedures used by clinical psychologists. All psychologists had a much lower accuracy rate than those trained in the HRB method. Unfortunately, the data were not presented in such a way that it could be placed in an operating characteristics table. There was no normal control group. Since that time, this high accuracy rate has not been equaled in any clinical judgment study of the HRB.

Table 9.5 indicates that the accuracy of clinical judgment in assessing the existence and lateralization of brain damage. The scores for the existence of brain damage were averaged so that a more adequate understanding could be obtained. The sensitivity scores ranged from 70.8% to 100%, with a mean of 87.6%. The specificity ranged from 93.7% to 69.0%, with a mean of 77.0%. The overall predictive power ranged from 72.5% to 95%, with a mean of 84.0%. Note that the very high sensitivity and specificity from the Goldstein, Deysach, and Kleinknecht, (1973) study was done with surgical subjects in which there were excellent criteria, probably 100% correct. None of the subsequent studies have had this accuracy when sensitivity and specificity were included. Examining the overall averages of this table indicated that the accuracy of neuropsychologists, especially those with considerable experience, for assessing the existence of brain damage is generally in the mid-80% range, with sensitivity being about 10 points greater than specificity.

Judging Lateralization of Damage

The ability to lateralize brain damage generally requires more clinical acumen than determining the existence of damage. Most neuropsychological tests in a battery have been designed to determine the existence of brain damage so their scores can be summed and a mere cutting point can be used. Throughout his career, Reitan (1964) has demonstrated that neuropsychological tests could be used in combination to indicate many other aspects of an organic lesion than just its existence, such as the location of the lesion and diagnosis of the pathology. Although still relatively basic, the accuracy of lateralization is an indication of the accuracy of neuropsychological expertise. Thus, studies of this ability are more indicative of clinical ability than those concerned with diagnosing the existence of brain damage.

A moderate number of studies were completed that claimed to examine the accuracy of laterality. However, several of them did not present enough data to construct their operating characteristics, so their accuracy could not be determined. As such, they were not included in these tables. For this reason, only three studies seem to have fully examined the accuracy of clinical judgment regarding lateralization. These are presented in Table 9.5. Only one study (Russell et al., 1970) presented the data directly in enough detail to determine the operating characteristics of the clinical judgment without describing problems that reduced the reliability of the results. In two other cases (Reitan, 1964; Wedding, 1983a). the data could be reconstructed. The "hit rate," which apparently meant sensitivity, for two clinicians in the study by Heaton et al. (1981) are provided without specificity measures or the *N*s for the three lateralization groups. Although this study was well known, it did not present enough data to construct all of the operating characteristics.

The results in Table 9.5 are so scanty and diverse that it appeared pointless to average the results. With such diversity, a fairly large number of studies needs to be examined before a determination can be made as to the accuracy of clinical judgment regarding lateralization of brain damage. Nevertheless, gross examination indicated that the accuracy for lateralization by clinical judgment in this table ranged from a sensitivity of 43.7% to 100%. As expected, the diffuse group was less accurate, with a sensitivity of 43.7% to 95.8%. Specificity again does not appear to be quite as accurate as sensitivity. It ranged from 57.0% to 91.3%. The overall power for these four groups ranged from 69.3% to 88.4%.

The clinical judges in these studies, with the exception of the Reitan (1964) and Boyar and Tsushima's (1975) neurosurgical patients studies, were about 70% accurate in predicting the neurological criterion of lateralization. Thus, these results support the estimate that, when the patient data involve relatively unambiguous subjects, the lateralization accuracy is about 65% to 70% when the diffuse category is included. The probability for a three-way division is 33.3%. Lateralization accuracy increases to from 93% to 100% when only the right and left categories are involved.

Individual Studies of Formal Methods

Concerning accuracy, the evaluation methods have varied from study to study. Only this current review has fully applied the concept of operating characteristics across all studies with complete data to determine the accuracy of various studies. Despite the use of such methods to obtain consistency, there is a great variation in the nature of the studies. They vary in the type of patients who are used and in the procedures themselves. Performing such studies requires a the great amount of time for clinical judges to examine the data. In Wedding's (1983a) study, the judges averaged 6.5 h to examine the 30 cases.

The result has been that one of two approaches has been chosen for validating clinical judgment. Either there has been an insufficient number of judges and an adequate number of cases or an adequate number of judges but an insufficient number of cases. Many judgment studies had only one judge, whereas others had two judges such as in the study by Heaton et al. (1981). The alternative can be seen in Faust et al. (1988) and Wedding (1983a).

Obviously, a large validity study is needed that will have both enough cases and enough judges to produce an adequate result. The problem is to obtain the resources to complete such a study, particularly now when almost no studies of this kind are being attempted. As a result, the studies have varied to such an extent that it is difficult to compare their accuracy even using formal methods and consistent statistical evaluation methods. For this reason several of the outstanding individual studies of neuropsychological accuracy will be examined to determine their particular characteristics and what they can contribute to an understanding of neuropsychological assessment accuracy. In a few instances, studies that were not included in the tables of this chapter will be examined. This is primarily because of their importance in the field of neuropsychological assessment.

Development of Formal Neuropsychological Methods

Beginning with Halstead's and Reitan's work and augmented by Russell et al.'s (1970) neuropsychological key, neuropsychological assessment became involved in developing formal methods for assessment. Except for the work by Halstead and Reitan, few formal or actuarial methods had been applied to neuropsychology before 1970.

Reitan, 1964

After his initial work, Reitan (1955) demonstrated that various diagnoses of brain damage and its location could be determined using only neuropsychological tests. Thus, the earliest clinical study of localization, as with so many other types of studies, was performed by Reitan (1964). It has not been duplicated. In this study, 64 focal cases and 48 diffuse cases were selected from Reitan's files. The neurological criteria and neuropsychological reports were separately rated according to the location and diagnosis. The location ratings were given by quadrants of the brain. These data, which were provided in Reitan's paper (1964, Table 14.4, p. 301), required some reconstruction to provide lateralization measures. The results are provided in Table 9.5.

These results show an 88.4% overall predictive power of the right, left, and diffuse groups and a 93% correct identification of the right and left groups when examined separately. This is the highest accuracy for any study that included the diffuse cases but not for the right-versus-left groups. Although, to some extent, the high accuracy rate was the result of Reitan's expertise, it may also be because of the initial selection of clear-cut neurological cases. Apparently, someone on Reitan's staff selected the cases. The fact that Reitan wrote the original reports was not a factor in this study because the rating was done from the original reports, which were written when Reitan was unaware of the history or diagnosis of the case. All of Reitan's reports during this time were written blind.

Russell et al. 1970

The Russell et al. (1970) study was the initial study in which there was an attempt to use a formal algorithm for assessment of neuropsychological data. The study used a computer program for assessment. It was modeled after a biological *taxonomic key*—that is, a formalized method used to ascertain the identity of a particular plant or animal specimen. The concept of a biological key is relatively old in terms of science ever since the first key was described by Nehemiah Grew in 1682 (Russell et al., 1970, pp. 16–17). Since then, keys have been thoroughly developed in biology so that they have become quite sophisticated. In the Russell et al. (1970) study, this method was applied to neuropsychological data derived from the HRB to differentiate patients into normal, diffuse, and right- and left-hemisphere–impaired groups and also to separate acute, chronic, and congenital patients. With time, it became obvious that the key was basically a decision-tree algorithm.

Of the 104 subjects in this study, 21 had left-hemisphere damage, 16 right-hemisphere damage, 43 had diffuse damage, and 24 had a negative neurological examination. The subjects were obtained by consecutively selecting all available subjects with a clear organic diagnosis from the files in Gerald Goldstein's laboratory at the Topeka, Kansas, VA hospital.

Initially, the key was not a computer program but a series of decision rules. In the study, the rules were applied by an intelligent patient who knew nothing about neurology. Later, Carolyn Shelly wrote the computer program in Fortran, and it was published with the book (Russell et al., 1970, pp. 142–153). Subsequent studies evidently used the computer program instead of running the key by hand.

The original validation of the key (Russell et al., 1970) was fairly successful. The accuracy rate for assessing brain damage is given in Table 9.2, and the accuracy of the lateralization categories—right, diffuse, and left—is given in Table 9.3. Across the lateralized cases, the overall predictive power is 54.7%. However, if the subjects are restricted to only the right- and left-hemisphere cases, the predictive power becomes 88%.

Regarding the clinical judgment used in the study, Gerald Goldstein assessed the lateralization and existence of brain damage entirely from the neuropsychological record. Although he had seen many of these cases previously, he did not remember them. At the time that he participated in this study, he had had only a few years of experience. Nevertheless, the prediction of clinical judgment across the three categories was almost as accurate as the well-experienced neuropsychologists in the Heaton et al. (1981) study. The predictive power in the Russell et al. study was 69.3%, whereas the Heaton et al. study, when the two judges were averaged, was 69.9%. When only the right and left cases were used, the clinical judgment had an overall predictive power of 96.3%. The relatively large number of diffuse cases, which are often ambiguous regarding lateralization, apparently reduced the overall predictive power to 69.3 when the three groups were included.

Unpublished Computer Programs

In the years following the publication of the neuropsychological key, several other programs were constructed. Although these were never published, they are presented here because they are discussed in the literature. The research on Adams revised program (ARP) (Adams et al., 1984) was published. The program apparently was Adams's dissertation (1975) revised for the Adams et al. (1984) study. In addition to the ARP, these programs include the System for Analysis and Interpretation of Neuropsychological Tests (SAINT) (Swiercinsky, 1978), Brain 1 (Finkelstein, 1976), Knights program (Knights, 1973), and the Eclectic Neuro Score (ENS) (Bernard, 1988) program. Of these, only SAINT and Brain 1 were used in studies by other neuropsychologists. Their concepts were discussed favorably in at least three other publications (Adams & Brown, 1986; Anthony et al., 1980; Lynch, 1988). Much later, a promising computer program was designed to both administer and score the SAINT. Initially, this appeared to have acceptable validity, but no further work appears to have been done with this battery.

The Critique of Formal Methods

This burst of creativity activity in neuropsychological assessment that was concerned with the development of formal methods existed until the 1980s. The reaction, however, disparaged formal methods. Much of the initial excitement and the criticism tended to center on the neuropsychological key. An examination of the studies used to discredit formal methods and particularly the key is quite enlightening. As discussed in Chapter 1, the leaders in this critique were Heaton and Adams (Adams & Heaton, 1985). Consequently, the adequacy of their work as the basis for the criticism will primarily be discussed.

Anthony et al. 1980

In 1980 and 1981, Heaton and Anthony were the principal authors of a study that was published in two papers. In the first paper, Anthony et al. (1980) examined the accuracy of the key and Brain 1, whereas the second paper compared the programs to clinical judgment (Heaton et al., 1981). Brain 1 was found to be largely lacking in accuracy. Concerning the meuropsychological key, Anthony et al. (1980) implied that their results were much worse with the same program than the results found in the original study so that "little confidence can be placed in most of the 'finer' diagnostic distinctions" made by the key. As such, the program had "limited clinical value" (p. 322).

Anthony et al. (1980) presented the entire matrix for their calculations (Table 4, p. 322). This enabled Goldstein and Shelly (1982) to demonstrate that Anthony et al. (1980) used a measure of sensitivity whereas Russell et al. (1970) used a measure of specificity. This change had created the impression that the Anthony et al. (1980) study provided more accurate results. This difference in method could explain all of the differences between the Russell et al. (1970) and Anthony et al. (1980) studies. The matrix provided by Anthony et al. (1980) provided sufficient data so that all of the operating characteristics for both the original neuropsychological key study (Russell et al., 1970) and Anthony et al. (1980) study could be directly compared. These operational characteristics are placed in Table 9.3. In this direct comparison, the original key study demonstrates that its accuracy is essentially the same as the application of the key in the Anthony et al. (1980) study. The overall predictive power of the Russell et al. (1970) validation across three categories—right, diffuse, and left—of the key was 54.7%, whereas the overall predictive power of the Anthony et al. (1980) study was 56.6%. When the diffuse category is removed and only right and left categories were considered, the overall predictive power of the Russell et al. (1970) study was 88.0%. In contrast, the Anthony et al. (1980) study was 85.7%.

Anthony et al. (1980) also examined the neuropsychological process key in Russell et al. (1970). Although their own work was not as accurate as that of Russell et al. (1970), they nevertheless said that the program was not statistically significant.

In conclusion, this examination of the data from both studies provides no support for Anthony et al.'s (1980) statement, "Unfortunately, it appears that both of these programs in their current forms are of limited clinical value.... Furthermore, our results indicate that little confidence can be placed in most of the 'finer' diagnostic distinctions [i.e., lateralization] made by these programs...."

Heaton et al. 1981

Because the study by Anthony et al. (1980) did not demonstrate a lack of accuracy for determining the existence and lateralization of brain damage, the crucial determination was whether clinical judgment was more accurate than the neuropsychological key. This comparison was provided by the other part of the study published by Heaton et al. (1981). This study, which is one of the most quoted study on neuropsychological clinical judgment, examined the accuracy of two experienced judges. The judges had more than 8 years of clinical and research experience and had collaborated in doing clinical ratings during the previous 3 years. Their ratings were highly correlated: $r = 0.95$.

In spite of a rather lengthy and detailed presentation that discussed the various aspects of the rating and faults of the key, this study failed to provide enough of the original data to determine the operating characteristics of the two judges. The entire presentation of data is provided in one paragraph and a limited table (p. 126). Only the hit rate of the two clinician judges are presented. This is essentially a measure of sensitivity. Not presented are the measures of specificity or the *N* for each lateralized group. Consequently, it is not possible to construct the total operating characteristics of these judges. Because a fully adequate statistical table of test results was provided by one of the authors—Anthony in Anthony et al. (1980, p. 322)—these authors could have provided the data needed to reconstruct the total operating characteristics of the clinical judgment. For this reason, the few data on lateralization presented in this study were not included in Table 9.5. It is quite possible that these judges, while being quite accurate in determining the existence of lateralized cases—that is, true positives—had a tendency to overestimate the existence of a lateralized condition and had a high portion of false negatives. This cannot be determined because the data were not provided. The result is that the accuracy of these judges is not determined and consequently is not reliable.

Goldstein and Shelly, 1982

In addition to showing the difference between using measures of sensitivity and specificity, Goldstein and Shelly (1982) completed another validation study of the lateralization and process parts of the key, which is presented in Table 9.3. Generally, this study did not rate the key as highly for accuracy as either the original study (Russell et al., 1970) or the Anthony et al. (1980) study. The lateralization study had a total predictive power for right, diffuse, and left of 48.2% and a right-versus-left total power of 75%. In part, this was because of a large proportion of diffuse cases: 300 diffuse cases out of 390. Diffuse cases are more likely to be misdiagnosed than lateralized cases. Base rates affect this type of study when one condition is preponderant. Nevertheless, Goldstein and Shelly (1982) found the accuracy of the lateralization part of the key to be relatively stable across studies.

Wedding's Studies, 1983

During the period of intense investigation of the accuracy of various neuropsychological procedures, including clinical judgment, the neuropsychological key, and discriminant analysis, one meticulously described study was often overlooked in the controversy. This was the Wedding study, which was published in two parts (1983a, 1983b).

In the first study (Wedding, 1983b), the key, Brain 1, and a discriminant analysis were compared. The HRB and the WAIS constituted the test battery that was administered. The study was well designed, and great care was used to select the subjects. There were 30 subjects, six in each of five categories. The categories were normals, schizophrenics, and right, left, and diffuse brain damage. Because the key was not designed to handle schizophrenia, the schizophrenics were grouped with normals when the key was used.

The only major error in the study was to use schizophrenics as subjects. Previous studies had demonstrated that they could not be distinguished from brain-damaged subjects (Goldstein, 1986; Watson, Thomas, Anderson, & Felling, 1968). For the key, they were grouped with the normals as a non–brain-damaged group. The result was that, even though the schizophrenics were grouped with the normals, the key was 60% correct and the discriminant analysis was 63% correct in Wedding's calculations. In the current study, the separation of brain-damaged and normals (with schizophrenics), the key had a total predictive power of 88.0% (Table 9.3), whereas the discriminant analysis had a power of 95.8%.

A lateralization study was performed on the key using only the data for lateralized subjects (Wedding, 1983b, Table 6, p. 19). This eliminated the problem of schizophrenic subjects. The normal subjects were also not included. The total *N* was reduced by the number of cases left out. The results are given in Table 9.3. In this study, the key had a total predictive power of 64.3% across all three lateralization categories and a predictive power of 85.7% when only the right and left subjects were used. This finding was equivalent to the original key study, which had a predictive power of 54.7% for the three categories and 88.0% for right and left categories alone. Thus, the accuracy rate in this study, although with a restricted *N*, was better than the rate in either the original study or the Anthony et al. (1980) study.

In the second study (Wedding, 1983a), 14 clinicians using clinical judgment were compared to each other, the accuracy of the key, and discriminant analysis. Of these 14 clinicians, one was considered to be an expert, the head of a laboratory who had published extensively and had years of experience interpreting the HRB. The other 13 were labeled inexperienced, although 10 were licensed practicing neuropsychologists with several years of experience; 3 were graduate students. All of the clinicians had been trained in the HRB and were comfortable giving it.

Because the complete data were provided in Table 9.1, the schizophrenic subjects could be eliminated. None of the schizophrenics along with those wrongly called *schizophrenic* were counted.

In the clinical judgments, concerning the existence of brain damage in order to increase the *N*, the reanalyzed data counted the number of judgments that the 14 judges made. There were 198 judgments when the wrong schizophrenics were eliminated. The total predictive power was 88.2%, which was equivalent to the original judgment of 88.5% and the judges in Heaton et al.'s (1981) study. One judge had a predictive power of 91.2%, and the other had 87.6%.

Concerning lateralization, the expert was separated from the nonexperts. The expert had a total predictive power of 80.0%, with a right-versus-left power of 100%. In contrast, the 13 nonexperts had a total predictive power of 67.4%, with a right-versus-left power of 95.2%. The total predictive power of the key in Wedding's (1983b) study (Table 3) for three categories was 69.2%, which was slightly better than the nonexperts. Across the full set of scores, Wedding found the accuracy of the key to be 60% and that of discriminant analysis 63%, whereas the expert was 63% and the nonexperts only 53.8%.

Russell, 1984

Because of problems with its original format, the key was reworked (Russell, 1984). The original key was weak on the left hemisphere, so that aspect was strengthened. The lateralized scores were summed to form a new lateralization index. This lateralization index was applied to 191 subjects who had been definitely diagnosed by medical university staff neurologists. As Table 9.3 demonstrates, this new lateralization index was more accurate than the original key in any previous study. The overall predictive power of this index was 78.1% accurate, and no errors were made regarding the right-versus-left discrimination. To date, this lateralization index does not appear to have been cross validated in any other study, in spite of its apparent high rate of accuracy.

As a note, an unpublished study was completed, concerning the two cases in the Heaton et al. (1981) study that the key missed but which the clinicians assessed correctly (Heaton et al., 1981, Tables 6 and 7, pp. 135–136). When the first case was run on the new lateralization index, the subject was correctly assessed using the HRNES–R program as having lateralized left-hemisphere brain damage. The other example was still incorrectly identified as not being brain damaged when the subject did have damage.

Adams et al. 1984

The study by Adams et al. (1984). reported data that were not complete enough to compute all of the statistics required for Table 9.3. This study reported the results of three experiments, two of which compared the key and Brain 1 (Finkelstein, 1977) to the ARP. The study concluded that the "lateralization… predictions are not done well by these programs" (Adams et al. 1984, p. 413). It was on the basis of this conclusion as well as the Heaton and Anthony (Anthony et al., 1980; Heaton et al., 1981) studies that computerized programs in the area of neuropsychology were considered to be relatively inaccurate.

Although all three experiments in the Adams et al. (1984) study report the proportion of brain-damaged subjects who were not diagnosed as brain damaged, there was no normal control group. Consequently, there is no adequate indication of the accuracy of these programs in separating normals from brain-damaged subjects. Obviously, the operating characteristics of this study could not be determined. The only meaningful comparisons were the lateralization investigations.

Experiments 1 and 2 used 63 of Halstead's original subjects. There were 21 cases each for the left hemisphere, the right hemisphere, and the diffuse condition. Experiment 1 compared Adams's original program with the ARP that used Reitan's cutting points instead of those originally developed by Adams. This experiment found that the original program lateralized cases better than the ARP.

The accuracy of experiment 2 also could not be determined. In regard to the key, the results are quite anomalous. The key was reported to have classified all of the subjects as right-hemisphere damaged. Possible reasons for this unusual occurrence, which was completely different from the results of any other study, were never discussed. In this experiment, the results for Brain 1 were rather inaccurate, as in other studies (Anthony et al., 1980; Wedding, 1983b). The ARP also provided a reasonable distribution of cases and performed a little better than the other two programs.

Experiment 3 in the Adams et al. (1984) paper has apparently been reported three times (Adams, 1986; Adams & Brown 1986; Adams et al., 1984), thus increasing its impact in the literature. This experiment used a new sample of subjects with 30 in each group—right, left, and diffuse. In this experiment, 26 of the 30 subjects had either a transient ischemic attack (TIA) or an episode of reversible ischemic neurological deficit (RIND). By definition, these are patients who neurologically recover completely from their episodes. In neurology, a TIA is diagnosed by lateralized motor, sensory, or speech problems that disappear within 24 h and leave no residual. The deficits in a RIND resolve within 3 weeks (Netter, Jones, & Dingle, 1985, p. 54). Consequently, one would expect that a large portion of the subjects in Adams's study would have such minimal residuals that they would be classified as normal by the programs. Adams states that the subjects had confirmed demonstrable causative lesions. However, he does not state how the lesions were confirmed. Because the usual TIA or RIND is diagnosed neurologically by motor or sensory deficits that resolve, few residual impairments would be expected for confirmation unless a patient's history was used. In any case, these subjects were very specialized and so were completely inappropriate for examining the general accuracy of any neuropsychological procedure.

Because there were no normal control subjects in this study, there was no means to determine how many normal subjects would have been misclassified as brain damaged or vice versa. Although, by diagnosis, these subjects should have been normal, all three programs indicated that many of these subjects had impairments.

Regarding lateralization, TIAs, RINDs, or strokes are not diffuse because they are diagnosed by lateralized symptoms. How then were the diffuse cases determined? In any case, TIAs and RINDs have effects that, when they exist at all, are so mild that they would seldom lateralize. Because only the percentage correctly classified for each category was presented, there was no way to decide where the errors were made. It is probable that most of the errors were made by classifying lateralized cases as diffuse. This is exactly what would be expected for patients with these kinds of diagnoses. It would also explain the unusually high rate of misdiagnosis in this study when compared to other studies.

No clinical judgment evaluations were presented, so there was no way to decide whether clinical assessment would have been any more accurate with this population. Other studies (Table 9.3) have shown that with an adequate sampling, the key at least is much more accurate in distinguishing lateralized cases than it was in this study. Consequently, because the key does not vary from one study to the next, it is apparent that this sample was flawed. All three of these neuropsychological programs were criticized for not lateralizing types of subjects that generally do not show lateralized impairment. At best, this study should have concluded that these programs do not lateralize TIA and RIND subjects with any great accuracy. As such, the study has no relevance to other kinds of brain damage and thus to brain damage in general. Consequently, it ascertained nothing about the accuracy of any formal programs applied to brain damage.

Faust et al., 1988

The 1988 study by Faust, Guilmette, Hart, Arkes, Fishburne, and Davey used a method of examining the accuracy of neuropsychological clinical assessment in which the number of judges was increased while the number of cases was reduced. They mailed test results selected from 10 cases to 600 neuropsychologists selected at random from several major neuropsychology organizations. Each neuropsychologist received only one of the 10 cases. The 155 usable cases that were returned thus represented a random sample of neuropsychologists in the United States.

In regard to assessing the existence of brain damage (Table 9.5), Faust et al. (1988) was inline with other studies. Their overall predictive power was 80.0%, whereas the average for the 10 studies was 84.0%. As in many of the studies, sensitivity at 85.8% was higher than specificity at 60.0%. The average sensitivity across all of the studies was 87.5%, with a specificity that was 10 points lower at 77.0%.

Unfortunately, the data provided in Faust et al. (1988) could not be placed in a form that permitted a lateralization measure. The closest category was the *general localization* category, although this category included anterior versus posterior areas as well and right, left, and diffuse. Because such a judgment is much less accurate than simple lateralization, the low accuracy score of 54% probably reflects the relative poor ability of neuropsychologists to classify the anterior versus posterior location of damage.

Russell and Starkey, 2001a, Russell, 2004

The work by Russell (1984) has gradually evolved, eventuating in a method to produce standardized scale scores using linear regression (Russell, 1987) to create the HRNES–R computer program (Russell & Starkey, 2001a). This is described in more detail elsewhere (Russell, 2000). This program contains two indexes of brain damage the AIS and PII. The accuracy of the AIS and PII were presented previously in Table 9.2.

The lateralization index that was designed for Russell's 1984 study was improved and validated and its operational characteristics determined. It is presented in Table 9.3 as the HRNES–R lateralization index. The HRNES–R had more than four times as many subjects as were in the 1984 study. The new subjects increased the number of diffuse cases: head trauma subjects were considered to be diffuse because experience had indicated that even when there were neurological localizing symptoms, neuropsychological examinations found more scattered impairment in other areas of the brain.

In this study, the lateralization index had considerably better accuracy than the first neuropsychological key. It had an overall predictive power across the three categories of 65.6% as opposed to 54.7% for the key. This was also better than the Anthony et al. (1980) results, which were 56.6%. Because the specificity of the Heaton et al. (1981) study is not known, the accuracy of the lateralization may very well be better than the Heaton et al. (1981) study.

Conclusion of Formal and Clinical Validity Studies

This review of the accuracy of formal neuropsychological batteries derived from a comprehensive review of the existing studies provides the basis for several conclusions about the validity and accuracy of neuropsychological testing.

The review has been fairly comprehensive in regard to examining the validation and accuracy of batteries. It used the Bayesian statistics of operating characteristics for this examination (Retzlaff & Gibertini, 1994; Slick, 2006). (More sophisticated methods were not used because the work that neuropsychologists have produced does not permit such sophistication.)

The first finding of this review was that neuropsychology has devoted relatively little effort to the development of unified batteries. This effort has been almost entirely limited to those who use the HRB or versions of that test. As Chapter 1 emphasized, since the 1980s and until very recently, other than the work of Reitan and his followers, almost no effort was devoted in the field to the creation, validation, and examination of the accuracy of batteries. In addition to this lack of effort, there has been very little in the way of reviews of batteries as a whole. To fill this gap, this writing has been devoted to examining the validation and accuracy of the studies that have been performed on formal neuropsychological methods related to batteries.

Neuropsychology Accuracy and Meehl's Contention

This review makes a major contribution by enlarging the information about the relative accuracy of formal methods related to clinical judgment. An ongoing argument in neuropsychology from its beginning has been whether an intuitive clinical judgment methodology is more accurate than formal methodologies. This has become a major contention in neuropsychology. In part, this review attempted to examine the accuracy of formal methods in neuropsychology in order to determine whether Meehl's (1954) findings could be applied to neuropsychology. Meehl found that, when applicable, formal or actuarial methods were as accurate or more accurate in predicting psychological characteristics of people than clinical judgment. Except for neuropsychology, Meehl and his associates (Dawes, Faust, & Meehl, 1989; Grove & Meehl, 1996; Grove, Zald, Lebow, Snitz, & Nelson, 2000) continued to confirm the accuracy of formal methods. Although Halstead and Reitan began to develop formal methods in the 1940s and 1950s, a comparison of these methods with clinical judgment has been neglected even though neuropsychological criteria was more concrete than that of other areas of psychology (Wedding, 1983a, p. 49). Since Meehl's original work, there have been repeated studies up to the present that have verified his initial results (Dawes et al., 1989; Grove et al., 2000; Grove & Meehl, 1996).

Although Meehl's findings were discussed by some neuropsychologists (Wedding, 1983a), Adams and Heaton, who wrote almost all of the critiques of computerized test scoring, particularly the neuropsychological key, seldom mention this work. Rather, they state that their research found clinical judgment to be far superior to formal methodologies. Typical of their statements is the following by Adams and Heaton (1985): "researchers have found programs such as the Russell et al. (1970) key to be significantly less accurate than human judges in predicting presence and lateralization of cerebral function" (p. 797). In the Adams and Heaton (1987) paper, they again state, "In the initial work on neuropsychological interpretation [primarily the neuropsychological key], the results have provided an unintended, but powerful, demonstration of human superiority over computer algorithms" (p. 363).

Apparently, determining the accuracy of the examination formal battery has not been applied to neuropsychological assessment results primarily because it was generally thought that the formal methods of determining the accuracy of neuropsychological conditions were less effective than clinical judgment. However, this current examination found their contentions to be highly questionable.

Index Accuracy

The first formal method to be examined were indexes of existing brain damage. In regard to the indexes (Tables 9.1 and 9.2), the HI, AIR, and other indexes closely approach the accuracy of a clinical evaluation by experts. The accuracy of all of these indexes was about 80%. Clinical judgment was found to be approximately 85% accurate. Because the 85% rate was that of experts, the rate of nonexperts would probably be equal to or not as accurate as indexes. Considering that these indexes use a simple single cutting point, with no complex decisions such as clinical methods assume, they were surprisingly accurate.

Heaton et al. (1981) admitted that the accuracy of the AIR, which was part of the neuropsychological key, was equivalent to that of human judgment. Consequently, in this discussion the lateralization part of the key became the primary area of contention. The process key was found to be less accurate than would be desirable. Later, Goldstein et al. (1996) demonstrated that the process key would accurately distinguish the acute and chronic condition for certain kinds of vascular lesions but not others.

Crucial Lateralization Studies

Examination of the individual writings by Adams and Heaton showed that they referred to only three studies: Adams et al. (1984) and the two parts of Heaton et al., which were Anthony et al. (1980) and Heaton et al. (1981).

Concerning the Adams study, a close examination of this work found that this analysis was evidently invalid. First, it had no control subjects so that operating characteristics could not be obtained. Second, the subjects primarily consisted of patients with TIAs and episodes of RIND. These are neurological diagnoses in which subjects completely recover. Therefore, they would not produce any amounts of brain damage, much less evidence of lateralization. As such, no adequate results of damage or lateralization could have been obtained from this group of subjects.

The Heaton study was published in two parts using the same set of subjects. One part of the study (Anthony et al., 1980) compared the neuropsychological key with Brain 1 using data generated in Heaton's laboratory. The results of this comparison demonstrated that Brain 1 was rather inaccurate. The situation with the key was different. It separated brain-damaged from non–brain-damaged subjects at an acceptably high level. Concerning the lateralization part of the key, the researchers presented the right, diffuse, and left results in their Table 4 (Anthony et al. 1980, p. 322).

Because the actual data were placed in a table, operating characteristics could be determined. These are described in Table 9.3. The table also contains the data from the original Russell et al. (1970) study. Direct comparison of the two studies demonstrates that they are overall of approximately equal accuracy. When only the right and left subjects are considered, the original key was more accurate. Thus, the Anthony et al. (1970) study provided no evidence that the key was "of limited clinical value."

Because these two studies did not provide any substantial grounds for stating that the key was inadequate, particularly in relationship to clinical judgment, the second study by Heaton et al. (1981) becomes the only basis for condemning the accuracy of computerized algorithms. In this study, the two "experts," who were described as having been trained in Reitan's laboratory and having had about 8 years of clinical experience with the HRB, provided the clinical judgments. The clinicians judgments had a high agreement rate with a correlation of 81.3%.

The results of the judgments are presented in the Heaton et al. (1981) paper on p. 126 in a paragraph and brief table. The text and table present the percentage of correct predictions (hit rate). This presents the measure of sensitivity or the percentage of true positive clinical judgments. However, the specificity rates or true negatives are missing as well as the *N*'s for three categories of left, right, and diffuse. Because both types of data are necessary to determine specificity rates, these rates could not be constructed. Thus, the operational characteristics are not known and the rate of true negatives might be low, which would reduce the total accuracy or overall predictive power. As a result, in spite of all the discussion in the rest of the paper, the accuracy of the Heaton et al. (1981) study is undetermined. This means that the only three studies that Adams and Heaton used to criticize the neuropsychological key are all incapable of determining the accuracy of clinical judgment compared to a formal method.

Finally, in Adams's and Heaton's writings there is evidently no mention of two papers that are important in regard to the question of the accuracy of formal methodologies. One of these is Goldstein and Shelly's (1982) paper, which demonstrated that the Anthony et al. (1980) cross-validation study made their application of the key to their data look worse than the original study (Russell et al., 1970) because of the way that they calculated their results. This is also true in the current analysis (Table 9.2).

The second omission was more egregious in that it consisted of a study comparing judgment and several formal methods, including the key. This study arrived at a different conclusion than that expressed in Adams's and Heaton's papers. Wedding's study was published in two papers (Wedding, 1983a, 1983b). In these papers, Wedding compared 14 clinical judges with the neuropsychological key, Brain 1, and a discriminant analysis. One of the judges was an expert who had had extensive experience with the HRB. The rest of the judges, who were designated as "nonexperts," had used the HRB but did not have years of experience.

It is not possible to compare Wedding's results with those of Heaton et al. (1981) because the accuracy of the Heaton et al. results could not be determined. Within Wedding's study, the key was almost as accurate as the expert and more accurate than the nonexperts. As Wedding stated, "The results offer strong support of the efficacy of actuarial and (particularly) statistical approaches to discrete decision making in clinical psychology" (1983a, p. 52).

In 1993, Russell and Starkey published a computer scoring program, the HRNES, which was revised in 2001 (Russell & Starkey, 2001b). It contained two indexes of brain-damage existence and a lateralization index (Table 9.2). The *N* had been increased to 200 normals and 715 brain-damaged subjects. The indexes of brain damage remained approximately the same with a total predictive power of 85% for the AIS and 83% for the PII.

In contrast, the accuracy of the lateralization index increased from 54.7% in the original key (Table 9.3) to 65.6%. The right-versus-left comparison increased from 88.0% to 96.9%. This was less than the 1984 study, but it was a more stable index. These increases in accuracy demonstrate that the accuracy of formal methods, including algorithms can be improved. The accuracy of the right-versus-left comparison at 96.9% was probably greater than the judgments in Heaton et al. (1981) or the Wedding judgments by expert clinicians.

Thus, the key was evidently accurate enough to be used clinically by inexperienced psychologists and as an initial appraisal by experienced neuropsychologists. In addition, the new HRNES–R lateralization index (Russell, 1984; Russell & Starkey, 1993) may be as accurate as the clinical judgment of experts. Certainly, experienced neuropsychologists could use the program as a first approximation to an assessment and then examine the context to form their final conclusions.

Thus, although neuropsychological studies have not appeared in most of the review studies of actuarial versus clinical methodologies, it is highly possible that Meehl's finding that formal (actuarial) methodologies are as accurate or more accurate than clinical judgment will eventually apply to the field of clinical neuropsychology. The tragedy is that the critical studies in this area have not been conducted. Consequently, this question cannot yet be answered.

Criterion Problems

Another important aspect of this review was to examine the accuracy of neuropsychological methods to determine their reliability. However, the accuracy of valid neuropsychological procedures depends on the accuracy of the criterion.

As discussed elsewhere, the purpose of neuropsychological procedures is to determine functioning, including pathological functioning of the brain. Individual tests are tests of brain functions. As such, although construct validity underlies neuropsychological interpretation and practice, the validity of assessment procedures is primarily predictive validity. In predictive validity, the purpose of a procedure is to predict a particular criterion related to brain functioning. Thus, the adequacy of the criterion determines the maximum accuracy of assessment methods. The measured accuracy of a procedure cannot be greater than the accuracy of the criterion.

Using the same battery and same conditions, the study by Boyar and Tsushima (1975) found a considerably higher rate of accuracy in judging neurosurgical patience than neurology patients. The neurosurgical patients were evidently far more distinctive as a criterion because of a more thorough methodology than were neurology patients who only had a neurological clinical interview and minimal testing such as

EEGs. It is tragic that, in the history of neuropsychology, this appears to be the only study in which there was a direct comparison of two criteria.

In addition, there are very few studies that compared a neuropsychological procedure, usually the HRB, to neurological procedures including a CT scan—and most of these early studies were in the 1970s. Apparently, neuropsychologist have been so awed by the accuracy of the CT scan, the MRI, and other scanning techniques that they have failed to realize that even these methods are far from infallible, even in relationship to localization. Although neurology is more accurate in diagnosing brain conditions today, its results are still far from being perfect criteria.

Criterion Sample Variability

One advantage of using a formal procedure, whether it is an index or a more complex procedure such as the neuropsychological key, is that the procedure remains consistent across studies. Therefore, the variation between studies depends on other factors than the form of the procedure—for example, the patient sample. This difference in samples is particularly evident in the lateralization studies in which there are three criteria: the right, diffuse, and left lesion sites. An examination of the studies demonstrates that the right-versus-left designation is far more accurate when the diffuse condition is not introduced. Not only are right and left lesions more definite but also the diffuse condition may contain unrecognized lateralized areas of damage. For instance, Alzheimer's disease may be lateralized, but it is usually included in the diffuse condition. Thus, it is evident that the diffuse category is much more unpredictable than the right and left lateralized categories. For instance, the Sherer and Adams (1993) study is well designed according to their paper, nevertheless its results are well below that of most of the other studies (Tables 9.1 and 9.2). Consequently, one may question the researchers' method of selecting their sample.

The Accuracy Ceiling

One major conclusion derived from the current examination of neuropsychology accuracy is that the accuracy of neuropsychological procedures for all operational characteristics tapers off rapidly after about 80%. In addition, it is often found that the accuracy of new procedures is reduced when they are cross validated. This ceiling on accuracy is one reason why the HRB has maintained its accuracy compared to other methods of testing for almost a half century. In fact, it is highly probable that the accuracy of neuropsychological procedures will not be greatly increased until the accuracy of the neurological procedures has increased. In addition, great attention should be devoted to the criterion in designing neuropsychological studies.

Comparing Procedures

Another finding is that procedures can only be reliable compared using the same sample because of the difference in criteria. There is so much variation from sample to sample that without using the same sample, the comparisons often are simply comparisons of the normative samples. This is quite evident in the relatively large studies of the HI and AIR. Comparisons using clinical judgment are even more variable, because their accuracy is affected by differences in both the sample and differences between the judges.

The Development of Procedures

Another finding, which is quite apparent, is that a great deal more work needs to be done to validate neuropsychological procedures. In comparison to the work that has been done on various intelligence tests, the work on battery procedures to determine aspects of brain damage is minimal. The only two procedures that have a substantial amount of cross validation are the HI and the AIR (Russell et al., 1970) The HI is still used in several batteries, although these are relatively few compared to use of clinical judgment with unstandardized batteries. The AIR has been replaced by the AIS and PII (Russell & Starkey, 2001a; Russell, 2004). These are quite adequate for clinical use and appear to be more accurate than the AIR.

The Most Accurate Programs

Currently, the NDS appears to be the most accurate procedure for determining both the existence of brain damage (Table 9.2) and its lateralization (Table 9.3). However, the HRNES–R, AIS, and PII are almost as accurate (Table 9.2) as well as for lateralization (Table 9.3). The accuracy of the MNB cannot be determined at this point because it used discriminant analysis and has not been cross validated. However, its discriminant analysis score at 92.4% is excellent. As such, it is certainly an adequate instrument for assessment.

Mathematical Sophistication

It is also evident that the mathematical sophistication that is relevant to neuropsychology has increased dramatically during the last decade. However, such sophistication has usually been applied only to individual tests and not to entire batteries. Thus, the mathematical procedures have far outstripped the development of neuropsychological batteries. The exception is the intelligence tests that are often used with a neuropsychological battery. The improvement in methodology, particularly operating characteristics, is evident as we examine the studies of accuracy. The complete operating characteristics are not found in any of the neuropsychological studies to the present. This appears to be the first paper in this area that has examined the complete operating characteristics of all of these studies.

The development of neuropsychological procedures obviously lags far behind the mathematics that has been developed. Since about 1990, accuracy studies were not applied to any batteries until quite recently. Co-normed batteries have just recently begun to be created after more than 20 years. The exception to the lack of application of sophisticated procedures does not apply to the use of discriminant analysis. As previously discussed, however, the transition from the initial application of discriminant analysis to an index that is easily scorable has not yet happened. This transition would help make formal methodologies more psychometrically scientific and reliable.

Comparative Accuracy of a Nonstandard Battery

The accuracy of nonstandard batteries is unknown. It is not possible to determine the accuracy of a nonstandardized battery because the tests are variable. In essence, they appear to be untestable. The studies that have just been reviewed seem to indicate that clinical judgment is as accurate as formal methods. This was the conclusion that Lezak (1995) championed in her critique of the HRB (pp. 710–711). She apparently forgot that the studies to which she was referring were all performed on the HRB, a fixed battery (see Chapter 13).

By contrast, a large proportion of neuropsychologists do not use a standardized or fixed battery (Sweet, Nelson, & Moberg, 2005). Their claim is that they use clinical judgment to compose the battery and to interpret it (American Academy of Neurology, 2007). This raises the question, what are the necessary components for a reliable clinical judgment?

Clinical Judgment Requirements

As discussed previously, clinical judgment can be scientifically validated, so it could be reliable. However, in a particular case such as a forensic assessment, three requirements exist. First, psychometric studies must demonstrate that a procedure can be accurately judged to be accurate. This requires measures of concordance between judges as well as validation studies that demonstrate the accuracy of the procedure. Second, it must be demonstrated that the procedure or condition of interest is the same as the one that was validated. Finally, it must be demonstrated that the clinician using this procedure can make accurate judgments with this procedure. This generally requires evidence of training or considerable experience using the procedure. An alternate method would be to demonstrate that one can make correct judgments in a blind analysis using this procedure. Because the latter possibility is never used in neuropsychology, only the existence of training in the procedure can be presented.

The Context of a Brain-Function Analysis

Before we reach a conclusion, we need to review the importance of context, which was discussed previously. In any situation, but particularly in forensic cases, a neuropsychological examination or brain-function analysis is limited to what has been discovered and validated. This limits the area to which neuropsychological brain-function analysis can be applied scientifically. Currently, when using a formal or fixed procedure, the accuracy of the method may be examined and its area of application determined. This review of the accuracy of neuropsychological testing quite clearly describes the area to which it applies. The knowledge that the clinician has of psychology and neurology can be applied to understanding the context of the analysis. In addition, a known context can be used to support the findings of the neuropsychological analysis. However, information related to the context is not scientific but a matter of common sense in applying knowledge of neurology and psychology.

Finally, as has been mentioned elsewhere, the area in which neuropsychology has demonstrated a scientific understanding is limited. In other words, only a limited area of neuropsychology has been investigated and a valid understanding of the area has been established. Opinions beyond that area must be handled with clinical judgment based on a psychological and neurological understanding of the subject.

Reliability of Unstandardized Batteries

Clinical judgment when using a standardized battery has been examined in this review, and the results have been discussed. They are obviously quite sufficient for clinical and forensic practice. Evidence of a person's ability to use these methods can be presented in the form of experience and training in the methods. Thus, whether formal methods or clinical judgment is used, these standard battery methods are adequate for clinical and forensic practice.

Concerning unstandardized batteries, without meeting the requirements for valid clinical judgments for a procedure and using that particular procedure reliably, one cannot credibly use that procedure in court. With this understanding, the unstandardized or flexible battery may be examined. First, concerning the validation of such a procedure, which consists of more than one test, no validating research has been published. Consequently, it is obvious that no indications of the validity and accuracy of an unstandardized battery can be produced, particularly in court.

Second, obviously if no procedure has been validated, no one can claim they are using a validated procedure. At best, we can present individual tests. However, the researcher has no way of determining the relationship of one test to another and consequently of determining the meaning of the entire group of tests. The only evidence the researcher can present is that from experience he or she knows what these tests mean. However, if the researchers are continually changing the tests in the battery, they cannot build experience with the battery. Thus, most neuropsychologists who use an unstandardized approach use a consistent core battery. If they use their own core battery, they need to present evidence that it is valid and accurate.

Finally, how can someone claim to have training in or experience with a battery of tests is continually changing or that no one else uses? At best, he or she can state what a particular test in the battery means but not how it is related to other tests and how they are all related to a final interpretation. Any such interpretation of an unstandardized battery may be questioned on the basis of the lack of a psychometrically reliable procedure that has been validated to accurately indicate a particular interpretation. Finally, the neuropsychologist will lack of training with the particular battery because only he or she uses it. Experience in what has been called a *core* battery is limited to one's own experience that is unvalidated. Interrelationships between tests have not been objectively studied and are only repeatable if the battery remains consistent—that is, it becomes a fixed battery.

To summarize, the validity and accuracy (the rate of error) of an unstandardized battery is unknown. It consists of many tests with relationships that are unstudied and unvalidated, so the information they represent is unreliable. Consequently, a validated overall interpretation of the battery cannot be presented, nor can the reliability of an unstandardized battery be demonstrated in practice or in court.

References

Adams, K. M. (1975). Automated clinical interpretation of the neuropsychological test battery: an ability based approach. *Dissertation Abstracts International, 35*, 6085B, (University Microfilms No. 75-13, 289).

Adams, K. M. (1986). Concepts and methods in the design of automata for the neuropsychological test interpretation. In S. B. Filskov & T. J. Boll (Eds.), *Handbook of clinical neuropsychology* (pp. 561–575). New York: Wiley.

Adams, K. M., & Brown, G. G. (1986). The role of the computer in neuropsychological assessment. In I. Grant & K. M. Adams (Eds.), *Neuropsychological assessment of neuropsychiatric disorders* (pp. 87–99). New York: Oxford University Press.

Adams, K. M., & Heaton, R. K. (1985). Automated interpretation of neuropsychological test data. *Journal of Consulting and Clinical Psychology, 53*, 790–802.

Adams, K. M., & Heaton, R. K. (1987). Computerized neuropsychological assessment: issues and applications. In J. N. Butcher (Ed.), *Computerized psychological Assessment* (pp. 355–365). New York: Basic Books.

Adams, K. M., Kvale, V. I., & Keegan, J. F. (1984). Relative accuracy of three automated systems for neuropsychological interpretation. *Journal of Clinical Neuropsychological, 6*, 413–431.

American Academy of Neurology. (2007). Baxter v. Temple brief.

American Educational Research Association, American Psychological Association, & National Council on Measurement in Education (AERA et al.), (1999). Standards for educational and psychological testing, Washington, DC: Author.

Anthony, W. Z., Heaton, R. K., & Lehman, R. A. W. (1980). An attempt to cross-validate two actuarial systems for neuropsychological test interpretation. *Journal of Consulting and Clinical Psychology, 48*, 317–326.

Barth, J. T., Gideon, D. A., Sciara, A. D., Hulsey, P. H., & Anchor, K. N. (1986). Forensic aspects of mild head trauma. *Journal of Head Trauma Rehabilitation, 1*, 63–70.

Bernard, L. C. (1988). *Eclectic Neuro Score (ENS) Version 2 [Computer program]*. Los Angeles: Loyola Marymount University.

Bigler, E. D. (1991). Neuropsychological assessment, neuroimaging, and clinical neuropsychology: a synthesis. *Archives of Clinical Neuropsychology, 6*(3), 113–132.

Boyar, J. I., & Tsushima, W. T. (1975). Cross-validation of the halstead–reitan neuropsychological battery: application in Hawaii. *Hawaii Medical Journal, 34*, 94–96.

Dawes, R. M., Faust, D., & Meehl, P. E. (1989). Clinical versus actuarial judgment. *Science, 243*, 1668–1674.

Dodrill, C. B. (1999). Myths of neuropsychology: Further considerations. *Clinical Neuropsychologist, 13*, 562–572.

Dikmen, S. S., Machamer, J. E., Winn, H. R., & Temkin, N. R. (1995). Neuropsychological outcome at one year post injury. *Neuropsychology, 1*, 80–90.

Faust, D., & Ahern, D. C. (in press). Clinical judgment and prediction. In D. Faust (Ed.), Coping with Psychiatric and Psychological Testimony (6th ed.). New York: Oxford University Press.

Faust, D., Grimm, P. W., Ahern, D. C., & Sokolik, M. (2010). The admissibility of behavioral science evidence in the court room: the translation of legal to scientific concepts and back. *Annual Review of Clinical Psychology*, *6*, 49–77.

Faust, D., Guilmette, T. J., Hart, K., Arkes, H. R., Fishburne, F. J., & Davey, L. (1988). Neuropsychologists' training, experience, and judgment accuracy. *Archives of Clinical Neuropsychology*, *3*, 145–163.

Faust, D., Ziskin, J., & Hiers, J. B. (1988). *Brain damage claims: Coping with neuropsychological evidence* (Vol. 1, pp. 186–188). Los Angeles: Law and Psychology Press.

Filskov, S. B., & Goldstein, S. G. (1974). Diagnostic validity of the Halstead–Reitan neuropsychological battery. *Journal of Consulting and Clinical Psychology*, *42*, 382–388.

Finkelstein, J. N. (1977). BRAIN 1: A computer program for interpretation of the Halstead–Reitan neuropsychological test battery. *Dissertation Abstracts International*, *37* B (University Microfilms No. 77-8, 8864).

Garb, H. N. (1998). *Studying the clinician: Judgment research and psychological assessment.* Washington, DC: American Psychological Association.

Gass, C. (2011, July 10). Personal communication.

Golden, C. J., Hammeke, T. A., & Purisch, A. D. (1980). *Manual for the luria–nebraska neuropsychological battery*. Los Angeles: Western Psychological Services.

Goldstein, S. G., Deysach, R. E., & Kleinknecht, R. A. (1973). Effect of experience and amount of information on identification of cerebral impairment. *Journal of Consulting and Clinical Psychology*, *41*, 30–34.

Goldstein, G. (1986). The neuropsychology of schizophrenia. In I. Grant & K. M. Adams (Eds.), *Neuropsychological assessment of neuropsychiatric disorders* (pp. 147–171). New York: Oxford University Press.

Goldstein, G. (1993, October). Personal communication.

Goldstein, G., & Shelly, C. H. (1972). Statistical and normative studies of the Halstead neuropsychological test battery relevant to a neuropsychiatric setting. *Perceptual and Motor Skills*, *34*, 603–620.

Goldstein, G., & Shelly, C. (1982). A further attempt to cross-validate the Russell, Neuringer, and Goldstein neuropsychological keys. *Journal of Consulting and Clinical Psychology*, *50*, 721–726.

Goldstein, G., Shemansky, W. J., Beers, S. R., George, T., & Roberts, K. (1996). A clarification of the Russell, Neuringer, and Goldstein process key: implications for outcome. *Archives of Clinical Neuropsychology*, *11*(7), 581–587.

Gouvier, W. D. (1999). Base rates and clinical decision-making in neuropsychology. In J. Sweet (Ed.), *Forensic psychology: fundamentals and practice*. Lisse, Netherlands: Swets and Zeitlinger.

Gouvier, W. D. (2001). Are you sure you're telling the truth? *NeuroRehabilitation*, *16*, 215–219.

Grove, W. M., & Meehl, P. E. (1996). Comparative efficiency of informal (subjective) impressionistic and formal (mechanical, algorithmic) prediction procedures: the clinical-statistical controversy. *Psychology, Public Policy, and Law*, *2*(2), 293–323.

Grove, W. M., Zald, D. H., Lebow, B. S., Snitz, B. E., & Nelson, C. (2000). Clinical versus mechanical prediction: a meta-analysis. *Psychological Assessment*, *12*(1), 19–30.

Guilford, J. P. (1965). *Fundamental statistics in psychology and education* (4th ed.). New York: McGraw-Hill.

Halstead, W. C. (1947). *Brain and intelligence*. Chicago: University of Chicago Press.

Heaton, R. K., Grant, I., Anthony, W. Z., & Lehman, A. W. (1981). A comparison of clinical and automated interpretation of the Halstead–Reitan Battery. *Journal of Clinical Neuropsychology*, *3*, 121–141.

Heaton, R. K., Miller, S. W., Taylor, M. J., & Grant, I. (2004). *Revised comprehensive norms for an expanded Halstead–Reitan Battery: Demographically adjusted neuropsychological norms for African American and Caucasian adults [Professional manual and computer program]*. Odessa, FL: Psychological Assessment Resources.

Kane, R. L., Sweet, J. J., Golden, C. J., Parsons, O. A., & Moses, J. A. (1981). Comparative diagnostic accuracy of the Halstead-Reitan and Standardized Luria-Nebraska Neuropsychological batteries in a mixed psychiatric and brain-damaged population. *Journal of Consulting and Clinical Psychology*, *49*, 484–485.

Kiernan, R. J., & Matthews, C. G. (1976). Impairment index versus T-score averaging in neuropsychological assessment. *Journal of Consulting and Clinical Psychology*, *44*, 951–957.

Knights, R. (1973). Problems of criteria in diagnosis: a profile similarity approach. *Annuals of the New York Academy of Science*, *205*, 124–131.

Larrabee, G. J., Millis, S. R., & Meyers, J. E. (2008). Sensitivity to brain dysfunction of the Halstead–Reitan vs. an ability-focused neuropsychological battery. *Clinical Neuropsychologist*, *22*(5), 813–825.

Lezak, M. D. (1995). *Neuropsychological assessment* (3rd ed.). New York: Oxford University Press.

Lezak, M. D., Howieson, D. B., & Loring, D. W. (2004). *Neuropsychological assessment* (4th ed.). New York: Oxford University Press.

Loring, D. W., & Larrabee, G. J. (2006). Sensitivity of the Halstead and Wechsler test batteries to brain damage: evidence from Reitan's original validation sample. *Clinical Neuropsychologist*, *20*(2), 221–229.

Lynch, W. (1988). Computers in neuropsychological assessment. *Journal of Head Trauma and Rehabilitation*, *3*, 92–94.

Mapou, R. L. (1988). Testing to detect brain damage: an alternative to what may on longer be useful. *Journal of Clinical and Experimental Neurology*, *10*, 271–278.

Matarazzo, J. D. (1990). Psychological assessment versus psychological testing: validation from binet to the school, clinic, and courtroom. *American Psychologist*, *45*, 999–1017.

Meyers, J. E., & Rohling, M. L. (2004). Validation of the meyers short battery on mild TBI patients. *Archives of Clinical Neuropsychology*, *19*(5), 637–651.

Meehl, P. E. (1954). *Clinical versus statistical prediction: A theoretical analysis and a review of the evidence*. Minneapolis: University of Minnesota Press.

Mitrushina, M. N., Boone, K. B., Razani, J. L., & D'Elia, L. L. F. (2005). *Handbook of normative data for neuropsychological assessment* (2nd ed.). New York: Oxford University Press.

Mutchnick, M., Ross, L. K., & Long, C. J. (1991). Decision strategies for cerebral dysfunction IV: determination of cerebral dysfunction. *Archives of Clinical Neuropsychology*, *6*, 259–270.

Netter, F. H., Jones, H. R., & Dingle, R. V. (1985). *The ciba collection of medical illustrations*. West Caldwell, NJ: Ciba.

Nunnally, J. C., & Bernstein, I. H. (1994). *Psychometric theory* (3rd ed.). New York: McGraw-Hill.

Reitan, R. M. (1955). Investigation of the validity of Halstead's measures of biological intelligence. *Archives of Neurology and Psychiatry*, *73*, 28–35.

Reitan, R. M. (1962). Psychological deficit. *Annual Review of Psychology*, *13*, 415–444.

Reitan, R. M. (1964). Psychological deficits resulting from cerebral lesions in men. In J. M. Warren & K. Akert (Eds.), *The frontal granular cortex and behavior* (pp. 295–312). New York: McGraw-Hill.

Reitan, R. M. (1991). *The neuropsychological deficit scale for adults computer program [Users manual]*. Tucson: Neuropsychology Press.

Reitan, R. M., & Wolfson, D. (1985). The Halstead–Reitan neuropsychological test battery. *Theory and Clinical Interpretation*, 347–397. Tucson Neuropsychology Press.

Reitan, R. M., & Wolfson, D. (1993). *The Halstead–Reitan neuropsychological test battery: Theory and clinical interpretation* (2nd ed.). Tucson: Neuropsychology Press.

Reitan, R. M., & Wolfson, D. (1993). Neuropsychological deficit scale. In R. M. Reitan & D. Wolfson (Eds.), *The Halstead–Reitan neuropsychological test battery: Theory and clinical interpretation* (pp. 347–397) (2nd ed.). Tucson: Neuropsychology Press.

Retzlaff, P. D., & Gibertini, M. (1994). Neuropsychometric issues and problems. In R. D. Vanderploeg (Ed.), *A guide to neuropsychological practice* (pp. 185–210). Hillsdale, NJ: Erlbaum.

Rojas, D. C., & Bennett, T. L. (1995). Single versus composite score discriminative validity with the Halstead–Reitan Battery and the Stroop Test in mild brain injury. *Archives of Clinical Neuropsychology*, *10*, 101–110.

Ross, L., Thrasher, M., & Long, C. J. (1990). Decision strategies in neuropsychology I: determination of lateralized cerebral dysfunction. *Archives of Clinical Neuropsychology*, *5*, 273–285.

Russell, E. W. (1981). The chronicity effect. *Journal of Clinical Psychology*, *37*, 246–253.

Russell, E. W. (1984). Theory and developments of pattern analysis methods related to the Halstead–Reitan Battery. In P. E. Logue & J. M. Shear (Eds.), *Clinical neuropsychology: A multidisciplinary approach* (pp. 50–98). Springfield, IL: Charles C. Thomas.

Russell, E. W. (1987). A reference scale method for constructing neuropsychological test batteries. *Journal of Clinical and Experimental Neuropsychology*, *9*, 376–392.

Russell, E. W. (2000). The application of computerized scoring programs to neuropsychological assessment. In R. D. Vanderploeg (Ed.), *Clinician's guide to neuropsychological assessment* (pp. 483–515) (2nd ed.). Hillsdale, NJ: Lawrence Erlbaum Associates.

Russell, E. W. (2003). The critique of the HRNES in the "Handbook of normative data for neuropsychological assessment." *Archives of Clinical Neuropsychology*, *18*(2), 165–180.

Russell, E. W. (2004). The operating characteristics of the major HRNES–R measures. *Archives of Clinical Neuropsychology*, *19*(8), 1043–1061.

Russell, E. W. (2005). Norming subjects for the Halstead–Halstead–Reitan Battery. *Archives of Clinical Neuropsychology*, *20*(4), 479–484.

Russell, E. W. (2009). Commentary on Larrabee, Mills, and Meyer's paper "Sensitivity to brain dysfunction of the Halstead–Reitan vs an ability-focused neuropsychology battery.". *Clinical Neuropsychologist*, *23*, 831–840.

Russell, E. W., Neuringer, C., & Goldstein, G. (1970). *Assessment of brain damage: A neuropsychological key approach*. New York: Wiley.

Russell, E. W., Russell, S. L. K., & Hill, B. D. (2005). The fundamental psychometric status of neuropsychological batteries. *Archives of Clinical Neuropsychology*, *20*(6), 785–794.

Russell, E. W., & Starkey, R. I. (1993). *Halstead–Russell neuropsychological evaluation system [Manual and computer program]*. Los Angeles: Western Psychological Services.

Russell, E. W., & Starkey, R. I. (2001). *Halstead–Russell neuropsychological evaluation system—revised [Manual and Computer program]*. Los Angeles: Western Psychological Services.

Russell, E. W., & Starkey, R. I. (2001). *Halstead–Russell neuropsychological evaluation system—Revised [Appendix F]*. Los Angeles: Western Psychological Services.

Russell, E. W., Starkey, R. I., Fernandez, C. D., & Starkey, T. W. (1988). *Halstead, Rennick, Russell Battery [Manual and Computer program]*. Miami: Scientific Psychology.

Sherer, M., & Adams, R. L. (1993). Cross-validation of Reitan and Wolfson's neuropsychological deficit scales. *Archives of Clinical Neuropsychology*, *8*, 429–435.

Sherer, M., Scott, J. G., Parsons, O. A., & Adams, R. L. (1994). Relative sensitivity of the WAIS–R subtests and selected HRNB measures to effects of brain damage. *Archives of Clinical Neuropsychology, 9*, 427–436.

Slick, D. J. (2006). Psychometrics in neuropsychological assessment. In E. Strauss, E. M. S. Sherman & O. Spreen (Eds.), *A compendium of neuropsychological tests: Administration, norms, and commentary* (pp. 3–43) (3rd ed.). New York: Oxford University Press.

Snow, W. G. (1981). A comparison of frequency of abnormal results in neuropsychological vs. neurodiagnostic procedures. *Journal of Clinical Psychology, 37*, 22–28.

Spreen, O., & Benton, A. L. (1965). Comparative studies of some psychological tests for cerebral damage. *Journal of Nervous and Mental Disease, 140*, 323–333.

Steinmeyer, C. H. (1986). A meta-analysis of Halstead–Halstead–Reitan test performances on non-brain damaged subjects. *Archives of Clinical Neuropsychology, 1*, 301–307.

Stern, R. A., & White, T. (2001). *Neuropsychological assessment battery (NAB)*. Lutz, FL: Psychological Assessment Resources.

Sweet, J. J., Nelson, N. W., & Moberg, P. J. (2005). "Salary survey" professional practices, beliefs, and incomes of U.S. neuropsychologists. *Clinical Neuropsychologist, 20* 325–300.

Swiercinsky, D. P. (1978, September). *Computerized SAINT: System for analysis and interpretation of neuropsychological tests*. Paper presented at the meeting of the American Psychological Association, Toronto.

Swiercinsky, D. P., & Leigh, G. (1979). Comparison of neuropsychological data in the diagnosis of brain impairment with computerized tomography and other neurological procedures. *Journal of Clinical Psychology, 35*, 242–246.

Swiercinsky, D. P., & Warnock, J. K. (1977). Comparison of the neuropsychological key and discriminant analysis approaches in predicting cerebral damage and localization. *Journal of Consulting and Clinical Psychology, 45*, 808–814.

Tsushima, W. T., & Wedding, D. (1979). A comparison of the Halstead–Reitan neuropsychological battery and computerized tomography in the identification of brain disorder. *Journal of Nervous and Mental Disease, 167*, 704–707.

Vega, A., & Parsons, O. A. (1967). Cross-validation of the Halstead–Reitan tests for brain damage. *Journal of Consulting Psychology, 31*, 619–625.

Volbrecht, M. E., Meyers, J. E., & Kaster-Bundgaard, J. (2000). Neuropsychological outcome of head injury using a short battery. *Archives of Clinical Neuropsychology, 15*, 251–265.

Watson, C. G., Thomas, R. W., Anderson, D., & Felling, J. (1968). Differentiation of schizophrenics from organics at two chronicity levels by use of Reitan-Halstead organic test battery. *Journal of Consulting and Clinical Psychology, 32*, 679–684.

Wedding, D. (1983a). Clinical and statistical prediction. *Clinical Neuropsychology, 5*, 49–55.

Wedding, D. (1983b). Comparison of statistical and actuarial models for predicting lateralization of brain damage. *Clinical Neuropsychology, 4*, 15–20.

Wedding, D., & Faust, D. (1989). Clinical judgment and decision making in neuropsychology. *Archives of Clinical Neuropsychology, 4*, 233–265.

Wheeler, L., Burke, C. J., & Reitan, R. M. (1963). An application of discriminant functions to the problem of predicting brain damage using behavioral tests. *Perceptual and Motor Skills, 16*, 417–440.

Wheeler, L., & Reitan, R. M. (1963). Discriminant functions applied to the problem of predicting cerebral damage from behavioral tests: a cross-validation study. *Perceptual and Motor Skills, 16*, 681–701.

Wolfson, D., & Reitan, R. M. (1995). Cross-validation of the General Neuropsychological Deficit Scale (GNDS). *Archives of Clinical Neuropsychology, 10*, 125–131.

Section IV

Application to Forensics

10 The Admissibility of Neuropsychological Expert Testimony Under the *Daubert* and *Frye* Evidentiary Standards

Lyndy Lambert and Cary Aronovitz

Federal courts and the majority of state courts in the United States follow Federal Rule of Evidence 702 and the Supreme Court's decision in *Daubert v. Merrell Dow Pharmaceuticals* in determining whether proffered medical expert testimony is admissible at trial. In *Daubert,* the Supreme Court transformed the trial court's role into that of a gatekeeper that ensures that only *reliable* and *relevant* expert opinion reaches a jury. However, to withstand an evidentiary challenge, *Daubert* does not require that a plaintiff or defendant retain the best expert who applies the best methodology for a given situation; instead, the party offering the witness must meet its burden by showing that the expert used a reliable methodology in reaching his or her opinion. Thus, regarding a neuropsychologist, the party must establish that the expert used a reliable methodology in completing his or her neuropsychological assessment.

Courts understand neuropsychology as "a specialty of psychology concerned with the study of the relationships between the brain and behavior, including the use of psychological tests and assessment techniques to diagnose specific cognitive and behavioral deficits and to prescribe rehabilitation strategies for their remediation."[1] Often, a neuropsychologist is used at trial to provide evidence establishing—or refuting—the existence of a traumatic brain injury. In certain situations, a qualified neuropsychologist can provide the only objective basis to determine brain damage as a result of subtle deficits that are undetectable in either a magnetic-resonance imaging (MRI) or computed tomography scan (Stern, 2001, pp. 93–94). A United States district court cited a report by the American Psychological Association that "neurological examinations are very limited in their capacity to detect brain damage." Neuropsychological testing, on the other hand, "is the only means of diagnosing some forms of brain damage."[2]

As the field of neuropsychology has developed, two approaches have emerged as the primary training and practice models: the *standardized battery*[3] and the *flexible battery* (or *variable battery*).

[1] *Baxter v. Temple*, 157 N.H. 280, 297 (2008) (Quoting *Hoskins v. State*, 702 So. 2d 202, 209 n.5 (Fla. 1997)).

[2] *Bado-Santana v. Ford Motor Co.*, 482 F. Supp.2d 192, 195 (D.P.R. 2007).

[3] The standardized battery is also referred to by neuropsychologists as a *fixed battery*. For the purposes of this chapter, we will use *standardized battery*.

The Scientific Foundation of Neuropsychological Assessment. DOI: 10.1016/B978-0-12-416029-3.00010-5

Under the standardized-battery approach, the neuropsychologist administers a uniform battery of tests such as the Halstead–Reitan Battery (HRB) or uses scale scores for all of his or her patients. The approach allows the neuropsychologist to identify the presence or absence of brain damage or impairment, identify the area of the brain involved, and validly compare test results with hundreds of patients who have undergone similar testing under the same battery.

Under the flexible-battery approach, a more individualized test battery is administered by the examiner, who selects from a myriad of published tests that he or she believes to be specific to a patient's characteristics, complaints, and symptoms. Because the neuropsychologist can choose specific tests to administer, the flexible-battery approach is ultimately more subjective than the standardized-battery methodology. Recently, a report from the American Academy Clinical Neuropsychology noted that 76% of practicing neuropsychologists now align with the flexible-battery approach.[4]

Under the evidentiary rules, *Daubert*, and the case law interpreting *Daubert*, "[t] here is no mechanical formula for determining whether an expert is qualified to offer opinion evidence in a particular field."[5] Thus, experts who are best prepared to defend their methodologies and prove the reliability of their opinions are most likely to withstand evidentiary challenges. Although state and federal courts have upheld the admissibility of neuropsychologist expert testimony using both the standardized-battery and flexible-battery approaches, the objective nature of the standardized battery lends itself to *Daubert*'s ultimate requirement of reliability. Because the entire battery is co-normed and subject to peer review, proponents of the standardized battery have the strong argument that the standardized battery is scientifically constructed in a manner that is inherently more reliable than the variable approach.

The Federal Rules of Evidence, *Daubert*, and the Court's Role as Gatekeeper

In federal courts, Federal Rule of Evidence 702 governs the admissibility of expert testimony at trial. Many state courts have adopted Rule 702 or a similar rule. Rule 702 provides the following:

> *If scientific, technical, or other specialized knowledge will assist the trier of fact to understand the evidence or to determine a fact in issue, a witness qualified as an expert by knowledge, skill, experience, training, or education, may testify thereto in the form of an opinion or otherwise, if (1) the testimony is based upon sufficient facts or data, (2) the testimony is the product of reliable principles and methods, and (3) the witness has applied the principles and methods reliably to the facts of the case.*[6]

[4] The American Academy of Clinical Neuropsychology submitted an amicus brief in favor of admitting the testimony of a neuropsychologist who used a flexible battery in her assessment. In the case, the Supreme Court of New Hampshire approvingly cited the amicus brief and determined the expert's testimony to be admissible for trial.

[5] *Bado-Santana*, 482 F. Supp.2d at 192.

[6] Fed. R. Evid. 702.

The Federal Rules of Evidence were drafted by Congress and first approved by the U.S. Supreme Court in 1972. Before adoption of these rules, the generally accepted test for the admissibility of expert testimony was the *Frye* test, which was derived from the decision of the Court of Appeals for the District of Columbia in 1923 in the case of *Frye v. United States*.[7] The *Frye* test, also known as the *general acceptance test*, focused exclusively on whether scientific testimony had gained general acceptance in the particular field in which it belonged. However, in 1993, the Supreme Court determined that the Federal Rules of Evidence had overridden the "rigid" ruling of *Frye* and affirmed "[n]othing in the text of this Rule establishes 'general acceptance' as an absolute prerequisite to admissibility."[8] The Court also reasoned that *Frye*'s pure regard for "general acceptance" did not comport with the liberal standards of the Federal Rules of Evidence.

Thus, in accordance with Rule 702, *Daubert v. Merrell Dow Pharmaceuticals* now provides the standard for the admissibility of expert testimony in federal court. Also important is that the analysis and findings of *Daubert* have also extended to the majority of state courts in the country that model their own evidentiary rules on the Federal Rules of Evidence.

In *Daubert*, the Supreme Court imposed two distinct prerequisites to the admission of expert testimony: (1) the evidence must be *reliable*—that is, the underlying methodology from which the evidence is derived (and not the conclusion drawn) must be based on "scientific knowledge"; and (2) the evidence must be *relevant*—that is, the proposed expert testimony should assist the trier of fact to understand or determine a fact in issue.

Daubert and its progeny[9] identified four factors useful in determining whether proposed expert testimony is based on valid principles and methodology: (1) whether the theory or technique can be and has been tested; (2) whether the theory or technique has been subjected to peer review and publication; (3) the known rate of error of the technique and the existence and maintenance of standards controlling the technique's operation; and (4) whether the technique is generally accepted in the scientific community.[10] Although none of these factors alone is dispositive, the party offering the expert opinion has the burden of laying the foundation for admission of the testimony and showing "that the expert's findings are based on sound science."[11]

For example, on remand (i.e., sending a case back to a trial court), the Ninth Circuit Court of Appeals analyzed how the standards in *Daubert* should be applied by the trial court:

> *Under Daubert, we must engage in a difficult, two-part analysis. First, we must determine nothing less than whether the experts' testimony reflects "scientific*

[7] *Frye v. United States*, 293 F. 1013 (D.C. Cir. 1923).

[8] *Daubert v. Merrell Dow Pharmaceuticals, Inc*, 509 U.S. 579, 588 (1993).

[9] The *Daubert* progeny are the cases that followed *Daubert* and further solidified the law relating to the admissibility of expert testimony. In *Kumho Tire Co v. Carmichael* (1999), the Court affirmed that the standards expressed in *Daubert* extended to both scientific and nonscientific experts. Further, *General Electric Co v. Joiner* (1997) now determines the standard of review for an appellate court over a trial court's determination of expert opinion admissibility.

[10] *Daubert*, 509 U.S. at 593–96.

[11] *U.S. v. Williams*, 95 F.3d 723, 729 (8th Cir. 1996).

> *knowledge," whether their findings are "derived by the scientific method," and whether their work product amounts to "good science." ... Second, we must ensure that the proposed expert testimony is "relevant to the task at hand" ... ; i.e., that it logically advances a material aspect of the proposing party's case.*

The Ninth Circuit continued: "something doesn't become 'scientific knowledge' just because it's uttered by a scientist; nor can an expert's self-serving assertion that his conclusions were 'derived by the scientific method' be deemed conclusive ... [I]t is our responsibility to determine whether those experts' proposed testimony amounts to 'scientific knowledge,' constitutes 'good science,' and was 'derived by the scientific method.'"[12]

Thus, both practitioners and experts must be aware when confronted with a *Daubert* challenge to proffered expert testimony that it is the role of the trial court—that is, the trial judge—to serve as gatekeeper to ensure that only relevant and reliable expert opinion reaches the jury. The judge will not require perfection, but the expert must demonstrate that he or she employed "in the courtroom the same level of intellectual rigor that characterizes the practice of an expert in the relevant field."[13]

Relating specifically to medical expert testimony, the Eighth Circuit Court of Appeals outlined the following standards for admission:

> *A party may present expert medical testimony if the expert's opinion is scientifically valid and it will assist the jury. Daubert described the district court as a gatekeeper. In exercising its gatekeeping function, a district court must make "a preliminary assessment of whether the reasoning or methodology underlying the testimony is scientifically valid and of whether that reasoning or methodology properly can be applied to the facts in issue." An expert opinion "must be supported by appropriate validation—i.e., 'good grounds,' based on what is known." In sum, the district court's gatekeeping role separates expert opinion evidence based on "good grounds" from subjective speculation that masquerades as scientific knowledge.*[14]

Although not required in the Federal Rules of Evidence, judges in practice have found that particular scrutiny can be placed on medical expert testimony, particularly expert opinion relating to brain injuries or brain damage, because of its highly persuasive—or perhaps prejudicial—impact on a jury.[15] In addition, federal court judges are often considered to use their gatekeeper function and deny the admissibility of expert testimony at a higher rate than in state court.

Finally, in considering the seriousness of its gatekeeping functions, courts have commonly reiterated that scientific reasoning, at a minimum, is a method of

[12] *Daubert v. Merrell Dow Pharmaceuticals Inc.*, 43 F.3d 1311, 1315–16 (9th Cir. 1995) (citations omitted), cert. denied, 516 U.S. 869 (1995).

[13] *Kumho Tire*, 526 U.S. at 152.

[14] *Glastetter v. Novartis Pharmaceuticals Corp.*, 252 F.3d 986, 988–89 (8th Cir. 2001).

[15] *See, e.g., Warner v. Rossignol*, 538 F.2d 910, 912–13 (1st Cir. 1976).

reasoning from the known to a conclusion, not vice versa. In excluding a purported expert's testimony, the Eighth Circuit found in one instance:

> *Here, the hypothesis presented by plaintiffs' experts follow no scientific principles. Those opinions reason that, because [plaintiffs] sustained birth defects ... and their parents used [defendant's] alfalfa tablets, and because some alfalfa tablets had contained an EtO residue, the parents must have ingested the EtO residue tablets. That inference turns scientific analysis on its head. Instead of reasoning from known facts to reach a conclusion, the experts here reasoned from an end result to hypothesize what needed to be known but what was not.*[16]

The decision underscores that a judge can, and often will, scrutinize an expert's subjective opinion based on uncertain science that appears predestined to reach a sought-after result. In the context of forensic neuropsychological testing, the court might view with more suspicion an expert's opinion regarding brain damage based on a flexible-battery approach, especially where the expert selects specific tests to help support an opinion that will favor the party who retained the expert.

The *Frye* Test

In *Daubert*, the U.S. Supreme Court determined that the Federal Rules of Evidence had displaced the antiquated *Frye* test in determining the admissibility of expert testimony. Thus, in all federal courts and the majority of state courts, *Daubert* now establishes the analysis in allowing or excluding expert opinion. The reason the decision applies to many state courts is that many states have expressly modeled their own evidence code after the Federal Rules of Evidence and have specifically adopted Rule 702.

A minority of states such as Florida, however, have not expressly adopted the Federal Rules of Evidence and therefore still adhere to their common law acceptance of the *Frye* standard. For instance, in contrast to federal Rule 702 quoted above, Florida's version of the evidentiary rule of admissibility of testimony of experts provides:

> *If scientific, technical, or other specialized knowledge will assist the trier of fact to understand the evidence or to determine a fact in issue, a witness qualified as an expert by knowledge, skill, experience, training, or education, may testify about it in the form of an opinion; however, the opinion is admissible only if it can be applied to the evidence at trial.*[17]

Rule 90.702 omits the remaining portions of federal Rule 702 that gave rise to *Daubert*: "(1) the testimony is based upon sufficient facts or data, (2) the testimony

[16] *Sorenson v. Shaklee Corp.*, 31 F.3d 638, 649 (8th Cir. 1994).
[17] Florida Rule of Evidence 90.702.

is the product of reliable principles and methods, and (3) the witness has applied the principles and methods reliably to the facts of the case." For this and other reasons, Florida and a minority of other state courts apply *Frye* principles to the admissibility of expert testimony.

Unlike the four-pronged approach outlined in *Daubert* to determine reliability, *Frye* demands that proffered scientific testimony have gained "general acceptance by the relevant scientific community."[18] Thus, *Frye* does not require the judge to look as closely at the method used by the scientific expert; instead, it only asks if the underlying principle has been accepted by the scientific community. Under *Frye*, therefore, the judge is not reviewing the specific methodology used, only whether the methodology as a whole has gained scientific acceptance (*see*, for example, Luyster, 2007).

The *Frye* case involved the admissibility of expert opinion based on the results of a systolic blood-pressure deception test, a crude precursor to the polygraph machine. The court concluded that the systolic blood-pressure deception test had not yet gained such standing and scientific recognition in the relevant scientific community that would allow the admissibility of the defendant's expert testimony on the test results. The court affirmed the exclusion of the expert's testimony, thereby allowing a murder conviction to stand.

State courts that still adhere to *Frye* have held that it only applies when an expert attempts to render an opinion that is based on new or novel scientific techniques.[19] Medical expert testimony concerning the causation of a medical condition that is based solely on an expert's training and experience is not considered by the courts to be "novel scientific evidence" subject to a *Frye* analysis.[20] The Florida Supreme Court has held that where a plaintiff's experts determined that the plaintiff's fibromyalgia was caused by trauma, based on a review of her medical history, clinical physical examinations, their own experience, published research, and differential diagnosis, their testimony was admissible as "pure opinion" and a *Frye* analysis was not required.[21] The court concluded that even if a *Frye* analysis was applicable, a lack of studies conclusively demonstrating a causal link between trauma and fibromyalgia did not preclude admission of the testimony.

There are many examples of scientific evidence that has been excluded under a *Frye* analysis because it was not proven to be sufficiently reliable: dog-scent–discrimination lineups in criminal cases,[22] polygraph evidence,[23] the results of a sodium butathol test in a criminal prosecution,[24] a clinical psychologist's reliance on a "sexual abuse legitimacy scale,"[25] and thermography to determine whether plaintiff

[18] *Frye v. United States*, 293 F. 1013, 1014 (D.C. Cir. 1923).

[19] *U.S. Sugar Corp. v. Henson*, 823 So. 2d 104, 109 (Fla. 2002); *see also Trach v. Fellin*, 817 A.2d 1102, 1109 (Pa. Super. Ct. 2003) (reiterating Pennsylvania's evidentiary standard that *Frye* only applies when a party seeks to introduce novel scientific evidence).

[20] *Marsh v. Valyou*, 977 So. 2d 543, 547–48 (Fla. 2007).

[21] Ibid.

[22] *Ramos v. State*, 496 So. 2d 121, 123 (Fla. 1986).

[23] *Walsh v. State*, 418 So. 2d 1000, 1002 (Fla. 1982).

[24] *Zeigler v. State*, 402 So. 2d 365, 373 (Fla. 1981).

[25] *Page v. Zordan*, 564 So. 2d 500, 502 (Fla. 2d DCA 1990).

sustained a permanent injury.[26] On the other hand, there are many more examples of scientific opinion testimony that has been allowed into evidence in states that still rely on the *Frye* standard. This is mostly because it was either "pure opinion" and a *Frye* analysis was not required, or it was not based on a new scientific technique.

Applying *Daubert* to the Standardized Battery and Variable Battery

Proponents of the standardized battery, such as the accepted and peer-reviewed HRB, defend their methodology because of its dependability. Those who favor the standardized battery begin with the premise that dependability is the most fundamental concept related to a scientific methodology because it ensures that "information will be invariant from one situation to another" (Russell, Russell, & Hill, 2005, pp. 785–794) By applying the same battery of tests to each patient, the neuropsychologist's methodology, experience, and objectivity cannot be questioned.

A battery is defined as "two or more tests that are related by an assessment method, such as by combination or comparison, which is used for a neuropsychological interpretation" (Russell et al., 2005, p. 787). Thus, under the HRB method, for example, each patient receives the same set of tests that are compared with one another to reach an interpretative conclusion of the individual's brain damage. Because the patient is psychometrically compared to hundreds of other patients subjected to the same tests and procedures, an attorney cannot challenge that an expert's findings were predetermined (Russell et al., 2005, p. 787).

Thus, for purposes of courtroom admissibility, the use of a peer-reviewed battery is extremely persuasive. If administered properly, the battery establishes each of the *Daubert* factors: (1) it has been tested and cannot be considered novel science; (2) it has been subject to peer review and publication; (3) as a psychometrically validated test, the battery will have a known error rate; and (4) the battery has gained general acceptance in the scientific community.

On the other hand, if a proponent of the variable battery is subjected to a *Daubert* challenge, he or she might not be able to convince the judge that his or her methodology can meet any of these four factors. Even though each individual test had received general approval, the combination of tests together—that is, the battery—as a whole is unique and would not have been validated and, as such, it could not receive general acceptance or have been subject to peer review. Thus, the reliability of the standardized battery will be considered highly persuasive to a court, but the subjective variable battery might face a more difficult challenge.

These principles are well defined in *Baxter v. Temple*, a case heard on appeal to the Supreme Court of New Hampshire.[27] In that case, the defendant contested the

[26] *Crawford v. Shivashankar*, 474 So. 2d 873, 876 n.4 (Fla. 1st DCA 1985).

[27] *See Baxter*, 157 N.H. 280 (2008). Notably, the court in *Baxter* applied the principles of *Daubert* because New Hampshire had adopted the Federal Rules of Evidence and the legislature had specifically codified the four factors of admissibility outlined in *Daubert*.

methodology used by the plaintiff's neuropsychologist—a flexible battery to test the plaintiff's child for a brain injury. The trial court conducted a six-day *Daubert* hearing and concluded that the neuropsychologist's variable battery was unreliable and thus inadmissible. The plaintiff appealed; following a 34-page opinion by the appellate court, the expert and her variable battery were eventually deemed admissible.

In *Baxter*, the parents of a child subjected to lead-paint contamination sued the owners of an apartment building. The plaintiff alleged that the high levels of lead paint in the apartment caused her to suffer from lead-paint poisoning and its effects, including reduced life expectancy, brain damage, and past and future pain and suffering. To prove that the child had sustained brain damage and would continue to suffer from its effects, the plaintiff's attorney retained a neuropsychologist who evaluated the child plaintiff for neurological issues potentially associated with her exposure to lead paint.[28]

In response, the defendants sought to exclude the plaintiff's expert testimony on the ground that she had used a flexible battery that was devised specifically to the patient and had failed to use an accepted standardized battery such as the Halstead–Reitan Battery.[29] The trial court held a six-day *Daubert* hearing to determine if the testimony or findings of plaintiff's expert could be considered by the jury. The plaintiff's expert was a neuropsychologist who had supervised, reviewed, and tested more than 200 children with lead-paint exposure at the time of trial. She specialized in child brain injuries, and she followed the same variable battery for each child—the Boston Process Approach (BPA). The trial court found that the BPA was generally accepted in the appropriate scientific literature to evaluate a brain injury but that there was insufficient evidence to support that the BPA "had gained general acceptance in the making of a forensic assessment." Because the plaintiff had not met her burden to show that the BPA was generally accepted or could be tested for a potential rate of error, the trial court found the expert's opinion and report inadmissible.

In a lengthy opinion, the appellate court reversed and allowed the expert to testify at trial. The appellate decision reiterated that the field of neuropsychology has gained acceptance by the Academy of Psychology. The court cited findings by the American Academy of Clinical Neuropsychology, submitted in the form of an amicus brief to the court, that reliance on a flexible-battery approach to neuropsychological testing is now a mainstream practice. The court found persuasive that 68% of practicing neuropsychologists use the flexible-battery approach.[30]

After conducting this broad overview of the flexible battery, the appellate court then analyzed the BPA and specifically the individual methodology of the plaintiff's expert in assessing patients. The court reviewed a number of the tests and procedures used by the plaintiff's expert and reiterated that she conducted the same procedure for each of her child patients affected by lead-based sickness. Thus, the court found

[28] *Baxter*, 157 N.H. at 288.

[29] Ibid. at 293. It must be noted that this "general acceptance" factor lends itself better to the minority of courts that adhere to the *Frye* standard. Under *Daubert*, such general acceptance is just one of several factors to be considered in the court's analysis.

[30] Ibid. at 300.

"when the BPA is administered in a manner consistent with the flexible battery approach … it is generally a reliable approach to neuropsychological assessment and is thus a reliable methodology for determining a person's cognitive status."[31]

The court reiterated that "[r]egardless of whether the standardized-battery approach was a better approach to evaluating the plaintiff, the relevant inquiry is whether [the plaintiff's expert] used a reliable methodology to conduct her neuropsychological assessments."[32]

Baxter provides an important glimpse into the judicial analysis of both standardized- and variable-battery methodologies. Under the guidelines of *Daubert*, the court must analyze each expert's methodology on a case-by-case basis and determine that the methodology was used properly and that the methodology as a whole is reliable. Following a six-day *Daubert* hearing at the trial level, a 34-page opinion at the appellate level, and the neuropsychologist's years of experience and hundreds of patients to compare, her variable battery methodology was deemed admissible. If the plaintiff's expert had used a standardized battery instead of the flexible battery, perhaps the parties could have avoided a lengthy *Daubert* hearing and an expensive and time-consuming appeal.

Applying *Frye* to the Standardized Battery and Variable Battery

Courts and commentators have debated whether the *Daubert* standard is more lenient or stricter than the *Frye* test (Bernstein & Jackson, 2004, pp. 351–352): "Courts and commentators disagreed, however, regarding whether this 'revolution' in how judges were to go about deciding whether to admit scientific evidence would lead to more permissive or more restrictive admissibility rulings." Some have questioned whether a state's adoption of *Frye* or *Daubert* makes any practical difference (Cheng & Yoon, 2005, pp. 471, 510). When analyzing "new or novel scientific techniques" both *Frye* and *Daubert* have rigorous requirements for meeting the burden of proof as to reliability. But where the methodology is not novel, jurisdictions that use a *Frye* standard will conclude that a *Frye* analysis is not warranted and will allow expert testimony based on widely accepted scientific techniques.[33]

The authors were unable to locate any case law applying the *Frye* standard to neuropsychological testing, but an analysis of decisions pertaining to the *Frye* test reveals that the courts would probably determine that standard neuropsychological testing would not be subject to a *Frye* test, regardless of whether the expert used a standardized battery or a flexible battery. Neither the standardized battery nor the flexible battery is considered to be a novel scientific technique. Both methods have

[31] Ibid.

[32] Ibid. at 184 quoting *Minner v. Am. Mort. & Guaranty*, 791 A.2d 826 (Del. 2000) (finding that a neuropsychologist that utilized a variable battery was reliable and admissible, even if the standardized battery was preferable).

[33] *Marsh v. Valyou*, 977 So. 2d 543, 547 (Fla. 2007).

been used for decades by thousands of experienced neuropsychologists in forensic settings. Although attorneys might challenge neuropsychological testimony for other reasons under the rules of evidence, such as an expert's lack of proper qualifications, it is unlikely they will be able to make a strong argument that a *Frye* analysis should even be conducted on neuropsychological testing unless the expert uses new tests that have not gained any scientific acceptance.

Causation, Hearsay, and "Weight of the Evidence"

Forensic neuropsychological experts and the litigants who retain them face other evidentiary considerations besides admissibility under *Daubert*. In many states, the courts preclude psychologists from testifying about the cause of cognitive deficits, reasoning that experts who are not medical doctors are unqualified to render opinions on medical causation. Experts and litigants must also beware of rules that disallow using experts as conduits of inadmissible hearsay. Lastly, even in cases where *Daubert* issues are raised, the courts often will allow a jury to hear expert testimony, reasoning that effective cross-examination will root out any deficiencies, thereby allowing the jury to reject the opinion or properly weigh it in light of all of other evidence.

Courts generally will allow medical doctors in appropriate specialties to testify about the cause of cognitive deficits. But courts in certain jurisdictions still maintain that a neuropsychologist may not opine on the *cause* of a brain injury or brain damage, only its current and future *effects*.[34]

A majority of the state courts in the United States have refused to draw a bright-line rule regarding whether a psychologist without a medical doctor degree may testify on causation. Florida is one state in which neuropsychologists may not render an opinion on the cause of brain injury. For example, *Grenitz v. Tomlian* is a case involving a child born with cerebral palsy whose attorney attempted to use a neuropsychologist to opine that the injury was caused by oxygen deprivation at birth. In *Grenitz*, the Florida Supreme Court noted that in Florida and many other states, the courts draw a bright-line rule that a psychologist who is not a medical doctor is not qualified to render an opinion as to the cause of brain damage.[35] Although the court in *Grenitz* acknowledged that Florida has receded from its limitation on psychologist expert testimony in general, it still held that neuropsychologists may not testify regarding medical causes of organic brain damage. The court acknowledged that neuropsychologist testimony is permissible with regard to the etiology (brain damage) of observable behavior, but he or she may not testify as to medical causation of the injury.[36]

The justice who authored the dissenting opinion in *Grenitz* recognized that the majority of courts that have ruled on this issue have refused to extend a bright-line

[34] *Grenitz v. Tomlian*, 858 So. 2d 999, 1008 (Fla. 2003) (Wells, J., dissenting).
[35] Ibid. at 1000; *see also McCarthy v. Atwood*, 2005 WL 937271 (Va. Cir. Ct. Apr. 18, 2005).
[36] *Grenitz*, 858 So. 2d at 1003.

rule that neuropsychologists are per se unqualified to speak to the causation of organic brain injury. Thus, many courts will allow a properly trained and experienced neuropsychologist to testify as to the cause of the observed cognitive deficits—that is, an injury to the brain caused by an accident or medical malpractice. In light of this judicial split, it is critical for the practitioner to understand whether neuropsychologist expert testimony is permissible in his or her state to opine about causation of brain injury. If the state has an outright bar, then additional experts such as neurologists and psychiatrists are required to establish the cause of the subject behavior.[37]

A second issue confronted by forensic neuropsychologists occurs when an expert's testimony is premised on improper hearsay. This objection is particularly relevant to neuropsychologists because in completing his or her review, the expert will often interview family members to further understand the patient's past and current behavior. Generally, if the neuropsychologist seeks to opine about statements made by the family members, then such opinions will generally be objected to as improper hearsay evidence.[38]

In *Stallings v. Werner Enterprises, Inc.*, for example, a neuropsychologist was retained by the plaintiff to render an opinion on whether the plaintiff was likely to develop dementia or Alzheimer's disease. There the defendant challenged the neuropsychologist's report because the doctor had interviewed several family members and friends of the plaintiff in reaching his opinion—evidence that the defendant viewed as inadmissible hearsay. However, the court found the testimony admissible because (1) it would be helpful to a jury; (2) the doctor was qualified to express the opinion in his report; (3) the method used was the product of reliable methods supported by published and peer-reviewed materials; and (4) the method is generally accepted in the field. Thus, even though the neuropsychologist may have relied on hearsay evidence in rendering his opinion, the suggested hearsay did not render his opinion inadmissible.[39]

Another issue arises when judges reject a *Daubert* or *Frye* challenge and instead determine that any perceived shortcoming in a neuropsychologist's methodology or testing battery should be countered through cross-examination rather than an outright ban on the testimony. Courts often reason that good cross-examination will uncover discrepancies, poor methodology, and other weaknesses in the test data and other evidence relied on by an expert witness, and that juries are smart enough to properly weigh an expert's opinions after effective cross-examination.

For example, in *United States v. Williams*, the defendant was placed on trial for murder and a neuropsychologist was retained for his defense to testify whether the defendant was mentally capable to form the *mens rea* required to be found guilty

[37] *Huntoon v. T.C.I. Cablevision of Colorado, Inc.*, 969 P.2d 681, 689 (Colo. 1998); *Hutchison v. Am. Family Mut. Ins. Co.*, 514 N.W. 2d 882, 87–88 (Iowa 1994).

[38] Under the Federal Rules of Evidence, hearsay evidence is a "statement, other than one made by the declarant while testifying at the trial or hearing, offered in evidence to prove the truth of the matter asserted." Fed. R. Evid. 801(c).

[39] 2009 WL 424583, at *5 (D. Kan. April 28, 2009).

of the crime. The federal government challenged the psychologist's assessment for, among other reasons, failing to administer a functional MRI scan and the psychologist's lack of particularized expertise in forensic neuropsychology. The court determined that because the psychologist's methods and testing procedures appeared to be generally accepted in the field and sufficiently reliable, any perceived deficiencies in her assessment could be questioned on cross-examination. Thus, the testimony was deemed admissible.[40]

Moreover, in *Bado-Santana v. Ford Motor Company*, the court found the retained neuropsychologist qualified to testify as an expert on mild traumatic brain injury (MTBI). There the defendants challenged the neuropsychologist on the basis that she had not done extensive research or published articles on MTBI. However, as in *Williams*, the court reiterated that any flaws in the expert's opinion could go to the weight of the evidence at trial rather than its admissibility. Thus, any prejudice to the defendant could be counterbalanced on a proper cross-examination.[41]

The case of *Chapple v. Ganger* provides an excellent example of how the trier of fact viewed conflicting testimony from neuropsychologists who employed different testing methodologies.[42] In the *Chapple* case, the parties waived their right to a jury trial and agreed to a bench trial in which the U.S. magistrate judge assumed the jury's typical role by making findings of fact and determining the appropriate amount of damages. This case involved an automobile accident in which the plaintiff's wife died and his 10-year-old son sustained head and other injuries. Following the accident, the child remained unconscious for 24 h. The neuropsychologists retained by the plaintiff and the defense differed in their assessments as to whether the child's brain injury was permanent and would eventually prevent him from attending college, thereby resulting in a loss of earning capacity.

The defendant retained Ralph M. Reitan, PhD, one of the developers of the HRB of neuropsychological tests. The plaintiff retained his own neuropsychologist to conduct evaluation and testing. There was no *Daubert* challenge to the testimony of either retained expert, although the plaintiff argued that Dr. Reitan's methodology was viewed by some experts as outdated. Unlike the plaintiff's retained expert, Dr. Reitan administered the Halstead–Reitan Battery and determined that most of the test scores fell in the normal range. He found only a few mild deviations that could be of significance regarding minor brain dysfunction.

Unlike Dr. Reitan, the plaintiff's expert found some "moderate" cognitive deficits, and she concluded the child was likely to be left with permanent residual problems with attention, memory, and executive functions. The court noted that Dr. Reitan rejected the assessment of the plaintiff's expert because "it was not what he described, a 'neuropsychological' examination, but instead 'was the kind of ability and cognitive testing that might be used to assess a normal child.'" Dr. Reitan reported that the majority of the boy's test results from the testing conducted by the plaintiff's expert were never compared with those of brain-damaged children.

[40] *United States v. Williams*, 2009 WL 424583 (D. HI. February 20, 2009).

[41] *Bado-Santana*, 482 F. Supp.2d. at 195.

[42] *Chapple v. Ganger*, 851 F. Supp. 1481 (E.D. Wash. 1994).

The court explained that "in contrast, under the Reitan method, the standard scientific procedure for developing neuropsychological tests is to perform research on brain-damaged and normal controls and then to determine how the test results differ."

The court carefully considered the conflicting opinions of the neuropsychologists, as well as other evidence regarding the boy's rapid physical recovery, his school records before and after the accident, and demographic and job availability information from the area where the plaintiff lived. Based on the evidence presented, as well as the lack of medical evidence as to long-term prognosis, the court was unable to conclude that the boy sustained permanent, organic brain damage. The judge specifically stated:

> *The court accepts the test results as they indicate normal scores in most areas. As to those areas which show below normal scores, there is not sufficient scientific evidence to support the conclusion those scores are indicative of permanent organic brain damage in children.*

Thus, the judge preferred to rely on the standardized-battery approach of Reitan rather than the methodology employed by plaintiff's retained expert to conclude that there was no evidence the boy sustained a permanent brain injury that would adversely affect his earning potential. As a result of these findings, the court made no award for lost earning capacity or employment opportunities.

The *Chapple* case illustrates that even where there is no challenge to the admissibility of neuropsychological testimony, the use of a standardized battery of tests might be more persuasive to the trier of fact than the results of a flexible battery.

Conclusion

The field of neuropsychology has greatly expanded and gained acceptance as a useful, and in certain situations necessary, element to prove or disprove a plaintiff's claim of brain damage and the extent of the plaintiff's cognitive deficits. Because of the individual tests and battery of tests administered, a neuropsychologist's report is quantitative and particularly apt to draw a *Daubert* objection. However, as the debate between the standardized battery versus the variable battery has continued, it is noteworthy that the standardized battery lends itself better to withstanding an evidentiary challenge under *Daubert*. By administering a standardized and validated set of tests, the standardized battery offers an objective assessment that passes the "reliability" overview.

Proponents of the variable battery, on the other hand, make the argument that tests should at least be individualized to a specific set of damages or a specific group of individuals. For example, a child suffering from lead-paint poisoning might require a separate group of tests than an elderly man or woman suffering from dementia.

From a legal standpoint, and within the confines of Rule 702 and *Daubert*, the standardized battery is a more objective and validated procedure that will have an easier time meeting the judge's reliability requirements. Although *Baxter* shows that a qualified and experienced neuropsychologist using a variable battery of tests can withstand a *Daubert* challenge, the subjective nature of the variable battery is likely to draw more scrutiny from the court. Even if there is no *Daubert* challenge to the forensic testing, the results of a standardized battery might prove to be more persuasive to a judge or jury than those of a flexible battery.

Neuropsychologists conducting cognitive testing in a forensic setting should consider all of the factors described in this chapter when determining which types of tests to administer. Use of a standardized battery is more likely to prevent a *Daubert* challenge, thereby streamlining and reducing the costs of litigation. And the jury is likely to give greater weight to expert opinions based on standardized-battery test results, leading to better results for the party who retains the expert using the best methodology.

References

Bernstein, D. E., & Jackson, J. D. (2004). The *Daubert* trilogy in the states. *Journal of Jurimetrics*, *44*, 351–352.

Cheng, E. K., & Yoon, A. H. (2005). Does *Frye* or *Daubert* matter? A study of scientific admissibility standards. *Virginia Law Review*, *471*, 510.

Luyster, J. (2007, Spring). *Frye* and *Daubert* challenges: Unreliable options v. unreliable science. *Trial Advocate Quarterly*.

Russell, E. W., Russell, S., & Hill, B. D. (2005). The fundamental psychometric status of neuropsychological batteries. *Archives of Clinical Neuropsychology*, *20*, 785–794.

Stern, B. H. (2001). Admissibility of neuropsychological testimony after *Daubert* and *Kumho*. *NeuroRehabilitation*, *16*, 93–94.

11 The Usefulness of a Validated Neuropsychological Test Battery in Scientifically Supporting and Communicating Forensic Evaluation Results

Brent P. Kolitz and Sally Kolitz Russell

Our practice has been administering neuropsychological evaluations using the Halstead–Russell Neuropsychological Evaluation System (HRNES; Russell & Starkey, 1993) or the revised version (HRNES–R; Russell & Starkey, 2001) for the past 18 years. One key reason why we have consistently been retained by both plaintiff and defense attorneys is that we are able to substantiate our neuropsychological findings with sound psychometric science. Because the HRNES–R average impairment score (AIS) and percent impaired index (PII) have been validated (Russell, 2004), attorneys can be confident that we have minimized bias and maximized science in our findings. Those attorneys who understand and appreciate the research behind this test battery can proceed with their cases, confident that, from the neuropsychological perspective, they have the weight of science behind them. Educating attorneys about the science behind the HRNES–R is a large part of our responsibility to their cases.

We are often deposed by some of the same attorneys who have retained us in the past, and the science behind the HRNES–R is rarely, if ever, attacked by an opposing attorney, particularly one who has previously learned and supported the value of this standardized neuropsychological battery. Every neuropsychological report we send out is accompanied by a printout of the HRNES–R computerized test report. Therefore, not only the attorneys can view the actual scores and normative corrections made for age and educational level but also the opposing neuropsychologist is able to do so.

The HRNES–R is a co-normed battery, in which all of the tests in the battery have been normed on the same population of subjects. This permits making comparisons among tests against a constant background (Russell, 2000). When using a co-normed battery of tests, one is able to compare the various test scores in the battery with one another, knowing that differences across an examinee's test performances represent real differences in the person's abilities and not simply differences among the normative samples of each test (as is typically the case in a neuropsychological battery that does not use coordinated norming).

The Scientific Foundation of Neuropsychological Assessment. DOI: 10.1016/B978-0-12-416029-3.00011-7

The HRNES–R battery is designed to assess the following major areas of neuropsychological functioning: executive, cognitive–intellectual, language, memory, motor–psychomotor, and sensory–perceptual. In addition to coordinated norming and complete coverage of brain functions, the HRNES–R also provides for redundancy of coverage—that is, multiple tests are administered that relate to each area of brain functioning. This is critical because an examinee may perform poorly on a test simply because he or she is hungry or fatigued or the area is not one of strength or interest.

The principle of *normal variation* refers to the finding that even for normal examinees, a certain percentage of test scores in a larger battery will fall within the impaired range. In fact, a study demonstrated that greater than half of normal subjects had at least four out of 40 scores on a battery impaired, and there was a greater than 30% probability that at least seven out of 40 tests would be impaired for normal subjects (Heaton, Grant, & Matthews, 1991). The redundancy of the HRNES–R helps protect against finding spurious impairments of entire domains of neuropsychological functioning. Knowledge of normal variation further permits the neuropsychologist to assess whether a few impaired scores within the context of a normal HRNES–R profile is evidence of actual neuropsychological impairment (generally, it is not).

Although we certainly use educated clinical judgment in our case formulations, our interpretations rest most firmly on the more accurate and reliable scientific findings provided by a standardized, validated test battery such as the HRNES–R (Russell, 2004). Moreover, we routinely administer at least two well-validated tests of effort and motivation to assess the possibility of incomplete effort on testing. Such assessment of symptom validity is necessary, particularly in forensic examinations (Bush et al., 2005; Heilbronner et al., 2009). If the examinee has not put forth adequate effort, then the results of the neuropsychological test battery must be considered invalid, and the scores can only be said to reflect at least the examinee's minimum level of performance. In addition, we add at least one comprehensive objective psychological measure (including response bias scales) to the neuropsychological test battery to evaluate the contribution of psychopathology and personality factors to the overall test profile.

The seven cases described below illustrate the usefulness of a validated test battery (such as the HRNES–R) in determining the presence or absence of neuropsychological impairment and in communicating these results with scientific rigor to the retaining attorneys, both plaintiff and defense. The cases are presented with the real details of the litigation and the actual neuropsychological test results, but all names and identifying information have been changed.

Description of Case 1 and Test Results (Robert Taylor)

Robert Taylor (age 54) was sent to us by the plaintiff attorney subsequent to his client's exposure to high levels of carbon monoxide 1 year previously. Taylor was a guest in a major hotel chain when he collapsed in the shower, suffering severe respiratory failure. His son, who had accompanied him on this business trip, died in bed. Taylor was unresponsive at the scene and had been diagnosed with a toxic effect of carbon monoxide and an acute respiratory failure. He received CPR at the scene, as well as intubation, and was administered oxygen. He was immediately transported to a hospital, where he was placed in a hyperbaric chamber.

Taylor had no preexisting medical or psychological problems and had earned both an MBA and a CPA degree. He had been employed for the past 20 years in the human resources department of a major corporation. He had no history of substance abuse.

At the time of Taylor's neuropsychological evaluation, 1 year postincident, he had been able to return to work in a much reduced capacity. His major complaints were difficulty with speech (he often slurred his words), as well as problems with coordination and balance. In addition he reported that, "I seem to have momentary blackouts, and my brain goes into freeze."

Since the incident, Taylor had been diagnosed with an irregular heartbeat. When questioned as to what he had remembered prior to his loss of consciousness, Taylor explained that he remembered being in the shower and falling, as well as yelling out to his son. He then got up and fell down again, and this is the last thing he remembered until he awoke in the hyperbaric chamber. He was informed of his son's death that same morning. Taylor also reported memory problems, difficulty with focusing and concentrating, and difficulty with his organizational abilities. He admitted being extremely depressed because of his son's death. He reported that he was in a very supportive marriage and had no problems in the relationship.

Taylor was administered the HRNES–R. His verbal IQ on the Wechsler Adult Intelligence Scale 3 (WAIS-III) was 128 (97th percentile), his performance IQ was 102 (55th percentile), and his full-scale intelligence quotient (FSIQ) was 117 (87th percentile). Taylor's vocabulary and information age-scaled subtest scores were 16 (98th percentile) and 13 (84th percentile), respectively. Therefore, it was determined that his premorbid abilities were most likely in the superior range, and his intellectual functioning was somewhat compromised in comparison to his preincident level. Taylor's nonverbal or performance IQ was considerably lowered by those tests known by research to be most sensitive to brain damage [digit symbol coding age-scaled score = 5 (5th percentile) and block design age-scaled score = 7 (20th percentile)]. These tasks relate to processing speed and were performed considerably lower than what would have been anticipated premorbidly. Most notable was the fact that Taylor's processing speed index score was only at the 18th percentile, which was consistent with the anoxia he experienced.

Taylor's performances on tests of executive functioning were all mildly to moderately impaired based on the HRNES–R norming. Executive function tests are among those known to be most sensitive to the effects of brain impairment, and Taylor's performance was not within normal limits for any of these tests [Halstead category test–Russell revision, Trails B, and tactual performance test (TPT)].

In the area of language functions, although the aphasia screening test (a very basic test of language abilities) was within normal limits, his performance on a word-naming test (Boston Naming Test) was moderately impaired. This is consistent with Taylor's report of word-finding problems. Interestingly, on tests of pure frontal-lobe functions, his performance was moderately impaired for both left-hemisphere and right-hemisphere functioning. Frontal-lobe functions are known to be readily compromised by both carbon monoxide poisoning and other anoxic events.

Motor functions were not compromised for this man, nor were sensory–perceptual functions. In the area of memory, long-term memory was impaired on all of the tests administered but recognition memory (a much less demanding type of memory) was well intact. Taylor readily passed two well-validated, objective tests of effort and motivation, which was consistent with his pattern of results across the overall neuropsychological test battery, as well as observations of his test-taking behavior.

On objective psychological testing [using the Millon Clinical Multiaxial Inventory-III (MCMI-III) and the Trauma Symptom Inventory], Taylor was found to meet criteria for an adjustment disorder with depressed mood, a generalized anxiety disorder, and posttraumatic stress disorder. Obviously, Taylor's depression resulted not only from his own cognitive deficits but also from the unexpected loss of his son.

On the HRNES–R, Taylor's AIS revealed that he had mild to moderate neuropsychological impairment, with a 64% probability of brain damage. The pattern of impaired functions quantifiably demonstrated that he had diffuse or bilateral problems (i.e., in both hemispheres of the brain). Of note was the fact that neuropsychological deficits demonstrated in this validated test battery were consistent with both carbon monoxide poisoning and anoxia in general. Studies have noted that carbon monoxide is especially toxic to the brain and the heart, and that patients with severe acute exposure may develop brain damage and severe mental impairments in both hemispheres of the brain, particularly in the frontal lobes. In addition, carbon monoxide poisoning often results in impaired processing speed. These patterns were entirely consistent with the pattern of deficits revealed by the HRNES–R.

The validated neuropsychological battery normed all of Taylor's test scores for both his age and his educational level of 18 years. Because Taylor's postincident verbal IQ was equal to 128, this number also was entered into the HRNES–R as a premorbid IQ score because his preincident verbal intellectual functioning was certainly at least as high as was measured in the examination. This high premorbid IQ score thus served to override the variable of 18 years of education, thus norming his raw scores at a more stringent level. Because all tests in the HRNES–R are co-normed, direct comparisons of Taylor's test performances could be made, safe in the knowledge that differences between test scores represented actual differences in ability, as opposed to differences in normative samples.

Outcome of Case 1

After our report was issued, the defense elected to dispense with its own neuropsychological examination. Several months later, a deposition was held in our office with 25 defense attorneys present. A good number of them had retained our practice in the past and therefore offered no critiques of either credentials or the HRNES–R. The deposition lasted approximately 5 h. Two months later, the case was settled in favor of the plaintiff.

We were advised by the plaintiff attorneys that using a validated test battery such as the HRNES–R made a case that seemed clear from the beginning even stronger. This particular plaintiff law firm had retained us in the past because of its ability to understand the scientific method used in our validated neuropsychological testing, as well as the research that underpinned the battery.

Description of Case 2 and Test Results (Mary Ross)

Mary Ross was a 60-year-old woman whose preincident history included headaches, ringing in the ears, some hearing loss, anxiety, a herniated disc, depression and suicidal thoughts, as well as surgery for a right cerebellopontine angle meningioma. This surgery occurred several years before the incident in suit.

It appears that Ross had been on a combination of medications that included Paxil twice a day and Serzone once a day for the past 5 years. As a result of an error by the pharmacy, Ross was given Seroquel instead of Serzone. Ross took one dose of the Seroquel and was claiming brain damage on the basis of having taken this one pill. In fact, when interviewed in our office, she stated, "I hurt my brain, and I used to be very smart, and I had an important job, and I feel dumb and make mistakes." She claimed that since taking this one pill her vision had changed, her hearing had become worse, she was losing her balance, her right hand shook, she often said words backward, and she often forgot what she was saying. In addition, she claimed that she could not remember what she had eaten for breakfast the same day, that she was unable to write coherently, and that she was now unable to drive because of confusion. Ross stated that she had done extensive reading on the effects of Seroquel and that all the problems she was experiencing were related to this single dose.

Her neurologist had written in his report, "I am not familiar with a single dose of Seroquel causing such residual sequelae." Ross underwent a magnetic resonance imaging (MRI) of the brain, which was unremarkable. She was tested by another neuropsychologist a year before our examination; he administered one test of effort and motivation, which Ross failed. However, this neuropsychologist determined that the failure meant that she was "severely demented from the medication." This neuropsychologist also administered a nonvalidated test battery in which the tests were not co-normed.

When interviewed in our office 2 years postincident, Ross did not demonstrate any amnesia for the events prior to taking the single dose of Seroquel, and there was no evidence for posttraumatic amnesia. In fact, after having taken the medication, she commuted from Ft. Lauderdale to her job in Miami 5 days a week for several months. When questioned in the interview, however, she stated that she was now unable to recite the alphabet or count to 10.

The validated, co-normed HRNES–R battery was administered to Ross over 3 days. All testing compared her abilities to persons of her own age and educational level (high school). IQ testing revealed her to be functioning at the fifth percentile overall. When normed for her age and educational level, this corresponded to a performance in the moderately impaired range. It was noted that her IQ had decreased from the time of the first neuropsychologist's testing 1 year previously.

On tests of executive functioning, Ross's overall performance ranged from profoundly impaired to well within normal limits. Also of interest was that she had performed successfully 1 year earlier on the Trails B test but was now unable to perform this test at all. In addition, her errors on the category test increased from 80 the year before to 140 on our examination.

Nevertheless, of great significance was that her performance was well within normal limits on a task involving spatial skills, memory, and nonverbal problem solving (the TPT). This test is known to be extremely sensitive to brain injury. In fact, research performed on the HRNES–R has demonstrated that the total time score on this test has the greatest overall predictive power for brain injury of any other test in the battery (Russell, 2004). This type of scientific knowledge about a neuropsychological test battery is only available in the case of a standardized, validated test battery. Notably, Ross had also performed well within normal limits on previous testing with the TPT, but the neuropsychologist failed to mention the significance of this. Even more significant was that her TPT memory score was within normal limits on both administrations. Notably, this test of incidental memory is often not perceived by examinees as a memory test.

On our examination, Ross performed very poorly on tests of psychomotor speed, as well as on tests relating to attention. Motor and sensory perceptual functions were also performed in the profoundly impaired range.

Her basic language skills on the aphasia screening test were found to be in the profoundly impaired range, as was her vocabulary ability. Ross had noted on interview that she was unable to recognize her own name on a bank statement. Nevertheless, despite her extremely poor performance on language testing, she completed the 1½ h interview flawlessly, with no word-finding problems or any receptive language problems.

Ross was also administered three well-validated, objective tests of effort and motivation, and she failed all three of them. These tests should only be failed if someone has extremely severe brain injury or severe dementia.

On objective psychological testing (MCMI-III), Ross denied any problems whatsoever, despite the fact that she had an extensive documented history of depression and anxiety. This pattern of responding was consistent with the results of the Minnesota Multiphasic Personality Inventory 2, which had been administered to her 1 year previously. It was noteworthy that Ross was even able complete these psychological tests, considering her profoundly impaired language test scores.

Our conclusions were that the results of the current neuropsychological evaluation were inconsistent with brain injury or psychological injury as a result of the medication incident. There were numerous inconsistencies in her behaviors, test performances, and test failures. As described earlier, Ross performed unrealistically poorly on many relatively "easy" tests, yet she scored within normal limits on some tests within the validated battery that are known to be extremely sensitive to brain impairment. Moreover, out of 35 common test scores that were compared between our testing and that of the previous neuropsychologist, 22 were performed significantly more poorly than during the initial evaluation. Such an extreme regression in cognitive functioning certainly did not make sense in the context of her alleged injury.

Outcome of Case 2

After testifying about our neuropsychological evaluation in federal court for approximately 8 h across 2 days, the jury issued a verdict for the defense, despite the fact that the pharmacy had clearly given the wrong medication to Ross.

The jury was allowed to be interviewed at the end of the trial, and the consensus was that jury members were so angry at the blatant malingering of this individual that they decided to award nothing to her, completely absolving the pharmacy of liability. Although we had considerable "soft" data and behavioral observations supporting this woman's malingering, it was more important that we could present to the jury the results of a validated battery of tests that had been co-normed and researched, and we could explain by the use of prepared exhibits that the pattern of test results was totally inconsistent with brain injury. The jury independently commented that this scientific approach to assessment had convinced them that this was a blatant case of malingering as opposed to "severe dementia" as claimed by her own neuropsychologist.

Description of Case 3 and Test Results (Linda Grant)

In contrast to the preceding case, Linda Grant, a 67-year-old woman, was referred by a plaintiff attorney for a neuropsychological evaluation subsequent to a pharmacy error in which she was given Coumadin at 10 times the prescribed dose. This resulted in a stroke several weeks later. She had been taking Coumadin for a heart condition for approximately 5 years.

A computed tomography (CT) scan of the brain indicated that Grant had sustained a right-sided acute subdural hematoma with a small right-temporal parenchymal hemorrhage. Grant underwent a right-frontal temporal parietal craniotomy for the subdural hematoma, as well as a cranioplasty. A postsurgery CT scan of the brain revealed postoperative changes, with a right-sided craniotomy defect as well as small residual subdural hematomas that were similar to those seen in the previous study. The intraparenchymal hemorrhages in the right temporal lobe were unchanged since the prior examination, with a small amount of edema noted. There was no significant mass effect and no midline shift.

Several days later, Grant suffered a generalized seizure, which was noted to be left focal. An EEG revealed slight diffuse slowing.

Grant's educational history was reported as graduating high school with honors. She won several college scholarships to pursue an artistic career but never attended college. When relating her history during the clinical interview, Grant tended to be somewhat tangential, frequently lost her train of thought, and demonstrated significant word-finding problems. She reported that her current problems were confusion, particularly when trying to cook and follow directions; difficulty dressing herself;

comprehension problems, particularly with reading; memory problems for recent but not remote memory; and difficulty with coordination to the extent that she was unable to paint as she had done before.

Grant was administered the HRNES–R battery in addition to objective tests of effort and motivation and an objective psychological–personality testing. Her FSIQ was found to be 89 (29th percentile). Her verbal IQ was 92 (30th percentile), and her performance IQ was 85 (16th percentile). Notably, the vocabulary and information subtests were performed within normal limits for her age and educational level, suggesting that Grant's premorbid IQ was most likely within the average range and was now significantly reduced.

Tests of executive functions were found to be mildly to moderately impaired; Grant had some difficulty with both the Trails B test and the category test. On the TPT, her performance was moderately impaired. As previously discussed, the total time score on this test is known to have the greatest overall predictive power for brain injury in the HRNES–R validated neuropsychological battery. Although she performed within normal limits for her dominant (right) hand, her performance was in the moderately impaired range for her nondominant (left) hand, consistent with her right-hemisphere cerebrovascular accident (CVA).

Basic language functions on the aphasia screening test were within normal limits, but on a test of word naming, her performance was mildly impaired for her age and educational level. Grant's rote reading ability was just at the borderline range.

Her frontal-lobe functions ranged from within normal limits to moderately impaired. On a word-fluency test, Grant's performance was well within normal limits relating to the left frontal area of her brain. However, on a design-fluency task relating to right-hemisphere frontal-lobe functioning, her performance was moderately impaired, consistent with the right-hemisphere insults she sustained.

Although Grant's basic spatial perceptual functions were spared, more complex spatial perceptual functioning (such as on the WAIS-III block design subtest) was moderately impaired, as were tests for psychomotor speed. Motor functions tests also followed the pattern of Grant's stroke, with clear evidence of consistent left-sided motor problems. Using her dominant (right) hand, Grant was found to be within normal limits on a test of simple motor speed (index finger tapping), as well as on a test of complex motor speed (grooved pegboard). However, her left-hand performance was moderately impaired for simple motor speed and severely impaired for complex motor speed. On a test of grip strength as measured by a hand dynamometer, Grant's performance was just within the borderline range for her right hand but moderately impaired on the left. Her sensory–perceptual functions were within normal limits.

Memory testing also revealed a pattern of right-hemisphere deficits. Grant's verbal memory for both immediate and delayed recall showed only borderline problems, whereas nonverbal memory (which involves spatial–perceptual functions) was impaired.

Tests of effort and motivation were administered orally because of Grant's reading problems, and she passed all three tests, demonstrating that she was giving good effort.

Psychological testing was administered using the publisher's audiotaped version and revealed a woman who was, not surprisingly, suffering from major depression. It was clear that the results of Grant's neuropsychological evaluation were consistent with overall moderate cognitive deficits and more pronounced for right-hemisphere brain functions. This was clearly consistent with the CVA she suffered, as well as with the effects of her craniotomy.

On the HRNES–R, Grant's AIS placed her within the moderate range of impairment on those tests in the battery that are known to be the most sensitive to brain injury. Her performance was found to be impaired on the vast majority of the AIS tests (PII of 70%), and the probability of brain damage was 65%. The remaining tests that comprise the HRNES–R also demonstrated clear brain injury, with almost 50% of those test scores impaired. The HRNES–R lateralization index indicated strong right impairment.

Although Grant did have major depression, if all of her problems had been entirely emotionally based, she would not have performed as well as she did on the majority of the left-hemisphere tests, including tests of verbal memory. By administering a validated, co-normed neuropsychological battery, we could report with a high degree of scientific accuracy that Grant did have neuropsychological impairment and that her cognitive deficits were consistent with her CVA and ensuing craniotomy.

Outcome of Case 3

Our neuropsychological report resulted in a clear settlement for the plaintiff. In fact, no deposition was taken in this case relating to our assessment because the report stood on its own merits. The report was reviewed by another neuropsychologist who was retained by the defense, and the defense consequently declined to pursue its own neuropsychological examination. By using the HRNES–R, we were able to clearly present findings that were consistent with prior objective neurological measures and were further substantiated by the CT and MRI scans of the brain. The pattern of Grant's brain injuries were much easier to discern against the constant background provided by a co-normed, validated test battery, and the scientifically based results certainly lent themselves to being communicated in a logical and reasonable fashion.

Description of Case 4 and Test Results (David Harris)

David Harris (age 36) was referred by a defense attorney, who stated there was no question that Harris had sustained a significant brain injury. The insurance carrier, however, requested that he be evaluated to confirm and substantiate the findings of the plaintiff neuropsychologist.

Harris had been involved in a head-on motor vehicle accident. There was major entrapment in the vehicle, and it took 30 min to extricate him. He sustained major facial trauma and had a Glasgow Coma Scale score of 3 at the scene. A noncontrast CT scan of the brain taken on admission to the emergency department revealed contusions in the right temporal lobe and high right-frontoparietal region, with a small right subacute hematoma in the high right-parietal convexity. It was also noted that there may have been minimal contusion in the left frontal lobe. Harris had therefore sustained a significant closed head injury. In addition, he had experienced hypoxia. Harris's injuries were so severe that one of the neurologists did not think he would survive. The hospital records documented global unresponsiveness, and recovery was not anticipated. Nevertheless, Harris did survive, but a CT scan of the brain taken several months after the accident revealed significant brain atrophy, which was noted to be too advanced for his age. Harris was discharged from the hospital after several months and transferred to a rehabilitation center.

Eighteen months after the accident, Harris was tested by a neuropsychologist, who diagnosed dementia secondary to severe traumatic brain injury and found him to be unemployable. He was reevaluated by the same neuropsychologist 3 years later and was found to have very little improvement in his cognitive functioning.

More than a year later, the defense attorney contacted our office and requested that we perform neuropsychological testing. Harris was administered as much of the HRNES–R as was possible given his considerable cognitive deficits. Our IQ testing was generally comparable with that of the other neuropsychologist, demonstrating that Harris's FSIQ was only at the first percentile. All executive function tests were moderately impaired, as were his language and spatial–perceptual functions. Psychomotor speed, motor functions, and sensory–perceptual functions were found to be mildly impaired. Harris's memory test results were generally moderately impaired. Tests of effort and motivation were administered to Harris, although it was anticipated that he might score poorly as a result of his very severe brain injury. The results indeed fit into that category, not because Harris was not well motivated but because he was too brain damaged to even be able to complete these tests successfully.

As we administered the HRNES–R, which covers all testable neuropsychological functions and provides redundancy in coverage by means of several tests for each brain function, our examination underscored Harris's severe brain damage even more clearly than did the previous two neuropsychological evaluations. Because all of the HRNES–R tests are co-normed, we also could scientifically support between-test comparisons. It was concluded that Harris would not be capable of performing any type of financially productive work in the future and that he required a guardian because he was not competent to make decisions regarding his personal care or finances.

Outcome of Case 4

It was notable that in this case we were of significant help to the opposing attorney, who took a videotaped deposition to be used in court in support of the plaintiff's claims. This attorney decided to use our findings in court, rather than those of his own expert, because he realized that our validated neuropsychological test battery was more comprehensive and scientifically based than the one administered by his own expert. The case was settled for the plaintiff before the trial began.

Description of Case 5 and Test Results (Ralph Smith)

Ralph Smith was administered a neuropsychological evaluation in our office approximately 3 years after he was struck by a car while he was riding a scooter. Smith lost consciousness on impact and was subsequently found on CT scan to have sustained numerous facial fractures. His Glasgow Coma Scale score at the scene was initially 6, increasing to 10 while in transit to the hospital. One week later, another CT scan of the brain was administered, revealing a contusion of the left frontal lobe.

Significantly, Smith had a preaccident history of depression relating to combat in the Gulf War. He had noted, "I did the worst thing—I killed an enemy soldier, and that was big for me. I didn't have a problem going to war—I just had a problem killing this person." The only treatment he ever had for this event was seeing a military psychiatrist for two sessions.

Two years after the motor vehicle accident, a neuropsychologist evaluated Smith and reported that he had word-finding problems and severe depression. The neuropsychologist concluded that Smith had severe brain injury, severe personality changes, difficulty with emotional control, aggression, and poor judgment. He stated that Smith would never be able to work again (previously, he had been working as an auto mechanic). Significantly, despite dedicating several paragraphs in the report to a description of Smith's preinjury depression, the neuropsychologist failed to administer any objective measures of psychological functioning.

The neuropsychological test battery he administered was not validated; as a result, there was no published research demonstrating the ability of his battery of tests to differentiate brain damage from a non–brain-damaged condition. Furthermore, neither the report nor the raw test data indicated what normative system was used to interpret the test scores, and it was not reported whether Smith's test scores had been corrected for both his age and educational–premorbid intellectual level (Smith had dropped out of high school after the 10th grade). The tests in this neuropsychologist's battery were not co-normed, so there was no scientific basis for making comparisons among the scores obtained. The test battery was also quite brief and did not comprehensively cover all domains of neuropsychological functioning. Entire areas of brain functioning (motor, executive, sensory–perceptual, spatial–perceptual) were omitted.

More than 1 year later, we administered the HRNES–R to Smith. When questioned about his educational history, he said that he had left school in the middle of the 11th grade because of failing grades, particularly in English. He reported that he had served in the army for 11 years and then was a mechanic in the reserves for 3 years. It was notable in the clinical interview that Smith had a rambling style of speaking and would sometimes lose his train of thought. He reported having no memory of his motor vehicle accident and also appeared to have some retrograde amnesia.

Smith's FSIQ on the WAIS-III fell within the average range, with no significant difference between his verbal and performance IQ scores. However, his performance was moderately impaired on the working memory and processing speed indexes of the WAIS-III.

Executive function tests ranged from within normal limits to mildly impaired. On the TPT, which he had never been administered previously, Smith's performance was entirely within normal limits for his age and educational level. As discussed previously, the total time score on this test is known to be one of the most sensitive indicators of brain impairment in the HRNES–R.

In the area of language, Smith's performance was mildly impaired on a test of verbal fluency, although on an expressive vocabulary test his performance was within normal limits for his age and educational level. His performance on a word-finding test was mildly impaired. All tests of spatial–perceptual functions were within normal limits, and there were no problems noted for sensory–perceptual or motor functions. Complex psychomotor speed was mildly impaired. Memory functions ranged from within normal limits to mildly impaired for both verbal and nonverbal material. Smith passed all objective tests of effort and motivation.

Objective psychological testing was consistent with someone who was experiencing clinically significant depression and anxiety, including some symptoms of posttraumatic stress disorder. Although his posttraumatic stress symptoms may well have been initiated by his experiences in the Gulf War, it is likely that his recent brain injury had exacerbated the disorder.

Smith obtained a completely normal average index score on the HRNES–R (AIS (Average Index Score) = 103; 96 and above is considered normal). He actually performed extremely well, and above average, on all but one of the nine index tests administered. As Smith had achieved an average FSIQ score on our testing, we elected to norm him not at his attained 10th-grade educational level, but rather at the high-school level, which is equivalent to an average premorbid IQ. This conservative approach to norming ensured that Smith's neuropsychological profile had every reasonable opportunity of demonstrating any cognitive deficits he might have. It was concluded that his neuropsychological test results were consistent with some mild, specific deficits in the areas of processing speed and verbal–nonverbal fluency, as well as some traumatic brain-injury–related changes in personality functioning, all within the greater context of generally intact to above-average neuropsychological functioning.

Outcome of Case 5

In deposition, we asserted that although Smith did have some specific cognitive deficits and changes in personality, this did not preclude that he might be able to return to work. Out of the more than 60 scores obtained on the HRNES–R, he actually demonstrated impaired performance on only a small handful of them, and these impairments were in the very mild to mild range. We testified that an individual able to achieve such a profile should not necessarily be sidelined from the workforce, as was concluded by the plaintiff's neuropsychologist. It was our testimony that Smith's ability to maintain successful employment would likely depend more on his emotional controls than on the few mild cognitive deficits he demonstrated. Most important from a psychological perspective was that Smith needed a course of consistent psychotherapeutic treatment, as well as a thorough and objective psychiatric review of his current psychopharmacological treatment regimen. We also recommended a vocational assessment and counseling as preparation for a return to work.

Several weeks later, the defense attorney told us that this case had settled, and the award had been significantly reduced from the plaintiff's original demand. The attorney explained that this settlement had been reached because our thorough, validated neuropsychological evaluation demonstrated that Smith was certainly not totally disabled. More than a year later, when working on a different case for the same defense attorney, we incidentally learned that Smith had ultimately received psychological treatment and had indeed returned to work as a mechanic.

Description of Case 6 and Test Results (Martin Langford)

Martin Langford (age 62) was referred by a defense attorney, related to the plaintiff's claim of brain injury, after a suitcase allegedly fell from the overhead compartment of an airplane, striking his head. Our review of the medical records revealed that he did not report any cognitive symptoms to his physicians until 2 years postincident. During the intervening period of time, Langford continued to work in his previous capacity as an insurance adjuster. His premorbid medical history was positive for hypertension and hyperlipidemia. In addition, 4 years before the alleged injury, Langford had been involved in a motor vehicle accident in which he had sustained a closed head injury with subsequent postconcussive symptoms.

Another neuropsychologist examined him 1 year postincident. On receipt of the raw test data, we were unable to determine what normative system this neuropsychologist had used to interpret the test scores or whether the norms made adjustments for both Langford's age and educational level. The test battery was not validated, and none of the tests were co-normed. The battery did not provide complete coverage of brain functions, omitting the areas of motor and sensory–perceptual functioning. The battery also did not provide for good redundancy; language functioning, for example, was covered by only a single test. No objective tests of effort and motivation were administered. No objective psychological test was administered—only one checklist that did not have any response bias scales was given. In addition, the report made no mention of the prior motor vehicle accident with closed head injury.

The neuropsychologist concluded that Langford, being 2 years postinjury, met the diagnosis of "mild cognitive impairment" and that his thinking and memory dysfunction interfered with his ability to work. He also opined that Langford's mild cognitive deficits left him more susceptible to Alzheimer's disease as he aged.

In our clinical history and interview, Langford reported no prior history of head injury, which was inconsistent with the medical records reviewed. He also denied any problems with hypertension or hyperlipidemia. He related that his main problems were with memory and orientation while driving, noting that he often became lost. When questioned more specifically about his memory difficulties, Langford stated that he had lost memory for events in the past, and people frequently had to remind him about important family events in his history. When questioned about whether he remembered anything from his college days, he said that he could not and that his "mind was a blank."

Langford's neuropsychological testing on our evaluation demonstrated that he had an average IQ, with performances on the digit symbol coding and block design subtests (two of the WAIS-III tests most sensitive to brain injury) that fell in the average to high average range. Executive function tests were all within normal limits, as were all of the language function tests. Psychomotor and processing speed tests were within normal limits, as were motor functions and sensory–perceptual functions. Only the memory function tests were consistently moderately to severely impaired. In addition, three objective, well-validated tests of effort and motivation were administered to Langford, and he failed all of them.

Outcome of Case 6

The deposition related to our examination focused on Langford's lack of effort and motivation, as well as the considerable deficiencies in the other neuropsychologist's test battery. Shortly after the deposition, the plaintiff's attorney dropped the case. The plaintiff's attorney reported informally that he had been completely unaware of the existence of objective tests of effort and motivation. When he learned the reasons why we considered his own expert's neuropsychological testing to be totally invalid and was presented with various nationally recognized position papers and journal articles, he quickly realized that he had no reasonable justification for pursuing this case in court.

Description of Case 7 and Test Results (Bruce Kramer)

Bruce Kramer (age 80) was referred by a defense firm for a neuropsychological evaluation. He had been involved in a bicycle versus automobile accident 2 years earlier. At the scene of the accident, Kramer had a Glasgow Coma Scale score of 15, although he had reportedly sustained a blow to the head and was dazed. He also sustained pelvic and hip fractures and a laceration to his face.

The emergency department report noted "minor closed head injury without loss of consciousness (cerebral contusion)." A CT scan of the head, while revealing no fractures, indicated "probable small areas of contusion with associated parenchymal hemorrhage involving right temporal and right thalamic regions, no mass effect."

In reviewing the preaccident records, it was discovered that Kramer had an extensive preaccident medical history, including myocardial infarction, bypass surgery, uncontrolled hypertension, transient ischemic attacks, a stroke that caused "focal atrophy in the right posterior frontal lobe," hypercholesteremia, anxiety, and depression. Of particular interest was the fact that the neurologist who evaluated Kramer for the plaintiff reported that his premorbid medical history was unremarkable.

The plaintiff's neuropsychologist performed an evaluation 2 years postaccident using a nonvalidated battery in which the test scores were corrected for age but not educational level. Kramer had only completed a seventh-grade education. The neuropsychologist also failed to administer any objective tests of effort and motivation or of psychological–personality functioning. This neuropsychologist concluded that Kramer's test score profile was consistent with traumatic brain injury. However, no mention was made of his significant preaccident brain insults, underlying vascular disease, open heart surgery with postoperative complications, hypertension, or history of anxiety and depression. There was also no mention that Kramer had been taking hydrocodone daily during the time of the evaluation.

When Kramer was sent to us for neuropsychological evaluation, the HRNES–R was administered, and his IQ was found to be overall within the average range, consistent with his employment history. It was concluded that there had been no significant decline in overall intellectual functioning from his estimated premorbid level.

Executive function tests were performed in the borderline to mildly impaired range for his age and educational level. Language functions were basically within normal limits except for rote reading, which showed him to be well below average for his age level and at the 19th percentile with a sixth-grade reading level. Reading is a well-learned skill that is usually not affected by all but the most severe of brain injuries. Kramer's performance on the vocabulary subtest of the WAIS–III also was moderately impaired for his age and educational level. Vocabulary also is typically preserved in cases of mild to moderate traumatic brain injury. Kramer passed all objective tests of effort and motivation that were administered.

Our conclusions were that this 80-year-old man had mild to moderate memory problems that were consistent with an individual who had sustained significant preaccident neurological insults, including a severe premorbid coronary arterial sclerotic problem, stroke, and transient ischemic attacks. Interestingly, despite all of Kramer's preaccident medical problems, his AIS on the HRNES-R revealed only mild cognitive impairment, with the probability of brain damage at 64%. This was entirely anticipated, given his premorbid medical history. In addition, an MRI taken 7 years before the accident showed exactly the same right-hemisphere insults as the MRI taken postaccident. Our report also included references to studies describing cognitive decline among older adults with cardiovascular disease, the effect of coronary bypass surgery on neurocognitive functioning, and, of course, the effect of a prior stroke and transient ischemic attacks on neuropsychological performance. We recommended counseling for his anxiety and depression, noting that his physical injuries and preexisting emotional problems were likely exacerbated by the accident.

Outcome of Case 7

Courtroom testimony related to our examination lasted more than 5 h. The majority of the cross-examination dealt with quite superficial aspects (fees, etc.), as the plaintiff attorney clearly wanted to avoid discussion of the limitations of her own expert's evaluation or dialogue about her client's extensive preaccident medical history. However, the judge allowed considerable latitude in discussing these areas.

The neurologist for the defense had been allowed to produce Kramer's pre- and postaccident MRI films of the brain, and it was pointed out to the jury that our validated neuropsychological test results were entirely consistent with the preaccident MRI findings, primarily demonstrating a right-frontal brain injury. The jury came back with a verdict for the defense as related to the brain-injury claim, and Kramer was compensated only for his physical injuries. We were later informed that a validated, co-normed test battery, with scores corrected for both age and educational level, was a significant factor in the jury's verdict.

Discussion

The preceding case descriptions illustrated the usefulness of a validated neuropsychological test battery (such as the HRNES-R) in communicating test results to attorneys, judges, and juries, as well as in establishing scientific support for the diagnoses and conclusions reached.

Validated neuropsychological test batteries designed with complete coverage of brain functions, redundancy of coverage, coordinated norming, and age- and education-corrected norms offer a rigorous background against which an examinee's cognitive functioning can be measured. Complementing a validated battery with the administration of objective tests of effort and motivation, objective psychological tests containing response bias scales, and knowledge of the principle of normal variation permits the neuropsychologist to reach a level of scientific confidence in his or her conclusions that is otherwise unavailable. Only the user of a validated neuropsychological test battery can respond to questions about the battery's predictive power, sensitivity, and specificity, as well as the ability of the battery as a whole to scientifically differentiate conditions of brain impairment and no brain impairment.

These benefits, of course, are by no means limited to the forensic setting and should be equally important to physicians, psychologists, and patients seeking scientifically based evidence to rule in or rule out neuropsychological deficits.

References

Bush, S. S., Ruff, R. M., Tröster, A. I., Barth, J. T., Koffler, S. P., Pliskin, N. H., et al. (2005). NAN position paper: Symptom validity assessment: Practice issues and medical necessity. *Archives of Clinical Psychology*, *20*, 419–426.

Heaton, R. K., Grant, I., & Matthews, C. G. (1991). *Comprehensive norms for an expended Halstead–Reitan Battery*. Odessa, FL: Psychological Assessment Resources.

Heilbronner, R. L., Sweet, J. J., Morgan, J. E., Larrabee, G. J., Millis, S. R., & Conference Participants. (2009). American academy of clinical neuropsychology consensus conference statement on the neuropsychological assessment of effort, response bias, and malingering. *Clinical Neuropsychologist*, *23*, 1093–1129.

Russell, E. W. (2000). The cognitive-metric, fixed battery approach to neuropsychological assessment. In R. D. Vanderploeg (Ed.), *Clinician's guide to neuropsychological assessment* (2nd ed.). Mahwah, NJ: Lawrence Erlbaum.

Russell, E. W. (2004). The operating characteristics of the major HRNES–R measures. *Archives of Clinical Neuropsychology*, *19*, 1043–1061.

Russell, E. W., & Starkey, R. I. (1993). *Halstead–Russell Neuropsychological Evaluation System [Manual and computer program]*. Los Angeles: Western Psychological Services.

Russell, E. W., & Starkey, R. I. (2001). *Halstead–Russell Neuropsychological Evaluation System—Revised [Manual and computer program]*. Los Angeles: Western Psychological Services.

Section V

Formal Neuropsychological Methods

12 In Defense of the Halstead–Reitan Battery: A Critique of Lezak's Review

In a section of her recent book *Neuropsychological Assessment*, Lezak (1995) reviews the Halstead–Reitan Battery (HRB) and some of its derivative methods. Lezak's book is widely referenced and consequently quite influential. However, the review often misrepresents the rationale and validity of the HRB as it exists today. Because a fairly high proportion of neuropsychologists use at least portions of the HRB (Butler, Retzlaff, & Vanderploeg, 1991; Lees-Haley, Smith, Williams, & Dunn, 1996), it is important to present a rebuttal to Lezak's review.

As part of the rebuttal, some of the rationale for the HRB will be presented. This is necessary because much of Lezak's criticism is derived from a misunderstanding of the methods used by the HRB. These methods arc often not well understood by many neuropsychologists, especially those using the approach that Lezak advocates.

In addition, several of the methods derived from the HRB will also be discussed because of Lezak's strong criticisms. These include Reitan's Neuropsychological Deficit Scale (NDS; Reitan, 1987), the Comprehensive Norms for an Expanded Halstead–Reitan Battery (CNEHRB; Heaton, Grant, & Matthews, 1991) and the Halstead–Russell Neuropsychological Evaluation System (HRNES; Russell & Starkey, 1993).

Background Discussion

Lezak's book is excellent in discussing the hypothesis-testing method and reviewing the research on single tests from that perspective. However, Reitan's method is basically not a hypothesis-testing method but a pattern-analysis method. This pattern-analysis method is generally misunderstood by Lezak and many other neuropsychologists. Because many of Lezak's criticisms are derived from this misunderstanding, a discussion of her review must involve an explanation of the method used by Reitan.

Pattern Analysis Versus Hypothesis Testing

The major underlining division in neuropsychology assessment methods appears to be between what are called the *hypothesis-testing* and *pattern-analysis* approaches. A large proportion of the other differences between approaches, methods, and types

The Scientific Foundation of Neuropsychological Assessment. DOI: 10.1016/B978-0-12-416029-3.00012-9

of assessment is derived from this distinction. These differences, such as that between flexible and fixed batteries, have been argued over the years. Although this division will be briefly presented here, a more thorough explanation of it has been presented elsewhere (Russell, 1994, 1997).

Hypothesis Testing

In the hypothesis-testing approach, the neuropsychologist selects and uses tests to answer a particular question framed as a hypothesis (Bauer, 1994; Lezak, 1995, pp. 111–113, 125; Russell, 1994). The neuropsychologist begins with a question, and then a hypothesis is constructed to answer the question. A test is then selected to test the hypothesis. The score that the patient obtains on a particular test, or the way in which the patient obtained the score, answers the hypothesis. Thus, the hypothesis-testing method is basically a one-question, one-test method, although the examiner might use additional tests to support the first test. The procedure of asking a series of questions may be called *multistage*, *serial*, or *ongoing hypothesis testing*. Such neuropsychological batteries become lengthy when there are many questions to be answered.

The hypothesis may not simply refer to externally derived questions but may be used as a method for clarifying the nature of deficits within the test battery. An example might be determining the reason for a slowed performance on block design. This is a type of exploratory questioning or hypothesis testing. It assumes that the neuropsychologist knows the relationships between tests and brain functions.

The hypothesis-testing process almost always requires a flexible battery. Various tests are selected according to their relation to a series of questions or hypotheses and not according to their relation to each other. As such, this method employs a group of tests that have no intrinsic relationship to each other. They are only related to the various hypotheses. Consequently, in the pure hypothesis-testing approach, one does not begin with a group of tests that are related to any hypothesis.

However, many neuropsychologists recommend a modified form of this method using a fixed or relatively fixed *core* (Bauer, 1994) or *basic battery* (Lezak, 1995, pp. 121–123). In this method, the neuropsychologist is looking for impaired test scores to provide an indication as to the condition of the patient, which will then provide hypotheses to test. This method is a rudimentary form of pattern analysis with a partially fixed battery.

Pattern Analysis

The pattern-analysis method is primarily concerned with the relationships between tests rather than with the individual scores or level of functioning on particular tests. This method compares tests with each other to discover a pattern that reveals information about a cognitive condition (Russell, 1994, 1997). Probably Reitan's most important contribution to neuropsychology will be his development of the pattern-analysis method on an inferential basis. The method and value of pattern analysis has been discussed in several places (Bauer, 1994; Russell, 1984, 1986, 1994).

Neuropsychologists using a pattern-analysis method may, of course, use the hypotheses testing method, but it is secondary to that of analyzing patterns. Pattern analysis requires certain design constituents for its application (Russell, 1984, 1986, 1994). Many neuropsychologists apparently are not aware of these requirements or how they are related to pattern analysis.

Lezak's Understanding of the Pattern Approach

Although Lezak's book correctly presents some of the basic concepts related to pattern analysis (Lezak, 1995, pp. 165–166, 168), Lezak appears to lack an understanding of the implications and requirements of that method for designing test batteries. The method that Lezak calls *pattern analysis* does not correctly describe Reitan's method. She identifies pattern analysis with test scatter, either intratest or intertest (Lezak, 1995, pp. 166–168). Although strong intratest scatter may indicate an organic problem, this is generally not a form of pattern analysis. The scatter may involve no comparisons between individual tests, but only a comparison of several tests to the person's overall level of cognitive ability. In the pattern-analysis method employed in Reitan's work, comparisons to a general level of normal functioning are not the central procedure. The tests are compared to each other, often without regard as to whether any of the tests are in the normal range. For instance, in a case in which all of the scores are abnormal, if the right-hemisphere scores are consistently more impaired than the left-hemisphere scores, then the person is considered to have right-hemisphere damage. Neuropsychologists who are experienced with a set battery know that a large proportion of the scores of patients who have even moderate brain damage are impaired to some extent—that is, the patterns occur on a background of generalized impairment.

The Fixed Battery

To use pattern analysis, it is necessary to establish a fixed battery. This has been designated as a set of tests or a set battery (Russell, 1995, 1997). The HRB is a set of tests designed for pattern analysis, not an uncoordinated group of tests. Patterns between tests cannot be observed when tests are continually changed. One cannot observe a relationship between tests A and B when sometimes only A is included in the battery and sometimes only B is included. Consequently, in a flexible battery, no stable basis for comparisons exist. In addition, the formal set battery requires coordinated norms and a consistent form of scale scores. This ensures equivalent test scores, which produces a constant background (Russell, 1994).

Without mentioning the HRB directly, Lezak disparages fixed batteries in several ways. She calls them "ready made batteries" (Lezak, 1995, pp. 123–125) that presumably do not require any expertise to assemble. An examiner using a fixed battery has "a general lack of knowledge about how to…" conduct neuropsychological testing. As such an examiner is "naive" or "inexperienced" (Lezak, 1995, pp. 123–125). Although these comments would be relevant to batteries using a hypothesis-testing approach, they demonstrate an ignorance of the nature of the pattern-analysis method, in that pattern analysis requires a set battery.

The competent use of a fixed or set battery to perform pattern analysis actually requires more expertise than the use of a flexible battery. In addition to using the same neurological and assessment knowledge that a hypothesis-testing method uses, pattern analysis requires more extensive knowledge of psychometrics and particularly knowledge of how tests interact with each other.

Coordinated Norms

One of the great advantages of a fixed or set battery is that it uses coordinated norms. All of the tests are either normed on the same sample or statistical methods are used to equate the measures. In such a battery, the scores may be directly compared to observe patterns. Lezak appears to understand and appreciate this advantage. She states that the Wechsler batteries are used for pattern analysis "because of their obvious statistical comparability" (Lezak, 1995, p. 168). In addition, the CNEHRB uses a "single standard score system" (p. 168).

She also recognizes that uncoordinated norms derived from various tests normed on divergent populations present problems. In regard to norms from different populations, Lezak writes, "although this situation results in less than perfect comparability between the different tests ... these 'mixed bag' norms generally serve their purpose" (Lezak, 1995, p. 157). She presents no research to support this claim.

In Lezak's presidential address for the International Neuropsychological Society (Lezak, 1988), after criticizing the concept of an IQ, she indicates that "subtest profile is an invaluable aid in conceptualizing the multiplicity of mental abilities and cognitive functions" (p. 360). She ends this speech by saying "the development of a well-standardized, neuropsychologically sound, and practically relevant set of mental abilities tests lies before us as the next major challenge for neuropsychological assessment" (p. 360). That statement was made in 1988. Now there are four batteries that have met this challenge: the HRNES (Russell & Starkey, 1993), the CNEHRB (Heaton et al., 1991), the NDS (Reitan, 1987) and the Luria–Nebraska Neuropsychological Battery (LNNB) (Golden, Purisch, & Harnmeke, 1985). Of these, three are derived from the HRB. Profiles can be derived for the HRNES, CNEHRB, and LNNB.

The Individual Approach

One of Lezak's rules (Lezak, 1995, p. 110), and one that she believes a fixed battery violates, is that a battery should be individualized or tailored to a patient's needs, abilities, and limitations. Contrary to her understanding, a fixed battery is designed to examine the individual person. As Lezak states, "The concept of behavioral deficit presupposes some ideal, normal, or prior level of functioning against which the patient's performance may be measured" (Lezak, 1995, p. 98). In other words, the attributes that make a person different from other people result from variations from a normal brain.

This implies that the way to assess a patient's individuality is to compare a person's responses against a standard fixed background that represents a normal brain.

This is what an individual test does. The test is fixed in that it cannot be changed each time it is administered, and it is normed and validated to represent a standard background. If one changes the construction of a test each time it is given, then there is no basis for distinguishing the person's individual responses. The need for this constancy is the basis for the requirements of reliability and validity in regard to an individual test (American Psychological Association, 1985).

The fixed battery extends this concept of a constant standard to the entire battery. As such, a fixed battery represents the normal brain. The battery provides a constant background against which individual differences become evident (Russell, 1994). A pure flexible battery changes the tests each time a person is examined so that the person's overall individual pattern of responses cannot be adequately examined. Thus, the fixed battery provides a consistent "prior level of functioning against which the patient's performance may be measured" (Lezak, 1996, p. 98).

If a person has major problems, such as the loss of an arm or a lack of ability in speaking English, the fixed battery must be modified, just as a flexible battery must be modified. These problems do not affect the fixed battery to any greater extent than a flexible one. In fact, scoring and prescribed changes in the testing procedure are incorporated into the HRB. These modifications handle most of the more common problems because of sensory and motor impairments.

In the usual neuropsychological examination situation, the hypothesis-testing approach using a flexible battery is not tailored to the whole person but to the referral questions. In most cases, the pure hypothesis-testing method does not even attempt to examine the whole individual person. Rather, it attempts to answer a series of specific referral questions (Russell, 1984).

In addition, a battery that is developed during the pressure of an examination will almost inevitably lack tests for some aspects of the person. This danger can be countered if the examiner has a group of tests in mind prior to the examination that covers all areas of brain functioning; but then this is an informal fixed battery. In addition, most neuropsychologists who use a fixed battery are not opposed to adding a few tests or modifying the battery to some extent as the situation and the patient's condition dictate. Nevertheless, the major portion of the battery is "fixed" so that the individuality of the patient can be assessed.

Fallacy of Nonrefutation

Because this is a discussion of a critical review, it is important to examine a type of fallacy that critiques often make. The type of fallacy, which often occurs in neuropsychology reviews and arguments, will be called the *fallacy of nonrefutation*. The fallacy is committed when a writing implies that if a test or battery has not been shown to be invalid, then it is valid. This is so obviously false that its theoretical base need not be discussed.

However, in a subtle form, this fallacy[1] is rampant in the critical writings of neuropsychology. The fallacy occurs in the following manner. A critic presents research

[1] The term *fallacy* is commonly used in philosophy to indicate a general type of erroneous thinking rather than a specific error. This usage of the term *fallacy* appeared appropriate to the intentions of this chapter.

studies that show that a test, battery, method, or approach has not been impressively validated and concludes or implies, on the grounds of the research studies that have been performed, that one should not use this test or battery. At another point in the writing, the same critic advocates the use of a different test, battery, method, or approach for the same purpose. No validation or reliability studies have ever been performed on this alternative procedure. The critic states or implies that this alternative procedure is highly valid and should be used. The implied basis for this belief is that no one can point to a study that shows the procedure to be invalid.

Application to Lezak's Work

Lezak's book is full of such arguments, especially in the review of the HRB and its derivative tests and batteries. The review seemingly demonstrates the faults of the HRB, implying that one should not use this battery. Elsewhere in the same book, she advocates using her battery. Not one study in the entire book is concerned with the validation of the method proposed in Lezak's book, thus every review statement using research results that implies that the HRB or the HRNES is too invalid to be used clinically, commits this fallacy. Both of these methods have been validated as batteries.

Battery Validity

The fallacy of nonrefutation implies validation. The contention in this chapter is that, because batteries are used to assess human performance as well as individual tests, the batteries should be validated as rigorously as are single tests. If a battery is, in fact, only a group of unrelated tests, then this requirement does not apply and each test must be evaluated on its own. However, any method or battery that claims to have merit as a unified entity, rather than as a group of unrelated tests, should be statistically treated as a unit. This is the manner in which the WAIS–R battery has been treated. The rules related to norming, reliability, and validity must be applied to such units as well as to individual tests (Russell, 1995). In her critiques, Lezak jumps from extreme concern with reliability, validity, and norming for individual tests to an almost complete disregard for these psychometric requirements when groups of tests are concerned, even though she believes that the use of test batteries for assessment is necessary.

In failing to examine battery validity, Lezak overlooks the rule for determining the validity of a battery when a battery has not been validated as a unit. If the battery has not been validated as a unit, then its known validity is only equivalent to the validity of the most accurate single test that is used in the battery. Consequently, to determine the most valid answer to any question or hypothesis, one need administer only that test. Administering other tests does not increase the known validity and may decrease it. The examiner may presume that administering more tests increases validity, but when there is no evidence for this presumption, the only validity that can be presented to a court in litigation is the validity of the individual tests.

The validation of batteries is complex, but it may be accomplished through several methods. The most basic method is the use of clinical judgment. Studies using clinical judgment have demonstrated that, in fact, clinicians using a particular battery or method can make valid assessments (Russell, 1995). In addition, objective methods may be used. The preliminary and most common objective method is to use an index. Indexes include the Halstead Index, the HRNES AIS, and the Wechsler IQ scores, among many other indexes. Indexes of lateralization (Adams, 1986; Russell, 1984; Russell, Neuringer, & Goldstein, 1970; Russell & Starkey, 1993) begin to refine the construct validation of neuropsychological batteries. Other actuarial methods, such as discriminant function, may also make a contribution to validation.

Lezak's Review of the HRB and Derivative Batteries

Halstead–Reitan Battery

In her book, Lezak (1995) devotes a number of pages to reviewing the HRB and some derivative batteries. However, she fails to apply any understanding of pattern analysis to her review of the HRB. She makes no mention of pattern analysis (pp. 709–715). Elsewhere she states, "By and large, the use of pattern analysis has been confined to tests in the Wechsler batteries" (p. 168). However, the primary method used by Reitan is that of an inferential pattern analysis (Reitan & Wolfson, 1986). In this regard, without mentioning the HRB, Lezak states, "Probably the most common approach to the psychological evaluation of organic brain disorders is through comparison of the test score levels…, in other words, through analysis of interest score scatter" (p. 167). To support this statement, she references four neuropsychologists, all of whom use the HRB.

Halstead's Original Work

In her review of the HRB, an extraordinary amount of space was devoted to discussing Halstead's original work (Halstead, 1947). Lezak painstakingly examined the norming of this original work, apparently to show that the "norms" were inadequate, at least for the Halstead Index. In this regard she is correct. They were inadequate by present-day standards. Unfortunately, for the review, Halstead's original work is about as relevant to the present-day HRB as saying that jet liners are deeply flawed because the Wright brothers first plane only flew 120 ft. This emphasis on the origin of the HRB is probably because of an inability to understand that a test battery can be developed over time. Obviously, flexible batteries cannot develop.

Reitan's Method

The crux of Lezak's critique was an evaluation of Reitan's method. This consisted of an attempt to demonstrate that what she calls the *clinical* method is superior to Reitan's method (Lezak, 1995, pp. 710–711). The means she used was an attempt to use HRB studies to discredit the HRB method. Although somewhat difficult to follow, her argument evidently follows these steps.

First, she asserts that Reitan uses an "actuarial" method for interpretation. She states, "A distinctive feature of Reitan's handling of the examination data of the HRB has been reliance on test scores for predicting the nature and the site of the lesion as well as its presence" (Lezak, 1995, p. 710). "Predictions about the site of the lesion and its nature (diffuse or focal, static or changing) are based on statistically identified relationships between test scores" (Lezak, 1995, p. 710). She calls such usage an "actuarial approach" (p. 710).

Second, she affirms that several HRB-computerized interpretative programs have been developed that use this actuarial method. "This actuarial approach has encouraged development of computerized interpretations of Halstead–Reitan test protocols" (Lezak, 1995, p. 710).

Third, she quotes studies that used the HRB, which maintain that the "actuarial" method used in the computerized programs is not as accurate as the "clinical" method. Here she quotes G. Goldstein and several studies that found that the clinical method was superior to the actuarial method. From this reasoning, Lezak implies that the "clinical" method is more accurate than Reitan's "actuarial" method. Lezak, of course, espouses the clinical method.

When this argument is examined closely, it is apparent that the argument involved two gross definition shifts. First, Lezak labels Reitan's method an "actuarial" method, when it is, in fact, a clinical method in that clinical inference based on test scores is used to make interpretations. Her statement "Predictions about the site of the lesion and its nature (diffuse or focal, static or changing) are based on statistically identified relationships between test scores" (Lezak, 1995, p. 710) is absolutely wrong. Such a statement indicates her lack of understanding of Reitan's work over the years. Reitan has only used statistics to verify HRB clinical lore, which was derived from clinical experience. He never used statistics to create an actuarial system.

The interpretative computer programs based on the HRB do use "actuarial" or "quasiactuarial" (Heaton, Grant, Anthony, & Lehman, 1981; Russell, 1995) methods, but these actuarial programs should not be confused with the "clinical" method that Reitan uses. The two methods are quite distinct. Reitan's clinical method uses clinical inference based on test scores, whereas an algorithm makes the interpretative decisions in the actuarial computer programs.

Anthony, Heaton, and Lehman (1980), Heaton et al. (1981), and the other HRB studies used the term *clinical* to refer to Reitan's inferential method, which Lezak had relabeled in her review as an *actuarial* method. Thus, Lezak's misapplies the term *actuarial* to Reitan's inferential method.

Lezak's second shift occurs when she implies that the "clinical method" that Goldstein and Shelly (1982), Anthony, Heaton, & Lehman, 1980), Heaton et al. (1981), and other HRB studies used was the same as the clinical method that she advocated in her book. Lezak's method includes the patient's history, medical records, and qualitative analysis of tests as well as test scores, whereas the Reitan clinical method, used in these studies, employed only test scores. In fact, none of these quotes or studies to which Lezak refers use the term *clinical* in Lezak's sense. They all used Reitan's inferential method. (In practice, as opposed to studies, HRB neuropsychologists use patient histories and so on.) Thus, Lezak's attempt to discredit the HRB method is groundless because she does not understand the way that the terms *actuarial* and *clinical* are used in regard to these studies.

In addition, Lezak could not have compared studies of her method with those of Reitan's method because no comparison studies have ever been made between the HRB and her method. In fact, no comparison studies have ever been made between the HRB and any other neuropsychological approach except the LNNB (Golden et al., 1985). (Both methods were approximately equally accurate in assessing the existence of brain damage.) Lezak's clinical method has never been validated, much less compared to Reitan's method. Because no comparative studies were cited, this part of Lezak's review has no relevance to the comparative validity of the HRB.

In addition, out of the vast HRB literature, Lezak picked out the studies and quotes, usually out of context, that were the most damaging to the HRB. A thorough review of the validity of the HRB using both clinical judgment and actuarial programs was later completed by Russell (1995) and found that a large proportion of Lezak's statements in her book concerning the accuracy of the HRB were wrong, inaccurate, or distorted. An example of such distortion is Lezak's use of a study by Klesges, Fisher, Pheley, Boschee, and Vasey (1984).

Review of Klesges et al. (1984)

In regard to validity, Lezak described only one study that reported any low validity rate for the HRB. This was the Klesges et al. (1984) study. It was used to show that "one study found many of the HRB tests to be relatively weak discriminators" (Klesges et al., 1984). The Klesges et al. study found a low correspondence between the diagnosis of brain damage based on a computerized axial tomography (CAT) scan examination (and one other unspecified neurological test) and a discriminant function analysis of the HRB. The results were completely at variance with all of the other 26 studies that have been done (Russell, 1995).

A close investigation demonstrated some very questionable aspects of this study. The diagnosis of only 94 of the 141 "brain-damaged" cases was provided. Thus, the diagnosis of 47 cases was unspecified. Although the average age of the subjects in this study was 35 for the "normals" and 37.5 for the brain-damaged subjects, the classification *trauma* was not included among the diagnostic categories. In any general hospital, head trauma patients compose a large proportion of neurological patients in this age range.

These unusual results are completely accounted for when one realizes that, along with several other diagnostic categories, the *CAT scan will miss head trauma* (when there is no hematoma or skull fracture), especially during the time the data for this study were collected. Thus, the CAT scan would have found no evidence of brain damage for a major proportion of patients who had actually sustained head trauma. This is common knowledge for neurologists and some neuropsychologists (Barth, Gideon, Sciara, Hulsey, & Anchor, 1986; Bigler, 1991). Because these patients were relatively young and obtained from a general hospital, it is apparent that many of the patients in this study had suffered head trauma. Table 4 in the Klesges et al. (1984, p. 32) study, indicates that only 54% of the subjects who were called normal by the CAT scan were designated as normal by the HRB. The HRB was correctly identifying the head trauma cases that the CAT scan missed. Consequently, the Klesges et al. (1984) study was completely defective in regard to the overall accuracy of the HRB and should never have been referenced. The neurological criterion for a neuropsychology validation study should never rely on any single neurological test, even the MRI scans, because every neurological procedure will miss certain kinds of cases. Rather, the neurological criterion for brain damage should be the diagnosis of a qualified neurologist who uses the history and all relevant tests.

Validity of the HRB

What then can be stated about the validity of the HRB method? Contrary to Lezak's review, the validity of the HRB is well established and high. The first demonstration of the validity or effectiveness of the Halstead battery as a clinical instrument was performed by Reitan in 1955 (Reitan, 1955). Again, in a paper published almost 50 years ago, Reitan (1964) produced the most thorough demonstration of the clinical accuracy of the HRB that has been accomplished. In fact, no other study since then has so well demonstrated the clinical validity of any battery or approach. These two papers were completely neglected in Lezak's review. Nor was Reitan's, 1962 *Annual Review* paper referenced. This paper laid out the method of validating a test battery, as well as discussing the validity of the HRB.

Subsequently, a large number of studies have validated the HRB and the computer programs based on it. More recently, the use of clinical judgment with the HRB has been reviewed by Garb and Schramke (1996). All of the validation studies concerned with the HRB have also been exhaustively reviewed by Russell (1995). Russell's review found that the HRB has been validated for the existence of brain damage 39 times: 24 times using indexes, seven times using discriminant function, and eight times using clinical judgment. Because several of these methods were often used in the same study, there have been 26 individual validation studies done on the ability of the HRB to discriminate brain-damaged subjects from normal subjects.

Consequently, the review was able to decisively establish the accuracy of the HRB. The accuracy of indexes varied from 58% to 92%, depending on the conditions, but overall an index was about 80% correct. Clinical judgment in predicting brain damage varied from 72% to 92%, but when the quality of the studies was taken into consideration, the accuracy was about 85%. The accuracy of discriminant function was essentially the same as the accuracy of clinical judgment. Thus, the accuracy of the actuarial programs, including indexes, although not quite as accurate as the clinical judgment of experts, was acceptable for clinical purposes.

The accuracy of most nonexpert neuropsychologists can be estimated from a paper by Garb (1989), who identified the experience level of the participants in a study by Wedding (1983). The Wedding study, which concerned the validity of the HRB, compared the accuracy of 14 judges, the neuropsychological key (Russell et al., 1970) (a computer program), and a discriminant function program. The accuracy was determined through the relative ability of these methods to separate diffuse, right-hemisphere, and left-hemisphere brain-damaged subjects from normals and schizophrenics. The judges included one expert and 13 nonexperts with varying degrees of experience.

The expert was somewhat more accurate than the actuarial neuropsychological key, 63% to 60%. However, the average of the nonexperts was 54%, definitely below that of the key. (The discriminant function had the same accuracy as the expert.) The neuropsychological key was more accurate than all but two of the 13 nonexperts. Thus, this study presents data indicating that at least one neuropsychology actuarial program is more accurate than nonexpert clinical judges using test scores. This finding contradicts the conclusion by Anthony et al. (1980) and echoed by Lezak that the neuropsychological key's accuracy was "...unacceptably low for clinical purposes..." (Lezak, 1995, p. 710).

From this review of the HRB studies, it is evident that Lezak's review of the HRB validity studies distorted the data derived from HRB studies and failed to compare the HRB to any other method. Not one sound research study has demonstrated that the HRB has low validity (Russell, 1995). As such, Lezak's review concerning the validity of the HRB must be considered fallacious.

Except for the LNNB, no validation studies of any assessment methods use batteries other than the HRB. This includes flexible batteries, Benton's battery, the Boston Process Approach, and Lezak's individualized approach. Although these methods are probably fairly accurate, their accuracy is not known; in particular, it is not known whether their accuracy is as great as that of the HRB. They probably are not as accurate, because more work has been devoted to improving the accuracy of the HRB than to any other battery. In addition, undoubtedly the validity of a flexible battery is highly variable and depends on the expertise of the psychologist. Lezak's recommendation of the use of her own battery while she discredits the HRB is an obvious example of the fallacy of nonrefutation.

Factor Structure

Lezak also questions the factor structure of the HRB: "Recent studies of the HRB factor structure produced differing results" (Lezak, 1995, p. 712). In spite of the many factor studies that have been performed on the HRB, the results of only three studies were presented. Examination of these studies found that they did not produce differing results. Even Lezak states, "Replicating this study [two of the three studies referenced]... gave the same set of factors" (p. 712). The results of the third study are obscure in Lezak's review, but they were in no way "differing." From the many factor studies of the HRB (Casey, 1991), it is evident that the HRB provides a consistent set of factors across studies. Except for the LNNB, where are the factor analyses of other batteries, especially Lezak's battery?

Reliability

Lezak also questions the reliability of the HRB Halstead Index and, by implication, the whole battery. "The reliability of the Impairment Index summary score appears to be questionable" (Lezak, 1995, p. 711). This statement was based almost entirely on one study (Matarazzo, Wiens, Matarazzo, & Goldstein, 1974) in which the test–retest reliability was reported as being $r = 0.08$. Russell (1992), in a study conveniently not mentioned by Lezak, reanalyzed these data and demonstrated that this low correlation was because of an artifact, that of a restricted range. When the range was corrected, the correlation became 0.88%.[2]

Other reliability studies using other populations have shown the reliability to be acceptably high (Garb & Schramke, 1996; Russell & Starkey, 1993, pp. 5–6). Only one reliability study has been done on a battery other than the HRB, and it was found to have acceptable interrater reliability (Brown, Del Dotto, Fisk, Taylor, & Breslau, 1993).

Presumed Disadvantages

Lezak states that some of the disadvantages of the HRB are that it "is unwieldy [and] takes relatively long to administer, and is not suitable for the thorough examination of patients with sensory and motor handicaps" (Lezak, 1995, p. 713). In fact, the HRB, including the WAIS–R, can be completed in about 6 h by a technician. Lezak's battery takes "two three-hour examination sessions" (Lezak, 1995, p. 122). At times, the first session may take as long as 6 h (Lezak, 1995, p. 121). Half of Lezak's battery is given by the neuropsychologist. As such, her battery requires considerably more time from the neuropsychologist than the HRB. Thus, one could say of Lezak's battery that it "is unwieldy and takes relatively long to administer."

In regard to patients with sensory and motor handicaps, measurement of these deficits is a forte of the HRB. The measurement procedure related to these deficits is, for the most part, handled by established adjustments in the battery and is accounted for in the scoring system. As such, the scoring makes use of such sensory and motor problems to aid in the interpretation. This usage of the HRB might not be known to a person who has never been trained in the use of the battery. As with every battery, some problems are too severe to be handled without modifying the battery. In this case, there are often established methods that are familiar to a neuropsychologist trained in the use of the HRB.

Batteries Derived from the Halstead–Reitan Battery

There have been several variations on the HRB, some of which Lezak reviews. In particular, a major development related to the HRB has been the creation of three major computerized scoring systems using new sets of norms: the NDS (Reitan, 1987), the CNEHRB (Heaton et al., 1991), and the HRNES (Russell & Starkey, 1993). In regard to these significant developments, Lezak's book is completely inadequate. As far as her book is concerned, Reitan's NDS does not seem to exist because it was not mentioned. In addition, one would not know that the CNEHRB uses a computer scoring program or that the HRNES is primarily a computer scoring program.

[2] I invite any neuropsychologists who knows of a validity or reliability study of any battery, method, or approach other than those related to the HRB or LNNB to inform me of the studies. Such studies will be referenced in any related future publication that I write.

In a footnote (Lezak, 1995, p. 15) Lezak states that the subject of computer programs will not be dealt with in her book except in a few cases where computer use is related to the material she is covering. Although a computer program has been produced for the CNEHRB to aid in scoring, the program was not central to the norms. Consequently, a review of this HRB method falls within the purview of Lezak's book, so the CNEHRB should have been reviewed. However, without providing an explanation, Lezak does not review it. The CNEHRB was recently reviewed (Russell, 1997) and found to have the same problems as the HRNES. Nevertheless, both provide a better scoring procedure for the HRB than any other norms. Because Lezak does not review either the NDS or the CNEHRB, her review of these batteries cannot be discussed.

Halstead–Russell Neuropsychological Evaluation System

Lezak's review devotes a fair amount of space in her book to reviewing the HRNES (Lezak, 1995, pp. 714–715). This is unexpected in that the HRNES, which is entirely a computer scoring program, falls outside the purview of Lezak's book (p. 15). Nevertheless, because she reviews it, her review *will* be examined.

Other Reviews of the HRNES

There have been several reviews of the HRNES that were generally favorable (Lynch, 1995; Mahurin, 1995; Retzlaff, 1995). These reviews were accurate in their description of the program. Although mainly supportive, they had some criticisms that were generally correct. Some of the criticisms were answered in a paper by Russell (1997), and some remain problems. However, the other three existing scoring programs also had these or other problems (Russell, 1997). In the only study so far published of the HRNES, which used airline pilots, Kay, Morris, and Starbuck (1993) found the corrections for educational level to be adequate for both the HRNES and CNEHRB. In a recent article, Heaton, Matthews, Grant, and Avitable (1996) demonstrated that age and education corrections do improve the accuracy of the HRB, especially at the extremes of age and education.

Lezak's Review of the HRNES

Although Lezak's review of the HRNES severely criticizes the battery, almost every statement she makes that was not purely descriptive was incomplete, misleading, or erroneous. Even the most basic description of the HRNES was inadequate in that the review did not mention that the HRNES is a computerized scoring program. This is like reviewing a Microsoft Windows program without telling the reader that the review concerns a computer program. There are also various specific errors and misrepresentations that will be examined in some detail because they concern important but erroneous information concerning the system.

WAIS–R Comprehension

Lezak states that the HRNES will not accept the WAIS or WAIS–R comprehension subtest (Lezak, 1995. p. 714). This is incorrect. During norming, the *N* for comprehension was not as large as for the other subtests because it was not routinely used in Russell's laboratory. It was found to be redundant for neurological patients. The manual (Russell & Starkey, 1993) was not clear on this point. However, if a person had run the WAIS–R portion of the program, then he or she would have immediately perceived that comprehension was included. Consequently, it is quite evident that Lezak only examined the program manual and reviewed this computer program for a professional book without even perusing the actual program.

WAIS and WAIS–R

The review states that the difference between the WAIS and WAIS–R was not equated (Lezak, 1995, p. 714). Again, the manual was not clear in regard to this operation. The computer program allows one to use either test. The HRNES transforms the WAIS scores into WAIS–R equivalent scores by adding the difference between the tests to the WAIS–R norms. This method was demonstrated to provide an acceptable equivalence (Russell, 1992).

Examination Time

Lezak's review estimated that the time required for the battery was 10 h for normal subjects (Lezak, 1995, p. 714). In our laboratory, it takes about 6 h to administer this examination. Patients are regularly scheduled for 8 h, during which time they receive the whole battery, the MMPI–2, and a half-hour interview. The total time is about the same as that required by Lezak's battery (see Lezak, 1995, pp. 121–123).

Coordinated Norms

The review questions whether the norms are "coordinated" because the *N* varies for some of the tests (Lezak, 1995, p. 714). As the manual states, the reference scale norming procedure was designed, among other things, to provide equivalent norms for tests that were not part of the original norming group (Russell & Starkey, 1993, p. 33). This problem does not seem to bother the reviewer when it occurs in the CNEHRB, even though the CNEHRB has no method of producing equivalent norms when the *N* varies.

Norming

Lezak's review questions the norming procedures used in the HRNES because the subjects came from the Veterans Administration system and the normal control or comparison patients were medical patients (Lezak, 1995, p. 714). These procedures are thoroughly discussed in the HRNES manual (Russell & Starkey, 1993) and in a more recent publication (Russell, 1997). With the exception that about nine tenths of the veterans are men, they represent a cross section of the country because a majority of them were drafted. The draft, which supplied most of the veterans in the United States, provided the most representative group of subjects used in any norming program. During the time the draft was actively used, all men in the United States between ages 21 and 45 were subject to the draft. Only those with physical disabilities, mental retardation, or psychosis or who had occupations essential to the war effort were eliminated. Otherwise, they were selected from the general population on a random basis. Thus, these veterans provide the most unbiased sample of the American male population in existence. The representativeness of this selection is supported by the mean IQ of the normal veteran subjects in the HRNES sample. This was a WAIS–R FSIQ of 102. In regard to females, studies have found that only motor tests demonstrate a significant gender difference (Heaton, Grant, & Matthews, 1986; Russell, 1997).

Lezak censures the HRNES for using medical patients as normal controls. This issue is hotly debated in neuropsychology, but in some studies medical patients have been found to better represent the population that is to be assessed clinically than norms using selected normal subjects (Russell, 1988). In addition, Lezak does not mention that the CNEHRB manual avoids stating whether patients with negative neurological examinations were used for norming, raising the suspicion that a portion of their norming subjects were also patients with negative neurological examinations.

The HRNES manual and Russell's (1997) paper discuss the problems that every other attempt at norming the HRB has had. There is no problem with the norming of the HRNES that is not found in all other sets of norms.

After studying the two batteries, Russell (1997) concluded that the norming for both the HRNES and the CNEHRB is more adequately accomplished than any other norms for the HRB tests. Because only the HRB derivative batteries and the LNNB have been normed as batteries, the HRNES and CNEHRB, along with perhaps the LNNB, represent the most acceptably developed norms that are available.

Lateralization Tables

Lezak's review questions the accuracy of the lateralization tables in the manual because the MRI was not used as criterion. True, as with the norming for almost all of the tests reviewed in her book, most of the subjects were tested before the MRI was developed (Lezak, 1995, p. 714). However, is the reviewer so unsophisticated in neurology as to think that neurologists were unable to accurately lateralize focal damage, using autopsies, surgery, and CAT scans, prior to the advent of the MRI? In the HRNES tables, lateralized cases were not used unless there was unequivocal evidence that the patient had lateralized damage. In this regard, the HRNES manual has some of the most accurate and extensive neuropsychology tables in existence. These indicate the ability of various HRB and related tests to detect both lateralization and the existence of brain damage.

Location Charts

Lezak's review labels the two charts of proposed test localization that are in the HRNES manual as "phrenology maps" (Lezak, 1995, p. 714). This critique is unnecessary, unwarranted, and unprofessional. It is unnecessary because the validity of the program itself had no direct relation to the diagrams. They could have been left out of the manual without any effect on the understanding or use of the program. They were included because some neuropsychologists had found them useful. In the caveats provided in the HRNES manual, their character and the cautions for their use were carefully explained.

The criticism is unwarranted because the best neurologists and neuropsychologists use functional diagrams of the brain (Geschwind, 1979; Goodglass, 1980). Lezak's book uses two such "phrenology maps" (Lezak, 1995, pp. 57, 70). One might say the charts in Lezak's book are different because they show functions and not tests. However, phrenology used the term *faculties,* which was simply another name for functions. Thus, the maps of brain functions in Lezak's book are more similar to phrenology faculty maps than are the maps in the HRNES manual.

Lezak's review provides no rationale for criticizing these location maps but substitutes scorn for rationality. Nowhere is a reasoned basis for the scorn presented. Had a rational explanation been attempted, the justification for the review's ridicule of these neuropsychological test location maps would have been seen as weak.

Presumably, the problem with the charts in the HRNES manual was that tests rather than functions were used. A rational criticism might go like this: it is obvious that functions, not tests, are related to various areas of the brain. The brain, after all, does not contain tests. The areas to which tests are related are too poorly known to locate them on a brain map, even when cautions are stated. Further, neuropsychology does not know enough about tests to determine which functions a test represents because a test generally represents several functions. Consequently, "The examiner looks for… evidence of impairment on tests involving function or skills that are associated neuroanatomically, in their cognitive expression" (Lezak, 1995, p. 167). This argument, that Lezak might have presented, appears to be reasonable. Reports are written in terms of functions. As such, Lezak might assume that knowledgeable, professional neuropsychologists describe the functioning of the brain, not test results (Adams, 1986). The difficulty with this reasoning is that research relates tests to areas of the brain, not functions. In support of this contention, almost every test reviewed in Lezak's (1995) book will have studies relating the tests to brain areas. The relation of functions to the brain is only secondarily derived from these studies using tests. In this regard, almost no research has been designed to determine what specific functions are measured by particular tests. In support of this, again examine Lezak's (1995) book. There are almost no research studies demonstrating the functions that particular tests represent. Most of the ideas that people have concerning the functions that a test is measuring are "intuitive" or derived from lore, not research. Consequently, we really do not know what functions particular tests represent. This is the missing link in the argument that functions and not tests can be represented in brain maps. Some neuropsychologists have the temerity to believe that when there is no research relating tests to functions, they, in their infinite wisdom, can disentangle the relationships between functions and tests so as to determine which "functions or skills are associated… *neuroanatomically. in* their cognitive expression" (Lezak, 1995, p. 167).

This is an example of the fallacy of nonrefutation. No research has demonstrated that these intuitive ideas are wrong, so if the ideas have not been proved to be wrong, then they must be right. In fact, our knowledge concerning the location relationship of tests to the brain, especially HRB tests, is better established than that related to functions. Thus, there is more justification for relating tests to areas of the brain than locating cognitive functions to areas. Consequently, the review was unprofessional because lacking a legitimate rational, it stooped to name-calling rather than offering a reasoned critique.

Reliability

The review states that the entire HRNES battery was not subjected to a reliability study (Lezak, 1995, p. 714). This is true. The reliability indications were derived from previous studies (Garb & Schramke, 1996; Russell & Starkey, 1993, pp. 35–36). Incidentally, there have been no reliability studies of other HRB batteries and certainly not of Lezak's method and battery.

Validation

The review questioned the validation studies of the HRNES (Lezak, 1995, p. 714). Such studies, in fact, were extensive (Russell & Starkey, 1993. pp. 35–41). In addition, the validity of the HRNES was supported by the validity studies of the HRB (Russell, 1995). Lezak's attack appears rather hypocritical when her book reports no validation studies of either her method or her battery.

To justify her questioning of the validity of the HRNES, Lezak's review states that, as an example of the inaccurate "level of cognitive functioning of the population contributing to these scores" (Lezak, 1995, p. 714), the cutting point between normality and brain damage for the category test was "10 points higher" than the cutting point of the one that Halstead had derived, which was 51. The HRNES cutting point was given in the manual as 61 (Russell & Starkey, 1994, p. 37, Table 6).

Lezak had previously criticized Halstead's original norms for being based on a sample that had a mean of only 28.3 years (Lezak, 1995, p. 711). She then failed to notice that the mean age for the HRNES sample was 47.1 (p. 32). When corrected to the age of Halstead's sample, the category score cutting point was approximately 48, which was almost the same as Halstead's original score and slightly more stringent. (Prorating was necessary to produce a score at the 28-year age level.) This is rather good agreement for norms that were gathered almost 50 years apart.

Interpretation

The review states that the HRNES has a "rather naively programmed set of recommended interpretations" (Lezak, 1995, p. 714). What this statement is referring to is rather obscure. There was no intention in the HRNES manual of providing an interpretative system (p. 19). The manual does provide some aids for interpretation. Any thorough test or battery will have a similar section—for instance, the WAIS–R manual pages 26–50 cover similar types of material (Wechsler, 1981).

Any attempt at a thorough discussion of neuropsychological interpretation using the HRNES would require a full book in itself. The HRNES is a scoring system with statistical aids that can be used to help interpretation. These include the AIS index and a lateralization index, both of which have been validated (Russell, 1997; Russell & Starkey, 1993). In addition, to provide a statistical basis for interpretation, the manual does present probably the most extensive analyses of the lateralization and diagnostic ability of various neuropsychological tests that have been published.

From this examination of Lezak's review, it is evident that the eloquent peroration advice of her review is based on a critique in which almost every item is wrong, misleading, or pejorative and as such lacks credibility.

Conclusion

From this extensive examination of Lezak's review of the HRB in the most recent edition of her book (Lezak, 1995), it is evident that she has a limited understanding of Reitan's method. Most of her criticisms would be appropriate to a hypothesis-testing approach but not to a pattern-analysis approach. Consequently, much of the critique was misplaced. She failed to understand the reason for a fixed battery in pattern analysis, such as its providing a constant background to reveal the individual characteristics and diagnoses of the patient.

Even then the review was plagued by inaccuracies. Lezak's attempt to question the validity of the HRB confused the meaning of the terms *clinical* and *actuarial* as used in regard to the HRB studies. In addition, Lezak was unable to present a single sound study that questioned the validity of the HRB. The only study that appeared to show a low validity for the HRB was fatally flawed. To the contrary, the validity of the HRB has been thoroughly established, and it is quite appropriate for clinical purposes. When scrutinized, almost no criticism in Lezak's review of either the HRB and HRNES was confirmed. Ultimately, Lezak's review falters on the fallacy of nonrefutation, which asserts that it is a fallacy to condemn methods that have been validated while recommending alternate methods that have not been validated. Lezak questions the reliability, validity, norming, and factor structure of the HRB without presenting a single study concerning any of these aspects of the battery she advocates. In this regard, some of Lezak's criticisms of the HRB or the HRNES might have had some cogency if she had presented any evidence that the method and battery that she advocates had a single study supporting its norming base, its reliability, or its validity.

Summary

Because many neuropsychologists use the HRB, it is important to answer a critical review contained in Lezak's (1995) book. Lezak understands hypothesis testing but not HRB pattern analysis or the use of fixed batteries. A fixed battery provides a constant background that reveals individual characteristics of the patient. Issues discussed include, types of batteries, legitimate review methods, and Reitan's method.

This writing demonstrates that almost all of Lezak's criticisms of the HRB and the HRNES are incomplete, misleading, or erroneous. Her critique of the Reitan method involved a confusion of terms. In spite of attempts to discredit the HRB, not a single sound study questioning the validity of the HRB was presented, whereas many studies have demonstrated its validity. The fallacy of nonrefutation asserts that it is a fallacy to condemn methods that have been validated while recommending procedures that have not been validated. Lezak questions Reitan's method, the HRB, and the HRNES, which have been thoroughly validated, while presenting no validating studies of her own recommended methods.

References

Adams, K. M. (1986). Concepts and methods in the design of automata for the neuropsychological test interpretation. In S. B. Filskov & T. J. Boll (Eds.), *Handbook of clinical neuropsychology* (pp. 561–575) (2nd ed.). New York: Wiley.

American Psychological Association (1985). *Standards for educational and psychological testing*. Washington, DC: Author.

Anthony, W. Z., Heaton., R. K., & Lehman, R. A. W. (1980). An attempt to cross-validate two actuarial systems for neuropsychological test interpretation. *Journal of Consulting and Clinical Psychology*, *48*, 317–326.

Barth, J. T., Gideon, D. A., Sciara, A. D., Hulsey, P. H., & Anchor, K. N. (1986). Forensic aspects of mild head trauma. *Journal of Head Trauma Rehabilitation*, *1*, 63–70.

Bauer, R. M. (1994). The flexible battery approach to neuropsychological assessment. In R. D. Vanderploeg (Ed.), *A guide to neuropsychological practice* (pp. 259–290). Hillsdale, NJ: Lawrence Erlbaum Associates.

Bigler, E. D. (1991). Neuropsychological assessment, neuroimaging, and clinical neuropsychology: a synthesis. *Archives of Clinical Neuropsychology*, *6*, 113–132.

Brown, G. G., Del Dotto, J. E., Fisk, J. L., Taylor, H. G., & Breslau, N. (1993). Analyzing clinical ratings of performance on pediatric neuropsychological tests. *Clinical Neuropsychologist*, *7*, 179–189.

Butler, M., Retzlaff, P., & Vanderploeg, R. (1991). Neuropsychological test usage. *Professional Psychology: Research and Practice*, *22*, 510–512.

Casey, C. J. (1991). *Factor analysis of the Halstead–Reitan neuropsychological battery to investigate the generalized and lateralized effects of brain damage*. Unpublished doctoral dissertation. University of Miami, FL.

Garb, H. N. (1989). Clinical judgment, clinical training, and professional experience. *Psychological Bulletin*, *105*, 387–396.

Garb, H. N., & Schramke, C. J. (1996). Judgment. research and neuropsychological assessment: a narrative review and meta-analysis. *Psychological Bulletin*, *120*, 140–153.

Geschwind, N. (1979). Specializations of the human brain. *Scientific American*, *241*, 180–199.

Golden, C. J., Purisch, A. D., & Harnmeke, T. A. (1985). *Luria–Nebraska neuropsychological battery: Forms I and II*. Los Angeles: Western Psychological Services.

Goldstein, G., & Shelly, C. (1982). A further attempt to cross-validate the Russell, Neuringer, and Goldstein neuropsychological *keys*. *Journal of Consulting and Clinical Psychology*, *50*, 721–726.

Goodglass, H. (1980). Disorders of naming following brain injury. *American Scientist, 68*, 647–655.

Halstead, W. C. (1947). *Brain and intelligence*. Chicago: University of Chicago Press.

Heaton, R. K., Grant, I., Anthony, W. Z., & Lehman, R. A. W. (1981). A comparison of clinical and automated interpretation of the Halstead–Reitan Battery. *Journal of Clinical Neuropsychology, 22*, 121–141.

Heaton, R. K., Grant, I., & Matthews, C. G. (1986). Differences in neuropsychological test performance associated with age, education, and sex. In I. Grant & K. M. Adams (Eds.), *Neuropsychological assessment of neuropsychiatric disorders* (pp. 100–120). New York: Oxford University Press.

Heaton, R. K., Grant, I., & Matthews, C. G. (1991). *Comprehensive norms for an expanded Halstead–Reitan Battery [Norms manual and computer program]*. Odessa, FL: Psychological Assessment Resources.

Heaton, R. K., Matthews, C. G., Grant, I., & Avitable, N. (1996). Demographic corrections with comprehensive norms: An overzealous attempt or a good start. *Journal of Clinical and Experimental Neuropsychology, 18*, 121–141.

Kay, G. G., Morris, S., & Starbuck, V. (1993). *Age and education based norms control for the effects of occupation on pilot test performance*. Paper presented at the annual meeting of the National Academy of Neuropsychology, Phoenix.

Klesges, R. C., Fisher, L., Pheley, A., Boschee, P., & Vasey, M. (1984). A major validational study of the Halstead–Reitan in the prediction of CAT-scan assessed brain damage in adults. *International Journal of Clinical Neuropsychology, 6*, 29–34.

Lees-Haley, P. R., Smith, H. H., Williams, C. W., & Dunn, J. T. (1996). Forensic neuropsychological test usage: an empirical survey. *Archives of Clinical Neuropsychology, 11*, 45–51.

Lezak, M. D. (1988). IQ: R.I.P. *Journal of Clinical and Experimental Neuropsychology, 10*, 351–361.

Lezak, M. D. (1995). *Neuropsychological assessment* (3rd ed.). New York: Oxford University Press.

Lynch, W. J. (1995). Microcomputer-assisted neuropsychological test analysis. *Journal of Head Trauma Rehabilitation, 10*, 97–100.

Mahurin, R. K. (1995). Review of the halstead russell neuropsychological evaluation system. In J. C. Conoley & J. C. Impara (Eds.), *The twelfth mental measurements yearbook* (pp. 448–451). Lincoln: University of Nebraska Press.

Matarazzo, J. D., Wiens, A. N., Matarazzo, R. G., & Goldstein, S. G. (1974). Psychometric and clinical test–retest reliability of the Halstead impairment index in a sample of healthy young, normal men. *Journal of Nervous and Mental Disease, 158*, 37–49.

Reitan, R. M. (1955). An investigation of the validity of Halstead's measures of biological intelligence. *Archives of Neurology and Psychiatry, 73*, 28–35.

Reitan, R. M. (1962). Psychological deficit. *Annual Review of Psychology, 13*, 415–444.

Reitan, R. M. (1964). Psychological deficits resulting from cerebral lesions in men. In J. M. Warren & K. Aken (Eds.), *The frontal granular cortex and behavior* (pp. 295–312). New York: McGraw-Hill.

Reitan, R. M. (1987). *The neuropsychological deficit scale for adults [Computer program, users manual]*. Tucson: Neuropsychology Press.

Reitan, R. M., & Wolfson, D. (1986). The Halstead–Reitan neuropsychological test battery. In D. Wedding, A. M. Horton & J. Webster (Eds.), *The neuropsychology handbook* (pp. 134–160). New York: Springer.

Retzlaff, P. D. (1995). Review of the Halstead Russell neuropsychological evaluation system. In J. C. Conoley & J. C. Impara (Eds.), *The twelfth menial measurements yearbook* (pp. 451–453). Lincoln: University of Nebraska Press.

Russell, E. W. (1984). Theory and developments of pattern analysis methods related to the Halstead–Reitan Battery. In P. E. Logue & J. M. Shear (Eds.), *Clinical neuropsychology: A multidisciplinary approach* (pp. 50–98). Springfield, IL: Charles C. Thomas.

Russell, E. W. (1986). The psychometric foundation of clinical neuropsychology. In S. B. Filskov & T. J. Boll (Eds.), *Handbook of clinical neuropsychology* (Vol. 2, pp. 45–80). New York: Wiley.

Russell, E. W. (1988). Renorming russell's version of the wechsler memory scale. *Journal of Clinical and Experimental Neuropsychology, 10*, 235–249.

Russell, E. W. (1992). Reliability of the halstead impairment index: a simulation and reanalysis of Matarazzo et al. (1974). *Neuropsychology, 6*, 251–259.

Russell, E. W. (1994). The cognitive-metric, fixed battery approach to neuropsychological assessment. In R. D. Vanderploeg (Ed.), *Clinician's guide to neuropsychological assessment* (pp. 211–258). Hillsdale, NJ: Lawrence Erlbaum Associates.

Russell, E. W. (1995). The accuracy of automated and clinical detection of brain damage and lateralization in neuropsychology. *Neuropsychology Review, 5*, 1–68.

Russell, E. W. (1997). Developments in the psychometric foundations of neuropsychological assessment. In G. Goldstein & T. M. Incagnoli (Eds.), *Contemporary approaches to neuropsychological assessment* (pp. 15–65). New York: Plenum.

Russell, E. W., Neuringer, C., & Goldstein, G. (1970). *Assessment of brain damage: A neuropsychological approach.* New York: Wiley.

Russell, E. W., & Starkey, R. I. (1993). *Halstead–Russell neuropsychological evaluation system [Manual and computer program].* Los Angeles: Western Psychological Services.

Wechsler, D. (1981). *WAIS—R. wechsler adult intelligence scale (revised) [Manual].* San Antonio, TX: Psychological Corporation.

Wedding, D. (1983). Clinical and statistical prediction in neuropsychology. *Clinical Neuropsychology, 5*, 49–55.

13 In Defense of the Halstead–Reitan Battery—Revisited

The latest edition of Lezak's classic book (Lezak, Howieson, & Loring, 2004) has again disparaged the Halstead–Reitan Battery (HRB) and the Halstead–Russell Neuropsychological Evaluation System (HRNES) (Russell & Starkey, 1993). This current critique entails a comparison with Lezak's general method. Lezak et al. (2004) have devoted more than 100 pages (pp. 3–38, 86–156) to describing her methodology as the ideal method for assessment. In contrast, in their critique of the HRB and HRNES, Lezak et al. (2004) advise the reader as to how neuropsychological assessment should not be performed. The implication was that the HRB and HRNES methods were faulty and should not be used. As such, a comparison of the two methodologies becomes imperative. This comparison would permit the judicious neuropsychologist to select his or her assessment method.

The Archaeological Fallacy

In regard to Lezak et al.'s (2004) review, as in Lezak's (1995) previous review, much of the criticisms are irrelevant primarily because of what may be called the "archaeological fallacy," because this material belongs to neuropsychology's distant past. Lezak et al. (2004) appear to go to great lengths to excavate ancient work to present negative points concerning the present HRB program (pp. 670–672). They spend more than 20% of the review discussing Halstead and Reitan's early contributions. In this regard, Lezak has an *idée fixe* concerning the original study presented by Halstead in 1947, which was published well over a half century ago (Lezak, 1995, pp. 711–712; Russell, 1998). Although this work was an excellent research study, it was long ago replaced by subsequent research, so it is no longer relevant to the contemporary validation of the HRB.

True, the Halstead Index (HI) (Halstead, 1947) is still being used (in its seven-item form). However, none of its current utility was derived from Halstead's original 1947 study (Russell, 2008). Rather, it is derived from a great number of subsequent studies supporting its validity. There are far more studies supporting its validity than any other neuropsychological procedure (Chapter 9).

Consequently, the statement made in the previous critique (Russell, 1998) concerning Lezak's review remains pertinent: "Unfortunately for the review, Halstead's original work is about as relevant to the present day HRB as saying that jet liners are deeply flawed because the Wright brothers first plane only flew 120 feet" (Russell, 1998, p. 371).

The Scientific Foundation of Neuropsychological Assessment. DOI: 10.1016/B978-0-12-416029-3.00013-0

When Is a Method Outdated?

A possible reason that Lezak et al. (2004) emphasize this old study is that this gives the impression that the HRB is out of date. The term *outdated* is used repeatedly in neuropsychology. Unfortunately, this produces the impression that neuropsychology as a whole has no durable knowledge. In the eyes of many scientists, this in itself stigmatizes neuropsychology as a "soft science."

In the Sciences Nothing Is Outdated by Time Alone

Galileo's observation of moons circling Jupiter is still accepted even though those observations were made in 1610. In science, a concept or methodology may be replaced by more recent studies that produce more accurate information or a more efficient methodology. However, these published studies that revise science must generally be "peer reviewed."

In regard to outdated methodology, Lezak's method is only a slight improvement on that used in 1941 by Goldstein and Scheerer. She would still find the following statement by them acceptable:

> *[T]he usual scoring method based on a scale of difficulty which has been standardized on a statistical basis offers no adequate instrument for determining the nature or degree of impairment of a patient. Unless one takes into account the entire procedure, the specific reasons for the difficulty the patient encounters, one cannot simply read off from a score which task represents a greater difficulty and which a lesser. Any statistical evaluation has to be based upon a qualitative analysis of test results* (Goldstein & Scheerer, 1941, p. 19).

It was more than a decade after this publication that Reitan (1955b) introduced his new method in which the results of an entire fixed battery were validly used to analyze results of a patient's brain functioning and pathology.

Subsequently, Lezak incorporated into her assessment method the use of a battery of tests and also used psychometrically derived individual test scores. Otherwise, her method is similar to the 1941 work of Goldstein and Scheerer. Thus, more than 60 years after Goldstein and Scheerer's work, Lezak et al. (2004) wrote, "A test-score approach to psychological assessment that minimizes the importance of qualitative data can result in serious distortions in the interpretations, conclusions, and recommendations drawn from such one-sided data base" (p. 136). Which method—Lezak's or Reitan's—is outdated?

The Rejection of "Primitive" Neurology

Also, in regard to being out of date, Lezak et al. (2004) consider that before magnetic resonance imaging (MRI), neurology was so primitive and inaccurate that all previous studies could be dismissed as essentially worthless: "A problem for early HRB research—or any other neuropsychological studies performed at that time—was the 'primitive' state of neurological diagnostic tools" (p. 672). Apparently, Lezak et al.

(2004) believe that because neurological diagnostic tools were too "primitive" for an accurate diagnosis before the MRI, no previous valid scientific neurological research existed.

This consigns more than a half century of neuropsychological work to the wastebasket. But, more critically, it also means that three centuries of neurological research is largely worthless. As such, all neurological findings in the "before the MRI era," such as the work of Broca, Wernicke, Luria, Head, Teuber, and Geschwind, should be dismissed.

In contrast to this emphasis on scanning procedures, neuropsychologists, who did not work with neurologists before the development of scanning techniques, continually fail to consider that, along with many relatively accurate neurological methods such as neurosurgery, angiograms, and autopsies, the most accurate basis of diagnosis was as fully usable then as today. This basis of diagnosis is *time*. Almost all progressive lesions eventually manifest themselves and can ultimately be accurately diagnosed, even if it is from an autopsy. In addition, scanning techniques remain unable to diagnose many conditions such as Alzheimer's disease, certain vascular pathologies, and closed head trauma unless a condition involves a hemorrhage (Bigler, 1991; Russell, 1998).

The great advantage of scanning techniques is that, along with not being invasive, they provide a diagnosis and localization of focal progressive lesions at an earlier point in their progression than was previously possible. This enables treatment to begin more rapidly and precisely. However, there is a real question as to whether the scanning techniques have greatly increased the ultimate accuracy of careful neurological diagnostic methods.

The Clinical and Research Basis for the HRB

Nevertheless, the primary failure of Lezak et al.'s (2004, p. 671) critique is that it confuses Reitan's clinical work with his research. Reitan retains this distinction quite consistently (Reitan, 1966; Reitan & Wolfson, 1993, pp. 30–36). Lezak et al. (2004) state, "The original goal of the HRB protocol was to collect research data, not to provide clinical information" (p. 671). Lezak et al.'s (2004) implication is that because the HRB was a research project, it is not clinically adequate. To support this contention, Lezak et al. (2004, p. 671) excavated Reitan's 1966 review of his scientific research.

Although neuropsychologists can still benefit from reading this review of Reitan's research methodology, the chapter was not intended to describe the clinical use of the HRB. If Lezak et al. (2004) intended to discuss the HRB as it has been used clinically, they should have referred to the most recent manual by Reitan and Wolfson (1993). In this work, the experimental and clinical methods are clearly differentiated (pp. 30–32) and the clinical use of the HRB is clearly described.

Reitan's Clinical Method

Although Lezak et al. (2004) stated that Reitan's 1966 work was a research protocol, they treated it as if it were a description of Reitan's clinical method. They state that

Reitan interpreted the findings of the HRB "without knowledge of patient history or neurological findings, and apparently, feedback was not given to the referral source much less the patient" (p. 672). Because this blatantly misrepresents his clinical method, it is necessary to describe Reitan's actual method (1970, 2007a).

Reitan's method was simultaneously threefold: (1) it performed a valuable clinical service to the hospital, (2) it enabled the development of an inferential clinical understanding of neuropsychological findings, and (3) it provided the basis for the research that supported the clinical assessment of his battery.

To accomplish these purposes, Reitan's method was to write the report based entirely on test results. He made a very deliberate attempt to ensure that the results of his neuropsychological testing were not influenced by knowledge of the patient's history or neurological diagnosis (Reitan, 2007b). The initial assessment was written "blind"—that is, without knowing a patient's history or neurological findings (Reitan, 1962). Thus, Reitan and his protégées had no knowledge of the patient, except the test results, age, education, and gender, before writing their report.

An assistant in his laboratory who had no contact with patients worked with the referring physician (usually a neurologist or neurosurgeon) to complete a full record of each patient's history, neurological findings, and diagnosis (including whether the diagnosis was firmly and unequivocally established). A diagrammatic representation of the lesion that the surgeons or neuropathologists observed at surgery or autopsy was included when possible. Funds were available to finance a neurosurgeon who summarized the complete medical record of patients who were tested. These results were then presented to Reitan to compare with the assessment report and included in the files of each patient.

In regard to the HRB's clinical function, many areas of the hospital, but primarily neurology and neurosurgery, referred patients to Reitan's laboratory. Reitan and his protégées did not see patients before writing their reports. A staff assistant handled the intake and the technician's work. The technician administered and scored the test results. Because several technicians were used, at times as many as 15 patients were examined per week.

After testing was complete, each report was written based entirely on test results. Only then did Reitan and his colleagues compare his report to the neurological findings. This report was used in the patient's treatment. The neuropsychological findings, along with the neurological record, became part of the hospital neurological workup. This information was presented to patients and their families by their doctors.

The hospital staff knew that Reitan's reports were "blind." Consequently, they also knew that they were obtaining an unbiased report of neuropsychological test findings, not simply a recapitulation of the results, that the neurologist had already placed in the progress notes and reports. Of course, Reitan was mistaken at times, but his contribution was so often correct and valuable that he was given complete cooperation by the hospital.

The research aspect of Reitan's work had two aspects. First, the blind analysis of records provided the discovery part of science that provided the clinical lore on which the HRB clinical assessment is based. Second, the patient's files became the basis for published research studies.

In terms of discovery, after issuing his report, Reitan received the neurological feedback just described about the patient's condition, which he compared to his neuropsychological findings and report. This enabled him to discover when he was correct and when and how he made mistakes. The blind-analysis method enabled Reitan and his students to develop a clinical acumen that was unparalleled in its accuracy.

Studies of clinical judgment have found that feedback, unbiased by prior knowledge of a patient's condition but subsequently compared to clinical judgment, is the only fully effective method of learning how test results are related to brain functioning (Garb, 1998, pp. 201–204). This method completely avoids confirmatory bias (Lezak et al., 2004, p. 140).

Lezak et al. (2004, p. 674) attempted to attack Reitan's blind-analysis method by comparing a patient's diagnosis from (Reitan, 1959) to the same case in Reitan and Wolfson's manual (1993), which they describe as having a different diagnosis. They wrote that Reitan's second diagnosis was "neoplasm." They stated that the patient was "(WC # 20)" (no page reference was given). However, on examining Reitan and Wolfson's manual (1993), the case was W.R.C., not W.C. (p. 673), and "# 20" refers to the case number in Reitan and Wolfson's book. This patient was, in fact, diagnosed this way: "his test results are fairly typical of a patient with a primary neuronal degenerative disease" (p. 680). This patient was definitively diagnosed from a biopsy as having Alzheimer's disease (Reitan & Wolfson, 1993, p. 677). Because it was 39 years since the first report (Reitan, 1959), it could not have been the same patient. If Lezak et al. (2004) were going to use a case as an example of the inadequacy of Reitan's method, then they at least ought to get the case right.

Reitan's Research

The 1966 chapter by Reitan, which was critiqued by Lezak et al. (2004, pp. 670–676), presents the first lengthy description of the research program that Reitan used to validate his clinical approach. Although Reitan's research (1962, 1966) was separated from his clinical work, it was integrated with that work and supported the judgments used in his clinical reports.

The data from Reitan's files were the basis of his research. Somewhat simplifying the situation, Reitan collected most of his cases from the hospital patients who were tested in his laboratory. The control cases were generally patients who had no neurological condition. When their neurological examinations showed that they had no past or current evidence of brain damage, they were assigned to the control group (Reitan, 2007b). Other control cases consisted of persons hospitalized for various non-neurological conditions and complaints, including paraplegia, spinal problems, emotional disturbances (excluding psychosis), and other medical illnesses.

Thus, the control group subjects were equivalent to the experimental group because the control and the neurological patients were generally derived from the same initial subject pool, which consisted of patients who were suspected of having brain damage. Such volunteers did not come from a "volunteer" group that had no connection to the experimental patients, and on average they had a full-scale intelligence quotient (FSIQ) almost one standard deviation (1 SD) above the brain-damaged group (Russell, 2004, and Chapter 14).

When enough pathology cases of a certain type had been collected for an adequate research study, Reitan and students could assemble a group of patients with a particular condition or lesion location to match the control group. With this arrangement, he could statistically test an inferential concept that was derived from his clinical work.

Because Reitan used the same battery of tests over the years, he was able to obtain groups of subjects for research who had many various neuropsychological conditions. Examination of these groups enabled him to directly compare their patterns of impairment both to other conditions and control subjects.

This work demonstrated the utility of using a fixed battery for both research and clinical purposes. The findings from research were directly applicable to clinical assessment (Reitan & Wolfson, 1993, pp. 33–35; Russell, 2005). Research, then, was a second form of feedback that increased the accuracy of the HRB. Thus, clinical and research were closely integrated forms of work that supported each other. In contrast, even the most recent tome by Lezak et al. (2004) is largely lacking in the type of research designed to discover and verify patterns of damage found in assessment, which Reitan demonstrates in this 1966 writing.

In their book, Lezak et al. (2004) do not describe research projects or laboratory work designed to validate the procedures for examining relationships between tests and diagnoses derived from her method. Whereas Reitan and his followers emphasized accuracy derived from research, Lezak emphasized clinical judgments that were subjectively related to results derived from voluminous and largely unintegrated research studies using a myriad of unrelated tests. Undoubtedly, she and other users of this method could build some clinical judgment experience over the years, but such experience remains subjective, difficult to teach, and almost entirely unvalidated (Garb, 1998, pp. 155–170).

The Psychometric Adequacy of the HRB

Much of the critique by Lezak et al. (2004) is devoted to criticizing various psychometric aspects of the HRB. There are so many inaccuracies in their review that they cannot be described in detail. However, one of the most egregious misrepresentations is the quotation of Reitan's statement that Halstead's instructions were inadequate (p. 673). Lezak et al. (2004) used this statement to support their concept that "[t]he HRB does not meet the basic requirements of test standardization" (p. 673). This is a gross example of an archaeological excavation. Halstead wrote his book in 1947 as a research study. He never intended to establish "norms." In regard to instructions, it is noteworthy that Lezak et al. (2004) did not refer to the 192 pages of instructions in Reitan and Wolfson's manual (1993, pp. 119–311) or to the extreme care given to the training in administration procedures used in Reitan's laboratory.

In line with this misrepresentation, Lezak et al. (2004) apparently did not know the instructions for administering the HRB and did not consider or heed Russell's (1998) previous appraisal and critique of Lezak's earlier criticisms of the battery. Consequently, many misrepresentations are repeated. For instance, the HRB can easily be administered to people with various disabilities, although, just as with Lezak's own assessment method, the HRB must be modified. Often the modifications are built into the instructions.

Another example is Lezak et al.'s (2004) continued overestimation of the length of time it takes to give the HRB and HRNES (p. 676) and underestimation of the time required to give the Lezak battery (Russell, 1998). The HRB requires roughly 5 to 6 h for patients who are relatively intact, whereas the HRNES–R for forensic evaluations is administered in three 3-h sessions in our laboratory. This includes the interview and psychological testing such as the Minnesota Multiphasic Personality Inventory and Millon Clinical Multiaxial Inventory as well as the HRNES–R battery.

Examination of the administrative time given in Lezak's previous book (1995, pp. 121–123) indicates that the individual tests in the basic battery require 3 to 4 h and the paper and pencil tests another 3 to 4 h. This is 6 to 8 h of testing for the basic test battery. Then the examiner may administer a number of other tests that probably require an additional few hours. As such, the total testing time may easily reach 8 to 10 h. The new volume (Lezak et al., 2004, p. 111) retains the same testing format, so presumably the time is similar.

The fact is that adequate neuropsychological batteries require approximately the same length of time. It is just not possible to perform a comprehensive examination of human brain functioning in less than 6 to 8 h, whether using a fixed or flexible battery. Unlike passive physiological tests such as a blood sample or MRI, the neuropsychological examinations require the patient to perform tasks for each test, and reliable performance requires considerable time. Thus, to obtain an adequate score requires time. Of course, screening procedures require less time (Reitan, 2006), but they are less accurate and certainly less comprehensive. Consequently, they often provide insufficient information. A single test for "brain damage" can be given in less than 15 min and, according to Spreen and Benton in 1965, they were about 71% correct. Today the digit symbol, which is given in 5 to 10 min, has a total predictive power of about 78% (Russell, 2004).

Alternate Versions of the HRB

Lezak et al. (2004) spent much of two pages (pp. 672–673) discussing alternate versions of the HI and the HRB. These versions generally have little relevance to Reitan's HRB. With the exception of the General Neuropsychological Deficit Scale (GNDS) (Reitan, 1991), this section of the review applies the label "HRB" indiscriminately to any number of sets of tests that contain HRB tests, many of which have little connection with Reitan's work. Obviously, they do not constitute an evaluation of the HRB.

In this regard, it is almost unbelievable that Lezak et al. (2004) would make the following statement about the various HRB related norms: "With so many available norms, it is possible to choose ones based on desired outcomes" (p. 673). This is precisely the concern in regard to any flexible battery. The large number of available tests and norms (Lezak et al., 2004; Mitrushina, Boone, & D'Elia, 1999; Mitrushina, Boone, Razani, & D'Elia, 2005) enable the neuropsychologist to choose tests and norms to obtain any "desired outcomes."

In addition, after their cursory examination of test batteries that have little relationship to the HRB, Lezak et al. (2004) come to the astounding conclusion that the HRB is not a "fixed" battery (p. 673). This is completely illogical. Reitan accepts only one form of his battery (Reitan & Wolfson, 1993). Although other people have added tests to obtain additional information, these batteries are not "the HRB" but some other battery using parts of the HRB. Reitan has not changed his battery so that the HRB is fixed. Obviously, none of the conclusions derived from this irrelevant critique of unrelated batteries are applicable to the HRB. If the concern is with these variations of the HRB, then each one should be evaluated.

As an example of this lack of relevance, as well as grave robbing, Lezak et al. (2004) devote one-quarter of a page (p. 672) to discussing the average impairment rating (AIR) index, which was derived from a book by Russell, Neuringer, and Goldstein, published in 1970. The AIR was never part of the HRB. It was initially devised by Philip Rennick without any input from Reitan. Although this scale may still be used by some neuropsychologists, it was extensively revised in Russell's laboratory many years ago (Russell, 1984) as part of the development of the HRNES and the HRNES–R (Russell & Starkey, 2001). Consequently, any discussion of the AIR has no relevance to either the HRB or the HRNES–R or any other battery.

The HRB Norms

Again Lezak et al. (2004) demonstrate their complete lack of understanding of Reitan's HRB method in the section on HRB norms (pp. 673–675). In regard to Lezak's penchant for archaeology, Lezak et al. (2004, p. 673) begin the section on normative data by again digging up Halstead's original sample with the implication that it constitutes norms for the HI or HRB. To repeat (Russell, 1998), this work by Halstead, which was a research study, was never intended to be a normative sample and was never used by Reitan or anyone else. Later studies demonstrated the accuracy of the seven-test version of the HI.

In regard to the GNDS scales, Lezak is completely incorrect when she describes them as being derived from norms (p. 674). The study that Lezak et al. (2004, p. 674) refer to (Reitan, 1985) was not a "norming" study but a "preliminary validation study" (Reitan & Wolfson, 1993, p. 353). Reitan's research studies were designed to measure relationships between brain-damaged and non–brain-damaged subjects on neuropsychological variables rather than to provide general norms (Reitan, 2007a). Rather than depending on the results of a single large sample or a few unrelated samples, as is customarily done in neuropsychological normative studies, Reitan reviewed many studies that he and his colleagues had published to determine the cutting points that consistently differentiated brain-damage and control groups. From this work, he identified the scores that most accurately separated the brain-damaged and control groups.

Next, four categories of performances were designated: (0) above average, (1) normal, (2) mildly to moderately impaired, and (3) severely impaired. The crucial separation is between categories 1 and 2. The scores of 0 and 4 were based on Reitan's judgment. Many other validation studies have been completed and published that support these cutting points. They are reviewed in Chapter 9 in this book, which Lezak et al. (2004) do not mention in their reference list.

The Psychometric Reliability of the HRB

The reliability of the HRB and later the HRNES (p. 677) was also discussed by Lezak et al. (2004), who stated, "Findings of studies examining the reliability of the Halstead Impairment Index have been mixed" (p. 675). Again this is a misrepresentation. As their *only* example of short time poor reliability, Lezak et al. (2004) mention one test–retest reliability study, which was the Matarazzo, Wiens, Matarazzo, and Goldstein (1974) study. This study found almost no test–retest correlation for the HI ($r = 0.08$). However, these meticulous reviewers of the literature failed to mention a reexamination of this study published in 1992 by Russell. This reexamination found that the low test–retest correlation resulted from an artifact of range restriction. Without this artifact, the correlation would have been 0.88.

More recent studies (Dikmen, Heaton, Grant, & Temkin, 1999) have found high 10-month test–retest reliabilities for the HI (0.88) and other HRB tests. As expected, reliabilities become lower as the time between testings increased. These results represented the same reliabilities that occur with the individual tests used in Lezak's methodology. Consequently, the results of the reliability studies were not mixed. They support the reliability of the HI and HRB tests.

The Validity of the HRB

In reporting studies on the validity of the HRB (p. 675), the author's review (Lezak et al., 2004) generally ignored supporting material. The section titled "Neuropsychological Findings" begins, "Tests of HRB effectiveness in identifying lesion laterality have produced equivocal results" (p. 675). Committing the "the fallacy of biased selection," the authors only selected studies that supported their contention. Lezak et al. (2004) quote selected studies indicating that the HRB only lateralizes lesions because of its inclusion of sensory and motor tests. They ignore the huge literature beginning with Reitan's (1955a) study indicating that Wechsler batteries, which are included in the HRB, can lateralize lesions without any sensory or motor tests (Barron & Russell, 1992; Lezak, 1995, pp. 696–698). Although disparaging the lateralization ability of the HRB, these conscientious reviewers again do not mention the review by Franzen (2000, pp. 125–126) or the most complete review and evaluation of lateralization studies available (Russell, 1995), which—to repeat—is not even in their index. Russell's review found that if only right and left lesions are involved, then the lateralization ability of the HRB was between 85% and 90% correct. There is nothing "equivocal" about these results. By contrast, Lezak et al. (2004) do not mention a single study in their tome that supports the ability of Lezak's methodology to lateralize lesions.

In regard to the existence of brain damage, Lezak et al. (2004, p. 675) provide a number of studies in an attempt to show that the Wechsler tests were as accurate in diagnosing brain damage as the HRB. The authors failed to mention the comparison by Russell and Starkey (1993, pp. 38–39, Table 7). This table demonstrated that when using the same sample, the HRNES indexes, which were largely composed of HRB tests, were considerably more accurate than the Wechsler IQ scales.

Recently, Loring and Larrabee's (2006) archeological study of Reitan's two 1955 studies on the HRB (1955a, 1955b) and the Wechsler–Bellevue Intelligence Scale (Wechsler, 1944) attempted to demonstrate that the intelligence test was as sensitive to the existence of brain damage as the HRB. To do so, they used the relatively new statistical concept of effect sizes.

Unfortunately, when these statistics were reexamined leaving out the three tests from the original HI that are not sensitive to brain damage (Russell, 2008), the HI effect size was very strong at 1.77, whereas the FSIQ was only 0.96. Thus, the HI as normally used in 1955 (Reitan, 1955b) was considerably more accurate in assessing the existence of brain damage than the Wechsler intelligence test.

It is not surprising that Wechsler tests are often relatively accurate in diagnosing brain damage because they are cognitive measures like the HRB. The advantage of the HRB tests is that they. are primarily fluid intelligence tests, whereas the Wechsler (1944) tests, especially the verbal tests, are generally crystallized. Fluid-ability tests are simply more sensitive to brain damage (Barron & Russell, 1992; Russell, 1979, 1980, 2008).

To support their contention that the HRB is not highly accurate, Lezak et al. (2004, p. 675) again cite the Klesges, Fisher, Pheley, Boschee, and Vasey study (1984, p. 675) as evidence of the questionable validity of the HRB, even though this study was demonstrated to be completely fallacious in Russell's (1998) previous review of Lezak's work. Perhaps the authors have continued to cite this study because it is the *only* study of the HRB that questioned the battery's validity.

Questioning the Validity of the HRB: A Pointless Task

Over the years, the HRB has accumulated a far greater amount of research that supports its validity than any other neuropsychology assessment procedure. At least three fairly thorough general reviews of these studies support the accuracy of the HRB and HI: Franzen (2000) and Russell (1995) and, for clinical judgment, Garb (1998). Again, it is rather surprising that such meticulous literature researchers as Lezak and her coauthors did not include any of these major references in the Lezak et al. (2004) index, much less in the text "(See Chapter 9 for a complete new review of these studies).

This material was previously reviewed in the critique (Russell, 1998) of the HRB in Lezak's third edition (1995).

Based on Russell's review in Chapter 9, it was found that the HRB has been validated for the existence of brain damage at least 39 times: 24 times using indexes, seven times using discriminant function, and eight times using clinical judgment. Because several of these methods were often used in the same study, by 1995 there had been 26 individual validation studies performed that support the validity of the HRB.

The General Neuropsychological Deficit Score (GNDS) was also discussed in Lezak et al. (2004, pp. 672–673). After describing the computer program, a number of supposed problems with it were presented. However, Lezak et al. (2004) did not reference any of the studies that have evaluated the GNDS.

The GNDS validation study reported in the manual (Reitan & Wolfson, 1993, pp. 350–364) compared a group of 41 control subjects with a group of 169 subjects representing a broad range of diseases and injuries. The overall results found that only about 10% of the controls earned scores that fell in the brain-damaged range for a 90% sensitivity and about 10% of the brain-damage sample earned scores that were in the control range for 90% selectivity. Cutoff points for the lateralization scales were also evaluated. Finally, a cross validation of the brain-damage, non–brain-damaged cutoff score was accomplished (Wolfson & Reitan, 1995) using entirely separate groups, which confirmed the originally study. The validation studies of the GNDS, which had been performed prior to 1995, are presented in a paper by Russell (1995, p. 11) that Lezak et al. (2004) somehow did not mention even in the book's index. This examination of several studies found the GNDS to be 80% correct and somewhat more accurate than the HI, which was 76% correct (p. 9). These are not equivocal results.

The HRNES and the HRNES–R

In addition to reviewing the HRB, Lezak et al. (2004) reviewed the HRNES (Russell & Starkey, 1993). Almost every criticism was the same as that in Lezak's previous edition (1995), which was answered by Russell (1998). This review is almost completely flawed in that a large portion of the reviewers' statements were not just biased but also factually incorrect.

However, the authors were apparently unaware that 3 years prior to the recent publication of the Lezak et al. (2004) book, the HRNES had been expanded and revised as the HRNES–R (Russell & Starkey, 2001).

Actuarial Evaluations

The reviewers begin their criticism of the HRNES in much the same way that Lezak (1995) had previously criticized the HRB (Russell, 1998): by stating that the HRNES "is an expanded system relying solely on actuarial evaluations" (p. 676). If this statement means that the entire battery is standardized and co-normed so that it is psychometrically designed to obtain accurate and valid interpretations from comparisons between tests, then they are correct. However, this statement apparently means that they consider psychometric thoroughness and validly derived interpretations to be a fault.

The authors indicate that the HRB does not provide information about many important brain functions (p. 676). However, although the HRNES–R is built around the HRB, its tests are not restricted to the HRB. It covers all areas and functions that are covered by the Lezak et al. (2004) system as presented in pages 22–38. Also, the HRNES–R procedure does not preclude an examiner from using additional tests to measure specific functions when no direct procedures in the battery are available.

HRNES-R Norms

Lezak et al. (2004) attempted to attack the HRNES norming by stating, "The different numbers of subjects contributing to the norms of different tests, however, raise questions about how 'coordinated' and comparable scores can be across tests" (p. 677). The reviewers appeared to be completely unaware of the various forms of bridge statistics used to join sets of norms and individual tests to the basic coordinated norm sets. These bridge statistics are explained in the HRNES manual (Russell & Starkey, 1993, 2001); in Appendix F of the HRNES–R; in a chapter by Russell in Rourke, Costa, Cicchetti, Adams, and Plasterk (1991, pp. 399–415); and in this book in Chapter 4. For instance, the norming procedure linear transformation is used to equate tests to the index used in creating the HRNES–R norms. This method is used to derive the scale scores from the AIS index for all tests, including tests with reduced *N* (Russell & Starkey, 1993, pp. 33–35). As a specific example of a poor understanding of co-norming, the reviewers state that the HRNES system would "accept either the WAIS or the WAIS–R without regard to differences between these batteries in raw score values" (p. 676). However, a correction value is built into the system (Russell, 1992; Russell & Starkey, 1993). For the HRNES–R, similar forms of bridge statistics are used to equate the Wechsler Adult Intelligence Scales 3 (WAIS–III) and Wechsler Memory Scales 3 (WMS–III) scores with the earlier versions of the Wechsler tests. This method had previously been described by Russell (1992) but was ignored by Lezak et al. (2004).

The result of using bridge statistics is that the HRNES–R is the only battery that has added tests to the HRB in such a way that all of these scores are statistically equivalent. The tests that were added to the Revised Comprehensive Norms for an Expanded Halstead–Reitan Battery (RCNEHRB) (Heaton, Miller, Taylor, & Grant, 2004) were simply given *t*-scores without equating them to the original normative sample. Thus, the RCNEHRB no longer exists as a set of coordinated norms but is rather like the norms in Mitrushina et al. (1999, 2005). They are often simply a collection of unrelated norms.

Lezak et al. (2004) also criticize the type of subjects used in the HRNES. They state that the HRNES norms were derived from a hospital population. Again, rather than being a fault, this is exactly the way that norms should be gathered. According to the *Standards for Educational and Psychological Testing* [American Educational Research Association, American Psychological Association, & National Council on Measurement in Education (hereafter, AERA et al.), 1999; Reitan & Wolfson, 1993, pp. 33–35; Russell, 2005], *the norming sample should correspond to the population representing such subjects*—that is, a neuropsychology subject suspected of having brain damage (AERA et al. 1999, p. 55) should be compared to norms derived from people who were suspected of having brain damage. In addition, the norms should be collected under the same conditions as they will be tested (AERA et al. 1999, p. 63). This is precisely the situation in regard to both medical and especially forensic subjects.

Lezak deprecates using volunteers (Russell, 2003). In this regard, Russell (2005) found that every set of volunteer norms for the HRB that could be located and which contained an IQ measure had an FSIQ that was approximately 1 SD above the national average. Thus, in accordance with the normal distribution, one-half of these patients in volunteer standardization samples have an intelligence level 1 SD above the national average. This means that one-half of the national population would be impaired if less than 1 SD is considered to indicate impairment. Thus, volunteer norms do not represent a "normal" population. All of these issues raised serious questions for volunteers about the original cutting-score recommendations, such as a *t*-score of 40.

Consequently, most sets of norms derived from the HRB and probably a large portion of individual norms in Mitrushina et al. (1999, 2005) and Strauss, Sherman, and Spreen (2006), being composed of volunteers, are not representative of a normal population.

Also, the HRNES–R provides detailed normative information for the type and source of patients, whereas such vital details are often lacking in other large sets of norms such as the RCNEHRB (Heaton et al., 2004) and most of the tests in Mitrushina et al. (1999, 2005).

Finally, Lezak et al. (2004) questioned the categorization of the brain-damaged subjects used in the HRNES and thus the HRNES–R because only the most recently examined subjects could have their classification checked by an MIR (p. 677). Earlier, this writing demonstrated how accurate neurological diagnosis was obtained before scanning techniques were introduced. Nevertheless, in regard to the HRNES, the CT scan was introduced in 1973, fairly early in the collection of Russell's data. According to records retained for these subjects (Russell, 2009), 193 (96%) of the 200 neurologically normal control group were tested after the introduction of the CT scan, and 483 (84%) of the 576 brain-damaged subjects had neurological examinations after the introduction of the CT scan.

As a further verification of their condition, all subject's records were reexamined at least 1 year after their neurological examination before being accepted for the norms. Patients who had a questionable diagnosis concerning the type of neuropathology were not used. Only 65% of the subjects who were administered a full battery were accepted as having an unambiguous neurological diagnosis. In very few of the norming studies reported by Mitrushina et al. (1999) in their book were the subjects so carefully selected.

The HRNES: Expanding the HRB

Another grievous lack in the Lezak et al. (2004) review is that these authors criticized certain deficiencies in the HRB and then fail to mention that these lacks were remedied in the HRNES–R (Russell & Starkey, 1993, 2001). They criticize the HRB for not having changed but do not mention that the HRNES has changed. Lezak et al. (2004) do list the various tests that the HRNES added so as to provide a relatively complete coverage of the brain. However, Lezak et al. (2004) did not review the revised version of the HRNES in which even more tests were added. The HRNES–R enables the examiner to use the WAIS–III and WMS–III as well as the older versions of these scales, along with the newer versions of many of the common tests included in the battery.

Lezak et al. (2004) criticize the HI for not having been changed and being too brief, but they did not mention that the HRNES has two different indexes based on recent norming (Russell & Starkey, 1993). These use 10 tests instead of 7. Lezak et al. criticize the HRB for a lack of formal memory tests (2004, p. 676) but fail to mention that the HRNES has an extensive group of co-normed memory tests so that the coverage is roughly equivalent to the WMS–III.

They state that the HRB, and by implication the HRNES, language assessment consists of a rudimentary aphasia language screening test (p. 676). They apparently mean the aphasia screening test, which was never intended to be a complete aphasia examination. The speech perception test and Wechsler verbal tests provide the HRB with several tests used to examine language.

The HRNES and HRNES–R have added a number of language tests such as the Boston Naming Test, the Peabody picture vocabulary test, expressive vocabulary test, and wide range achievement test. As such, its general language assessment is quite adequate for a general neuropsychological examination.

Lezak et al. (2004) criticize the HRB "norms" but do not emphasize that the HRNES has well-developed norms (Mahurin, 1995; Retzlaff, 1995; Russell & Starkey, 1993, 2001) based on both normal controls and brain-damaged subjects. They criticize the HRB for a lack of age and education corrections without mentioning that the HRNES has age, ability (IQ or education corrections), and gender corrections.

Phrenology

Lezak et al. (2004) again attack the use of test location maps in the HRNES manual (Russell & Starkey, 2001, p. 22) as an example of "phrenology." This was adequately dealt with in the previous review (Russell, 1998), which specifically states that the locations are only approximate and are based on lore as well as research. However, extensive use of figures illustrating well-known neurology and neuropsychology books are standard practice. In this regard, Damasio (2003) states, "The brain uses a number of dedicated regions working in concert to portray aspects of the body's activities in the form of neural maps" (p. 7). He repeatedly employs the concept of neural maps in his books (p. 351). In addition, almost every neurology book that discuses cognition, motor control, or perception contains location neural maps. For instance, Kolb and Whishaw (1990) present neural maps on pages 173, 269, 426, and 570, among others. More recently, Gazzaniga, Ivry, and Mangun (2002) place maps on pages 65, 196, 358–359, 451, 470, and 510, as well as many more.

Also, Chapter 3 of the newest edition of Lezak et al.'s (2004) classic (titled "Behavioral Geography"—*geography* is a spatial term), unlike most functional neuroanatomy works, has only a few figures localizing functions. Rather, the text has a considerable verbal discussion of function locations. Tests are seldom mentioned in this section, although when tests are described in the body of the book their apparent locations are usually included. Thus, the chapter on behavioral geography in Lezak et al. (2004) provides only a left-hemisphere description of brain functioning. As such, this chapter will be of minimal help to neuropsychologists attempting to gain a spatial understanding of the relationship of specific tests to areas of the brain.

Validity of the HRNES–R

The critique of the validity of the HRNES and consequently the HRNES–R (Lezak et al., 204, p. 677) is completely inaccurate. The HRNES, like the HRB, is both a clinical and research instrument. Thus, the HRNES–R (Russell & Starkey, 2001) was gradually developed from the HRB and the HRNES, almost entirely on the basis of research studies, only some of which have been published. The construct validity of the HRNES–R is based on the HRB and a 35-year history beginning with the *Assessment of Brain Damage* (Russell, Neuringer, & Goldstein, 1970). Its construct validity is documented in many subsequent studies (Russell, 1975, 1984, 1986, 1992, 1995, 1998, 2000a, 2000b, 2004; Russell & Starkey, 1993, 2001). Its validity was reviewed favorably in *The Twelfth Mental Measurements Yearbook* (Mahurin, 1995, pp. 448–451; Retzlaff, 1995, pp. 451–453). In addition, its validity is specified in a study providing operational characteristics of its major indexes and scores (Russell, 1995, 2004). No other battery has had the cutting points and operational characteristics of its tests so thoroughly delineated.

In this regard, Lezak et al.'s (2004) penchant for irrelevant ancient norms found that the HRNES category test average cutting score was 10 points higher than Halstead's (1947) cutting point (p. 677). However, as a reminder of the information originally presented in the first review of Lezak's critique (Russell, 1998), if the difference in the ages of Halstead's and Russell's norms is taken into consideration, then the cutting points were only three points apart.

Conclusion of the HRNES–R Review

In conclusion, Lezak et al.'s (2004) summary of the HRNES and so the HRNES–R is so erroneous and misrepresented that it is useless as a guide to neuropsychologists. Thus, rather than acceding to Lezak et al.'s (2004) prepossession, neuropsychologists should carefully compare the HRNES–R (Russell & Starkey, 2001) and the studies that support it with the completely unvalidated Lezak assessment method (Lezak et al., 2004). If this is done, then test-wise examiners who understand psychometric test development will discover a standardized scoring system for a whole battery that is scientifically derived and thoroughly validated. Experienced clinicians who understand the nature of brain-behavior variability will be interested in a sophisticated and reliable program for examining patterns of brain functioning for interpretations. Practical examiners will want to spend their time on a battery of standard length that is normed on a population with an average intelligence and whose results can be directly generalized to subjects referred for a possible organic condition, including medical patients and forensic clients.

Problems Concerning Lezak's Methodology

To be balanced, a critique should examine the statistics of both contending parties, so it is now appropriate to examine Lezak et al.'s methodology using the same criteria that they applied to the HRB and HRNES–R.

First, not only are no studies presented in their book (Lezak et al., 2004) that support Lezak's method, but a psychometric examination of her method demonstrates a number of problems that question the dependability or forensic reliability of interpretations derived from that method.

Lezak et al. (2004) emphasize the importance of examining many functions in a neuropsychological assessment. This method requires a group or battery of tests rather than a single test (Lezak et al., 2004, pp. 17–18, 111–118). To compare tests, Lezak et al. (2004) state, "In evaluating a patient's performance on a variety of tests, the examiner can only compare scores from different tests when the standardization populations of each of the tests are *identical* [italics mine] or at least reasonably similar, with respect to both demographic characteristics and scored distribution" (p. 144). This requirement is psychometrically correct only if there is co-norming. Accuracy requires co-norming.

The HRB, HRNES–R, and some other batteries conform to this requirement because their tests are fixed or equated using a standardized population so that the relationships between tests remain the same.

The difficulty with this statement in regard to Lezak et al.'s (2004) method becomes obvious when studies indicate that "reasonably similar" is completely insufficient for accurate comparisons. Scales that are not fixed or equivalent cannot be psychometrically compared because it is not clear whether a difference between scores is the result of a difference between the individual's abilities or the result of a difference between norms.

In this regard, Lezak et al. (2004) attempt to dismiss the importance of such variability: "Although this situation results in less than perfect compatibility between the different tests, in most cases the examiner has no choice but to use norms of tests standardized on an undefined mixed or nonrandom adult sample. Experience quickly demonstrates that this is usually not a serious hardship, for these 'mixed bag' norms generally serve their purpose" (p. 147).

First, it is not true that "the examiner has no choice but to use norms of tests standardized on an undefined mixed or nonrandom adult sample." Several batteries use standardized norms. Obviously, the HRB is one but there are also the HRNES–R, the Meyers Neuropsychological Battery (MNB) (Volbrecht, Meyers, & Kaster-Bundgaard, 2000), and the Luria–Nebraska Neuropsychological Battery (Golden, Purisch, & Hammeke (1991).

However, more critical is that in recent years the incompatibility of various norms has become common knowledge. A comparison of the norms in Mitrushina et al. (1999) demonstrate this problem, which Mitrushina et al. (1999) recognize and discuss (pp. 6–7). Even Lezak (2002) reports this as a problem by comparing norms from Mitrushina et al. (1999).

The discrepancies between norms were thoroughly examined in a study by Soukup, Ingram, Grady, and Schiess (1998) as well as in a well-known paper by Kalechstein, van Gorp, and Rapport (1998). Thus, it is now quite clear that various sets of norms may provide incompatible scale scores. More crucially, there is no psychometric method of knowing the amount of incompatibility because the norms have not been statistically compared.

In spite of Lezak et al.'s (2004) assurances, without a fixed battery or standardization to ensure the equivalence of tests, there is no scientifically valid way of determining whether a difference between test scores results from a difference in norms or a difference in an individual's abilities (Russell, Russell & Hill, 2005, Chapters 7 and 8 above). If the expert witness cannot ensure the equivalency of the tests in a comparison used to support an interpretation, then that interpretation will not be forensically reliable.

Combining Tests

As discussed in Russell et al. (2005) and in previous chapters, certain problems occur when tests are used in a group without statistically combining them. There is the statistical probability that any test may be impaired by chance, and there is no way of determining whether an impaired test is impaired by chance or by pathology. When tests are employed in a battery, the probability that a certain number of tests will be impaired depends on the number of tests and the cutting points used to indicate impairment. Although several impaired tests in a flexible battery are more likely to indicate brain damage than just a few tests, the number required to accurately indicate brain damage cannot be known without the employment of a validated index. There is not even a way of determining whether any single test is more accurate than a group of tests. There is no way of determining which of two or more contradictory tests or groups of tests are correct. Thus, unless one combines test scores into a validated index, a group of tests is statistically no more accurate in indicating the existence of brain damage than one test (Russell et al., 2005, Chapters 7 and 8 above).

Forms of Validation

The two forms of psychometric procedures that can be used to validate a battery are formal analysis and clinical judgment. Formal methods such as indexes, except for individual tests, are not used by Lezak or any flexible method (Lezak et al., 2004, pp. 3–38, 86–156). In fact, Lezak is very strongly opposed to the use of even the simplest form of formal indexes such as IQs (Lezak, 1988). Apparently, she is not aware that a test score itself is an index of test items.

The result of this failure to use formal methods is that, as with all flexible methodologies, no part of Lezak's methodology has been formally validated, except for individual tests. As such, the combinations and comparisons of tests used in her battery are forensically unreliable. By contrast, the dependability or forensic reliability of the various formal assessment methods used in the fixed or standardized batteries can be directly determined and validated. Such validity has been demonstrated for the HI, NDS, HRNES–R, and MNB indexes (Reitan & Wolfson, 1993; Russell, 1995; Volbrecht et al., 2000).

Clinical Judgment

Because Lezak's methodology eschews the use of formal scientific methods, except for individual tests, her method depends completely on clinical judgment. As such, it is crucial to examine the accuracy of clinical judgment. Clinical judgment has been thoroughly discussed (Franzen, 2000; Garb, 1998; Russell, 1995).

In regard to clinical judgment, inter-rater reliability of judgment is particularly important because this statistic measures the consistency of a judgment across neuropsychologists (Garb, 1998, pp. 10–14). If neuropsychologists do not agree, then their method cannot be validated. Clinical judgment of batteries, including reliability, was reviewed for neuropsychology by Garb (1998, pp. 155–156), who found that the inter-rater reliability for clinical judgments using batteries varied from good to excellent in various studies.

However, *none* of these studies were performed on Lezak's or any other flexible battery. They were mostly performed on the HRB (See Chapter 9 above). In regard to flexible batteries, including Lezak's approach, Garb states, "Unfortunately, reliability has not been described for the flexible battery and flexible approaches" (p. 157). Thus, the psychometric reliability of a flexible battery, including Lezak's methodology, has never been tested and so remains unknown and unreliable.

In regard to clinical judgment using the HRB, the validity of Reitan's clinical judgment using a fixed battery has been ensured by means of blind analysis (Reitan, 1962, 1964). In the review in Chapter 9 of clinical judgment, eight studies were located concerning the existence of brain damage based on the HRB. The sensitivity to brain damage in percentages varied from 68.7 to 94.4, with an average of 85.7. Selectivity varied from 52.9 to 100 with an average of 90.4. A meta-analysis by Garb and Schramke (1996) found the sensitivity of clinical judgment for the HRB to be essentially the same at 84% (Garb, 1998, p. 159; Garb & Schramke, 1996) as Russell (1995) had found at 85% (p. 31).

Conclusion of the Review

As demonstrated in this chapter, the multitude of studies establishes the validity and rate of error of the HRB and HRNES–R. In contrast, there are no published studies examining the validity of Lezak's method, which uses a whole battery, and there is no information concerning experimental control procedures or rate of error for that methodology. As such, Lezak's method, as with all clinical judgments based on flexible methods, cannot be defended as forensically reliable.

Consequently, the fallacy of nonrefutation (Russell, 1998) applies to Lezak et al.'s (2004) review of the HRB and HRNES–R. (This fallacy consists of criticizing a validated procedure while advocating the use of an unvalidated one because the unvalidated one has not been shown to be invalid.) In the same book in which Lezak et al. (2004) implied that the HRB and HRNES, which would include the HRNES–R, should not be used because they had so many problems, Lezak's method is presented as the ideal procedure. However, nowhere in this vast book (Lezak et al., 2004) are any studies cited that provide any indication of the validity or accuracy of the Lezak method. As such, the entire description of Lezak's methodology (Lezak et al., 2004, pp. 3–38, 86–156) should be considered as an unvalidated position paper rather than as a validated methodology. By contrast, the HRB and HRNES–R are validated methodologies.

Summary

The latest edition of Lezak's classic book, now with coauthors (Lezak et al., 2004), advocates her methodology while criticizing the HRB and the HRNES–R. In regard to the HRB studies, much of Lezak et al.'s critique is irrelevant. Their critique confounds Reitan's clinical assessment method with his scientific research methodology. Nevertheless, Reitan's assessment method was thoroughly supported by his research. The review by Lezak et al. (2004) devotes a considerable amount of space to criticizing nonexistent normative studies because Reitan did not use norms for the HRB and the test scales for the NDS are based on research studies that differentiated pathological and normal subjects and not norms. The HRB's and the HRNES's reliability is criticized for using the same methods employed by Lezak et al. (2004). The criticism of the HRB's validity is largely based on studies that did not use Reitan's HRB but other psychologist's variations of it. Major literature reviews that support the validity of the HRB and HRNES–R were ignored. The critique of the HRNES does not mention that its new version, the HRNES–R, incorporates neuropsychology measures, such as extensive memory tests, that Lezak et al. (2004) fault the HRB for lacking. Both the HRB and HRNES–R are thoroughly validated through extensive research literature, whereas no research studies are provided that validate Lezak's battery methodology in the 105 descriptive pages of the method.

References

Barron, J. H., & Russell, E. W. (1992). Fluidity theory and the neuropsychological impairment in alcoholism. *Archives of Clinical Neuropsychology*, *7*(2), 175–188.

Bigler, E. D. (1991). Neuropsychological assessment, neuroimaging, and clinical neuropsychology: a synthesis. *Archives of Clinical Neuropsychology*, *6*(3), 113–132.

Dikmen, S., Heaton, R. K., Grant, L., & Temkin, N. R. (1999). Test–retest reliability and practice effects of expanded Halstead–Reitan neuropsychological test battery. *Journal of the International Neuropsychological Society*, *5*, 346–356.

Franzen, M. D. (2000). *Reliability and validity in neuropsychological assessment* (2nd ed.). New York: Kluwer Academic/Plenum.

Garb, H. N. (1998). *Studying the clinician: Judgment research and psychological assessment.* Washington, DC: American Psychological Association.

Garb, H. N., & Schramke, C. J. (1996). Judgment research and neuropsychological assessment: a narrative review and meta-analysis. *Psychological Bulletin*, *120*, 140–153.

Golden, C. J., Purisch, A. D., & Harnmeke, T. A. (1985). *Luria–Nebraska neuropsychological battery: Forms I and II.* Los Angeles: Western Psychological Services.

Goldstein, K., & Scheerer, M. (1941). Abstract and concrete behavior: an experimental study with special tests. *Psychological Monographs*, *53*(2), whole issue No. 239.

Halstead, W. C. (1947). *Brain and intelligence.* Chicago: University of Chicago Press.

Heaton, R. K., Miller, S. W., Taylor, M. J., & Grant, I. (2004). *Revised comprehensive norms for an expanded Halstead–Reitan Battery [Norms, manual, and computer program].* Odessa, FL: Psychological Assessment Resources.

Kalechstein, A. D., van Gorp, W. G., & Rapport, L. J. (1998). Variability in clinical classification of raw test scores across normative data sets. *Clinical Neuropsychologist, 12*(3), 339–347.

Kolb, B., & Whishaw, I. Q. (2003). *Fundamentals of human neuropsychology* (5th ed.). New York: W. H. Freeman.

Klesges, R. C., Fisher, L., Pheley., A., Boschee, P., & Vasey, M. (1984). A major validational study of the Halstead–Reitan in the prediction of CAT-scan assessed brain damage in adults. *International Journal of Clinical Neuropsychology, 6*, 29–34.

Lezak, M. D. (1988). IQ: R.I.P. *Journal of Clinical and Experimental Neuropsychology, 10*, 351–361.

Lezak, M. D. (1995). *Neuropsychological assessment* (3rd ed.). New York: Oxford University Press.

Lezak, M. D., Howieson, D. B., & Loring, D. W. (2004). *Neuropsychological assessment* (4th ed.). New York: Oxford University Press.

Loring, D. W., & Larrabee, G. J. (2006). Sensitivity of the Halstead and Wechsler test batteries to brain damage: evidence from Reitan's original validation sample. *Clinical Neuropsychologist, 20*(2), 221–229.

Mahurin, R. K. (1995). Review of the halstead russell neuropsychological evaluation system. In J. C. Conoley & J. C. Impara (Eds.), *The twelfth mental measurements yearbook* (pp. 448–451). Lincoln: University of Nebraska Press.

Matarazzo, J. D., Wiens, A. N., Matarazzo, R. G., & Goldstein, S. G. (1974). Psychometric and clinical test–retest reliability of the Halstead impairment index in a sample of healthy young, normal men. *Journal of Nervous and Mental Disease, 158*, 37–49.

Mitrushina, M. N., Boone, K. B., & D'Elia, L. F. (1999). *Handbook of normative data for neuropsychological assessment*. New York: Oxford University Press.

Mitrushina, M. N., Boone, K. B., Razani, J., & D'Elia, L. F. (2005). *Handbook of normative data for neuropsychological assessment* (2nd ed). New York: Oxford University Press.

Reitan, R. M. (1955a). Certain differential effects of left an right cerebral lesions in human adults. *Journal of Comparative and Physiological Psychology, 48*, 474–477.

Reitan, R. M. (1955b). Investigation of the validity of Halstead's measures of biological intelligence. *Archives of Neurology and Psychiatry, 73*, 28–35.

Reitan, R. M. (1959). The comparative effects of brain damage on the Halstead impairment index and the Wechsler-Bellevue scale. *Journal of Clinical Psychology, 15*, 281–285.

Reitan, R. M. (1962). Psychological deficit. *Annual Review of Psychology, 13*, 415–444.

Reitan, R. M. (1964). Psychological deficits resulting from cerebral lesions in men. In J. M. Warren & K. Akert (Eds.), *The frontal granular cortex and behavior* (pp. 295–312). New York: McGraw-Hill.

Reitan, R. M. (1966). A research program on the psychological effects of brain lesions in human beings. In N. R. Ellis (Ed.), *International review of research and mental retardation* (pp. 156–218). New York: Academic Press.

Reitan, R. M. (1970). Personal communication and experience.

Reitan, R. M. (1985). Relationships between measures of brain functions and general intelligence. *Journal of Clinical Psychology, 34*, 245–253.

Reitan, R. M. (1991). *The Neuropsychological Deficit Scale for adults [Computer program, manual]. From Traumatic brain injury. Vol. II: Recovery and rehabilitation*. Tucson: Neuropsychology Press.

Reitan, R. M. (2006). *Screening procedures for neuropsychological impairment, using subtests from the Halstead–Reitan Battery*. Paper presented at the Third Annual Convention of the Coalition of Clinical Practitioners in Neuropsychology, Las Vegas.

Reitan, R. M. (2007a). Personal communication, 11 January.

Reitan, R. M. (2007b). Personal communication, 6 December.

Reitan, R. M., & Wolfson, D. (1993). *The Halstead–Reitan Neuropsychological Test Battery: Theory and clinical interpretation* (2nd ed.). Tucson: Neuropsychology Press.

Retzlaff, P. D. (1995). Review of the halstead russell neuropsychological evaluation system. In J. C. Conoley & J. C. Impara (Eds.), *The twelfth menial measurements yearbook* (pp. 451–453). Lincoln: University of Nebraska Press.

Rourke, B. P., Costa, L., Cicchetti, D. V., Adams, K. M., & Plasterk, K. J. (Eds.), (1991). *Methodological and biostatistical foundations of clinical neuropsychology*. Berwyn, PA: Swets & Zeitlinger.

Russell, E. W. (1975). A multiple scoring method for the assessment of complex memory functions. *Journal of Consulting and Clinical Psychology, 43*, 800–809.

Russell, E. W. (1979). Three patterns of brain damage on the WAIS. *Journal of Clinical Psychology, 35*(3), 611–620.

Russell, E. W. (1980). Fluid and crystallized intelligence: effects of diffuse brain damage on the WAIS. *Perceptual and Motor Skills, 51*, 121–122.

Russell, E. W. (1984). Theory and developments of pattern analysis methods related to the Halstead–Reitan Battery. In P. E. Logue & J. M. Shear (Eds.), *Clinical neuropsychology: A multidisciplinary approach* (pp. 50–98). Springfield, IL: Charles C. Thomas.

Russell, E. W. (1986). The psychometric foundation of clinical neuropsychology. In S. B. Filskov & T. J. Boll (Eds.), *Handbook of Clinical Neuropsychology* (Vol 2, pp. 45–80). New York: Wiley.

Russell, E. W. (1992). Reliability of the Halstead impairment index: a simulation and reanalysis of Matarazzo et al. (1974). *Neuropsychology, 6*, 251–259.

Russell, E. W. (1995). The accuracy of automated and clinical detection of brain damage and lateralization in neuropsychology. *Neuropsychology Review, 5*(1), 1–68.

Russell, E. W. (1998). In defense of the Halstead–Reitan Battery: a critique of Lezak's review. *Archives of Clinical Neuropsychology, 13*(1), 365–381.

Russell, E. W. (2000a). The application of computerized scoring programs to neuropsychological assessment. In R. D. Vanderploeg (Ed.), *Clinician's Guide to Neuropsychological Assessment* (pp. 483–515) (2nd ed). Hillsdale, New Jersey: Lawrence Erlbaum Associates.

Russell, E. W. (2000b). The cognitive-metric, fixed battery approach to neuropsychological assessment. In R. D. Vanderploeg (Ed.), *Clinician's Guide to Neuropsychological Assessment* (pp. 449–481) (2nd ed). Hillsdale, New Jersey: Lawrence Erlbaum Associates.

Russell, E. W. (2003). The critique of the HRNES in the "Handbook of Normative Data for Neuropsychological Assessment". *Archives of Clinical Neuropsychology, 18*(2), 165–180.

Russell, E. W. (2004). The operating characteristics of the major HRNES–R measures. *Archives of Clinical Neuropsychology, 19*(8), 1043–1061.

Russell, E. W. (2005). Norming subjects for the Halstead–Reitan Battery. *Archives of Clinical Neuropsychology, 20*(4), 479–484.

Russell, E. W. (2008). Commentary on Loring and Larrabee's reanalysis of Reitan's original studies. *Clinical Neuropsychologist, 22*(3), 519–523.

Russell, E. W. (2009). Commentary on Larrabee, Mills, and Meyer's Paper "Sensitivity to brain dysfunction of the Halstead Reitan Vs an Ability-focused Neuropsychology Battery. *The Clinical Neuropsychologist, 23*, 831–840.

Russell, E. W., Neuringer, C., & Goldstein, G. (1970). *Assessment of brain damage: A neuropsychological key approach*. New York: Wiley.

Russell, E. W., Russell, S. L. K., & Hill, B. (2005). The fundamental psychometric status of neuropsychological batteries. *Archives of Clinical Neuropsychology*, *20*(6), 785–794.

Russell, E. W., & Starkey, R. I. (1993). *Halstead–Russell neuropsychological evaluation system [Manual and computer program]*. Los Angeles: Western Psychological Services.

Russell, E. W., & Starkey, R. I. (2001). *Halstead–Russell neuropsychological evaluation system—revised [Manual and computer program]*. Los Angeles: Western Psychological Services.

Soukup, V. M., Ingram, F., Grady, J. J., & Schiess, M. C. (1998). Trail Making Test: Issues and normative data selection. *Applied Neuropsychology*, *5*, 65–73.

Spreen, O., & Benton, A. L. (1965). Comparative studies of some psychological tests for cerebral damage. *Journal of Nervous and Mental Disease*, *140*, 323–333.

Strauss, E., Sherman, E. M. S., & Spreen, O. (2006). *A compendium of neuropsychological tests: Administration, norms, and commentary* (3rd ed.). New York: Oxford University Press.

Wechsler, D. (1944). *The measurement of adult intelligence* (3rd ed.). Baltimore: Williams & Wilkins. [Includes manual for the Wechsler-Bellevue Intelligence Scale]

Wolfson, D., & Reitan, R. M. (1995). Cross-validation of the General Neuropsychological Deficit Scale (GNDS). *Archives of Clinical Neuropsychology*, *10*, 125–131.

14 Norming Subjects for the Halstead–Reitan Battery

Neuropsychological test norms typically come from one of two sources: volunteer participants and clinical patients who are found to be neurologically normal. There are arguments criticizing subjects who are not volunteers. In part, Mitrushina, Boone, and D'Elia (1999) selectively eliminated a major set of norms from their handbook (Russell, 2003) who were not volunteers. On the other hand, Reitan and Wolfson (1993, pp. 33–35; 1997) contended that neurologically normal subjects represent the ideal group for neuropsychological assessment controls.

Nevertheless, this volunteer population presents a number of confounds that limit the usefulness of their data in interpreting neuropsychological test scores collected from persons with known brain pathology. These confounds include differences in data-collection methods, screening out pathological cases from the volunteers, self-selection biases among the volunteers, and a restriction of range in volunteer-based norms that lead to inappropriately low cutoff scores for identifying defective performances.

The main argument in favor of using volunteer subjects is that their screened and confirmed "normalcy" contrasts with neurologically normal subjects who had enough problems to warrant referral for neuropsychological evaluation. Regrettably, this screening ensures that the volunteer normative populations are never truly random, and the deviation from random selection is in the direction of raising the bar for normalcy. In Dodrill's (1987) control group, nearly one-third of the original sample was excluded when screened for evidence of organic or psychiatric dysfunction. Similarly, Fastenau (1998) excluded nearly a quarter of randomly selected older participants who had no known neurological history because many had possible histories of undiagnosed cerebrovascular problems.

Volunteer normative participants select themselves for studies and are often encouraged to do so with compensation for participation. They may not always have the motivation to perform optimally, and effort measures to ensure their effortful performance have never been done (Green, Rohling, Lees-Haley, & Allen, 2001). Lacking evidence of poor effort, some normative studies have reported unexpected results showing greater impairment among normal than among patient groups in the domains of memory (Haaland, Linn, Hunt, & Goodwin, 1983), psychomotor functions (Pauker, 1981), complex acoustic functions (Bornstein, 1985), or speeded information processing (Gronwall, 1977).

The Scientific Foundation of Neuropsychological Assessment. DOI: 10.1016/B978-0-12-416029-3.00014-2

Thus, one set of variables causes volunteers to provide data that raise the ceiling for normalcy, whereas another set of variables may cause the performance of volunteers to underrepresent "normal" performance. What is the empirically driven neuropsychologist to do? One solution might be to use a well-established method for judging the general ability level of the normative sample, a procedure outlined by Anastasi and Urbina (1997) under the rubric "national anchor norms" (p. 70). Of all the tests in our armamentarium, none is a better candidate for universal standard than the Wechsler tests.

In the meta-analysis reported by Stanczak, Stanczak, and Templer (2000), significant differences were observed in the Wechsler scores of volunteer participants when compared with psychiatric, neurological, and normal neurological comparison groups. These differences came about because of the superior intellectual performance of the volunteer participants, and not because of defective performance among the other groups. The mean Wechsler Adult Intelligence Scale—Revised full-scale intelligence quotient (FSIQ) score for the self-report volunteer group was almost 112 (111.6) (Stanczak, 2003). Not surprisingly, the volunteer participants averaged nearly 3 years more education than the referral participants.

The higher-than-average FSIQ for volunteers was also supported by a reexamination of a review of smaller studies (Steinmeyer, 1986). For the norms with IQ scores, the nine volunteer groups had a mean FSIQ of 116.9, whereas the five neurologically normal groups had an FSIQ of 103.6. The observation that the volunteer participants in these studies had considerably higher IQ scores than the referral participants raises the possibility that a similar bias exists in other norming studies that used volunteer participants.

To test this possibility, the participants in the five large-scale normative studies of the Halstead–Reitan Battery (HRB), with an $N > 200$ and that had Wechsler (1955, 1981) IQ measures for the sample were examined. The specific hypothesis tested was that volunteer normative participants have considerably higher IQ scores than normal neuropsychological subjects who are referred as part of a neurological examination.

Methods and Results

Subject demographics reported in the normative studies of Fromm-Auch and Yeudall (1983); Heaton, Grant, and Matthews (1991); Pauker (1981); Russell and Starkey (2001); and Yeudall, Reddon, Gill, and Stefanyk (1987). Of these, only the norms of Russell and Starkey (2001) are composed entirely of neurologically normal subjects; the remaining four studies used at least a large portion of volunteers in their norming. The norms for Heaton et al. (1991) were used in this examination because the revision by Heaton, Miller, Taylor, and Grant (2004) did not provide IQ levels for its Caucasian subjects. Because the Heaton et al. (1991) data were used for the Heaton et al. (2004) norms, the IQ levels of the Heaton et al. (2004) norms are probably approximately the same. These data are presented in Table 14.1.

Table 14.1 Descriptive Statistics for the Co-Normed Halstead–Reitan Battery Studies

	Sets of Norms				
Characteristics	**Pauker**	**Fromm-Auch & Yeudall**	**Yeudall et al.**	**Heaton et al.**[a]	**Russell and Starkey**[b]
Date Published	1981	1983	1987	1991	2001
N	363	193	225	378	200
Age: 0	39.0	25.4	24.7	41.8	44.6
Age range	19–76	15–32	15–40	20–8I	18–89
Education: 0	12.5	14.8	14.6	13.6	12.7
FSIQ: 0	1 15, WAIS	119, WAIS	112, WAIS–R	1 14, WAIS	102, WAIS–R
Norming method	Stratified	Stratified	Stratified	Regression	Regression
Demographic categories	IQ, age: 4 × 3	Age, sex: 4 × 2	Age, sex: 4 × 2	Education, age, sex: 6 × 9 × 2	Education, age, sex[c]: 4 × 6 × 2
Location[d]	Canada	Canada	Canada	CO, W I, CA[e]	FL, OH
Subject type	Volunteer	Volunteer	Volunteer	Unclear	Negative neurological
Tests covered[g]	HRB (8)	HRB (13)	HRB (13)	HRB (12) + W + 9	HRB (12) + W + 12

[a]The revised Heaton et al. (2004) norms were not placed in this table because the FSIQ for the Caucasian subjects was not provided.
[b]The HRNES (Russell & Starkey, 1993) has the same demographic statistics as the HRNES–R (Russell & Starkey, 2001).
[c]The division by sex was restricted to tapping, grip strength, and pegboard.
[d]U.S. state or Canada.
[e]Only three areas are fully represented (see Russell, 1997, and Chapter 8).
[f]Manual is not clear as to *type* of subjects.
[g]HRB (x): number of HRB tests; W: WAIS or WAIS–R subtests + number of non-HRB tests added.

This demonstrates that the mean FSIQ of the volunteer subjects was 115, one full standard deviation above average. Clearly, then, these "normal" volunteer participants were not normal but represented the upper one-sixth of the population. Only the norms of Russell and Starkey (2001), using referred but neurologically normal participants, showed a more average IQ of 102.

Discussion

Much of the controversy concerning the appropriate groups to use for normative studies comes from a failure to differentiate between the demands of the research laboratory versus those of clinical practice. Rigorous exclusion and scrubbing of participants in research projects helps to ensure that a rigorous comparison between brain-damaged and control subjects is possible. When applied to the development of norms, however, the clinical assessment question becomes one of differentiating between persons with a neurological condition and those without. For this, the most appropriate reference group is persons who are neurologically evaluated and found to be neurologically normal.

In addition, the use of referred but neurologically normal participants in normative studies is mandated by the *Standards of Educational and Psychological Testing* [American Educational Research Association, American Psychological Association, & National Council on Measurement in Education (hereafter, AERA), 1999]. It specifies that norms should represent the same population as their intended use (p. 55), and norms should be collected under the same testing conditions as will be used in the intended assessment procedure (p. 63).

Some might argue that referred but neurologically normal participants may actually be abnormal with some undiagnosed pathology. This issue was addressed by Russell (1990, 2009), who described a series of 200 referred but neurologically normal subjects who were followed for more than a year after their initial presentation and evaluation. More than half were initially diagnosed with psychological or minor physical ailments, but no one in this group showed evidence of neurological problems at any point during the following year. These data suggest that concerns about undiagnosed pathology among neurologically normal subjects might rarely be correct, and is largely a red herring that draws attention away from the relevance and importance of using such a group of patients for comparison purposes.

As this study indicates, volunteer subjects are not representative of the "normal" person who undergoes clinical evaluation. Although this finding is surprising, the full import of it is not immediately obvious. It is evident that norms based on volunteer subjects run the risk of increasing false diagnoses of pathology by increasing the criteria of what is normal. However, the great import of this increased IQ greatly increases the proportion of normal subjects that would be considered as impaired. Furthermore, the scrupulous scrubbing and selecting of volunteer participants apparently leads to a more homogenous group with a restricted range of variation. This range restriction further increases the likelihood of false-positive diagnoses whenever cutting scores are derived from the performance of volunteer participants. Reliance on volunteer norms increases the chances that a neurologically normal person of average intelligence will be misdiagnosed as brain damaged. This concern is important in the clinical arena and even more important in the forensic setting.

References

American Educational Research Association, American Psychological Association, & National Council on Measurement in Education (AERA et al.), *Standards for educational and psychological testing*. Washington, DC: American Educational Research Association.

Anastasi, A., & Urbina, S. (1997). *Psychological testing* (7th ed.). Upper Saddle River, NJ: Prentice Hall.

Bornstein, R. A. (1985). Normative data on selected neuropsychological measures from a nonclinical sample. *Journal of Clinical Psychology, 41*, 651–659.

Dodrill, C. B. (1987). *What constitutes normal performance in clinical neuropsychology?* Paper presented at the 97th annual convention of the American Psychological Association.

Fastenau, P. S. (1998). Validity of regression-based norms: an empirical test of the comprehensive norms with older adults. *Journal of Clinical and Experimental Neuropsychology, 20*, 906–916.

Fromm-Auch, D., & Yeudall, L. T. (1983). Normative data for the Halstead–Reitan neuropsychological tests. *Journal of Clinical Neuropsychology, 5*, 221–238.

Green, P., Rohling, M. L., Lees-Haley, P. R., & Allen, L. M. (2001). Effort has a greater effect on test scores than severe brain injury in compensation claimants. *Brain Injury, 15*(12), 1045–1060.

Gronwall, D. M. (1977). Paced auditory serial-addition task: a measure of recovery from concussion. *Perceptual and Motor Skills, 44*(2), 367–373.

Haaland, K. Y., Linn, R. T., Hunt, W. C., & Goodwin, J. S. (1983). A normative study of Russell's variant of the Wechsler memory scale in a healthy elderly population. *Journal of Consulting and Clinical Psychology, 51*, 878–881.

Heaton, R. K., Grant, I., & Matthews, C. G. (1991). *Comprehensive norms for an expanded Halstead–Reitan Battery [Norms, manual, and computer program]*. Odessa, FL: Psychological Assessment Resources.

Heaton, R. K., Miller, S. W., Taylor, M. J., & Grant, 1. (2004). *Revised comprehensive norms for an expanded Halstead–Reitan Battery [Norms, manual, and computer program]*. Odessa, FL: Psychological Assessment Resources.

Mitrushina, M. N., Boone, K. B., & D'Elia, L. F. (1999). *Handbook of normative data for neuropsychological assessment*. New York: Oxford University Press.

Pauker, J. D. (1981). *Adult norms or standards for the Halstead–Reitan neuropsychological test battery*. Unpublished manuscript, Clarke Institute of Psychiatry and University of Toronto, Canada.

Reitan, R. M., & Wolfson, D. (1993). *The Halstead–Reitan neuropsychological test battery: Theory and clinical interpretation* (2nd ed.). Tucson: Neuropsychology Press.

Reitan, R. M., & Wolfson, D. (1997). Emotional disturbances and their interaction with neuropsychological deficits. *Neuropsychological Review, 7*, 3–9.

Russell, E. W. (1990). *Three validity studies for negative neurological criterion norming*. Paper presented at the 98th annual convention of the American Psychological Association, Boston.

Russell, E. W. (1997). Developments in the psychometric foundations of neuropsychological assessment. In G. Goldstein & T. M. Incagnoli (Eds.), *Contemporary approaches to neuropsychological assessment* (pp. 15–65). New York: Plenum.

Russell, E. W. (2003). The critique of the HRNES in the "Handbook of Normative Data for Neuropsychological Assessment". *Archives of Clinical Neuropsychology*, *18*, 177–180.

Russell, E. W. (2009). Commentary on Larrabee, Millis, and Meyers' paper "Sensitivity to brain dysfunction of the Halstead Reitan vs an ability-focused neuropsychology battery." *The Clinical Neuropsychologist*, *23*, 831–840.

Russell, E. W., & Starkey, R. I. (1993). *Halstead–Russell Neuropsychological Evaluation System [Manual and computer program]*. Los Angeles: Western Psychological Services.

Russell, E. W., & Starkey, R. I. (2001). *Halstead–Russell Neuropsychological Evaluation System—Revised [Manual and computer program]*. Los Angeles: Western Psychological Services.

Stanczak, D. E. (2003, March 27). Personal communication.

Stanczak, E. M., Stanczak, D. E., & Templer, D. I. (2000). Subject-selection procedures in neuropsychological research: a meta-analysis and prospective study. *Archives of Clinical Neuropsychology*, *15*(7), 587–601.

Steinmeyer, C. H. (1986). A meta-analysis of Halstead–Reitan test performances on non-brain damaged subjects. *Archives of Clinical Neuropsychology*, *1*, 301–307.

Yeudall, L. T., Reddon, J. R., Gill, D. M., & Stefanyk, W. O. (1987). Normative data for the Halstead–Reitan neuropsychological tests stratified by age and sex. *Journal of Clinical Psychology*, *43*(3), 346–367.

Wechsler, D. (1955). *Wechsler Adult Intelligence Scale [Manual]*. New York: Psychological Corporation.

Wechsler, D. (1981). *WAIS–R, Wechsler Adult Intelligence Scale [Revised manual]*. San Antonio, TX: Psychological Corporation.

15 The Major Halstead–Reitan Battery Norm Sets

> *In order to ascertain more precisely the individual's exact position with reference to the standardization sample, the raw score is converted into some relative measure. These derived scores are designed to serve a dual purpose. First, they indicate the individual's relatives standing in the normative sample and thus permit an evaluation of her or his performance in reference to other persons. Second, they provide comparable measures that permit a direct comparison of the individual's performance on different tests.*
>
> ***Anastasi and Urbina (1997, p. 49)***

Although there have been several major attempts to review and catalog norms for neuropsychological tests, all of these attempts have neglected the group of Halstead–Reitan Battery (HRB) (Reitan & Wolfson, 1993) norms that use simultaneous norming or co-norms. The omission of such batteries is a significant deficiency in the literature because co-norming is now well established in psychology.

In neuropsychology, co-norming is used by the Halstead–Russell Neuropsychological Evaluation System—Revised (HRNES–R) (Russell & Starkey, 1993), the Neuropsychological Deficit Scale (NDS) for adults (Reitan, 1986), the Meyer's Neuropsychological Battery (MNB) (Meyers & Rohling, 2004), and the Neuropsychological Assessment Battery (NAB) (Stern & White, 2001). Co-norming is also used by the Wechsler tests such as the Wechsler Adult Intelligence Scale (WAIS–III) and the Wechsler Memory Scales 3 (WMS–III) (Wechsler, 1997, pp. 13–14). Several other tests also use co-norming such as the Wide Range Achievement Tests (WRAT) (Wilkinson, 1993), the Peabody Picture Vocabulary Test (3rd ed.) (Dunn & Dunn, 1998) along with the expressive vocabulary test (Williams, 1997) and the Luria–Nebraska Neuropsychological Battery (LNNB)(Golden, Purisch, & Hammeke, 1991).

In addition, the development of computerized scoring of whole batteries (Kane & Kay, 1992, 1997; Kane, Winter, Bleiberg & Kane, 2007), which generally uses co-norms, represents one of the recent advances in neuropsychological assessment.

Although neuropsychological norms have been examined in three major books, none of these reviews discussed co-norming or computerized norming. The fourth revision of Lezak's *Neuropsychological Assessment* (Lezak, Howieson, & Loring, 2004) provided a relatively complete coverage of individual neuropsychological tests but provided norms for only a few of the individual tests. Concerning computerized scoring, Lezak et al. (2004) stated, "Computer assessment programs have been

The Scientific Foundation of Neuropsychological Assessment. DOI: 10.1016/B978-0-12-416029-3.00015-4

proliferating and may be on the verge of assuming a dominant place in the neuropsychological assessment repertory" (p. 13). However, there was no further discussion of such programs.

A Compendium of Neuropsychological Tests (3rd ed.) (Strauss, Sherman, & Spreen, 2006) provided norms for a fairly extensive number of individual neuropsychological tests. The book provided a profile system for evaluating individual tests. Although this implied simultaneous use of norms for individual tests, the norming problems that arise with the comparison of tests are only briefly mentioned.

In 1999, a massive compendium of selected neuropsychological tests was published as the *Handbook of Normative Data for Neuropsychological Assessment* by Mitrushina, Boone, and D'Elia (1999). It provided an almost exhaustive cataloging of the published norms for 17 neuropsychological tests, 15 of which are widely used. Of these tests, 7 were in the HRB (Reitan & Wolfson, 1993), and 11 were included in the HRNES–R (Russell & Starkey, 1993). Nevertheless, some of the norms derived from this computer-scoring program were eliminated whereas, with no consistency, others were not (Russell, 2003). This handbook did not cover any co-normed batteries as batteries or discuss the theory related to co-norming.

Selection Criteria for Batteries

Of the major fixed batteries that have been used in neuropsychology for a number of years, only the HRB has had any norming studies. Consequently, this chapter will be limited to the HRB and batteries derived from it.

At least 24 norming studies of the HRB have been published. These are listed by Dodrill (1987), Fromm-Auch and Yeudall (1983), and Steinmeyer (1986). Most of these studies suffered from a small sample size or were incompletely reported. With all of these norms available, certain criteria for selecting the major studies to be reviewed were formulated.

First, if the initial data pool was much less than 200, the study was eliminated. The desirable size of the pool depends on the standard error (SE) of the sample (Guilford, 1965, pp. 144–146). The *rule of diminishing returns* means that the advantage of adding new subjects decreases as the size increases. For instance, using an index with a standard deviation (SD) of 8.7 and an N of 10 produces a SE of 2.9, or almost 3 score points. With an N of 200, the SE is 0.62 points, less than 1 score point. Adding 300 more subjects reduces the SE to 0.39, a difference of one-third of a point. Thus, the size of the norming sample, more than 200, is not as important as the procedure for subject selection. In other words, a group of 20,000 college graduates is not representative of the general population even if it is a huge sample.

The second criterion was that the study must at least norm the core tests of the HRB. For instance, Bornstein (1985) normed a group of tests derived from the HRB using a large sample of 365 volunteers. However, his norms included only five tests, and some of the missing tests include such major tests as the category test.

Finally, only the most complete version of a set of norms was examined. For example, apparently the data from the well-known Fromm-Auch and Yeudall (1983) norms were incorporated into the Yeudall, Reddon, Gill, and Stefanyk (1987) norms.

Although the latter set of norms is less well known, a few new cases were added and the norms were presented in a more complete form. As such, only the Yeudall et al. study (1987) was examined here.

Types of Battery Norms

Three methods have been used to create norms for fixed batteries. The first method used stratified scores in which a proportion of the total sample was included in each of the various age, education, and sex categories. This was equivalent to gathering a small set of norms for each composite set of stratified levels or cells.

The second method used linear regression to predict the mean scores for the age, intelligence or education, and sex of each subgroup or cell.

The third method was used by Reitan to set the norms for the NDS (Reitan, 1986). These scale-score norms were derived from his long clinical experience rather than from a data-norming study (see Chapter 13). His norms were similar to those gathered directly from a sample (see Table 15.2), and the NDS has been thoroughly validated (Russell, 1995).

Normative Characteristics of the Batteries

After applying the selection criteria, only five sets of coordinated norms remained to be reviewed. In temporal order, these norms were Pauker (1981a), Dodrill (1987), Yeudall et al. (1987), the HRNES–R (Russell & Starkey, 2001), and the Revised Comprehensive Norms for an Expanded Halstead–Reitan Battery (RCNEHRB) (Heaton, Miller, Taylor, & Grant, 2004). Reitan's (1986) NDS is reviewed separately because the norms were based on Reitan's clinical experience and not psychometric procedures.

The descriptive statistics for the five co-normed HRB normative studies are provided in Table 15.1. The NDS is not included because its norms were not directly psychometrically derived. This table provides the *N*, mean age and range, mean full-scale intelligence quotient (FSIQ), education, norming method, demographic categories covered, location, subject type, tests covered, and whether the scoring was computerized.

In this table, the mean number of subjects whose data were used to create the norms is from 120 to 634. The norms fall into two groups of age ranges. The mean age for the Yeudall et al. (1987) study was 24.7, and that for the Dodrill study was 27.8, whereas the mean ages for the Pauker study was 39, the RCNEHRB was 44.4, and the HRNES–R was 44.6.

Evaluative Criteria

These criteria for evaluating the various sets of norms represented the requirements provided in the *Standards for Educational and Psychological Testing* [American Educational Research Association, American Psychological Association, & National Council on Measurement in Education (hereafter AERA et al.), 1999]. These include the size of the sample, the representative location of the sample, and whether the

Table 15.1 Descriptive Statistics for the Co-Normed Halstead–Reitan Battery Studies

Characteristics	Sets of Norms				
	Pauker (1981a)	**Yeudall et al. (1987)**	**Dodrill (1987)**	**CNHRB (2004)**	**HRNES–R (2001[a])**
N	363	225	120	634	200
Age: 0	39.0	24.7	27.8	44.4	44.6
Age Range	19–76	15–40	16–40	20–85	18–89
Education: 0	12.5	14.6	12.3	13.8	12.7
FSIQ: 0	115 WAIS	112 WAIS–R	100 WAIS–R[b]	114[c]	102 WAIS–R
Adjustment Method	Stratified	Stratified	Not Stratified	Regression	Regression
Demographic Categories	IQ & Age: 4 × 3	Age & Sex: 4 × 2	Not Given	Education, Age, Sex: 6 × 9 × 2	Education, Age, Sex[d]: 4 × 6 × 2
Location	Canada	Canada	WA[e]	CO, WI, CA[f]	FL, OH[e]
Subjects Type	Volunteers	Volunteers	Volunteers	Unclear[g]	Neg. Neuro.
Tests Covered[h]	HRB (8)	HRB (13)	HRB (13) + W + 5	HRB (12) + W + 9	HRB (12) + W + 12
Computerized	No	No	No	Yes	Yes

[a]The HRNES has the same descriptive statistics as the HRNES–R.
[b]Dodrill's norms were adjusted so that the FSIQ was 100. The original sample was more than 200.
[c]FSIQ. was not provided, so the WAIS FSIQ for CNEHRB(1991) was substituted.
[d]Sex adjustments were restricted to tapping, grip strength, and pegboard for HRNES–R.
[e]U.S. state.
[f]Only three areas are fully represented (see text).
[g]Manual is unclear as to the type of subjects.
[h]HRB(*N*) = number of Halstead–Reitan Battery tests; W = Wechsler adult subtests (see text); + = number of non-HRB tests.

norms were composed of volunteers or neurologically normal patients. In addition, the type, completeness, and method of co-norming were examined. Finally, adjustment procedures for demographic characteristics were considered.

Stratified Batteries

In a stratified battery, a proportion of the total sample is represented in each of the various age, education, and sex categories. In this way, a person's score is compared only with someone from the same age, education, and sex group. However, each division separates the total *N* into smaller units or cells. Consequently, the individual cells are reduced by the number of divisions that are incorporated into the set of norms. Because norming data usually fall into a normal distribution, this means enough data for the extreme cells, those at the ends of the age and education range, are greatly attenuated. The extreme cells often do not contain enough subjects to produce an accurate mean for the cells. For instance, in Pauker's (1981a, p. 931) norms, there were only four subjects in the cell for ages 53 to 71 and FSIQ 89 to 102. With such a low *N* for the different cells, the variability at the extremes was often high from cell to cell.

The only direct methods for overcoming this problem while still using stratification would be to collect several times as many subjects as reported in the largest studies. An alternative to a very large *N* is combining cells into a few large groups as Bornstein (1985) did. However, if only a few representative groups are used, then the comparison with an individual examinee's scores becomes less accurate. For instance, in Bornstein's study, education was divided into two groups: (1) less than high school and (2) high school and above. Consequently, college graduates fall into the same group as high-school graduates, many of whom have a below-average intelligence.

Another method of dealing with the small cell problem is to sacrifice one of the three demographic characteristics of age, cognitive ability (education or IQ), and sex. The result is that no stratified normative sample would have included all three major demographic characteristics.

A final method of handling small *N*'s is to statistically smooth the variations between cells. Pauker (1988) achieved this directly for his battery by creating overlapping intervals from which he constructed a table of *t*-scores. As such, these norms can be used without great concern for irregularities because of small cells.

The final problem with stratification is that this method requires such an extensive amount of time to gather test data that it has been impossible to obtain data for a large number of the HRB tests. This is clearly seen in Table 15.1. No stratified set of norms includes all of the HRB tests. In conclusion, the *N* required for a co-normed battery is so great that every form of stratified norms has sacrificed one of the demographic characteristics.

Pauker's Norms (1981a, 1981b)

Pauker (1977) developed the first set of norms for the HRB that was relatively comprehensive. Unfortunately, the norms were never published, although the norms are available in either raw form (Pauker, 1981a) or in *t*-score form (Pauker, 1981b).

Evaluation

Pauker's work (1981a) is still one of the most adequately normed studies that are based on volunteers. The norms were derived from paid volunteers from an area in Canada near Toronto. The sample consisted of the mean raw scores of 363 subjects who ranged in age from 19 to 76 years, with a mean age of 39. The mean education was 12.5 years, and the mean WAIS FSIQ was 114.7. Thus, the sample appears to be a representative of adults, with the exception that the FSIQ is almost 1 SD above average. The norms covered the basic HRB tests, and the raw scores were stratified by IQ and age but not by sex. The author stated that there was no significant difference between the scores of men and women. This may have reflected the large proportion of females (211 women to 152 men). It is the only co-normed sample to have a strong preponderance of women and the only one to find no difference between genders on pure motor tasks.

Based on the description of the data-collection process, the norms should represent one of the most adequately composed sets of volunteer norms to be assembled. The study met all of the requirements for selecting participants usually specified for persons volunteering. However, these norms tended to be lower than traditional norms. In particular, the finger tapping speed was slower than commonly expected. The low tapping scores may have occurred because the proportion of women was particularly high. In summary, these were excellent norms according to all the usual criteria.

Yeudall et al. (1987) Norms

The Yeudall et al. (1987) norms provided mean raw scores for age and sex without creating scale scores. Their volunteer norms were evidently an expansion of the Fromm-Auch and Yeudall (1983) norms by adding 32 subjects. Although the Fromm-Auch and Yeudall (1983) norms were widely used, the Yeudall et al. (1987) data not only included a few more subjects but also were more detailed. The descriptive statistics for Yeudall et al.'s (1987) study demonstrated almost no variation from the earlier set.

Evaluation

The subjects for the Yeudall et al. (1987) raw-score norms were 225 Canadian volunteers with a slight preponderance of men (127 men, 98 women). The age range extended only from 15 to 40 so that the full adult age range is not represented. Both the mean education of 14.6 years and the mean WAIS–R FSIQ of 112.2 indicate that the sample scored at an intelligence level that approached 1 SD above the mean. The sample was stratified by age and sex but not by ability (IQ or education). Thus, these norms would be suitable only for a population less than 40 years old and of college intellectual ability.

Dodrill's Norms (1987)

Dodrill (1987) published many studies in which he evidently used the data from his set of norms. A relatively complete form of the data was presented in the 1987 study. Unfortunately, these norms were never published, although they may be obtained from the author. Complete scale scores were not constructed, although Dodrill created "ranges" of raw scores that indicated the severity of impairment.

Evaluation

Within its restricted limits, the 1987 study by Dodrill is in many ways the best designed normative study that has been completed, even though its final *N* was 120. The age range was limited to the range from 16 to 40. The battery is fairly extensive in that the full HRB, WAIS–R, and five other neuropsychological tests were included. Dodrill selected his subjects so they formed a normal distribution with an FSIQ of 100 and an SD of 14.4. His paper does not describe the method used to obtain the normal distribution. Apparently, data that had been collected from 61 subjects with above-average intelligence were not used (Dodrill, 1987, p. 3). Thus, the original sample of 181 was close to 200 and had an above-average IQ. However, if a random method was used to eliminate cases that did not fit a normal distribution, then the procedure had an acceptable outcome. As such, it probably provides the best norming population at this time within its age range.

Dodrill's "norms" were neither stratified nor adjusted for demographic characteristics other than for IQ. The norms have a mean age of 27.8 years and a WAIS–R FSIQ of 100. There are equal numbers of men and women in the sample. However, these norms can only be used for the age range of 16 to 40.

Computerized Programs

Three currently published sets of norms for the HRB use computerized scoring: the NDS (Reitan, 1986), the RCNEHRB (Heaton et al., 2004), and the HRNES–R (Russell & Starkey, 2001).

The computerized norming process has a number of distinct advantages for the clinical neuropsychologist. Such a norming process increases efficiency. The amount of time and effort required of an examiner to use normative tables for batteries as extensive as these batteries (with corrections for age, education, and sex) is almost prohibitive without such a scoring program. Generally, computerized norming programs permit scale scores to be obtained as rapidly as the test raw scores can be entered into the program (Russell, 1997, p. 25).

In addition, if the scores are entered correctly, the scoring computations for these programs are 100% reliable (Russell, 2000a, p. 486). The scores can be printed to help interpretation and to arrange the data in an orderly manner. The computer printout displays the neuropsychologist's evidence for forensic case reports in a professional manner. Finally, computer programs are useful in gathering data for research (Russell, 2000a, p. 510).

The Neuropsychological Deficit Scale

The NDS (Reitan, 1986) overcomes several major problems that plague stratified norms by creating a set of scale scores based on Reitan's clinical experience

(Russell, 2000b, pp. 489–490; Chapter 14). Reitan's computer program (Reitan, 1986; Reitan & Wolfson, 1993) is a partially interpretative program that is designed to computerize the initial aspects of an analysis of data from the HRB. The NDS follows the classical HRB methodology in detail. Using the Halstead–Reitan method, neuropsychologists have found the program to be of great value. The program norms have scale scores that represent Reitan's four levels of interpretation. Interpretative analyses more detailed than the NDS findings can use the more traditional HRB methods, which are based on raw scores (Reitan & Wolfson, 1993).

The NDS has been validated in many studies (Russell, 1995, 2000b, pp. 497–498, Chapter 9) and has been found to be as accurate as or even more accurate than any other procedure in measuring the existence of brain damage in the middle age range. This is true to the present. (No other major comparative study appears to have been performed since 1955). Apparently, one reason for the great accuracy of this program is that Reitan combined an index level of performance with a lateralization score. The lateralization procedure identifies brain-damaged cases missed by a single brain-damage index.

Transformation of Battery Scores

Two norming studies have used regression norming to obtain their norm tables. These are the Comprehensive Norms for an Extended Halstead–Reitan Battery (CNEHRB) (Heaton, Grant, & Matthews, 1991) and the Halstead–Russell Neurological Evaluation System (HRNES) (Russell & Starkey, 1993). Both have been revised as the RCNEHRB (Heaton et al., 2004) and the HRNES–R (Russell & Starkey, 1993, 2001). Because regression norming was the method for overcoming the major problems of small cell size and irregular norm scores that occur with stratification, these transformation methods should be discussed.

The regression method is used both to calculate scale scores and to produce score adjustments for the entire range of age and cognitive ability. This means that each of the various categories of age and ability (IQ or education) is predicted from the entire normative population (Heaton et al., 1991; Russell, 1997). This method also smooths the norms so that irregular variations do not occur as with stratified data.

In addition, regression norming permits larger co-normed batteries than can be obtained from stratified batteries. The two regression normed batteries, the RCNEHRB (Heaton et al., 2004) and the HRNES–R (Russell & Starkey, 1993, 2001), have considerably larger number of demographic characteristic categories and have included a greater number of tests than any stratified battery (see Table 15.1).

Linear Regression Versus Linear Transformation

The use of regression for creating test scores is a venerable procedure in psychometrics, but it has only recently been applied to neuropsychological norms. Versions of linear regression were employed to create scale scores in the renorming of Russell's (1988) version of the Wechsler Memory Scale (Wechsler, 1945). The first full neuropsychological battery with which the regression method was used was the

Halstead–Rennick–Russell Battery (Russell, Starkey, Starkey, & Fernandez 1988). In 1991, the CNEHRB (Heaton et al., 1991) was published using a multiple linear-regression method to obtain the scaled scores. The HRNES was published by a national company in 1993 (Russell & Starkey, 1993). In 2001, the HRNES was revised as the HRNES–R (Russell & Starkey, 2001). Most recently, a revised version of the CNEHRB was published as the RCNEHRB (Heaton et al., 2004). All of these battery norms use regression norming to create their scores and to adjust scores for age and ability.

Intellectual Ability

Many neuropsychological tests are affected by a patient's intellectual ability because there is a strong correlation between measures of intelligence and many neuropsychological test scores (Heaton, Grant, & Matthews, 1986; Dodrill, 1999; Russell, 2001). With the exception of those of Yeudall et al. (1987) and Dodrill (1987), all co-normed sets have stratified or adjusted categories of subjects by intellectual ability, using either a measure of intelligence or education level.

The most direct method of estimating a person's intellectual ability is by means of the FSIQ. However, in testing people with brain damage, the direct prediction of intelligence using an intelligence test is generally inaccurate because the acquired brain damage affects that performance. This means that norms that are directly based on IQ cannot be used to assess the existence of brain damage or the amount of impairment associated with brain damage.

To overcome the difficulty of using IQs in norming, one of the methods that indicate the subject's premorbid intelligence can be applied. Of all the single predictors of premorbid ability, the measurement most closely related to premorbid ability is a person's educational attainment (Schinka & Vanderploeg, 2000). Consequently, the RCNEHRB norms are based on a regression method to adjust for education.

The HRNES–R norms also are based on a regression method, but they can be adjusted for either education or premorbid IQ. If available, an actual premorbid FSIQ can be used. Otherwise, several formulas for predicting premorbid IQ have been developed (Schinka & Vanderploeg, 2000). Thus, the predicted premorbid IQ score from any of these methods, including education, a prediction formula, or an actual premorbid IQ when available, can be used in the HRNES–R program to adjust scores for intelligence.

Criticisms of Norming with Regression

The use of linear regression for norming has generally been supported in neuropsychology (Crawford & Howell, 1998; Moses, Prichard, & Adams, 1999; Vanderploeg, Axelrod, Sherer, Scott & Adams, 1997), although the way in which it has been applied has been criticized (Fastenau, 1998; Fastenau & Adams, 1996; Golden & Van den Broek, 1998). Thus, there appears to be a general agreement that linear regression in some form is a legitimate means of overcoming the problem of having small *N*'s in the extreme cells of norms.

A thorough examination of the way regression methods in norming were used in neuropsychology appeared in a review of the CNEHRB (Heaton, Grant, & Matthews,

1991) by Fastenau and Adams (1996). They described several problems. Most criticisms were not very important and were answered by Heaton, Matthews, Grant, and Avitable (1996). The only criticism that should be mentioned was the contention by Fastenau and Adams (1996) that there were so many cells in the Heaton et al. (1996) table of norms that there would have been only one or two subjects in many cells. This point indicates that Fastenau and Adams (1996) completely misunderstood the statistical nature of linear regression. Although this criticism would be quite appropriate for a stratified sample, it does not apply to norming by linear regression because linear regression uses the whole sample to predict the entire range of scores. Linear regression, as Crawford and Howell (1998) stated, is the most adequate method of avoiding the problems produced by low *N*s per cell. In normative regression studies, the only parameters that affect norms would be those that apply to the whole sample such as the total sample size, distribution of the sample, and the mean FSIQ.

With regard to the use of linear-regression methods to correct for age and education, at least four studies have now demonstrated that such corrected scores are more accurate in diagnosing brain damage than are uncorrected scores (Heaton et al., 1996, 1999; Moses et al., 1999; Vanderploeg et al., 1997). This contention holds at least in the middle age range. Even authors who accepted this method reported reduced accuracy at the extremes using standard stratified norms (Fastenau, 1998).

A study by Golden and Van den Broek (1998) was designed to evaluate whether the regression and *t*-score correction methods used in the CNEHRB are an improvement over the traditional use of raw scores. Data from a group of 68 patients with lesions localized in the four quadrants of the brain (17 subjects per quadrant) were used to compare raw scores and *t*-scores. The raw scores were observed to be as sensitive as or in some cases more sensitive to localization than the *t*-scores.

However, this study had one very serious problem. The average age of patients in the study was 42.2, with a range from 37.7 to 44.7 or 7 years. The average educational level was 13.1 years, with a range from 12.6 to 13.7 or 1.1 years. These are quite narrow ranges for both characteristics, and this range occurs in the exact center of the CNEHRB norms where the computer program makes almost no adjustments to the scores. Consequently, the statistical performance of the raw scores in this range is almost exactly equivalent to that of the *t*-scores. An assessment of the effect of using corrections for age and education is significant only when the extremes of the age and education ranges are used. Thus, the selection of subjects made it almost impossible to obtain significant differences between the raw and scaled scores.

Revised Comprehensive Norms for an Extended Halstead–Reitan Battery

The CNEHRB (Heaton et al., 1991; Heaton et al., 2004) was revised in 2004. The revised battery (Heaton et al., 2004) is essentially two sets of norms. The first was an expansion and continuation of the original CNEHRB norms. The second set consists of the largest set of neuropsychological norms for African American subjects available. Because a critique of the norms for African American subjects requires special expertise and an analysis beyond the scope of this chapter, the current examination focuses on the section of the norms derived from the Caucasian subjects (Heaton et al., 2004).

This RCNEHRB (Heaton et al., 2004) includes the HRB tests, variations of the WAIS–III, and nine other tests. An extensive set of normative tables is used to manually norm scale scores; a computer-scoring program is available. The manual (Heaton et al., 2004) is quite extensive, but most of the manual consists of the tables for converting a raw score into a corrected scale score. The manual scoring procedure is quite time consuming and even tedious. Consequently, most neuropsychologists who use the battery for more than a few tests use the scoring program.

The CNEHRB has been reviewed several times (Fastenau,1998; Fastenau & Adams, 1996; Fuerst, 1993; Golden & Van den Broek, 1998; Moses et al., 1999; Russell, 1997). The critical reviews have generally been refuted (Heaton, Avitable, Grant, & Matthews, 1999; Heaton et al., 1996).

Norming Method

The description of the statistics used in creating the norms for both the Caucasian group and the African American group in the revised battery was comprehensive (Heaton et al., 1991, pp. 17–34). The raw scores from the normative sample were normalized and then transformed into corrected *t*-scores through several steps (Heaton et al., 1991, pp. 17–18). This procedure transformed the norms into normal distributions, equated the scales, and converted them to attainment scales with three points for each SD. Multiple regression was used to create *t*-score norms with adjustments for age, education, and sex.

In this procedure, the normalization process in the first step influenced the final *t*-score method so that the *t*-scores were also normally distributed. This has several implications for the test construction and interpretation.

Scores from brain-damaged subjects typically form extremely skewed distributions on most neuropsychological tests (Dodrill, 1987; Russell, 1991). In the RCNEHRB, these skewed distributions were forced to fit a normalized distribution. This is evident in Figure 1 of the manual (Heaton et al., 1991, p. 30). Both the normal and the brain-damaged subjects' scores show an approximately normal distribution. Consequently, the scales do not reflect the amount of impairment produced by relatively severe brain damage (Moses et al., 1999, p. 952).

Golden and Van den Broek (1998) also correctly pointed out that the range for the scale scores on the RCNEHRB is limited to three intervals for each standard deviation. This number of intervals is transferred to the *t*-scores (Russell, 1997). Thus, although the *t*-scores have 10 numbers per SD, these scores are grouped so that the actual number of *t*-score intervals is only three.

In addition, this limited number of scale scores means that the entire range of scale intervals is only 19 points, with nine intervals above the mean and nine below. Nine intervals above the mean is generally sufficient, given the way in which neuropsychological raw test scores are skewed (Russell, 2001). They generally have a low ceiling that extends less than two standard deviations above the normal population mean. However, nine intervals or three standard deviations below the mean are quite inadequate to measure the severity of impairment for many individuals with brain damage.

Co-norming

The initial CNEHRB (Heaton et al., 1991) was relatively well co-normed, with only two exceptions. The data for the Boston Naming Test and the Boston Diagnostic Aphasia Examination (Heaton et al., 2004, p. 7) were collected in Goodglass's laboratory (Goodglass & Kaplan, 1983) and were not co-normed with the rest of the tests. Except for the HRB and WAIS, the various additional tests were added to the battery at different times and apparently from different laboratories, although this is not described in the discussion of the sample. Thus, the new tests were not co-normed with the original sample. The WAIS–R data came from the national standardization sample (Heaton, 1992), which had no connection to the original data for the CNEHRB (Heaton et al., 1991) other than that the scores were converted to *t*-scores. For the RCNEHRB (Heaton et al., 1991, pp. 9–10), the WAIS–III scores were also derived from the national standardization sample and were unrelated to the original data for the CNEHRB. The data for the California Verbal Learning Test, which was added to the battery, were apparently gathered in another laboratory in California (Heaton et al., 2004, p. 7). The locations for gathering data for the letter and category fluency test and the paced auditory serial addition test, which were also added after the original data were collected was not specified (Heaton et al., 2004, p. 11). Consequently, a large proportion of the tests in the revised battery were not co-normed with the original sample. This means that, although they all use *t*-scores, the normative scores come from different samples, so they are not equivalent. Consequently, the RCNEHRB is no longer a co-normed battery.

Coverage

The RCNEHRB scores represent the entire HRB except for the lateral dominance examination. The RCNEHRB does not use the WAIS–III norms directly. These norms, derived from the national sample, provide scores that are demographically corrected in the WAIS–III/WMS–III/WIAT-II scoring assistant or writer. The individual neuropsychologist may use the WAIS–III scores along with the RCNEHRB scores with the understanding that the former scores are not co-normed with the latter scores, so differences between these test scores may be because of differences between norm sets.

In addition to the HRB tests, the RCNEHRB contained several well-known tests such as the Wisconsin Card Sorting Test, paced auditory serial addition test, Boston Naming Test (Goodglass & Kaplan, 1983), Peabody Individual Achievement Test, and the California Verbal Learning Test. The RCNEHRB also contains several tests that were either constructed for this battery or were less well known, including the Thurstone (Written) Word Fluency Test, Letter and Category (Oral) Fluency Tests, Digit Vigilance Test, Complex Ideational Material Subtest of the Boston Diagnostic Aphasia Examination, and the Figure Memory Test (Heaton et al., 2004, pp. 1–14). These tests provide good coverage of brain functions because they include a number of excellent tests. Research needs to be done to evaluate how these tests in this battery are related to each other.

Interpretation Aids

The RCNEHRB contains several interpretation aids that may help neuropsychological analysis. Deficit scores are used to indicate the severity of an impairment. Remember that scores for brain damage on this battery have been normalized to be equivalent to an average distribution, so they do not correspond to the actual amount of impairment that occurs on a test.

The average impairment rating (AIR) from the Russell, Neuringer, and Goldstein (1970) neuropsychological key was retained because it appeared to be a fairly accurate measure of brain damage. In addition, the RCNEHRB contains another general index of brain damage, the Global Deficit Score (Heaton et al., 2004, pp. 14–15), which averages the deficit scores of the 21 measures (it requires 18 measures to be used). It was only partially validated because the normal and brain-damaged subjects were not derived from the same sample (Heaton et al., 2004, pp. 31–33). Their Figure 4 (p. 33) indicates that the Global Deficit Score was more sensitive than the AIR. Although the sensitivity of the Global Deficit Score was provided, its selectivity and its overall predictive power were not (Russell, 2004). When sensitivity is high, selectivity is often low. Thus, the description of the operating characteristics of the Global Deficit Score is quite incomplete and so its comparison to the AIR is unknown.

Descriptive Statistics

The descriptive statistics for the RCNEHRB (Heaton et al., 1991) are provided in Table 15.1. The basic norms applicable to the HRB include 634 Caucasian subjects, of whom 486 came from the original battery sample. Each of the other tests has a different number of subjects (Heaton et al., 2004, p. 8). The basic sample for the revised battery was 65.9% male, which is essentially the same as in the original battery (69.6% men). The proportion of women was then 34.1%.

The age range for the normative tables is from 20 to 85. The sample had a mean age of 44.4 (SD = 17.9). The mean education level is 13.8 years (SD = 3.1). This is somewhat higher than high school of 12 and the average for the country.

In the CNEHRB, all 486 subjects were administered the WAIS. The sample had an average WAIS FSIQ of 113.8 (SD = 12.3), which approached one full SD above the national average (Russell, 2005). The manual for the revision (Heaton et al., 2004, p. 20), unlike every other major battery, does not provide data concerning the mean FSIQ of the subjects, although the subjects in the sample were presumably given an intelligence test because WAIS–III data appear to have been available. As such, there is no way to determine whether the FSIQ for the revised battery was as high as in the original battery.

An indirect method of judging whether the new subjects added to the CNEHRB norms have reduced the FSIQ is to examine the scaled scores for HRB tests derived from the battery's norming procedure (Appendix D, p. 92). For instance, in the original battery the category test scaled score for education of 12 years and ages 40–44 years, which was the mean of the sample, was 51. In the RCNEHRB (Appendix D, p. 140), the scale score for category test using the same demographic group was also

51. Other scales demonstrate similar equivalencies. Thus, apparently the ability of the revised battery has remained considerably above average.

Sample Representation

The descriptions of the CNEHRB and the revised battery's norming samples are incomplete according to the *Standards for Educational and Psychological Testing* (AERA et al., 1999, pp. 54–56). In contrast to the discussion of the statistical norming methods, the description of the representation of the sample provided in both the original and the RCNEHRB manuals is unusually meager for such an extensive program. The revised battery has six paragraphs and one table (pp. 7–9). By contrast, the WAIS–III devotes 27 pages to the description of its sample (Wechsler, 1997, pp. 19–46). Thus, the CNEHRB provides relatively little information about the selection of subjects, which could be used to judge the adequacy of these norms. This lack of detail is unfortunate because this is one of the most commonly used norming programs in neuropsychology.

According to the *Standards* (AERA et al., 1999), two major criteria for judging the accuracy of the representation of a sample are a through specification of the location from which the norms were drawn and a description of the type of subjects tested.

Locations of Sample Subjects

The description of the locations represented by the norming sample for the original and the RCNEHRB (Heaton et al., 2004, p. 7) is inadequate (Russell, 1997, pp. 38–40). The manuals give the impression that the norms were representative of 11 locations, including part of Canada. The revised norms manual states that members of the sample "were recruited and tested in a number of U.S. states, including California, Washington, Colorado, Texas, Oklahoma, Wisconsin, Illinois, Michigan, New York, and Virginia, as well as the Canadian province of Manitoba" (Heaton et al., 2004, p. 7). However, neither the original nor the revised manual provides the *N* for these locations, although this is also required by the *Standards* (AERA et al. 1999, p. 55). This requirement was also clearly stated in the previous version of the *Standards* (AERA et al., 1985. p. 33), which was in effect at the time that the original battery sample was published (Heaton et al., 1991).

The reason for this lack of the *N* by location becomes apparent when the RCNEHRB data are examined in detail. A fairly accurate estimation of the *N* for various locations in the sample is possible. Essentially the same sample was described three times in the literature. The first time was in the Heaton et al. (1986, pp. 103–104) descriptive study. The second time was in the CNEHRB manual (Heaton et al., 1991, pp. 5–6). The third description, given in the manual for the revision (Heaton et al., 2004, pp. 7–9), was almost exactly the same as that in the 1991 manual.

In the 1986 study, the norming group of 553 was stated as being derived from only three locations: "the University of Colorado (N = 207), University of California at San Diego (N = 181), and University of Wisconsin (N = 165) Medical Schools"

(Heaton et al., 1986, p. 103). When describing the subjects in the CNEHRB manual, Heaton et al. (1991, p. 9) stated, "Although all subjects in the Heaton et al. (1986) study were initially included in the present project [CNEHRB] some had to be removed from the sample" [those below age 20; p. 7]. According to this statement, only those subjects ages 15 through 19 were removed from the sample described in the 1986 study. The manual does not state how many of these younger subjects were removed. In the manual (Heaton et al., 1991), the number of subjects for the norms was stated to be 486. This meant that there were 67 fewer subjects in the 1991 set of norms than in the 1986 study. This would be approximately the number of subjects ages 15 through 19 who had been removed. Thus, the *N* of 486 for the CNEHRB is the number that would be expected *if almost no other subjects had been added to the subject pool from all other eight locations* listed in the manual. Thus, the number of added subjects must have been quite small. It is quite conceivable that, from some of the locations, only one subject was contributed to the total pool. Even though at least one subject was undoubtedly obtained from each of the other sites, it is also quite evident that the CNEHRB norms are not representative of the 11 sites. They are representative of only three sites, which were university areas in the northern and western part of the United States. This inaccurate representation of the sample locations was repeated without qualification in the RCNEHRB Handbook of Normative Data for Neuropsychological Assessment (Mitrushina et al., 1999, pp. 51–52). The *N* for each location was still not provided.

Apparently, the 148 Caucasians in the revised norms (Heaton et al., 2004) who were added to the subjects from the original norms came from the San Diego area. That was the location of the author's laboratory and where the African American subjects in the same study resided (Heaton et al., 2004, p. 7). Because apparently 181 of the original norms also came from San Diego, 329 of the Caucasian subjects in the revised norms (Heaton et al., 2004) came from this city. Thus, it is apparent that more than half of the subjects in the RCNEHRB (Heaton et al., 2004) came from the San Diego area, so this normative sample is primarily representative of the Western United States, especially the San Diego area, and not 11 areas spread over the United States and the Canadian province of Manitoba.

Type of Subjects

Many neuropsychologists believe that volunteers are the only adequate type of subjects for norming (Mitrushina et al., 1999, pp. 36–37; Russell, 2003, 2005). As such, we would expect that a statement that all of the subjects were volunteers would be included in these manuals. However, neither the CNEHRB (Heaton et al., 1991, pp. 5–6) nor the RCNEHRB (Heaton et al., 2004, pp. 7–9) manuals specifically state that the subjects were volunteers. The subjects were called *participants* in both manuals (Heaton et al., 1991, pp. 5–6; Heaton et al., 2004, pp. 7–9). The term *participants* does not rule out the use of "neurologically normal" patients as subjects. Such subjects are patients who were referred for a possible neurological condition but who had no brain damage as determined by neurological examination.

Very little information is provided about the subjects in the manual for the revised norms. The only information provided is that "All participants completed structured interviews" (Heaton et al., 2004, p. 7) and "Most individuals were paid for their participation in the various research studies" (Heaton et al., 2004, p. 7). Again, no *N*s are provided.

The "structured interview" may have been approximately the same questionnaire that many of Reitan's students have given patients when administering the HRB (Jarvis & Jeffrey, 1984, pp. 80–83; and personal experience). Such a questionnaire was also administered to the neurologically normal patients tested in the HRNES–R norming study (Russell & Starkey, 1993, 2001) and for the neurologically normal patients used in the neuropsychological key (Russell et al., 1970). As such, a "structured interview" does not indicate that the subjects were volunteers.

Presumably, volunteers would be paid. Thus, the word *most* in the preceding quotation could refer to any number above 50%. So perhaps as many as 49% of the subjects may not have been volunteers. It is simply not clear how many of the subjects in the RCNEHRB norms were neurologically normal patients and how many were volunteers.

It is known that of the original authors, Matthews, who was at the University of Wisconsin Medical School (Heaton et al., 1986, p. 103; Heaton et al., 1991, p. 5), usually included patients referred for neuropsychological testing in composing his norms (Matthews, 1988). His subjects would have been neurologically normal persons, not volunteers.

In summary, it appears that the norming subjects in the RCNEHRB were a mixture of volunteers and neurologically referred patients with no neurological problems, largely from three university hospital areas in the northern and western parts of the United States, especially San Diego.

Halstead–Russell Neurological Evaluation System—Revised

From its beginning, the HRNES–R (Russell & Starkey, 1993, 2001) was designed not only to provide co-norms for the HRB but also to extend the method pioneered by Reitan (Russell et al., 1970). This would create a psychometrically integrated system of assessment using a whole battery. This system was designed for pattern analysis (Russell & Starkey, 1993). In this regard, most of the comparisons that Reitan made using raw scores can be performed employing scaled scores, and often the comparisons can be direct without the specific corrections for age and ability that raw scores require.

Reviews

HRNES (Russell & Starkey, 1993) was reviewed several times. Although one review by Lezak (1995) was highly critical, many of her statements and evaluations were incorrect (Russell, 1998). The other reviews have been favorable (Lynch, 1995; Mahurin, 1995; Retzlaff, 1995). The reviews by Mahurin and Retzlaff were published in *The Twelfth Mental Measurements Yearbook*.

Descriptive Statistics

The means and SDs of the HRNES–R (Russell & Starkey, 2001) are the same as those of the original version (Russell & Starkey, 1993), although the demographic adjustments were revised. This information is fully presented in the manual (Russell & Starkey, 1993, pp. 27–32, and Table 1, pp. 28–29 and Table 7, pp. 38–41).

In addition, the operating characteristics, such as sensitivity and selectivity and predictive power of the major tests and indexes in this battery have been published (Russell, 2004). The overall predictive power of the average impairment index was 85% when the base rate was 50%. An addendum (Appendix F) published with the revised edition of the battery contains the scale-score norms.

Subjects

All subjects were referred as part of their medical workups through the normal hospital referral process, except for 12 normal unpaid volunteers. Subjects for the norm sample were mostly patients from the Cincinnati ($N = 98$) and Miami Veterans Administration (VA) medical centers ($N = 678$), which were part of university hospital medical school centers. There were 200 "normal" control subjects and 578 brain-damaged subjects. These patients were diagnosed by neurologists, neurosurgeons, and neuropathologists who were faculty members of the medical schools. As such, they constitute among the best neurology, neurosurgery, and neuropathology doctors in the United States. All of the brain-damaged subjects received whatever neurological procedures the neurologist or neurosurgeon deemed necessary, such as angiograms, cranial surgery, and even some autopsies. Of the brain-damaged subjects, 87.4% were given computed tomography (CT) scans. All of the controls, except the 12 normal volunteers, received the CT scan if the consulting neurologists thought it would aid in ruling out a neurological diagnosis.

Patients from the Miami VA medical centers seem to represent a fairly cosmopolitan population because Miami is a retirement location. Although the representation of the sample was limited, this is true of all major batteries. These subjects are more thoroughly described than the subjects in any other major study using HRB tests (Russell, 2009).

The brain-damaged patient's medical records were examined to determine whether there was a clear diagnosis of neuropathology and the location and type of damage. At least a year after administering the examination, each subject's medical file was reexamined to determine whether there was evidence that the original diagnosis had been incorrect.

Of the 1,538 subjects who were administered the complete battery by Russell's laboratory, 623 (40.5%) were rejected as having a diagnosis that was either too vague or too complicated (multiple diagnoses).

Most of the 200 neurologically negative control group subjects were patients with a possible neurological condition who were found to be without brain damage (12 were volunteers). These patients are more fully described in Russell (2009).

They had been referred for a neurological examination that proved to be negative. All schizophrenia and severe acute bipolar disorders were eliminated. The sample was mostly composed of mildly depressed and neurotic subjects with memory or somatic complaints or mild personality disorders. The personality disorders were primarily manifested by subjects with episodes of functional uncontrolled behavior that might have indicated a seizure disorder. The primary types of symptoms were memory complaints, somatic symptoms, and alcoholism. (The alcoholics were derived from a treatment program but had been cleared of brain damage by neurology.) Some patients had mild head trauma or controlled seizures that had not produced any cognitive impairment, according to their neurological examinations.

All of these subjects, except for the 12 unpaid volunteers, were referred to rule out a neurological condition. Thus, this type of patient depicts the type of population that a neuropsychological assessment generally must distinguish from authentic brain-damaged subjects (AERA et al., 1999, p. 55, Standard 4.5; Reitan & Wolfson, 1993, pp. 33–35).

The control sample's mean demographics were 177 males, 23 females, 188 Caucasians, and 12 African Americans. The average age for the neurologically normal subjects was 44.6 years (SD = 13.3), with an average education of 12.8 years (SD = 2.9). The mean FSIQ was 102.1 (SD = 12.5). In the normal sample, 24 (12%) were women, which is approximately the proportion of females in the VA medical system. The tests showing differences between men and women—grip strength, tapping, and grooved pegboard—were compared with those of other samples from the literature to ensure that there was no significant deviation from the average US population (Dodrill, 1978; Heaton et al., 1986; Mitrushina et al., 1999; Yeudall et al., 1987).

Reference Scale Norming

The HRNES and the revised battery scale-score norms were designed to reflect the skewed distribution of a brain-damaged sample using a scaling method called *reference scale norming* (Russell, 1991; Russell & Starkey, 1993, pp. 33–34).

The scaled scores and corrections were derived from raw scores without normalization. Essentially, digital (*D*) scores for every test in the battery were obtained by predicting the raw scores from an index using linear regression. These *z*-scores were transformed into *D*-scores with a mean of 100 and an SD of 10. Thus, they were equivalent to *t*-scores except the mean is 100 instead of 50. The *D*-score distribution is equivalent to distributions of mean test raw scores, which can extend to 5 SDs below the mean. This method produced scaled scores that model the mean distribution of the test scores that are skewed (Moses et al., 1999).

Reference scaling also provided a method for co-norming tests that were added to the battery after the original group was normed. This was a form of co-norming bridge statistics. When new tests were added to the battery, their scaled scores were created by either predicting them from the AIS (Russell, 2004) or using linear transformation (Russell & Starkey, 2001, Appendix F, pp. 1 & 11). Consequently, the additional tests were directly coordinated with the rest of the co-normed battery.

Because the WAIS–III and the WMS–III were themselves co-normed, a form of bridge statistics integrated them with the HRNES–R so that they were co-normed with the entire battery (Russell & Starkey, 2001, Appendix F, pp. 17–19, 24–25). The result of this statistical bridge was that the entire HRNES–R is a single co-normed unit that included the WAIS–III and parts of the WMS–III.

Demographic Corrections

The demographic correction method for the HRNES–R was supplied by data from the 200 normal subjects. The correction was made directly to the raw scores, not the scaled scores. The correction essentially adjusts the raw scores to those age 45 and with an education of 12 years. The methods for correction were different for age, premorbid ability, and sex. The method is described in detail elsewhere (Russell, 2000b, pp. 491–492).

Age corrections were derived by linear regression based on the entire normal sample and presented for each decade from 20 to 90 by predicting the test scores at the middle of the interval (e.g., 25, 35, and 45).

The method of obtaining the corrections for an estimated premorbid ability was based on the average WAIS–R FSIQ for each major education category. An unpublished study by the author found that the major changes in IQ tended to occur in steps at each graduation level rather than being linearly related to a person's years of education. For instance, subjects who did not obtain a college degree but had several years of college were not statistically different from those who graduated from high school with 12 years of education.

In this set of norms, the FSIQ for each education category was corrected based on the difference between each education graduation category and the 12-year category for each test (Russell & Starkey, 2001, Appendix F). Corrections then occur in steps: less than high school graduation, high school graduates, college graduates, and graduates with advanced degrees.

Thus, in the HRNES–R computer program, an estimate of premorbid IQ for the battery may use education, a formula for estimating premorbid intelligence, or an IQ score from actual premorbid intelligence test.

The correction for sex on the HRNES–R did not use a regression method but rather the ratio between the ability of men and women (Russell & Starkey, 2001, Appendix F, pp. 2, 5, 9). For the correction by sex, the women's scores were corrected to be equivalent to men's scores on tests in which there was a gender difference. This correction was restricted to three measures: grip strength, tapping speed, and grooved pegboard. Women were somewhat faster than men on the grooved pegboard, whereas men had higher scores on the other two tests.

Coverage of Functions

The tests for HRNES–R were selected to provide complete coverage of the brain functions by area and type (Russell, 2000a, pp. 501–510). This was accomplished as completely as the understanding of brain functioning allowed. To accomplish this, a number of tests were added to the HRB and the Wechsler intelligence tests. These will be described by functional area. (References for these tests are in the HRNES–R manual and Appendix F, so they will not be enumerated.)

Executive function tests of attention include the rhythm test, digit span, and Corsi board. Fluency is measured by the H-words, figure fluency, and FAS. Mental or psychomotor speed is examined by trail-making test speed and the digit symbol. Planning is tested by block design and the category test. The trail-making Test B tests mental efficiency, and judgment was indicated by the category test and analogies. Coverage in this area was not as adequate as for some other areas.

Cognitive functions are assessed by analogies, arithmetic, similarities, picture completion, and the category test. Intelligence is assessed by the WAIS, WAIS–R, or WAIS–III. Spatial relations are examined by trail-making test A, block design, object assembly, gestalt objects, and the aphasia test cross. Social intelligence is partially tested by picture arrangement.

Language is tested by the aphasia screening test, Boston Naming Test (Goodglass & Kaplan, 1983), H-words, information, vocabulary, Peabody picture vocabulary test—revised and III (Dunn & Dunn, 1997), and the expressive vocabulary test (EVT; Williams, 1997). Academic achievement is measured by the WRAT-R and WRAT–3 reading, spelling, and arithmetic (Jastak, Jastak, & Wilkinson, 1984).

The coverage of memory in this battery is roughly equivalent to that of the WMS–III. Memory is examined as working memory, recent memory, and crystallized memory. Working memory is measured by digits forward, digits backward, the Miami selective learning test [a modified version of the Buschke memory test (Buschke, 1973)], immediate recall, and the Corsi board. Recent memory is examined by Wechsler Memory Scale (Revised or III) logical memory one-half hour and visual reproduction one-half hour, and Miami selective learning test, one-half hour recall and recognition. Learning is measured by information, vocabulary, tactual performance test, memory, and location.

Motor ability is examined by tapping speed, right and left hands; grip strength, right and left hands; and the grooved pegboard, right and left hands.

Sensory perception is examined by gestalt objects and gestalt words, finger agnosia, and fingertip writing examination. Spatial and body schema and stereognosis are assessed by tactual performance test time—right, left, both, and total time.

Finally, the lateralization examination from the HRB and the name writing test speed, which is in the lateralization examination, has been normed.

Thus, the entire HRB, except for the tactile form recognition test, is included. Although some modifications in scoring were used, scoring does not differ from Reitan's method in any essential manner (Reitan & Wolfson, 1993). Consequently, the HRB scores can be interpreted either in the traditional manner using raw scores using the NDS (Reitan & Wolfson, 1993) or the HRNES–R (Russell, 2000a; Russell & Starkey, 2001) corrected scale scores.

Interpretation Aids

The HRNES–R contains a number of interpretative aids that are intended for judicious use. These were formal pattern-analysis procedures such as indexes and formalization of intuitive interpretative methods (Russell, 2000a, p. 464; 2000b, pp. 495–501). Such formal aids change prior interpretative concepts based on clinical experience and intuition into a more objective formal procedure. All aids included in this battery have been validated (Russell & Starkey, 1993, 2001).

The battery has two summary index scores: the average index score (AIS) and the percent impaired score (PIS). These two indexes are described in the manual (Russell & Starkey, 1993, pp. 21–20, 37, 38, 90). The PIS is similar to the Halstead Index because it indicates the proportion of the index test scores in the brain-damaged range. The AIS is the mean of the index test scores.

The revised battery also has a probability of brain-damage index (Russell, 1997; Russell & Starkey, 2001) that provides a measure of the probability that an individual with a certain AIS has brain damage.

The lateralization index, which is a revised version of the lateralization index in the neuropsychological key (Russell et al., 1970; Russell & Starkey, 1993), provides an indication of the extent that brain damage is lateralized. The method has been revised from the neuropsychological key (Russell et al., 1970).

An Alzheimer's index, based on a study by Russell and Polakoff (1993), provides an indication of whether a patient may have Alzheimer's disease (the cutting point of >1.2 indicates the possible presence of Alzheimer's disease). Because the index is also sensitive to the effects of alcoholic brain damage, the assessments may be confused without reviewing the patient's history. Finally, a temporal lobe damage index was derived from studies by Dobbins and Russell (1990) and Russell and Russell (1993). This indicates the possibility of temporal lobe damage when the subject has left lateralized brain damage.

Comparisons

The six major norming programs of HRB are compared in Table 15.2. Because the mean age and ability varies from battery to battery for adequate comparison, the norms must be equated for age and ability levels (FSIQ or education). This was achieved by adjusting scores to a common age and ability category. All sets of norms were adjusted to age 45 and an education category of 12 years or FSIQ of 100. For three batteries—Pauker's, the RCNEHRB, and the HRNES–R—scores can be directly obtained for any adult age and ability levels. However, because the Yeudall norms do not extend beyond age 40 and the Dodrill norms are not stratified, the norms needed to be adjusted to a common age and ability. This was accomplished through applying the HRNES–R corrections (Russell & Starkey, 2001, Appendix F, pp. 12–17) to the Yeudall et al. (1987) and Dodrill (1987) batteries. All sets of norms were adjusted to age 45 and an education of 12 years or FSIQ of 100. NDS (Reitan, 1986) scores were derived from the central score in level 1 because these represented an average person. The effects of sex were not examined in Table 15.2 because they varied considerably from one research study to another (Heaton et al., 1986; Pauker, 1981a; Yeudall et al., 1987).

This comparison indicated that, in general, scores are fairly similar across all sets of formal norms, and the NDS (Reitan, 1986) scores were generally similar to the normed scores. The RCNEHRB tended to be somewhat higher than the other norms. By contrast, the HRNES–R norms were somewhat lower. This difference might be

Table 15.2 Comparison of Mean Scores for Neuropsychological Norms for Approximately Age 45 and High School Education or FSIQ = 100)

Test	(Norming Studies: Adjusted to Age 45, Education 12, or FSIQ 100)					
	HRNES–R Adjustment[a]		Stratified[b]	Program Adjusted[c]		
	Yeudall[d]	Dodrill[e]	Pauker[f]	RCNHRB[g]	HRNES–R[h]	NDS[i]
	Age 45	Age 45	Age 45	Age 45	Age 45	
Category Test (err)	54	45	54	35	48	36
Trails A (s)	25	25	—	28	34	33
Trails B (s)	74	72	—	62	84	75
Rhythm (correct)	25	25	27	27	26	26
Speech Perception (right)	7	6	6	4	7	8
TPT Tot Time (min)	14.7	14.8	16.0	12.0	16.3	12.0
TPT Memory (correct)	7	7	7	8	7	7
TPT Location (correct)	5	5	4	4	4	6
Tapping[j] (per 10 s)	48	51	42	54	45	52
Grip[j] (kg)	51	—	—	54	45	—
Pegboard[j] (per 3 min)	—	—	—	65	72	—

[a]HRNES–R corrections were used to make adjustments to age 45 and education 12 years or FSIQ 100.
[b]Stratified or adjusted by age and FSIQ.
[c]Adjustments made using the norms or program of the norm set.
[d]Yeudall et al. (1987): adjusted from age range 21–25 and FSIQ 112.
[e]Dodrill (1987): adjusted from age 27.7 and FSIQ 100.
[f]Pauker (1981): scores used FSIQ of 103–112 and age 35–52.
[g]RCNEHRB (Heaton et al., 2004) norms for men: education 12, age 45, *t*-score about 50.
[h]HRNES–R (Russell & Starkey, 2001) norms for men: education 12, age 45 (Appendix–F4, pp.18–23).
[i]NDS; numbers equivalent to average score (Reitan, 1986, p. 79).
[j]Dominant hand for men.

expected because all of the norms other than the HRNES–R and the Dodrill norms had FSIQs that approached 1 SD above average (Russell, 2005). Dodrill had forced his norms into a normal distribution with an FSIQ of 100. The HRNES–R may have had more average scores because this norming group consisted of patients who presented with symptomatology requiring neuropsychological evaluation (Russell, 2003), whereas the other norms were largely derived from volunteers with higher-than-average IQ ability levels (Russell, 2005).

Summary

This review of the major HRB norms examines six major sets of norms. All of the stratified batteries were incomplete in their representation of some demographic characteristics or subtests. Of the unstratified batteries, the NDS used norms that were derived from Reitan's experience and previous research control groups. Nevertheless, his norms were thoroughly validated. The RCNEHRB was normed using linear regression, and the scores were adjusted for age, ability, and sex. It was not completely co-normed, and the norms are considerably above average. The HRNES–R norms used linear regression, and the scores are demographically adjusted. It was largely normed on neurologically normal subjects. It is fully co-normed. The domain coverage of these latter two batteries was extensive. Both included the HRB tests, versions of the adult Wechsler tests, memory, and most major types of cognitive functions.

References

American Educational Research Association, American Psychological Association, & National Council on Measurement in Education (AERA et al.), (1985). *Standards for educational and psychological testing*. Washington, DC: Author.

American Educational Research Association, American Psychological Association, & National Council on Measurement in Education (AERA et al.) (1999). *Standards for educational and psychological testing*. Washington, DC: Author.

Anastasi, A., & Urbina, S. (1997). *Psychological testing* (7th ed.). Upper Saddle River, NJ: Prentice Hall.

Bornstein, R. A. (1985). Normative data on selected neuropsychological measures from a non-clinical sample. *Journal of Clinical Psychology, 41*, 651–659.

Buschke, H. (1973). Selective reminding for analysis of memory and learning. *Journal of Verbal Learning Behavior, 12*, 543–550.

Crawford, J. R., & Howell, David C. (1998). Regression equations in clinical neuropsychology: an evaluation of statistical methods for comparing predicted and obtained scores. *Journal of Clinical and Experimental Neurology, 20*, 755–762.

Dobbins, C. T., & Russell, E. W. (1990). Left temporal lobe brain damage pattern on the Wechsler Adult Intelligence Scale. *Journal of Clinical Psychology, 46*, 863–868.

Dodrill, C. B. (1978). The hand dynamometer as a neuropsychological measure. *Journal of Consulting and Clinical Psychology, 46*(6), 1432–1435.

Dodrill, C. B. (1987). What constitutes normal performance in clinical neuropsychology?. Paper presented at 97th Annual Convention of the American Psychological Association, Atlanta.

Dodrill, C. B. (1999). Myths of neuropsychology: further considerations. *Clinical Neuropsychologist, 13*, 562–572.

Dunn, L. M., & Dunn, L. M. (1997). *Peabody picture vocabulary test (PPVT-III)* (3rd ed.) [Manual]. Circle Pines, MI: American Guidance Service.

Fastenau, P. S. (1998). Validity of regression-based norms: an empirical test of the comprehensive norms with older adults. *Journal of Clinical and Experimental Neuropsychology, 20*, 906–916.

Fastenau, P. S., & Adams, K. M. (1996). Heaton, Grant, and Matthew's comprehensive norms: An overzealous attempt. *Journal of Clinical and Experimental Neuropsychology*, *18*, 444–448.

Fromm-Auch, D., & Yeudall, L. T. (1983). Normative data for the Halstead–Reitan neuropsychological tests. *Journal of Clinical Neuropsychology*, *5*, 221–238.

Fuerst, D. R. (1993). A review of the Halstead–Reitan Neuropsychological Battery norms program. *Clinical Neuropsychologist*, *7*, 96–103.

Golden, C. J., Purisch, A. D., & Hammeke, T. A. (1991). *Luria–Nebraska Neuropsychological Battery: Forms I and II* [Manual]. Los Angeles: Western Psychological Services.

Golden, C. J., & Van den Broek, A. (1998). Potential impact of age-and education-corrected scores on HRNB score patterns in participants with focal brain injury. *Archives of Clinical Neuropsychology*, *13*, 683–694.

Goodglass, H., & Kaplan, E. (1983). *Boston naming test* [Booklet]. Philadelphia: Lea & Febiger.

Heaton, R. K. (1992). *Comprehensive norms for an expanded Halstead–Reitan Battery: A supplement for the wechsler adult intelligence scale—revised* [Manual]. Odessa, FL: Psychological Assessment Resources.

Heaton, R. K., Avitable, N., Grant, I., & Matthews, C. G. (1999). Further cross validation of regression-based neuropsychological norms with an update for the Boston Naming Test. *Journal of Clinical and Experimental Neuropsychology*, *21*, 572–582.

Heaton, R. K., Grant, I., & Matthews, C. G. (1986). Differences in neuropsychological test performance associated with age, education and sex. In I. Grant & K. M. Adams (Eds.), *Neuropsychological Assessment of Neuropsychiatric Disorders* (pp. 100–120). New York: Oxford.

Heaton, R. K., Grant, I., & Matthews, C. G. (1991). *Comprehensive norms for an expanded Halstead–Reitan Battery* [Norms, manual, and computer program]. Odessa, FL: Psychological Assessment Resources.

Heaton, R. K., Matthews, C. G., Grant, I., & Avitable, N. (1996). Demographic corrections with comprehensive norms: an overzealous attempt or a good start. *Journal of Clinical and Experimental Neuropsychology*, *18*, 121–141.

Heaton, R. K., Miller, S. W., Taylor, M. J., & Grant, I. (2004). *Revised comprehensive norms for an expanded Halstead–Reitan Battery: Demographically adjusted neuropsychological norms for African American and Caucasian adults* [Professional manual and computer program]. Odessa, FL: Psychological Assessment Resources.

Jarvis, P. E., & Jeffrey, T. B. (1984). *Halstead–Reitan Test Battery: An interpretive guide*. Odessa, FL: Psychological Assessment Resources.

Jastak, J. F., Jastak, S. R., & Wilkinson, G. S. (1984). *Wide range achievement test—revised (WRAT-R)* [Manual]. Wilmington, DE: Jastak Associates.

Kane, R. L., & Kay, G. G. (1992). Computerized assessment in neuropsychology: a review of tests and test batteries. *Neuropsychology Review*, *3*, 1–117.

Kane, R. L., & Kay, G. G. (1997). Computer applications in neuropsychological assessment. In G. Goldstein & T. M. Incagnoli (Eds.), *Contemporary approaches to neuropsychological assessment* (pp. 359–392). New York: Plenum.

Kane, R. L., Winter, K. P., Bleiberg, J., & Kane, R. L. (2007). DoD contributions to computerized neurocognitive assessment: the ANAM Test System. In R. L. Kane (Ed.), *Archives of Clinical Neuropsychology* [Supplement], S2S1, S1–S144.

Lezak, M. D. (1995). *Neuropsychological assessment* (3rd ed.). New York: Oxford University Press.

Lezak, M. D., Howieson, D. B., & Loring, D. W. (2004). *Neuropsychological assessment* (4th ed.). New York: Oxford University Press.

Lynch, W. J. (1995). Microcomputer-assisted neuropsychological test analysis. *Journal of Head Trauma Rehabilitation*, *10*, 97–100.

Mahurin, R. K. (1995). Review of the Halstead–Russell neuropsychological evaluation system. In J. C. Conoley & J. C. Impara (Eds.), *The twelfth mental measurements yearbook* (pp. 448–451). Lincoln: University of Nebraska Press.

Matthews, C. G. (1988). Personal communication.

Meyers, J. E., & Rohling, M. L. (2004). Validation of the Myers short battery on mild TBI patients. *Archives of Clinical Neuropsychology*, *19*(5), 637–651.

Mitrushina, M. N., Boone, K. B., & D'Elia, L. F. (1999). *Handbook of normative data for neuropsychological assessment*. New York: Oxford University Press.

Moses, J. A., Prichard, D. A., & Adams, R. L. (1999). Normative corrections for the Halstead–Reitan neuropsychological battery. *Archives of Clinical Neuropsychology*, *14*, 445–454.

Pauker, J. D. (1977, February). Adult norms for the Halstead–Reitan neuropsychological test battery: Preliminary data. Unpublished paper presented at the Annual Meeting of the International Neuropsychological Society, Santa Fe, NM.

Pauker, J. D. (1981a). Adult "norms" or "standards" for the Halstead–Reitan neuropsychological test battery. Unpublished manuscript, Clarke Institute of Psychiatry and University of Toronto, Canada.

Pauker, J. D. (1981b). T score conversion tables for Halstead–Reitan neuropsychological test battery for adults. Unpublished manuscript, Clarke Institute of Psychiatry and University of Toronto, Canada.

Pauker, J. D. (1988). Constructing overlapping cell tables to maximize the clinical usefulness of normative test data: rationale and an example from neuropsychology. *Journal of Clinical Psychology*, *44*, 930–933.

Reitan, R. M. (1986). *The neuropsychological deficit scale for adults: Computer program.* Tucson: Neuropsychology Press.

Reitan, R. M., & Wolfson, D. (1993). *The Halstead–Reitan neuropsychological test battery: Theory and clinical interpretation* (2nd ed.). Tucson: Neuropsychology Press.

Retzlaff, P. D. (1995). Review of the Halstead–Russell neuropsychological evaluation system. In J. C. Conoley & J. C. Impara (Eds.), *The twelfth mental measurements yearbook* (pp. 451–453). Lincoln: University of Nebraska Press.

Russell, E. W. (1988). Renorming Russell's version of the Wechsler Memory Scale. *Journal of Clinical and Experimental Neuropsychology*, *10*, 235–249.

Russell, E. W. (1991). A reference scale method for constructing neuropsychological test batteries. In B. P. Rourke, L. Costa, D. V. Cicchetti, K. M. Adams & K. J. Plasterk (Eds.), *Methodological and biostatistical foundations of clinical neuropsychology* (pp. 399–415), Berwyn, PA: Swets & Zeitlinger.

Russell, E. W. (1995). The accuracy of automated and clinical detection of brain damage and lateralization in neuropsychology. *Neuropsychology Review*, *5*(1), 1–68.

Russell, E. W. (1997). Developments in the psychometric foundations of neuropsychological assessment. In G. Goldstein & T. M. Incagnoli (Eds.), *Contemporary approaches to neuropsychological assessment* (pp. 15–65). New York: Plenum.

Russell, E. W. (1998). In defense of the Halstead–Reitan Battery: a critique of Lezak's review. *Archives of Clinical Neuropsychology*, *13*, 365–381.

Russell, E. W. (2000a). The application of computerized scoring programs to neuropsychological assessment. In R. D. Vanderploeg (Ed.), *Clinician's guide to neuropsychological assessment* (pp. 483–515) (2nd ed.). Hillsdale, NJ: Lawrence Erlbaum Associates.

Russell, E. W. (2000b). The cognitive-metric, fixed battery approach to neuropsychological assessment. In R. D. Vanderploeg (Ed.), *Clinician's guide to neuropsychological assessment* (pp. 449–481) (2nd ed.). Hillsdale, NJ: Lawrence Erlbaum Associates.

Russell, E. W. (2001). Toward an explanation of Dodrill's observation: high neuropsychological test performance does not accompany high IQs. *Clinical Neuropsychologist, 15*, 423–428.

Russell, E. W. (2003). The critique of the HRNES in the "Handbook of normative data for neuropsychological assessment." *Archives of Clinical Neuropsychology, 18*(2), 165–180.

Russell, E. W. (2004). The operating characteristics of the major HRNES-R measures. *Archives of Clinical Neuropsychology, 19*(8), 1043–1061.

Russell, E. W. (2005). Norming subjects for the Halstead–Reitan Battery. *Archives of Clinical Neuropsychology, 20*(4), 479–484.

Russell, E. W. (2009). Commentary on Larrabee, Mills, and Meyer's paper "Sensitivity to brain dysfunction of the Halstead–Reitan vs an ability-focused neuropsychology battery.". *Clinical Neuropsychologist, 23*, 831–840.

Russell, E. W., Neuringer, C., & Goldstein, G. (1970). *Assessment of brain damage: A neuropsychological key approach*. New York: Wiley.

Russell, E. W., & Polakoff, D. (1993). Neuropsychological test patterns in men for Alzheimer's and multi-infarct dementia. *Archives of Clinical Neuropsychology, 8*, 327–343.

Russell, E. W., & Russell, S. L. K. (1993). Left temporal lobe brain damage pattern on the WAIS: addendum. *Journal of Clinical Psychology, 49*, 241–244.

Russell, E. W., & Starkey, R. I. (1993). *Halstead–Russell neuropsychological evaluation system*. Los Angeles: Western Psychological Services. [Manual and computer program]

Russell, E. W., & Starkey, R. I. (2001). *Halstead–Russell neuropsychological evaluation system—revised*. Los Angeles: Western Psychological Services. [Manual and computer program]

Russell, E. W., Starkey, R. I., Starkey, T. W., & Fernandez, C. D. (1988). *Halstead–Rennick–Russell Battery*. Miami: Scientific Psychology. [Manual and computer program]

Schinka, J. A., & Vanderploeg, R. D. (2000). Estimating premorbid level of functioning. In R. D. Vanderploeg (Ed.), *Clinician's guide to neuropsychological assessment* (pp. 39–67) (2nd ed.). Mahwah, NJ: Lawrence Erlbaum Associates.

Strauss, E., Sherman, E. M. S., & Spreen, O. (2006). *A compendium of neuropsychological tests: Administration, norms, and commentary* (3rd ed.). New York: Oxford University Press.

Steinmeyer, C. H. (1986). A Meta-analysis of Halstead–Reitan test performances on non-brain damaged subjects. *Archives of Clinical Neuropsychology, 1*, 301–307.

Stern, R. A., & White, T. (2001). *Neuropsychological assessment battery (NAB)*. Lutz, FL: Psychological Assessment Resources.

Vanderploeg, R. D., Axelrod, B. N., Sherer, M., Scott, J., & Adams, R. L. (1997). The importance of demographic adjustments on neuropsychological test performance: a response to Reitan and Wolfson (1995). *Clinical Neuropsychologist, 11*(2), 210–217.

Wechsler, D. (1945). A standardized memory scale for clinical use. *Journal of Psychology, 19*, 87–95.

Wechsler, D. (1997). *WAIS–III, WMS–III.* San Antonio, TX: Psychological Corporation. [Technical manual]

Wilkinson, G. S. (1993). *Wide Range Achievement Test (WRAT3): Administration manual* (3rd ed.). Wilmington, DE: Wide Range.

Williams, K. T. (1997). *Expressive vocabulary test (EVT).* Circle Pines, MN: American Guidance Services. [Manual]

Yeudall, L. T., Reddon, J. R., Gill, D. M., & Stefanyk, W. O. (1987). Normative data for the Halstead–Reitan neuropsychological tests stratified by age and sex. *Journal of Clinical Psychology, 43*(3), 346–367.

Made in the USA
Monee, IL
13 September 2026

62977354R10256